14 75 MN

DATE DUE

Jan 28 80			

GAYLORD

PRINTED IN U.S.A.

INCOME DISTRIBUTION THEORY

ALDINE TREATISES IN MODERN ECONOMICS

edited by Harry G. Johnson
University of Chicago and
London School of Economics

INCOME DISTRIBUTION THEORY

Martin Bronfenbrenner

Carnegie-Mellon University

Aldine · Atherton

Chicago and New York

First published 1971 by
Aldine · Atherton, Inc.
529 South Wabash Avenue
Chicago, Illinois 60605

Library of Congress Catalog Card Number 77–131045
ISBN 202–06037–3
Printed in the United States of America

To my brilliant failures
this book is dedicated

Foreword

The purpose of the Aldine Treatises in Modern Economics is to enable authorities in a particular field of economics, and experts on a particular problem, to make their knowledge available to others in the form they find easiest and most convenient. Our intention is to free them from an insistence on complete coverage of a conventionally defined subject, which deters many leading economists from writing a book instead of a series of articles or induces them to suppress originality for the sake of orthodoxy, and from an obligation to produce a standard number of pages, which encourages the submergence of judgment of relevance in a pudding of irrelevant detail. The Aldine Treatises seek to encourage good economists to say what they want to say to their fellow economists, in as little or as much space as they consider necessary to the purpose.

The present volume treats the economics of the distribution of income. That subject was the heart of Ricardo's contribution to the development of English classical economics and remained the backbone of the science of economics until contemporary times. But the two "revolutions" of the 1930's—the "monopolistic competition" revolution and the Keynesian revolution—produced widespread skepticism about the relevance of traditional distribution theory to the circumstances of contemporary society. Monopolistic competition theory, particularly in its "imperfect competition" variant, raised doubts about both the efficiency and the justice of the determination of factor prices under contemporary competitive conditions. However, the dismissal of microeconomic theory in favor of macroeconomic analysis associated with the Keynesian Revolution gave rise to a variety of efforts to replace the marginal productivity theory of distribution by various kinds of macroeconomic substitutes, some of Marxian and some of Keynesian origin. The result has been a noticeable nervousness of contemporary economists in dealing with the theory of distribution, in marked contrast to the confidence with which they are prepared to deal both with the microeconomic theory of prices and production and with the macroeconomic theory of aggregate output and employment. In the view of many the microeconomic approach to distribution theory is not to be trusted, but no satisfactory macroeconomic approach has taken its place. Yet problems of distribution remain of great importance to the economist concerned with public affairs, in contexts ranging from the problem of poverty and its remedification to the feasibility and requirements of an "incomes" or "guidelines" policy.

A treatise on the precise subject of income distribution, which deals with it as the central theme and not as a peripheral afterthought, should therefore prove useful to students, teachers, and policy-involved economists. The author of the present treatise is admirably qualified for his task. He has, contrary to prevailing fashions, taught a course on this subject over a long period of years, in nine American universities and one Japanese university, and in the course of that time has both acquired an intimate knowledge of the literature—some familiar, some arcane, but all relevant—and had the opportunity, both on his own and through his students, to work intensively on some of the puzzles, paradoxes, and superficially empty theoretical boxes that constitute a test of the power of theory but that are all too often ignored or glossed over when distribution theory is taught as a small segment of a course with another subject as its main theme. Moreover, while he was brought up in the strict school of traditional marginal productivity theory that ruled at the University of Chicago during the 1930's, he is distinguished by a wide-ranging intellectual curiosity combined with scholarly dispassionateness, and has consistently attempted to sort out and treasure whatever grains of truth there may be in alternative approaches to the theory of distribution, be they Keynesian, Marxian, French institutionalist, or whatever.

To the best of my knowledge, this is the only book available that ranges —and ranges authoritatively—over the whole field of distribution theory. The author treats, boldly and not gingerly, the ideological issues involved in income distribution. He is concerned with the personal as well as the functional distribution of income. He has devoted appropriate attention to problems of statistical measurement of the income distribution. The core of the book is, naturally, the traditional theory of marginal productivity and its application to the special cases of wages, interest, rent, and profits. But it is an extensive treatment of the criticisms of marginal productivity theory and the allegation that under imperfect competition marginal productivity payments involve exploitation of the factors of production. It also includes reviews of the extensive Keynesian literature on distribution, particularly the Keynesian theory of wages and employment and the Keynesian theory of interest. And it concludes with a discussion of a subject that is extremely relevant to contemporary problems of economic policy formation, the use of guidelines and incomes policy as an instrument for containing inflation.

In his own Preface to the volume, Professor Bronfenbrenner characterizes the book as "old fashioned," in the sense that it places a heavy emphasis on "reformulation and restatement." This in my judgment is a virtue rather than a fault. Knowledge is painful to acquire and too easy to forget; and in a busy and bustling profession, it is too easy to be fascinated by each new wave as it rolls in and to overlook the fact that the tide is ebbing out (or flowing in, as the case may be). The purpose of the Aldine Treatises is precisely to enable an author to take stock of a particular field of knowledge and to express his own judgments on what is currently relevant and what has been transitory in importance. In that context, a reformulation and restatement in contemporary terms of the past contributions that have proven valuable by the test of time renders an important service to the current generation of economists.

Harry G. Johnson

Preface

This is an old-fashioned income distribution book. It was written by a theoretical economist and concentrates on economic theory. It follows the tradition of John Bates Clark's *Distribution of Wealth* (1899), Sir John Hicks' *Theory of Wages* (1932), and my teacher Paul Douglas' *Theory of Wages* (1934); these names lead a long list of intellectual creditors.

What makes the book old-fashioned is, primarily, its content of "reformulation and restatement," which also makes it long. I am unwilling to discard neoclassical economics, either marginalism or the production function, either at the micro-economic or the macro-economic level. Unlike the ultra-Keynesians, I do not believe that distribution is determined wholly or even primarily in output markets, making the input markets shadow-boxing arenas. At the same time, I try to understand those who think otherwise and to present their positions with a modicum of fairness and a minimum of vituperation. As a result, some sections may sound like a minor Mozart essaying rock and roll.

But my main excuse for length is "balance" between distributional ideology (Chapters 1 and 5), distributional statistics (Chapters 2 to 4), distributional micro-economics (Chapters 6 to 10, 12, and 14 to 15), and distributional macro-economics (Chapters 11, 13 and 16). Chapter 17, on incomes policies, is something of an afterthought.

Felix Klein prided himself on his ability to present various branches of elementary mathematics "from an advanced standpoint," i.e., with maximum rigor, elegance, and generality. My aim is almost precisely the opposite; I attempt to present advanced economics "from an elementary standpoint," i.e., retaining some tenuous contact with intuitional "soul" and with matters of interest outside the economics profession. The price of "soul" is often verbosity.

Paul Douglas, Frank Knight, Oskar Lange, Abba Lerner, Henry Schultz, Henry Simons, and Jacob Viner, each in his own way, interested me as a Chicago student in one or another distributional problem in the Dark Ages when Keynes' *General Theory* (1936) was peering over the horizon. I have taught distribution periodically since 1947 at nine American universities (Wisconsin, Washington, Michigan State, Minnesota, Colorado, Carnegie-Mellon, Pittsburgh, Stanford, and Harvard, in temporal order) and one Japanese university (Kobe). My pedagogical start, and therefore the start of this book, was however a curmudgeonly revolt on two fronts: against the conventional "theory" course that was concentrated on output markets until the last week, when "oh yes, input prices aren't really given after all;" and against the conventional "labor" course in which "democratic business unionism" is an American Institution and can therefore do no wrong.

In nine American and one Japanese universities, one accumulates a number of colleagues. Some are sympathetic and some are not. From colleagues interested in distribution, both more or less sympathetic to my biases, I have learned a good deal and suffered frequent correction of my errors. Some of the results are reflected here. My principal creditors on colleague account are James Earley, Harold Groves, Robert Lampman, Walter Morton, Selig Perlman, and Eugene Rotwein (Wisconsin); Charles Killingsworth, Thomas Mayer, and Victor Smith (Michigan State); O. H. Brownlee, John Buttrick, Leonid Hurwicz, Anne Krueger, and N. J. Simler (Minnesota); Myron Joseph, Morton Kamien, Michael Lovell, Robert Lucas, Allan Meltzer, and Leonard Rapping (Carnegie-Mellon); Otto Eckstein, John Gurley, Harold Lydall, and Melvin Reder (Stanford, including the Center for Advanced Study in the Behavioral Sciences).

Happy the book that is not badly timed, meaning that no major contributions appeared too late to mention, while the manuscript was going through the press. This volume is not among the happy ones. The principal authors unfairly neglected in consequence include Charles E. Ferguson on neoclassical distribution theory, Friedrich Lutz on interest theory, Harold Lydall and Joseph Stiglitz on personal income distribution, and Lester Thurow on the problem of poverty.

While distributing kudos, I cannot forget Harry Johnson, Aldine's official economics editor, and Sidney Weintraub, my personal unofficial one. Neither lets any nonsense get by him; to add to my worries, one is a neoclassicist and the other an ultra-Keynesian, so they occasionally disagree on the definition of nonsense. Among my several graduate-student assistants, Shigeo Minabe at Kobe and Toshihisa Toyoda at Carnegie-Mellon have been real gems. Of the secretaries who have strained their eyes over the manuscript, Mrs. Mary Jo McClure (Carnegie-Mellon) and Mrs. Helena A. Smith (Center for Advanced Study in the Behavioral Sciences) have been both most hardworking and most forgiving.

It is usual to absolve all listed persons from complicity in remaining errors. This is difficult to justify in this case. Some listed persons have tempted me beyond my intellectual depth, and should bear part of the consequences. Had I sought rigor sufficient to satisfy other listed persons, not one line would ever have been written. This might have been a good thing, and no "remaining errors" would have existed.

On the side of finance *cum* leisure, much of the writing was done during my tenure of a Ford Foundation Research Professorship at Carnegie-Mellon and of a National Science Foundation Fellowship at the Center for Advanced Study in the Behavioral Sciences. I am duly grateful for these misallocations of funds.

Every married man's wife improves his professional acumen, his scholarship, his mathematics, his statistics, his English, or at least his typing. Or so it seems. Teruko Okuaki Bronfenbrenner, however, is not singularly competent in any of those respects. My main reason for thanking her is that she has been a better-than-average psychiatric nurse. Need I say more?

The book is dedicated to the brilliant failures among 25 years of graduate students. One always learns from one's better students, but such is not the point of this dedication. The point is, rather, the disturbingly low correlation between the amounts individual students taught me and the professional statures they later achieved. The unanticipated successes I had best write off as mistakes in my own judgment. The brilliant failures, however, are another matter. Collectively, and combined with others' brilliant failures, they represent a real loss to "intellectual eminence and scholarship sublime."

What happened to them? Some, perhaps, I overestimated even as students. Some burned themselves out, like Olympic swimmers. Others concentrated their talents on playing one or another speculative market or on climbing one or another organizational pyramid. Some found their greatest comparative advantages in action agencies, in social reform, in pure teaching unadulterated by research, or in raising families. Some were victims of poor physical or mental health, or accidents in various forms. This dedication is to them and their work, as they might have been.

Contents

CHAPTER ONE

The Disputed Importance
of Distribution

Is distribution a sufficiently important problem for serious study, and if so, why? The views of economists have varied widely, both in the historical development of economic thought and in the writings of at any given period. At one extreme, some see the distribution of income, wealth, and power as *the* economic problem, far outranking "scarcity" or "efficiency." At the opposite extreme, some see distribution as a totally uninteresting problem—the outcome of more basic decisions "up the line." This chapter aims to provide a representative sample of economists' divergent views.

Distribution Is Fundamental

1.   One of the earliest and best known affirmations of the importance of distribution comes from Ricardo's *Principles* of 1819,[1] with rumbling undertones of class conflict rather than universal harmony:

> The produce of the earth—all that is derived from its surface by the united application of labour, machinery, and capital, is divided among three classes of the community; namely, the proprietor of the land, the owner of the stock or capital necessary for its cultivation, and the labourers by whose industry it is cultivated.

1. David Ricardo, *Principles of Political Economy,* in Piero Sraffa (ed.) , *Works and Correspondence of David Ricardo* (Cambridge: Cambridge University Press, 1951) , vol. i, p. 5.

But in different stages of society, the proportions of the whole produce of the earth which will be allotted to each of these classes, under the names of rent, profit, and wages, will be essentially different . . .

To determine the laws which regulate this distribution, is the principal problem in Political Economy.

The "readable Ricardo" of John Stuart Mill makes the point more strongly and succinctly in a passage dating from 1848 and paraphrased ever since by "economy of abundance" writers, to whom classical economics is supposedly anathema:[2]

It is only in the backward countries of the world that increased production is still an important object; in those most advanced, what is economically needed is a better distribution.

A half century later, John Bates Clark reasserted the "supreme importance" of distribution, including his characteristic ethical note:[3]

For practical men, and hence for students, supreme importance attaches to one economic problem—that of the distribution of wealth among different claimants . . . The welfare of the laboring classes depends on whether they get much or little; but their attitude toward other classes—and therefore, the stability of the social state—depends chiefly on the question, whether the amount they get, be it large or small, is what they produce. If they create a small amount of wealth, and get the whole of it, they may not seek to revolutionize society; but if it were to appear that they produce an ample amount and get only a part of it, many of them would become revolutionists, and all would have the right to do so.

During the same period, Clark's British contemporary John A. Hobson was developing in volume after volume a maldistribution theory of business depressions, combining materials from underconsumptionists (Lauderdale, Malthus, Sismondi) and Socialists (Marx, Engels, Rodbertus). Maldistribution theories themselves, which we shall examine in Chapter 5, have never achieved wide acceptance among professional economists[4] because they do not explain *recovery* from economic depression in any sys-

2. Mill, *Principles of Political Economy*, ed. by W. J. Ashley (London: Longmans, 1900), p. 749. A second heretical aphorism of Mill on distribution, that it is "a matter of human institution solely," whereas the laws of production "partake of the character of physical truths," is found *ibid.*, pp. 199 f.

3. Clark, *The Distribution of Wealth* (New York: Macmillan, 1899), pp. i, 4.

4. Gottfried Haberler, in his standard *Prosperity and Depression*, 3rd ed. (Lake Success: United Nations, 1946), p. 119, comments on maldistribution theories generally: "It is difficult to summarize these theories because . . . their scientific standard is lower than the standard of those reviewed earlier . . . it is only in regard to certain phases of the cycle that these theorists have anything original to contribute. The under-consumption theory is a theory of the crisis and depression rather than a theory of the cycle."

tematic or convincing way. But within the trade union and Socialist movements, the British Labour party and the American New Deal, maldistributionism entered nevertheless into an unquestioned social and economic gospel, and maintained interest in the distribution problem as such.

Social reformers have also harped constantly on distributional themes, not only because they found in maldistribution the explanation of depressions but also because of ethical reasons. Galbraith has restated their case:[5]

> If people were poor, as in fact they were, their only hope lay in a redistribution of income. Much though Ricardo and his followers might dissent, there were always some who believed that redistribution might be possible. All Marxists took a drastic redistribution for granted. Throughout the nineteenth century the social radical had no choice but to advocate the redistribution of wealth and income. If he wanted to change things, this was his only course. To avoid this issue was to avoid all issues.
>
> The *formal* liberal attitude toward inequality has changed little over the years. It is a trifle uncouth to urge a policy of soaking the rich. Yet on the whole the rich man remains the natural antagonist of the poor. Economic legislation continue to be a contest between the interests of the two. No other question in economic policy is ever so important as the effect of a measure on the distribution of income. The test of the good liberal is still that he is never fooled and that he never yields on issues favoring the wealthy. Other questions occupy his active attention, but this is the constant.

The classical-economist and classical-Socialist concern with distribution and redistribution has become especially marked in India. It is not easy to determine the precise meaning of the Indian government's "socialist pattern of society . . . not rooted in any doctrine or dogma." One element is, however, stated to be "a progressive reduction of the concentration of incomes, wealth, and economic power," and it was listed as one of four paramount goals of the Second Five-Year Plan. Eventually, the Indian people are to receive incomes at advanced-country standards, largely in public employment. In the public sector, not only will property incomes be minimal, but skilled workers and managers will receive relatively small differentials over common labor. As for private industry, it is seen as a composite mass of small proprietorships, partnerships, and cooperatives, "function[ing] in unison with the public sector."[6] "Unison with the pub-

5. John Kenneth Galbraith, *The Affluent Society* (London: Pelican, 1962), pp. 73, 76 (running quotations).

6. Government of India, *Second Five Year Plan, A Draft Outline* (National Planning Commission, 1956), pp. 9, 7; *Third Five Year Plan, A Draft Outline* (National Planning Commission, 1960), p. 2. During the Himalayan conflict of 1962–63 with China, a "ceiling on emoluments" of Rs. 3000 ($600 approx.) per month was imposed in public employment, and a ceiling Rs. 5000 was proposed in the Indian Parliament. See H. K. Paranjape, "Ceiling on Emoluments," *Economic Weekly* (March 30, 1963).

lic sector" includes distributive equalitarianism, if the cream of India's technical and managerial skills is not to be drawn into private industry.

Pandit Nehru's personal position on distribution was stronger than that of the government he led. The running quotation below, from *Glimpses of World History*, may owe a special flavor to having been written in prison:[7]

> Democracy, if it means anything, means equality; not merely the equality of possessing a vote, but economic and social equality. Capitalism means the very opposite: a few people holding economic power and using this to their own advantage . . . there is no equality under this system, and the liberty allowed is only within the limits of capitalist laws meant to preserve capitalism.
>
> The conflict between capitalism and democracy is often hidden by misleading propaganda and by the outward forms of democracy, and the sops that the owning classes throw to the other classes to keep them more or less contented . . . when there are no more sops left to be thrown, the conflict comes to a head. When that stage comes, all the supporters of capitalism band themselves together to face the danger to their vested interests. Liberals and such-like groups disappear, and the forms of democracy are put aside.
>
> Some people imagine that all this could be avoided if a few sensible persons were in charge. This is a very misleading idea, for the fault does not lie with individuals, but with a wrong system. Groups that occupy dominant or privileged positions convince themselves by an amazing self-deception and hypocrisy that their special privileges are a just reward of merit. It is impossible to convince a dominant group that its privileges are unjust. And so, inevitably, come clashes and conflicts and revolution, and infinite suffering.

Distribution is Unimportant

2.   Reaction against what we have called the classical stress on distribution seems to have set in shortly before World War II and to have progressed further in the United States than in Europe. A clear statement, with no claims to originality, is found in the first formal work on welfare economics.[8]

> It is evident that, provided the dividend accruing to the poor is not diminished, increases in the size of the national income, if they occur in isolation without anything else happening, must involve increases in economic welfare.

Let us explore the implications of this doctrine, which became for a time conventional in welfare economics. In an extreme case, where all of

---

7. Saul K. Padover (ed.) , *Nehru on World History* (Bloomington: Indiana University Press, 1962) , pp. 284–286.

8. A. C. Pigou, *Economics of Welfare,* 4th ed. (London: Macmillan, 1932) , p. 82.

a given increase in national income accrues to the rich, or to the owners of property, while the relative share of the poor, or the working classes, is reduced, conventional welfare economists would nonetheless maintain that economic welfare has risen. (Students of Marxism will recall that such a decline in the labor or proletarian share is, on one interpretation, precisely what *Das Kapital* calls "increasing misery.")

Pigou's point is made again a generation later by Simons in the United States, in protest against the maldistributionism of the New Deal:[9]

> Our primary problem is production. The common man or average family has a far greater stake in the size of our aggregate income than in any possible redistribution of income.

The Affluent Society gives a new twist to the argument, since to Galbraith the relevant "production" or "growth" alternative to redistribution includes primarily public goods and leisure (financed by sales taxation), rather than private goods and services.

The anticlassical reaction has progressed so far in America that, in Galbraith's words,[10] "as pornography has become more popular, inequality has become obscene. Ours is a classless society. We must not set the poor against the rich, or possibly vice versa." Other eminent economists have expressed astonishment that intelligent persons should concern themselves seriously with such meaningless abstractions as the "labor share" and the "rate of exploitation."[11] It is also symptomatic in Western Europe that some economic policy programming models call the existing distribution a condition of "social equilibrium," and impose the restriction that it not be disturbed. At the same time, within the Socialist world, as early as 1920 the U.S.S.R. was denouncing that petty-bourgeois heresy, concern with *uravnilovka* ("equality").[12]

9. Henry C. Simons, *Economic Policy for a Free Society* (Chicago: University of Chicago Press, 1948), pp. 5 f. Compare also Henry C. Wallich: "From a dollars-and-cents point of view it is quite obvious that over a period of years, even those who find themselves at the short end of inequality have more to gain from faster growth than from any conceivable income redistribution." (Quoted in Galbraith, *op. cit.*, pp. 86 f.)

10. Galbraith, "Let Us Begin: An Invitation to Action on Poverty," *Harper's* (March 1964), p. 24.

11. "I find it hard to see why anybody is interested in the particular figure of the percentage of aggregate income that goes to wages." Milton Friedman, in David Mc Cord Wright (ed.), *The Impact of the Union* (New York: Harcourt Brace, 1951), p. 69.

12. Jan Tinbergen, *On the Theory of Economic Policy* (Amsterdam: North Holland, 1952), pp. 15, 20, 48, 75. Also not to be displaced (downward) is the real wage rate. For Soviet practice, plus citations from Marx, Lenin, and Stalin, see Harry Schwartz, *Russia's Soviet Economy*, 2nd ed. (Englewood Cliffs, N.J.: Prentice-Hall, 1954), pp. 90 ff., 534 f. In the post-Stalin period, a Czech economist, Antonin Bruzek, claims that "it is necessary in the socialist countries to maintain and even increase a certain differen-

3.   Table 1.1 presents in paradigm form three leading positions on the
distribution problem. These are the Capitalist, Social Democratic, and
Communist, of which the second system has retained the most interest in
income distribution as such. The table separates positions as to the desirable size of the private property share in functional distribution and the

Table 1.1.   Three Leading Positions on Distribution Problems

	Importance of Distribution	Desirable Property Share	Desirable Wage Differentials
Capitalist	Minor	Finite	Large
Social Democratic	Major	Infinitesimal	Small
Communist	Minor	Infinitesimal	Large

desirable size of wage differentials in personal distribution. Here, interestingly enough, the Capitalist position differs from the Social Democratic
more completely than from the Communist. Capitalistic wage differentials, often relatively large, are determined by market forces including
collective bargaining, giving rise to complaints of "labor aristocracy." Under Communism, on the other hand, at least in its Socialist stage prior to
"full Communism," these differentials may be kept large as matters of
policy. High differentials are expected to encourage the formation and
supply of human capital and thereby increase production.

Criteria for Judging Economic Systems

4.   To speak of the distribution problem as being major or minor means,
of course, major or minor relative to some other economic problem or to
some other criterion for judging an economic system. Such criteria are
subjective matters. The writer's personal predilections have crystallized
along six lines, four of them (including the distributional) purely eco-

---

tiation of income according to the work done . . . If this condition is not fulfilled,
economc growth is slowed down and . . . incomes cannot rise sufficiently." "The Main
Factors and Methods of the Income Distribution of the Population in the Czechoslovak
Socialist Republic," (Marchal and Ducros, *The Distribution of National Income* (New
York: St. Martin's Press, 1968) , pp. 246 f.
    At the same time, a major Soviet wage-structure reform was carried out during the
decade 1956–1965, featuring "reduction in occupational and industrial differentials in
basic wage rates. The number of grades and the range of rates . . . were reduced and
generally the increase in basic rates was larger for the lower grades and in the lower-
paying industries." Janet G. Chapman, "Wages," in *The Soviet System and Democratic
Society: A Comparative Encyclopedia* (Freiburg: Harder, forthcoming)

nomic,[13] the other two semieconomic. The "judgment criteria" topic is not part of distribution theory proper, but helps assess its importance.

The first criterion is a conventional one. What average or per capita level of living does the economic system provide at the present time?

The second criterion introduces issues of economic growth and resource conservation. What prospects for improvement in the level of living does the economic system provide for the foreseeable future?

The third criterion introduces the issues of economic stability. How stable is the average level of living against pressures in a downward direction? (Short-term pressures are associated with business recession and depression; long-term ones are associated with various phenomena from aging to automation.)

The fourth criterion is the distributional one. How equitably does the economic system allocate levels of living among its economic citizens?

Passing on to the semieconomic criteria, the fifth is as much political

13. Many economists have drawn up other sets of criteria. Three sets are summarized below:

(a) Sumner Slichter, in *The American Economy* (New York: Knopf, 1948), pp. 187 ff., lists seven economic and four semieconomic tests against which to measure American performance; all eleven tests are substantive rather than formal. (1) Is the economy good at increasing output per man-hour? (2) Has the economy provided people with reasonable security and abundant opportunities? (3) Does the economy adjust itself effectively to new conditions? (4) Does the economy distribute its product widely and fairly? (5) Does the economy provide a reasonable balance between the interests of consumers and the interests of producers? (6) Does the economy distribute enough income on the basis of need? (7) Does the economy permit a substantial amount of income to be acquired in uneconomic ways—misrepresenting goods, restricting production, shifting real costs to workers or the community, or wasting resources? (8) Is industry operated with proper regard for its workers and their needs as human beings? (9) Are economic institutions favorable to the development of great work in noneconomic fields—art, literature, religion, science, philosophy, etc.? (10) Does the economy furnish a favorable environment for democratic institutions? (11) Do the economic institutions help build a satisfactorily balanced scale of values?

(b) Bela Balassa's criteria are more formal (*The Hungarian Experience in Economic Planning* [New Haven: Yale University Press, 1959], pp. 5–24). He has five criteria: (1) static efficiency in resource allocation; (2) dynamic efficiency "indicated by the hypothetical growth rate . . . attainable . . . under a given resource use and saving ratio;" (3) the actual income growth rate; (4) consumer satisfaction; (5) income distribution.

(c) Peter J. D. Wiles goes all out, deflating all alternative criteria in favor of growth alone. To Wiles, growth is "better than the optimum allocation of resources . . . or even full employment, . . . a cuckoo in the nest of economic topics." This single-criterion position he develops in "Growth Versus Choice," *Ec. J.* (June 1956). For the opposite extreme, downgrading growth, see Tibor Scitovsky "What Price Economic Progress?" in *Papers on Welfare and Growth* (Stanford: Stanford University Press, 1964), no. 13; W. Arthur Lewis, "Is Economic Growth Desirable?" in *Theory of Economic Growth* (Homewood, Ill.: Irwin, 1955), pp. 424–435; M. Bronfenbrenner, "The High Cost of Economic Development," *Land Econ.* (May and August 1953).

as economic. To what extent is the economic system compatible with general civil liberties, in the sense of the Bill of Rights of the United States
Constitution? Putting the issue in the negative: To what extent does the
economic system depend on the forced labor of slaves, prisoners, or class
enemies? Upon the suppression of opinions in opposition to a sacred
Plan? Upon "cruel and unusual punishments" for economic offenses like
evasion of rationing, speculation in inventories, private entrepreneurship
in commodity production, or attempted "voting with one's feet" by escape
abroad?

The sixth and last criterion is as much medical and psychological as
economic, and in its psychiatric aspects builds upon the views of Erich
Fromm, Jules Henry, and Herbert Marcuse:[14] To what extent is the economic system compatible with the physical and mental health of its economic citizens? Are people systematically worked to death before their
time, as through neglect of safety considerations, or insufficient food and
sleep? Are people systematically poisoned by polluted environments? Are
they systematically deprived of privacy, or of the companionship of other
family members, particularly their wives and children? Are they first alien-
ated, then driven to alcohol, drugs, ulcers, and nervous collapse by artificial competition for artificial goals—the "squirrel cage" and "rat race"
depicted by anticapitalist social psychology?

5.   Of these six criteria or dimensions, let us concentrate, in Figure 1.1,
upon two dimensions only. These are the average level of living and the
equity of distribution. Let us also go a long step further, and use as proxy
for the average level of living the national income per capita, and as proxy
for the *equity* of distribution some simple statistic of its equality with no
regard to "claims" or "merit," such as the inverse of the coefficient of variation of personal incomes. Let us plot the average level of living alone the
vertical axis, and the equity of distribution along the horizontal one, and
indicate by points (A, B) the current positions of two societies (America
and Britain) with respect to these variables. The United States has the
higher level of living, and Britain the more equitable distribution.

To show the subjectivity of the question "How important is distribution?" we can add two indifference maps for two hypothetical individuals
I and *J*—interplanetary Crusoes, perhaps, selecting terrestrial habitats. Individual *I* (indifference curves I_1) resembles the conventional welfare
economist or Midwestern Republican, out of Shylock or Harpagon by
Gradgrind, Bounderby, or Soames Forsyte. His indifference curves are

14. Innocent of psychological or psychiatric training, the writer owes his appreciation of the psychological implications of economic systems to Walter A. Weisskopf.

horizontal; in selecting between societies he considers only levels of living, without regard to distribution. He will prefer America to Britain, since point A lies on indifference curve I_3 and point B on indifference curve I_1.

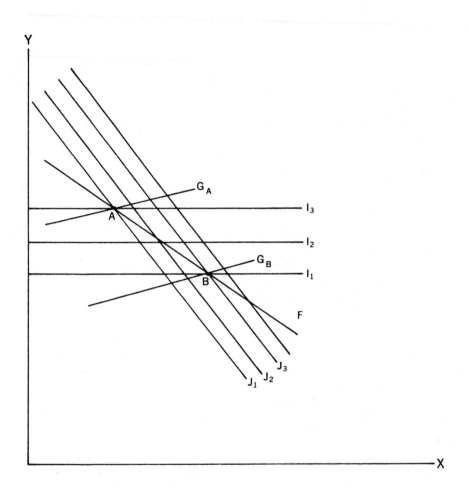

Figure 1.1

He may also maintain that the two points A and B lie on a production-possibility function like F, whose downward slope implies that increased distributional equity lowers output in the long run—by reducing saving and capital formation, "killing the goose that lays the golden eggs."

Individual *J* (indifference curves *J*ᵢ) is an unreconstructed Social Democrat, New Dealer, or follower of Pandit Nehru.[15] His indifference curves are drawn diagonally, meaning that to him equity is indeed important. In extreme cases, the J_i may be vertical. Quite generally, the more nearly vertical the J_i curves, the more important is equity to *J*. *J* will prefer Britain to America if his indifference curves are steep enough, as they are in Figure 1.1. Here, point *B* lies on indifference curve J_3 and point *A* on indifference curve J_1. The well-meaning and well-financed appeals for "the American way of life" leave *J* completely cold, because of his concern with income distribution.

As for production possibilities, *J* will probably deny the existence of such a function as *F*, passing through *A* and *B*. He will rather ascribe the difference between the living levels of America and Britain to considerations of population, of resources, of history ("Who suffered most in recent warfare?") or of such abstractions as "stage of development" or "economic structure." If he is maldistributionist in his theorizing, *J* may envisage *different* production possibility functions G_A and G_B for the two societies. Each of these functions probably slopes upward because, in *J*'s view, equitable distribution increases effective demand and keeps the economy working at high pressure and full capacity.

Actual positions are occasionally more extreme than those of our hypothetical *I* and *J*. On the side of *I*, the conservative economist Hayek introduces antitotalitarian considerations to deny the relevance of distributional equity:[16]

> That the concept of justice is so commonly and readily applied to the distribution of incomes is entirely the effect of an erroneous anthropomorphic interpretation of society as an organization rather than a spontaneous order . . . Nobody distributes income in a market order . . . and to speak of a just or unjust distribution is therefore just nonsense . . . All efforts to secure a

15. A quaint example of this type of thinking is Sontoku Ninomiya (1787–1855), the "peasant sage" of Tokukawa Japan. "In a community in which its members are faithful followers of Ninomiya's teaching, none will be excessively rich or inordinately poor, and though the private properties of individual persons may not increase in a striking manner, living conditions of all people will be stabilized and they will be able to lead a happier and fuller life. One is safer to live in one-storeyed house, 15 metres high, built on a solid table-land 90 metres high, than to live in a many-storeyed house, 100 metres high, standing on frail ground of sand with a depth of one metre. Likewise, one who lives in a community where there is nobody too rich or too powerful, will feel safer and happier than one who lives in a community where only a few are exceptionally rich and the prepondering (*sic*) majority are poor." Hyoji Sugawara, "Life, Character, and Teaching of Sontoku Ninomiya," in Tadaatsu Ishiguro (ed.), *Ninomiya Sontoku, His Life and "Evening Talks"* (Tokyo: Kenkyusha, 1955), pp. 73 f. (running quotation).

"just" distribution must therefore be directed towards turning the spontaneous order of the market into . . . a totalitarian order.

On the side of J, the revolutionary philosopher Marcuse regards further extensions of private (noncollective) consumption as responses to "false" needs and "products of a society whose dominant interest demands repression," leading not to satisfaction but merely to "euphoria in unhappiness."[17]

Leaving to later chapters the problem of decision between the rival production-possibility estimates F and G, we may say here that no objective basis for choice exists as between the indifference maps I_1 and J_1. It follows that we cannot say objectively whether or not point A is socially preferable to B, or whether or not the American system is preferable to the British.[18] Nor is it completely safe to say that either country necessarily gets the distribution it desires.

At the same time, an important objective point should be made. Our several criteria are not independent of each other, but interrelated. It is difficult—it may even be impossible—to operate on one of them, or on a subset of them, without undesired repercussions upon the others. If rapidity of economic growth and increase in the labor share, for instance, are our principal desiderata, and we accept a "Keynesian" (or Kaldorian) theory of aggregative income distribution,[19] we face an uncomfortable dilemma. We must face (if we cannot modify) its conclusions—that a rising growth rate lowers the labor share relative to the share of property (or, under Socialism, the share of the state), and that a rising labor share will decelerate economic progress.

One solution of this dilemma is to regard growth as valuable primarily for permitting redistributive amelioration of poverty at little or no *absolute* cost to rich classes and nations. Upward trends on diagrams are, in this view, only slightly less relevant than a third car in every garage or a second television set in every bedroom. If an increasing growth rate in-

16. Friedrich A. von Hayek, "Principles of a Liberal Social Order," (mimeographed: Mont Pelerin Society, Tokyo, 1966), pp. 9 f.

17. Herbert Marcuse, *One-Dimensional Man* (Boston: Beacon, 1964), pp. 4 f.

18. Nicholas Rescher, in *Distributive Justice* (Indianapolis: Bobbs-Merrill, 1966), pp. 35–38, proposes, as a basis for comparison, the "effective averages" of the two distributions. If the mean (income) of a distribution be M and its standard deviation σ, the effective average E is $\left(M - \dfrac{\sigma}{2} \right)$. This suggestion, while ingenious, does not escape bias. In Figure 1.1, it would require the poorer country (Britain) to have only half the σ of the richer one (U.S.) for the same E value.

19. See Chapter 16, sections 32–36. The implications cited in the text refer only to full-employment conditions, as does the Kaldor theory itself.

terferes with the alleviation of poverty, then, for nearly every finite trad-off, it is the growth rate that should go. A rising labor share, however, is but an imperfect proxy for the alleviation of poverty; labor aristocracies on the one hand, widows and orphans on the other, prevent any one-to-one correspondence between the two.

Another solution is to argue, with Harry Johnson, that the relative importance of income distribution should decrease as a country develops, although the case of India suggests that it does not always do so in practice. Johnson argues.[20]

> There is . . . a conflict between economic efficiency and social justice. The extent or importance of this conflict is likely to vary according to the state of economic development. The more advanced a country is, the more likely are its citizens to have consciences about the distribution of income, and to accept the high taxation necessary to correct it . . . ; the higher the level of income reached, the less serious will be any slowing down of the rate of growth brought about by redistribution policies. An advanced country can afford to sacrifice some growth for the sake of social justice. But the cost of greater equality may be great to any economy at a low level of economic development, . . . particularly, as it is evident that historically the great bursts of economic growth have been associated with . . . big windfall gains; it would therefore seem unwise for a country anxious to enjoy rapid growth to insist too strongly on policies aimed at ensuring economic equality.

The Dormancy of Distribution: Trend or Long Swing?

6. In developed democracies (with few exceptions), professional and popular interest in distribution tended to be dormant during the half century ending in 1960. (The depressed 1920s in Britain and 1930s in America represent intermissions in the process toward dormancy.) This tendency was precisely contrary to the fears of conservative philosophers during the classical period of political economy. These philosophers had doubted the compatibility of political democracy with economic recognition of talents and ability. This section speculates about why interest in distribution was blunted, and on the likelihood that this change may be permanent.[21]

---

20. H. G. Johnson, *Money, Trade, and Economic Growth*, 2d ed. (London: Unwin, 1964), p. 159.

21. I have spelled out these views more fully in "Some Neglected Implications of Secular Inflation," in Kenneth K. Kurihara (ed.), *Post-Keynesian Economics* (New Brunswick: Rutgers University Press, 1954); and in "The American Distribution and Inflation Problems," *Annals of the Hitotsubashi Academy* (April 1959).

Three examples of conservative fears of democracy, and of the economic lynching to follow, are provided by the three running quotations that follow, all dealing primarily with the United States. The first is by John Adams, second President; the second is by Benjamin Watkins Leigh, a Virginia senator of the Jacksonian period; the third is by the early Victorian historian, poet, and critic, Lord Macaulay:[22]

President John Adams: Suppose a nation, ten millions in number, all assembled together; not more than one or two millions will have lands, houses, or any personal property. Would [you] be responsible that, if all were to be decided by a vote of the majority, the eight or nine millions who have no property would not think of usurping over the rights of the one or two millions who have? Perhaps, at first, prejudice, habit, shame or fear, principle or religion, would restrain the poor from attacking the rich, and the idle from usurping on the industrious; but the time would not be long before courage and enterprise would come, and pretexts be invented by degrees, to countenance the majority in dividing all the property. Debts would be abolished first; taxes laid heavy on the rich, and not at all on the others; and at last a downright equal division of everything be demanded, and voted. What would be the consequence of this? The idle, the vicious, the intemperate, would rush into the utmost extravagance of debauchery, sell and spend all their share, and then demand a new division of those who purchased from them. The moment the idea is admitted into society, that property is not as sacred as the laws of God, anarchy and tyranny commence.

Senator Benjamin Watkins Leigh: Power and property may be separated for a time by force or fraud—but divorced, never. For so soon as the pang of separation is felt, property will purchase power, or power will take over property. And either way, there must be an end to free government.

Lord Macaulay: Institutions purely democratic must, sooner or later, destroy liberty or civilization, or both. In Europe, where the population is dense, the effect of such institutions would be almost instantaneous. In 1848 a pure democracy was established [in France]. There was reason to expect a general spoliation, a national bankruptcy, a new partition of the soil, a maximum of prices, a ruinous load of taxation laid on the rich for the purpose of supporting the poor. Happily the danger was averted; and now there is a despotism, a silent tribune, an enslaved press. Liberty is gone, but civilization has been saved. If we had a purely democratic government [in Great Britain], the effect would be the same. Either the poor would plunder the rich, and civilization

22. President Adams: *The Works of John Adams* (Boston: Little Brown, 1850–1856), VI, pp. 508 f., reprinted in Massimo Salvadori (ed.), *The American Economic System* (Indianapolis: Bobbs-Merrill, 1963), pp. 19 f. Senator Leigh: Quoted by Leonard Silk, "Business and Government: A New Balance of Power?" *Business Week* (July 17, 1965). Lord Macaulay: Letter to Henry S. Randall, published as "Lord Macaulay on American Institutions," *Harper's Magazine* February 1877), reprinted in Horace Knowles (ed.), *Gentlemen, Scholars, and Scoundrels* (New York: Harper, 1959), pp. 90–92.

would perish, or order and prosperity would be saved by a strong military government, and liberty would perish.

Your fate is deferred by a physical cause. As long as you have a boundless extent of fertile and unoccupied land, the Jeffersonian politics may continue without any fatal calamity. But the time will come when New England will be as thickly populated as Old England. You will have your Manchesters and Birminghams, and in those Manchesters and Birminghams hundreds of thousands of artisans will assuredly be sometimes out of work. Then your institutions will be fairly brought to the test. Your government will never be able to restrain a distressed and discontented majority. For with you the majority is the government, and has the rich, who are always a minority, absolutely at its mercy.

The day will come when in the State of New York, a multitude of people, none of whom has had more than half a breakfast, or expects to have more than half a dinner, will choose a Legislature. On one side is a statesman preaching patience, respect for vested rights, strict observance of public faith. On the other is a demagogue ranting about the tyranny of capitalists and usurers, and asking why anybody should be permitted to drink champagne and ride in a carriage when thousands of honest folk are in want of necessaries. Which of the two candidates is likely to be preferred by a working-man who hears his children cry for more bread? There will be, I fear, spoliation. The spoliation will increase the distress. The distress will produce fresh spoliation. There is nothing to stop you. Your Constitution is all sail and no anchor. Either civilization or liberty must perish. Either some Caesar or Napoleon will seize the reins of government with a strong hand, or your republic will be as fearfully plundered and laid waste by barbarians in the twentieth century as the Roman Empire was in the fifth, with this difference, that your Huns and Vandals will have been engendered within your own country by your own institutions.

The question is not whether Adams and Macaulay were wrong. They have been thus far, egregiously wrong. The question is, rather, why they were wrong, and what the longer-term significance is of their having been wrong.

7.   The main reasons they were wrong about the economic impact of political democracy have been economic affluence and the failure of inequality to increase as predicted. Much of the pre-1914 egalitarian literature turns out, on examination, to be as much about poverty and social minima as about equality. It went without saying that such minima were unobtainable except by redistribution where growth per capita was slow, and that redistribution had to be revolutionary to reverse an assumed trend in the opposite direction. In the twentieth century, however, progress has combined with distributional near-stability to provide an alternative route to social minima, less revolutionary than anticipated. Lamp-

man, writing in the 1950s, envisaged the proportion of Americans living in poverty being halved in a generation by economic progress alone, without changes in the distributive mechanism.[23]

8. Affluence, plus disconfirmation of gloomy predictions about the course of inequality, may have suffered to mute our ancestors' passionate concern with distributional issues to a polite and perfunctory chant.[24] Other factors, however, have operated in the same direction and should not be forgotten.

The most important of these other factors has probably been social mobility in the upward direction. It was easy for an eighteenth- or nineteenth-century writer, on either side of the barricades, to see society as composed of classes with rigid barriers between them. These lines have apparently become more fluid in the advanced countries, possibly due to economic growth, to geographical imperialism (opportunities abroad), and to the prevalence of small families in the upper classes. Class lines have not disappeared sufficiently to eliminate "class" political parties, but voting along existing, objective class lines has been diluted by voting along potential, subjective ones. These potential, subjective lines are determined by the classes to which people have traditionally belonged in the past, or by the classes they expect their children or grandchildren to attain in the future. The vision of a representative poor man regarding himself as a potential capitalist or the ancestor of a capitalist family, and voting accordingly, does not seem to have occurred to Adams, Macaulay—or Marx. (It did occur to Lenin later on.) This vision makes a difference, for however long it endures; especially when it is the potential leadership group of the revolutionary proletariat who see themselves as having a choice between rising out of their class (in Eugene Debs' words) and rising with it.[25]

---

23. For citation (and disagreement), see Michael Harrington, *The Other America* (New York: Macmillan, 1962), pp. 159–163. Subsequent discussion has been voluminous. Two points at issue have been the rate at which the poverty line will itself rise with the national income, and the magnitude of the lower tail of the personal income distribution, consisting of irremediably handicapped persons immune to economic progress. Among the more influential contributions to this literature have been W. H. Locke Anderson, "Trickling Down," *Q.J.E.* (November 1964) and Lowell E. Gallaway, "The Foundations of the 'War on Poverty'," *A.E.R.* (March 1965). Eugene Smolensky speaks of the residual need for "de-tailing" the personal income distribution in "Poverty and Pennsylvania" (mimeographed: Pennsylvania Conference of Economists, 1966).

24. Galbraith certainly believes so, as per his *Affluent Society, op. cit.*, ch. 7.

25. Two widespread beliefs—that social mobility has been rising in America, and that it is significantly higher there than in Western Europe—are difficult to support by quantitative sociological research. Bernard Barber, *Social Stratification* (New York: Harcourt Brace, 1959), ch. 16; also Reinhard Bendix and Seymour Martin Lipset (eds.),

The antidemocratic prophets of economic lynching also exaggerated the unity of the proletarian majority in other ways. This majority has been divided and subdivided along racial, linguistic, religious, and occupational lines. In most advanced countries, it is also divided by types and degrees of skill as well. Like affluence and social mobility, the disunity of the proletariat has been most egregious in the United States, where two or three centuries of mass migration from Europe and Latin American have been superimposed upon an approximate 12 per cent minority descended from black slaves. The United States developed, not surprisingly, a tradition of high skill differentials for its labor aristocracy, who were functionally literate in the English language and adapted to urban life, in contrast with "greenhorns" from overseas, "hicks" and "hillbillies" from the countryside, and "niggers" from the South. However, mutual recrimination between racial and religious segments of the working class, between peasants and urban workers, and between blue- and white-collar groups, are by no means confined to America. Soviet and Chinese Communist leaders have inveighed against "great Russian" and "Han" chauvinism respectively, and have attempted to increase proletarian solidarity by requiring manual labor from intellectuals and farm labor from factory workers.

Antidemocratic pessimists also failed to reckon in their forecasts with liberal societies' fear of the one-party dictatorships and the abridgements of personal liberty that have thus far accompanied, for one or more "Stalinist generations," any drastic changes in distributive arrangements. This fear is not confined to the wealthy or the intellectuals, but extends deeply into the working classes. In all historical cases of capitalist overthrow and socialist establishment, the ousted capitalist, precapitalist, or semicapitalist regime was itself highly dictatorial, or else the revolution was made under the aegis of a socialist army of occupation.

To some indeterminate extent, of course, fear of social revolution and acceptance of the status quo, particularly within the working class, have themselves been more or less deliberately induced by the upper-class minority. The private agencies of mass communication (newspapers, magazines, motion pictures, television, radio) are costly to operate and sometimes highly profitable. They are, like other businesses, owned and managed by individuals who were either wealthy in advance or become wealthy through success in these enterprises. One need deny neither the existence of substantial freedom of the press, nor the impartiality of many individual editors and publishers, nor the struggling survival of radical organs to assert that a certain effective antiredistributionist bias exists in

---

Class, Status and Power (Glencoe, Ill.: Free Press, 1953), pp. 442–453 (Rogoff), pp. 454–464 (Lipset and Bendix), pp. 577–587 (Rogoff).

the aggregate content of the mass media as a whole. Much the same is true of educational institutions, both public and private, and of publicly operated radio and television, although the mechanisms of private influence, sometimes amounting to control, are more complex and indirect. And if we include the political and electoral processes as separate "mass media," the high and rising cost of campaigning has also operated with a similar "pluto-democratic" bias. (The term is Adolf Hitler's.)

9. Consider, finally, the role of creeping inflation. Economic demands, by majorities and minorities alike, are expressed directly and initially as demands for higher money prices, wages, salaries, and incomes, but seldom for benefits so abstruse as larger income shares.[26] With the unplanned demise of the full gold standard in the 1930s, and its replacement by the monetary management of what Marxists call "fictitious values," has evolved a substitute for redistribution quite unrelated to production, growth, or affluence generally. This is inflation of the price level which, unless and until it is overdone (as in Germany and China after two World Wars), permits simultaneous satisfaction of conflicting demands for money income, and thereby acts as a social mollifier or lubricant. So long as money illusion holds its sway, *i.e.*, so long as inflation is held within some such bounds as 5 or 10 per cent per year and perhaps 50 per cent per decade, people continue to think and calculate in conventional money terms. So long as people continue to think and calculate in such terms, a society can solve its distribution problems by inflationary sleight of hand, pretending to distribute 105 or 110 per cent of whatever is produced. The reason hyperinflation exercises, by contrast, an exacerbating effect on distributional tensions is that such inflation dissipates money illusions quickly, imparts to fixed income consumers some consciousness of their losses, and brings on new calculations and demands in real rather than monetary terms.

Creeping inflation also assuages the particular distribution problem of one strategic disadvantaged group. This group includes the untrained (or mistrained) unskilled worker, who is often handicapped by the "wrong" race, religion, age, sex, national origin, or education. In normal times, an employer does not find it worthwhile either to train such workers on the job or to subsidize their training elsewhere, in view of their higher mobility after training. In normal times, also, skilled workers and

26. The most effective American "redistributionist" of the twentieth century was Huey Long. His heyday coincided with the Depression, and he did not speak of income shares directly. His "Every Man a King" gospel proposed an income floor of $5000, financed by higher income and estate taxes ($1 million ceiling on post-tax income, $3 million on post-tax inherited wealth).

their unions object to upgrading potential competitors, and taxpayers see no overriding value in spending public funds to increase underemployment. Only under inflationary disequilibrium, with labor shortages at current wage rates, are employers more willing to take training risks, unions less restrictive, and taxpayers more friendly to vocational education. Normally, as Minsky puts it, "high wage workers, and other affluent citizens, have been subsidized, by way of low product prices, by the poor,"[27] but over-full employment removes the subsidy at the same time that it raises the measured price level.

10.   Adams, Macaulay, and their fellow pessimists were not fools. The possibility must be faced squarely of their being more correct for the future than for the past. In this case, the hibernation of interest in distribution will have been only temporary, and the contradiction between political equality and economic inequality will become more acute. What are the prospects for such a contradiction, to be followed by the economic lynching of the rich, or alternatively, by substantial suppression of the political rights of the majority?

Turning primarily to affluence, there is no certainty that it will continue to outrun aspiration, even in developed democracies. True, it has done so in the past, despite the best efforts of advertising and salesmanship, which black arts are also in a constant process of development. There is, furthermore, no certainty that affluence will continue as an exclusive prerogative of capitalist nations with unequal distributions of income and wealth. What if, for example, the Communists of the U.S.S.R. make good their promises to surpass capitalist living standards by 1980 or 1990, and the shoe passes to the other foot?

11.   In connection with social mobility and its probable future, no less an economist (and no less a conservative) than Frank W. Taussig worried, on the basis of survey research in 1928, that "by the middle of the [20th] century more than two-thirds of the successful businessmen in the United States will be recruited from the sons of business owners (large or small) and business executives (major or minor)." A later critic has inquired: "Are the seats of authority permanently reserved for those born

---

27. Hyman P. Minsky, "The Role of Employment Policy," in Margaret S. Gordon (ed.), *Poverty in America* (San Francisco: Chandler, 1965), p. 184. (Note that inflationary disequilibrium, not inflation itself, is the responsible factor.) At the same time, shortages of unskilled workers are created and the skill differential declines as inflation progresses. (*Ibid.*, p. 184, citing Lloyd Ulman, "Labor Mobility and the Industrial Wage Structure in the Postwar United States," *Q.J.E.* [February 1965]) .

to the purple or the long green? Is it time to throw Horatio Alger out of the library and substitute an industrial version of Burke's Peerage?"[28] The brute statistics, comparing the origins of business leaders in 1928 and 1952 (uncorrected for changes in the underlying population), indicate no major changes. Table 1.2, for example, indicates no cause for acute concern.

Table 1.2. Social Origins of American
Business Leaders, 1928 and 1952

Occupation of Father	1928		1952 (percentage)		Change	
Laborer (unskilled, semi-skilled)	2		5		+3	
Laborer (skilled)	9		10		+1	
Laborer (total)		(11)		(15)		(+4)
Clerk, salesman	5		8		+3	
*Minor executive	7		11		+4	
*Major executive	17		15		−2	
Salariat (total)		(29)		(34)		(+5)
*Owner (small business)	20		18		−2	
*Owner (large business	14		8		−6	
Professional	13		14		+1	
Total		(47)		(40)		(−7)
Farmer	12		9		−3	
Other	1		2		+1	
Grand Total	100		100		0	
Subtotal, Starred Groups	58		52		−6	

SOURCE: W. Lloyd Warner and James C. Abegglen, *Big Business Leaders in America* (New York: Atheneum, 1963), p. 25.

Our concern, however, is less with statistical indicators of upward mobility, with other measures developed by empirical sociologists, or with possible flaws therein, than with the *quality* of mobility, which sociologists cannot yet measure effectively. More important than either the amount or the speed of upward mobility is the distinction between what might be called "competitive" and "bureaucratic" mobility. Competitive mobility features the outsider winning his way to equality with the Establishment, but joining it only after conquest, usually during middle age. Carnegie, Ford, Rockefeller, and Vanderbilt were all examples. Bureaucratic mobil-

28. F. W. Taussig and C. S. Joslyn, *American Business Leaders* (New York: Macmillan, 1932), p. 235, cited by W. Lloyd Warner and James C. Abegglen, *Big Business Leaders in America* (New York: Atheneum, 1963), p. 4; A. H. Raskin, review of Warner and Abegglen, *Saturday Review of Literature.*

ity, by contrast, features the outsider being co-opted into the Establishment at or below the age of thirty by personal favoritism (marrying someone's daughter), by passing examinations (as in Imperial China), or by taking academic degrees.

This difference is important. Potential proletarian leaders could formerly choose the alternative path of direct competition and win out at almost any age short of senility. Today such rough-and-ready types are unlikely to enter prestige colleges, to pass muster as upper-division in-laws, or to impress personnel offices with their paper qualifications until their age for bureaucratic mobility has passed.[29] With reduced opportunities for competitive mobility, they gravitate into leadership positions in the Opposition, as witness John L. Lewis, Walter Reuther, and James R. Hoffa in the American labor movement. Their audience too will be on hand, among their fellows who have also failed to qualify.

Meanwhile, the men on the make who do achieve bureaucratic mobility simultaneously lose their common touch, if they ever had any. They are not "potential proletarian leaders." Their talents seldom endear them to the classes out of which they have risen. Neither their successes nor their means to success characteristically will reconcile unsuccessful competitors to "the system." Quite the contrary, they may brand the system as one where the wrong man, "with a smile and a shoeshine," is upwardly mobile,[30] and the right man damned forever by his name, his accent, his manners, or his late educational start.

---

29. The tendency of middle-class and managerial families to increase in relative size should also be remembered. It may be only temporary, but for so long as it lasts, the rising relative numbers of upper-class sons, nephews, and in-laws will impose an additional quantitative block to upward mobility from "across the tracks" and "back of the yards."

30. The conservative economist David McCord Wright and the neo-Marxian sociologist C. Wright Mills have both made this point. "Wright's Law of Deterioration of Self-Perpetuating Groups" reads:

Where access to the top is conditioned on the consent of those already there, promotion is likely to go to the agreeable conformist rather than the able explorer. The group in power increasingly surrounds itself with yes men. The caliber of the "palace guard" rapidly declines. ("Income Redistribution Reconsidered," in Lloyd A. Metzler and Evsey D. Domar [eds.], *Income Employment, and Public Policy* [New York: Norton, 1948], p. 163.)

Mills is concerned more immediately with the abstract "merit" of the American self-made man:

Even if . . . 90 per cent of the elite were sons of wage workers—but the criteria of co-optation remained what they now are—we could not from that mobility necessarily infer merit . . . In a world of corporate hierarchies, men are selected by those above them in the hierarchy . . . Men shape themselves to fit them, and thus are made by the criteria, the social premiums that prevail. If there is no such thing as

12. A greater measure of working-class unity seems also on its way.[31] The concurrent decline of immigration and illiteracy in advanced countries seems already to be breaking down distinctions. Knots of intractability and prejudice may remain for years—Negroes and Latin Americans in the United States, Arabs and Africans in France, Greeks and Italians in Germany, Koreans and "New Citizens" in Japan—but the trend is clear. As for the dread of communes, Red Guards, and concentration camps inhibiting interest in distributional reform, this depends on the long-term progress of the Soviet "thaw," not to mention how soon the "hundred flowers" will put forth new buds in China. We assume that these changes, if they occur, cannot be concealed for long.

13. This leaves long-term inflation to be considered, meaning a slow and irregular upcreep of the price level, serving as a social lubricant and an evasive agent against income distribution problems. The effectiveness of inflation in this role depends upon its slowness, which in turn depends significantly on money illusion. (Without money illusion, each economic pressure group takes account of predicted further inflation in framing its own demands over a particular period. Under these circumstances, satisfaction of all active claimants may sooner or later—probably sooner—accelerate the inflation beyond the rate tolerable to those passive claimants, the fixed income groups.) Or, alternatively, the effectiveness of inflation as a social lubricant requires some sort of automatic escalation in the incomes of previously fixed-income receivers. Eventually this leads in its turn to a Blondinian tightrope walk between hyperinflationary chaos on the one hand, and, on the other, some restraint on wage and price increases, which reexcites the distributional disputes the inflation initially cured.

---

a self-made man, there is such a thing as a self-used man, and there are many such men among the American elite.

Under such conditions of success there is no virtue in starting out poor and becoming rich . . . In a system of cooptation from above, whether you began rich or poor seems less relevant in revealing what kind of man you are when you have arrived than in revealing the principles of those in charge of selecting the ones who succeed. (Mills, *The Power Elite* [New York: Oxford University Press, 1957], p. 348 f.)

Ralph Turner, "Modes of Social Ascent through Education: Sponsored and Contest Mobility," in A. H. Halsey, Jean Flood, and C. Arnold Anderson (eds.), *Education, Economy, and Society* (New York: Free Press, 1961), ch. 12, ascribes to British education (even) more stress on cultivating "sponsored" mobility than is the case for America.

31. Likewise, an increased measure of cooperative activity between the underdeveloped countries as a group, focused in the United Nations Council for Trade and Development established in 1964.

It seems impossible to prove that this tightrope cannot be walked, or that (even if it cannot) inflation may not yield useful temporary respites from distributional haggling. The writer conjectures, however, that in most countries the chances of success are too small, and the gain of time too brief, to make "stability through inflation" a promising policy. If distributional issues must eventually be met head on to hold an inflation within bounds of some kind, there is something to be said for meeting these issues immediately, before inflation has despoiled the country's fixed-income groups or before the best economic brains have been directed to the creation of not-quite-foolproof escalation schemes for the incomplete protection of one or another subgroup.

14. There is, therefore, reason to anticipate revived public and professional interest in problems of the distribution of income and wealth. Galbraith has spoken, but too soon—or perhaps too late. From the vantage point of the coming generation, the revival has perhaps already set in. In the United States, a landmark was the "Income Revolution" thesis of the National Bureau of Economic Research (see Chapter 3) or rather, the sharp retorts of its critics. In Britain, revival set in initially on the theoretical side, with "monopoly" and "structural" theories of aggregate distribution in relation to capital accumulation and economic growth. These theories have in turn stirred up the ashes in other countries, including the United States, Germany, Holland, and Scandinavia.[32] (For France, we shall cite in Chapter 2 the incomplete economic-sociological treatise of Marchal and Lecaillon; internationally, we have cited already the Marchal-Ducros edition of the Palermo papers of the International Economic Association.)

Distribution and Policy Paralysis

15. For the present, however, distributional issues affect policy decisions mainly by indirection. Their indirect influence typically takes the form of a policy paralysis. Thus, when deflation or disinflation is called for, ac-

---

32. Sidney Weintraub, *Approach to the Theory of Income Distribution* (Philadelphia: Chilton, 1958) and *Keynesian Theory of Employment, Growth and Distribution* (Philadelphia: Chilton, 1966); Paul Davidson, *Theories of Aggregate Income Distribution* (New Brunswick N.J.: Rutgers University Press, 1960); National Bureau of Economic Research, *Studies in Income and Wealth*, vol. 27 (Princeton: Princeton University Press, 1964), and vol. 33 (New York: Columbia University Press, 1969); Wilhelm Krelle, *Verteilungstheorie* (Tübingen: Mohr, 1962); J. G. M. Hilhorst, *Monopolistic Competition, Technical Progress, and Income Distribution* (Rotterdam: Rotterdam University Press, 1965); Karl G. Jungenfelt, *Löneandelen och den Ekonomiska Utvecklingen* (Stockholm: Almqvist and Wiksell, 1966).

tion is delayed because of distributional disagreement about the resulting size and speed of price, wage, and profit changes, or about the timing of any direct wage and price controls. (It is difficult to explain to workers, for example, why wage increases are more inflationary than tax- or interest-rate increases, and almost equally difficult to induce most organized groups to leave such issues, which involve their relative positions so fundamentally, to the apparent randomness of impersonal market determination.) Should tax changes be decided upon, these too will be delayed by distributional arguments about alternative changes in taxes as between income and sales taxes, personal and corporate taxes, and (in graduated schedules) lower and higher brackets. When adjustments to passive trade balances in the international economy are required, there is again distributional delay: should pressure fall on labor costs or profit margins in the industries affected? Is the larger national income obtainable from improved international resource allocation really worth its distributional cost, in terms of relative changes in the prices of labor and capital inputs? If a war on poverty is to be waged, how should costs be distributed between income classes above the poverty line? Even in bloodless technical issues like public-utility pricing, distributional issues can intrude. They may be set off by issues of "democratic pricing," *i.e.*, the subsidy of services used primarily by the poor, or forms of "peak-load pricing" that raise rates at times when and places where the poor use them most heavily.

16. Other situations come readily to mind, particularly in developing areas where distributional considerations are essential elements in political disputes. Palestine is a Middle Eastern case in point. Zionists profess themselves surprised at the intense opposition of the ordinary Arab (as distinguished from the Arab leader) to the expansion of their settlements. They had anticipated no such response, since Jewish capital was simultaneously raising the Palestinian Arab's economic status to the highest in the Arab world of 1919–1939. The apparent explanation is that Zionism also raised both the share of Palestinian income going to "foreigners" (non-Arabs) and the absolute income of the representative Palestinian "foreigner" relative to that of the representative Palestinian Arab. Much the same was true of Palestinian wealth; the share held by foreigners rose, both absolutely and per capita, as a consequence of Zionism.

Similar problems are associated with European settlements and capital exports in Asia and Africa, and with "Yanqui" equivalents in Latin America. In most or all of these cases, foreign capital raises the absolute levels of "native" living—the exceptions are associated with population explosions. At the same time, the "natives'" relative shares in their countries' income and wealth decline, both in the aggregate and per capita. When it comes to determining political reactions, the relative decline normally outweighs the absolute increase. This may lead to anomalous results within developing countries. For example, urban labor, even when its level of living is rising rapidly—both absolutely and relative to the peasantry—is typically more revolutionary and antiforeign than the peasantry—is typically more revolutionary and antiforeign than the peasantry, because labor's living level still remains so low relative to that of the foreigners with whom the workers come increasingly into contact, but whom the peasants seldom see.

CHAPTER TWO

Variations on the
"Distribution" Theme

Economics vs. Business: Income vs. Wealth

1. The *distribution* of income, of wealth and of such related entities as "wages" or "liquid assets," means, in economics, its division among various social groups and classes, usually in consequence of the workings of an economic system. This usage contracts in a confusing way with the meaning of the term *distribution* in business administration. There it relates to the physical process of distributing goods from their point of production to their points of consumption, and may be used synonymously with "marketing." In these chapters, we follow the economic usage; from this viewpoint, such questions as "Does distribution cost too much?" are meaningless.

It is important to distinguish between the distribution of income and that of wealth, although academic practice used "wealth" in both senses as recently as World War I, and popular practice still does so. Income is conventionally regarded as a *flow* of returns from human and nonhuman assets alike, while wealth is a *stock* of nonhuman assets (plus slaves, a human asset, where the institution of slavery survives) and an *increment* of wealth is a *component* of income.[1] The distributions of income and wealth differ widely, depending (chiefly) on the importance of "human

1. In economic research studies, human wealth is sometimes estimated as the capitalized earnings from labor, and included in total wealth. In that case, income is an increment of wealth and consumption a decrement of wealth.

capital" as an income-earning asset, and on the rate of return obtained as income in different societies.

Comparing the United States and the United Kingdom, for example, the distribution of income, as commonly measured, is more unequal in the United States, while the distribution of wealth is more equal there.[2] An incomplete and superficial explanation of this disparity is the greater concentration of British wealth in residential housing and other forms of "consumer capital" whose returns, if any, are not recorded as income. Comparing capitalist and socialist states, the major differences in distribution seem to apply to wealth and, on the income side, to the property income directly derived from wealth. These differences result from the drastic restrictions imposed under socialism upon private opportunities to hold earning assets in "commodity production," and to retain income from this source.[3]

Distribution Bases

2.   There is a wide variety of distribution problems in economics, each corresponding to a different division of society into social groups, classes, or regions. Economists have traditionally concentrated their attention on two bases for such division; we continue in this tradition.

The major distribution problem, for general economists (economic theorists) past and present, has been *functional*. By *functional distribution* we mean the division of income as between income from labor (human capital, wealth, or assets) and income from property (nonhuman capital, wealth, or assets).

Often each of these broad categories is broken down further. Labor incomes are subdivided into wages (income of manual workers), salaries (income of white-collar workers), and executive compensation (income of managerial workers). In France, the income of *cadres* is sometimes classified separately; it combines the higher reaches of the salariat with the lower reaches of the managerial stratum. Likewise, property income is frequently subdivided into income from rents, interest, and dividends. There is also a third, or mixed, category—the income people receive from

2. Compare Robert J. Lampman, *The Share of Top Wealth-Holders in National Wealth, 1952–1956* (Princeton: Princeton University Press, 1962), pp. 210–214. Also Harold Lydall and J. B. Lansing, "Distribution of Personal Income and Wealth in the United States and Great Britain," *A.E.R.* (March 1959).

3. Private ownership of earning assets in commodity production, and retention of their income, seems generally tolerated on a small scale in socialist countries, particularly in agriculture and handicrafts, provided that only family labor is "employed." It is also permitted on a larger scale when a number of small owners form a producers' cooperative or *artel*, and divide total returns among the members.

the businesses that they own, either by themselves or in partnership with others. This category is called in America "proprietors' income" or "income of unincorporated enterprises." It is frequently tabulated separately from pure labor or property incomes, but it may be divided between them by one or another ingenious statistical device. (See section 4-f of this chapter.)

The "proper" breakdown of functional income categories is still unsettled. Departure from economic conventions, for the sake of conformity with accounting practice, is advocated as a main thesis of a leading French treatise on income distribution.[4]

The secondary distribution problem for general economists has been *personal*. By *personal distribution* we mean division of income (or wealth) by size, or more precisely, by size brackets of the income or wealth of economic units. Tables 2.1 and 2.2 are examples, respectively, of American functional and personal income distributions.

3.　　We shall have little to say about distribution problems of other sorts, but can indicate the existence and nature of some of the more pervasive varieties.

　　a.　　*Occupational* distribution involves the division of income by different industries (or for occupational groups). Occupational distribution problems have been most important in connection with agriculture. Considerations of the agricultural share in national income, as well as comparisons of average incomes on and off the farm, are used to support demands for farm parity, floors under farm prices, and the like. The "farm problems" of various countries have been largely problems of the occupational distribution of income and sometimes also, indirectly, of wealth.[5]

　　b.　　*Geographical* or *regional* distribution involves division of income or wealth by regions within a given country. In the 75 years between the close of the Civil War and the onset of World War II, the South was, for example, "America's no. 1 economic problem," because of its low share in the national income and wealth. (More recently, interest has shifted to less well-defined low-income pockets like "Appalachia.") During the in-

---

4. Jean Marchal and Jacques Lecaillon, *La répartition du revenu national* (Paris: Librairie de Médicis, 1958), vol. i. The earlier reference to *cadres* as a separate income category refers also to Marchal and Lecaillon, "Is the Income of the 'Cadres' a Special Class of Wages?" *Q.J.E.* (May 1958).

5. Thus, solutions of farm problems that would allow farm prices to fall, but then rely on falling farm land values to reduce production costs, are opposed by farmers. They shift the distribution of *wealth* against farmers and other farm landowners by imposing heavy capital losses upon them, even though they may not shift the *income* distribution against farmers.

*Table 2.1.   Functional Distribution of
Personal Income (United States, 1964)*

	Billions of Dollars	Percentage of Total
Labor income		
Wage and salary disbursements	333.5	
Other labor income	16.5	
Subtotal	350.0	70.7
Proprietors' income		
Business and professional	39.1	
Farm	12.0	
Subtotal	51.1	10.3
Property income		
Rental income of persons	18.2	
Dividends	17.2	
Personal interest income	34.3	
Subtotal	69.7	14.1
Transfer payments		
Total receipts	36.6	
Less: Personal contributions	−12.4	
for social insurance	24.2	4.9
	495.0	100.0

SOURCE: *Economic Report of the President* (1966), Table C-13, pp. 224 f.
NOTE: Figures are rounded and may not add to totals.

*Table 2.2   Personal Distribution of Spending
Units and Total Money Income before Taxes,
by Income Groups (United States, 1960)*

Income of Spending Units	Spending Units (per cent)	Total Money Income (per cent)
Under $1,000	6	1
$1,000–$1,999	10	2
$2,000–$2,999	10	4
$3,000–$3,999	10	6
$4,000–$4,999	11	9
$5,000–$5,999	13	12
$6,000–$7,499	15	17
$7,500–$9,999	13	19
$10,000 and over	12	30
Total	100	100

Median income, $5,170; Mean income, $5,830

SOURCE: George Katona, Charles A. Lininger, James N. Morgan, and Eva Mueller, *1961 Survey of Consumer Finances* (Ann Arbor: Survey Research Center, University of Michigan, 1962), table 1.1, p. 8.

terwar generation, Great Britain had similar problems in its blighted areas of South Wales and the industrial Midlands. More recent geographical distribution problems, of special interest to regional scientists and development economists, have involved the Italian *Mezzogiorno* (the mainland south of Naples, plus the islands of Sicily and Sardinia) and the Brazilian *Noroeste* (the lower Amazon Valley and the "bulge" into the Atlantic Ocean).

c. The *international* distribution problem is the regional one writ large. There is evidence, presented most forcefully by Myrdal,[6] that the world's income has been redistributed since the Industrial Revolution in favor of the "advanced" countries where industrialization was early, despite alleged "factor-price-equalization" tendencies to equalize input prices. The advanced countries include Western Europe, North America, Australasia, and perhaps South Africa. These countries, plus a few others like Russia and Japan, have advanced, while the rest of the world has struggled with the "Malthusian devil" of "population explosion." The gap between rich and poor countries has apparently increased. If this is true, the Marxian "principle of increasing misery" (interpreted to mean a falling income share for the poor) can be asserted as operating between rich and poor countries on the international scene, even if not between rich and poor classes within individual countries.

d. *Racial* distribution problems become important in regions of racial conflict. It seems significant, for example, that the earliest (colonial period) income distributions for present-day Indonesia and Malaya, when these countries had European upper classes, Chinese middle classes, and Malay working classes, were broken down along racial lines (Malays, Europeans, Chinese, and "others"). In the United States, the first substantial study of the Negro's share[7] in the national income was prepared in the 1940s as background material for Myrdal's *American Dilemma*. Many more studies were made in connection with the War on Poverty twenty years later. Because the American Negro family structure is supposedly more unstable and more matriarchal than the white, separate distributions for Negro males and females have been estimated. The results suggest that gains in Negro income (relative to white) were concentrated among females during the 1950s and 1960s.[8]

6. Gunnar Myrdal, *The International Economy* (New York: Harper, 1956), ch. 1. For statistical details over the century ending in 1960, see L. J. Zimmerman, *Poor Lands, Rich Lands: The Widening Gap* (New York: Random House, 1965), pp. 30–42.

7. Richard Sterner, *The Negro's Share* (New York: Harper, 1943).

8. "Negro family incomes in the rural South still average less than 45 per cent of white family incomes. In the urban South the gap is only slightly less, with Negro incomes averaging about half of white incomes. In the urban North, Negro incomes average about 70 per cent of white incomes. There does not appear to have been any significant change in these ratios since the end of World War II. During periods of

e. The *sexual* distribution (primarily of wealth), as distinguished from the related issue of "equal pay for equal work," has become a subject of interest under the special circumstances existing in the United States and Canada. These are prosperous countries where women have longer life expectancies than men, where men normally marry women younger than themselves, and where wealthy decedents often bequeath the bulk of their earning assets to surviving spouses. As a result of all these factors, exaggerated accounts are sometimes heard about the trend to "petticoat control" of the country's wealth and, to a lesser extent, of its income from interest, rent, and dividends. The facts of economic growth, with new capital predominantly in male hands, actually operate against so extreme an outcome. Even without growth, however, the algebra of Markoff chains[9] will normally set definite limits to its validity.

f. Under conditions of rapid or continuous rise or fall in the purchasing power of money, the distribution of income by *variability* groups (explained immediately below) becomes important for economic policy. Let us define *fixed* income as arising from assets, or from long-term contracts fixed in monetary terms, or from prices and other payments (salaries, pensions, utility rates) that are in practice revised only with long lags behind price-level changes. Other incomes we call *variable*. Under inflationary conditions, the declining relative position of fixed-income receivers prompts demands to "escalate" their incomes, which may be met with the reply that escalation will accelerate the underlying inflation.

---

declining unemployment, Negroes tend to catch up slightly. When unemployment rises, they lag behind. The fluctuations are, in other words, cyclical; there is no sign of long-run improvement. And while the competitive position of the Negro family as a whole has remained stable, the competitive position of the Negro male has deteriorated. Only the relative improvement in the position of Negro women has kept the total income of Negro families relatively stable compared to whites." Christopher Jencks and David Riesman, *The Academic Revolution* (Garden City: Doubleday, 1968), pp. 410 f. (running quotation). A major source of these conclusions is Alan B. Batchelder, "Decline in the Relative Incomes of Negro Men," *Q.J.E.* (November 1964). See also U.S. Bureau of Labor Statistics, *The Negroes in the United States: Their Economic and Social Situation* (Washington: Government Printing Office, 1966), ch. 4; and U.S. Department of Health, Education, and Welfare, *Toward a Social Report* (Washington: Government Printing Office, 1969), pp. 41–47.

9. See Chapter 3 in this book. Briefly, the mathematical argument is this: If p per cent of the wealth held by men will pass (by bequest) to women, and p' per cent of the wealth held by women will also pass to other women by the same process, p and p' both being approximately constant in the range .50 to 1.00, the sexual distribution will tend, after n generations, to the nth power of the matrix:

$$\begin{bmatrix} p & 1\text{-}p \\ p' & 1\text{-}p' \end{bmatrix}$$

which will eventually approach identity with the $(n\text{-}1)$st power: For the percentage held by women to increase steadily, there must be a rising trend of p or p' or both.

Under conditions of deflation or "currency reform," on the other hand, the "dead hand of the *rentier*" is feared as endangering prosperity and growth, and there may be moves to reduce the fixed-income share of the national income. In all these cases, it is difficult to justify any line that we are apparently forced to draw between the recipients of the fixed and the variable components of income.

Statistical Conundrums

4. In comparing distributions of income or wealth at different times and places, the student or research worker is constantly threatened by statistical fallacies and non-comparabilities. "Things are seldom what they seem, Skimmed milk masquerades as cream" among the distribution statisticians as well as aboard *H.M.S. Pinafore.*

Thirteen points of frequent non-comparability, perhaps even of bias, in income-distribution statistics are touched on below. (Most of them relate to the *concept of income* used as the basis for analysis; for example, is it national, personal, or disposable income that is being distributed?) We can indicate in most cases the choices made in preparing the American data on Tables 2.1 and 2.2. We can also indicate in many cases the probable consequences for measured inequality or income shares if different choices had been made.

a. Is income limited to the value of commodity production and services directly related thereto, like public utilities and transportation, or does it include also the value of consumer services and general public services? The more limited concept is the Marxian "value of output," which, however, includes as "constant capital" and nonlabor income, *all* raw materials used up in production processes. The Western concept is broader; it includes consumer services of all kinds, but treats as income only net *additions* to the society's stock of raw materials and intermediate products. The choice made here affects the measured labor share significantly. As one might expect, it comes out higher in the Western than in the Marxian concept.

b. Is income measured gross or net of depreciation (1) on physical capital goods, and (2) on "human capital"? The usual measures of net income or product, the "totals" of tables like our Table 2.1, deduct depreciation on physical but not on human capital, thereby raising the measured labor share.[10] Measures of gross output, income, or product include no depreciation allowances; they are less commonly used as totals in distribution estimates.

10. An exception to this generalization is Rasool M. H. Hashimi, *Studies in Functional Income Distribution* (East Lansing: Michigan State University Press, 1960) .

c.　Is income measured gross or net of the "personal taxes" levied on personal incomes, real and personal property, estates, and on a per capita basis (poll taxes)? The data of our tables are taken gross of such taxes. The effect of deducting them depends, of course, upon their nature. If they are primarily payroll and poll taxes, their deduction lowers the measured labor share and raises most measures of income equality. If personal taxes are primarily progressive income and succession taxes, the effect of taking them into account is in the opposite direction, although it may be surprisingly small when the effect of loopholes and "dipping deeply into large fortunes with a sieve" are also taken into consideration.[11]

Soviet-type distribution schemata and statistics go further along this line. They distinguish between *primary* and *secondary* distributions.[12] The former are taken prior to personal taxes, and can be made roughly comparable with Western pre-tax statistics. Secondary distributions are not only taken net of taxes, but include a wide variety of other state redistributive activities. The "shares" are also defined differently than in Western practice, although there are similarities to the standard macroeconomics of $Y = C + I + G$. A diagrammatic schema by a Soviet economist, using percentages for 1959, is adapted as Figure 2.1.

d.　Does income include the undistributed profits of private corporations? Personal income does not include this item, and it is not considered in Tables 2.1 and 2.2. Inclusion of some allowance for it would increase the measured shares of wealthier groups and of property owners.

---

11. For a statistical illustration, see Joseph A. Pechman, *Distribution of Income Before and After Federal Income Taxes, 1941 and 1947,* Studies in Income and Wealth, vol. 13 (New York: National Bureau of Economic Research, 1951).

12. The distinction is applied to capitalist economies as well. A Soviet textbook, P. Nikitin, *Fundamentals of Political Economy,* trans. Violet Dutt and Murad Saifulin (Moscow: Foreign Languages Publishing House, n.d.) puts it this way (running quotation from pp. 133–135):

"A distinction should be made between *primary* and *secondary* distribution of the national income. [It] first falls into the hands of the capitalists. Primary distribution consists in its being distributed between capitalists and workers. The workers receive wages, the capitalists surplus value.

After the national income has been distributed among the basic elements of capitalist society, a secondary distribution or redistribution takes place. [I]n the non-productive branches of the economy no national income is created. But the capitalists who control these enterprises and institutions pay salaries, cover the cost of maintaining premises, and make a profit. The capitalists cover these items of expenditure out of the national income created in the sphere of material production by charging for the services provided. Part of the income of the working people is [also] redistributed through the state budget in the interests of the ruling class.

The bourgeois state has its army, police, administrative apparatus, and so on. All are maintained out of the state budget, *taxes* levied upon the population being its main source of revenue. After working people have received wages through the primary distribution of the national income, they have to pay taxes. In this way, the part of the national income at the disposal of the working people is reduced."

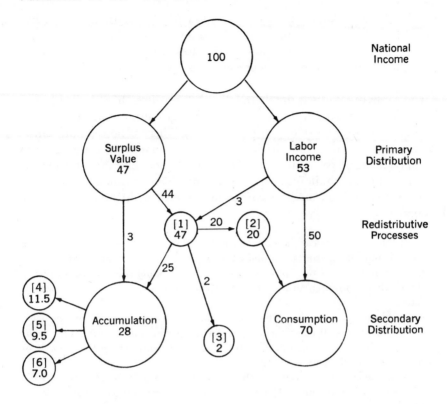

NOTES: [1], Redistribution Fund; [2], Derivative Income, corresponding roughly to Transfer Payments; [3], Materials Used in Research and Administration; [4], Increase in Fixed Productive Funds, corresponding to Plant and Equipment Investment; [5], Increase in Non-productive Funds, corresponding to Housing and Public Investment; [6], Increase in Current and Reserve Funds, corresponding to Inventory Investment.

SOURCE: A. I. Petrov, "Distribution of National Income in the U.S.S.R." in Marchal and Ducros, *op. cit.*, p. 221.

Figure 2.1. Primary and Secondary Distributions of Soviet National Income (Percentages, 1959)

On the other hand, national income includes this item in the profit share, and alternative functional distributions are often made that allow for its influence. Allowance for undistributed profits is more ·difficult in personal income distribution, because of technical difficulties in its allocation between income brackets.

e. Does income include capital gains, whether "realized" (by actual sale of assets) or not? In general it does not, except when total "taxable income" is considered in a country that taxes realized capital gains. No distribution data known to this writer allow for the "constructive" or hypothetical realization of such gains. Inclusion of capital gains in income would obviously increase the published shares of wealthier groups and of property owners, except in depression years of net decline in capital values.

f. We have discussed the share labeled "Proprietorship" in Table 2.1. This form dominates (in America) family agriculture, independent retailing, and the practice of many professions. There is no easy and unexceptionable way to divide the income of a farm family, a corner grocer, or a practicing physician between the return to labor and the return to investment in land, buildings, equpiment, and so on. A number of alternative rules have been used by statisticians to deal with this problem. Six examples are given here:[13]

(1) The property earnings of the self-employed may be imputed on the basis of industry-specific rents and interest rates, and the residual assigned to labor. This is called the "property method," but underestimates the property share when entrepreneurial property earns more than the market rate of return.

(2) The labor earnings of the self-employed may be imputed on the basis of the earnings of hired workers in similar industries. This is called the "labor method," but underestimates the labor share when entrepreneurial labor is of higher quality than hired labor.

(3) An aggregative variant of the property method is the "asset method," which imputes economy-wide rates of return to assets owned by the self-employed. (The corresponding aggregation of the labor method does not seem to be used widely.)

(4) The income of the self-employed may be divided on the same basis as the current labor income/property income ratio in the corporate sector of the economy. This is called the "economy-wide basis."

(5) A simplification of the economy-wide basis substitutes a single long-run average labor income/property income ratio for a series of current ratios. This is called the "proportional basis."

(6) The income of the self-employed may be left completely out of account, only the remainder being distributed. Thus, functional distributions of income in the manufacturing sector alone are sometimes used, this being the

---

13. For critical discussion of the strengths and weaknesses of these methods, see Edward C. Budd, "The State of Income Distribution Theory," in *Income Distribution Analysis* (Raleigh: North Carolina State University Press, 1966), pp. 7–9. Budd himself uses the labor method; see his "Factor Shares, 1850–1910" in *Trends in the American Economy in the Nineteenth Century*, Studies in Income and Wealth, vol. 24 (Princeton; Princeton University Press for N.B.E.R., 1960). Terminology is from Irving Kravis, "Relative Income Shares in Fact and Theory," *A.E.R.* (December 1959), pp. 924 f.

sector in which proprietorship is least important. Such a device can hardly be recommended for developing economies dominated by peasant proprietors and small retailers.

g. Another difficult item in Table 2.1 is "Transfer payments." How can such an item be allocated functionally between labor and property? Since the great bulk of such payments go to working people, the item can be combined with "other labor income" and added to the labor share. It may also be omitted, making the income distributed functionally to this extent closer to national than personal income.

h. Is income measured nationally or domestically? If it is on a national basis, as in the United States, incomes received by local residents from foreign sources are included, but incomes paid to foreigners from local production are excluded. If income is measured on a domestic basis, incomes received by local residents from abroad are excluded, but incomes paid to foreigners from local production are included. The domestic basis, as widely used in developing countries, raises the apparent property share by including net rents, interest, and dividends paid abroad, which may be a significant portion of the country's income. The change of basis would probably not affect the American figures in any significant way.

i. Is income limited to sums received in money, or does it include imputed income received in kind, a category ranging from food raised by farmers for home consumption and "rent" on owner-occupied homes to the "expense-account way of life" of corporate officials in high-tax countries? Here the American data are imperfectly consistent. Table 2.1 (functional distribution) attempts to include nonmoney items, although its coverage is incomplete.[14] Table 2.1 (personal distribution) is derived from survey data, and is limited to money income because few respondents can estimate their imputed incomes. Margaret Reid has estimated that under American conditions, total income is distributed somewhat more equally than money income.[15] In developing countries with large nonpecuniary sectors, the difference is probably larger than in the United States, but in the same direction. In socialist countries, the difference is in the opposite direction, since the salaries of the party *cadres* and other members of the elite are lower than in America, relative to their nonmonetary perquisites.

14. Two important failures of coverage at the upper tail of the personal distribution are incomes received in the form of unrealized accretions to wealth (by capital gains, etc.) and incomes divided over long periods for tax-avoidance purposes.

15. Margaret G. Reid, "Distribution of Non-money Income," in Conference on Research in Income and Wealth, *Studies in Income and Wealth*, vol. 13 (New York: National Bureau of Economic Research, 1951).

j. How have the data been derived, particularly those for personal income distributions? If they are taken from tax returns, there are probably more serious problems of understatement and concealment than if sample surveys are used, although some interviewees suspect connections between surveying and tax-collecting agencies when none exist. The American data of Table 2.1 rely on sample surveys made under the auspices of the Survey Research Center of the University of Michigan, which may be biased by exclusion of informants who do not understand what "income" is, or are incompetent to estimate their own even within broad limits. (Such people tend to be extremely poor.) Use of survey material is the usual practice. One ambitious Japanese study[16] has not (even after translation) been used widely outside Japan, because it was based largely on tax return data.

k. What are the "units" whose income is being measured or compared? Some studies, perhaps most notably Simon Kuznets' *Shares of Upper Groups in Income and Saving*[17] (for the United States), work with income per head. The results are sensitive to changes in average family size in different income classes, and also to changes in the number of income earners in a family. Thus, for example, some part of the declining share of the top 5 per cent and 1 per cent of income receivers in total income, over the period 1929–1946, results from a differential rise in the number of children in high-income families relative to low-income families. This may itself reflect the movement of wealthy families to the suburbs and exurbs rather than any "income revolution."

Most contemporary studies, however, use composite units of some sort. In the United States, one standard unit is the family. "A family unit consists of all related persons living in the same dwelling unit. A single person who is unrelated to the other occupants of a dwelling unit or who lives alone is a family unit by himself."[18] The Survey Research Center uses a spending unit, defined as "all related persons living together who pool their incomes." Other surveys have used "consumer units" of persons living together and pooling significant items of expenditures, whether or not they are related. Many other units are also possible and have been

16. Chotaro Takahashi *et al.*, *Dynamic Changes in Income and Its Distribution in Japan* (Tokyo: Kinokuniya, 1959).

17. New York: National Bureau of Economic Research, 1953. The term "income revolution" was applied to Kuznets' results by Arthur F. Burns in a National Bureau report entitled "Looking Forward," and reprinted in Burns, *Frontiers of Economic Knowledge* (New York: National Bureau of Economic Research, 1954). See Chapter 3, section 2 in this book.

18. Katona *et al.*, *1961 Survey of Consumer Finances* (Ann Arbor: Survey Research Center, University of Michigan) p. 3. "Relationship" may for purposes of these definitions be by blood, marriage, or adoption.

used. One such is the "adult unit," which ignores children. Others are the "adult equivalent" and "adult male equivalent," per capita units adjusted by treating women and children as fractions whose sizes depend on age and sex. In countries where the "large" or "undivided" family system prevails, this family may be used as a unit rather than the smaller "nuclear" household.

l. Over what time period should income be measured? The conventional period is the twelve-month calendar or fiscal year. It appears that with shorter periods the personal distribution is more unequal, and with longer periods less unequal. Statistical evidence on this point is furnished by studies that compare and combine the income tax returns of identical taxpayers in successive years. Such studies have been conducted, for example, with data from the state of Wisconsin.[19] The result is not unexpected; longer periods tend to average out periods of unusually high earning power (as for athletes and actors) with periods of unusually low earning power (as during illness or unemployment). Distributions of both "age-specific" and "lifetime" incomes have been constructed in considerable number.[20] They show greater equality than distributions for shorter periods, but statistical comparability with short-period distributions has not been easy to achieve in a turbulent world of fluctuating business activity and price levels.

m. What statistic should be used to measure equality or inequality (in the case of personal distribution) or to allocate income between functional types (in the case of functional distribution)? We leave to Chapter 3 formal discussion of the measurement of inequality. It suffices to point out here that results will vary according to the weight given the extreme values of a distribution, particularly the high incomes of its upper tail. For this reason, quartile and other positional measures, which ignore the values of extreme items,[21] sometimes move in the opposite direction from standard deviations and coefficients of variation, which include them.

19. Frank A. Hanna, Joseph A. Pechman, and Sidney M. Lerner, *Analysis of Wisconsin Incomes;* Studies in Income and Wealth, vol. 9 (New York: National Bureau of Economic Research, 1948), part III, ch. 4 (by Hanna).

20. Much of this work through 1961 has been summarized critically by James N. Morgan, "The Anatomy of Income Distribution," *Rev. Econ. and Stat.* (August 1962), pp. 272–274.

21. The quartiles of an income distribution with n discrete items are the values of those items ranked $(n + 1)/4$, $(n + 1)/2$, and $3(n + 1)/4$, respectively, from the bottom. They are often denoted by the symbols q_1, Md (median), and q_3. A measure of variation involving these values, and ascribed to the British statistician Arthur Bowley, is: $(q_3 - q_1)/(q_3 + q_1)$. This ignores precise values of items below q_1 and above q_3.

The coefficient of variation equals the standard deviation of a distribution divided by its arithmetic mean. It takes account of the values of all items in both its numerator and its denominator.

As for the labor share, the prime problem of functional income distribution, conventional Western statistics show labor income as a percentage of total personal or national income. They have tended in recent years to show increases in many countries, for reasons we shall consider later. At the same time the favorite Marxian statistic, the rate of surplus value (sometimes called "the rate of exploitation"), has also tended upward in the same countries! Paradoxical as this result may seem, it has a simple explanation. In the Marxian scheme, only direct manual labor is commodity production is defined as "variable capital," so that only its income is labor income, forming the denominator of the rate-of-surplus-value statistic. The numerator of this same statistic is neither total output nor total income but only total *surplus value.* Surplus value includes not only property income (in the same industries) but also all income paid to white-collar workers in these industries. A rise in the rate of surplus value can and has come about by such anomalous forms of "exploitation" as the shift of the labor force (with advancing technology) from blue-collar to white-collar occupations. For example, when a ditchdigger is retrained to become a shipping clerk, or when a machine tender is replaced by a computer programmer, the rate of surplus value rises!

Defining Poverty

5.   An important problem, this time in personal distribution, has been to estimate the number and proportion of the population living in poverty. Poverty is like an ugly woman, easier to recognize than to define. And on second thought, even recognition is a problem when we transcend the boundaries of time and space. Was St. Francis of Assisi's "Lady Poverty" comparable to the poverty of modern Kamagasaki, Calcutta, or East Harlem, or only a distant country cousin, several centuries removed?

Social workers and social economists have attempted many statistical definitions of poverty, without avoiding elements of arbitrariness. Sometimes these are frank and open; as an example, a historian wrote,[22] "I will abandon the commonly accepted $2000 a year—a criterion unchanged despite the postwar inflation—and take the more realistic $3000."

More often, the arbitrary element is concealed under one or another more sophisticated approach. One traditional procedure, associated with wealth or assets rather than with income, has been to draw up a list of commonplace amenities—so many square feet of floor space per person, so many calories of food per day, etc. When a family lacks a certain proportion of these items, it is defined as living in poverty, even if the family's income would permit their purchase (as in the case of a miser). Con-

22. Gabriel Kolko, *Wealth and Power in America* (New York: Praeger, 1962), p. 73.

versely, if the family has enough of these amenities, it is not poverty-stricken, even if it subsists by depending on the charity of friends and relatives, by selling assets and drawing down savings, or by incurring debt. Rowntree's study of English poverty at the turn of the twentieth century[23] exemplifies the use of this method. It is also used to question the realism of results achieved by other means.[24]

6. Current practice in defining poverty runs commonly in terms of income and ignores wealth.[25] The lowest 10 per cent of the population, for example, may be defined as living in poverty. (Why not 1, 5, or 50 per cent? This is a matter of contemporary plausibility.) Under this usage, no war on poverty can ever be won, short of some egalitarian millennium, and 10 per cent of the population will remain poor "by definition," regardless of the growth rate of the economy and the measures taken to alleviate poverty. "When everyone else has a spaceship, a man with one Cadillac can reasonably be called poor."[26] A less extreme suggestion would classify as poor anyone whose income is below 50 per cent of the median income of his society.[27] (Why not 10, 25, or 90 per cent? This

23. B. Seebohm Rowntree, *Poverty: A Study of Town Life* (London: Macmillan, 1901). As of 1899, Rowntree found that one-half of the inhabitants of York lived below his poverty standards. When his study was repeated in 1935 and 1950, however, "poverty" as he had orginally defined it was almost nonexistent in York. See also Clifton R. Wharton, Jr., "The Economic Meaning of 'Subsistence,'" *Malayan Econ. Rev.* (October 1963), p. 50.

24. Thus, Herman P. Miller and Simon Rottenberg cite U.S. Census data for 1960: Of families with incomes below the "official" $3000 poverty line, 79 per cent own a television set, 51 per cent own both a television set and a telephone, 73 per cent own a washing machine, 19 per cent own a home freezer, 65 per cent have a dwelling unit that is not dilapidated, and has hot running water and a toilet and bath for their exclusive use, and 14 per cent bought an automobile (not necessarily new) during the preceding year. Miller, "Major Elements of a Research Program for the Study of Poverty," in *The Concept of Poverty* (Washington: U.S. Chamber of Commerce, 1965), p. 122; Rottenberg, "Misplaced Emphasis in Wars on Poverty," *Law and Contemporary Problems* (Winter 1966), pp. 65 f.

25. A welcome exception is Burton A. Weisbrod and W. Lee Hansen, "An Income—Net Worth Approach to Measuring Economic Welfare," *A.E.R.* (December 1968). They convert net worth into income flow, with adjustments for life expectancy. Inclusion of net worth *lowers*, in particular, the statistical incidence of poverty among the aged.

26. John Johnston, *Chicago Daily News*, quoted by Rose D. Friedman, *Poverty: Definition and Perspective* (Washington: American Enterprise Institute, 1965), p. 14. This example is fanciful, but by rough comparison of poverty studies in different years, R.A. Gordon suggests that the poverty line may have doubled between 1900 and 1950, and risen by between 40 and 75 per cent in the quarter century following 1935 (when American real disposable income per capita was rising by 85 per cent.) "An Economist's View of Poverty" in Margaret S. Gordon (ed.), *Poverty in America* (San Francisco: Chandler, 1965), pp. 4 f.

27. The implications of this criterion are developed for the United States by Victor R. Fuchs, "Toward a Theory of Poverty," in *The Concept of Poverty* (Washington: U.S. Chamber of Commerce, 1965), pp. 74–77. See also Fuchs, "Redefining Poverty and Redistributing Income," *Public Interest* (Summer 1967).

again is a matter of plausibility.) Here again, the outcome of war on poverty depends solely upon income redistribution, to the exclusion of economic growth, but the war is less hopeless. More common, and therefore more "practical," is the procedure of preparing and pricing a minimal food budget, applying some (presumably) realistic multiplier (such as 3, in the United States), and rounding off.[28] Or a total budget, including nonfood expenditures, can be estimated directly. The multiplier step is then avoided, but we do not have for non-food components any relatively well-developed standards corresponding to the "nutritional adequacy" criterion used to judge food.

The American Council of Economic Advisers (C.E.A.) relied on a Social Security Administration "economy-plan" budget for a nonfarm family of four ($3165 in 1962 prices) to set its own poverty line of $3000 for 1963.[29] Families with incomes below $3000, regardless of size, were classified as poor, whatever their actual living conditions might have been (thanks to past savings, accumulated assets, private gifts, loans, etc.). Families with incomes above the crucial amount were placed above the poverty line, despite actual living levels that might have been depressed by the pressure of accumulated debt or the penury of family members.

On this basis, the C.E.A. determined:[30]

28. The American system is explained in Betty Peterkin, "S.S.D.A. Food Plans and Costs," *Family Econ. Rev.* (March 1965). Rose Friedman (*op. cit.,* pp. 18–25) believes the multiplier to be too high, arguing that the representative low-income family obtaining an adequate diet actually spends less than one-third of its income on food.

29. Council of Economic Advisers, *Economic Report of the President* (1964). pp. 58 f. (The corresponding figure for single persons was $1500.) In a more extended study, James N. Morgan *et al., Income and Welfare in the United States* (New York: McGraw-Hill, 1962), pp. 188–190, use a schedule prepared by the Community Council of Greater New York. They define "families with inadequate income" as "those whose incomes are less than nine-tenths of thier budget requirements." The ratio of a family's disposable income to its needs (as computed from this standard), Morgan and his colleagues call it, "welfare ratio." They estimate that 28 per cent of all adult units, including 20 per cent of all families had welfare ratios below 0.9 in the United States as of 1959.

30. *Economic Report of the President* (1964), p. 59 (running quotation). In partial justification of certain of these rough-and-ready procedures, a later C.E.A. study noted that 69 per cent of those classified as poor in 1962 remained so in 1963. For two overlapping subgroups, families headed by persons 65 and over and by persons not at work, the percentage remaining poor was 80 per cent. (*Ibid.* [1965], p. 164.)

A series of subsequent studies by Mollie Orshansky (*Soc. Sec. Bull.,* January and July 1965; April and May 1966) subdivided "families" more carefully by size and type. Her 1963 estimate was of 7.2 million families and 5 million single persons in poverty—34.5 million in all, including 15 millon children and 5 million "senior citizens." The major impact of the Orshansky revisions was to raise the estimates of the number of poverty-stricken children, and reduce the estimates of the number of aged poor. Miss Orshansky also faces up to, but cannot solve, statistical problems raised by the dilemma of "privacy in poverty." (How do we classify large, tenuously related, "sub-families" huddled together to pool expenses slightly above the poverty line? Or single persons and broken families isolated below the poverty line because prosperity permits their relatives to dispense with their meager incomes?)

There were 47 million families in the United States in 1962. Fully 9.3 million, or one-fifth of these families—comprising more than 30 million persons—had total money incomes below $3000. Over 11 million of these were children, one-sixth of our youth. 5.4 million families, containing more than 17 million persons, had total incomes below $2000. Serious poverty also exists among persons living alone or in boarding houses. In 1962, 45 per cent of such "unrelated individuals"—5 million persons—had incomes below $1500, and 29 per cent—or more than 3 million persons—had incomes below $1000. Thus, by the measures used here, 33 to 35 million Americans were living at or below the boundaries of poverty in 1962—nearly one-fifth of our nation.

Several critics have found the C.E.A. "standard" budgets too niggardly, and their estimates of the number of poor people too low. Harrington's poverty-stricken, semi-invisible "Other America"[31] numbers nearly 50 million, approximately 25 per cent of the total population. (His poverty lines are one-third higher than the C.E.A. ones.) Keyserling[32] has presented a series of still higher ranges (from $6200–$9600 for large families to $2300–$3100 for single individuals, depending primarily on considerations of age and place of residence.) On the other hand, Rose Friedman[33] estimates only 4.8 million families as poor, from a series of poverty lines for different sizes of families that average to $2200 for the total population. Who is right? It depends primarily upon one's choice of standard budget.

7. Somewhat less arbitrary might be a different approach in terms of break-even points, sometimes called "wolf points," in consumption functions. Using income and consumption-expenditures data for a society as a whole, or for different income brackets and family compositions, we can estimate the income level at which an average household no longer saves, and below which it draws on past savings, sells assets, or incurs debt to maintain consumption. This level is called the break-even, or wolf point. (The "wolf" is the one at the door, not any economist or statistician named Wolf.)

We have made three such break-even point estimates. One uses a time-series approach for an entire economy. It uses per capita disposable income and consumption expenditures data for the United States from 1947 through 1961, in 1962 prices.[34] The other two are from Japanese data for the year 1958 and the month of September, 1961. They are cross-section

---

31. Michael Harrington, *op. cit.*, pp. 179–191.

32. Leon Keyserling, *Progress or Poverty* (Washington: Conference on Economic Progress, 1964), pp. 16 f.

33. Rose Friedman, *op. cit.*, pp. 34 f.

34. *Economic Report of the President* (1963), Table C-16, p. 191. Use of longer-term or even "permanent" income and consumption data might have improved our studies.

studies, relating to income and consumption of urban workers' families, broken down by average monthly income classes at 1958 and 1961 prices respectively.[35]

These are our numerical results:[36]

U.S.A.: Time-series data, in dollars; wolf point, $1146 per capita per year.

Japan: Cross-section data, in thousand yen; wolf points: Y26,770 per family per month, or $892 per family per year (1958) ; Y25,860 per family per month, or $862 per family per year (September, 1961) .

This numerical result for the United States suggests a poverty line, at least for families, that is somewhat higher (less conservative) than the official one. For a median-sized family of 3.8 persons, for example, our wolf point is $4354 in 1962 prices, as against $3000.[37] The Japanese poverty line is, as expected, below the American, although the disparity is exaggerated by the official exchange rate of Y360 to the dollar. Comparing the two Japanese figures with each other, the fall of the wolf point between 1967 and 1961 is surprising, since prices rose in the meantime. Decreased income tax burdens may have been responsible, in addition to sampling variance.

35. Institute of Economic Research, Hitotsubashi University, *Economic Statistics of Japan for Postwar Years* (Tokyo: Hitotsubashi University, 1960) , table XI-2-a, p. 148; and *Kakei Chosa Nempo* (Tokyo, 1961) , table 3, pp. 30–33. These income figures cover personal income before taxes. No imputed items are included. The "annual" figures omit the month of December, when substantial year-end bonuses are paid. Omision of December (a standard Japanese practice) raises our computed wolf points as much as one-third above Japanese "common-sense" estimates, since many families go into debt for 11 months with the expectation of balancing their budgets in December. Compare *Economic Statistics of Japan, op. cit.,* p. 149.

36. To estimate the wolf point of any consumption function $C = C_0 + cY$ means to find the value of Y such that C and Y are equal. This value is $C_0 / (1 - c)$. We estimate C_0 and c by ordinary least squares.

37. For *urban* families, however, the U.S. Bureau of Labor Statistics has assumed an "adequate" budget of approximately $4,000 per year for four persons at 1957 prices, as against an AFL-CIO estimate of $4,800. (Harrington, *op. cit.,* p. 81) . Our figure of $4,584 for four persons (at somewhat higher prices) falls approximately half-way between these two.

CHAPTER THREE

Topics in Personal
Income Distribution

Statistical Measurement of Inequality

1. To measure the degree of *inequality* of a personal income distribution —a frequency distribution of incomes by size—we have mentioned two statistics, the standard deviation and the coefficient of variation, defined as the standard deviation divided by the arithmetic mean. (To measure the degree of *equality,* we could have used the reciprocals of the same statistics.) The attraction of these particular statistics is their simplicity, but they are not widely used in practical work. The coefficient of variation, for example, takes no account of the skewness of the income distribution; it has a lower bound (at zero) but no finite upper bound; and it is influenced by extreme values.

Of the infinite variety of conceivable measures of personal income equality and inequality, many of those used in Western Europe and America have been compared and summarized by Bowman.[1] The most familiar of these are the Pareto α and the Gini coefficient of concentration, R. We consider these in order.

---

1. Mary Jean Bowman, "A Graphical Analysis of Personal Income Distribution in the United States," reprinted in American Economic Association, *Readings in the Theory of Income Distribution* (Philadelphia: Blakiston, 1946), no. 4. (This volume will be referred to as *Readings.*) Soviet statistics tend to compare incomes in the top and bottom deciles of the distribution. Harold F. Lydall, in *The Structure of Earnings* (Oxford: Oxford University Press, 1968), eschews any single measure in favor of a *series* of comparisons of percentiles 99, 98, 95, 90, 80, 25, 15 and 5 (from the bottom) with their common median.

2.   Pareto's "Law of Income Distribution" appeared in 1897 in his *Cours d'économie politique;*[2] at that time, supporting statistical data were still widely scattered, unreliable, and difficult to obtain. Pareto's generalization relates only to the upper tail of the personal income distribution, to values above the mode. Its overall usefulness is reduced by its omission of the lower income brackets.

Pareto's law is in two parts, one relating to the mathematical form of the income distribution's upper tail and the other to the arithmetical value of one of its coefficients. Let Y be a level of income (above the mode), and let N be the proportion of income receivers with incomes equal to or greater than Y. Then, Pareto found, the upper brackets of the distributions of his data could all be represented accurately by the formula:

$$N = AY^{-\alpha}, \text{ or in logarithmic form, } \log N = A - \alpha \log Y$$

The A and α are statistical parameters, determined by the method of least squares in fitting the function (in logarithmic form).

It is easy to determine whether a given distribution follows the Pareto law by plotting its points on double-logarithmic paper. If the plotted points follow a straight line with a negative slope, the distribution is Paretian. Thus, the upper tail of the data of Table 2.2 (incomes of $4000 and above) is plotted as Figure 3.1. The fit is a good one, except for the two lowest points (income below $4000). The good fit of the Pareto distribution, of course, does not in itself rule out alternative forms.

The value of A has no economic significance; it is not independent of the units in which N and Y are measured. The value of α is, however, independent of the choice of units. On this value Pareto concentrated his attention. In his data, which covered a wide range in both time and space, the absolute values of α clustered around 1.5–1.7. The values of α would have been larger in absolute value for highly equal distributions, smaller for highly unequal ones. Pareto believed that he had discovered an economic constant comparable in significance to the gravitational constant in physics; hence the expression "Pareto's Law."

Subsequent data, some of it reproduced in Table 3.1, cast doubt upon this uniformity.[3] The American mathematician H. T. Davis, a follower of Pareto, has recast the law into a condition for social stability in what he calls a mathematical interpretation of history.[4] Davis conjectures that

2. Vilfredo Pareto, *op. cit.*, vol. 2 (Lausanne: Rouge, 1897).

3. For the data of Figure 3.1, the absolute value of α is 1.87. This is higher than the original "Paretian range," but is not unusual in twentieth-century observations.

4. Davis, *Analysis of Economic Time Series* (Bloomington: Principia Press, 1941), ch. 9.

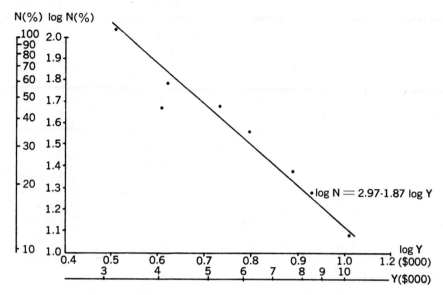

SOURCE OF DATA: See Table 2.2.

Figure 3.1. Illustration of Pareto's Law (United States, 1960)

α-values substantially greater than 1.5 in absolute value lead to aristocratic revolutions from the Right because they indicate insufficient scope for special abilities, whereas values substantially smaller than 1.5 inspire proletarian revolutions from the Left. In framing these conjectures, Davis has generalized from a few European instances. (There is, on the other hand, considerable evidence, largely from Asian countries, that development tends eventually to reduce inequality, so that absolute values of α tend upward over time; Oshima has summarized this evidence,[5] although not in Paretian terms.) Temporarily at least, Pareto's Law of Income Distribution has been suspended, if not officially repealed.

3. Consideration of the concentration ratio begins with the joint cumulative distribution function of total income and recipient units. This function is known in English-speaking countries as the Lorenz curve, and in Latin countries as the Gini curve. It was applied to distribution prob-

5. Harry T. Oshima, "The International Comparison of Size Distribution of Family Incomes with Special Reference to Asia," *Rev. Econ. and Stat.* (November 1962), pp. 443 f. In earlier writings Oshima considered the evidence insufficient. See his controversy with Theodore Morgan, *Ec. J.* (March 1956), and sections 10–11 of the next chapter.

Table 3.1. Specimen Estimates of Pareto α—Statistic

Country	Year	Value	Country	Year	Value
U.S.A.	1866–71	1.40–1.48	Canada	1939	1.84
	1914	1.54		1944	1.92
	1919	1.71		1946	2.28
	1924	1.67			
	1929	1.42	Brazil	1942	1.27
	1934	1.78			
	1938	1.77	Venezuela	1945	1.24
	1941	1.87			
	1945	1.95	Peru	18th cent.	1.79
U.K.	1688	1.58	Argentina	1942	1.2–1.3
	1812	1.31			
	1843	1.50	Germany	1471	1.43 (Augsburg)
	1867	1.47		1526	1.13 (Augsburg)
	1893	1.50		1852	1.89 (Prussia)
	1918	1.47		1872	1.82 (Prussia)
	1937–38	1.57		1890	1.60 (Prussia)
	1944–45	1.75		1913	1.56 (Germany)
				1928	1.78 (Germany)
				1936	1.67 (Germany)
France	Middle Ages	1.57			
	1894	1.68	Hungary	1935	1.86
	1931	1.75			
	1934	1.82	Denmark	1935	1.94
Switzerland	Middle Ages	1.41 (Basle)	Sweden	1944	2.15
Italy	Time of Cireco	1.5	Finland	1926	1.88
	Middle Ages	1.41 (Florence)		1934	2.03
				1942	2.13
Netherlands	1935	1.83			
			Russia	1910	1.39
Palestine	1944	2.22 (Arabs)		1924	1.96
	1944	1.9 (Jews)			
			Burma	1928–29	1.32
India	1913	1.45			
	1923	1.13	Japan	1890	1.67
	1929	1.48		1913–14	1.89
	1945–46	1.79		1930	1.66
			New Zealand	1933–34	2.29
Australia	1896	1.53		1938–39	2.35
	1931–32	2.11			
	1943–44	2.12	South Africa	1944–45	2.03 (Whites)

SOURCES: Colin Clark, *Conditions of Economic Progress*, 2d ed. (London: Macmillan, 1951), pp. 533–537. Includes several of Pareto's original estimates, which have been assembled by Francesco Brambili, "Sull' invarianza della forma della distribuzione dei redditi," *L'Industria* (1950). Also includes results of Norris O. Johnson, "The Pareto Law," *Rev. Econ. Stat.* (February 1937), a fundamental study for the United States.

lems at approximately the same time, and apparently independently, by two economic statisticians, the American Max Lorenz and the Italian Corrado Gini.

The cumulative percentage of income receivers is plotted from 0 to 100 on the horizontal axis of a diagram such as Figure 3.2, and the cumulative percentage of total income received is plotted on the vertical axis. When the relevant observations have been connected, the result is called a Lorenz or a Gini curve. Among this curve's interesting mathematical

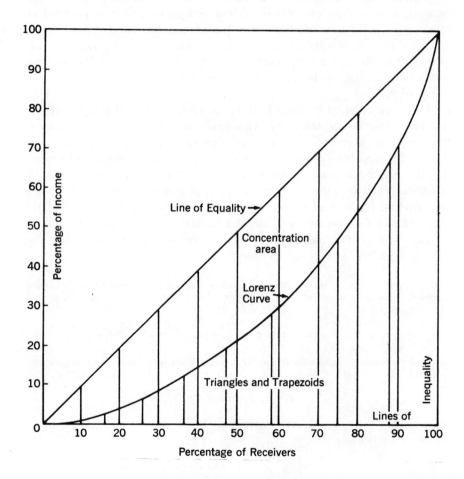

SOURCE: Katona *et al.*, *1961 Survey of Consumer Finances* (Ann Arbor: Survey Research Center, University of Michigan, 1962), Table 1.1, 1.3, pp. 8, 10.

Figure 3.2. Lorenz Curve, Money Income (U.S. Spending Units, 1960)

properties is that its slope at every point is the ratio of the corresponding income to the mean income.[6] (Its statistical use is not limited to distributions of income or wealth; for example, it has been employed in studies of industrial concentration and oligopoly.) If the distribution plotted is entirely equal, the Lorenz curve will be a 45-degree line through the points (0, 0) and (100, 100) at two vertices of Figure 3.2, since any percentage of recipients N will by hypothesis have received N per cent of the total income. At the opposite extreme, if all the income goes to one recipient, the Lorenz curve will degenerate into a pair of perpendicular straight lines, namely the horizontal base line and the right-hand vertical base line. On the diagram these two special cases have been labeled lines of equality and inequality, respectively. Unless there are negative incomes, the observed Lorenz curves pass through the points (0, 0) and (100, 100) but otherwise lie entirely between the lines of equality and inequality.

The more unequal the distribution, the larger will be the area between the Lorenz curve and the line of equality (the region labeled "concentration area" in Figure 3.2) as a proportion of the isosceles right triangle under this same line of equality. In cases approaching complete inequality, the two areas (concentration area and triangle) will include almost identical regions, so that their ratio will approach unity. In extreme cases of equality, the concentration area will approach zero both in absolute size and as a fraction of the triangular area.

The ratio of the concentration area to the triangular area under the line of equality is precisely the concentration ratio R. Barring negative

---

6. If the Lorenz curve is a continuous function, the cumulative percentage of income receivers (abscissa) of any observation at any income level Y_1 is the quotient of two definite integrals:

$$\int_{-\infty}^{Y_1} N(Y)\, dY \Big/ \int_{-\infty}^{\infty} N(Y)\, dY$$

while the cumulative proportion of income received is the quotient of two other definite integrals:

$$\int_{-\infty}^{Y_1} Y N(Y)\, dY \Big/ \int_{-\infty}^{\infty} Y N(Y)\, dY,$$

each denominator being a constant. The slope of the Lorenz curve is, then, removing the indefinite integral signs, simply:

$$\frac{Y_1 N(Y_1)}{N(Y_1)} \Bigg/ \frac{\int_{-\infty}^{\infty} Y N(Y)\, dY}{\int_{-\infty}^{\infty} N(Y)\, dY}$$

The numerator of this expression reduces to Y_1, and the denominator to the arithmetic mean income $\bar{Y}$, so that we have, finally, the result that the slope of the Lorenz curve equals $(Y_1 / \bar{Y})$.

incomes, its limits are zero and unity. Observed values of R for the distribution of pre-tax money incomes by spending units have been between 0.35 and 0.42 in the United States, somewhat lower in the United Kingdom. We owe to the University of Michigan study of *Income and Welfare in the United States* our most systematic analysis of the variability of this ratio as units of analysis and income measures are changed. The Michigan group's adjustments and refinements have operated generally to lower the measured concentration ratio for the United States in 1959 (Table 3.2), in passing from "Gross factor income" to "Welfare ratio." These terms are explained in the table.

Table 3.2.   Concentration Ratios for Various Units of Analysis and Measures of Income (United States, 1959)

	Adult Units	Spending Units	Families
Gross factor income (Deduct imputed items and transfer payments) . Result is:	.485	.431	.419
Money income (Deduct personal taxes) . Result is:	.448	.393	.385
Disponsable money income (Add back imputed items, and irregular private transfers) Result is:	.422	.363	.355
Gross disposable income (Divide by budget standard) . Result is:	.402	.353	.346
Welfare ratio	.346	n.a.	.309

SOURCE: James N. Morgan *et al., Income and Welfare in the United States,* (New York: McGraw-Hill, 1962) , table 20.2, p. 315. For definitions of certain of the terms used, cf. *ibid.,* pp. 188–190, or chapter 2 of this book.

Certain disadvantages of the Lorenz curve–concentration ratio approach to the measurement of inequality have been indicated by many statisticians, most fully by Garvy.[7] The ratio is insensitive to changes in income distribution and to errors of measurement. Its observed range of variation within a country over time seems small, as compared with possible sampling errors. The ratio does not distinguish between different *locations* of inequality within the income range; for example, between the effects of unemployment increasing inequality at the low end during depressions, and the effects of dividends increasing it at the high end during prosperity. More useful base lines than the line of equality can be

7. George Garvy, *Inequality of Income: Causes and Measurement,* in Studies in Income and Wealth, vol. 15, esp. pp. 27–30, 36–39. Compare also Morgan *et al., op. cit.,* pp. 311–313.

conceived. In analyzing spending units of different sizes, Garvy proposes to substitute the hypothetical Lorenz curve that would result from an equal distribution of per capita income. The result would, in all probability, be a lower value of R. Finally, no algebraic formula is computed for the Lorenz curve, and the computed approximations of the concentration ratio have a bias that makes the computed values of R systematically too low. The more observations are available, and the more evenly they are spread along the Lorenz curve, the smaller is this bias.

A simple method of computing concentration ratios is illustrated by Table 3.3. It involves summation of areas double those of the triangles and trapezoids in Figure 3.2, and subtracting the sum from 10,000 (double the area of the triangle under the line of equality). Division of the difference by 10,000 gives an estimate of R. The sample computations of the table, using American data for 1960,[8] illustrate our statements regarding bias in such estimates. The data for income groups, with observations bunched near the high end of the Lorenz curve, give an underestimate of R (section a). The data for income deciles are less biased (section b), because observations are spaced more evenly. Combining the data of both parts into a single section c, we have the unusual result of a fall in R as compared with section b. (This anomaly we ascribe to rounding of the original data.)

Distribution Formulas and Their Generation[9]

4. The Pareto line of section 2 is an example of a *distribution formula*. It fits the upper tails of many personal income distributions very well, but the remainder very badly. We shall now consider some other formulae that fit the overall distributions better. We shall also consider briefly (stating many results without proof) some of the statistical processes that might generate some of these empirical functions.

A simple example of a statistical process generating a function is the Central Limit Theorem of probability theory. Suppose a variable, distributed in any way we please. If random samples of size n are taken and the mean of each sample computed, then the theorem says, among other things, that these sample means will be distributed normally if n is sufficiently large. In this example, the statistical process is called sampling for

8. In Table 3.3 the "dummy" rows permit triangles to be treated as trapezoids (with one altitude of zero length) for the purpose of computing their areas. The "paired sum" columns are sums of the two altitudes of each of the series of trapezoids by which the Lorenz curve is approximated.

9. An introductory treatment of this subject, aimed at the statistical economist rather than the economic statistician, is Lawrence R. Klein, *An Inroduction to Econometrics* (Englewood Cliffs, N.J.: Prentice-Hall, 1962), ch. 4.

Table 3.3 Concentration Ratios, Money Incomes (U.S. Spending Units, 1960)

Income Bracket ($000)	Percentage of Receivers / Income (1)	Percentage of Income (2)	Cumulative % of Income (3) = Cum. (2)	Paired Sums of (3) (4)	Trapezoidal Areas (5) = (1) × (4)
a. By Income Groups					
Dummy	0	0	0	—	—
Under 1	6	1	1	1	6
1–1.99	10	2	3	4	40
2–2.99	10	4	7	10	100
3–3.99	10	6	13	20	200
4–4.99	11	9	22	35	385
5–5.99	13	12	34	56	728
6–7.49	15	17	51	85	1,275
7.50–9.99	13	19	70	121	1,573
10 and over	13	30	100	170	2,210
Total	100	100			6,517
b. By Income Deciles					
Dummy	0	0	0	—	—
Lowest (0–1.39)	10	1	1	1	10
Second (1.40–2.39)	10	3	4	5	50
Third (2.4–3.29)	10	5	9	13	130
Fourth (3.30–4.21)	10	6	15	24	240
Fifth (4.22–5.00)	10	8	23	38	380
Sixth (5.10–5.91)	10	9	32	55	550
Seventh (5.92–6.79)	10	11	43	75	750
Eighth (6.80–8.01)	10	13	56	99	990
Ninth (8.02–10.50)	10	16	72	128	1,280
Highest (> 10.51)	10	28	100	172	1,720
Total	100	100			6,100

For part a:

$$R = \frac{10,000 - 6,517}{10,000}$$

$$R = .348$$

For part b:

$$R = \frac{10,000 - 6,100}{10,000}$$

$$R = .390$$

Table 3.3.—(Continued)

c. (a) + (b) Combined

Income Bracket ($000)	Percentage of Receivers (1)	Percentage of Income (2)	Cumulative % of Income (3) = Cum. (2)	Paired Sums of (3) (4)	Trapezoidal Areas (5) = (1) × (4)
Dummy	0	0	0	—	—
0–1	6	0.5	0.5	0.5	3
1.0–1.39	4	0.5	1	1.5	6
1.39–1.99	6	2	3	4	24
2.0–2.39	4	1	4	7	28
2.4–2.99	6	3	7	11	66
3.0–3.29	4	2	9	16	64
3.3–3.99	6	4	13	22	132
4.0–4.21	4	2	15	28	112
4.22–4.99	7	7	22	37	259
5.0–5.09	3	1	23	45	135
5.1–5.91	9	9	32	55	495
5.91–5.99	1	2	34	66	66
6.0–6.79	10	9	43	77	770
6.8–7.49	55	8	51	94	470
7.5–8.01	5	5	56	107	535
8.02–9.99	8	14	70	126	1,008
10.0–10.50	2	2	72	142	284
10.51 and over	10	28	100	172	1,720
Total	100	100			6,177

$$R = \frac{10,000 - 6,177}{10,000}$$

$$R = .382$$

SOURCE: See Figure 3.2.

the mean, and the function generated is the normal or Gaussian law of error.

5. Income and wealth distributions are usually skewed to the right, meaning that they include a relatively few extremely large values. In technical terms, they are positively skewed, rather than normal, distributions. A simple process that generates a skew distribution is the law of proportional effect, which has in fact been applied to income distributions by Gibrat.[10] Suppose that a number of individuals each have at the outset an income y_o, and that each individual's income undergoes a series of random proportional changes r_i—capital gains and losses, perhaps. The r_i may be either positive or negative. After t periods, with one such shock per period, each original income y_o will become

$$y_t = y_o (1 + r_1) (1 + r_2) \ldots (1 + r_t)$$

whose logarithm is

$$\log y_t = \log y_o + \sum_1^t \log u_i$$

where u_i equals $(1 + r_i)$.

If the u_i are independent of each other, the Central Limit Theorem implies that both their sum and their mean will tend toward normality in large samples. This implies that the distribution of $\log y_t$ will tend toward normality in large samples. Converting from logarithms to ordinary numbers, we get the log-normal or Gibrat curve, which does in fact fit many income distributions quite closely (see the references in fn. 10), although it does not do as well as the Pareto disirubtion in the upper ranges.

Another statistical process generating the Pareto distribution was worked out by Simon for executive salaries and by Lydall for employment incomes.[11] Suppose that employees within each representative firm

10. Robert Gibrat, "On Economic Inequality," *International Economic Papers* (1957). See also J. Aitchison and J. A. C. Brown, *The Lognormal Distribution* (Cambridge: Cambridge University Press, 1957), ch. 11, and C. Takahashi *et al., Dynamic Changes in Income and Its Distribution in Japan* (Tokyo: Kinokuniya, 1959) *passim.*

11. Herbert A. Simon, "The Compensation of Executives," *Sociometry* (March 1957), developed by Robin Marris, *The Economic Theory of "Managerial" Capitalism* (New York: Free Press, 1964), pp. 89–99. Also Harold F. Lydall, "The Distribution of Employment Income," *Econometrica* (April 1959). A more significant "pyramid variable" than the number of bodies supervised is often the value of assets for which responsibility is assumed. Either sort of pyramid explains the observed tendency for executive compensation to be correlated more closely with firm size than with profitability, as per David R. Roberts, "A General Theory of Executive Compensation," *Q.J.E.* (May 1956) and *Executive Compensation* (Glencoe: Free Press, 1959). Thomas Mayer, in "The Distribution of Ability and Earnings," *Rev. Econ. and Stat.* (May 1960), speaks of a general "scale-of-operations effect," which correlates positively the number of units of a man's "production" and the probability of successful completion of each unit to explain quite generally for skewness phenomenon in the size distribution of incomes.

form a pyramid. Each man in each grade (except, of course, the bottom one) has q subordinates, and the income paid to this man is p times the total paid to his q subordinates in the grade below. Both p and q are positive constants independent of i; q is greater than unity, but p need not be.

If y_i is the average income in any grade, these assumptions give us

$$\frac{y_{i+1}}{q\,y_i} = p, \quad \text{or} \quad \frac{y_{i+1}}{y_i} = p\,q; \quad \text{also} \quad \frac{n_i}{n_{i+1}} = q, \quad \text{or} \quad \frac{n_{i+1}}{n_i} = \frac{1}{q}$$

A double-logarithmic graph of the number of persons n_i in each grade, plotted against the grade income level y_i, will now produce a negatively sloping Pareto line. Its slope is defined as

$$\frac{\log n_{i+1} - \log n_i}{\log y_{i+1} - \log y_i} = \frac{\log \,(n_{i+1}/n_i)}{\log \,(y_{i+1}/y_i)} = \frac{\log \,(1/q)}{\log pq} = \frac{-\log q}{\log pq}.$$

With p and q constant, this slope is likewise constant, and equal to the Pareto α.

Several writers have worked out more complex distributions, tending to the Pareto form for higher incomes only.[12] Lydall, for example, attaches a Pareto upper tail to a log-normal distribution for the "standard form" of his *Structure of Earnings*.

6.   A more general approach uses the Markoff chain to generate income distributions with no reference to any particular formula or curve type. This method may be regarded as expressing quantitatively the facts of social mobility as applied to incomes; some of its results illustrate a popular theory that "if everyone started out equal tomorrow, in a few years we would have just as much inequality as we have today."

Suppose that all income receivers are divided into n size brackets, and that we have two distributions for identical income receivers in successive time periods. From this information we can compute the "transition probability" p_{ij} that an individual in class i at time t will be in class j (which may of course be the same as class i) at time $t+1$. We can then tabulate the p_{ij} into a matrix of non-negative transition probabilities or vectors $p_{i,t}, p_{i,t+1}, p_{i,t+2}, \ldots, p_{i,t+k}$ which is called a Markoff chain. Eventually a stationary solution may be reached, quite independent of the original distribution $p_{i,t}$, such that the $p_{i,t+k}$ are identical with the $p_{i,t+k+1}$. Table 3.4 includes an example. Indeed, such a result is general,

12. D. G. Champernowne, "A Model of Income Distribution," *Ec. J.* (September 1953) ; Herbert A. Simon, *Models of Man* (New York: Wiley, 1958) , ch. 9; Klein, *op. cit.*, pp. 156 f.; Benoit Mendelbrot, "The Pareto-Levy Law and the Distribution and Income Maximization," *Q.J.E.* (February 1962) ; Josef Steindl, *Random Process and the Growth of Firms: A Study of the Pareto Law* (New York: Hafner, 1965) , ch. 6.

provided only that the matrix of transition probabilities is not *partitioned;* that is, that there are no classes i and j between which movement is impossible. (A hypothetical partitioned transition matrix with four income

Table 3.4.   Matrices of Personal Income
Transition Probabilities

a. Notation
Income Bracket, Period t + *1*

Income Period Period t	1	2		n	Total	$p_{i,t}$
1	p_{11}	p_{12}	$\ldots$	p_{1n}	1	$p_{1,t}$
2	p_{21}	p_{22}	$\ldots$	p_{2n}	1	$p_{2,t}$
.	.	.		.	.	.
.	.	.		.	.	.
.	.	.		.	.	.
n	p_{n1}	p_{n2}	$\ldots$	p_{nn}	1	$p_{n,t}$
Total	$p_{1,t+1}$ $(= \Sigma p_{i1} p_{i,t})$	$p_{2,t+1}$ $(= \Sigma p_{i2} p_{i,t})$	$\ldots$	$p_{n,t+1}$ $(= \Sigma p_{in} p_{i,t})$	1	1

b. Hypothetical Illustration of Convergence

Transition probabilities:

	Rich	Middle Class	Poor
Rich	.60	.30	.10
Middle class	.20	.40	.40
Poor	.10	.20	.70

Initial distributions (at time t_o):

	(1) Equal	(2) Unequal
Rich	.00	.40
Middle class	1.00	.20
Poor	.00	.40

Subsequent distributions in first and fifth periods (t_1, t_5):

	t_1		t_5	
	(1) Equal	(2) Unequal	(1) Equal	(2) Unequal
Rich	.20	.32	.25488	.26098
Middle class	.40	.28	.28170	.28342
Poor	.40	.40	.46342	.45561

classes is constructed as Table 3.5. It is clearly impossible to move from classes 1 or 2 to classes 3 or 4, or vice versa. There is a steady-state result, but it is not independent of the initial distribution.)

Empirical testing of this explanation for the British income distribution of 1954 has been carried out by Vandome in the course of an Oxford savings survey. Transition probabilities between 1953 and 1954 incomes

Table 3.5. Partitioned Matrix of Income Transition Probabilities

Income Bracket Period t	Income Bracket Period t + 1				
	1	*2*	*3*	*4*	*Total*
1	.70	.30	0	0	1
2	.40	.60	0	0	1
3	0	0	.50	.50	1
4	0	0	.25	.75	1

were calculated to form a 12- by 12-square array of income brackets.[13] Although more than half of the 144 possible p_{ij} were zero, the matrix of transition probabilities was not partitioned. Table 3.6 gives Vandome's results for both 1953 and 1954 distributions, together with the stationary state that would result from a Markoff chain of income distributions for 1955, 1956, . . . , using the same p_{ij}. This steady state was surprisingly close to the actual 1954 distribution, except in the highest brackets.

The transition probability–Markoff chain approach is, we have said, independent of any particular algebraic formula for the income distribu-

Table 3.6. Pre-Tax Income Distributions (United Kingdom, 1953–54) and Stationary Distribution (Percentages of Receivers)

Income Bracket (Pounds Sterling)	1953	1954	Stationary
0–99	3.5	3.4	3.4
100–199	13.6	14.1	13.9
200–299	12.5	12.4	11.5
300–399	15.3	15.8	15.3
400–499	17.1	13.0	11.4
500–599	11.2	15.5	14.6
600–699	13.3	13.5	13.3
700–799	4.5	3.5	3.1
800–999	5.1	4.5	3.7
1,000–1,499	2.6	3.0	4.3
1,500–1,999	0.5	0.4	0.9
2,000 and over	0.8	1.0	4.6

SOURCE: Vandome, *op. cit.*, reproduced in Klein, *op. cit.*, table 4.8, p. 169.

13. Peter Vandome, "Aspects of the Dynamics of Consumer Behavior," *Bull. Oxford Inst. Stat.* (1958). Vandome's 1953 incomes were multiplied by 1.09 for increased comparability with 1954 incomes in a period of economic growth and price inflation. (Omission of this adjustment would have exaggerated the degree of upward mobility.)

tion itself. Special conditions on transition probabilities, however, may force the stationary distribution at time $(t + k)$ into some definite form, such as the Pareto or the Gibrat distribution. For example, Champernowne considers transition probabilities p_{ij} whose sizes depend on the *spread* between the two classes i and j:

$$p_{ij} = q\ (j - i) \qquad\qquad (j \neq i)$$

where q is a constant, where the upper limit of each class is a fixed multiple of the lower limit, and where the unit interval is specially defined for each value of i (each row of a matrix like Table 3.3) so as to make

$$p_{ij} = 1 - \sum_j q\ (j - i) \qquad\qquad (j \neq 1)$$

Champernowne then shows, under these restrictions, that the stationary income distribution approaches the Pareto formula. Other writers, using the quotient (j/i) where Champernowne used the difference $(j - i)$, derive the log-normal (Gibrat) formula instead.[14]

7. What are the social implication of all this algebra? At first glance, it bears out the conservative claim that once-and-for-all income redistribution, being ineffective in the long run, is seldom worth the trouble it involves. It is also subject, however, to a quite different interpretation, namely, that effective redistribution should not only "turn the rascals out," but also change people's chances of getting rich or poor (that is, the matrix of transition probabilities). Specifically, effective redistribution should increase the probability that any individual, wherever he stands at time t, will be closer to the mean income class m at time $t + 1$. All the p_{in} with n close to or equal to m should be raised somehow, and other transition probabilities lowered. Of course, these changes in transition probabilities may react unfavorably on production, growth, or other desiderata. The algebra itself, however, provides no evidence that effective redistribution is (or is not) worth attempting. It is entirely neutral.

Explanations for Skewness

8. Many basic human attributes and abilities are apparently distributed normally. These include height, weight, muscular strength, and intelligence quotients.[15] It seems anomalous to many writers on the Left that

14. Klein, *op. cit.*, p. 170, and references cited there.

15. The normality of the I.Q. distribution is, however, contrived. Any distribution of I.Q. test scores can be skewed to the right by making the test questions more difficult, or to the left by making them easier. The normal, unskewed distribution is easiest to manipulate, and test construction strives to achieve it. The results, however, tell us nothing about the actual shape of the mental-ability distribution. Lydall, *Structure of Earnings, op. cit.*, pp. 76–79, and references cited there.

the distributions of income and wealth (positive values only) should be skewed so obviously to the right. With little reference to such algebra as we have just considered, critics have assumed from the mere fact of skewness that the distributional pattern cannot be based on ability alone. It reflects, they maintain, the cumulative consequences of economic institutions, particularly the inheritance of property and of "connections" leading to lucrative employment.

A number of "natural" or "statistical" explanations for the skewness of the income distributions have, however, been advanced. One, which can be related to transition probabilities, has been considered above. Several other explanations have been summarized by Staehle and later by Lebergott.[16] Most formally, income may depend upon the value of the *product* (not the sum) of a number of independent abilities, each distributed normally. This would bring income within the scope of the law of proportional effect, in which case it is the logarithm of income that one would expect to be normal—and lo, we have the Gibrat distribution. It is also possible to find a number of complex or compound abilities distributed, like income, in a skewed fashion. Examples are skill at shooting billiards and scholarly creativity in the production of mathematical papers. Another conservative suggestion is that the economic system may give high rewards for supernormal abilities, while exacting relatively low penalties for subnormal ones. In this case, the observed skew distribution results from the combination of two normal semidistributions. The left-hand distribution (subnormal abilities) has a low standard deviation, and the right-hand distribution (supernormal abilities) has a high standard deviation.

Since the publication of Staehle's pioneering paper, a number of economic explanations for skewness of the income distribution have been adduced. Milton Friedman, for example, suggests that people differ in their attitudes toward uncertainty-bearing:[17] A large number prefer security, and their incomes follow normal distribution *a* in Figure 3.3; a smaller number are gamblers by disposition, and their incomes follow normal distribution *b,* which has a somewhat higher mean and a much higher standard deviation. Adding the two distributions vertically, we get distribution *c,* which is clearly skewed to the right.

Similar arguments apply when attention is concentrated on investment in human capital. Becker and his associates have related the inequality of the income distribution both to inequality in schooling and to the

16. Hans Staehle, "Ability, Wages, and Income," *Rev. Econ. Stat.* (February 1943); Stanley Lebergott, "The Shape of the Income Distribution," *A.E.R.* (June 1959).

17. M. Friedman, "Choice, Chance, and the Personal Distribution of Income," *J.P.E.* (August 1953). For criticism, see Lebergott, *op. cit.,* pp. 332 f.

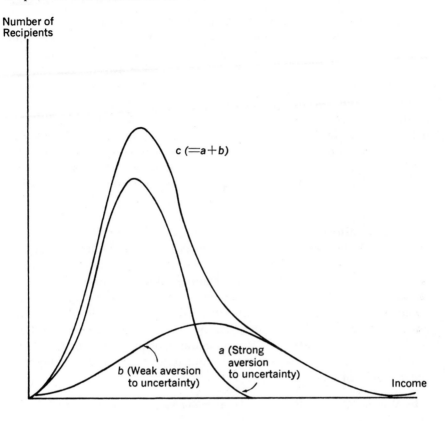

Figure 3.3

estimated rate of return to investment in education.[18] That is to say, in those American states where education is unequally distributed, both the estimated rate of return to additional education and the degree of income inequality are high. (These results are not particularly surprising.) Mincer has gone furthest in the direction we are considering here, relating the skewness of the income distribution to differences in expenditure on human capital formation, primarily education.[19] His results can be assimilated to Friedman's by treating "investment in education" as a form of "preference for uncertainty."

18. Gary S. Becker, *Human Capital* (New York: Columbia University Press, 1964), pp. 61–66; Becker and Barry R. Chiswick, "Education and the Distribution of Earnings," *A.E.R.* (May 1966), pp. 365–368.
19. Jacob Mincer, "Investment in Human Capital and Personal Income Distribution," *J.P.E.* (August 1958).

Another treatment of the skewness problem is the "standardization approach." By breaking down the population of income receivers into cells of identical or near-identical age, education, race, sex, geographical location, occupation type, and incidence of unemployment, one can reduce substantially the degree of skewness of the income distribution within each cell, and then explain the skewness of the entire distribution as the result of adding numerous normal distributions with different means and standard deviations, as in the "Friedman" case of Figure 3.3. Miller, for example, argues that sex and occupational differences are primarily responsible for skewness in the United States.[20] Adams, also using American data, employs a complex scaling system to derive a forecasting equation for incomes of white males in a single year (1949).[21]

9. The maldistributionist critic, whether socialist or reformer, tends to explain both the skewness and the upper tail of the personal distribution as consequences primarily of the institution of inheritance of income-bearing property. Irving Fisher, no flaming radical, described the entire wealth distribution (which, as we have seen, is more unequal than that of incomes) as the result of "inheritance, constantly modified by thrift, ability, industry, luck, and fraud," and the more conservative Edwin Cannan has said that "inequality in the amounts of property which individuals have received by way of bequest and inheritance is by far the most potent cause of inequality."[22]

20. Herman P. Miller, *Income of the American People* (New York: Wiley, 1955), ch. 3.

21. F. Gerard Adams, "The Size of Individual Incomes: Socio-Economic Variables and Chance Variation," *Rev. Econ. and Stat.* (August 1958). His variables are:

$A = 1$, 18–24 years of age
$= 2$, 25–35 years
$= 3$, 35–44 years
$= 4$, 45–54 years
$= 5$, 55–64 years
$= 6$, 65 and over
$L = 0$, southern region
$= 1$, non-southern region
$C = 0$, open country.
$= 1$, community of fewer than 50,000.
$= 2$, community of 50,000 or more.

$E = 1$, low education (less than college for white-collar, less than high school for blue-collar workers).
$= 2$, high education.
$J = 0$, unskilled and service occupations.
$= 2$, high education.
$= 1$, semiskilled, skilled, clerical, and sales occupations.
$= 2$, managerial and professional.
$P = 0$, worked fewer than 11 months in 1949
$= 1$, worked full year in 1949.

His forecasting equation is:

$$\log\ Y = 2.65 + 20\,A - .027\,A^2 + .056\,E + .14\,J + .055\,L + .060\,C + .21\,P$$

A similar study for Great Britain is T. P. Hill, "An Analysis of the Distribution of Wages and Salaries in Great Britain," *Econometrica* (July, 1959). See also Klein, *op. cit.*, pp. 171–178. Lebergott (*op. cit.*, pp. 339–343) supplements a "standardization" approach with credit-rationing considerations. These truncate the lower tail of the distribution by limiting the amounts of (borrowed) money people can lose.

22. Fisher, *Elementary Principles of Economics* (New York: Macmillan, 1912), p. 513; Cannan, *The Economic Outlook* (London: Unwin, 1912), p. 249.

We do not yet know how great may be the element of exaggeration in such statements as these, or indeed, whether they are inflated at all. Stigler, however, has developed an elementary schema for working out the distributional consequences of varying assumptions about the process of inheritance.[23]

Let the growth rate of the stock of property, in value terms but deflated for price-level changes, be g. (Under full equilibrium, g will be equal to the interest rate after proper allowance for imputed income. Stigler does not make this assumption.) Then, if present property owners have held their capital an average of n years, the estimated value of the inherited portion at the time of inheritance can be computed by a discounting formula. Call the inherited proportion k. Assume further that inherited and personally accumulated property earn, in the aggregate, equal rates of return. Then k is also the proportion of property *income* derived directly from inheritance. By the discounting formula,

$$k = \frac{1}{(1 + g)^n}$$

whose results are presented in Table 3.7 for a few values of g and n. Clearly, the relative importance of inheritance moves inversely to both these variables. Multiplying further by the proportion of income from property to total income, we might obtain a further series of estimates of the influence of inheritance on total income.

Such estimates would, however, have a downward bias. They make no allowance for the indirect inheritance of labor income through superior educational opportunities and superior access to higher-paid jobs, as by Henry Ford II in the Ford Motor Company, David Rockefeller in the

*Table 3.7. Percentage of Property Income
Derived from Inheritance*

Average Growth Rate of Capital Value (g)	*Average Holding Period by Present Owners* (n)			
	10 yrs.	*15 yrs.*	*20 yrs.*	*25 yrs.*
2.0 per cent	0.82	0.74	0.67	0.61
2.5	0.78	0.69	0.61	0.54
3.0	0.75	0.64	0.55	0.48
3.5	0.71	0.60	0.50	0.42
4.0	0.68	0.56	0.46	0.38
5.0	0.61	0.48	0.38	0.30
6.0	0.56	0.42	0.31	0.23
8.0	0.46	0.32	0.21	0.15

23. George J. Stigler, *Theory of Price*, 3rd ed. (New York: Macmillan, 1966), pp. 309 f.

Chase Manhattan Bank, the doctor's son in medical school, the bricklayer's son in the bricklayers' union, and indeed the entire congeries of factors summarized in classical economics under the heading of "noncompeting groups."

Neither should the "outright robbery" explanation of the distribution's skewness and upper tail be entirely forgotten. A particularly forthright explanation along these lines comes from Gamal Abdel Nasser of Egypt, speaking as a socialist and recognizing as legitimate only income derived from labor:[24]

> How can a man gather a million pounds, two, three, 10 or 20 million pounds? How did he get all his money? Any man living in this world, if he remained throughout his working lifetime, and if we gave him the largest possible return for his work, could not possibly manage to gather a million pounds for his work. Only through exploitation, chicanery, skulduggery, theft, and virtual enslavement of workers can a person acquire a million pounds.

Poverty: Islands and Cases

10. Many studies have been made, from icily statistical to heatedly passionate, on the question, "Who and why the poor?" Are our Lower Depths really different from our Upper Reaches? Was Wesley, in point of fact, sociologically correct to assert of a drunkard: "There, but for the Grace of God, goes John Wesley"?

A popular classification of poverty types comes from Galbraith. His division is into "island" and "case" poverty; the "islands" refer to "pockets of poverty" and the "cases" to individual or group handicaps:[25]

> If the head of a family is stranded deep in the Cumberland plateau, or if he never went to school, or if he has no useful skill, or if his health is broken, or if he succumbed as a youngster to a slum environment, or if opportunity is denied him because he is a Negro, then he will be poor and his family will be poor, and that will be true no matter how opulent everyone else becomes.

Galbraith has been interpreted as claiming that his "islands" are, or can be reduced easily to, Robinson-Crusoe specks in the Antipodes, and his "cases" to two-headed freaks in medical museums. The burden of his critics' argument has been that his islands are as large as the Australian continent, his cases as frequent as the common cold.

---

24. Nasser, quoted in *Muhammad Speaks* (Chicago, October 28, 1966).

25. The division was made in Galbraith's *Affluent Society*, ch. 23. The quoted passage is from his "Let Us Begin," *Harper's* (March 1964), p. 16. Of the six illustrations included, the first and fifth are "islands," while the other four are "cases." (The two types may, of course, overlap.)

We will review here the methods and conclusions of five statistically sophisticated studies of poverty on the American scene, which are of the sort criticized from the Left for understatement. (Harrington's *Other America,* for example, argues that most of the poor are hidden away in side-street slums, furnished rooms, or rural back roads that researchers seldom visit, and that they venture out only in "ordinary" clothes. For these reasons, he continues, detached professionals understate the problem and ignore its human aspects. A foreign critic, Gunnar Myrdal, goes further. He calls poverty "an ugly smell rising from the basement of the stately American mansion."[26])

11. Using a conventional definition (which we have criticized earlier in Chapter 2, section 5), the Council of Economic Advisers (with Lampman as principal consultant) has estimated the low-income population at 20 per cent of the total in 1962. This compares with 23 per cent in 1956, 28 per cent in 1952, and 32 per cent in 1947. The council anticipates a further decline to 10 per cent by 1980, on the assumption that poverty declines at the same annual rate as it did in the delade 1947–1956.[27] More important for our present purposes, the council divides the poor according to handicapping and descriptive characteristics; the writer has used their data to compute some "poverty coefficients," which are presented in Table 3.8. The largest such coefficient (2.75) is associated, to no one's surprise, with the absence of an income earner in the family. The next three are for closely related attributes: family head female, not in the labor force, or aged (2.50, 2.44, 2.43). Then comes a gap of several points, followed by rural farm residence (2.29) and nonwhite color (2.20). By contrast, the lowest coefficient is 0.35, not shown in the table, for families whose heads have had education beyond high school.

We also owe to Lampman another presentation, Table 3.9, that indicates qualitatively how susceptible many important causes of poverty may be to the "disease" of economic growth. They will all be ameliorated substantially, in his view, although he would agree with Galbraith that the complete elimination of poverty "won't be accomplished simply by stepping up the growth rate, any more than . . . by incantation or ritualistic washing of the feet. Growth is only for those who can take advantage of it."[28]

26. Myrdal, *Challenge to Affluence* (New York: Pantheon, 1962), p. 49.

27. *Economic Report of the President* (1964), pp. 59 f.

28. Galbraith, "Let Us Begin," *op. cit.,* p. 16. The Lampman and Galbraith positions are less easily reconciled at budget time than in this study. Lampman is a spokesman for economists and others who stress an "aggregative" or "growth" approach in the "war on poverty." Galbraith is a spokesman for the "case" or "structural" approach, which is more elaborate and more directly expensive, but may involve less inflationary pressure.

Table 3.8.   Poverty Coefficients for Selected
Characteristics (United States, 1962)

Characteristics	Poverty Coefficient
Age of family head:	
14–24 years	1.60
65 years and over	2.43
Education of family head: 8 years or less	1.74
Sex of family head: female	2.50
Labor force status of family head:	
Not in civilian labor force	2.44
Unemployed	1.50
Color of family: nonwhite	2.20
Number of earners in family: none	2.75
Regional location of family: south	1.57
Residence of family	
Rural farm	2.29
Rural nonfarm	1.36
Number of children under 18 in family: none	1.30

SOURCE: *Economic Report of the President* (1964), Table 4, p. 61.

NOTES: 1. A "poverty coefficient" is defined as

$$\frac{\% \text{ of poor families with given characteristic}}{\% \text{ of all families with given characteristic}}$$

2. It is not legitimate to combine poverty coefficients for single characteristics in estimating poverty coefficients for multiple characteristics. For example, these data do not permit estimation of coefficients for persons both elderly and with poor education.

Table 3.9.   Importance of Selected Characteristics
in Future Trend of Low Income Population
(United States)

Characteristic	Percentage with This Characteristic 1957	Probable Changes over Time	Immunity to Economic Growth
Low education	67	Fall	High
Old age	25	Rise	High
Nonwhite color	20	Rise	Low
Female headship	25	Constant	High
Disability (all types)	n.a.	Constant	High
Large family size	33	Constant	Low

SOURCE: Lampman, "The Low Income Population and Economic Growth," *op. cit.*, p. 29.

Lampman's exception, as the table shows, is poverty among the aged. This may actually become more acute if the American economy grows more rapidly—"only this, and nothing more." In the first place, growth should increase postretirement life expectancy. In the second place, "useless" oldsters stay with their families in poor societies, because they cannot keep alive by themselves. In wealthier societies, they can eke out marginal existences in separate households and make the poverty statistics look bad, unless special pains are taken in their cases. This illustrates what is called the "privacy in poverty" dilemma.

Returning to statistical matters, the Survey Research Center has conducted its own survey of poverty, independently of any government agency. The center's estimate of 14.8 million family heads and single individuals living in poverty (1959) is based on a sample of 2800 families. This includes unusually detailed cross-classifications of principal causes of poverty; an example is Table 3.10. (Not reproduced are further breakdowns of physical and mental disability by type, and of the determinants of withdrawal from the labor force, the so-called voluntary unemployment.)

More current are the Social Security Administration studies under Miss Orshansky's direction, cited in Chapter 2. They use larger samples than others, and finer breakdowns can therefore be significant statistically. They are also repeated annually on comparable bases. Over and above these improvements, the main substantive "Orshansky contribution" is demographic. She underlines the old saw that "the rich get richer and the poor get children," stressing the larger-than-average family, possibly including one or more subfamilies, as a cause of poverty. Her results naturally provide support for family planning and allied social movements.

Thurow has used a *geographical* cross-section study of the incidence of poverty in the fifty American states (ranging from a high of 51.6 per cent for Mississippi to a low of 9.8 per cent for Connecticut in 1960) for another estimate of the causes of poverty, based on an econometric model.[29] His results do not permit ranking the causes in order of importance, but do include seven causes that, taken together, account for some 98 per cent

29. Lester C. Thurow, "The Causes of Poverty," *Q.J.E.* (February 1967). Thurow's variables for 1960 are listed and explained on p. 40:

P = percentage of families in poverty (income less than \$3000).
F = percentage of families living on farms.
N = percentage of families headed by a nonwhite.
L = percentage of families with no one in the labor force.
P = percentage of population 14 and over who worked 50–52 weeks per year.
I = index of state industrial structure: higher for states with concentrations of high-wage industry, and vice versa.
D = dummy variable = 1 for Alaska and Hawaii, 0 for other states.

Table 3.10.   Heads of Poor Families with Characteristics Related to Poverty (United States, 1959)

Likely Cause of Poverty	Aged	Disabled	Single, with Children	Unemployed in 1959	Nonwhite	Self-Employed Businessman or Farmer	None of These	Percentage With Other Indications of Poverty
1. Aged	100% 2.8 mill.	32% 0.9 mill.	1% 0.04 mill.	2% 0.04 mill.	22% 0.6 mill.	8% 0.2 mill.	0%	65%
2. Disabled, not (1)		100% 0.8 mill.	15% 0.1 mill.	4% 0.03 mill.	26% 0.2 mill.	17% 0.1 mill.	0%	62%
3. Single with children, not (1–2)			100% 1.1 mill.	14% 0.1 mill.	43% 0.5 mill.	3% 0.01 mill.	0%	60%
4. Usually employed. Worked < 49 weeks in 1959, not (1–3)				100% 0.9 mill.	29% 0.2 mill.	0%	0%	29%
5. Nonwhite, not (1–4)					100% 1.4 mill.	14% 1.4 mill.	0%	14%
6. Self-employed business man or farmer, not (1–5)						100% 1.0 mill.	0%	0%
7. Not (1–6)							100% 2.4 mill.	0%
Total	2.8 mill.	1.7 mill.	1.2 mill.	1.1 mill.	2.9 mill.	2.7 mill.	2.4 mill.	

SOURCE: Morgan et al., *Income and Welfare in the United States*, Table 16–3, p. 195.

of the interstate variation in the incidence of poverty. These are the percentage of the state's families on farms, the percentage headed by a nonwhite, the percentage with no member in the labor force, the percentage completing less than eight years of school, the percentage of the state's population underemployed, an index of the state's industrial structure, and a dummy variable correcting for the peculiar circumstances of Alaska and Hawaii.

An Income Revolution?

12. The thesis that America has had an "income revolution" arises from Kuznets' study of the declining share of upper income groups (the top 1 and 5 per cent) in American income and saving. It was stated more directly and controversially by Arthur F. Burns than by Kuznets himself.[30] The income revolution thesis immediately became a major element in propaganda for "modern," "enlightened," "responsible," or "people's" capitalism:

> Few Americans and still fewer Europeans are aware of the transformation in the distribution of our national income that has occurred within the past 20 years—a transformation that has been carried out peacefully and gradually, but which may already be counted as one of the great social revolutions of history.
> In 1929 the highest 5 percent of the income recipients obtained 34 percent of the total disposable income of individuals—that is, the total of personal income, inclusive of any capital gains but after deducting federal income tax payments. By 1939 their share had dropped to 27 percent of total income, and by 1946 to 18 percent . . . . If we now compare 1929 and 1946, we find that the share going to the top 5 percent groups declined 16 points. Had perfect equality of incomes been attained in 1946 the share would have dropped from 34 to 5 percent, that is, by 29 points. In other words, the income share of the top 5 percent stratum dropped 16 points out of a maximum possible drop of 29 points; so that, on the basis of this yardstick, we may be said to have trav-

---

A specimen equation (equation [1], p. 42) shows the first three dependent variables entering positively and the last three entering negatively, in accordance with expectations:

$$P = 96.51 + .2978\,F + .1133\,N + .5410\,L + .4345\,E - .5368\,W - .7600\,I - 10.38\,D.$$

All the explanatory variables are significant to at least the 5 per cent level, and the coefficient of determination is .98 after adjustment for loss of degrees of freedom. Thurow notes, however, the presence of intercorrelation among the independent variables.

30. Burns, "Looking Forward," in *Frontiers of Economic Knowledge* (New York: National Bureau of Economic Research, 1954), pp. 135 f. The "Kuznets" references are to Simon S. Kuznets, *Shares of Upper Income Groups in Income and Savings* (New York: National Bureau of Economic Research, 1953).

,elled in a bare two decades over half the distance separating the 1929 distribution from a perfectly egalitarian distribution. If we turn to the top 1 instead
of the top 5 percent group, the results are still more striking. The share of the
top 1 percent group in total income was 19.1 percent in 1929 and 7.7 percent
in 1946. Since the share of this group dropped 11.4 points out of a total possible drop of 18.1 points, we have traveled since 1929 on the basis of this yardstick almost two-thirds of the distance towards absolute income equality. Re-
grettably, the "iron curtain" precludes comparison of our achievement with
that of the vaunted "people's democracies," but it is permissible to wonder
whether many of them can point to so vast a democratization of the distributive process in their own countries.

13.   Responses were not long in coming. Starting with a frankly partisan
Labor Research Association pamphlet on *The Income "Revolution"* and
Lampman's article "Recent Trends in Income Inequality."[31] they have
continued ever since. Debate has questioned both the *uniqueness* and the
genuineness of the American "democratization of the distributive process"
during the period 1929–1946. Is it related specifically to American institution of "people's capitalism," or is it an expected consequence of short-
term recovery from depression, or a result of long-term economic growth?
To what extent has the National Bureau relied on statistical artifacts, resulting from various devices to avoid income taxes and from changes in
the relative sizes of rich and poor families?
14.   The question of uniqueness has not been explored thoroughly, but
Solow has made a systematic comparison with a number of European industrial nations over a twenty-year period ending in the mid-1950s. A
running quotation lists his principal conclusions:[32]

> In all cases the movement over time has been toward equality; in all cases
> (except possibly Sweden) the movement has been slight. One important differ-
> ence shows up between American and European experience. In [European
> countries] there is some evidence that the process of equalisation has continued
> past the end of the war. In this country after 1947, only very small changes
> took place in the pre-tax distribution of income. Sweden started in 1935 with
> the most unequal distribution of any we have recorded and wound up in
> 1954 with one of the least unequal. One is tempted to connect this with the
> fact, that, of all the countries represented, real personal income per head
> increased fastest (between 1938 and 1954) in Sweden.

31. Victor Perlo "The Income 'Revolution'" (New York: International Publishers,
1964); Lampman "Recent Trends in Income Inequality," *A.E.R.* (June 1956). A
vehement summary is given by Perlo (*op. cit.*, p. 7): "Kuznets measured the wrong
things, and he measured them wrongly. Correct measurement would show no decline
in the share of the top 1 percent or top 5 percent of the population. And measurement
of the right things would show a marked increase in the control over income and
wealth by the top handful who run big business in the United States."

32. Robert M. Solow, "Income Inequality Since the War," in Ralph E. Freeman (ed.),
Postwar Economic Trends in the United States (New York: Harper, 1960), pp. 113 f.

Contrasting this country with Europe, we started off in the thirties with a slightly less equal distribution than the United Kingdom, about the same as the Netherlands, and a more equal distribution than either Germany or Sweden. By 1954, we had more equal distribution than the Netherlands and Western Germany, about the same as the United Kingdom, and a trifle less than Sweden. In recent years the lowest quantile has had a noticeably smaller share of total income in the United States than in the United Kingdom or in Sweden.

Unlike the Kuznets volume, Solow's international comparison considers the entire personal distribution rather than its upper tail. Strict comparability between the two studies is therefore not achieved. At the same time, Solow has touched upon a rebuttal point, which we shall consider later, to the effect that "the only significant rises [sic] in income distribution have occurred in the second- and third-richest income tenths . . . This group is largely made up of . . . professionals, small businessmen, top clerical workers, and lesser managers, with rising salary or wage incomes and no unemployment, and by no means was in urgent need of a greater share of the national income."[33]

15. The most vehement attack upon the income-revolution thesis charges statistical legerdemain. These charges relate to both individual and corporate "adjustments" to the rising personal and corporate income taxes of the New Deal and World War II. The lower personal income share of upper income groups reflects, say the critics, little more than tax avoidance and evasion.[34] They point to lower pay-out rates of corporate dividends (avoiding personal income taxes for wealthy stockholder), the so-called "expense-account way of life," the spreading of income over time in deferred compensation and executive retirement plans, the conversion of personal income into capital gains (which need never be realized) by stock-purchase options for executives, and outright evasion through underreporting of property income. Another statistical problem arises from Kuznets' choice of per capita income as his basic measure. This is affected by changes in family size, and also in the number of income earners per family. According to basic tables by Selma Goldsmith,[35] the number of

33. Gabriel Kolko, *Wealth and Power in America* (New York: Praeger, 1962).

34. A brief but vitriolic attack on the grounds mentioned here, citing many basic sources, is found in Kolko, *op. cit.*, pp. 16–23. In connection with capital gains, Kuznets' "basic variant" of income, source of the controversial Burns quotation, is unusual in *including* such gains (when realized).

35. Selma F. Goldsmith *et al.*, "Income Distribution" supplement to *Survey of Current Business* (Washington: Government Printing Office, 1953); Selma F. Goldsmith *et al.*, "Size Distribution of Income Since the Mid-Thirties," *Rev. Econ. and Stat.* (February 1954); Selma Goldsmith, "Size Distribution of Personal Income," *Survey of Current Business* (April 1958). Much of the Goldsmith data is collected and condensed in Solow, *op. cit.*, table X, p. 117.

persons per family has, in the generation since 1935–36, fallen much less in the top quintile of families than elsewhere in the income distribution. At the same time, the number of income earners per family in the top quintile seems to have risen absolutely as well as relatively to the remainder of the population.

Nor should we forget to consider the other 95 or 99 per cent of the income distribution. Assembling imperfectly comparable estimates by deciles from several sources for the half century beginning in 1910,[36] Kolko concluded, as quoted above, that the income share of the lowest 20 per cent has fallen, and that the large relative gains have been in the second and third deciles from the top. Figure 3.4, reproducing his data for 1929 and 1959 as Lorenz curves, illustrates this conclusion.

We have computed concentration ratios for Kolko's data and fitted time trends to them. Over the entire half century, the slope of this trend is practically zero (insignificantly positive). This bears out Kolko's antithesis of unchanging income inequality, but the results rest heavily on highly equalitarian (and statistically questionable) distributions for 1910 and 1917. For the subperiod since 1929 there is a downward trend of .00105 (0.105 per cent) per year in the concentration coefficient, and the issue is more dubious.

It is often admitted that any American "income revolution" had run its course by the end of World War II. *Business Week* commented in 1963:[37]

> In 20 years, the sharing of income among rich, middleclass, and poor has scarcely changed. Indeed, Herman P. Miller, Census Bureau . . . specialist on trends in the distribution of income, foresees [the possibility of] more inequality, with relatively less income going to low-productivity workers . . . left behind by rapid technological advance.

Kravis has also surveyed the estimates of overall American income inequality for selected periods from 1888 to 1958. He finds two periods of decline in inequality, ending with World Wars I and II respectively. Like other students, he finds inequality essentially constant since 1945. Certain of his conclusions are reproduced as Table 3.11.

16.   Turning briefly to the British scene, sharp reductions in income inequality were also reported by the Board of Inland Revenue for the decade

36. Kolko, *op. cit.*, table I, p. 14. Data for 1910–1937 are from the National Industrial Conference Board, and for 1941–1959 from the Survey Research Center. (We have added 1960 Survey Research Center results.)

37. Unsigned article, "Income Revolution' Slows Up," *Business Week* (September 28, 1963), p. 144, based on advance proofs of Herman P. Miller, *Rich Man, Poor Man* (New York: Crowell, 1964). Compare also E. C. Budd, "Postwar Changes in the Size Distribution of Income in the U.S." (*A.E.R.*, May 1970).

1938–1948, although the term "income revolution" was not employed. During the early 1960s there arose in government circles a feeling that the equalizing movement had gone too far; certain reductions were made, beginning in 1961, in the relative burden of income taxes in the upper

Table 3.11. Indexes of Inequality (United States, Selected Years, 1888–1958)

(1950 = 100)	
Year or Period	*Index of Inequality*
1888–1890	137
1901	95
1918	89
1935–1936	116
1941	110
1944	98
1950	100
1956	97
1958	98

SOURCE: Irving Kravis, *The Structure of Incomes* (Philadelphia: University of Pennsylvania Press, 1962), p. 213.

brackets. Complacency regarding distributional issues was of long standing in Britain, since much traditional British economics anticipated automatic declines in inequality as development proceeded. The great name of Alfred Marshall, among others, had supported this position.[38] As in America, however, complacency has not gone unchallenged. A statistical rebuttal to the Board of Inland Revenue was drawn up by Titmuss while he was a member of the Labour party "shadow cabinet." Titmuss casts doubt on the alleged 1938–1948 reduction in inequality.[39] His arguments are much like those adduced for America by Lampman, Kolko, Perlo, and

38. Marshall's views are illustrated by a quotation from the penultimate chapter of his *Principles of Economics*, 9th ed. (London: Macmillan, 1961), p. 687:

The diffusion of education, and prudent habits among the masses of the people, and the opportunities . . . for the safe investment of small capitals, are telling on the side of moderate incomes. The returns of the income tax and the house tax, the statistics of consumption of commodities, the records of salaries paid to the higher and the lower ranks of employees of Government and public companies, all indicate that middle class incomes are increasing faster than those of the rich; that the earnings of artisans are increasing faster than those of the professional classes, and that the wages of healthy and vigorous unskilled labourers are increasing faster than those of the average artisan.

(This passage is followed by a sharp comment upon the American situation, which Marshall viewed as precisely contrary.)

39. Richard M. Titmuss, *Income Distribution and Society Changes—A Critical Study in British Statistics* (London: Allen and Unwin, 1962).

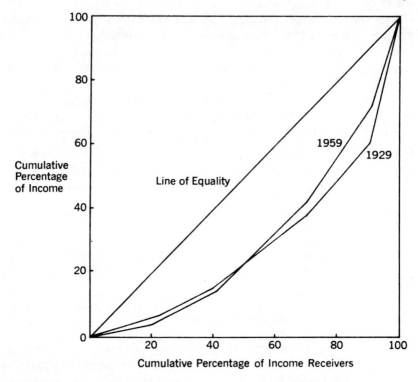

Source: Gabriel Kolko, *Wealth and Power in America,* Table 1, p. 14.

Percentage of Income Receivers	10	20	30	40	50	60	70	80	90	100
Percentage of Income, 1929	1.8	5.4	10.0	15.5	22.0	29.9	38.9	48.7	61.0	100
Same, 1959	1.1	4.0	8.6	14.9	22.7	31.9	42.6	55.3	71.1	100

Figure 3.4. Comparative Income Distribution Lorenz Curves (United States, 1929 and 1950)

others, with appropriate modifications for British tax laws and other institutional practices, particularly the traditional British leniency toward capital gains.

A Minatory Conclusion

17. The American income revolution, such as it was, largely ended by 1946, and may have reversed itself in some degree. Aggregative American distributional history in the subsequent fifteen years seems uneventful, but only because a number of individually significant changes happened to cancel each other out. A paper by Avril[40] summarizes a number of these

40. Wilbur L. Avril, "The Size Distribution of Income: 1947 to 1961" (mimeographed; Pennsylvania Conference of Economists, 1966) . See also B. F. Haley, "Changes in the Distribution of Income in the United States," Marchal and Ducros, *The Distribution of National Income* (London: Macmillan, 1968) , ch. 1.

developments, and points a more general moral: such sectorally significant developments should not be overlooked in the social critic's professional concern with the broad brush and the big picture.

The principal developments isolated by Avril are summarized below. They involve both the functional distribution of income by shares and the personal distribution of each share by total-income size groups. Several of the numerical conclusions, also, are unfortunately sensitive to choices made in connection with our "statistical conundrums" of Chapter 2, section 4.

(a) There was a substantial rise in the wage and salary share, from 63.3 to 69.9 per cent of the particular variant (family personal income as developed by the Office of Business Economics) used by Avril. This rise was due in turn to the migration of some 1.5 million families out of agriculture into wage-earning occupations, and to the increased importance of government civilian employment. This change alone would have *raised* the share of the top 10 per cent (who received 21.3 per cent of wages and salaries in 1947) by 0.6 points![41] In addition, however, the share of wages and salaries received by the top 10 per cent also rose to 24.9 per cent, reflecting the increasing numbers and importance of salaried managerial and professional workers. This shift in the distribution of wages and salaries would also, by itself, have raised the share of the upper 10 per cent by some 2.4 points.

(b) The share of self-employment income fell from 19.1 to 12.2 per cent of the total, and the share of the top 10 per cent of income receivers in self-employment income also fell from 55.7 to 51.8 per cent. Two main reasons for these declines were specifically agricultural—a decline both in farm prices and in the relative volume of farm sales. Avril also found evidence of profit squeeze in the construction, trade, and service industries, and claims that "high income salaried managers and professionals . . . replaced the self-employed as the dominant group in the upper 10 per cent."[42] These changes were the principal equalizing factors isolated in the Avril study.

(c) Pure property income rose from 11.4 to 13.8 per cent of family income. The major cause was the rise in personal interest income (up from 4.4 to 6.9 per cent in the period studied); the period from 1947 to 1961 was marked by both a rise in interest rates and a rise in the volume of interest-bearing debt relative to the gross national product. The dividend share also rose slightly, but net rental income declined, possibly in consequence of a shift to home ownership. Taking property income as a

41. This estimate ignores the correlative effects of declines in other functional shares, whose distribution was even more concentrated. It should, therefore, be taken with a grain of salt.

42. Avril, *op. cit.*, p. 20.

whole, the share of the top 10 per cent of income receivers declined, reducing the anti-equalitarian effect of the rise in property income itself.
The 1947 and 1961 figures for the upper-group share in property income
was 60.0 and 54.6 per cent respectively.

(d) Paradoxically, a small disequalizing influence is ascribable to the
rising importance of transfer payments from 6.2 to 8.2 per cent of the
total, going primarily to the aged. This statistical result reflects Avril's
choice of the family as his recipient unit, with single individuals included
as one-person families. "By receiving these transfer payments, the elderly
could now exist as [separate low income families] rather than living with
their children in [higher income units]. Thus the growth of transfers
would cause a greater percent of [income] recipients to be found in the
low income range."[43]

(e) It is difficult to reach firm conclusions about the distributional
importance of the increasing availability of education, and Avril does not
make the attempt. An economic argument for cheap public education has
been, from the outset to the present and at all levels of schooling, that it
would open up high-paying work to the children of the poor, thus equalize the personal income distribution. It is, however, uncertain to what extent education has worked out this way.

The relative compensation for the lower range of clerical jobs, particularly those open to women or to part-time workers, has fallen; it no longer
profits the poor boy to escape from low-level blue-collar work into low-
level white-collar work. Other offsets have included (1) maintenance of
qualitative differentials between private and public education; (2) loss
of earnings to poor families while children attend school; (3) raising of
job standards to keep pace with the quality of applicants;[44] and (4) increased relative compensation of manual occupations requiring unusual
strength, endurance, or dexterity but *not* intellectual ability, thus creating
a new labor aristocracy.

Even so, Lydall has found "a reasonably good positive relation between
inequality of education and inequality of earnings" in an international
comparison of fifteen countries.[45] France, Japan, and perhaps Chile are
exceptions; the U.S., Canada, and Britain are not. Further than this he
does not go. The sociologists Jencks and Riesman, however, express surprise, possibly unwarranted, that the effect has not been larger under
American conditions:[46]

43. *Ibid.*

44. The responsibility for the raising of job standards lies with minimum-wage regulations, trade union rules, and other defensive reactions of noncompeting groups to
competition "from below," rather than with the educational system itself.

45. Lydall, *Structure of Earnings, op. cit.*, pp. 210 f., 224 f.

46. Jencks and Riesman, *op. cit.*, p. 151 (running quotation).

Whether education makes people more or less equal has not been much debated in recent years, though Jefferson and other pre-industrial political philosophers were much concerned with it. Yet it is in some ways the central problem posed by the academic revolution. If we revert to income distribution as a measure of equality, it seems clear that the spread of education has not brought anything like a revolution. Yet it could be argued that the modest redistribution that took place during the Depression and World War II was in some way causally related to the enormous jump in the median educational attainment of the young during the 1920's and 1930's. Conversely, it could be claimed that the stability of income distribution since World War II reflected the relatively slow rise in median attainment since then. If this hypothesis were correct—and we are rather skeptical—it would provide a strong argument for attempts to make higher education as nearly universal as secondary education became a generation ago.

CHAPTER FOUR

Topics in Functional
Income Distribution

Much of this chapter resembles a "gay quarter" revisited by daylight, without its nocturnal glamor. We shall be reexamining several firmly held, even emotionally held, parts of the income distribution folklore in the cold gray light of pedantic scholarship. Most of the ideas will turn out to be half-truths rather than fallacies, but true believers will not be satisfied.

Relations to Personal Distribution

1. Among the myths of functional distribution are two propositions that involve personal distribution as well. These are (1) the larger the individual's income on the average, the smaller the proportion that is derived from wages and salaries; and as a loose corollary, (2) any measure that increases the labor share of the functional distribution will increase the equality of the personal one. Both these propositions are half-truths. The difficulty with the first relates to the "widows and orphans" at the lower tail. The difficulty with the second relates to distributional changes over the business cycle.

2. Table 4.1, taken from American tax statistics for 1953, verifies proposition (1) only for incomes above $5,000, well above the mean income for that year. Below the mean, the relationship is rather the reverse, due to the importance of low-income property holders. These are not only widows and orphans, but pensioners and retired folk generally, not to men-

Table 4.1. Functional Distribution of Income, by Personal Income Brackets (United States, 1953)

Adjusted Gross Income ($000)	Wages and Salaries	Property Income	Entrepreneurial Income	Capital Gains	Misc.
		(Percentage of Income)			
Under 1.0	83.7	3.2	12.0	0.0	1.0
1.0–1.5	85.2	3.3	11.1	0.0	0.6
1.5–2.0	82.8	4.6	11.5	0.2	0.8
2.0–2.5	85.3	3.8	10.2	0.2	0.4
2.5–3.0	86.9	2.9	9.5	0.3	0.4
3.0–3.5	88.5	2.4	8.5	0.2	0.4
3.5–4.0	90.4	2.1	7.1	0.2	0.2
4.0–4.5	91.4	1.9	6.3	0.2	0.2
4.5–5.0	91.5	1.9	5.9	0.3	0.3
5.0–6.0	91.7	2.1	5.8	0.2	0.2
6.0–7.0	90.2	2.6	6.6	0.3	0.3
7.0–8.0	88.4	3.1	7.7	0.5	0.3
8.0–9.0	84.9	4.1	10.2	0.5	0.3
9.0–10.0	79.9	5.4	13.5	0.7	0.3
10.0–15.0	66.0	9.5	22.7	1.4	0.5
15.0–20.0	49.6	14.8	33.1	2.1	0.5
20.0–30.0	42.7	18.3	36.2	2.3	0.5
30.0–50.0	40.0	22.5	33.7	3.3	0.5
50.0–100.0	34.6	30.4	28.8	5.7	0.5
100.0–200.0	26.2	41.1	21.3	10.9	0.4
200.0–500.0	16.4	52.8	11.1	19.5	0.2
500.0–1000.0	6.4	65.4	0.8	27.3	0.1
1000 or more	1.5	72.2	0.7	25.5	0.0
Total	82.1	5.8	10.8	0.9	0.4
Subtotal (under 5.0)	88.7	3.4	3.4	0.3	0.4
Subtotal (over 5.0)	76.2	8.0	14.1	1.4	0.4

SOURCE: U.S. Treasury, Internal Revenue Service, *Statistics of Income for 1953* (Preliminary Report), part I, table 2, pp. 11 f.

NOTES: 1. Percentages rounded, may not add to 100.0.
2. "Property Income" represents sum of "Dividends," "Interest," "Annuities," "Rents and Royalties," and "Estates and Trusts."
3. "Entrepreneurial Income" represents sum of "Individual Proprietorships" and "Partnerships," minus "Operating Losses."
4. "Capital Gains" represents income from sales of both capital and noncapital assets.
5. The fine breakdown by income classes includes taxable returns only. The total and subtotals include nontaxable returns.

tion working people who receive supplementary incomes from rental of house property or interest on past savings.

The same table shows property income, which forms the second major functional component, falling in relative importance until the $5,000 income level is reached, and rising rapidly thereafter. This pattern is roughly complementary to that of labor income. Capital gains (realized gains only) rise more steadily in importance, to second rank at the high end of the scale. Entrepreneurial income, a mixed entity as we know, shows a complex bimodal pattern. One concentration (of small farmers and retailers) is at the bottom of the distribution. Another concentration (high-earning professionals for the most part) is in brackets from $15,000 to $100,000.

The poor man largely dependent on property income is by no means an exclusively Western or advanced-country phenomenon. Schemes for land reform in developing countries, which are drawn up on the assumption that all landlords—or at least, all absentee landlords—are rich, face the reality that many landlords suffering partial confiscation are in fact white-collar workers little better off (even allowing for the supplementary rental incomes) than the peasantry that is supposedly benefited by the reforms.

3.   It is quite true, turning to proposition (2), that an increase in the labor share, *ceteris paribus,* increases equality. The *ceteris paribus* clause is, however, of great importance. The concrete content of this clause is: "provided total income distributed does not fall at the same time."

The most volatile of the functional shares, if we compare prosperous with depressed conditions, is the profit residual. As a result primarily of the fluctuations of profit, the labor share falls in good times and rises in bad times. It is easy to argue from this fact, as maldistribution theorists of the cycle usually do, that the falling labor share of the prosperity period brings on a cyclical downturn due to shortages of purchasing power, and that the rising labor share in the depression period checks the decline and may even be conducive to recovery.

A few stubborn statistical difficulties, however, get in the way. The labor share is itself distributed more equally in prosperity than in depression, because part time work and unemployment increase the coefficient of concentration of labor incomes. The other shares, at the same time, are distributed somewhat more equally in depression, because there are fewer windfalls at the very top. (See Table 4.2.)

The net result of all these changes in coefficients of concentration within functional shares can easily be a movement of the overall coefficient parallel to the labor share—upward in prosperity, downward in depression.[1] Fragmentary studies for the United States, covering the great depression of the 1930s, indicate that equality moved with and not against the cycle

----

1. This point was explored by Milton Friedman in a "Foreword" to Hanna, Pechman, and Lerner, *Analysis of Wisconsin Incomes, op. cit.,* pp. 10–15.

Table 4.2. Concentration Ratios of Functional
Shares in Prosperity and Depression
(Wisconsin, 1929–1936)

Type of Receipt	Concentration Ratio		
	Prosperity 1929	Depression 1935	1936
Wages and salaries	.335	.356	.343
Business income	.496	.488	.467
Net rent	.603	.573	.568
Net interest	.746	.730	.706
Capital gains	.821	.793	.766
Dividends	.875	.813	.854

SOURCE: Frank Hanna, Joseph A. Pechman, and Sidney Lerner, *Analysis of Wisconsin Incomes, op. cit.,* p. 120 (by Pechman).

in at least one important instance.[2] We do not know how general this outcome may be.

4.   An essay by Stiglitz[3] applies economic-modeling techniques to the interrelation between personal and functional income distributions. We limit ourselves here to three paraphrases (by Robert Lucas) of Stiglitz' simplest model.

Consider two individuals 1 and 2. Individual 1, a representative poor man, has w of wage income and rK_1 of property income from his stock K_1 of nonhuman capital. Similarly, individual 2, a representative rich man, has $w + rK_2$. The wage rate w and the interest rate r are taken (perhaps unrealistically) as uniform, and income differences are due only to the size of the two capital stocks. Specifically $K_2 > K_1$ implies $(w + rK_2) > (w + rK_1)$, and the course of inequality depends on the course of capital formation. Three simple assumptions lead to different results.

(1)   All types of income are subject to a uniform saving ratio s. Individual 1 saves S_1 and individual 2 saves S_2:

$$S_1 = s(rK_1 + w) = \frac{dK_1}{dt} \text{ and } S_2 = s(rK_2 + w) = \frac{dK_2}{dt};$$

$$\frac{dK_1}{dt}/K_1 = s\left(r + \frac{w}{K_1}\right) \text{ and } \frac{dK_2}{dt}/K_2 = s\left(r + \frac{w}{K_2}\right).$$

$$\text{Since } K_2 > K_1, \frac{w}{K_1} > \frac{w}{K_2} \text{ and } \frac{dK_1/dt}{K_1} > \frac{dK_2/dt}{K_2}.$$

2. Horst Mendershausen, *Changes in Income Distribution During the Great Depression* (New York: National Bureau of Economic Research, 1946), ch. 2 and pp. 114–120. Results for numerous individual American cities are tabulated separately on p. 29.

3. Joseph Stiglitz, "Distribution of Income and Wealth Among Individuals," Cowles Foundation Paper 208 (mimeographed: Yale University, 1967).

In words, the growth rate of the poor man's capital exceeds that of the rich man's capital. The two capital stocks, and therefore the two incomes, tend to eventual equality.

(2)   Only property income is subject to the uniform saving ratio s. All wage income is consumed.

$$S_1 = srK_1 = \frac{dK_1}{dt} \text{ and } S_2 = srK_2 = \frac{dK_2}{dt}$$

$$\frac{dK_1}{dt}/K_1 = \frac{dK_2}{dt}/K_2 = sr$$

The two capital stocks grow at the same rate. Therefore the distribution of income remains unchanged.

(3)   Wage and property income are subject to separate (positive) saving ratios (s_w, s_k), whose relative sizes are immaterial to the argument. This case, in the limit $(K_1, K_2$ increasing without bound) reduces to that of assumption (1).

$$S_1 = s_k rK_1 + s_w w = \frac{dK_1}{dt} \text{ and } S_2 = s_k rK_2 + s_w w = \frac{dK_2}{dt}$$

$$\frac{dK_1}{dt}/K_1 = s_k r + s_w \frac{w}{K_1} \text{ and } \frac{dK_2}{dt} K_2 = s_k r + s_w \frac{w}{K_2}.$$

Our argument under (1) applies for sufficiently large values of K, although the rate of convergence of the two income is slower than in (1) if $s_k > s_w$. In the special case of $s_w = 0$, this case converges to case (2).

Constant Relative Shares?

5.   "The stability of the proportion of the national dividend accruing to labour is one of the most surprising yet best-established facts in the whole range of economic statistics. It is the stability of this ratio for each country which is chiefly remarkable, and this appears to be a long-run, and not merely a short-run phenomenon."[4] Not one but two articles of economic faith and folklore cluster about the "mystery" of constant relative shares, which has been called Bowley's Law.[5]

4. J. M. Keynes, "Relative Movements of Real Wages and Output," *Ec. J.* (March 1939), p. 48 (running quotation). Sidney Weintraub informs me that the Polish economist Michal Kalečki brought Bowley's Law to Keynes' attention.

5. The hypothesis of constant share ratios (40 per cent for wages in Great Britain, 60–65 per cent for wages and salaries in the U.S.) rested originally on Arthur L. Bowley's researches on the functional distribution of British incomes in the prewar generation 1880–1913. See J. R. Hicks, *Theory of Wages* (London: Macmillan, 1932), pp. 130–133.

6. The initial article of faith is that Bowley's Law is both correct and unexplained, at least in the private sector of Western economics. Klein lists constancy of the labor share as one of the five "great ratios of economics," which he goes on to treat as constants in framing a growth model.[6] The alleged failure of economic theory to explain Bowley's Law adequately has been called (by Joan Robinson) a "reproach" to the entire discipline.

The second article of faith is that trade unionism raises the labor share. This faith, often transposed into the belief that unionism *should* raise the labor share under proper economic institutions, implies that Bowley's Law is false when organized labor is strong. Evidence to the contrary may be rejected outright as "bourgeois statistics," or transposed into evidence that the labor share would have fallen except for the power of labor organizations.

In actual fact, the great depression of the 1930s, and the great inflation that followed it, have called Bowley's Law into serious question. Over the period 1945–1960 in the United States, Machlup computed labor shares varying between 63.6 and 68.9 percent; over the longer period 1929–1960, the range was even wider, between 58.2 and 73.4 per cent. He therefore concluded that "there is really not quite so much to explain after all."[7] The same record suggests a slowly rising labor share, whether we use standard measures, as did Kravis, or follow Weintraub in his preference for a measure he calls k (gross revenue from sales divided by total payrolls).[8] At the same time, a path-breaking statistical analysis by Solow pointed out that the labor share was by no means constant either within or between individual industries, and questioned the need for a special theory to explain the squeezing of "a number of unruly microeconomic markets" into "a tight-fitting size 65 straitjacket," which did not fit too well anyway.[9]

Solow's statistical skepticism involved sampling theory of a relatively

6. L. R. Klein, *Introduction to Econometrics, op. cit.*, pp. 183–186; also Klein and R. F. Kosobud, "Some Econometrics of Growth: Great Ratios of Economics" (*Q.J.E.*, May, 1961). The other "great ratios" are the average propensity to save, the capital-output ratio, the velocity of circulation of money (or more precisely, its reciprocal), and the proportions between factors in production.

7. Fritz Machlup, "Micro- and Macro-Economics," in *Essays on Economic Semantics* (Englewood Cliffs, N.J.: Prentice-Hall, 1963), p. 112.

8. Irving Kravis, "Relative Income Shares in Fact and Theory," *A.E.R.* (December 1959); Sidney Weintraub, *Some Aspects of Wage Theory and Policy* (Philadelphia: Chilton, 1963), ch. 3–4. Weintraub's k, of course, rises as the labor share falls, and vice versa.

9. Solow, "A Skeptical Note on the Constancy of Relative Shares," *A.E.R.* (September 1958). The phrases quoted are from p. 628.

elementary order. If a frequency distribution of n observations has a mean M and a standard deviation σ, the standard error of M is given by the formula:

$$\sigma_M = \frac{\sigma}{\sqrt{n-1}}$$

In Solow's study, an industry's labor share, observed over time, has a mean and standard deviation of its own, which we call M_i and σ_i respectively. Let the weighted mean of the M_i be the grand mean M, derive the overall σ from the several σ_i using methods associated with the analysis of variance,[10] and go on to compute σ_M. The statistic σ_M is an indirect or "pure chance" estimate of the standard deviation of the labor share for the economy as a whole.

From the time series of the labor share in the aggregate economy, including all n industries, it is easy to compute the standard deviation of the labor share directly. It will generally differ from the indirect estimate. Solow's statistical test involves a comparison of the indirect (pure chance) and the direct estimates of standard deviation of the aggregate labor share. Had the second (or direct) value been significantly smaller than the first (or indirect) estimate, we should require a special theory to explain the difference. But in fact, no such significant difference appeared between the direct and indirect estimates of the standard deviation of the labor share. Hence the "skepticism" in Solow's title.

"Skepticism" is too mild a term to describe the reaction Bowley's Law elicits from Simon Kuznets, the most patient, detailed, and critical American student of international distribution statistics.[11]

> Stability of the wage share, like the stability of many other economic statistics, if and when observed, is due to the balancing of conflicting effects of the underlying determinants; and its occurrence and continuity depend upon the occurrence and continuity of that balancing. It is clear . . . that the stability of the wage share in the United Kingdom, if present, was an exceptional

10. The formula involved, in our notation, is:

$$n\sigma^2 = \sum_i \frac{n_i}{n}\sigma_i^2 + \sum_i n_i\,(M_i - M)^2$$

where n_i is the weight of the i-class (industry) and $n = \sum_i n_i$. If X_i is a single observation of a labor share in the i-th industry; the derivation of this formula requires that the $(X_i - M_i)$ be independent of the $(M_i - M)$. See, for instance, Taro Yamane, *Statistics: An Introductory Analysis* (New York: Harper and Row, 1964), pp. 622–635.

11. Kuznets, "Quantitative Aspects of the Economic Growth of Nations, IV: Distribution of National Income by Factor Shares," *Econ. Dev. and Cult. Change* (April 1959), part ii, p. 56. (Kuznets' first sentence could serve as a trumpet blast against "structuralism" in many another form.)

and temporary phenomenon; that the apparently stable share in the United States was that of *wages and salaries*—and it has been replaced in subsequent revision by a long-term rise; and that long-term stability of the wage share has not been observed for any other country.

The Role of Unionism

8. Turning to the role of unionism, a useful starting point is Denison's essay, "Income Types and the Size Distribution."[12] Denison begins by breaking down the observed rise in the American labor share between 1929 and 1952, in order to determine the economic sectors in which it occurred, and particularly, how much of the increase was in ordinary business (private enterprise). His results, which we reproduce partially as Table 4.3, show that most of it was not in this sector at all. The overall rise in the labor share was from 58.1 per cent of the national income in 1929 to 64.3 per cent (1948–1952 average). In ordinary business, however, the rise was much smaller, from 61.7 to 62.9 per cent. In the further sub-division of nonfarm corporations, where unions are strongest, the rise was negligible, *i.e.*, from 74.1 to 74.2 per cent.[13] The most startling rise came in "all other sectors"—meaning, especially in later years, governmental units of all kinds[14]—where unionism was generally weak. In this sector, the rise in the labor share was from 45.2 to 69.9 per cent.

As the second part of his analysis, Denison breaks down the rise in the labor share within "ordinary business" according to whether it should be ascribed to the relative increase in the importance of industries with high labor shares in 1929, or to relative share shifts within individual industries. Examples of industries with high labor shares in value added are

12. Edward F. Denison, "Income Types and the Size Distribution," *A.E.R.* (May 1954), pp. 257 f. Since Denison's denominator is national rather than personal income, it includes undistributed corporate profits and excludes transfer payments of all kinds. His labor shares are accordingly lower than are ordinary distributions of personal income. They do not, however, include capital gains.

13. By limiting analysis to the corporate sector, one avoids biases that occur when a proprietorship or partnership incorporates, or is purchased by a corporation. In these cases, one or more "proprietors" often become salaried employees, and the measured labor share is almost certain to rise, whatever happens to the remuneration of the people affected. (The reverse is true, of course, when a corporation becomes a proprietorship or partnership.)

14. In American national income accounting, the government's contribution to national income is defined as the government payroll, so that the government's labor share is 100 per cent by definition. The rise in the relative importance of government agencies, particularly those of the federal government, is probably the main reason for the rise in the measured American labor share. (Government *enterprises*, like electric plans or bus lines, produce salable output and are treated more like private business firms.) For an elementary explanation of these peculiarities, see Gardner Ackley, *Macroeconomic Theory* (New York: Macmillan, 1961), pp. 49–51.

steel, automobiles, construction, and heavy industry generally. The trade union movement hopes to achieve share shifts within industries by raising wages "out of profits" by collective bargaining.

Denison's results imply that, even when they are of the "right" (positive) sign, relative share changes due to share shifts, possibly influenced by collective bargaining, were less significant than share changes due to industry weight changes, with which unions had little if anything to do.

Table 4.3. Compensation of Employees as Percentage
of National Income, by Economic Sectors
(United States, Selected Years, 1929–1952)

Sector	1929	1948	1952	Average 1948–52
Entire economy	58.1	62.7	66.3	64.3
Ordinary business	61.7	61.3	64.8	62.9
Nonfarm corporations	74.1	74.2	75.2	74.2
Nonfarm noncorporate	48.4	49.0	51.9	50.0
Farming	16.5	14.4	16.1	16.0
All other sectors	45.2	68.9	71.4	69.9

Further Breakdown of "Ordinary Business"

		Due to	
Year	Actual Change from 1929	Shifts in Industry Weights	Share Shifts within Industries
------	------	------	------
1948	−0.4	0.4	−0.8
1949	1.7	1.2	0.5
1950	0.8	1.6	−0.8
1951	0.8	1.8	−1.0
1952	3.1	2.3	0.8
Average 1948–52	1.2	1.5	−0.3

SOURCE: E. F. Denison, "Income Types and the Size Distribution," *A.E.R.* (May 1954) .

Denison's method can be explained quite simply. Let s_i be the labor share in industry i in 1929, and let it change by ds_i during the period under consideration. Let the relative weight of industry i in national income of 1929 (measured by value added) be w_i, and let it change by dw_i during the period we are considering. The column "Due to Shifts in Industry Weights," which assume shares constant at their 1929 levels, may then be derived as

$$k \left(\sum_i s_i \, dw_i \right) .$$

The column "Due to Share Shifts Within Industries," assuming industry weights constant, may be derived as

$$k \left(\sum_i w_i ds_i \right).$$

We must explain the constant k in these formulas. If it were absent (or equal to unity), the sum of Denison's two columns would not be the actual changes unless the two sorts of changes (ds and dw) were independent of each other. The constant k is an adjustment factor to insure (force) such equality.

9. Contemporaneously with the Denison study, Levinson carried on a similar investigation with one significant methodological difference.[15] He divided "private national income," a broader category than Denison's "ordinary business," into union and nonunion sectors, and worked out his results for the sectors separately as well as in combination. Levinson's "union sector" covers categories in which American unionism is generally strong and aggressive, namely manufacturing, mining, construction, transportation, and public utilities. His "nonunion sector," on the other hand, covers categories in which American unionism is generally weak or passive, namely, agriculture, trade, services, and finance. Some of his results are reproduced as Table 4.4.

On this table, Levinson's "inter-industry shifts" are analogous to Denison's "shifts in industry weights," and his "intra-industry shifts" to Denison's "share shifts within industries." Perhaps because of a different choice of beginning and ending years, Levinson's results are more "friendly" to the unionist position than Denison's. For example, there is a positive "intra-industry" shift in the "employee compensation" row of the union sector, but not the nonunion sector. His figures, in fact, suggest a hypothesis about the distributional effects of the American wartime and postwar inflation. It injured the rentier elements throughout, but in the union sector benefited mainly employees, and in the nonunion sector, mainly profit receivers and individual entrepreneurs.

10. Both of these studies, insofar as they include both corporate and noncorporate enterprise, exaggerate somewhat any increase of labor shares ascribable to collective bargaining, since they commingle such an increase with other factors increasing the percentage of income receivers who are employees. Two such factors are the relative increase of the corporate

15. Harold M. Levinson, "Collective Bargaining and Income Distribution," *A.E.R.* (May 1954). An earlier and longer study by Levinson used, of necessity, an earlier ending date (1947): *Unionism, Wage Trends, and Income Distribution* (Ann Arbor: University of Michigan Press, 1951), pp. 80–110.

*Table 4.4.   Inter- and Intra-Industry Redistribution
of Private National Income (United States, 1929–1952)*

Type of Income Payment	Percentage of Income Originating 1929	1952	Inter-Industry Shift	Intra-Industry Shift	Total Shift	Per Cent Shift
a. Union Sector						
Employee compensation	34.0	39.5	+4.0	+1.5	+5.5	+16.2%
Proprietors' income	2.2	2.2	+0.5	−0.5	0.0 ⎫	+13.0
Corporate profits	10.1	11.7	+1.9	−0.3	+1.6 ⎬	
Interest and rent	1.2	0.4	−0.1	−0.7	−0.8 ⎭	−66.7
Total	47.5	53.8	+6.3	−	+6.3	
b. Nonunion Sector						
Employee compensation	21.6	21.9	+0.3	0.0	+0.3	+1.4%
Proprietors' income	15.8	14.4	−1.7	+0.3	−1.4 ⎫	−0.5
Corporate profits	3.0	4.3	−0.4	+1.7	+1.3 ⎬	
Interest and rent	12.1	5.6	−4.5	−2.0	−6.5 ⎭	
Total	52.5	46.2	−6.3	−	−6.3	
c. Total (a) + (b)						
Employee compensation	55.6	61.4	+4.3	+1.5	+5.8	+10.4
Proprietors' income	18.0	16.6	−1.2	−0.2	−1.4 ⎫	+4.8
Corporate profits	13.1	16.0	+1.5	+1.4	+2.9 ⎬	
Interest and rent	13.3	6.0	−4.6	−2.7	−7.3	−54.9
Grand total	100.0	100.0	−	−	−	

SOURCE: Harold M. Levinson, "Collective Bargaining and Income Distribution," *op. cit.*, p. 309. Compare Levinson, *Unionism, Wage Trends, and Income Distribution, op. cit.*, p. 106.

form and the movement of farmers to the city. Adjustment for the increasing percentage of income receivers who are employees has been attempted by J. D. Phillips, under the rubric of "wage parity." To obtain Phillips' "parity ratio," "the percentage of employee compensation in each year is divided by the percentage of employees in the labor force for the corresponding year."[16] Phillips' parity ratios exhibit a rising trend over the period 1929–1957, but 1929 was an unrepresentatively low year, and no upward trend seems apparent after 1940. When Phillips used wage parity ratios for the private sector only, they "showed no increase . . . over the 1920s, except for the cyclical rise in the Great Depression," contrary to the hypothesis "that unions have obtained gains for labor at the expense of other income."[17]

16. Joseph D. Phillips, "Labor's Share and 'Wage Parity'," *Rev. Econ. and Stat.* (May, 1960), p. 165.
17. *Ibid.*, p. 174.

Another questionable feature of the Denison and Levinson studies is that their results are influenced by arbitrary choices of beginning and ending years. (The Denison paper uses a number of alternative ending years, in addition to the average reproduced in Table 4.3. It is therefore somewhat preferable on this point to the Levinson one.) To avoid the difficulty, Simler has used statistical time series and correlation analysis. For thirty-six (in some cases, forty-nine) American manufacturing industries, he determined the average labor share ratios during two periods, a non-union one (1899–1935) and a union one (1935–1955) ; he also fitted trend lines to the share ratios for each industry in each period, and compared the slopes.[18] At the same time, Simler measured increases in union strength, taking the average percentage of "unionizable" (primarily manual) workers organized in both pre-union and union periods. Then he arranged his industries in rank order, regarding both increased labor shares and increased union strength, and correlated the ranks for the entire groups of industries. There was no marked positive correlation; in many cases the correlation was actually negative, and Simler summarizes:[19]

> There does not appear to be any significant correlation between union strength and/or changes in union strength and changes in labor's relative share. Those industries which reflected substantial advances in the average level of the wage-income ratio and/or marked relative increases in the slope of the regression line between the two periods tended to rank low on the scales measuring union strength, while those industries which ranked high on these scales tended to reflect only minor favorable-to-labor changes in income distribution.

The Simler study does not, of course, consider "externalities," meaning, in this case, the influence of unionization in some industries on wage movements in other industries or even "across the board" to the economy as a whole.

Distribution in Economic Growth

11. Our next topic is the historical one, whether economic growth does or does not tend to increase the labor share of the national income and product. We leave to later chapters the related analytical problem of whether or not such an increase would or would not react favorably upon the growth rate as conventionally measured.

The *classical* position is usually considered a pessimistic one: growth lowers the labor share, after correction by some such measure as Phillips'

18. N. J. Simler, "Unionism and Labor's Share in Manufacturing Industries," *Rev. Econ. and Stat.* (November, 1961) .

19. *Ibid.,* pp. 375 f. (running quotation) .

"wage parity." Ricardo, Malthus, and following them, Henry George, would find the principal cause in the rise of population and fixity of land, although they would almost certainly differ as to the division of the blame between concupiscence and landlordism. *Progress and Poverty,* the title of George's great book, indicates the viewpoint of these writers, although George goes further than the others in associating growth with increasing misery. When it comes to comparing the relative living standards of the representative worker and his representative landlord, the classical conclusions follow from the classical premises. It may be wrong, however, to leap to a further pessimistic conclusion about relative shares. If wages fall, but only slowly, as the labor force expands, the labor share may rise, even though both absolute and relative living standards of workers decline.[20]

Marx and the Marxists take a different stand. They find the cause of subsistence wages in unemployment, rather than in overpopulation (like Malthus) or in diminishing returns (like Ricardo). Progress means, to Marx, a rising organic composition of capital as a consequence of accumulation; accumulation also tends to raise the relative rate of surplus value. This process translates readily into "increasing misery" as defined earlier, since capitalist living standards presumably rise while working-class standards stagnate. What bourgeois economists call the "labor share" must also fall even though the relative number of workers rise. The argument is most easily explained in algebraic terms.[21]

20. Problems of substitution among labor, land, and capital might enter into this discussion, but we are not ready for them.

21. Marx's "organic composition of capital" is the number of labor-hours of value used up as raw materials, intermediate products, and the depreciation of fixed capital (constant capital, or C), divided by the number of hours consumed by production workers (variable capital, or V). As capital accumulates, the depreciation component of C, in particular, rises relative to the other components of $(C + V)$, and so (C/V), the organic composition of capital, increases.

The rate of surplus value is, in the Marxian system, the number of hours a production worker spends at work over and above the number required to produce his subsistence, divided by the number of "necessary" or subsistance hours. In symbols, the excess number of hours represents surplus value, or S, and the necessary number is V. The rate of surplus value is therefore the quotient (S/V). Increasing surplus value, in consequence of capital accumulation and technical progress, results from a fall in the denominator of this expression, *i.e.,* a fall in the number of hours' work required to maintain a worker at a constant level of subsistence. In Marxian terms, it is a rise in *relative* surplus value, as distinguished from the rise in *absolute* surplus value, which results from lengthening the working day. (Insofar as the workers' subsistence level rises, of course, the rate of surplus value may not rise, and may even fall over time.)

The preceeding paragraph has shown that both (C/V) and (S/V) tend to rise with economic growth. In Marxian terms, total value, or W, is defined as $(C + S + V)$. The bourgeois economists' "labor share" is approximately $V/(C + S + V)$. If both (C/V)

The *neoclassical* attitude on the probable course of the labor share was apparently involved in Bowley's Law. Prior to the enunciation of that law, the problems seem temporarily to have dropped from sight. For example, the most relevant reference in Marshall's *Principles of Economics* is the generalization: "It seems certain that the incomes of the working classes generally are increasing at least as fast as those of other classes."[22]

12. Much of the spadework in analyzing, and rendering comparable, the course of the labor share of national income in the fragmentary statistics of various countries has been done by Simon Kuznets. His presidential address to the American Economic Association[23] propounded a famous conjecture, namely, that growth may be divided tentatively into two stages with opposite distributional effects. In the earlier stage, capital is scarce and relatively unskilled labor is in almost unlimited supply. Under these conditions, classical and Marxism pessimism accords with the facts. Progress raises the demand for capital; unskilled labor is a poor substitute; the capital share rises. Subsequently capital accumulates, population growth slows down some-what, and the general level of skill and training improves, until labor rather than capital becomes a "scarce" or "strategic" factor. In these conditions, the labor share at first remains stable, then actually rises. It was the misfortune alike of Ricardo and Marx to have observed and extrapolated only the first of these periods, rather than to have forecast the change that followed.

In a later and more detailed statistical compilation, Kuznets shows that over the shorter period for which usable distribution statistics are available (for most countries, the "second period" of his earlier conjecture), the labor share tends quite uniformly to rise. "The share of compensation

---

and (S/V) rise, as Marx believes they will, $(C + S + V)/V$, or W/V, must rise too. Its reciprocal, the labor share, must fall.

There is a modicum of statistical legerdemain here, for which Marx is not responsible. We have not mentioned payments to unemployed workers, whose competition keeps wages down and surplus value up, in the Marxian system. Whatever they receive is, however, surplus value in Marxian terms, so that the algebra is not disturbed. In conventional statistics likewise, as we saw in Chapter 2, transfer payments are excluded from national income.

22. Alfred Marshall, *Principles of Economics*, 8th ed. (London Macmillan, 1920), p. 713 n.

23. Kuznets, "Economic Growth and Income Inequality," *A.E.R.* (March, 1955). On the other hand, Murray Brown bases his "endogenous" explanation of industrialization on a steady rise of wages, relative to capital costs, in Great Britain, commencing about 1600, which he interprets as indicating labor scarcity *ab initic.* "Toward an Endogenous Explanation of Industrialization," *Social Research* (Summer 1966), pp. 301–303, and references cited. For South and Southeast Asian evidence, compare Myrdal, *Asian Drama*, 3 vols. (New York: Pantheon, 1968), vol. i, pp. 563–572 and vol. iii, app. 14.

of employees in total income tends to be higher in countries with high income per capita, lower in the less developed countries . . . The range is somewhat narrower when we exclude the colonies and the small units . . . but it is still appreciable."[24] In these estimates salaried workers are included in the working class, and all salaries in labor income. When only wage earners and wage incomes are considered, the picture is less clear, and Kuznets is hesitant to reach a conclusion.[25]

Kuznets' comfortable global conclusions are not without their exceptions. These are sometimes explainable by special circumstances, usually connected with economic dualism. We cite three examples: Japan, Mexico, and Israel.[26] Japanese development seems to have involved a declining labor share in its "modern" sector for the period 1919–1962, and Japan is ordinarily thought of as advanced during most of this period. If one adds entrepreneurial income in primary industry—agriculture, forestry, and fisheries—to labor income in the total economy, calling the sum "proletarian income," there is also a declining trend for the period 1955–1962. A possible explanation runs in terms of the absorption, at low wages, of surplus labor from rural Japan—"disguised unemployment." In Mexico, the top 1 per cent of the gainfully employed population allegedly received 66 per cent of the national income in 1955, while the remaining 99 per cent received only 34 per cent! (In 1940, the distribution had been exactly the reverse.) Dualism may again be part of the answer here. As for Israel, immigration of unskilled workers from undeveloped regions of North Africa and the Middle East was mainly responsible for raising the concentration ratio from .18 in 1950 to .25 in 1956-57.

We also mention, as a pathological case from a developing country, the Dominican Republic under dictator Rafael Leonidas Trujillo. We have found no trended distribution data, either personal or functional, but:[27]

> In 1962, the Council of State . . . published the following data on the share of the national riches possessed by Trujillo at the moment of his death: 22 per cent of the bank deposits, 63 per cent of the production of sugar, 63 per cent of cement, 73 per cent of paper, 86 per cent of paint, 71 per cent

24. Kuznets, "Quantitative Aspects of the Economic Growth of Nations, IV: Division of Income by Factor Shares," *op. cit.*, pp. 8 f.

25. *Ibid.*, pp. 41–44.

26. For Japan, see K. Ohkawa, "Changes in National Income Distribution by Factor Shares in Japan," in Marchal and Ducros, *The Distribution of National Income* (London: Macmillan, 1968), ch. vi. The Mexican data are from Oscar Lewis, "Mexico since Cárdenas," *Social Research* (Spring, 1959), p. 26, citing Manuel Germán Parra; and the Israeli from Giora Hanoch, "Income Differentials in Israel," Falk Foundation for Economic Research in Israel, *Fifth Report* (1959–60), p. 47.

27. Vicente Girbau Leon, "Imperalism in the Dominican Republic," *Monthly Review* (September 1965), pp. 13 f.

of tobacco, 85 per cent of milk, 68 per cent of flour. Moreover, the Dominican airline was his, as were the principal newspapers and most of the radio and TV stations . . . Trujillo had deposited $200 million in Swiss banks and . . . $35 million in the Canadian Bank of Nova Scotia. He possessed . . . 30 per cent of the land and 25 per cent of the livestock. In addition, monopolies were created in 1954 to control all foreign and domestic commerce; 51 per cent of their stocks were the property of Trujillo.

Redistributive Effects of Inflation[28]

13. Two related hypotheses about the redistributive effects of inflation have become accepted conventionally, but shaken by more recent statistical analysis. These are: (a) In inflation, money wages tend to lag behind prices; real wages fall, real profits rise, and the income distribution shifts against labor; (b) Business firms as such gain, on balance, from inflation.

The wage-lag hypothesis has been advanced in many studies in economic history. Among the best known are Hamilton's thesis of profit inflation as a cause of industrialization in Western Europe,[29] and in accounts of the American Civil War and World War I. These studies agreed that real wages declined *during* and *because of* inflation, while real profits rose and distribution shifted accordingly.

These plausible conclusions have, however, been challenged, either for their arbitrary choices of beginning and ending years or because observed wage lags were explainable on other grounds. For example, Alchian and Kessel argue that Hamilton's 30 per cent *decline* in real wages in Spain during the "American treasure" inflation of 1520–1600 would become a 4 per cent *increase* if the period 1522–1602 were used.[30] As for another Hamilton study of Spanish inflation two centuries later, which shows declining urban wage rates, this was a period in which the Spanish population roughly doubled. Associated with this was a substantial migration to the cities. The wage-lag hypothesis for this episode cannot be accepted until the downward "demographic" pressure on wage rates has been taken into account more fully.[31]

28. This section leans heavily on M. Bronfenbrenner and Franklyn D. Holzman, "Survey of Inflation Theory," *A.E.R.* (September 1963), pp. 647–652 (written primarily by Holzman).

29. Earl J. Hamilton, "Price Inflation and the Industrial Revolution," *Q.J.E.* (February 1942) and "Prices and Progress," *Journ. Econ. Hist.* (Fall 1952).

30. Armen A. Alchian and Reuben A. Kessel, "Redistribution of Wealth through Inflation," *Science* (Sept. 4, 1959). Alchian and Kessel's rival theory is discussed below (section 14).

31. This argument follows David Felix, "Profit Inflation and Industrial Growth: The Historic Record and Contemporary Analogies," *Q.J.E.* (August 1956).

Several writers have examined in detail the functional distribution of both personal and national income in the United States during the several inflationary spurts that have occurred since the end of World War II. With regard to wages and profits only, the picture is mixed. Some periods, such as 1946–1948, apparently conform to the wage-lag hypothesis; other periods, such as 1955–1957, apparently do not. To whatever extent the distinction between "demand-pull" and "cost-push" inflations is usable, one might expect to find profits rising faster than wages in the first type of inflation but not the second.[32] This may explain the differences between the 1946–1948 and 1955–1957 inflation episodes, since the former was primarily demand-pull while the latter included, according to many writers, substantial elements of cost-push.

As far as other factor returns are concerned, postwar inflation seems quite unambiguously to have eroded the shares going to interest, to rent, and also to dividends. (The decline in dividends was compensated, to some extent, by capital gains.) The Hashimi study shows that what he calls "active" elements (wages and profits) gained relative to the "passive" ones (rent and interest) whenever prices rose in the United States during the 1929–1957 period.[33]

Perhaps more important, however, are the effects of inflation on the personal income distribution. Within each major economic category, particular individuals are left behind. Bach and Ando conclude that "the major losers from inflation on current income account—the relatively fixed income groups—[are] clearly scattered throughout the economy as pensioners, insurance recipients, college professors, and others, rather than concentrated in major income size or occupation groups."[34] In any case, the simple theory that places labor on the losing end seems largely outmoded once labor has become organized and money illusions have been evaporated by experience in long or repeated inflations.

14.   The second hypothesis, that "business" gains from inflation, involves elements of wealth along with income redistribution. It is based on at least two assumptions. First, if it were true that wages lag behind prices, it would follow (with rent and interest fixed in money terms) that business profits would rise during inflations. A more common assumption is that

32. This is the argument of Edmund S. Phelps, "A Test for the Presence of Cost Inflation in the United States, 1955–57," *Yale Econ. Essays* (Spring 1961). Compare Richard Selden, "Cost-Push versus Demand-Pull Inflation, 1955–57," *J.P.E.* (February, 1959), and Bronfenbrenner and Holzman, *op. cit.*, pp. 629 f.

33. R. M. H. Hashimi, *Studies in Functional Income Distribution* (East Lansing: Michigan State University Press, 1960), part II.

34. G. L. Bach and Albert K. Ando, "The Redistributional Effects of Inflation," *Rev. Econ. and Stat.* (February 1957).

business firms are debtors and gain during inflation by the right to repay debts in depreciated currency. (This would, however, be false if, when loans were made or bonds floated, interest rates anticipated or overanticipated future price increases.)

The Alchian-Kessel studies confirm this general analysis, but question the assumption that business firms are generally net debtors. This may have been true before 1914, but the Alchian-Kessel samples for the period since 1945 show business firms distributed approximately evenly between net debtors and net creditors.[35] Bach and Ando find, not surprisingly, that in relatively mild inflations, the operation of the debtor-creditor mechanism on the relative positions of business firms is often obscured by the effects of other factors, most significantly sales volume.[36]

A number of writers also analyze the effect of inflation on the *personal* distribution of *wealth* in terms of the net monetary (fixed-price) assets and liabilities of different population groups, including *income classes*.[37] Most income groups, except the "under $1,000" class, have a net monetary asset position of 13–15 per cent of their total assets; the lowest group records only 8 per cent. This suggests that the absolute losses from inflation are apt to be smallest for the low income group, with others about equally vulnerable. When the results are recomputed in percentage terms, however, the net losses from inflation are regressive, as compared with those from such inflation-control measures as tight money (higher interest rates) and increased taxes.[38] The most elaborate study suggests that (for 1957) inflation is also *absolutely* regressive, meaning that persons with incomes below $6,000 suffer on the average a real decline in net worth, while those with incomes above $7,000 gain on the average.

35. Alchian and Kessel, *op. cit.* See also Kessel and Alchian, "The Inflation-Induced Lag of Wages," *A.E.R.* (March 1960) .

36. Bach and Ando, *op. cit.*

37. The most relevant Alchian essay is "Inflation and the Distribution of Income and Wealth," in Marchal and Ducros, *op. cit.,* ch. 22.

38. O. H. Brownlee and Alfred Conrad, "Effects upon the Distribution of Income of a Tight Money Policy," *A.E.R.* (May 1961) ; also Boris P. Pesek, "Distribution Effects of Inflation and Taxation," *A.E.R.* (March 1960) .

CHAPTER FIVE

Maldistribution?

Under the heading of "Maldistribution" we shall examine three broad groups of issues. The first, or *ethical*, group of issues deals with the eternal unsolved problems of distributive justice. The second, or *economic*, group of issues deals with the maldistributionist form of the underconsumption theory of businss depressions and long-term tendencies toward economic stagnation.

Insofar as ethical maldistribution persists, it interferes with the *optimality* of the economic system. Insofar as economic maldistribution persists, it interferes with the *viability* of the economic system. Either type of maldistribution interferes with the social and political *stability* of the economic system.

The third, or *political*, group of issues to be discussed in this chapter is a classification of income-redistribution methods practiced and advocated in modern societies. (Chapter 17 will consider income policies, or wage-price guidelines, in more detail.)

Selection of Rich and Poor

1. The initial subhead of our ethical discussion is microeconomic in the extreme. Accepting for the moment as just, or alternatively as immutable, some overall distributions of income both personal and functional, do the "right" people rise to the top, or sink to the bottom? Leo Durocher's famous summary refers to the world of sports: "Nice guys finish last." Jonathan Swift, of *Gulliver's Travels*, put the case with equal harshness: "Mankind may judge what Heaven thinks of riches by observing those upon whom it has been pleased to bestow them." A more detailed summary of the prosecution's argument is by the Victorian critic John Ruskin. It applies to both ends of the scale:[1]

In a community regulated by laws of demand and supply, but protected from open violence, the persons who become rich are, generally speaking, industrious, resolute, proud, covetous, prompt, methodical, sensible, unimaginative, insensitive, and ignorant. The persons who remain poor are the entirely foolish, the entirley wise, the idle, the reckless, the humble, the thoughtful, the dull, the imaginative, the sensitive, the well-informed, the improvident, the irregularly and impulsively wicked. the clumsy knave, the open thief, the entirely merciful, just, and godly person.

What may be called the standard defense is little more than Social Darwinism, applying to human society the biological doctrine of survivel of the fittest. The rich deserve their income and wealth because they are the fittest, and they have proved themselves the fittest by becoming and remaining rich. Such is the circular theology of what Matthew Arnold, and following him R. H. Tawney, call the Religion of Inequality.[2] At the upper tail of the distribution, it implies that "the rich, the well-born, and the able" will be, by and large, the same people; or, if you prefer, that the union and intersection of the three sets will be nearly identical. At the lower tail, it implies likewise that poverty results from some fault or faults of the poor. Two fashionable Protestant divines of the American gilded age, Henry Ward Beecher and Russell Conwell, assuaged the understuffed consciences in their overstuffed congregations by such pronouncements as these:[3]

> The general truth will stand that no man in this land suffers from poverty unless it be more than his fault—unless it be his *sin*. (Beecher)
> The number of poor to be sympathized with is very small . . . To sympathize with a man whom God has punished for his sins, thus to help him when God will still continue a just punishment, is to do wrong, no doubt about it. (Conwell)

Senator Barry Goldwater more recently reacted in the same tradition, discussing the education and training aspects of the war on poverty:[4]

> We are told that many people lack skills and cannot find jobs because they did not have an education. That's like saying that people have big feet because they have big shoes. The fact is that most people who have no skill have had no education for the same reason—low intelligence or low ambition.

1. On Swift, see R. H. Tawney, *Equality,* 4th ed. (London: Allen and Unwin, 1952) , p. 26; on Ruskin, F. H. Knight, *The Ethics of Competition* (New York: Harper, 1935) , p. 66.

2. Tawney, *op. cit.,* ch. 1, esp. p. 19.

3. Quoted in Herbert G. Gutman, "Protestantism and the American Labor Movement: The Christian Spirit in the Gilded Age," *Am. Hist. Rev.* (October 1966) , p. 76 n.

4. Goldwater, quoted in *Time* (January 24, 1964) .

A bit of well-reported dialogue between major literary figures of the 1920s is in point here. F. Scott Fitzgerald remarked to Ernest Hemingway that the rich were, after all, very different from the rest of us. "Yes," replied Hemingway, "they have more money than we do." In our terms, Fitzgerald was upholding Social Darwinism, though in a milder form than such proponents as Herbert Spencer in England or William Graham Sumner in America, while Hemingway was contradicting it.

2.   The Swift and Ruskin passages in section 1 illustrate a paradox. Britain and, even more, America are called materialistic or business civilizations, and the paradox is a paradox of the business civilization. On the one hand, it is natural to think of fitness, in the Darwinian sense, in such a civilization as primarily the ability to make money. Success may come in many fields, not necessarily in business, but it must carry a certain financial validation in any event. Leading lights in every field, "The Army, the Navy, the Church, and the Stage," must be reasonably well off, if not positively wealthy, before we recognize them as unequivocally successful. The sneer, "If you're so smart, why aren't you rich?" silences the aberrant egghead, and not only about economic or business matters.

Yet, paradoxically, the pecuniarily successful man becomes the prime exemplar of the business society's way of life. He is the high priest and philosopher-king, as well as the doughty warrior of his society. He combines the first two Estates of the Realm in his collective person; he is Caesar's wife as well as Caesar. When he violates the accepted canons of morality, he bites, in a sense, the hand that feeds him. The peccadilloes of the artist, actor, athlete, intellectual, or even public man (below the pinnacle) we discount as we would the "temperament" of talented children. To recognize such pecadilloes in enclaves like Hollywood or Bloomsbury casts no aspersion on society as such. But the disclosed transgressions of business leaders face the severer half of our double standard. They arouse head-shaking, finger-wagging, and fears of decadence, precisely because our society is business or materialistic. The sternness of Ruskin's judgment above all, coupled with the notorious abnormalities of his own private life, reflects and illustrates the paradox of the business civilization.

The Pattern of Personal Income Distribution

3.   Leaving the selection problem in the realistic limbo of irresolution, we consider now the distribution as a whole, as a distribution of the incomes of a mass of anonymous and faceless spending units. It is for many economists and social critics self-evident that existing "capitalist" distributions are too unequal, so that "equity" and "equality" become synony-

mous. Only a pettifogging pedant would ask why they think so—or, for that matter, why their opponents think otherwise.

The older welfare economics of Marshall and Pigou, to look back no further into formal doctrinal history, included an "uneasy" case for income equalization, based upon two questionable propositions: (a) The utility functions of all individuals, i and j included, were cardinally measurable with continuous first derivatives, from which negatively sloped marginal utility curves for income could be derived. (b) The utility functions of any two individuals i and j were comparable, either because i and j were, to a sufficient approximation, identical, or because their differences themselves reflected inequalities of background and breeding that could hardly be allowed for without "poisoning the wells" against redistribution.

The logical consequence of these assumptions was a case for complete equalization of the incomes of i and j, as the means to maximize total social utility "for the contemplation of God." In fact, no responsible economist went so far, since "responsibility" involved concern with motivating labor, saving, risk-bearing, and other approved types of economic behavior. The dramatist George Bernard Shaw was among the few who passed beyond advocacy of more and better tax progression to propose complete equalization:[5]

> Socialism means equality of income or nothing . . . Under Socialism you would not be allowed to be poor. You would be forcibly fed, clothed, lodged,

5. Shaw, *The Intelligent Woman's Guide to Socialism and Capitalism* (New York: Brentano, 1928), p. 670. Shaw envisaged only seven distributive schemata (*ibid.*, p. xv and ch. 7): "1. To each what he or she produces. 2. To each what he or she deserves. 3. To each what he or she can get and hold. 4. To the common people enough to keep them alive whilst they work all day, and the rest to the gentry. 5. Division of society into classes, the distribution being equal or thereabouts within each class, but unequal as between the classes. 6. Let us go on as we are. 7. Socialism: an equal share to everybody."

With these categories may be compared an academic discussion (Nicholas Rescher, *Distributive Justice* [Indianapolis: Bobbs-Merrill, 1966], p. 73):

> In the course of the long history of discussions on the subject, distributive justice has been held to consist, wholly or primarily, in the treatment of all people: (1) as equals (except possibly in the case of certain "negative" distributions such as punishments); (2) according to their needs; (3) according to their ability or merit or achievement; (4) according to their efforts and sacrifices; (5) according to their actual productive contribution; (6) according to the requirements of the common good, or the public interest, or the welfare of mankind, or the greater good of a greater number; (7) according to a valuation of their socially useful services . . . in the essentially economic terms of supply and demand.

All these canons except the third, Rescher notes, have been applied to the special problem of a just wage or income by Fr. John A. Ryan in *Distributive Justice*, 3rd ed. (New York: Macmillan, 1942), ch. 14.

taught, and employed whether you liked it or not. If it were discovered that you had not character and industry enough to be worth all this trouble, you might possible be executed in a kindly manner, but while you were permitted to live, you would have to live well.

4.   After Marshall and Pigou became passé, the assumptions of cardinal measurability and interpersonal comparability of utility fell into increasing disrepute. A new welfare economics, following Kaldor and Hicks,[6] tended to argue instead that any measure that increased the total of available goods and services should be regarded as economically desirable, as giving rise to the "possibility in principle" that beneficiaries might compensate sufferers and leave all parties better off. A noneconomist critic argues against the Kaldor-Hicks compensation criterion (without provision for realization, as well as possibility, of compensation):[7]

> That this principle rests upon outright mythology is perfectly evident. There is no reason [to suppose] in theory, and little evidence in practice, that beneficiaries of a new economic arrangement are likely to compensate those who sustain losses thereby. If one is going to motivate economic measures on terms of a social-contract conception, one must assure in advance that the terms of this contract are reasonably realistic ones. [There is no justification for] reliance on the mythology of compensatory redistribution.

At the same time, the ethical case for equality relapsed for a time into a practical form, which had antedated marginal-utility economics. This form was the assurance of a "social minimum" of income for the poor. This, it was assumed more or less without evidence, could be obtained despite the Malthusian devil of overpopulation, but not without substantial redistribution involving absolute loss to the rich. Tawney, for example, shied away from complete equalitarianism, arguing:[8]

> Nobody [presumably excepting Shaw—M.B.] thinks it inequitable that, when a reasonable provision has been made for all, exceptional responsibilities should be compensated by exceptional rewards, as a recognition of the service performed and an inducement to perform it . . . What is repulsive is not that one man should earn more than others . . . but that some classes should be excluded from the heritage of civilization.

6. Nicholas Kaldor, "Welfare Propositions in Economics and Interpersonal Comparisons of Utility," *Ec. J.* (September 1939) ; Sir John Hicks, "The Foundations of Welfare Economics," *ibid.* (December 1939) .

7. Rescher, *op. cit.,* pp. 15 f. (running quotation) , citing I.M.D. Little, *Critique of Welfare Economics,* 2nd ed. (Oxford: Clarendon Press, 1957) and David Braybrooke, "Farewell to the New Welfare Economics," *Rev. Econ. Stud.* (Autumn 1955) .

8. Tawney, *op. cit.,* p. 118.

What is important is not that all men receive the same pecuniary income. It is that the resources of society should be so husbanded and applied that it is a matter of minor significance whether they receive it or not.

One consequence of this position, to repeat, would seem to make a major benefit of economic growth some lessening in the degree of sacrifice by the rich, both in money and utility, that is required to raise the poor to a given minimum income. (But what if the social minimum itself rises, as in the revolution of rising expectations, at least as rapidly as with national product per capita?) Another consequence might be, if Tawney's "husbandry and application" means all it implies, that the legal title of the rich to their income and wealth would be conditioned upon their utilizing these stocks and flows much as a Fabian "Great Society" would have done.

5. A sharpening of the older utility-theory argument was made by Lerner's *Economics of Control*, in the hope of generalizing assumption (b), above, involving interpersonal comparison of utilities. (He does not profess to dispense with this assumption completely.) [9] We develop Lerner's essentially probabilistic argument with the aid of Figure 5.1, which simplifies his own diagram.

A given income *YY* is to be divided optimally between individuals *i* and *j* whose marginal utilities of income are given by the curves *II* and *JJ* on the diagram. *II* is read from the left, *JJ* from the right. As these curves are drawn, individual *i* is a better "lightning calculator of pleasures and pains" than *j*; for this reason, or possibly from his superior innate sensibilities, *i* should get the lion's share of *YY* if social utility is to be maximized. (*X* is the maximum utility point, where the two individuals' marginal utilties are equal.)

Unfortunately, only God and Lerner know that *i* is a more efficient pleasure machine than *j*. The rest of us, including the free market, if we depart from equal division (at point *A*), are no more likely to give any increment *AB* or *AC* to *i* than to *j*. (On the diagram, *AC = AB*). If the increment *AB* were in fact given to *i*, the increase in social utility, as compared with equal distribution at *A*, would be the shaded area *G* (gain). If, as is equally likely, we gave the equal increment *AC* to *j* instead, the cor-

9. A. P. Lerner, *Economics of Control* (New York: Macmillan, 1946), pp. 30–32. Lerner says specifically (p. 25): "It is not meaningless to say that a satisfaction one individual gets is greater or less than a satisfaction enjoyed by somebody else."

An alternative derivation of Lerner's result, axiomatic rather than graphical, was developed by Milton Friedman, "Lerner on the Economics of Control," reprinted in *Essays in Positive Economics* (Chicago: University of Chicago Press, 1953), pp. 308 f., including note 7.

responding decrease in social utility would be the cross-hatched area *L* (loss) . It follows from the slopes of *II* and *JJ* that $G < L$. Therefore, if the gain and loss situations are equally probable, as Lerner maintains, the expected social utility of departure from equality is negative.

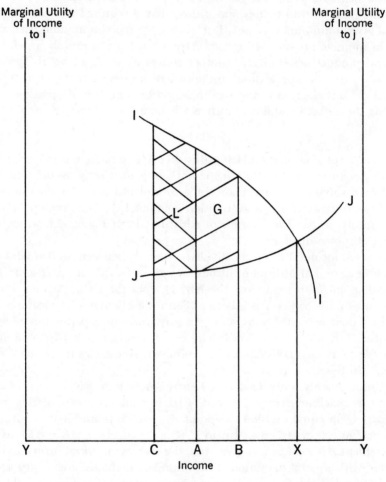

Figure 5.1

Two elementary objections may be made at once. First, since *YY* is given and fixed by hypothesis, no account can be taken of the almost necessary interconnection between income distribution and other aspects of economic performance. (Compare Chapter 1, section 5.) Second, within any social class or "noncompeting group," persons with a higher preference for income relative to the congeries of other amenities misleadingly labeled as "leisure" tend to choose high-income and high-risk occupations and investments, while those with marginal substitution rates more favorable to leisure are more prone to adopt high-leisure careers and portfolios. Choices between practice and teaching in professionl fields like law, medicine, business (and economics) are often made on some such bases by middle-class and upper-class students before their mid-twenties (and, unless reversible, are almost as often regretted at ages of thirty and above!). Choices between professional training as a whole and, say, unskilled labor as a whole are harder to explain on any similar basis. Social backgrounds are usually so different that little effective choice remains. Lerner's equiprobability argument is systematically wrong for choices such as those between teaching and private practice among trained professionals. It is less wrong, or at least less biased, for choices such as those between professional training and manual labor, which are often unreal choices anyway.

6.   Attempts to derive equalitarian or maldistributionist conclusions from utility analysis, without the crucial and questionable comparability and measurability assumptions, have thus far ended in failure. Strotz, in particular, has explored the problem along axiomatic lines.[10] We shall not attempt to summarize his analysis, but his results add to the "unease" of the equalitarian case. Without comparability and measurability, one can derive a preference for one distribution over another only by the circular method of inserting it into one's initial set of assumptions or axioms, as so many equalitarians do. This may be done either directly, by initially stating a preference for equality, or indirectly, by including in (ordinal) utility or preference functions some "benevolent concern" with the incomes of the poor. ("Benevolent concern" might mean that, with his own income given, each individual would feel better off if some or all persons had higher incomes than if they had lower ones, provided only that the rank order of incomes was not distributed.) [11]

10. Robert Strotz, "How Income Ought to Be Distributed: A Paradox in Distributive Ethics," *J.P.E.* (June 1958), the paradox being that "income should be distributed so that total income is a maximum" (p. 197), *i.e.*, that distribution is irrelevant! Objections and rebuttals are found in Franklin M. Fisher and Jerome Rothenberg, "How Income Ought to Be Distributed: Paradox Lost," *ibid.* (April 1961); Strotz, "How Income Ought to be Distributed: Paradox Regained," *ibid.* (June 1961); Fisher and Rothenberg, "How Income Ought to Be Distributed: Paradox Enow," *ibid.* (February 1962.)

11. "Malevolent concern" might then mean the opposite preference. Malevolent concern with the incomes of the rich would have the same implications for equality as benevolent concern with those of the poor, and vice versa. Certain of the policy consequences of distributional benevolence are developed by Harold M. Hochman and James D. Rogers, "Pareto Optimal Redistribution," *A.E.R.* (September 1969).

7. Marginal-utility agnosticism plays a negligible role in attempts to refute the ethical-maldistributionist position. Most of the leading elements in such attempts we have already met, in this and earlier chapters. There is praise for the rich as individuals and as a class, "the great oaks that shade a country and perpetuate their benefits from generation to generation."[12] This may be formalized into Social Darwinism. More commonly it is coupled with paeans to social mobility *à la* Horatio Alger, or explained by individual preferences related to hard work, risk-bearing, or investment in human capital. There is assimilation of the income distribution with the distributions of human abilities, and concern for both progress and stability if adequate scope and motivation are not provided for the more able. The "motivation" argument is extended, devoid of biological overtones, into the simple claim that people, whatever their innate characteristics, will not develop or apply their skills, and will not use either private or social property efficiently without commensurate return. As a converse argument, all forms of social minima are supposed to subsidize idleness and improvidence to some extent, so that the combined effects of penalties upon the rich and social minima for the poor are declining progress and productivity. "Everyone but an idiot knows that the lower classes must be kept poor, or they will never be industrious."[13]

Underlying these arguments are three tacit assumptions, which have from time to time been questioned. The first of these tacit assumptions is that no distinctions need be drawn between "earned" income from human capital and "unearned" income from nonhuman capital, or that dissipation of the second, like underdevelopment of the first, would result from equalitarianism. (The adjectives "earned" and "unearned" will suffice to point up the issue.) The second tacit assumption is that, in the natural course of events, the ordinary reasonable man or social animal, even one with somewhat less than ordinary endowment of capital of any kind, will in fact be able to earn a competence no lower than the accepted reasonable living standard of his place and time. (This is periodically doubted, whenever the pace of labor-saving innovation is accelerated.) The third and final assumption is that the incremental production and progress attributable to inequality is desirable in itself, for reasons over and beyond the mere provision of employment. This has been questioned in the twentieth century by "economy of abundance" writers in all advanced countries, but their doubts may be more apparent than real. That is to say, these writers' main contention, slips and exaggerations aside, is only that private production of material commodities has passed its apo-

12. Edmund Burke, cited by Tawney, *op. cit.*, p. 94.
13. *Ibid.*, quoting Arthur Young.

gee and that the wave of the future lies with the public provision of services, if not in pure leisure of the lotos-eating variety.

8. Certain more sophisticated arguments against equality have come more recently into vogue at a level comparable to marginal-utility agnosticism.[14] If, for example, all aspects of economic performance are in fact, interrelated, support of the private enterprise system on other grounds, such as traditional liberalism, should allegedly also involve reconciliation with the resulting distributions of income and wealth. This passes over into a negativistic position which maintains that, in an imperfect world, such practical equalizing devices as progressive taxation do more harm than good, either in the maldistribution of power and the inquisitorial impingements on personal liberty necessarily involved in efficient enforcement, or in the property holders' loss of the liberty to lead a life of leisure, or in the concentration of tax incidence upon the economic innovator. (Less hardship is involved when the top is lopped off a quiescent rentier's high income than when the new man is prevented from building up the underlying capital to found a family. The luck of Henry Ford is often mentioned, in building up his fortune before American surtax rates became steep.)

Critics of equality are also concerned about the future of science, art, and culture if their support is limited, by equalitarian measures, to the public authorities, and if "competition" from private philanthropy is lessened or eliminated. Will not all these aspects of life be censored or otherwise forced into a few orthodox modes approved by the government in power? Danger obviously exists, as may be seen from the example of centralized socialist regimes, but it should not be exaggerated. In large federal systems with separation and division of powers, the elimination of private philanthropy need not bring on dead-level orthodoxy. The universities of neighboring American states, for example, differ widely in character and emphasis. Within a single state, the same is true for the Cow

---

14. Representative traditional-liberal sources for one or more of these viewpoints include Bertrand de Jouvenel, *The Ethics of Redistribution* (Cambridge: Cambridge University Press, 1961); Milton Friedman, *Capitalism and Freedom* (Chicago: University of Chicago Press, 1962), ch. 10; John Jewkes, *Ordeal by Planning* (London: Macmillan, 1948), pp. 8 f., pp. 163–170, ch. 10; David McCord Wright, "Income Redistribution Reconsidered," in Metzler and Domar, *Income, Employment, and Public Policy* (New York: Norton, 1948).

Absolute elimination of some cultural forms may also be a problem. In an equalitarian regime, de Jouvenel fears (*op. cit.*, p. 41): "The production of all first-quality goods would cease. The skill they demand would be lost and the taste they shape would be coarsened. The production of artistic and intellectual goods would be affected first and foremost. Who could buy paintings? Who even could buy books other than pulp?"

College, the Teachers College, the Junior College, the Northern Branch, the Southern Branch, and so on throughout the "multiversity" systems. In other countries, various official ministries promote quite different patterns of scientific and cultural activities, not to mention the parallel bureaucracies under the aegis of the Party, the army, or the state police. Interstitial opportunities for the unorthodox may survive, or even flourish, under these sorts of competition as well as under competition between public and private purses, or between private philanthropists with no state activity whatever.

Economic Maldistributionism

9.   The economic string to the equalitarian bow is the maldistribution theory of business depression, which played so large a part in the ideology of British Labourism and the American New Deal. We do not call it "underconsumption theory," because underconsumption theories also include purely monetary variants, associated, for example, with the Social Credit movement in Britain and Canada. Neither should we say theory of "the business cycle," because this particular theory of depression has difficulty explaining any subsequent recovery or prosperity.

The maldistributionist case is deceptively simple in its essentials. The poor (or, in some versions, the workers) spend most of their incomes; the rich (or the capitalists, including corporate business entities) save most of theirs. In the simpler models, including the Marxian one, the working class does not save at all. The capitalist system, particularly with infusions of cartel and monopoly arrangements, produce an income distribution that limits total consumption expenditures to something below the maximum full employment output of consumption goods. For a time, the problem can be warded off, as by deepening of capital, extension of consumer credit to the poor, or artificial expansion of luxury consumption by high-pressure marketing, but the eventual outcome will be a fall of consumer goods production to some level that can be absorbed, but that can be produced at less than full employment. A stability condition, seldom stated explicitly except by professional economists, is that any fall in employment and income reduces output by a larger increment than it reduces consumer expenditures, and vice versa for any rise.[15] Were it not so, spiraling processes could proceed indefinitely in either direction.

The economic downturn from an assumed initial position of full em-

<hr/>

15. The best-known example of such a stability condition is John Maynard Keynes' "basic psychological law" of a marginal propensity to consume, out of income positive but less than unity. (If C represents aggregate consumption, and Y aggregate disposable income after personal taxes, $0 < (dC/dY) < 1$.

ployment will come sooner if the rich attempt to hoard their savings without investing them. It will be postponed if they invest them in plant, equipment, or inventories, since such investment maintains both employment and purchasing power.[16] Postponement, however, cannot be permanent, because the investment must result in eventual increase of the output of consumer goods, whereas purchasing power has at best been merely maintained at the full-employment level. Once the increment of consumption goods production reaches the market, recession will set in as before.[17] Investment, moreover, will become unprofitable, and will at least be reduced in volume, if not discontinued, once consumer goods output has expanded beyond purchasing power.

10. Say's Law, in the crude form of "Supply creates its own demand" (known more precisely as Say's Identity), was for years the standard textbook rebuttal to all forms of underconsumption heresy, including the maldistributionist variety. It never satisfied most of the heretics, although the great British maldistributionist John A. Hobson frequently professed fealty to the faith he never practiced.[18] Something more had to be added to Say's Law in serious discussions. That "something more" became increasingly, after the formulation of "Austrian" capital theory, an appeal to the rate of interest as reinforcement for Say's Law. Again we can paraphrase in elementary form.

Suppose some tendency toward maldistribution in a fully employed economy, of the type postulated by maldistributionist theory. This tendency will manifest itself not only in a fall of income and employment, but also in a rise of planned saving in excess of planned investment. This in its turn will cause interest rates to fall. The fall of interest rates will have at least five reactions, all operating to restore equilibrium at full employment and to correct automatically the tendency toward economic maldistribution.

(1) People, meaning primarily the rich, will consume a higher pro-

16. "Investment" in land, in existing securities, or on any goods carried over from past production, has no such effects of maintaining income and employment. It might well be called "hoarding on the wing."

17. A later writer has put the problem epigrammatically (Evsey D. Domar, "The Problem of Capital Accumulation," in *Essays in the Theory of Economic Growth* [New York: Oxford University Press, 1957], p. 118) : "If saving is not invested, we have a depression today. If it is invested, there will be an excessive accumulation of capital tomorrow, and a depression the day after." And again ("Expansion and Employment," *ibid.*, p. 101) : "As far as unemployment is concerned, investment is at the same time a cure for the disease and the cause of even greater ills in the future."

18. Hobson's vacillations with regard to Say's Law have been traced by Erwin E. Nemmers, *Hobson and Underconsumption* (Amsterdam: North Holland, 1956) , pp. 38, 70, 97 f.

portion of their income, and save less. In some cases, this will mean increased borrowing (negative saving).

(2) Other people, including corporations, will invest more because of the lower cost of money capital.

(3) The increased investment will raise labor productivity and physical output by providing labor with more and better capital to work with, and/or by lowering the prices of consumption goods through lower capital charges per unit of output. (Lower interest rates also may operate independently to lower capital charges, quite apart from the effects of increased investment.[19]) In either case, there will be an increase in real purchasing power and in the aggregate volume of sales.

(4) Increased investment will also increase the ratio of capital goods to consumption goods in the economy. It will become profitable to increase the volume of investment embodied in any given output of consumption goods, that is, to "deepen" the economy's capital. "Deepening of capital" will accordingly reduce the real volume of consumption goods to be purchased out of any given national income. Such deepening does not require overall displacement of labor, since investment goods are themselves products of labor along with other inputs, and since the deepening process accelerates the growth of the economy.[20] There need therefore be neither contraction of employment nor downward pressure on wage rates.

(5) If the weight of net interest receipts is higher algebraically (larger positively or smaller negatively) in higher incomes than in lower ones, any fall in interest rates will operate automatically in the direction of equalizing incomes and eliminating maldistribution. If the maldistribu-

---

19. The direct effect of interest rate changes on production cost is complex. The capital charges that enter into marginal cost are products of three terms: marginal physical use (depreciation) of capital goods (machines) when output expands; the price of machines per unit; the rate of interest. The first of these terms we assume unaffected in this footnote; the process of capitalization causes the second term to rise as the third falls, and vice versa, so that in short-term equilibrium the product of all three terms is uncertain.

In the interval *before* capitalization is reflected in machinery prices, however, capital charges move with the interest rate. The same result may hold in longer-run equilibrium, if production of new machines influences the price of existing ones, and provides capital gains (positive or negative) to their owners.

20. It will certainly shift labor from consumption to investment goods industries, however. If investment goods are themselves more capital-intensive than consumption goods, there may be some second-order downward pressure on both employment and wages. If wages rates are not uniform between economic sectors—because of, for example, the influence of noncompeting groups—or if labor is imperfectly mobile, there may be pressure (in either direction) on employment and wages. (Or the pressure may be simultaneously upward in investment goods industries and downward in goods industries.)

tionist theory of depression is correct, maldistribution is self-eliminating and prosperity is self-restoring.

To all such abstract and involved replies, the standard maldistributionist rebuttal runs in practical terms. For example, interest rates need not fall if they are "administered" by Wall Street, "the international bankers," or "one big union of the vested interests." Or, if rates fall on paper, hardened fringe terms of credit transactions will keep the real total cost of credit as high as ever.[21] Or, finally, if interest rates do fall more than nominally, the time required for them to do so, and for the effects of lower rates to make themselves felt, is too long and too costly—in terms of employment and income forgone—for any reliance to be placed upon them by hard-headed businessmen and voters.

11. Over and beyond the abstract, or at least the qualitative, realm of deductive economic theory, there has arisen a statistical, quantitative, and econometric reply to maldistributionism. This reply has tended to minimize the importance of differing consumption propensities as between different income size brackets and, in one important version, to deny their existence altogether in the long run.

By a consumption propensity, we may mean either an average or a marginal propensity to consume out of disposable income. It is often important to distinguish between the two. If C is real consumption and Y real disposable income (net of personal taxes), and the two are related by a consumption function $C = C(Y)$, the average propensity to consume is C/Y and the marginal propensity to consume is dC/dY. Moreover, in the standard Keynesian case, which fits actual data well, the consumption function is linear:

$$C = C_o + cY \qquad (C_o > 0, 0 < c < 1) \qquad (5.1)$$

As we saw in Chapter 2, the average propensity to consume is $c + C_o/Y$, and the marginal propensity simply c. It follows that the average propensity to consume exceeds the marginal one for all positive values of C_o and Y.

The plausibility of statistical skepticism about economic maldistribution has come to rest mainly upon three points:

(1) In the first place, the magnitude of the consumption effect of redistributing a unit of income, whether $1 or $1 billion, from class i (rich) to class j (poor), depends upon the *marginal* rather than the *average*

---

21. The related notion that an interest-rate fall in a depression period will be accompanied and offset by deflationary contraction in the total money supply is apparently alien to the maldistributionist outlook. It is probably of later origin than the pre-World War I pattern of argument that we are attempting to trace here.

consumption propensities in these two classes. This is because the changes occurring in the incomes of individuals are increments, positive in j and negative in i, that alter the average propensities with which they are associated.

(2) In the second place, marginal propensities to consume are not only smaller than average ones, at least in the short period, but fall more slowly as family income increases.[22] In fact, the marginal (although not the average) propensity to consume may be higher for some middle-class elements who would lose under equalitarian redistribution than for the poor who would gain by it. This paradox reflects the influence of the subsistence minimum, which raises the average consumption propensity of the poor to unity and above—the "wolf point" phenomenon—but affects their marginal propensity only slightly. Poor persons may devote substantial portions of income increments to paying off old debts and avoiding new ones, or use the increments as substitutes for drawing down savings, selling assets, or depending on friends and relatives. If so, their marginal propensity to consume is relatively low, although their average propensity may remain greater than unity.

(3) In the third place, there exist classes of consumer goods whose consumption may actually be reduced by income equality. These include, at the lower end of the scale, inferior goods[23] like turnips, dried eggs, and in some places, public transportation. They also include, at the upper end, such conspicuously consumed luxury items as diamonds, furs, and ocean-going yachts. Equalitarians of good will have concentrated their attention on the broad middle range of "desirable" consumption items like milk, warm clothing, and medical care, while neglecting both penurious and luxurious extremes.

For the United States, a pioneer essay in statistical skepticism, using 1941 data, was made by Lubell.[24] He worked out the effects of redistribution patterns that collapsed each point of the Lorenz curve of personal income distribution (Chapter 3, section 3) the same percentage of the

---

22. The consumption functions considered in this sentence are *family* consumption functions, relating family consumption to family income at a point of time, on a cross-section basis, rather than the standard national consumption functions like (5.1), derived from time series. The family consumption functions are s-shaped, whereas national consumption functions do tend to be linear.

23. The income elasticity of demand for any good, it will be remembered, is the relative change in the amount demanded, divided by the relative change in consumers' income, with prices constant. (Mathematically, it is the logarithmic partial derivative of amount demanded with respect to income.) This elasticity is normally positive. For inferior goods, however, it is negative, while for luxuries it may be substantially greater than unity.

24. Harold Lubell, "Effects of Redistribution of Income on Consumers' Expenditures," *A.E.R.* (March and December 1947), p. 930.

vertical distance separating it from the line of equality. For a 10 per cent shift toward equality, he estimated the effect as only a 0.52 per cent rise in consumer expenditures (or a 5.5 per cent fall in personal saving). For a 50 per cent shift toward equality, the corresponding figures were a 2.87 per cent rise in consumer expenditures (or a 30.5 per cent fall in saving). For a complete 100 per cent shift, he estimated a 5.82 percent rise in consumer expenditures (or a 61.5 per cent fall in saving). These results included no multiplier effects,[25] which would have raised income levels, and accordingly raised the estimates of expenditure increase while lowering those of saving decrease.

The epitome of statistical skepticism is reached with the permanent income hypothesis of Milton Friedman.[26] Previous studies related measured consumption to measured income with relatively minor adjustments. Friedman believes the underlying relation to be between permanent consumption and permanent income; this relationship, moreover, he believes to be invariant for income changes. (Permanent consumption differs from measured consumption in that reported expenditures for durable goods are distributed over the lifetime of their services, instead of being concentrated in the period when the goods are purchased. "Permanent income" is defined to exclude transitory variations. It is estimated in practice as a weighted average of present and past measured incomes. The weights diminish rapidly in a distributed-lag pattern, which we need not explain here, as one goes backward in time.) The constant proportion between permanent consumption and permanent income, approximately 0.88, leads Friedman to conclude that the high observed average consump-

---

25. In an elementary Keynesian model, income Y is the sum of consumption C and investment I, while consumption is a linear function of income:

$$Y = C + I, \quad C = C_o + cY, \quad I = I_o.$$

(The subscript o denotes a structural or autonomous parameter or variable.) Combining the above three expressions, and letting $(C_o + I_o)$ equal total autonomous expenditures A_o, we have

$$Y = A_o + cY \quad \text{or} \quad Y = \frac{A_o}{1-c}.$$

The Keynesian multiplier μ is the derivative dY/dA_o. In this simple model, it equals $1/(1-c)$.

For an extension of Lubell's analysis to include multiplier effects, see M. Bronfenbrenner, Taro Yamane, and C. H. Lee, "A Study of Redistribution and Consumption," *Rev. Econ. and Stat.* (May 1955). This essay also extends Lubell's method to allow for possible changes in individual spending patterns as a consequence of increases in income, resulting from the assimilation of individuals' consumption patterns to the habits of their new income classes.

26. Friedman, *A Theory of the Consumption Function* (Princeton: Princeton University Press, 1957), pp. 209 ff., 235. Other "permanent" concepts are developed more fully below (Chapter 10, section 17).

tion propensity of the poor reflects primarily the high proportion of poor (rich) people temporarily below (above) their permanent incomes. The implication of these results for the long period is that equalization of personal incomes will have no measurable effect on permanent consumption as a percentage of income.

This is not true for functional redistribution, however. The ratio of permanent consumption to permanent income is higher, the higher is the ratio of human wealth (capitalized labor income) to nonhuman wealth. It is therefore higher for workingmen than for property owners. It is also higher for property owners than for the self-employed, presumably because of the greater uncertainty in the incomes of the self-employed, their generally poorer access to credit, and their frequent ambition to rise by their own bootstraps.

Holbrook and Stafford quantify this "income-source effect" for the United States in the early 1960s.[27] Let (H, W, X, M, K) be six components of permanent income; labor income of family heads (H); labor income of other family members (W); transfer income (X); entrepreneurial income; (M); and income from capital assets, including imputed rent from owned houses (K), all "permanentized" by modifications of the Friedman method. If consumption is similarly "permanentized," the consumption function of the Holbrook-Stafford sample is

$$C = 508 + .875\,H + .862\,W + .593\,X + .463\,M + .769\,K.$$

Insofar as the permanent-income hypothesis is correct, one should redistribute income from capitalists and the self-employed to wage- and salary-earners, even from poor peasants to labor aristocrats, if one wishes to raise consumption from a given income. Relative incomes have little, if anything, to do with the case. It is difficult to find any ethical grounds to justify particular patterns of redistribution that operate to increase the propensity to consume.

On a different statistical front from any of the other economists mentioned, Mendershausen estimated that American income inequality, as measured by the concentration ratio, actually *increased* between 1929 and

27. Robert Holbrook and Frank Stafford, "The Propensity to Consume Separate Types of Income: A Generalized Permanent Income Hypothesis" (mimeographed: University of Michigan, 1968).

Japanese economists, seeking to explain the low Japanese consumption propensity, have attempted to account for *international* differences in saving ratios by differences in the relative shares of the self-employed popuation. See the discussion between Ryutaro Komiya and Miyohei Shinohara in Komiya (ed.), *Postwar Economic Growth in Japan*, trans. Ozaki (Berkeley: University of California Press, 1966), pp. 167–169, 178–181, 184–186.

1933.[28] This implies that the equalizing effect of the fall in profits (at the high end of the personal income distribution) on measured inequality was, in one important case, more than offset by the contrary effect of the rise in unemployment (at the low end of the same distribution). Figure 5.2 illustrates the point at issue. If Mendershausen's results hold generally, it is hard to claim that depression generates recovery by any such simple process as reducing overall inequality. Such a criticism, however, does not hit its mark if we interpret maldistributionism as exclusively a theory of recession or depression, with upturns explained by exogenous

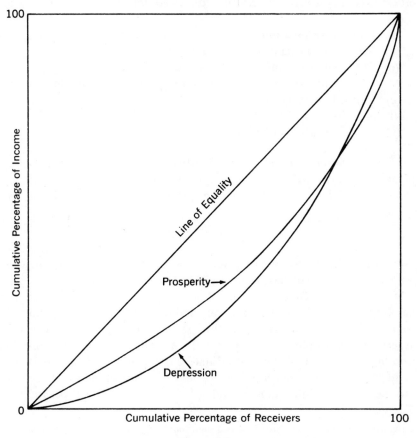

Figure 5.2

28. Horst Mendershausen, *Changes in Income Distribution During the Great Depression* (New York: National Bureau of Economic Research, 1946) pp. 25–36, 68–80.

shocks. (In the 1930s, both the New Deal program and the onset of World War II could qualify as "shocks" on the American scene.)

Principal Redistribution Measures

12.   Assume that "society has made, for whatever reasons, a decision in favor of equalitarian and/or pro-labor redistribution of income and wealth. There are some seven main types of measures available. Their order runs, in a very general way, from the less radical and revolutionary to the more radical and revolutionary. No set of measures excludes any other, except possibly by reducing the need for it. The seven sets are these:

(a) Progressive taxation.
(b) Regressive expenditures.
(c) Collective bargaining.
(d) Wage and price supports (including minimum wage legislation) .
(e) Multiple pricing and rationing.
(f) Socialization of the flow.
(g) Confiscation of wealth.

13.   If individual i is rich and individual j is poor, while Y is income prior to some tax and T is the receipts of this same tax, then the tax (or combination of taxes) is progressive, proportional, or regressive according as

$$T_i/Y_i \gtreqless T_j/Y_j$$

(Measuring the *degree* of progression is a more arcane matter, on which no general agreement has been reached.) [29]

Since the Lloyd George budget (1909) in Britain, progressive taxation has become the accepted neoliberal method for redistributing both income and wealth. Musgrave, in his general treatise on the economic aspects of public finance, has it primarily in mind in providing a "distribution branch" as one of three coordinate units in his ideal "Fiscal Department." [30] The taxes concerned are primarily direct or personal levies on incomes, estates, inheritances, and gifts *inter vivos*. [31] Corporate taxes

29. A standard treatment, indicating numerous alternative measures, is Richard A. Musgrave and Tun Thin, "Income Tax Progression, 1929–48," *J.P.E.* (December 1948) .

30. R. A. Musgrave, *The Theory of Public Finance* (New York: McGraw-Hill, 1959) , p. 5.

31. James Meade, in *Efficiency, Equality, and the Ownership of Property* (Cambridge: Harvard University Press, 1965) , proposes a restructuring of succession taxes on the dual basis of the size of the donor's estate and the amount of each donee's inherited or donated wealth from all sources.

(usually resulting in differential taxation of dividend payments) and special excises on luxury goods (somehow defined) may also be included marginally in the progressive category, as may capital levies at progressive rates.

There seem, however, to have developed, at least in advanced capitalist countries, certain limits on the effectiveness of tax progression as a redistributive device. Two dilemmas in particular affect progressive income taxation. The first dilemma is how simultaneously to close "loopholes" in the tax code and to preserve material incentives for investment in both human and physical capital (and also for efficient allocation of the stocks in existence). The second and related dilemma is how simultaneously to make progressive taxation "bite" on the beneficiaries of old fortunes and to avoid discouraging the accumulation of new ones. A common result of contradictions between the desire to redistribute income and the political power of the wealthy (including the acumen of their attorneys) has been the erosion of steeply progressive rate structures by the creation of special privileges, so that the tax system operates by "dipping deeply into large fortunes with a sieve." Corporate taxation, meanwhile, has failed to discourage the avoidance of taxes through retaining earnings for internal investment in closely controlled "corporate pocketbook" enterprises, while "luxury taxation" characteristically raises most of its revenue from items in inelastic demand, which the poor "should do without, but won't."

14. With progressive taxation approaching diminishing returns in some nontechnical sense of the term, redistributive energies have apparently shifted, tacitly and on balance, to regressive expenditures.[32] Reverting to the example of rich individual i and poor individual j, a public expenditure item G, whose benefits to i and j can be isolated to the extent of statistical estimation, is regressive, proportional, or progressive according as

$$G_i/Y_i \gtrless G_j/Y_j$$

Regressive expenditures ordinarily supply public services to the entire populace either free or well below their average and marginal cost, but these services are supposedly consumed mainly by the poor. The rich presumably prefer higher-cost and supposedly higher-quality alternatives, which they purchase on the market. (To whatever extent this presumption fails, as in the educational and other facilities of the more exclusive suburbs, redistribution may be abortive or even, when tax system are suf-

32. A number of public finance writers use the term "progressive" and "regressive" in the opposite senses from ourselves. Compare, for example, Walter W. Heller, *New Dimensions of Political Economy* (Cambridge: Harvard University Press, 1966), p. 153.

ficiently regressive, absolutely perverse.) [33] Education, medical care, urban transport, and public housing are examples of regressive expenditures, although income limitations on eligibility for public housing usually transfer it to another category of redistributive devices. Transfer payments for poverty, unemployment, illness, and the like are also regressive expenditures. More extreme cases are social dividend, negative income tax, guaranteed income, and family allowance proposals.

15. An entire monograph would be required to summarize these latter proposals, which have enjoyed a considerable vogue in the United States in consequence of the "War on Poverty" of the 1960s.[34] Six features are usually considered desirable, but must be traded off against each other:

(a) Coverage or efficiency: as many as possible of "the poor," however defined, should be covered by the plan.

(b) Economy: low administrative costs; small "leakage" of benefits to the nonpoor. (Universal social-dividend schemes rank low by this criterion.)

(c) Equity: as between different income levels, family sizes, etc.

(d) Carryover: this applies primarily to negative income taxes. (It implies reliance on the framework of the existing tax system, and exclusion of "cross-hauling" of payments to and from the same households.)

(e) Self-respect: minimizing the inquisitorial features of administration, as by making allowances payable to all residents.

(f) Incentive: this criterion opposes high marginal losses of allowances when the poor work. It is rejected by writers like Theobald, who regard the "work ethic" as obsolete.)

Several graphic devices to facilitate comparisons between alternative income-maintenance and allied proposals have been developed. We present one of these as Figure 5.3; it compares an "existing" and a "proposed" system.[35] On this diagram, the horizontal axis represents annual

33. Aaron Director, among others, has formulated the generalization that most redistribution schemes actually work out in practice to the benefit of the middle classes, and to the detriment of both the rich and the poor. This generalization has been christened "Director's Law" in George Stigler, "Director's Law of Public Income Redistribution" *J.L.E.* (April 1970).

34. A comprehensive and critical summary of proposals is found in Christopher Green, *Negative Taxes and the Poverty Problem* (Washington: Brookings Institution, 1967), chs. 3–9. More institutional material on Canadian and Western European practice is found in Martin Schnitzer, *Guaranteed Minimum Income Proposals Used by Governments of Selected Countries*, prepared for the Joint Economic Committee of the U.S. Congress (Washington: Government Printing Office, 1968).

35. Figure 5.3 is based on James Tobin, "On Improving the Economic Status of the Negro," *Daedalus* (Fall 1965); fig. 1, p. 893. Another type of figure is the so-called "break-even" chart; its horizontal axis is the same as that of Figure 5.3; its vertical axis measures "taxes" (positively) and "allowances" (negatively). Green, *op. cit.*, ch. 6.

family income prior to taxes and allowances; the vertical axis represents annual family "disposable income" net of taxes and allowances; a 45-degree line is a locus of break-even points where the two are equal. The existing system is represented by a broken line *OAB*. It implies no allowances whatever, and a proportional tax rate on all income over *OA*. Any income below OA ($3700, under the Tobin representation for a family with three children) is a "break-even" income and lies on the 45-degree line *OO'*. The proposed system is represented by the line *CEF*. It involves a maximum allowance of *OC* ($1000) to a recipient with no income whatever, and a tax rate (or allowance-reduction rate) higher than the existing bottom-bracket income tax rate. (In the Tobin plan, this rate is

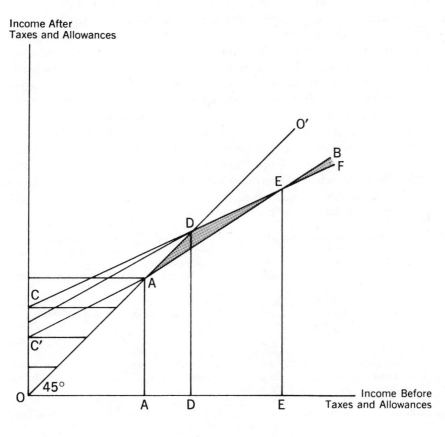

Figure 5.3

33 1/3 per cent, as against 14 per cent under the existing system.) Point *D* ($6000 for Tobin's family with three children) is the break-even point where income tax net of allowances is zero. Point *E* ($7963) is the point where net tax liability under the existing and the proposed systems is the same.

Income recipients below *OD* (horizontal shading) gain by receipt of allowances; income recipients in the range *AE* (diagonal shading) gain by reduced net tax liabilities; income recipents in the range *AD*, therefore, gain on both counts. Income recipients above *OE* (vertical shading) suffer increased tax liabilities; they receive no allowances and therefore lose on balance.[36]

A Friedman-type negative income tax proposal is illustrated also, the disposable-income function in this case being *C'AB,* with no gain to any income recipient with an income above *OA.* The reader can, if he so desires, experiment with a wide range of additional alternatives.[37]

16.   When regressive expenditures are financed by regressive taxation, redistribution either does not occur at all or occurs along unanticipated lines. (In this connection it is sometimes important to estimate and compare *degrees* of tax and expenditure progression.) One pattern, which is probably more important than generally realized, has been called "diagonal redistribution." It results from expanded regressive services financed by increased taxes on alcohol and tobacco products. Here, at the margin, redistribution from rich to poor may be less important than redistribution from poor smokers and drinkers to poor abstainers; hence the "diagonal" label. In at least one specific case, the United Kingdom during the 1940s, the effectiveness of regressive expenditures may have been cut drastically by diagonal redistribution, while the observed redistribution was due largely to other factors, including the rationing system.[38]

36. In the actual Tobin proposal (a more nearly pure regressive-expenditure plan than the one illustrated in Fig. 5.3), the post-tax disposable income function is the broken line *CEB* rather than *CEF,* and no taxpayer loses. The proposal was to be financed from other taxes, by debt, and by reduction of other expenditures, chiefly military.

37. Milton Friedman, *Capitalism and Freedom* (Chicago: University of Chicago Press, 1962), ch. 12. Green (*op. cit.,* pp. 57 f.) lists a number of American antecedents with similar views.

38. This point is stressed by Findley Weaver, "Taxation and Redistribution in the United Kingdom," *Rev. Econ. and Stat.* (August 1950). Weaver considers only "welfare state" expenditures. Allan Cartter, after estimating the benefits of all expenditures, comes to the opposite conclusion in *The Redistribution of Income in Postwar Britain* (New Haven: Yale University Press, 1955), chs. 7 and 11.

Another diagonal effect occurs when expansion is financed by general sales taxes, as proposed in Galbraith's *Affluent Society.* Here it is the large-family poor who help support the small-family poor, if the tax base includes food, clothing, and medicines.

17. A major element in the ideology of trade unionism and its agricultural equivalents has always been the redistribution of income from "rich" capitalists and landlords to "poor" workers and farmers. (To mention "labor aristocracy" in the presence of a union leader is to wave the proverbial red cape at the proverbial bull.) Accordingly, legislation to legitimize unionism, widen the range of the bargaining process, or increase the bargaining power of organized labor vis-à-vis employers and strikebreakers actual or potential, is redistributive in intent at least. There is, however, little evidence that such legislation, or indeed the entire trade union movement, has in practice had much redistributive effect. We have already seen some of the relevant statistics, and shall examine the subject again in Chapters 10 and 11.

18. Since redistribution by collective bargaining is usually a slow process at best, a number of policies have been designed to accelerate it. Where strong and viable bargaining agencies do not develop, legislation can substitute for bargaining. (Compare Chapter 17 below.) On the American scene, the two outstanding examples are minimum wage legislation for labor and minimum support prices for certain agricultural products. In many other countries, and in some American local units, small retailers and their associations are given parallel protection by minimum prices for service, minimum mark-ups for commodities, resale price maintenance, and so on. We may call this body of legislation "support for the prices of the goods and services supplied by the poor" or simply "wage and price supports."

The redistributive effectiveness of wage and price supports, taken by themselves, is open to question. Assume a minimum wage for unskilled labor, significantly above the going rate. Assume that it is enforced and is not passed on completely in higher prices. It clearly benefits those workers who continue to be employed. But what of those who are either unemployed from the start or who lose their jobs when wages rise? For them to share in the benefits, public employment must be offered at the new minimum wage, or relief of some kind made available at or above the former market level of wages. When one cannot find employment, it makes little difference what the going wage of the employed may be.

The redistributive case for agricultural price supports is weak for a different reason. The bulk of the poor farmers are not primarily commercial but subsistence farmers. They consume most of their produce and have little to sell on the market. The prices they might obtain for commercial crops are of little importance if they cannot raise enough to sell.

19. "Multiple pricing and rationing" is a generic term for a number of schemes to sell limited quantities of basic commodities below both cost and market price, to individuals who qualify for special treatment by reason of their poverty. Two American examples are urban public housing (usually managed directly by public authorities) and food stamp plans for the sale of agricultural produce (where retailers are compensated for their losses) . The subsidy element is common to both cases.

Even with no multiple-pricing feature, the frequent wartime device of rationing necessities at controlled prices during a suppressed inflation involves some redistribution. All, or nearly all, the income of the poor is devoted to rationed goods at controlled prices. The additional income of the rich is immobilized or, more accurately, it must be spent in free markets at high prices. Some rationing schemes also permit the poor to supplement their incomes by the sale of ration coupons that they cannot afford to utilize. This redistribution is particularly great if the control system can prevent shifts of production away from the controlled necessities and "utility models" to the luxury items that are joint or alternative outputs in production, escape controls by reason of initial unimportance, or are permitted higher profit margins.

Because controls and rationing were more thoroughgoing and were retained longer after World War II in Great Britain than in America, while fiscal redistribution in both countries was eroded by tax loopholes and diagonal effects, it may be reasonable to ascribe the greater shift toward equality in Britain largely to the multiple-pricing and rationing devices.[39]

20. Our last two redistribution methods are explicitly socialistic. "Socialization of the flow" is a term, apparently coined in Japan by Tsuru,[40] to describe a relatively mild process of socialization. In this process, the titles of owners of productive property are not disturbed, although expansion of the capital stock is presumably a public prerogative. All, or the major part, of the income the owners receive from such property is, however, taken by the public authorities; the owners' claims are reduced to what are known in courts of equity as "bare legal titles." Private rights in other forms of wealth are left undisturbed, except that the taxed "flow" of income may be defined to include some estimate of what idle or underemployed property might have produced if allocated properly. Socialization

39. Separate cost-of-living indexes for different income levels, family sizes, etc., were computed, compiled, and applied to British distribution data by Dudley Seers, *The Levelling of Incomes Since 1938* (Oxford: Blackwell, 1951) , pp. 19–28, 53–69. Seers interprets the price effects as concentrated in the wartime period 1939–1945, and as reversing themselves partially in 1946–1949.

40. Shigeto Tsuru (ed.) , *Has Capitalism Changed?* (Tokyo: Iwanami, 1961) , editor's introduction. The *idea* of socialization of the flow is, of course, much older.

of the flow should perhaps be regarded as a generalization of Henry George's single tax on unimproved land, to cover also such improvements as commercial buildings, machinery, equipment, inventories, and probably cash balances as well.

Confiscation or expropriation of property is the most extreme device considered. Private owners lose not only the income from their property but also their legal claim to it. The loss may be immediate or may occur after certain conditions are satisfied, such as the death of the present holder (abolition of inheritance) or the payment of a certain number of years' rent (a common land-reform scheme). In poor countries, such as Communist China in the 1940s and 1950s, confiscation may extend beyond productive capital, as defined above, to include consumers' capital in luxury goods and in "hoards" of food and clothing.

The terms "confiscation" and "expropriation" are too strong to describe accurately all redistributions under this head. The terms themselves imply either violence or the threat of violence; but the process may itself be largely or completely voluntary, as in religious or Utopian cooperative communities. Christian and Buddhist monasteries, Israeli *kibbutzim,* and the Indian *bhoodan yagna* are cases in point, the last being less complete than the others.

CHAPTER SIX

The Demand for
Productive Inputs

We have been postponing the crucial question of why the primary distribution of income—in a market economy—is what it is, before such secondary modifications as were considered in the closing sections of the last chapter. This question will dominate the remainder of this book.

Distribution and Pseudo-Distribution

1. Economists have for centuries answered this question of why the income distribution is what it is almost exclusively in terms of the functional distribution. We shall follow this convention, although it involves silence about the detailed interrelations between the several distributions discussed in Chapter 2.

Economists have then gone on to argue, first, that the total income to the suppliers of any productive input, service, or factor depends upon the quantity of that input employed and upon its price per unit; and second, that economics has little to say about the basic determinant of the quantity employed, which is the stock or quantity in existence. They concentrate their attention, accordingly, upon the determination of input prices. The first of the two propositions above is tautologous. The second is not, if we accept any notions of economic determination of either population or capital stock, which most economists do for the very long run.

Be that as it may, distribution theory has conventionally been telescoped into a theory of input prices, to which has more recently been appended a scheme of verification at the aggregative level. It is the theory of input prices that was called (by Edwin Cannan) "pseudo-distribution," because of its omissions.[1] We shall ourselves continue, however apologetically, in the pseudo-distribution tradition, as modified aggregatively since Cannan's day. We shall concentrate on the prices and employment of labor forces and physical capital stocks which are assumed to change only autonomously to the economic system. This leaves the endogenous aspects of their changes almost entirely to history, to the other social studies, or to one special branch of economics, the theory of economic growth and development.

Terminology and Notation

2. In this chapter and in those that follow, we shall generally use x to denote the quantity of some output per time period.[2] In cases of joint production, x is an index number. The units of x are chosen so that the price of x is unity; in joint production cases, unity will be the value of a price index number. This choice of units involves no loss of generality. In problems where output price *change* is central to the analysis, p will be the price of a unit of x.

Input quantities per period are denoted by $a,b,c, \ldots$, and their prices by $p_a, p_b, p_c \ldots$; all input and output quantities and prices are non-negative. In many cases, a will represent a number of man-hours of homogenous labor, or labor measured in "efficiency units"; b a number of dollars' worth of malleable capital or "meccano sets," and so on. These are, of course, only approximations to reality, by which one should not be misled. The unwary reader should be warned in advance that many eminent economists question their legitimacy, particularly as regards capital.[3]

The direct-consumption demand for inputs (the services of butlers and doctors, of land used for lawns, of machines for home carpentry) is governed by the major propositions of the economic theory of consumption. We concentrate, therefore, on the indirect demand for these inputs in productive processes.

1. The classical economists (Smith, Ricardo, Mill, Malthus) certainly considered labor endogenous in their population theories, but their treatments of income distribution concentrated on input prices.

2. This usage is most convenient for microeconomic analysis. In macroeconomic analysis (Chapter 16) it is convenient to think of x as a unit of *value added*. When x is a unit of output, we may treat intermediate products as inputs to production processes. When x is a unit of value added, the notion of input is confined to "factors of production."

3. See G. C. Harcourt, "Some Cambridge Controversies in the Theory of Capital," *J.E.L.* (June 1969), including references cited; for the uninitiated, secs. 1–1 through 1–6 (pp. 369–372) may suffice.

3. A microeconomic production process carried on by a single firm will be represented by a *production function:*

$$x = F(a,b,c, \ldots) \tag{6.1}$$

with the caveat that its existence, especially the existence of its macro-economic analogue, is called in question by the neo-Cambridge School. (See footnote 3.) All production functions like (6.1) are treated here as single valued, continuous and twice differentiable, although linear programming and input-output analysis focus attention on their short-run discontinuities. If $a,b,c, \ldots$ all equal zero, x also equals zero, for obvious economic reasons.

The first partial derivatives of (6.1) are the *marginal products* or *marginal productivities* of the inputs $a,b,c, \ldots$ They are non-negative in areas of economic interest; since they are partial derivatives, the marginal productivity of a requires that $b,c, \ldots$ be held constant, but it is not independent of the levels at which these other inputs are conceived as constant. Also, although the marginal productivity of, say, a, is positive, the inverse *total* derivative da/dx may be negative; if so, a is called a *regressive* input.[4] It is ordinarily assumed that any two inputs a and b can be substituted for each other in production, output x being held constant. This is called the *principle of substitution.* When this principle holds, the negative total derivative $-db/da$, with x held constant, is called the *marginal rate of substitution,* or simply m.r.s., between a and b; it need not be independent of the level at which x is being held constant.[5] (Some writers call this derivative the m.r.s. "of a for b," and others "of b for a"; our neutral usage is adequate for most purposes.) As the ratio a/b increases, with x or b remaining constant, input a ordinarily becomes a poorer substitute for the remaining b, and the m.r.s. $-db/da$ ordinarily falls. This (combined) postulate is called the principle of *diminishing marginal rate of substitution.* (It holds only within a certain *substitution area,* defined in section 9 below.)

The second partial derivatives of the production function (6.1) are ordinarily negative in the region of economic interest. This is one form of the principle of *diminishing returns to inputs.* The mixed second par-

4. A *regressive* input need not be *inferior.* If an input is inferior, a rise in its price may lead to increased output, but lower profits. An input cannot be inferior at all levels of output, and hence inferiority is inconsistent with homogeneity of the production function (section 4 below) . See Charles E. Ferguson, *The Neoclassical Theory of Production and Distribution* (Cambridge, England: Cambridge University Press, 1969) , ch. 9.

5. In linear programming and input-output terms, marginal productivities are zero, and m.r.s. are generally undefined. The principle of substitution does not hold, and no inputs are regressive.

tial derivatives of (6.1) may have any sign.[6] Inputs a and b are called *complementary, independent,* or *competitive* (substitutes) according to whether the sign of the mixed second partial derivative of x with respect to these two input quantities is positive, zero, or negative.

4.   A special case of (6.1), which we will use frequently as a first approximation, involves only two independent variables a and b and is *linear homogeneous*. That is to say, if (6.1) is of a form like

$$x = \alpha a + \beta b \quad \text{or} \quad x = a^\alpha b^\beta$$

such that, where λ is any positive number,

$$\lambda x = F(\lambda a, \lambda b) \tag{6.2}$$

the production function F is linear homogeneous in the inputs a and b.[7] The economic meaning of linear homogeneity, in the production function context, is that multiplying the quantity of each input by any positive factor (either greater or less than unity) will multiply the output x by the same factor. This condition is called *constant returns to scale*. It is obviously related to *constant cost*. It is perfectly consistent with diminishing returns to any or all *individual inputs*.

If the multiplicative factor λ in (6.2) is set equal to the reciprocal of a, we have at once:

$$\begin{aligned} x/a &= F(1, b/a) \\ x &= a f(\rho) \end{aligned} \tag{6.3}$$

where ρ is the ratio b/a, and the function f, while still a production function, depends only on this ratio but is no longer homogeneous. We also have the convenient result known as Euler's Theorem on Homogeneous Functions, or sometimes the "adding-up theorem":[8]

6. These second derivatives, both ordinary and mixed, do not exist for linear programming and input-output analysis.

7. More generally, and with any number of inputs,

$$\lambda^n x = F(\lambda a, \lambda b, \lambda c, \ldots)$$

implies that F is homogeneous of degree n, where n may be positive, negative, or zero. A linear homogeneous function is called homogeneous of first degree.

8. To derive (6.4), differentiate (6.2) with respect to λ:

$$x = \frac{\delta F}{\delta(\lambda a)} \frac{d(\lambda a)}{d\lambda} + \frac{\delta F}{\delta(\lambda b)} \frac{d(\lambda b)}{d\lambda}$$

which reduces to (6.4), since

$$\frac{\delta F}{\delta(\lambda a)} = \frac{\delta(\lambda x)}{\delta(\lambda a)} = \frac{\delta x}{\delta a}, \text{ etc.}$$

A longer, but more elementary, proof is found in R. G. D. Allen, *Mathematical Analysis for Economists* (London: Macmillan, 1938), pp. 317–319. A more complex formula applies to homogeneous functions of degree n other than unity.

$$x = a\frac{\delta x}{\delta a} + b\frac{\delta x}{\delta b} \qquad (6.4)$$

Both (6.2) and 6.4) may be extended mechanically to any number of variables, but (6.3) requires some notational modification.

We limit our analysis largely to cases where the adding-up theorem (6.4) holds. This restriction seems (and is) highly restrictive, particularly in the short period. Where it does not hold, however,

$$x = a\frac{\delta x}{\delta a} + \frac{\delta x}{\delta b} + u$$

where the residual u may have either sign. In such cases the distribution of the residual is left undetermined; under competitive conditions, at least, economic theory has little to say about it. (Compare Chapter 15, section 14.)

Diminishing Returns

5.   Our strategy in determining the amount of any input demanded by a competitive producer—who seeks to maximize his net returns, knows his production function perfectly, and cannot influence any of his input or output prices—will be to proceed by stages. First, assuming only two inputs, we shall assume input b to be technically or institutionally fixed, so that only input a and output x are variable. Then we shall permit variations in both inputs a and b. The next relaxation will involve knowledge of both input prices, which have hitherto been taken as unknown except for sign (positive). Following this, the output price will itself be introduced.

6.   If a is the only variable input and x is measured in real terms (which may refer to some "base period" prices), a conventional function is of the form F in Figure 6.1.[9] Points A, B, and C are particularly notable. At A, (with OA units of input a), the concavity of the function F shifts from upward to downward. This is the *inflection point* at which the marginal product F' or $\delta x/\delta a$ is at a maximum. (In many cases, point A corresponds with the origin O, so that F' is falling for all positive outputs and F is concave downward throughout.) At B (OB units of a), the *ray* or *radius vector* from O to F has its maximum value, and the marginal product F' equals the average product F/a or x/a. At C (OC units of a),

9. The detail of the function F, as well as of the other functions in the diagram, depends, as we shall see, upon the level at which input b is held constant.

As the diagram is drawn, the scale of x is different from the scale of $\delta x/\delta a$ and x/a, but the latter two variables are drawn to the same scale.

X, X/a, δx/δa

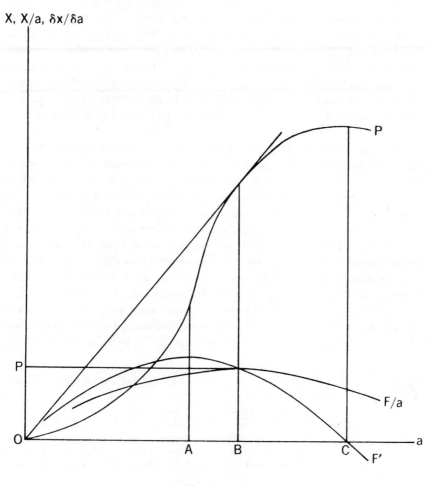

Figure 6.1

F itself has a maximum value and F' falls to zero. To the right of C, "too many cooks spoil the broth," and output x declines. (In many cases F is asymptotic to some maximal value, so that neither C nor the area to its right exists.) [10]

10. The underlying mathematics is not difficult. When, as at point A, the function F has a point of inflection, its derivative F' has a stationary value, here presumably a maximum. When, as at C, F has a maximum, F' is zero. When F is rising and concave upward, F' is positive and rising; where F is rising and concave downward, F' is positive and falling; when F is falling and concave downward, F' is negative and falling.
A change of variable will assist in justifying the attributes associated with point B.

7.   In the region *OA*, total product, average product, and marginal product are rising. This is a zone of *increasing* returns to input *a*. In the region *AB*, total and average products are rising but marginal product F' is falling. This is a zone of diminishing *marginal* returns to *a*. In the region *BC*, only total product F is rising. This is a zone of *diminishing average and marginal* returns to *a*. To the right of *C*, all the functions are falling. This is a zone of *diminishing average, marginal, and total* returns to *a*.

8.   In which zone (s) or region (s) would a rational producer operate, with all input and output prices positive but unknown? Hardly, it would seem, at *C* or to the right of it, where the marginal product of *a* is zero or negative. Nevertheless, the phenomenon of nonpositive marginal productivity has been diagnosed for unskilled agricultural labor in the rural areas of numerous densely populated underdeveloped countries on five continents.[11] The persistence of such labor redundancy is sociologically understandable. The excess workers are relatives, or other dependents, of the landlord or the farm operator, who does not maximize his own income at their expense. A more nearly "economic" explanation is that, with underdeveloped transportation, a farmer must support unproductive workers most of the year so that they will be available during the busy planting and harvesting seasons when their productivity is definitely posi-

---

Let G be F/a (the average product of *a*) , so that $F = Ga$ and the marginal product $F' = d (Ga)/da$. We then have

$$\frac{d (Ga)}{da} = G + a\, \frac{dG}{da}.$$

   When, as at *B*, G and F' are equal, $dG/da = 0$. This means that G is at a stationary value, here presumably a maximum. When, as to the left of *B*, $F' > G$, dG/da is positive, and the average product G is rising. When, as to the right of *B*, $G > F'$, dG/da is negative, and the average product G is falling.

   11. It is possible that disguised unemployment in this extreme sense may be largely a statistical illusion, due to underestimation of food consumed on farms. If additional workers add nothing or less than nothing to marketed supplies of *x*, this means only that they consume more than their marginal products, not that marginal products are themselves nonpositive. Accurate measurement of nonmarketed output is difficult but essential.

   Important proponents of the surplus labor hypothesis include W. Arthur Lewis, "Development with Unlimited Supplies of Labour," *Manchester School* (May 1954) , Ragnar Nurkse, *Problems of Capital Formation in Underdeveloped Areas* (New York: Oxford University Press, 1953) , John C. H. Fei and Gustav Ranis, *Development of the Labor Surplus Economy* (Homewood, Ill.: Irwin, 1964) , ch. 2. Opponents include Jacob Viner, "Reflections on the Concept of Disguised Unemployment," *Ind. Journ. Econ.* (July 1957) , Harry Oshima, "Underemployment in Backward Economies," *J. P. E.* (June 1958) , and T.W. Schultz, *Transforming Traditional Agriculture* (Chicago: University of Chicago Press, 1964) . Critical treatment and extensive bibliography are found in Gunnar Myrdal, *Asian Drama* (New York: Twentieth Century Fund, 1968) , vol. ii, ch. 21, and vol. iii, appendix 16.

tive. "Parkinson's Law" suggests that we should find considerable employment in excess of C in both the public sector and the private nonprofit sector of most economies; the "peacetime army" is a case in point.

Accepting C as the upper limit for rational employment of a, we inquire as to the lower limit. Here the condition is that the marginal product of input b not be rendered negative by insufficiency of the cooperant input a. If $\delta x/\delta b$ were negative, it would pay to throw some b away, despite its "fixed" status. The lower limit is not easy to find in the general case, unless the production function is linear homogeneous. If it is linear homogeneous in the neighborhood of point B, B is in fact the lower limit we are looking for.[12] The zone of operation is the range BC, in which diminishing returns to the variable input hold in both the marginal and the average senses of the term; popular usage is decidedly misleading here. (Linear homogeneity in the neighborhood of any point, such as B, does not imply linear homogeneity throughout the length of F. Only in very special cases is linear homogeneity consistent with the shape of F as drawn on Figure 6.1.) [13]

Optimal Employment

9. Many studies, particularly in agricultural economics, proceed with analysis along the lines of Figure 6.1. After introducing a known input price p_a, they show that the higher is p_a (within limits),[14] the closer will the employment of a approach B; and that the lower is p_a (while remain-

---

12. The simplest proof is indirect. Suppose we are to the left of B. The marginal product of a exceeds the average product, $\delta x/\delta a > x/a$. Within the linear-homogeneous range of the production function F, Euler's Theorem (6.4) holds:

$$x = a\,\frac{\delta x}{\delta a} + b\,\frac{\delta x}{\delta b} \quad \text{and} \quad \frac{x}{a} = \frac{\delta x}{\delta a} + \frac{b}{a}\frac{\delta x}{\delta b}$$

If $\delta x/\delta a > x/a$, $\delta x/\delta b$ is negative for positive a and b. Conversely, for points to the right of B, $x/a > \delta x/\delta a$ and $\delta x/\delta b$ is positive.

13. An example of such a mathematical curiosum is a modified Cobb-Douglas production function:

$$x = a^{\alpha_1} b^{\beta_1} + a^{\alpha_2} b^{\beta_2}$$

which is linear homogeneous for a particular value of λ, such that

$$\lambda = \lambda^{\alpha_1 + \beta_1} + \lambda^{\alpha_2 + \beta_2} \quad \text{or} \quad \lambda^{\alpha_1 + \beta_1 - 1} + \lambda^{\alpha_2 + \beta_2 - 1} = 1$$

This function also has a point of inflection where its partial derivatives with respect to a and b are both zero. At this point,

$$\frac{\alpha_1}{\alpha_2} = \frac{\beta_1}{\beta_2} = -a^{\alpha_2 - \alpha_1} b^{\beta_2 - \beta_1}$$

which has no obvious economic significance.

14. If p_a exceeds some upper limit, such as P in Figure 6.1, it does not pay to continue the enterprise at all.

ing positive), the closer will the employment of *a* approach *C*. If the variable input *a* is agricultural labor and the fixed input *b* is agricultural land, closeness to *B* may be interpreted as extensive agriculture, and closeness to *C* as intensive agriculture. Neither form is inherently more efficient than the other. Efficiency depends on relative input prices. Intensive agriculture is adapted to China and the Netherlands, extensive agriculture to the United States and Australia. Such are the conclusions drawn from this analysis.

We may also proceed by an alternate route, dispensing with the assumption that the supply of input *b* cannot be increased. In the upper panel of Figure 6.2, accordingly, quantities of *a* and *b* are shown on the two axes, and treated symmetrically. Output quantities x_i, on the other hand, are shown as contours or *isoquants;* their number is infinite, but only four are shown in the figure. No pair of isoquants need be parallel in any sense, but no two isoquants may cross, because the production function (6.1) is single valued. The isoquant slopes db/da are (negative) quotients of the marginal productivities of *a* and *b*, or $(\delta x/\delta a) \div (\delta x/\delta b)$.[15] They also reflect our postulates that $\delta^2 x/\delta a^2$ and $\delta^2 x/\delta b^2$ are both negative, so that the m.r.s. between *a* and *b* falls as the ratio a/b rises along any isoquant; that is, for any constant value of the output *x*. The *ridge line OA* is a locus of isoquant points such that the marginal product $\delta x/\delta a$ and the m.r.s. db/da are both zero; it may be called the *a* ridge line to distinguish it from the *b* ridge line *OB*, along which the marginal product $\delta x/\delta b$ and the m.r.s. da/db are both zero.

The region between the *a* and *b* ridge lines *OA* and *OB* is called the *substitution area*. It may be closed or open, and may include the entire quadrant of Figure 6.2. Within this area, the marginal products of all inputs are positive. On the diagram, with only two inputs, the marginal product of *a* is zero along the *a* ridge line *OA*, and negative to the southeast of this line; the marginal product of *b* is zero along the *b* ridge line *OB*, and negative to the northwest of this line.

Proceeding horizontally, which means holding *b* constant at b_1 or b_2 and adding *a*, the values of *x* increase (from x_1 to x_2 to x_3, etc.) until the *a* ridge line *OA* is reached. At the intersection with *OA*, the value of *x* is constant (a relative maximum); and to the right of *OA*, it falls. Proceeding vertically, which means holding *a* constant at $a_1, a_2, \ldots a_5$, and adding

15. For any continuous and differentiable function $x = f(a, b)$:

$$dx = \frac{\delta x}{\delta a}\, da + \frac{\delta x}{\delta b}\, db$$

a result not to be confused with the more restrictive Euler's Theorem. If *x* is held constant, *dx* is zero by definition, and the result in the text follows at once. A more detailed proof is found in Allen, *op. cit.*, pp. 326–328.

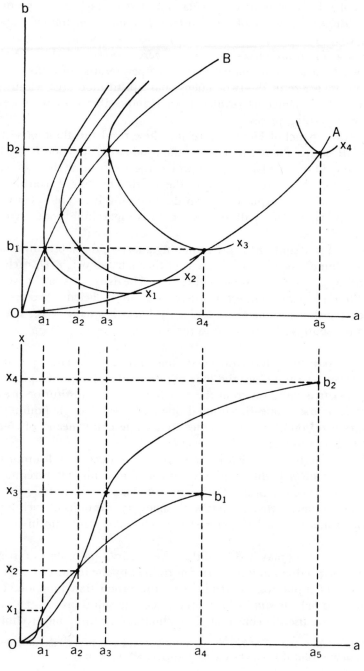

Figure 6.2

b, values of *x* increase until the *b* ridge line *OB* is reached. At the intersection with *OB,* the value of *x* is constant (a relative maximum) ; above
OB, it falls.

Assuming all input prices positive or zero, we repeat the question.
Where would a rational competitive firm operate? Its operation might
take place anywhere in the two-dimensional substitution area within the
ridge lines. Any further narrowing down is impossible without more information regarding prices.

The bottom panel of Figure 6.2 relates these results to those of section
8. It also illustrates the dependence of the production function *F* (of Figure 6.1) on the particular value at which the fixed input *b* is assumed
to be constant. We note that, near the origin, holding *b* constant at
b_2 produces a lower output of *x* than does holding it at the lower value
b_1; this apparent anomaly illustrates a negative marginal productivity of
input *b.*

In input-output and linear programming analyses, the substitution area
becomes a bundle or cone of linear rays through the origin *O,* each ray
representing a separate process or activity. The isoquants are a web of
parallel line segments connecting these rays. For "efficient" processes or
activities, the slopes of successive segments of any isoquant decrease as we
move to the southeast from the *b* to the *a* ridge line.

10.   By introducing information first about input prices and then about
output prices, we can reduce the zone of rationality for input employment
by a competitive employer from the two-dimensional substitution area of
Figure 6.2 to, first, a one-dimensional line and then, a single point.[16] Reduction of a region of rational choice to a single point means, of course,
complete determination.

The verbal argument is that if the marginal product of each input falls
as more is employed, the employer can maximize his net revenues by
equating the marginal productivities of a dollar's worth of each input—
not, as is sometimes stated carelessly, of some physical units of each input.
This conclusion is called the *marginal productivity principle* in its *proportional* form.

The mathematics may involve either the maximizing of output (represented by the production function) constrained by the input prices, or the
minimizing of input cost constrained by the production function. Each
problem is called the *dual* of the other, and the solutions are the same.
In each case we use the constrained maximum (or minimum) technique

16. With *n* inputs instead of two, the substitution area is a hyperplane of *n* dimensions, which are reduced to one by the knowledge of all input prices.

of the Lagrange multiplier.[17] We denote this multiplier by λ in the first case and by μ in the second, and only later consider their economic meanings. The relevant functions and partial derivatives with respect to a and b are

$$F(a,b,\ldots) - \lambda\,[ap_a + bp_b + \ldots) - c] = \max.$$

$$(ap_a + bp_b + \ldots) - \mu[F(a,b,\ldots) - x] = \min.$$

$$\frac{\delta F}{\delta a} - \lambda\,p_a = 0,\ \frac{\delta F}{\delta b} - \lambda p_b = 0,\ldots$$

$$p_a - \mu\frac{\delta F}{\delta a} = 0,\ p_b - \mu\frac{\delta F}{\delta b} = 0,\ldots$$

$$\frac{\delta F}{\delta a}\bigg/\frac{\delta F}{\delta b} = \frac{p_a}{p_b},\ldots$$

$$\frac{\delta F}{\delta a}\bigg/\frac{\delta F}{\delta b} = \frac{p_a}{p_b},\ldots \qquad (6.5)$$

where c and x are predetermined values of cost and output, respectively.

The corresponding geometry is shown for two inputs in Figure 6.3. Let us introduce, as a family of parallel straight lines, specimens of the infinite collection of iso-cost or *budget lines* facing the competitive employer:

$$ap_a + bp_b = C \qquad (6.6)$$

with C, the production budget, assuming a different value for each budget line. The slope db/da of any budget line (6.6) is $-(p_a/p_b)$. We already know that the slope of any isoquant, such as those transplanted here from Figure 6.2 is $-(\partial x/\partial a \div \partial x/\partial b)$ or $-(\delta F/\delta a \div \delta F/\delta b)$. The differential equation (6.5) is satisfied by the family or locus of tangency points between the families of budget lines and isoquants. The locus of tangencies, labeled OO' on Figure 6.3 is called the *expansion path* or *scale line* corresponding to the proportional marginal productivity condition (6.5).[18] The values of the multipliers λ and μ (λ being the reciprocal of μ) vary from point to point along the expansion path. The declining m.r.s. along the isoquants, insofar as it holds in the real world, insures against the path tracing out stationary values other than maxima of the employer's net revenue, and also insures against a plurality of paths.

Also, an expansion path may not turn back upon itself (to the northwest or southeast) without implying two values of, say, input a with the same values of both input b and the m.r.s. between a and b. This violates our assumption of a falling m.r.s. between a and b within the substitution area. If there are three or more inputs, however, there will be a multitude of isoquant maps on a two-dimensional diagram like Figure 6.3, each map

17. Allen, *op. cit.*, pp. 364–367. (We are considering only the first-order conditions for maximum or minimum.)

18. We have postulated that zero values of all inputs imply a zero value of output. This requires that the isoquant for $x = 0$ degenerate to a single point, namely the origin of the diagram, through which all expansion paths must pass.

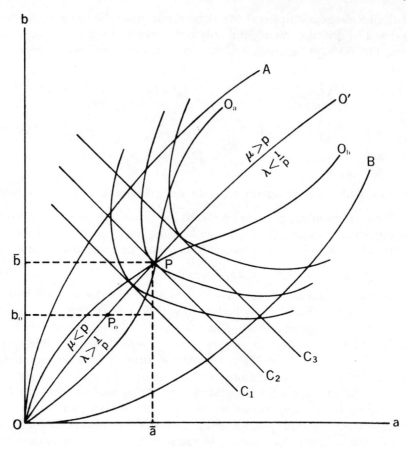

Figure 6.3

corresponding to a different value of, say, input c, and each with its own expansion path for the given prices ratio p_a/p_b. In such cases, with c variable, there is nothing to prevent the association of increases in x with decreases in a or in b, but not both, resulting from movements between expansion paths. In this case a or b would be a regressive input.[19]

If our isoquants are discontinuous, as in linear economic models, input-output and linear programming cases, equation (6.5) may never be satisfied as written. In this event, (6.5) is replaced by the condition that the

19. This treatment of regression, while stemming from Hicks, *Value and Capital,* 2d ed. (Oxford: Oxford University Press, 1946) pp. 93–98, differs from his primarily in limiting regression to instances of three or more inputs.

difference (slope of linear isoquant — slope of budget line) should shift from positive to negative as the ratio a/b is increased; the locus of the sign changes or *corner solutions* then defines the expansion path, which is also linear. That is to say, OO' is a ray from the origin O of the diagram.

If the production function is homogeneous throughout its length, the expansion path will be a ray through the origin. If any two points (a,b) and (a',b') lie on the same isoquant x, then $(\lambda a, \lambda b)$ and $(\lambda a', \lambda b')$ lie on the same isoquant $\lambda^n x$, n being the degree of homogeneity. If (a,b) is a lower cost combination than (a',b') in producing x units of output, it follows that $(\lambda a, \lambda b)$ is a lower cost combination than $(\lambda a', \lambda b')$ in producing $\lambda^n x$ units. In other words, the optimum input proportion is unaffected by the scale of operation if the production function is homogeneous. This fact is implied diagrammatically by a linear path through the origin.

11. Of the infinity of points on an expansion path, is there a single one that is optimal for the employer? If so, what are its characteristics? To answer these questions, we conceive of the output price p as free to deviate from its base period value of unity. Its actual value, however, is known to the employer in his capacity as demander of inputs. In the process of answering the two questions, we also interpret the Lagrange multipliers λ and μ of the development leading to equations (6.5).

Suppose, then, that in the development of (6.5),

$$\mu = \frac{p_a}{\delta F / \delta a} = \frac{p_b}{\delta F / \delta b} > p$$

which implies both

$$p \frac{\delta F}{\delta a} < p_a \quad \text{and} \quad p \frac{\delta F}{\delta b} < p_b$$

at some point on the expansion path. In this case the *value of the marginal product* (v.m.p.) of each input would be less than the respective input price. It would be in the employer's interest to reduce his output, that is, to move southwest along the expansion path in the direction of the origin O. Similarly, if our initial value of μ had been less than p, it would have been advantageous for the employer to increase the scale of his operations or, formally, to move northeast along the expansion path in the direction of O'. At the optimum point, where the employer is under no pressure to move in either direction, $\mu = p$. To put it differently, at the optimum point (with all prices known), the economic meaning of the Langrange multiplier μ is the output price. (Conversely, had we chosen to make comparisons involving the other multiplier λ, this would have been the reciprocal $1/p$ of the output price.) [20] In either case, we denote the optimum point by P on Figure 6.3, with coordinates a and b.

The economic principle involved is marginal productivity in its *absolute* form: with all prices known, the optimum employments of productive inputs are determined by equality between input prices and their respective v.m.p. values:

$$p_a = p \frac{\delta x}{\delta a}, \qquad p_b = p \frac{\delta x}{\delta b}, \ldots \tag{6.7}$$

Equations (6.7) can also be derived directly, by differentiating the employer's profit function π partially with respect to the input quantities. The function concerned is:

$$\pi = pF(a, b, \ldots) - (ap_a + bp_b + \ldots) = \text{max.}$$

with no constraints or Lagrange multipliers involved.

In adjusting to the equilibrium position where the marginal productivity principle holds in absolute form, the competitive employer is looked upon as adjusting the *quantities* of inputs demanded until point P, with coordinates a,b, is reached and (6.7) is satisfied. He is not looked upon as adjusting input *prices* arbitrarily to approach (6.7) for any initial or technologically determined volume of employment. (There remains some confusion on this point among the critics of marginal productivity analysis.)

12.   If the production function is homogeneous throughout its length, and the expansion path is a ray through the origin, economically meaningful location of the optimum point P is impossible. If the degree of homogeneity is less than unity (diminishing returns to scale), the optimum scale is the smallest possible, and the optimum point P approaches the origin O along the expansion path. If the degree of homogeneity is greater than unity (increasing returns to scale), the optimum scale is the largest possible, and the optimum point P goes to infinity along the expansion path. If the degree of homogeneity is precisely unity (linear homogeneity, constant returns to scale), any point on the expansion path is as profitable or unprofitable as any other, and the optimum point P is indeterminate.

What is the economic meaning, if any, of this anomaly? There may exist a range of inputs and outputs within which, for the reasons just suggested, our "standard" economic analysis gives indeterminate results, at the firm level. Within this range, some form of "linear economics" may be superior. On the other hand, common sense suggests that this range

20. It can also be shown that $\mu \gtrless p$ implies $\lambda \lessgtr \frac{1}{p}$, and vice versa.

of indeterminacy is seldom large. Outside this range, the use of linear analysis may be at least as misleading as the use of standard analysis within it. In addition, when we are considering a competitive industry whose size is determined by competitive forces, the indeterminacy (within limits) of firm size is not a serious obstacle.

13.   Before taking leave of Figure 6.3, let us reconsider, in a regime of known input and output prices, the assumption that one input, say b, is fixed in amount, and only a is variable. The employer will then adjust his demand for a so as to satisfy (6.7), but he cannot adjust his employment of b in the short run. Suppose that his fixed stock of b, which we call b_o, is below $\overline{b}$ and therefore incompatible with both point P and (6.7). Then the point P_o on the expansion path, corresponding to b_o, involves too low a value of a as well as of b. The value of a satisfying (6.7) lies to the right of the expansion path but remains less than $\overline{a}$, since the optimality of $\overline{a}$ requires $\overline{b} > b_o$ as cooperant input. Conversely, if we had located b_o in excess of $\overline{b}$, the optimal employment of a would have been to the left of the expansion path but in excess of $\overline{a}$.

Tracing out the locus of fixed "second-best" or "suboptimal" employments of input a, with b at different levels, we obtain a curve lying to the right of the expansion path when $b_o < \overline{b}$, to its left when $\overline{b} > b_o$, and intersecting it at P where $b_o = \overline{b}$. This curve is called the a *input line,* labeled OO_a in the diagram. Reversing our assumption as to the identity of the fixed input, we can also derive a b input line OO_b, below the expansion path when $\overline{a}_o < a$, above it when $\overline{a}_o > a$, and again intersecting it at P where $a_o = \overline{a}$. It follows that the input lines intersect each other at P, which is a point of full equilibrium.

14.   If each input price equals its v.m.p., as when (6.7) is satisfied across the board, the question arises whether the entire product is distributed and accounted for, or whether some positive or negative residual may not be left as pure profit, positive or negative, to be secondarily allocated among the input owners. Euler's Theorem (6.4) can be interpreted as an adding-up theorem, demonstrating the absence of a residual for linear homogeneous production functions. But we have just shown that this case is among those for which the marginal productivity equations (6.7) have only trivial solutions! Clearly, there is a dilemma here.

The dilemma was solved by Sir John Hicks in an appendix to his *Theory of Wages.*[21] The economics-cum-geometry of Hicks' solution is that, for a firm in long-term competitive equilibrium (with price equal to min-

21. Hicks, *Theory of Wages,* (London: Macmillan, 1932), pp. 233–239, acknowledging partial anticipation by Leon Walras and Knut Wicksell.

imum average cost), Euler's Theorem holds as though the firm's production function were, *at that point,* tangent to and identical with a linear
homogeneous function, whatever its general form may. be at other points.

We may reproduce Hicks' demonstration. Denote average cost by

$$C = \frac{ap_a + bp_b + \ldots}{x} = \text{min.}$$

The minimization is to be with respect to the input variables $a, b, \ldots$.
Taking partial derivatives with respect to these variables, and remembering that $(ap_a + bp_b + \ldots) = Cx$, or total cost, we obtain

$$\frac{1}{x^2}\left(xp_a - Cx\,\frac{\delta x}{\delta a}\right) = 0, \qquad \frac{1}{x^2}\left(xp_b - Cx\,\frac{\delta x}{\delta b}\right) = 0, \ldots$$

which reduce to forms closely resembling (6.7):

$$p_a = C\,\frac{\delta x}{\delta a}, \qquad p_b = C\,\frac{\delta x}{\delta b}, \ldots$$

Substitute these results in the definition of C above:

$$C = \frac{aC\,(\delta x/\delta a) + bC\,(\delta x/\delta b) + \ldots}{x}$$

Multiply by x or xp, cancel out the C terms, and we have the adding-up
theorem. There is no unexplained residual—in long-term competitive
equilibrium, at least.

Input Demand Functions

15.   Having determined optimal employment of an input by a competitive employer or firm under some given set of input and output prices,
the next step is to consider the consequences of price changes. The most
important single price, in the case of a single input, say, input a, is its own
price p_a; the response of the employer, changing his employment of a as
its price changes, *ceteris paribus,* constitutes his demand function for a.

If one accepts the argument that the optimal strategy for the employer
involves adjusting employment so that the v.m.p. of input a, or $p\,(\delta x/\delta a)$,
approaches p_a, it is natural to think of the v.m.p. function as the desired
demand function. Unfortunately, this is not completely consistent with
other branches of economic analysis. The inconsistency concerns the con-
tents of the *ceteris paribus* pound. Normally, in economic analysis, these
include the *prices* of all complimentary and competitive goods. Here, however, by differentiating the production function to obtain $\delta x/\delta a$, we im-

plicitly held the *quantities* of inputs b, c, ... constant instead. Unless we know that p_b, p_c, ... will not change, and also that b, c, ... are independent of such ratios as p_a/p_b, p_a/p_c, ... when p_a changes, inconsistencies may be involved in treating the v.m.p. and input demand functions for a as identical.

We can indicate the difference between v.m.p. and input demand functions for an important special case, the linear homogeneous Cobb-Douglas function for two inputs:

$$x = x_o \, a^a \, b^{1-a}$$

where x_o is a statistically determined constant. The v.m.p. function for input a is, by differentiation, with p taken as unity,

$$a x_o \, a^{a-1} \, b^{1-a} \qquad \text{or} \qquad a x_o \, (a/b)^{a-1}. \tag{6.8}$$

The independence of (6.8) from any input prices (except that the v.m.p. itself equals p_a where profits are maximized) warns us that something is amiss. The true demand function for a is

$$a = \frac{x}{x_o} \left(\frac{\alpha}{1-\alpha} \frac{p_b}{p_a} \right)^{1-a} \tag{6.9}$$

which is quite different from (6.8),[22] and is derived immediately below.

To derive (6.9), set up a profit, revenue, or objective function. This is maximized, as in previous sections of this chapter, by partial differentiation with respect to a and b. This process yields expressions for p_a and p_b in terms of a and b. These expressions in p_a and p_b give equilibrium values of a and b, and the value of b is substituted in the production function. The steps follow:

$$x_o \, a^a \, b^{1-a} - (a p_a + b p_b) = \text{max.}$$

$$p_a = \alpha x_o \, a^{a-1} \, b^{1-a}, \qquad p_b = (1-\alpha) \, x_o \, a^a b^{-a}$$

$$p_a/p_b = \frac{\alpha}{1-\alpha} \frac{b}{a}$$

$$a = \frac{b\alpha}{1-\alpha} \frac{p_b}{p_a}, \qquad b = \frac{a(1-\alpha)}{\alpha} \frac{p_a}{p_b}$$

$$\frac{x}{x_o} = a^a \left[\frac{a(1-\alpha)}{\alpha} \frac{p_b}{p_a} \right]^{1-a} = a \left(\frac{1-\alpha}{\alpha} \frac{p_a}{p_b} \right)^{1-a}.$$

The last expression yields (6.9) at once.

22. The expressions corresponding to (6.8) and (6.9) for input b are

$$\frac{\delta x}{\delta b} = (1-\alpha) \, x_o \, (a/b)^a \qquad \text{and} \qquad b = \frac{x}{x_o} \left(\frac{1-\alpha}{\alpha} \frac{p_a}{p_b} \right)^a.$$

16.   The demand function (6.9) for α slopes downward. With output x constant its slope is:

$$\frac{\delta a}{\delta p_a} = \frac{-a\,(1-\alpha)}{p_a}$$

which is negative when all the right-side terms are postive.[23]

If we also allow for output variation, with dx "incorporating" changes in both inputs:

$$\frac{da}{dp_a} = \frac{\delta a}{\delta p_a} + \frac{\delta a}{\delta x}\frac{dx}{dp_a} = -\frac{a\,(1-\alpha)}{p_a} + \frac{\delta a}{\delta x}\frac{dx}{dp}\frac{dp}{dp_a};$$

the added term is, however, non-negative:

$$\frac{\delta a}{\delta x} > 0,\ \frac{dx}{dp} > 0,\ \frac{dp}{dp_a} \geqq 0.$$

A downward slope (da/dp_a) can be shown to be general. It is, in fact, more general here than in the analysis of output demand in consumer theory. It is a stability condition of input-demand theory; output markets may in extreme cases be stable even when demand curves slope upward.

The proof that the input demand function must slope downward for stability is essentially mathematical, although literary and geometrical attemps have been made to distinguish between the input- and the output-demand cases.[24] (An economic difference is that in input demand theory we treat the employer's production budget as *variable*, ignoring difficulties of "finance"; the corresponding value in output demand theory, the consumer's income or assets, is held *fixed*. A geometric difference is that expansion paths may not turn back to the northwest or southeast, whereas the corresponding consumption-theory functions may.) The mathematics involved are second-order conditions for a maximum or minimum of a function of several variables.

Consider any function $x = F\,(a,\,b)$, whose maximum values are of economic interest. But if what we take to be a maximum is in fact a minimum or a saddle point,[24a] the vanishing of the partial derivatives—neces-

---

23. To show the plausibility of restricting both α and $1-\alpha$ to positive values, compute the relative share of input a in the Cobb-Douglas function, with $p_a = \delta x/\delta a = \alpha x_o\,(a/b)^{1-\alpha}$. The relative share ap_a/x then equals α. Similarly, the relative share of input b, or bp_b/x, equals $1-\alpha$. For both inputs to earn positive relative shares, both α and $1-\alpha$ must be positive.

24. Robert R. Russell, "A Graphical Proof of the Impossibility of a Positively Inclined Demand Curve for a Factor of Production," *A.E.R.* (September 1964) ; David M. Winch, "The Demand Curve for a Factor of Production," *ibid.* (September 1965.)

24a. A saddle point exists when a point on $F\,(a,\,b)$ is simultaneously a maximum with respect to a and a minimum with respect to b, or when there exists some intermediate "direction" between a and b, with regard to which the point is not a stationary value. Compare Allen, *op. cit.*, pp. 352–356.

sary conditions for the maximum—is no longer sufficient. There exist additional second-order conditions for a maximum (minimum) of F (a, b), which also guarantee that an equilibrium situation, once disturbed, will tend to reestablish itself.[25] The stability conditions for a maximum value of F (a, b) are:

$$\delta^2 F/\delta a^2, \quad \delta^2 F/\delta b^2 \quad \text{both} < 0 \qquad (\delta^2 F/\delta a^2)\,(\delta^2 F/\delta b^2) > (\delta^2 F/\delta a \delta b)^2$$

For a minimum, stability requires positive signs for the first inequalities above, the final one remaining unchanged.

In the case of equations (6.7);

$$p_a = p\,\frac{\delta x}{\delta a}, \qquad p_b = p\,\frac{\delta x}{\delta b};$$

these expressions may be differentiated totally with respect to an input price, say p_a.[26] The result is a pair of equations:

$$\frac{\delta^2 x}{\delta a^2}\frac{da}{dp_a} + \frac{\delta^2 x}{\delta a \delta b}\frac{db}{dp_a} = \frac{1}{p}$$
$$\frac{\delta^2 x}{\delta a \delta b}\frac{da}{dp_a} + \frac{\delta^2 x}{\delta b^2}\frac{db}{dp_a} = 0. \tag{6.10}$$

The determinant D of the coefficient matrix of these equations is:

$$D = \begin{vmatrix} \dfrac{\delta^2 x}{\delta a^2} & \dfrac{\delta^2 x}{\delta a \delta b} \\[2ex] \dfrac{\delta^2 x}{\delta a \delta b} & \dfrac{\delta^2 x}{\delta b^2} \end{vmatrix}$$

This determinant D must be positive for stability of the function $xp - (ap_a + bp_b)$ underlying (6.7), since it equals the strategic quantity $(\delta^2 x/\delta a^2)\,(\delta^2 x/\delta b^2) - (\delta^2 x/\delta a \delta b)^2$.

We can solve (6.10) for da/dp_a, the slope of the demand curve for input a. In terms of the determinant D, the solution is:

$$\frac{da}{dp_a} = \frac{1}{D}\begin{vmatrix} 1/p & \dfrac{\delta^2 x}{\delta a \delta b} \\[2ex] 0 & \dfrac{\delta^2 x}{\delta b^2} \end{vmatrix} = \frac{\delta^2 x/\delta b^2}{pD}. \tag{6.11}$$

For the stability conditions to hold (which they may not, in an imperfect world), the numerator of (6.11) must be negative and the denom-

25. This discussion limits itself to static stability in the sense of Hicks, *Value and Capital, op. cit.* It does not consider dynamic stability, which involves explicit consideration of speeds of adjustment.

26. Allen, *op. cit.*, pp. 481 f.

inator positive. The slope da/dp_a of the input demand function is accordingly negative as a stability condition.[27]

17.   A geometrical illustration, following the lines of our last two diagrams, is helpful in visualizing the mechanism of equations like (6.10) and (6.11). Such an illustration is provided by Figure 6.4. Here, let our original position be the long-run equilibrium point P_o, with input coordinates $\bar{a}_o$ and $\bar{b}_o$ and output x_o. Point P_o is also located on expansion path OO and on budget line BA_o. The production budget may be derived from any point on BA_o, if input prices are known. Three (equal) values are $Bp_b, A_o p_a$, and $(\bar{a}_o p_a + \bar{b}_o p_b)$.

Now introduce a substantial once-and-for-all change in one input price, namely p_a, with p_b and p remaining constant. The price line through point B is now BA'. Since BA' lies within BA_o, the amount of a obtainable for the sum Bp_b has been reduced for all positive values of b. In words, the price change of a has been upward. Corresponding to this higher price is a new expansion path OO'. It is drawn closer than OO to the b-axis; this reflects a falling m.r.s. along each isoquant and implies a more b-intensive pattern of production.

Had the production budget been fixed at OB, the new equilibrium position (corresponding to P_o) would have been at R. The path from P_o to R may be broken down into two effects, as in consumer theory: (a) A *scale effect* or *output effect* $P_o Q$, resulting from the reduced real value of the production budget and leading to reductions in total output and in both inputs;[28] and (b) A *substitution effect* QR, leading to reduced employment of a and increased employment of at least one competitive input b.[29] However, since the production budget is in general variable,

27. The cross-effect on input b depends upon the sign of $\delta^2 x/\delta a \delta b$, and may usually take either sign without prejudice to stability. In the two-input case, however:

$$\frac{db}{dp_a} = -\frac{\delta^2 x/\delta a \delta b}{p^D}$$

and the mixed derivative $\delta^2 x/\delta a \delta b$ is positive, within the substitution area. (If it were not, the productivity of each input would fall as the other was added, and only one would be used.) With $\delta^2 x/\delta a \delta b$ positive—and a and b complementary—db/dp_a must also be negative for stability.

28. If one input, say, a, were regressive, we might have a negative value of:

$$\frac{dx}{da} = \frac{\delta x}{\delta a} + \frac{\delta x}{\delta b}\frac{db}{da} \qquad \left(\text{and its reciprocal } \frac{da}{dx}\right)$$

but $\delta x/\delta a$ and $\delta x/\delta b$ would remain positive. The db/da term embodies substitution effects, considered immediately below.

With more than two inputs, the output effect of a rise in p_a might include a fall in the employment of b or c but not both.

29. An alternative treatment would locate point Q at the intersection of OO and BA', so that the substitution effect is drawn along a budget line instead of an isoquant. The mathematical issues between the two treatments need not concern us here, but are

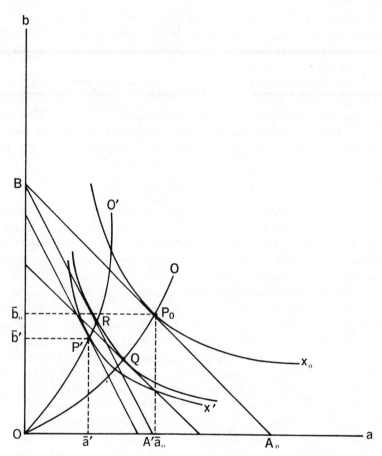

Figure 6.4

there is a third effect RP', which we may call a *budget effect*, toward the origin along the new scale line OO'. This third effect has no consumer theory counterpart, since it results from the change in the employer's optimum production budget if one or more input prices change in the

---

elucidated in Jacob L. Mosak, "Interpretation of the Fundamental Equation of Value Theory," in Oskar Lange *et al.* (eds.), *Studies in Mathematical Economics and Econometrics* (Chicago: University of Chicago Press, 1942).

A more radical alternative would assume, as an aspect of *ceteris paribus,* other input prices changing when p_a changed, so as to keep constant an index number of input prices. This would limit consideration to substitution effects. See M. Friedman, "The Marshallian Demand Curve," *Essays in Positive Economics* (Chicago: University of Chicago Press, 1953), pp. 50–65.

same direction relative to the output price. With the budget effect included on the diagram, the new equilibrium point is at P', with input coordinates $\bar{a}'$ and $\bar{b}'$ and output x'. (The price line through P' is parallel to BA'; it is not labeled on the diagram.)

Each of the three effects into which we have subdivided the movement P_oP' in Figure 6.4 includes some reduction in the employment of input a, whose price has risen. This confirms our mathematical result. The effect on the employment of b is also negative, but this will not be the case for more than two inputs if the substitution effect outweighs the other two.

The Elasticity of Substitution

18.   A logical next step after determining the slope of an input demand curve might be to consider its elasticity. Before doing so, however, a digression is required, to define the *elasticity of substitution* between any two inputs a and b. This elasticity will prove to be an important factor in estimating the elasticity of demand for either input taken separately.

The most elementary question that the elasticity of substitution was designed to answer is this: If p_a rises relative to p_b, and the employment of a consequently falls relative to that of b, what will happen to the relative income shares of the two inputs?[30] Clearly, if a 1 per cent rise in the price ratio leads to a 10 per cent fall in the employment ratio, the share of a (whose relative price rose) will fall, and the share of b (whose relative employment rose) will rise. If a 10 per cent rise in the price ratio leads to a 1 per cent fall in the employment ratio, the results of the previous sentence are reversed. If the percentage changes in the price and employment ratios are equal and opposite in direction, the relative shares will remain approximately constant. (Bowley's Law, which we considered

---

30. Before the development of the substitution-elasticity notion, the Cambridge economists answered this question somewhat clumsily in an important special case (a increasing in quantity, with p, b, and p_b all remaining constant). In our notation, their condition is

$$x\left(\frac{\delta x}{\delta a} + a\frac{\delta^2 x}{\delta a^2}\right) > a\left(\frac{\delta x}{\delta a}\right)^2.$$

If E represents the elasticity of demand for a, defined as

$$E = -\frac{\delta x/\delta a}{a\dfrac{\delta^2 x}{\delta a^2}}$$

the Cambridge condition may be written, in our linear homogeneity case, after some algebraic manipulation,

$$E > \frac{1}{1 - \dfrac{a\delta x/\delta a}{x}} = \frac{x}{b\dfrac{\delta x}{\delta b}}$$

or, in words, "the elasticity of demand [for a] is greater than the relative shares of all other [inputs] taken together." A.C. Pigou, *The Economics of Welfare*, 4th ed. (London: Macmillan, 1932), p. 665 n.

in Chapter 4, may be interpreted as an estimate that this is the general state of affairs.)

The economist's device for answering such questions, at least formally, has been, since Marshall's *Principles of Economics* (1890), some form of elasticity (logarithmic derivative) with the absolute value of unity the watershed between opposite results. Since we are dealing with *relative* prices and *relative* quantities, the elasticity of substitution, denoted by σ_{ab} or simply σ, also deals with these terms. As defined by Hicks[31] in 1932 to insure positive values,

$$\sigma = \frac{d(b/a)}{b/a} \div \frac{d(p_a/p_b)}{(p_a/p_b)} . \tag{6.12}$$

That is, verbally, the elasticity of substitution σ is the ratio of the proportionate change in the ratio (b/a) of relative quantities to the proportionate change in their relative prices (p_a/p_b).

In advanced economies the capital stock tends to grow more rapidly than the labor force, particularly when immigration and capital outflow are restricted more severely than their opposites. As an expected consequence, real wage rates have risen, while real interest rates may have tended downward on balance. The distributional result under competitive conditions, ignoring both interindustry shifts and technological progress, should be a rise in the property share if the elasticity of substitution exceeds unity. Capital has risen in employment more rapidly than labor, by more than enough to compensate for the fall in its relative price. The result should be a rise in the labor share if the elasticity of substitution is less than unity, since wages have risen more rapidly than returns per unit of capital, and by more than enough to compensate for the fall in the relative employment of labor. Finally, there should be no distributional change if the elasticity of substitution is unitary; Bowley's Law can therefore be rephrased as an empirical proposition that the elasticity of substitution is unitary. Since we observe rising labor shares, as commonly measured, we should expect estimates of the elasticity of substitution to be generally less than unity, as they appear to be.[32]

19. From the definitional formula (6.12), we cannot tell whether the elasticity of substitution of labor for capital equals that of capital for

---

31. *Theory of Wages, op. cit.*, pp. 117–120, 244.

32. Two American examples: In a sample of 22 industries in a period of falling property shares (1948–1960), Brown found only two with $\sigma > 1$, the range of his 22 estimates being 0.338 to 1.452. (Murray Brown, *The Share of Corporate Profits in the Postwar Period* [Washington: U.S. Dept. of Commerce Working Paper in Economics and Statistics, 11 (April 1965)], p. 110.) Over a shorter period (1953–57) in a sample of 20 industries, Kendrick found only one with $\sigma > 1$, the range of the estimates being −0.14 to 1.86. (John W. Kendrick, commenting on Solow, "Capital, Labor, and Income

labor, or, generally, whether $\sigma_{ab} = \sigma_{ba}$. The more common formula, which makes the symmetry obvious, applies strictly only in the linear-homogeneous ranges of two-input production functions. This formula is

$$\sigma = \frac{(\delta x/\delta a)\ (\delta x/\delta b)}{x\delta^2 x/\delta a \delta b}$$

or, using F_a for $\delta x/\delta a$, F_{aa} for $\delta^2 x/\delta a^2$, F_{ab} for $\delta^2 x/\delta a \delta b$, etc.:

$$\sigma = \frac{F_a F_b}{x\ F_{ab}}. \tag{6.13}$$

The Hicks-Allen derivation of (6.13) from (6.12) [33] while not particularly difficult, is long; we have relegated it to Appendix A of this chapter.

The Elasticity of Derived Demand

20.   The ordinary (price) elasticity of demand for either an input or an output is the quotient of the proportional change in the quantity demanded and the proportional change in the commodity's price, which is presumed to have led to movement along a demand function that is itself unchanged.[34] The *negative* of this quotient is frequently taken, so that the elasticity may itself be positive.

---

in Manufacturing," in Conference on Research in Income and Wealth, *The Behavior of Income Shares,* Studies in Income and Wealth, vol. 27 [Princeton: Princeton University Press, 1964], p. 140.) An "international cross-section" study for 24 industries in a single period also obtained $\sigma < 1$ in 23 of the cases. (Kenneth J. Arrow, Hollis B. Chenery, Bagicha Minhas, and Robert M. Solow, "Capital-Labor Substitution and Economic Efficiency," *Rev. Econ. and Stat.* [August 1961], p. 225.)

   Counterexamples also exist, however, and the issues are far from resolved. For example, by limiting the "capital" term in production functions to capital instruments in actual use (*i.e.*, to engineering rather than economic data) a value of 0.99 for σ in the American metal-machining industry was derived by Mordecai Kurz and Alan Manne ("Engineering Estimates of Capital-Labor Substitution in Metal Machinery," *A.E.R.* [September 1963], p. 676). Again, with "labor" figures adjusted for quality improvements over the period 1936–1960, a time-series study of the American fertilizer industry yielded 22 estimates of σ over all or part of these 25 years; of these, 16 were in excess of unity and 12 within the range 0.90–1.10 (G.S. Sahota, "The Sources of Measured Productivity Growth: U.S. Fertilizer Mineral Industries, 1936–1960," *Rev. Econ. and Stat.* [May 1966], p. 195.) Among international cross-section studies, Victor Fuchs replicated the Arrow-Chenery-Minhas-Solow study above, adding a dummy variable to separate more- from less-developed countries, obtaining σ estimates clustered closely about unity with a median of 1.04 ("Capital-Labor Substitution: A Note," *ibid.* [November 1963], p. 438).

   33. The most convenient reference (Allen, *op. cit.*, pp. 342 f.) is too condensed for many students.

   34. If e_{xy} be the elasticity of any arbitrary variable x with respect to any other arbitrary variable y, with some functional relationship existing between the two, we have:

$$e_{xy} = \frac{dx}{x} \bigg/ \frac{dy}{y} = \frac{dx\ y}{dy\ x} = \frac{d\ (\log x)}{d\ (\log y)}$$

For demand elasticities greater than unity, total expenditure for the commodity concerned is greater at low than at high prices, and the reverse is true for elasticities less than unity. For unitary elasticity, the expenditure is a constant. Since normally the proximate method of raising suppliers' incomes in the short run, when quantities supplied are inflexible upward, is to raise prices and restrict output, it is usually to suppliers' benefit that demand be price-inelastic.

The conventional supply-and-demand diagrams of our textbooks, with price and quantity (not their logarithms) on the vertical and horizontal axes (not the reverse), are extraordinarily adapted to the perpetuation of confusion regarding demand elasticities. It is natural to associate a steep slope with a high elasticity, and the constant slope of a straight line with a constant elasticity. Actually, for two functions intersecting at a point, the function with the shallower slope has the higher elasticity at that point. Unless its slope is zero (infinite elasticity) or infinite (zero elasticity), a straight line implies a different elasticity at each point, ranging from zero as it intersects the horizontal axis to infinity as it intersects the vertical one (with unity at the midpoint).[35] The general problem of comparing elasticities of two different functions at two different points on a diagram is perfectly soluble after appropriate manipulation, but visual comparisons are deceptive.

We propose to show initially that a v.m.p. function for an input normally provides a downward-biased estimate of the elasticity of demand for that input, and that the arithmetic sum of the demand functions of all employers provides a bias in the opposite direction for the elasticity of the market demand curve for the input. We shall then proceed to discuss Marshall's four determinants of the elasticity of derived demand[36] and their subsequent modification by Hicks.[37]

21. Let us review (from section 15 the distinction between a v.m.p. function for an input and the associated derived demand function. In the first

---

If the functional relationship involves other variables than x or y alone, the partial derivative equivalents of the last two expressions continue to hold. If more than one relationship exists simultaneously between x and y, as in the case of demand and supply relationships between a commodity's price and quantity, the resulting "identification problem" carries over to the elasticities.

35. A generalization of these results is due to Marshall. If the demand function be linear, intersecting the horizontal and vertical axes at X and Y respectively, the elasticity of demand at any point P between X and Y equals PX/PY. If the reader cannot vertify this general proposition, or recall the proof, its source is Marshall, *Principles of Economics*, 9th ed. (London: Macmillan, 1961), book iii, ch. 4, note 1, and Mathematical Note iii, pp. 102 f., 839).

36. *Principles of Economics*, 8th ed. (New York: Macmillan, 1920), book v, ch. 6, and Mathematical Note xv.

37. *Theory of Wages, op. cit.*, pp. 241–246.

case (v.m.p. function), we hold the *quantities* of other inputs constant; in the second (demand function), we hold constant their *prices,* and also the output price. It is not immediately apparent what bias is involved in estimating demand elasticity from the v.m.p. approximation rather than the derived demand function itself, but consider the left-hand panel of Figure 6.5.

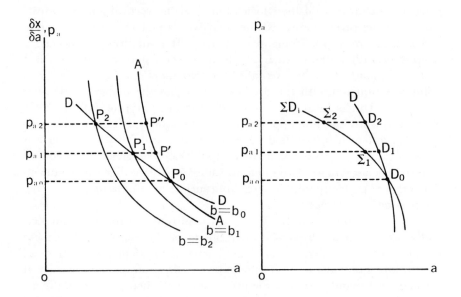

Figure 6.5

This diagram includes a family of v.m.p. functions for input a, with constant output price but with different levels of b $(b_0 < b_1 < b_2 \ldots)$. We assume as required for stability in the two-input simplification a complementary relation between a and b, so that increased amounts of b tend to increase the v.m.p. of a. We also assume no change in p_b. Then, it should be clear, a rise in the price of a will not only decrease its own employment and the output of x, but also the employment of the cooperant input b, whose price is constant by assumption. We therefore trace out (in Fig. 6.5) the path P_0, P_1, P_2, . . . forming the derived demand function DD, rather than the path P_0, P', P'', . . . along the original v.m.p. function AA, for successive rises in p_a. By the elasticity formula $(-da/dp_a \div p_a/a)$ the price elasticity of DD exceeds that of AA at their intersection P_0.

Therefore, in the "representative" condition of complementarity between inputs, demand functions tend to have higher elasticities than v.m.p. functions. If we take input b to represent the aggregate of all other inputs, with all their prices constant, the two-input example of the diagram can be generalized to cases of three or more inputs.

In the right panel of the same Figure 6.5, the vertical axis is unchanged, but the horizontal one represents demand for input a by the entire body of employers, present and potential. We may think of each millimeter as representing 100 or 1000 times as many units of a on the right-hand panel as on the left-hand one. The curve ΣD_i is the horizontal sum of all the demand functions DD (left-hand panel) of all present and potential employers for a. It is therefore a first approximation to the market demand function for a, but unfortunately suffers from elasticity bias.

We assume pure competition, so that no firm can affect any input or output price by changing its own employment or production and there can be no effective collusion on the market. In particular, ΣD_i therefore assumes constancy of the output price. If, however, all firms reduce their employment of a as its price rises, the decline in total output x will normally lead to some rise in its price. This will in turn raise the v.m.p. (value of marginal product) for all inputs, including a, all along the line. Any such rise in v.m.p. functions for a will also shift derived demand functions for a (such as DD in the left-hand panel) to the northeast. Their horizontal sums for the higher input prices $p_{a1}, p_{a2}, \ldots > p_{a0}$ will therefore lie northeast of ΣD_i; and each sum determines a point, such as $D_1 > \Sigma_1$ or $D_2 > \Sigma_2$, on the market demand function D. A converse development locates D to the southwest of ΣD_i when $p_a < p_{ao}$. The intersection of D and ΣD_i at D_0 corresponds to the original input price p_{ao}. This time, application of the elasticity formula shows the demand elasticity of ΣD_i systematically lower than that of D at D_0, because the slope of ΣD_i exceeds that of D at the intersection point.

No usable method has yet been developed of estimating the elasticity bias of Σ (v.m.p.) $_i$ (not shown on the diagram) as an approximation to D. We know only that the two elements of bias offset each other.

22. It is normally advantageous for the suppliers of inputs, or for their agents (such as trade unions), that the demands for these inputs be inelastic, to permit price increases without disemployment. Exceptions to this generalization occur, at one extreme, when input supplies are flexible upward (with low opportunity costs), so that low-price policies increase suppliers' total income. They also occur, at an opposite extreme, when some or all employers can be forced off their demand functions, by, for instance, what we shall call "all-or-none bargaining" (or by full-employ-

ment policies in their extreme forms),[38] and demand elasticities do not matter.

Marshall observed, and at least partially derived mathematically,[39] four conditions tending to reduce the elasticity of derived demand for inputs and intermediate products. We quote at length, omitting the examples drawn from building-trades labor:[40]

> Let us inquire what are the conditions, under which a check to the supply of a thing that is wanted . . . as a factor of production of some commodity, may cause a very great rise in its price. The first condition is that the factor itself should be essential, or nearly essential to the production of the commodity, no good substitute being available at a moderate price.
>
> The second condition is that the commodity in the production of which it is a necessary factor, should be one for which the demand is stiff and inelastic; . . . this of course includes the condition that no good substitutes for the commodity are available at a price but little higher than its equilibrium price . . .
>
> The third condition is that only a small part of the expenses of production of the commodity should consist of the price of this factor . . .
>
> The fourth condition is that even a small check to the amount demanded should cause a considerable fall in the supply prices of other factors of production; as that will increase the margin available for paying a higher price for this one . . .

Let us denote by E the derived demand elasticity for input a, by η the direct one for output x, by e the elasticity of supply of input b, and by k the relative share ratio ap_a/xp for a, while continuing to use σ for the elasticity of substitution between a and b. Translating Marshall's observations into these symbols, E varies directly with (1) the elasticity of substitution $(\delta E/\delta\sigma > 0)$; (2) the elasticity of demand for x $(\delta E/\delta\eta > 0)$; (3) the share ratio of a $(\delta E/\delta k > 0)$; and (4) the elasticity of supply of b $(\delta E/\delta e > 0)$. All the results are plausible, and were accepted for a generation without hesitation.

38. Extreme full-employment policies may place public agencies in the position of employers of last resort or "blank check" subsidizers of private employers. Forthright advocacy of guaranteed public employment at minimum wages well above the poverty line as an intrinsic part of the American poverty program may be found in Hyman P. Minsky, "The Role of Economic Policy," in Marget S. Gordon (ed.), *Poverty in America* (San Francisco: Chandler, 1965). See also Lester C. Thurow, *Poverty and Discrimination* (Washington: Brookings, 1969). ch. 4, pp. 155 f., and Appendix F.

39. Hicks (*Theory of Wages, op. cit.*, pp. 241 f.) is convinced that Marshall "derived his rules from mathematics," but in his mathematical notes Marshall "confines himself to a simplified case, that in which the proportions of factors employed remain constant. A more extended inquiry, he assures us, would lead to substantially the same results."

40. *Op. cit.* (8th ed.), pp. 385 f. More concise statements are found in Pigou, *op. cit.*, book iv, ch. 5.

Subsequent controversy has centered upon the third law, the so-called importance of being unimportant, whose plausibility seems as great as any of the others. Hicks derived (and we retrace his steps in Appendix B of this chapter[41]) a complex relationship between the five variables above, in the two-input linear homogeneity case:

$$E = \frac{\sigma (\eta + e) + ke\ (\eta - \sigma)}{(\eta + e) - k\ (\eta - \sigma)} \tag{6.14}$$

which can be differentiated partially with respect to σ, η, k, and e, thus testing Marshall's laws in turn. The first, second, and fourth of these derivatives are unquestionably non-negative for all reasonable (non-negative) values of the variables. The third law, however, seems to require for validity the additional condition $\eta > \sigma$. What, economists have inquired, is the common or economic sense of this? (Hicks did not tell us in 1932, but left the result in a mathematical black box.)

23. Despite several ingenious attempts to breathe sense into Hicks' exception to Marshall's third rule,[42] the answer seems to be that it is a blind alley and that Marshall was correct after all. The exceptions require that the share of an input be negative, and so may be ruled out of court.

To show the "instability" implications of the Hicks exceptions, solve (6.14) for k, the relative share of input a:

$$k = \frac{(e + \eta)\ (E - \sigma)}{(e + E)\ (\eta - \sigma)}$$

with all the elasticities positive. If $E > \sigma$, Hicks' exception $(\sigma > \eta)$ is seen at once to imply a negative k. We focus attention, therefore, on the opposite case $(\sigma > E)$. This, we may show, requires a negative marginal product of a, which not only is inconsistent with competitive equilibrium but leads in turn to a negative k. We have, in competitive equilibrium with a linear homogeneous production function,

$$E = - \frac{p_a}{a\ (\delta p_a / \delta a)} = - \frac{\delta x / \delta a}{a\ (\delta^2 x / \delta a^2)} \quad \text{and} \quad \sigma = \frac{(\delta x / \delta a)\ (\delta x / \delta b)}{x\ (\delta^2 x) / (\delta a \delta b)}$$

41. In filling the cavities of Hicks' elliptical derivation (*Theory of Wages, op. cit.,* pp. 242–244), I have required assistance from Sir John himself (by correspondence) and from Marcel K. Richter (in person).

Marshall's original approach to (6.14) (*op. cit.,* p. 853) is a special case $(\sigma = 0)$. Allen later explored a second special case (*op. cit.,* p. 373) in which $e = \infty$. For discussion, see M. Bronfenbrenner, "Notes on the Elasticity of Derived Demand," *Oxford Econ. Papers* (October 1961). Hicks subsequently derived a dual of (6.14) and considered yet a third special case $(e = 0)$ in "Marshall's Third Rule: A Further Comment," *ibid.,* p. 262.

42. For two examples (with citations to earlier literature), see the Bronfenbrenner and Hicks articles cited in note 41.

with all terms positive except $\delta^2 x/\delta a^2$. The condition $\sigma > E$ therefore implies

$$\frac{\delta x/\delta b}{x \; (\delta^2 x) \, / \, (\delta a \delta b)} > - \frac{1}{a \; (\delta^2 x/\delta a^2)} \; .$$

Over the homogeneity range of $F\,(a,b)$, as we derive (from the adding-up theorem) in Appendix A,

$$\delta^2 x/\delta a^2 = - \; (b/a) \; (\delta^2 x/\delta a \delta b) \, .$$

Using this result, the last inequality becomes

$$\frac{\delta x/\delta b}{x \; (\delta^2 x) \, / \, (\delta a \delta b)} > \frac{1}{b \; (\delta^2 x/\delta a \delta b)}$$

or, since the mixed derivative is positive,

$$b \; \delta x/\delta b > x.$$

But, from Euler's Theorem (6.4), over the homogeneity range of the production function,

$$x = (a \; \delta x/\delta a) \; + \; (b \; \delta x/\delta b)$$

so that $b \; \delta x/\delta b > x$ implies $a \; \delta x/\delta a < 0$, or, with positive a, a negative marginal product of a. This is inconsistent with competitive equilibrium. It also implies a negative share ratio $k \; [= (a \delta x/\delta a) \, /x]$, and involves us in a contradiction with our initial assumption that k was positive. This completes the demonstration.[43]

43. Professor Harry Johnson (in his editorial capacity) and the writer have had great difficulties with this section. Johnson has worked out algebraic, graphic, and arithmetic counterexamples, all indicating that Hicks was right and Marshall wrong with none of the anomalies suggested in the text. These examples, however, involve *shifting* production functions. As I wrote Johnson (July 14, 1969) :

"We are starting from a system of six equations, not all independent. There are demand and supply functions for two inputs, plus demand and production functions for output. Nothing in the subsequent mathematics . . . indicates explicitly which function or functions have shifted where there is, say, a change in the labor share k, such as is involved in Marshall's disputed third law.

"Marshall, however, and following him Hicks, was interested primarily in the consequences of a shift in labor supply. Marshall, and following him Hicks, wanted the system to answer questions like: Given a shift in the labor supply, would it encounter a demand elasticity greater or less than it does, had the original labor share k been larger than its original value? Hicks' mathematics answers this question, and answers others at the same time. One of the other questions it answers is: Had it been the production function whose shift had changed k, how would the elasticity of demand have varied as k changed? His apparatus, because of its generality, does not distinguish between these classes of cases. Fortunately for Marshall, only the third of his four laws of input demand seems affected by the mathematical generalization of his field.

"What I think [this section] shows is that, under the Marshallian assumptions as I understand them, with only the labor supply shifting and the other functions fixed,

Innovation, Neutral and Biased

24.   We have thus far assumed all production functions (6.1) to be static and unchanging over time. This is, of course, an oversimplification in a world of progress and change, invention and innovation. We may actually have:

$$x = \phi(t) F(a, b), \; x = F[\alpha(t) a, \beta(t) b], \; \text{or} \; x = \phi(t) F[\alpha(t) a, \beta(t) b] \quad (6.15)$$

where t (time) is a surrogate or proxy for all the forces of progress.

In the first alternative equation of (6.15), which is easiest to deal with and is most frequently assumed by economists, all progress is treated as *disembodied*. This means that the progress function $\phi(t)$ is separate from the production function $F(a,b)$; the inputs themselves do not change qualitatively, and the productivity of all inputs rises over time. In the second alternative equation, on the other hand, all progress is treated as *embodied;* there is no separate progress function $\phi(t)$; instead, inputs change qualitatively over time according to embodiment functions $\alpha(t)$, $\beta(t)$, so that we might have written

$$a = \int_{0}^{t} \alpha(t) \, a(t) \, dt \qquad \text{and} \qquad b = \int_{0}^{t} \beta(t) \, b(t) \, dt.$$

In the third alternative, elements of both embodied and disembodied progress are combined. While most realistic, this form of (6.15) presents the greatest statistical difficulties, and has not yet been applied empirically.

25.   In a diagram like Figure 6.1, technical progress implies upward shifts in the total and average product function F and F/a; technical regress implies the reverse. The marginal product function F' may, as we shall see, shift in either direction so long as the total area (integral) under it increases at all points for progress, and decreases for regress. In a diagram such as Figure 6.2 (upper panel), progress compresses the isoquants x_i toward the origin O, while regress stretches them further out.

Marshall is right and Hicks wrong. This implies no error in Hicks' mathematics, but points out that the Hicksian exception to Marshall's third law involves an economic anomaly. What I think you showed was that, with the production function also shifting, Hicks is right and Marshall wrong. The demand for labor need not be rendered inelastic by a large k, or by an increasing k, and no anomalies result if the elasticity effects are the other way. But is there anything extraordinary in a production-function shift simultaneously raising the labor share and lowering the elasticity of demand for labor? If anything, such a case seems less surprising than the opposite one, where share and elasticity move together. Surely, this case could not have been the one Marshall had in mind in maintaining 'the importance of being unimportant'?"

The patterns of compression or extension, however, need not be symmetrical. The isoquant x_i may at all points be compressed a larger part of the distance to the origin than the isoquant x_j. Also, one point on x_i may be compressed further than others, so long as the basic characteristics. of the isoquant are preserved; the m.r.s. at any point on x_i may shift in either direction.

Fei and Ranis decompose the effects of progress into *intensity* (symmetrical contraction of the relevant isoquant) and *bias* (departure from symmetry).[44] In their isoquant diagrams, intensity is a radial movement along a vector through the origin, and bias is a movement parallel to an input axis (in their case, labor).

26.   Fei and Ranis' graphic methods aid in visualizing these ideas.[45] The asymmetries of technical progress (including organization, morale, education, health, etc.), which they represent as departures from radial movement, may operate favorably or unfavorably to suppliers of any input *a,* whereas the symmetrical or radial movement necessarily operates favorably. If, with a constant output price, the relative share of *a* rises at the expense of some other input b $[d/dt\,(ap_a/bp_b)] > 0$, or $\{[d/dt\,(a/b)] \div (a/b) > [d/dt\,(p_b/p_a)] \div (p_b/p_a)\}$ as a result of innovation, the innovation is called *a*-using, *b*-saving, or *a*-biased.

Turning now to the suppliers of *b,* if the favorable radial or intensity effect of an innovation is more than offset by the unfavorable *a*-bias of the same innovation, in such a way that, to maintain constant employment of *b,* its price p_b must fall absolutely, the innovation is called *very a*-using, *b*-saving, or *a*-biased.

Schemata for greater precision in defining, and sometimes measuring, innovational bias have been devised by several economists. We shall here outline the most popular one, which is also best articulated with marginal-productivity economics, and then compare it with certain of the alternatives.

This "standard" schema is due to Hicks. In this system, an innovation is judged *a*-biased or *a*-using, and therefore *b*-saving, if, at pre-innovation equilibrium employment levels *a, b, c,* . . . , the marginal productivity of *a* is raised by the innovation relatively to that of *b;* the innovation is neutral if the ratio of the two marginal productivities is not changed by

44. Gustav Ranis and John C. H. Fei, *Development of the Labor Surplus Economy* (Homewood, Ill.: Irwin, 1964) pp. 77–80; also diagrams 6–7 (pp. 69, 93).

45. Another exposition is Murray Brown, *On the Theory and Measurement of Technological Change* (Cambridge: Cambridge University Press, 1966), ch. 2. Both Brown and Fei and Ranis build primarily on Hicks, *Theory of Wages, op. cit.,* pp. 121–127.

it; and it is *b*-biased (*a*-saving) if the ratio is shifted unfavorably to *a*.[46] Since the marginal rate of substitution (m.r.s.) between inputs *a* and *b* has been defined as the slope of an isoquant and as the ratio $\delta x/\delta a \div \delta x/\delta b$, the Hicks criterion can be rephrased in these terms: An innovation is *a*-biased and *b*-saving if it raises the m.r.s. and the slope of the isoquant at the point *a, b;* neutral if it leaves the slope and m.r.s. unchanged at this point; *b*-biased and *a*-saving if it lowers the m.r.s. and the slope of the isoquant at this point.

Let us assume an *a*-biased, *b*-saving innovation, and limit discussion to the two-input simplification. The innovation would be judged very *a*-biased (very *b*-saving) if the value of the marginal productivity of *b*, or $\delta x/\delta b$, not only declined relative to $\delta x/\delta a$, but also declined absolutely, at the pre-innovation equilibrium point $\bar{a}, \bar{b}$.

The common sense of this scheme is that ordinary *a*-biased and *b*-saving innovations should tend to increase both the absolute income and the relative share of the suppliers of *a*, but only the absolute income of the suppliers of *b*. Very (or "ultra") *a*-biased and *b*-saving innovations, on the other hand, should decrease both the absolute and the relative income of the suppliers of *b*. In addition to the difficulties consequent on the introduction of additional inputs, ambiguities arise from our choice of points of comparison. The point *a, b* is by hypothesis an equilibrium position before the innovation, but it is in general a position of disequilibrium after the innovation, so that we are comparing an equilibrium with a disequilibrium situation. If we had based our comparison on the post-innovation equilibrium position—call it *a', b'*—we might have obtained qualitatively different results as to innovational bias. There is as yet no easy way of combining or compromising away whatever anomalies may occur. (This is no problem in Hicks' original context of fixed input supplies.)

27. The graphics of the Hicks criterion are not difficult (Figure 6.6). The left panel is an isoquant diagram; x_0, x_1 are pre-innovation isoquants based on a pre-innovation production function; *x* is a post-innovation isoquant based on a post-innovation production function. In terms of output, $x > x_0 > x_1$. Three alternative points of equilibrium are presented, P_1, P_2, and P_3; the respective *a* and *b* coordinates are omitted for clarity. Had P_1 been the pre-innovation equilibrium point, we should

46. The Hicks criterion, like most of its rivals, was devised with a two-input case primarily in mind. With three or more inputs, an innovation may be at once *a*-biased relative to *b*, and *a*-saving relative to *c*. Unequivocal *a*-bias implies *a*-bias relative to all other inputs or, alternatively, relative to an index number summarizing all other inputs.

adjudge the innvoation a-biased and b-saving, since the slope of x_1 exceeds that of x at P_1 (the curve x_1 cutting x from above). Had P_2 or P_3 been the introductory equilibrium points, we should have adjudged the innovation neutral or b-biased, respectively, on analogous grounds; x and x_0 are tangent at P_2, while x_1 cuts x from below at P_3.[47]

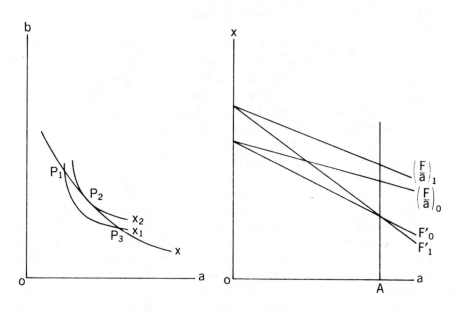

Figure 6.6

The right panel of Figure 6.6 is concerned with a very a-saving (b-biased) innovation. The coordinates are now a and x, as in an ordinary supply-and-demand function for input a terms of output x. F/a represents the average productivity of a, and F' the corresponding marginal productivity, as in Figure 6.1, while the subscripts 0,1 refer, respectively, to situations before and after the innovation. Since the functions are linear, the slope of each F' (marginal) function is double that of the corresponding F/a (average) function.[48] Since this is a true (progressive)

47. In Figure 6.5, the "new" isoquant has a larger radius of curvature than the "old" ones. This is not a necessary condition.

48. Let a linear average function be $y(x)$; the corresponding total function is xy, and the corresponding marginal function;

$$\frac{d(xy)}{dx} = y + x\frac{dy}{dx},$$

the derivative dy/dx being the slope of the average function.

innovation, $(F/a)_1 > (F/a)_0$ for all values of a; however, $F'_1 < F'_0$ to the right of A. This intersection is the feature that makes the innovation very b-biased; geometrically it arises from the fact that the slope of $(F/a)_1$ exceeds that of $(F/a)_0$. This twisting of the average productivity function results in a zone to the right of A in which we can call the innovation very b-biased and very a-saving. For initial employment of a in excess of OA, the marginal productivity of a is reduced by the innovation. Insofar as such cases exist for labor inputs, their relevance to the analysis of automation and technical unemployment should be clear; likewise, their relevance to the workability of guidelines, guideposts, income policies, and the like, based exclusively on consideration of average productivity. (Compare Chapter 17, sections 20–21.)

28. This standard schema can be compared with three others for the linear homogeneity range of the production function, following a method developed by Seeber.[49] The criteria to be compared are these:

a. Does the m.r.s. or the ratio $\delta x/\delta a \div \delta x/\delta b$ change (Hicks criterion)? The innovation is a-biased, neutral, or b-biased (as we have seen) according to whether the change is positive, zero, or negative, with a and b constant.

b. Does the capital-output ratio b/x change, with a representing labor and b capital, and with the rate of interest, which equals the v.m.p. of b, constant at r (Harrod criterion)?[50] The innovation is a-biased, neutral or b-biased according to whether the change is negative, zero, or positive.

c. When the average productivity of capital x/b rises for a given capi-

---

To determine the slope of the marginal function, take $d^2(xy)/dx^2$:

$$\frac{d^2(xy)}{dx^2} = \frac{d}{dx}\left(y + x\frac{dy}{dx}\right) = 2\frac{dy}{dx} + \frac{d^2y}{dx^2}$$

If the average function y is linear, its slope is a constant and the second derivative vanishes. Therefore, the slope of the marginal function is twice that of the average. It too is a constant, and so the marginal function is itself linear. Also, average and marginal functions cross when

$$y = y + x\frac{dy}{dx}.$$

Here, the intersection is at $x = 0$, since the slope dy/dx is a non-zero constant.

49. Norton C. Seeber, "On the Classification of Inventions," *So. Ec. J.* (April 1962). The alternative criteria considered do not include all that have been suggested. One important omission is contained in Oskar Lange, "A Note on Innovations," *Readings*, no. 10; the Lange criterion includes output as well as input considerations, in line with the man in the street's classification into output-increasing and cost-decreasing improvements. For a more detailed comparison, involving no fewer than 14 criteria of neutrality or bias, see Ryuzo Sato and Martin J. Beckmann, "Neutral Inventions and Production Functions," *R. E. Stud.* (January 1968).

50. R. F. Harrod, *Towards a Dynamic Economics* (London: Macmillan, 1952), p. 26 f.

tal-labor ratio b/a, does the rise involve a change in the elasticity of x/b with respect to b/a (Robinson criterion)?[51] The innovation is a-biased, neutral, or b-biased according to whether the elasticity change is negative, zero, or positive.

d. Does the output or productivity elasticity $\delta x/\delta a \div x/a$ change? The innovation is a-biased, neutral, or b-biased as the change is positive, zero, or negative. (The output or productivity elasticity can be seen from its formula to be the relative share $(a\,\delta x/\delta a)/x$ in elasticity disguise. This criterion is therefore tautologous under competitive conditions.)

Seeber goes about his reconciliation of comparisons by distinguishing between short-run and long-run conditions according to whether the employment of both inputs is constant or variable. He relates the "Robinson" elasticities to the ordinary ones we have encountered already. Beginning with the production function,

$$x = F\,(a, b)$$

and defining $y = (x/a)$, $\rho = (b/a)$, we have, in the homogeneity range of F,

$$y = f\,(\rho)\,.$$

If a is labor and b is capital, b/x $(= \rho/y)$ is an average capital-output ratio. Also, with constant a,

$$\frac{dy}{d\rho} = \frac{\delta x}{\delta b}\,.$$

Combining these results in elasticity terms,

$$\frac{dy}{d\rho}\frac{\rho}{y} = \frac{\delta x}{\delta b}\frac{b}{x} \qquad \text{or} \qquad E_{y\rho} = E_{xb}.$$

Similarly, if $z = (x/b)$ and $\gamma = (a/b)$, with constant b,

$$E_{z\gamma} = E_{xa}.$$

(E_{xb} and E_{xa} are also relative shares which, by the adding-up theorem, sum to unity, so that $E_{xa} = 1 - E_{xb}$, and vice versa.)

Now we are ready for Seeber's diagrams. They show that, in the short run, Robinson neutrality implies Hicks neutrality and Harrod capital-saving, but in the long run, Robinson neutrality implies Harrod neutrality and Hicks capital-saving.) (Robinson neutrality, therefore, emerges as a hybrid of the other criteria.)

The short-run analysis is confined to the left panel of Figure 6.7; the long-run analysis uses the right panel also. In the short run (left panel),

51. Joan Robinson, "The Classification of Inventions," *Readings*, no. 9.

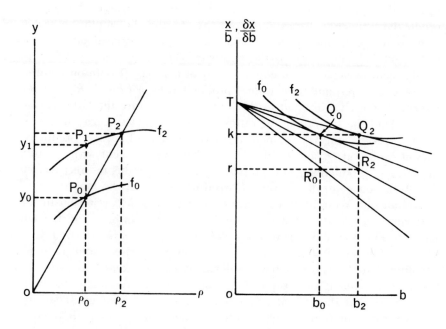

Figure 6.7

a and b are both fixed. Their quotient ρ is likewise fixed at the value ρ_0. We compare the pre-innovation production function f_0 at P_0 (an equilibrium position) with the post-innovation one f_2 at P_1 (which may not be an equilibrium position). If the elasticity of f_0 at P_0 equals the elasticity of f_2 at P_1 (Robinson neutrality), with constant ρ, the relative shares of a and b are unchanged. It follows that their marginal productivities have changed proportionately. Hicks neutrality is assured. Harrod neutrality, however, is violated; the capital-output ratio b/x, which equals ρ/y, is decreased from ρ_0/y_0 to ρ_0/y_1, and the innovation is capital-saving. (The ratio z/x also falls as y rises, but this does not make the innovation labor-saving. The capital-output ratio is all that matters; asymmetry detracts from the appeal of both the Harrod criterion and of a mirror image that considers only the *labor-output* ratio a/x or $1/y$, with constant *wage* rate p_a.) [52]

The long-run analysis, which utilizes both panels of Figure 6.7, is more involved. Here the quantity of capital b is measured along the horizontal

52. This is called the "Solow criterion" by Sato and Beckmann, *op. cit.*, pp. 59 f. See Robert M. Solow, "Technical Progress, Capital Formation, and Economic Growth," *A.E.R.* (May 1962).

axis of the right panel; both average and marginal products of capital are measured along the vertical one. The innovation has raised the average productivity function for capital from f_0 to f_2, and the employment of b from b_0 to b_2. (Appropriate adjustments of a are assumed off-stage, or rather, off-diagram.) The partial elasticity of f_2 at Q_2, corresponding to employment of b_2, is drawn equal to that of f_0 at Q_0 (Robinson neutrality).[53] The corresponding marginal productivities of capital, R_2 and R_0, are equal to each other and to the interest rate r, since the latter is constant.[54] Had the capital-output ratios not been equal to each other at a constant r, satisfying Harrod neutrality, isoelasticity of *average* productivities of capital at Q_0 and Q_2 would have been inconsistent with equality of *marginal* productivity of capital at R_0 and R_2. By this indirect reasoning, Robinson neutrality implies Harrod neutrality in the long run.

We can now reestablish a relationship with the Hicks criterion in the long run. The constancy of the capital-output ratio implies (on the left panel of Fig. 6.7) movement along the ray OP_0 to its intersection with f_2 at P_2. The value of the capital-labor ratio ρ has risen from ρ_0 to ρ_2, meaning that the rise in labor employment has not kept pace with the rise in employment of capital. The constant-elasticity conditions, however, imply that the capital and labor shares are unchanged. The only consistent explanation for these several changes, under competitive equilibrium, is a rise in $\delta x/\delta a$ relative to $\delta x/\delta b$. This makes the innovation labor-biased and capital-saving by the Hicks criterion, as expanded to cover changes in the ratio of the two inputs.

Constant relative-share production functions comprise a special class, for which all these criteria may be mutually consistent. An example is the Cobb-Douglas function, as modified by Solow to include disembodied technical progress:[55]

$$x = e^{gt} a^a b^{1-a}$$

53. The elasticities of f_0 and f_2 at Q_0 and Q_2 are equal to those of their tangents, as follows at once from elasticity formulas. If these tangents are themselves linear, and intersect on the vertical axis at some point T, their elasticities at Q_0 and Q_2 will each equal

$$\frac{kQ_i}{kT} \cdot \frac{Ok}{kQ_i} = \frac{Ok}{kT}$$

Since the slopes of linear marginal functions are twice those of corresponding linear functions, we can locate the marginal productivities R_0 and R_2 from knowledge of Q_0, Q_2 and T.

54. The statement in the text implies the applicability of marginal productivity analysis to the demand for capital and the theory of interest. This is a controversial proposition of neoclassical economics, which the writer accepts but which Mrs. Robinson (among others) considers meaningless and misleading. See Chapter 16, section 8.

55. Solow, "Technical Change and the Aggregate Production Function," *Rev. Econ. and Stat.* (August 1957).

in which

$$\frac{d}{dt}\left(\frac{a\,\frac{\delta x}{\delta a}}{x}\right)=\frac{d\alpha}{dt}=0$$

and similarly for the share of b, whatever may happen to y, to ρ, or to their elasticity. Also, the ratio of marginal productivities,

$$\frac{\delta x/\delta a}{\delta x/\delta b}=\frac{b}{a}\,\frac{\alpha}{1-\alpha}$$

is independent of technical progress as represented by gt. For such a production function, then, Harrod and Robinson neutrality imply Hicks neutrality as well.

Induced Innovation and Its Biases

29. Innovation is not merely a chance or spontaneous process. It is often, perhaps ordinarily, induced by deliberate expenditure on research and development.[56] Bias in spontaneous innovation may be equally likely in all input directions—not to mention innovations involving new or modified outputs—and neutrality is a usable neutral assumption. Labor-saving bias, by contrast, is ascribed so generally to the induced component of innovation as to make "labor-saving-machinery" a single word like "dam-yankee" and to arouse fears of the workman's following the workhorse into economic obsolescence. While the predominance of capital-biased, labor-saving, induced innovation has not been proved rigorously, economists have assumed its existence and sought to explain it.

Superficial explanations that labor is "dear" are unsatisfactory if the v.m.p. of labor equals its cost. Historical-institutional explanations have accordingly been the next line of defense.[58] Two examples of these are

56. This idea is at least as old as Marx, and perhaps even Ricardo. An exhaustive development, illustrated by four specific inventions, is Jacob Schmookler, *Invention and Economic Growth* (Cambridge, Mass.: Harvard University Press, 1966).

57. What we now call "labor-saving bias in innovation" was assumed by both Ricardo and Marx. In Marx, it forms one basis for the so-called "rising organic composition of capital," from which is derived "the falling rate of profit," sometimes called "Marx's Law."

58. As an unusually convincing sample of this historical evidence, see Richard R. Nelson, Merton J. Peck, and Edward Kalachek, *Technology, Economic Growth, and Public Policy* (Washington: Brookings, 1967), pp. 28–34. We quote from pp. 31–34, including comparisons of British with American conditions:

Habakkuk has argued that in England, where fuel was scarce and expensive, a much larger percentage of technological advances was aimed at saving fuel than in the United States. Watt's steam engine and Bessemer's hot blast process are instances

repeated here: (a) Wage rates have been rising relative to capital charges; labor saving is designed to substitute today's labor (embodied in capital instruments) for tomorrow's labor, with minimum risk of obsolescence. (b) When labor is organized into trade unions (with working rules, jurisdiction boundaries, etc.) , or is hired with long-term employment commitments, it cannot always be deployed so as to avoid situations where v.m.p. is systematically below wage rates for prolonged periods, and where v.m.p. cannot be raised, either by dismissals or output price rises, to keep pace with wage increases. In other words, except in labor-shortage periods, bargaining or humanitarian considerations may keep v.m.p. normally somewhat below present and (particularly) anticipated wage rates, thereby imparting labor-saving bias to induced innovation.

A stronger theoretical proposition along similar lines has been developed by Kennedy, Weiszäcker, and Samuelson,[59] at the cost of exaggerating the automatic and predictable character of induced innovation. It springs from an embodiment view of innovation as input-augmenting:

$$x = F[\alpha\,(t)\,a, \quad \beta\,(t)\,b]$$

where the augmentation factors α and β can be varied by deliberate inventive activity according to a concave innovation-possibility frontier like

---

where the record shows clearly that the inventors were interested in saving fuel. Habakkuk suggests that, in contrast, a much larger percentage of effort in the United States than in England was specifically aimed at saving labor.

The tendency toward labor saving inventions may be a continuing phenomenon in countries like the United States. As a result of general technological advance, . . . the cost of new machinery has tended to fall relative to the wage rate. This has raised substantially the profitability of technological advances which improve the terms at which machinery can be substituted for labor . . .

Thus efforts to advance technology will tend to be drawn toward saving on factors whose relative cost is rising . . . This does not necessarily mean that . . . factor-saving innovation will always be sufficiently strong to offset the growing scarcity of a particular factor—only that allocation of inventive effort will tend to move in these directions. However, Schmookler's convincing evidence that the number of patents awarded for capital equipment . . . is closely related to the lagged expenditures on capital equipment . . . suggests that [a] simple demand-pull model . . . explains much of the existing pattern of allocation of inventive effort, as well as changes in that pattern.

(References to "Habakkuk" refer to H. J. Habakkuk, *American and British Technology in the Nineteenth Century* [New York: Cambridge University Press, 1962]; references to citations of "Schmookler" refer to Jacob Schmookler, *Invention and Economic Growth, op. cit.*)

59. Good expositions and bibliographies are found in William Fellner, "Profit-Maximization, Utility-Maximization, and the Rate and Direction of Innovation," *A.E.R.* (May 1966) , and at a more advanced level in Paul A. Samuelson, "A Theory of Induced Invention along Kennedy-Weiszäcker Lines," *Rev. Econ. and Stat.* (November 1965) . Kennedy himself adjures the production function altogether: Charles Kennedy, "Induced Bias in Innovation and the Theory of Distribution," *Ec. J.* (October 1964) and "Samuelson on Induced Innovation," *Rev. Econ. and Stat.* (November 1966) .

II in Figure 6.8. (In terms of this production function, innovation is *a*-biased, neutral, or *b*-biased according to whether α is less than, equal to, or greater than β.)

The saving that arises from augmentation (economizing) of *a* rather than *b* is proportional to the existing relative shares k and $1\text{-}k$ in x, and can be indicated by two families of lines in Figure 6.8, corresponding to different relative shares. (In the diagram, only the optimal, tangential member of each family is shown, with the innovation-possibility frontier *II* pre-determined by, for example, past research and development activity.) Specifically, P_1 is an optimal innovation mix corresponding to a high *b*-share; the slope of the tangent (isosaving) line indicates that a small augmentation of *b* (small β) saves as much as a larger augmentation of *a* (large α). Also, induced innovation à la P_1 involves lowering the employment ratio b/a. Since $\beta > \alpha$ at P_1, this represents *a*-biased and *b*-saving innovation. Parallel results hold for P_2. Neutrality $(\alpha = \beta)$ would be found at P_0, where a 45-degree ray from the origin intersects the innovation-possibility frontier.

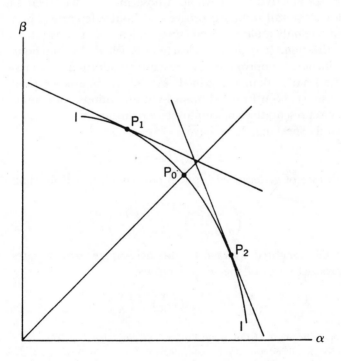

Figure 6.8

30. Assuming, as most writers do, inelastic capital-labor substitution ($\sigma < 1$) with the capital stock growing faster than employment, one would expect both a rising labor share in the absence of innovation and an increasingly capital-biased, labor-saving character of induced innovations as the labor share rises. The Kennedy-Weiszäcker theory accordingly modifies Bowley's Law (constant relative shares) to an argument that relative shares represent the outcome of conflict between inelastic substitution (raising the labor share) and induced innovation (offsetting this increase), with the outcome theoretically unclear but apparently relatively small in either direction. Brown's statistical estimates for the United States support this view.[60] Ignoring interindustry effects, he ascribes to technology an .077 per cent increase in the profit share during the decade 1950–1960, more than offset by a .178 per cent decrease due to real wage increases (with inelastic substitution).

Generalized Input Productivity

31. We close this chapter with a note on a generalized measure of input or "factor" productivity as a whole, whose increase has been suggested as an index of overall technical progress without reference to bias.[61] It is, as we shall see, only an *average* measure, which does not as yet lend itself to marginalization. It is defined clearly only when the functional distribution of income is approximately constant. In addition, since its value is consistently smaller than the growth rate of average labor productivity alone, its use has been frowned upon by trade union representatives and favored by representatives of employers' organizations.

Technically speaking, if we have

$$x = F(a, b, \ldots)$$

the growth rate of generalized input productivity, which we shall denote by

$$d\left(\frac{x}{a, b, \ldots}\right) \Big/ \left(\frac{x}{a, b, \ldots}\right),$$

is merely the weighted average of the percentage growth rates of the average productivities of the several inputs:

$$d\left(\frac{x}{a}\right) \Big/ \left(\frac{x}{a}\right), d\left(\frac{x}{b}\right) \Big/ \left(\frac{x}{b}\right), \ldots$$

60. Brown, "The Share of Corporate Profits," *op. cit.,* table 7, p. 124.

61. John W. Kendrick and Ryuzo Sato, "Factor Prices, Productivity, and Economic Growth," *A.E.R.* (December 1963), pp. 978, 983; Kendrick, *Productivity Trends in the U.S.* (Princeton: Princeton University Press, 1961), ch. 5.

where the weights are their respective relative shares

$$\frac{a}{x}\frac{\delta x}{\delta a}, \quad \frac{b}{x}\frac{\delta x}{\delta b}, \ldots$$

and are assumed approximately constant in the short run.

We know from elementary calculus that

$$\frac{d\,(x/a)}{x/a} = \frac{a}{x}\left(\frac{a\,dx - x\,da}{a^2}\right) = \frac{dx}{x} - \frac{da}{a}$$

and similarly

$$\frac{d\,(x/b)}{x/b} = \frac{dx}{x} - \frac{db}{b}.$$

Hence, translating into symbols our definition of the input productivity growth rate,

$$\frac{d\,(x/a,b,\ldots)}{x/\,(a,b,\ldots)} = \left(\frac{a}{x}\frac{\delta x}{\delta a}\right)\left(\frac{dx}{x} - \frac{da}{a}\right) + \left(\frac{b}{x}\frac{\delta x}{\delta b}\right)\left(\frac{dx}{x} - \frac{db}{b}\right) + \ldots \quad (6.15)$$

If the adding-up theorem (6.4) holds, the weights, or relative shares, add to unity, and (6.15) may be simplified:

$$\frac{d\,(x/a,b,\ldots)}{x/\,(a,b,\ldots)} = \frac{dx}{x} - \left(\frac{a}{x}\frac{\delta x}{\delta a}\frac{da}{a} + \frac{b}{x}\frac{\delta x}{\delta b}\frac{db}{b} + \ldots\right)$$

$$= \frac{1}{x}\left[dx - \left(\frac{\delta x}{\delta a}da + \frac{\delta x}{\delta b}db + \ldots\right)\right] \quad (6.16)$$

32. Letting a represent homogenized labor, b homogenized capital, and x homogenized value added, and assuming their respective growth rates to be in their usual or canonical order:

$$\frac{db}{b} > \frac{dx}{x} > \frac{da}{a}$$

it follows at once (since the relative share of labor must be a positive proper fraction) that:

$$\frac{d\,(x/a)}{x/a} = \frac{dx}{x} - \frac{da}{a} > \frac{d\,(x/a,b)}{x/\,(a,b,)} = \left(\frac{a}{x}\frac{\delta x}{\delta a}\right)\left(\frac{dx}{x} - \frac{da}{a}\right) + \left(\frac{b}{x}\frac{\delta x}{\delta b}\right)\left(\frac{dx}{x} - \frac{db}{b}\right)$$

because the quantity in the final right-side parenthesis is negative.[62] The

---

62. Kendrick and Sato's estimates (*ibid.*) spell the inequality out quantitatively for the United States. "Average labor productivity increased by 2.4 per cent a year over the long period [1919–1960] and by 2.8 per cent in the postwar period, on average, compared with increases in capital productivity of 1.3 and −0.1 per cent over the longer and shorter periods. When the two 'partial productivity' ratios are combined, the resulting measure of 'total tangible factor productivity' show an increase of approximately 2.1 per cent a year, on average, over both the long period and the shorter postwar period."

class-angles underlying both the support of the generalized input productivity notion and the opposition to it are accordingly easy to understand, in an economy where collective bargaining is important.

Guideposts, guidelines, and incomes policies usually use the growth rate of man-hour productivity (x/a) as an important policy benchmark. (See Chapter 17.) Were they to shift attention to the lower growth rate of general input productivity $x/a, b, \ldots,$ capital-labor substitution would be interfered with by the extension of input-price regulation from wages alone to inputs in general. "Guidepost" wage rates would be permitted to rise more slowly than under standard concepts. On the other hand, parallel rises would presumably be built into real interest rates, rents, and possibly profit margins as well. "Standard" incomes policies propose, at least, to maintain the labor share (this requires downward pressure on interest rates, if capital accumulates faster than the labor force grows, so that the capital-labor ratio rises). The general-input-productivity alternative, on the other hand, would operate to increase the relative share of the more rapidly growing inputs, that is, capital (in the advanced countries).

Appendix A

THE STANDARD FORMULA FOR THE ELASTICITY OF SUBSTITUTION

i. The Hicks-Allen derivation of (6.13) from (6.12) defines the price ratio p_a/p_b as r. (We have used this symbol previously for the interest rate; the two usages should not be confused.) Using the Hicks-Allen notation, (6.12) is

$$\sigma = \frac{(a/b)\, d\,(b/a)}{dr/r} = \frac{ar}{b}\, \frac{d\,(b/a)}{dr} \tag{6.i}$$

We know that both b/a and r depend on a and b, and begin by expressing the differentials $d\,(b/a)$ and dr in terms of da and db:

$$d\left(\frac{b}{a}\right) = \frac{a\,db - b\,da}{a^2}, \qquad dr = \frac{\delta r}{\delta a}\, da + \frac{\delta r}{\delta b}\, db$$

ii. Since r is defined as p_a/p_b, it also equals the m.r.s. $-db/da$, so that $db = -r\,da$. Using this relation to eliminate db,

$$d\left(\frac{b}{a}\right) = -\frac{(ar + b)\, da}{a^2}, \qquad dr = \left(\frac{\delta r}{\delta a} - r\, \frac{\delta r}{\delta b}\right) da$$

Substitute these results in the definition (6.i) of σ and manipulate algebraically:

$$\sigma = \frac{r}{ab}\, \frac{ar + b}{r\,(\delta r/\delta b) - (\delta r/\delta a)} \tag{6.ii}$$

iii.   The next step is to evaluate $\delta r/\delta a$ and $\delta r/\delta b$ in terms of the production function F and its derivatives. Along the expansion path, $r = F_a/F_b$ by (6.5). Differentiating this quotient with respect to a and b,

$$\frac{\delta r}{\delta a} = \frac{\delta}{\delta a}\left(\frac{F_a}{F_b}\right) = (F_b F_{aa} - F_a F_{ab})/F_b{}^2, \qquad \frac{dr}{db} = (F_b F_{ab} - F_a F_{bb})/F_b{}^2.$$

Substitute these expressions for $\delta r/\delta a$ and $\delta r/\delta b$ in (6.ii) and also the equilibrium value F_a/F_b for r. After some more algebra, (6.ii) becomes

$$\sigma = -\frac{F_a F_b\ (aF_a + bF_b)}{ab\ (F_a{}^2 F_{bb} + F_b{}^2 F_{aa} - 2F_a F_b F_{ab})} \tag{6.iii}$$

The Hicks-Allen simplification of (6.iii) requires the production function F to be linear homogeneous. The parenthetical expression in the numerator of (6.iii) reduces to x by Euler's Theorem (6.4):

$$x = aF_a + bF_b$$

Equation (6.4) can itself be differentiated with respect to a and b. This differentiation permits the rewriting of both F_{aa} and F_{bb} in terms of a, b, and F_{ab} alone, with x constant and $dx = 0$.

$$aF_{aa} + bF_{ab} = 0, \qquad \text{so that} \qquad F_{aa} = -\left(\frac{b}{a}\right) F_{ab}$$

$$aF_{ab} + bF_{bb} = 0, \qquad \text{so that} \qquad F_{bb} = -\left(\frac{a}{b}\right) F_{ab}$$

iv.   When these substitutions are made in (6.iii), the rest is easy except for some tedious algebra:

$$\sigma = \frac{xF_a F_b}{F_{ab}\ (a^2 F_a{}^2 + 2abF_a F_b + b^2 F_b{}^2)}. \tag{6.iv}$$

The parenthetical expression in the denominator of (6.iv) is precisely x^2 in the linear homogeneity case of (6.4). After this last substitution, (6.13) follows at once:

$$\sigma = \frac{F_a F_b}{xF_{ab}} = \frac{(\delta x/\delta a)\ (\delta x/\delta b)}{x\delta^2 x/\delta a \delta b} = \frac{p_a p_b}{xp^2\ \delta^2 x/\delta a \delta b}. \tag{6.13}$$

v.   An alternative system of coefficients and parameters, leading to an elasticity of substitution which is the reciprocal of that derived here, has been developed by Fei and Ranis as a portion of their theory of economic development.[1] Their formula, in terms of our symbols, is

$$\frac{1}{\sigma} = \epsilon_{aa} + \epsilon_{bb}$$

1. *Op. cit.*, pp. 76, 106.

where the ϵ terms are elasticities of input *shares* with respect to input *quantities*. As the Fei-Ranis algebra is fuller than Hicks', we need not retrace the derivation here.

Appendix B

THE HICKS FORMULA FOR THE ELASTICITY OF
INPUT DEMAND, WITH EXTENSIONS.

vi.   As a starting point, we collect a number of previous results:

$$x = F(a, b) \qquad\qquad \text{(production function)}$$

$$p_a = p \frac{\delta x}{\delta a}, p_b = p \frac{\delta x}{\delta b} \qquad \text{(v.m.p. functions)}$$

$$\eta = -\frac{dx}{dp}\frac{p}{x}, E = -\frac{da}{dp_a}\frac{p_a}{a} \quad \text{(output and input demand elasticities)}$$

$$e = \frac{db}{dp_b}\frac{p_b}{b} \qquad\qquad \text{(input supply elasticity)}$$

$$\sigma = \frac{(\delta x/\delta a)\ (\delta x/\delta b)}{x\ (\delta^2 x/\delta a \delta b)} \qquad \text{(elasticity of substitution)}$$

We shall use again, from Appendix A:

$$\frac{\delta^2 x}{\delta b^2} = -\frac{a}{b}\frac{\delta^2 x}{\delta a \delta b}, \qquad \text{and similarly} \qquad \frac{\delta^2 x}{\delta a^2} = -\frac{b}{a}\frac{\delta^2 x}{\delta a \delta b}. \qquad (6.\text{v})$$

Also, without regard to linear homogeneity:

$$dx = \frac{\delta x}{\delta a}\ da + \frac{\delta x}{\delta b}\ db$$

whence (using the v.m.p. functions) :

$$p\ dx = p_a da + p_b\ db \qquad\qquad\qquad (6.\text{vi})$$

vii: If the equilibrium equality between receipts and expenditures remains satisfied for small changes in input quantities:

$$d(xp) = d(ap_a) + d(bp_b)$$
$$p\ dx + x\ dp = (p_a\ da + a\ dp_a) + (p_b db + b\ dp_b)$$

which, by (6.vi) reduces to:

$$x\ dp = a\ dp_a + b\ dp_b \qquad\qquad\qquad (6.\text{vii})$$

Now introduce elasticity notions, assuming no exogenous changes in the demand for input b. The three terms of (6.vii) are (except for sign) the denominators of η, E, and e respectively, and (6.vii) may be written

$$\frac{p\ dx}{\eta} = \frac{p_a da}{E} - \frac{p_b db}{e}. \qquad\qquad (6.\text{viii})$$

viii. Next, laying (6.vii–6.viii) aside for future reference, substitute for db in these equations its value in supply-elasticity terms:

$$db = \frac{be}{p_b}\, dp_b = \frac{be}{p_b}\, d\left(p\, \frac{\delta x}{\delta b}\right)$$

and evaluate the differential $d\,(p\,\delta x/\delta b)$:

$$d\left(p\, \frac{\delta x}{\delta b}\right) = \frac{\delta}{\delta x}\left(p\, \frac{\delta x}{\delta b}\right)dx + \frac{\delta}{\delta a}\left(p\, \frac{\delta x}{\delta b}\right)da + \frac{\delta}{\delta b}\left(p\, \frac{\delta x}{\delta b}\right)db. \tag{6.ix}$$

The first term of (6.ix) is developed as follows:

$$\frac{\delta}{\delta x}\left(p\, \frac{\delta x}{\delta b}\right)dx = \left[p\, \frac{\delta}{\delta x}\left(\frac{\delta x}{\delta b}\right) + \frac{\delta x}{\delta b}\frac{\delta p}{\delta x}\right]dx = \frac{\delta x}{\delta b}\, dp = p_b\, \frac{dp}{p} = -p_b\, \frac{dx}{x\eta}.$$

(To justify the second step, we recall that $\delta\,(\delta x/\delta b)\,/\delta x$ vanishes, since $\delta x/\delta b$ is not a function of x. The third and fourth steps apply v.m.p. and output demand elasticity definitions, in that order.)

The other right-side terms of (6.ix) are combined, with p constant:

$$p\left[\frac{\delta}{\delta a}\left(\frac{\delta x}{\delta b}\, da\right) + \frac{\delta}{\delta b}\left(\frac{\delta x}{\delta b}\, db\right)\right]$$

$$= p\left(\frac{\delta^2 x}{\delta a\delta b}\, da + \frac{\delta^2 x}{\delta b^2}\, db\right) = p\, \frac{\delta^2 x}{\delta a\delta b}\left(da - \frac{a}{b}\, db\right).$$

(The last step uses [6.v].)

The left-hand side of (6.ix) is, from the equation before (6.ix), $p_b db/be$. Multiply both sides of (6.ix), in their new guises, by xp/p_b and rewrite completely:

$$\frac{xp\, db}{be} = \frac{xp^2}{p_b}\frac{\delta^2 x}{\delta a\delta b}\left(da - \frac{a}{b}\, db\right) - \frac{p\, dx}{\eta} \tag{6.x}$$

ix. The motivation for the development of (6.x) was to permit introduction of the elasticity of substitution σ and the share ratio k (for input a) into our derivation of the input demand elasticity E (also for a). This we can now accomplish, combining the definitions of σ and of v.m.p. for the two inputs:

$$\sigma = \frac{p_a\, p_b}{xp^2\, \dfrac{\delta^2 x}{\delta a\delta b}}, \qquad \text{whence} \qquad \frac{xp^2}{p_b}\frac{\delta^2 x}{\delta a\delta b} = \frac{p_a}{\sigma}.$$

Using this equation, collect terms in db from (6.x) :

$$\frac{p\, dx}{\eta} = \frac{p_a\, da}{\sigma} - \left(\frac{ap_a}{b\sigma} + \frac{xp}{be}\right)db$$

but:

$$\frac{ap_a}{b\sigma} = \frac{ap_a}{bp_b}\frac{p_b}{\sigma} = \frac{k}{1-k}\frac{p_b}{\sigma} \quad \text{and} \quad \frac{xp}{be} = \frac{xp}{bp_b}\frac{p_b}{e} = \frac{1}{1-k}\frac{p_b}{e}.$$

After these modifications, (6.x) becomes:

$$\frac{p\,dx}{\eta} = \frac{p_a}{\sigma}\,da - \frac{p_b}{1-k}\left(\frac{1}{e} + \frac{k}{\sigma}\right). \qquad (6.\text{xi})$$

x.   Collecting in matrix form (6.vi, 6.viii, and 6.xi), we obtain the matrix equation:

$$
\begin{vmatrix}
p & -p_a & -p_b \\
 & & p_b/e \\
p/\eta & -p_a/E & \\
p/\eta & -p_a/\sigma & \dfrac{p_b}{1-k}\left(\dfrac{1}{e}+\dfrac{k}{\sigma}\right)
\end{vmatrix}
\begin{vmatrix} dx \\ da \\ db \end{vmatrix}
=
\begin{vmatrix} 0 \\ 0 \\ 0 \end{vmatrix}
$$

This has a nontrivial solution (other than 0, 0, 0) in dx, da, and db only if the determinant of the left-side matrix is zero. Simplifying the determinant of the matrix through division by the three price terms $(p, -p_a, p_b)$ this condition may be written:

$$
\begin{vmatrix}
1 & 1 & -1 \\
1/\eta & 1/E & 1/e \\
1/\eta & 1/\sigma & \dfrac{1}{1-k}\left(\dfrac{1}{e}+\dfrac{k}{\sigma}\right)
\end{vmatrix}
= 0
$$

Develop this determinant by the minors of the first row:

$$\left(\frac{\sigma + ek}{Ee\sigma\,(1-k)} - \frac{1}{e\sigma}\right) + \left(\frac{1}{e\eta} - \frac{\sigma + ek}{\eta e\sigma\,(1-k)}\right) + \left(\frac{1}{E\eta} - \frac{1}{\eta\sigma}\right) = 0.$$

Multiply by the common denominator $[E\eta e\sigma\,(1-k)]$ and regroup, factoring out terms in E:

$$E[\,(1-k)\,(\sigma-\eta-e) - (\sigma+ek)\,] = -[\,ke\,(\eta-\sigma) + \sigma\,(e+\eta)\,].$$

Only minor simplifications are required in solving for E and obtaining Hicks' formula (6.14):

$$E = \frac{\sigma\,(e+\eta) + ke\,(\eta-\sigma)}{(e+\eta) - k\,(\eta-\sigma)} \qquad (6.14)$$

xi.   To test Marshall's four rules, differentiate (6.14) partially with respect to σ, η, k, and e in that order. If the rules hold, all derivatives should be positive. We let the denominator of (6.14) be y, and take all elasticities positive, as well as the share ratios k and $1\text{-}k$:

$$\frac{\delta E}{\delta \sigma} = \frac{1}{y^2}\,(1-k)\,(e+\eta)^2 \qquad\qquad > 0$$

$$\frac{\delta E}{\delta \eta} = \frac{1}{y^2}\,k\,(e+\sigma)^2 \qquad\qquad > 0$$

$$\frac{\delta E}{\delta k} = \frac{1}{y^2} (e + \eta) (e + \sigma) (\eta - \sigma) > 0 \quad \text{for } \eta > \sigma$$

$$\frac{\delta E}{\delta e} = \frac{1}{y^2} k (1 - k) (\eta - \sigma)^2 \qquad > 0$$

This bears out the first, second, and fourth of Marshall's laws, but apparently denies "the importance of being unimportant" when $\sigma > \eta$.

xii. Other interrelations can also be derived between the coefficients of (6.14). A perplexing extension involves relative shares and the elasticity of substitution. (In the two-input case, the share of each input appears higher, the higher the elasticity of substitution between it and the other input!)

In the homogeneity range of production functions:

$$x = F(a, b) = aF(1, b/a) = a f \left(\frac{b}{a} \right) = a f(\rho).$$

The marginal productivities of the two inputs are:

$$\frac{\delta x}{\delta a} = f \left(\frac{b}{a} \right) + a \frac{\delta}{\delta a} f \left(\frac{b}{a} \right) = f \left(\frac{b}{a} \right) - \frac{ab}{a^2} \frac{df (b/a)}{d (b/a)} = f(\rho) - \rho f'(\rho)$$

$$\frac{\delta x}{\delta b} = f'(\rho).$$

The complementarity inter-relation is:

$$\frac{\delta^2 x}{\delta a \delta b} = \frac{\delta}{\delta a} \left(\frac{\delta x}{\delta b} \right) = \frac{\delta f'(\rho)}{\delta a} = f''(\rho) \frac{\delta \rho}{\delta a} = -\frac{b}{a^2} f''(\rho) = -\frac{\rho}{a} f''(\rho).$$

The relative share of a, with p set at unity, is:

$$k = 1 - \frac{b \, \delta x / \delta b}{x} = 1 - \frac{b f'(\rho)}{a f(\rho)} = 1 - \frac{\rho f'(\rho)}{f(\rho)}.$$

The elasticity of substitution may now be rewritten in terms of ρ:

$$\sigma = \frac{(\delta x / \delta b) (\delta x / \delta a)}{x \, \delta^2 x / \delta a \delta b} = -\frac{f'(\rho) [f(\rho) - \rho f'(\rho)]}{a f(\rho) [\rho f''(\rho) / a]} = -\frac{f'(\rho) \left[1 - \dfrac{\rho f'(\rho)}{f(\rho)} \right]}{\rho f''(\rho)}$$

$$\sigma = -\frac{k f'(\rho)}{\rho f''(\rho)}$$

from which:

$$k = -\frac{\sigma \rho f''(\rho)}{f'(\rho)} \quad \text{and} \quad \frac{\delta k}{\delta \sigma} = -\frac{\rho f''(\rho)}{f'(\rho)}. \tag{6.xii}$$

Both these expressions are positive, if we have positive marginal productivities and diminishing returns to the capital-labor ratio ρ.[2]

2. For this derivation, see Hugh Rose, "Unemployment in a Theory of Growth," *Int. Econ. Rev.* (September 1966), p. 262, equation (8).

But (6.xii) proves too much, and involves us in contradictions. Since neither a nor b enters (6.xii) explicitly, does not the relative share of b also seem to rise with σ, although the two shares must not rise simultaneously? Indeed, a parallel development in terms of b begins with:

$$x = b \, \phi \, (1/\rho) \qquad \text{rather than} \qquad x = a \, f \, (\rho) \, .$$

The resulting equivalent of (6.xii) is:

$$1 - k = -\frac{(\sigma/\rho) \, \phi'' \, (1/\rho)}{\phi' \, (1/\rho)} \, , \qquad \text{or} \qquad k = \frac{\phi' \, (1/\rho) \, + \, (\sigma/\rho) \, \phi'' \, (1/\rho)}{\phi' \, (1/\rho)}$$

with $\delta (1 - k) / \delta \sigma$ positive and $\delta k / \delta \sigma$ negative! Since $af(\rho)$ and $b\phi (1/\rho)$ are equally legitimate equivalents of $F(a, b)$, we seem to be up a blind alley. To put the problem differently, k does not seem to be a single-valued function of σ.

xiii.   To avoid this blind alley, we work with the two shares k and 1-k, or rather with their ratio z. (We need no longer put homogeneity restrictions on the production function.) Unlike k, z is related unequivocally to σ:

$$\frac{ap_a}{bp_b} = \frac{a/b}{p_b/p_a} = \frac{k}{1 - k} = z \, .$$

To show how k, the share of a, changes with the employment ratio a/b $(= 1/p)$, when the input price ratio p_b/p_a is functionally related to a/b, we write:

$$\frac{dk}{d \, (a/b)} = \frac{dz}{d \, (a/b)} \Big/ \frac{dz}{dk} \tag{6.xiii}$$

and evaluate the right side of (6.xiii).

Taking account of the functional relationship between a/b and $p_b p_a$:

$$\frac{dz}{d \, (a/b)} = \frac{\delta z}{\delta \, (a/b)} + \frac{\delta z}{\delta \, (p_b/p_a)} \frac{d \, (p_b/p_a)}{d \, (a/b)}$$

$$= \frac{1}{p_b/p_a} - \left[\frac{a/b}{(p_b/p_a)^2} \frac{d \, (p_b/p_a)}{d \, (a/b)} \right] . \tag{6.xiv}$$

Now turn to a general definition of the elasticity of substitution:

$$\sigma = \frac{d \, (a/b)}{a/b} \Big/ \frac{d \, (p_b/p_a)}{p_b/p_a} = \frac{d \, (a/b)}{d \, (p_b/p_a)} \cdot \frac{1}{z} \, .$$

By analogy with ordinary marginal analysis, and thinking of $dz/d \, (a/b)$ as a marginal share function, introduce $1/\sigma$ (which equals $\{[d \, (p_b/p_a) / (p_b/p_a)] \div [d \, (a/b)]/ (a/b)]\}$ into (6.xiv):

$$\frac{dz}{d \, (a/b)} = \frac{1}{p_b/p_a} \left(1 - \frac{1}{\sigma} \right) = \frac{p_a}{p_b} \left(\frac{\sigma - 1}{\sigma} \right) .$$

The other derivative of (6.xiii) is evaluated directly:

$$\frac{dz}{dk} = \frac{d}{dk}\left(\frac{k}{1-k}\right) = \frac{1}{(1-k)^2}.$$

Substitute these solutions in (6.xiii):

$$\frac{dk}{d(a/b)} = \frac{(1-k)^2 (p_a/p_b) (\sigma - 1)}{\sigma}. \tag{6.xv}$$

Convert to an elasticity $Ek/E(a/b)$, remembering that $(a/b)(p_a/p_b) = k/(1-k)$:

$$\frac{Ek}{E(a/b)} = \frac{dk}{d(a/b)}\frac{a/b}{k} = \frac{(1-k)(\sigma - 1)}{\sigma}. \tag{6.xvi}$$

Both (6.xv) and (6.xvi) vanish when the elasticity of substitution is unitary, confirming our previous conclusion that a unit value of σ implies constancy of relative shares. When σ takes on other values, however, these expressions do not vary greatly from zero, particularly if $\sigma > 1$. Differentiate (6.xv–6.xvi) with respect to σ; the respective results are:

$$\frac{p_a}{p_b}\left[\frac{(1-k)}{\sigma}\right]^2 \quad \text{and} \quad \frac{1-k}{\sigma^2}.$$

These values are small for large relative shares (k close to unity) and for large values of the elasticity of substitution ($\sigma > 1$). These results help to explain the relative insensitivity of input shares to the elasticity of substitution.[3]

---

3. This argument rephrases Bronfenbrenner, "A Note on Relative Shares and the Elasticity of Substitution," *J.P.E.* (June 1960), pp. 284 f.; and Solow, "Relative Income Shares in Fact and Theory," *op. cit.*, pp. 629 f. Bronfenbrenner presents the results graphically, with units of a and b chosen to equalize the initial input prices.

CHAPTER SEVEN

The Antimarginalist
Backlash

This chapter retraces ground covered by Sir Dennis Robertson's 1931 essay on "Wage-Grumbles."[1] There Robertson was considering not the dissatisfaction of workers with their low incomes, but the dissatisfaction of their ideological spokesmen, to which we should join the bulk of the industrial-relations profession, with the marginalist or neoclassical tradition as applied to wage determination, a tradition that Chapter 6 has obviously followed.

Demand for Inputs versus Wage Theory

1. Marginal productivity analysis, a shorthand term for the theory presented in the last chapter, was developed in the last quarter of the nineteenth century from at least three points of view: (a) as a parallel to the marginal utility analysis of output demand, (b) as a generalization of the Ricardian theory of rent to inputs other than land, and (c) as a theory of wages. We present it only as a theory of input demand;[2] its wage-theory

1. D. H. Robertson, "Wage-Grumbles," *Readings*, no. 12. For a corresponding, but more advanced and analytical, introduction to "interest-grumbles," see G. C. Harcourt, "Some Cambridge Controversies in the Theory of Capital," *J.E.L.* (June 1969) . *op. cit.*

2. An intermediate stage is the so-called discounted marginal productivity theory of demand for land and labor (but not capital) inputs. The theory begins with the fact that inputs are commonly paid before their outputs are sold. Then, distinguishing

claims have not proved tenable. The modern formulation (theory of input demand) is at once more general and less useful than the initial formulation (theory of wages).

The modern form is more general because it applies not only to labor but also to land and capital.[3] It is less useful because, being limited to the demand side, it can serve as a theory of input prices (including wage rates) only in the extreme case of completely inelastic supply. This was the case the neoclassicals had in mind in presenting marginal productivity as wage theory, with a given stock of labor offering a given stock of effort at any positive wage rate. As is now recognized quite generally, this is a very special case, especially when burdened further with the assumption of full employment.

Moreover, the $p_a, p_b, \ldots$ of Chapter 6 are employer's costs per unit of $a, b, \ldots$. They may differ, sometimes sharply, from the returns per unit of $a, b, \ldots$ as direct wages, interest, or rent. We can indicate, for a labor input, certain causes of divergence that do not involve "exploitation" in the sense of Chapter 8, section 10 below. Input cost exceeds input remuneration when facilities on the job, or "fringe benefits" anywhere, are supplied to workers in addition to wages. Cost also exceeds remuneration in a regime of wage or payroll taxes; remuneration exceeds cost in a regime of wage or payroll subsidies. A more sophisticated sort of divergence is introduced, given cyclical or random fluctuations in a firm's employment, by the bookkeeping and other transfer costs of altering the labor force. This divergence can be explored in depth by the methods of inventory theory;[4] it causes purely competitive wage rates to fall systematically below the value of marginal product (v.m.p.) in seasonal or cyclical industries.

---

between "original factors" of land and labor, and other inputs that apply the original ones indirectly, the theory argues that the former are paid their m.v.p. discounted for futurity, while capital receives the discount factor determined in quite other grounds. (In this theory, capital has no productivity, other than those of the land and labor which it applies indirectly and which have already been paid.) A history and criticism of this view is found in Earl Rolph, "The Discounted Marginal Productivity Doctrine," *Readings*, no. 15.

We should ourselves modify the argument of Chapter 6 for futurity complications only to the extent of specifying p (the output price) in connection with the demand for all inputs indiscriminately, as the price as of the time the inputs are paid, *i.e.*, the anticipated market price discounted for futurity and perhaps uncertainty.

3. The application to capital is to the rent of capital goods, which is the numerator of the rate (or rates) of interest, the denominators being the values of the capital goods themselves. When the denominators themselves vary with the passage of time, with the rate of use of the capital services, or with interest rates, a theory of rent on capital may not be an adequate or complete theory of interest.

4. Solow, "Distribution in the Long and Short Run," in Marchal and Ducros, *The Distribution of National Income* (London: Macmillan, 1968), pp. 462–466.

Neoclassical Associations

2.   Even as a theory of input demand, and more specifically of demand for labor inputs, and however qualified, "marginalism" finds itself opposed viscerally and ideologically on two primary grounds. These are its association with a theory that unemployment is primarily or exclusively remediable by money wage and real wage reductions, and its implication that marginal productivity represents what workers and other input suppliers deserve, in some ethical sense.

Leaving ethical issues to section 17 of this chapter, two points may be made here. One is a general warning against "guilt by association." The marginal productivity theory of input demand and the high-wage theory of unemployment, however closely associated in the public mind and however often held or rejected together by economists, are by no means necessarily connected. Wage cuts to remedy unemployment were recommended and applied long before marginal productivity was ever heard of; Lord Keynes himself accepted a marginalist theory of the demand for labor, but concentrated his attention on ways and means of shifting it to the right. The sets of marginal economists and depression wage-cutters intersect but are not identical, either with each other or with a third set called "neoclassical economists."

3.   Part of our problem in relating marginal productivity to employment theory is the fashionable distinction between microeconomics and macroeconomics; or rather, with the difficulty of unifying them in workable fashion by methods less specialized than computer simulation. In Chapter 6, and for several chapters to come, we are moving in the microeconomy (the theory of the consumer, the firm, the industry, and so on), with individual input prices and employments determined against a background of constant national income and employment.[5] "Employment" will therefore mean (in these chapters) employment of workers of specific sorts in producing specific goods and services, while "unemployment" will include shifts to employment in other occupations, presumably less desirable to the workers affected. It should not surprise us if additional—but hopefully, not inconsistent—modifications are necessary when we move to the macroeconomy, with its relative unconcern for the precise composition of the aggregates of production, employment, and price levels with which it deals.

Pure Competition and Competitive Equilibrium

4.   Under this head we begin with two sets of criticisms, mutually contradictory and therefore difficult to meet simultaneously. One strain limits

5. The level of employment may be, but need not be, "full employment."

the theory to the special case of pure (or perfect) competition.[6] This objection is valid as against the position presented in Chapter 6, although its quantitative significance is questionable. The next chapter is devoted to modifications for cases of imperfect competition; subsequently, in discussing collective bargaining (Chapter 10), we shall recognize the power of unions to force employers off their free-market demand functions for labor by all-or-none bargaining and approaches thereto.

The second strain of criticism is inconsistent with the first, and represents an elementary misunderstanding of marginal productivity analysis. As we have already mentioned (Chapter 6, section 12), it represents marginalism as making the employer a pure monopoly buyer (monopsonist) who adjusts wage rates arbitrarily for a given employment but, out of the goodness of his heart, never lowers them below v.m.p.! From this misunderstanding have been derived important and influential bargaining and indeterminacy theories, which see wages varying between the subsistence level at the lower end and v.m.p. at the upper end of an interval, the precise point depending on bargaining considerations. The "marginalism" attacked by this theory is, of course, nonsense; more important, it is also a caricature.

5.   A deeper criticism, which may be regarded as anticipating contemporary "Keynesian" distribution theory, stresses the indeterminacy of wages in a different sense. What Dobb,[7] for example, means by indeterminacy is not only the penumbra of incomplete information and fringe benefits but also doubt as to the stability of competitive equilibrium, both in the large and the small. What shall we say if, for example, a rise in wages is reflected (after some lag) in a higher v.m.p. of workers whose health, strength, or morale have been raised by higher incomes? Or if redistribution against property owners has the eventual effect of forcing a decrease in their luxury consumption, so that they raise their saving and investment? The productivity of workers might then rise by the availability of additional complementary capital instruments, with no decline required in employment.[8]

6. Under pure competition (often called "atomistic"), no buyer or seller can affect any price by changing the amounts of his own purchases or sales, and there is no collusion between or among buyers and sellers. If, in addition, all traded goods and services are homogeneous at least within standardized grades, if "maximizing behavior" is carried on consistently with stable and continuous profit, utility, and related functions, and if all relevant information about *existing* prices and qualities is known by all market participants with certainty, we have perfect competition. (Perfect forecasting of *future* prices and qualities, by all participants is not required. We do, however, need "rational expectations," whose mean values converge to actual results.)

7. Maurice Dobb, "A Sceptical View of the Theory of Wages," *Ec. J.* (December 1929). A more elementary presentation may be found in Dobb's Cambridge Economic Handbook, *Wages* (London: Nisbet, 1928), chs. 4 and 5.

8. It is this aspect of Dobb's thinking that foreshadows Nicholas Kaldor's aggregative theory of distribution. (See Chapter 16, sections 32–36, below.)

The argument of Chapter 6, indeed, concealed elements of circularity at the aggregate level, and our original equilibrium position may have been neutral, if not positively unstable.[9]

Downward-Sloping Input Demand Functions

6.   At the microeconomic level of the individual firm, union spokesmen and labor intellectuals resent bitterly the marginalist conclusion that the demand for any type of labor input might slope downward. This proposition implies that whatever wage gains they achieve over and above the competitive labor market involve some cost in unemployment, at least within the plants and occupations where the gains are made. It is therefore not so, alternatively, if it is so, its only implication is that something must be done to "safeguard our [labor-using] technology."

Still postponing the complications of imperfect competition and all-or-none bargaining, let us consider the positive (as distinguished from the normative) arguments offered against the downward-sloping input demand function and its labor-market implications.

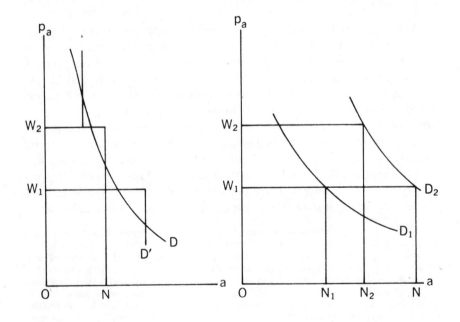

Figure 7.1

9. A "neutral equilibrium" may be stable at any point within a range or area.

The two simplest arguments contain elements of truth. They may be dealt with together by the assistance of Figure 7.1. (a) The input demand function, which we have treated as smooth and continuous, may be a broken or a step function, particularly for the individual firm in the short run, as per a well-known essay by Stigler.[10] Thus, in the left panel of Figure 7.1, p_a may take on any level between W_1 and W_2 while employment remains at N, since the smooth curve D is no more than a convenient approximation to the step function D', which represents the short-run state of affairs. (b) In a growing firm or industry (or, for that matter, economy), the employment loss may be entirely hypothetical and unobserved, as in the right panel of Figure 7.1. In this diagram, employment rises from N_1 to N_2 despite the wage rise from W_1 to W_2, because the demand for labor has concurrently shifted from D_1 to D_2. The disemployment due to the wage increase is the unobservable quantity N_2N.

Next, if visible reduction in employment is decided upon, it may be shifted to future "generations" so that no worker need lose his post. Reduction usually takes the initial form of not replacing workers who quit or retire. (This method is sometimes called "A and P," meaning not the Atlantic and Pacific Tea Company but "attrition and pregnancy."[11]) Stronger methods are sometimes prohibited by a regime of job tenure or lifetime employment guarantees, whether legislative or conventional.

Should actual dismissals be necessary, they may be concentrated on a minority of new employees (with low seniority), temporary employees, apprentices, foreigners, minority groups, or the employees of subcontractors. To the great bulk of the wage-raising union's membership, the (partial) demand function for their particular services, as seen by themselves, is completely inelastic. Should it be decided to spread the work rather than penalize the minority (or support this minority from union funds), the membership as a whole becomes more conscious of the economics of the demand for labor services.

Information, Motivation, and Timing

7. The major thrust of antimarginalist theories of input demand is not, however, any crude misconception or misinterpretation of the marginalist position. It lies in skeptical doubt that employers have either the informa-

---

10. George J. Stigler, "Production and Distribution in the Short Run," *Readings,* no. 6.

11. Unions' motives for objecting even to "A and P" employment reductions may range from considerations of the amount of dues collected to the nepotistic interests of members in employment for relatives and friends, and the fear that a local's picket lines may not be honored by other unions if it falls below a critical minimum size.

tion or the motivation to approximate the neo-classical economist's "irrational passion for dispassionate rationality" with sufficient closeness and single-mindedness to make the analysis realistic or useful. Doubt also exists about the calendar time period in which these reactions are supposed to occur.

As regards information first of all, it is commonly asserted that neither employer or employee knows the v.m.p. of any sort of labor.[12] Only the employer's knowledge, however, concerns us here; v.m.p. is a demand-side phenomenon, and the knowledge of the employee, if important at all, is a supply-side one.

8.   There are a number of special cases, involving what are called *limitational* inputs, in which v.m.p. is indeed irrelevant or indeterminate. Such cases may arise from either technical considerations (fixed coefficients of production) or social ones (including the working rules of individual enterprises). Limitational conditions of input demand, which have been taken as typical by many economists present and past,[13] are divided into two sorts. Their input-pricing consequences will be considered in Chapter 14 under the heading of "Paretian rents." In one sort of limitational condition, a production coefficient or input-output ratio like a/x is fixed; in a second sort, the ratio between two inputs, like a/b, is the fixed element.

In the first case, with fixed input-output coefficients, we should have, instead of our ordinary production function (6.1);

$$x = ka + F(b, c)$$

with the constant k equal to the marginal productivity of a, but having no direct connection with the demand for a. Given the prices and productivities of the substitutional inputs b and c, the employer determines a tentative optimal output of x and then demands either x/k of a or none at all (depending on the prices of x and a). There is no direct or immediate entrance of the marginal productivity k into the stair-step demand function for a.

In the second limitational case, there are fixed "input-input" coefficients like $b/a = k$ (where k is a constant differing from the k of the last paragraph). It may become impossible for the employer to estimate sep-

---

12. The late Edwin E. Witte, nearing the end of a long and useful lifetime as mediator and arbitrator of labor disputes, told the writer in the mid-1950's that no form of marginal analysis had ever been raised by either employer or employee representatives in any proceeding in which he had participated.

13. For a historical account, consult Stigler, *Production and Distribution Theories* (New York: Macmillan, 1941), ch. 12. In contemporary economics, input-output and linear programming writers, as well as institutionalists in the Veblen tradition, tend to assume fixed coefficients in the short period.

arate marginal productivities for a and b. He must hire only the composite (one unit of a *plus* k units of b) and can estimate only the productivity of that composite.

9. Even in the general case of substitutional inputs, the marginal productivity $\delta x/\delta a$ is a mathematical abstraction, to which the observable dx/da is often a poor approximation. We have

$$\frac{dx}{da} = \frac{\delta x}{\delta a} + \frac{\delta x}{\delta b}\frac{db}{da} + \frac{\delta x}{\delta c}\frac{dc}{da} \tag{7.1}$$

and it is seldom practical or efficient to hold inputs b, c, . . . constant while a is being varied. So how, the critics ask, can the marginal productivity of a be determined?

Production functions like (6.1) can ideally be estimated, of course, and derivatives taken, but the added precision and accuracy of this process is not yet ordinarily considered an adequate justification for the expense involved in making the estimate and keeping it up to date. A crude approximation is, however, available, using (7.1) Let $\bar{x}$, $\bar{a}$, $\bar{b}$, $\bar{c}$ be the mean values of x, a, b, c as observed at n different points in time. Let Δx_i, Δa_i, Δb_i, Δc_i represent deviations of the i-th observations of x, a, b, c from their respective means. Then we have, to a first approximation (the more accurate, the more closely the deviations approximate the differentials of the calculus):

$$\frac{\Delta x_1}{\Delta a_1} = \frac{\delta x}{\delta a} + \frac{\delta x}{\delta b}\frac{\Delta b_1}{\Delta a_1} + \frac{\delta x}{\delta c}\frac{\Delta c_1}{\Delta a_1}$$

$$\cdot \quad \cdot \quad \cdot \quad \cdot \quad \cdot \quad \cdot \quad \cdot \quad \cdot$$

$$\frac{\Delta x_n}{\Delta a_n} = \frac{\delta x}{\delta a} + \frac{\delta x}{\delta b}\frac{\Delta b_n}{\Delta a_n} + \frac{\delta x}{\delta c}\frac{\Delta c_n}{\Delta a_n}.$$

(The arguments $\Delta x_i/\Delta a_i$, $\Delta b_i/\Delta a_i$, etc. are computed from observed values.) The n equations above, one for each observation (lagged if necessary), can be solved for the unknown marginal productivities (partial derivatives) by the method of least squares. The normal equations in a simple three-input case are:

$$\Sigma\left(\frac{\Delta x_i}{\Delta a_i}\right) = n\frac{\delta x}{\delta a} + \Sigma\left(\frac{\Delta b_i}{\Delta a_i}\right)\frac{\delta x}{\delta b} + \Sigma\left(\frac{\Delta c_i}{\Delta a_i}\right)\frac{\delta x}{\delta c}$$

$$\Sigma\left(\frac{\Delta x_i}{\Delta a_i}\right)\left(\frac{\Delta b_i}{\Delta a_i}\right) = \Sigma\left(\frac{\Delta b_i}{\Delta a_i}\right)\frac{\delta x}{\delta a} + \Sigma\left(\frac{\Delta b_i}{\Delta a_i}\right)^2\frac{\delta x}{\delta b} + \Sigma\left(\frac{\Delta c_i}{\Delta a_i}\right)\left(\frac{\Delta b_i}{\Delta a_i}\right)\frac{\delta x}{\delta c}$$

$$\Sigma\left(\frac{\Delta x_i}{\Delta a_i}\right)\left(\frac{\Delta c_i}{\Delta a_i}\right) = \Sigma\left(\frac{\Delta c_i}{\Delta a_i}\right)\frac{\delta x}{\delta a} + \Sigma\left(\frac{\Delta b_i}{\Delta a_i}\right)\left(\frac{\Delta c_i}{\Delta a_i}\right)\frac{\delta x}{\delta b} + \Sigma\left(\frac{\Delta c_i}{\Delta a_i}\right)^2\frac{\delta x}{\delta c}$$

If estimation processes, too, are impracticably difficult, expensive, or inaccurate, the critic should recall that, with output and input prices

given, the efficiency-minded employers need only estimate the employment of a for which the quantity $(\delta x/\delta a) - (p_a/p)$ shifts from positive
to negative, that is, for which v.m.p. shifts from above to below input
price. He need not know any extended portion of the marginal productivity function.

10.   But, in fact, how efficiency-minded *are* employers? When "the employer" is an organization, corporate or otherwise, the question is particularly moot as to why it should be guided by productivity considerations
in demanding inputs, since the interests of individual members of the
organization vary. If the employer is a governmental agency, a philanthropic institution, a producers' cooperative, or some other body relatively disinterested in profit, what external or internal controls force efficiency in the economic sense rather than in some other sense, or in no
sense at all?[14] Indeed, the organization's stated purpose may be quite inconsistent with efficiency in practice—the maximization of physical output
(or its growth rate), by a factory, regardless of cost; of employment, by a
trade union or a public-works relief agency; of innovative progress, by a
research laboratory; of artistic quality, by an orchestra or *atelier*.[15] Even
in atomistic private enterprise, where marginalism is apparently decreed
by profit-maximizing considerations, questions are raised about the universal single-mindedness of the profit motive, and we speak of business
organizations as possessing "multiple goals," of which profit is *primus*
(perhaps even *secundus* or *tertius*) *inter pares?*

Focusing on the market for labor inputs, a company has to "live with"
its workers, organized or unorganized, in greater intimacy or amity than
with most of its customers, most of its stockholders, with "society," or with
other beneficiaries of efficiency expertise. It is frequently under legal or
social pressures, amounting sometimes to codetermination with employee
representatives, to increase employment or at least not to dismiss redun-
dant workers. Bookkeeping and other costs are involved in increasing or
decreasing staff.

There are also, within the organization itself, numerous "empire build-

14. It is, of course, true that these bodies, whatever their stated goals, are influenced
to varying degrees in their wage rates and hiring practices by the business firms with
whom they compete for staff.

15. We define efficiency, meaning economic efficiency, indifferently in the senses of
maximizing output at given cost and minimizing cost for a given output. These dual
criteria yield the same results if production functions, input prices, and output prices
are given, although not for comparing the efficiency of different enterprises with different production functions in different markets. For the single competitive enterprise,
economically efficient results differ from those of the competitive market only when
nonmarket prices—sometimes called "shadow prices"—are used in efficiency calculations
to express some social priority or to adjust for "externalities."

ers," including personnel managers and other intermediate bosses, whose comfort and status depend on maximizing the number and the paper qualifications of their subordinates and, in some cultures, on the number of relatives by blood or marriage whom they can add to the payroll. A common question on application forms for executive positions is "How many (and how well-qualified) people did you supervise in your previous employment?" At the other extreme, there exist bitterly antilabor and antiunion managements that accelerate automation at the expense of short-run profits to keep the remaining workers cowed and well-behaved. There are, in addition, a number of routines and rules of thumb in every organization, which govern employment and staffing practices and oper- ate to make inputs limitational that outside observers would consider quite substitutional.

These and similar phenomena have been summarized by psychologists and organization theorists under the rubric of "multiple goals" and "as- piration levels."[16] If an organization with multiple goals is satisfied with its profits, its size (measured in one or more of several ways, from book value to market share) , its growth rate, its technical advancement, its out- put quality, its public "image," and so on, it will tend to keep on doing or extrapolating whatever it has been doing in the recent past, preferring a quiet life to "rocking the boat" by resorting to efficient profit-maximiz- ing. Its input demands, specifically, will be less elastic than marginalist theory implies that they should be; labor is by no means the only input to take on the economic status of a "quasi-fixed factor" in Oi's sense.[17] Only insofar as its aspirations are raised or unsatisfied,[18] will there be the sort of "search" or rethinking that leads to marginalist outcomes. Even here, if the firm's profit position is satisfactory but other goals present problems, the adjustment may be away from marginalist solutions rather than toward them.

We conclude tentatively that the applicability of marginal productivity analysis to input demand is limited largely to the pirvate sector, although development of Lange–Lerner–Liberman "competitive socialism" and cost-benefit analysis may extend its future importance within public and semipublic bodies as well. Also, within the private sector, its applicability within individual firms may be significantly attenuated by nonprofit and

16. Compare Richard M. Cyert and James G. March, *A Behavioral Theory of the Firm* (Englewood Cliffs, N.J.: Prentice-Hall, 1963) , chs. 2 and 3.

17. Walter Y. Oi, "Labor as a Quasi-Fixed Factor," *J.P.E.* (December 1962) .

18. Or, as Melvin Reder reminds us in "A Reconsideration of Marginal Productivity Theory," *ibid.* (October 1947) , pp. 256–259, insofar as the "control" of the dominant managerial or stockholder group is threatened. (Much of the analysis in this section springs originally from Reder's work.)

antiprofit motives. Its overall applicability over time, or in cross-section studies of industries and economics, is a matter of the mutual offset of deviations, as per the law of large numbers; its prima facie validity is no better than its statistical verification.

11.   Verification-falsification problems lead directly into others involving timing. In a well-known questionnaire study. Lester secured reactions from a substantial sample of employers in the southern United States on a number of labor-market issues associated with the reduction of the North-South wage differential.[19] In this context, employers in Lester's sample replied, first, that their demand for labor depended on output rather than on wage rates (implying nothing more than low short-run elasticity of substitution between inputs), and second, that their initial response to wage increases would not be to reduce their scale of production. From these and related responses, Lester called for a complete re-formulation of the microeconomic theory of input demand as applied to labor markets.

Rather than cutting production following a wage increase or a cut in the North-South wage differential (the response of only 4.1 per cent of Lester's questionnaire sample),[20] or installing labor-saving machinery (26.1 per cent) which might also be expected to reduce their employment, 67.8 per cent of Lester's respondents proposed to stress "improved methods and efficiency," "price-product changes," and "increased sales efforts." These, in Lester's interpretation, would maintain both output and employment.

One may cavil, as did Machlup in replying to Lester,[21] about the details of his questionnaire construction. ("Output reduction" has antisocial connotations; Southern employers were particularly sensitive to charges of dependence on substandard wage scales as covers for entrepreneurial inefficiency.) Nevertheless, we need not question the validity and sincerity of the replies Lester received. They relate, however, to the initial "shock effects" of the anticipated wage increase. Seen as initial reactions, there is

19. Richard A. Lester, "Shortcomings of Marginal Analysis for Wage-Employment Problems," *A.E.R.* (March 1946). The North-South wage differential refers to the ratio of Northern to Southern wage rates in the United States for uniform occupations and plant sizes, which has fallen rapidly since 1940 and by 1967 approached unity in many fields covered by nationwide bargaining. (As Lester points out, several British, German, and Australian studies parallel one or more aspects of his own.)

20. *Ibid.*, table III, p. 78.

21. Fritz Machlup, "Marginal Analysis and Empirical Research," *A.E.R.* (September 1946), pp. 536–538, 547–553; the Lester-Machlup dialogue continued (*ibid.*, March 1947), with the participation of George Stigler. Machlup returned to the issue 20 years later in his presidential address to the American Economic Association, "Theories of the Firm: Marginalist, Behavioral, Managerial" (*ibid.*, March 1967).

nothing surprising about them: raising productivity, cutting down waste, raising output prices, and increasing sales effort to make the increases "stick" without cutting sales. Where marginalist adjustments enter the picture is at the next stage, if these initial reactions are inadequate. If efficiency cannot in fact be raised sufficiently to compensate for the wage increase, or if prices cannot be raised sufficiently without reductions in sales, how would the employer react? Would he *still* refrain from reducing output or from substituting machinery for labor? Questions about these "second-order reactions" may be harder to answer than questions about the initial, or first-order, ones. Marginalist theory, however, should be considered in second-order terms. If it can be tested effectively by attitudinal survey research, which Machlup doubts, the surveys should probe further than initial first-order reactions or shock effects.

Ambiguities and Misunderstandings

12. We combine in this catch-all section a number of ambiguities and misunderstandings not elsewhere classified, most of which have enjoyed long if subterranean lives in backlash literature. It has been easy, however unfair, to belabor the unfortunate orthodoxy with nonsense results that it does not claim, and that it need not imply.

Among the oldest such ambiguities has been the confusion of *specific* productivity with *marginal* productivity. According to the specific-productivity interpretation, economists believe that one may isolate specific units of output as having been produced solely by one or another input (land, labor, or capital). Examples of this erroneous interpretation are Bernard Shaw's "When a farmer and his laborers sow and reap a field of wheat, nobody on earth can say how much of the wheat each of them has grown"; and Bertrand Russell's, "Consider a porter on a railway . . . What proportion of the goods carried can be said to represent the produce of his labour? The question is wholly insoluble."[22] A sufficient answer is that marginal and specific productivity are two different notions that are often wrongheadedly confused, and that no qualified economist has maintained a specific-productivity theory of either input demand or input prices.

13. It is also easy to construct numerical examples involving production with increasing marginal productivities of one or another input, or production outside the substitution area in which all marginal productivities are non-negative and to which price-sector employers theoretically confine themselves. The usual purport of these examples is, that marginalism "distributes" more (or less) than is available, or that it maximizes losses

22. These examples are Robertson's (*op. cit.,* p. 225).

rather than profits. The instability cases are excluded in advance by the theory, which does not mean that they cannot occur.

As for unexplained residuals, positive or negative, they may, of course, persist except in the norvana of long-run competitive equilibrium, and their allocation lies outside the purview of marginal theory. Their existence does not, however, invalidate the marginal theory unless they are in fact both large and persistent enough to "swamp" rather than merely supplement it. This is difficult and perhaps impossible to demonstrate outside the arithmetical examples devised for the purpose.

(To construct an infinity of such examples, use a modified Cobb-Douglas function:

$$x = x_0 a^\alpha b^\beta$$

with the sum of α and β positive but close to zero [for large positive residuals] or far above unity [for large negative ones]. A negative α or β will yield negative marginal products of a and b, respectively.)

14.   Another old chestnut springs from the two senses of the term "marginal." In ordinary parlance, a "marginal worker" is one barely qualified for his job—and a "marginal economist" likewise. Ricardo's "margin of cultivation" and his followers' "marginal land" belong to this tradition. It is carried to the extreme in Stephen Leacock's fable of the marginal blacksmith working on marginal land with a marginal horseshoe, hammer, and nails. (To which factor should the product be imputed? The marginal horse dies before the marginal blacksmith makes up his marginal mind!) It is patently unfair to accuse the "conventional wisdom" of basing the demand for average workers on the productivity of marginal ones, as is occasionally done. The criticism has some marginal validity insofar as the grading of inputs is imperfect, and the first units hired are systematically better than average, or the last units worse than average. Neither, of course, does the theory assume, except in first approximations with two or three inputs, that all "labor" or "capital" is homogeneous in any sense, or readily reducible to homogeneity by such devices as "efficiency units."[23]

15.   For our next illustration we return to Lester's critique cited in section 11. Lester is only one of a number of writers who have found it absurd to think of obsolete hand-labor methods being substituted for modern labor-saving machinery whenever wages fall.[24] This absurdity is often

23. The pitfalls of the "efficiency unit" are discussed by Machlup, "On the Meaning of the Marginal Product," *Readings*, no. 8, pp. 160–163.

24. Lester, *op. cit.*, pp. 73 f. When northern plants established lower-wage southern branches, or moved south, they installed the same machinery as in the higher-wage North, or in some cases more modern (more labor-saving) varieties.

real, and it has been careless of economists to speak of labor-capital substitution in terms applicable to replacing steam shovels by wheelbarrows or water buffaloes. More typical are changes in the life span of machines, obsolescent or otherwise, changes in the size of the crews assigned to machines (or the number of machines tended by one worker), or changes in the number of apprentices and helpers to keep up production during absences, "breaks," and so on. An example may be taken from transportation. In the United States, most streetcars, buses, and taxis have one-man crews. Japan, with lower wage rates, uses similar but predominantly older vehicles (with a higher proportion of streetcars), but the two-man crew is the rule in streetcars and buses. India, with still lower wage rates, commonly has a helper accompanying the taxi-driver as well, and keeps its vehicles in use still longer. Also, in low-wage India, the Japanese *jinrikisha* survives, although it no longer pays in Japan except for ceremonial transportation in tourist areas.

16.   At a higher level of complexity are questions of grossness and netness, where, in the presence of considerable ambiguity, we content ourselves with indicating two usages. By the gross marginal product of input *a* in producing output *x,* we have meant $\delta x/\delta a$, and by the net marginal product, the same $\delta x/\delta a$ minus the value of nonpecuniary fringe benefits to the *a*-supplier, marginal hiring costs, etc. In the important case of labor, "marginalism" means adjusting employment so as to equate gross marginal product with the wage rate per period. A more common usage defines gross marginal product as dx/da, and net marginal product as either $\delta x/\delta a$ or

$$\frac{d}{da}\left[x - (bp_b + cp_c)\right] = \frac{dx}{da} - \left(p_b\frac{db}{da} + p_c\frac{dc}{da}\right)$$

which differs from $\delta x/\delta a$ insofar as other input prices depart from their respective v.m.p. An advantage of this system is its usefulness in demonstrating that pure competitive equilibrium maximizes the average net products of all inputs, as it minimizes the average costs of all outputs.[25]

Ethical Implications

17.   One may surmise that hesitancy to accept the positive economics of marginal productivity, or even to give it a fair hearing, arises from dissat-

25. Satisfaction of the adding-up theorem (6.4) may be indicated graphically in the conventional system by equality between the marginal net product of each input with its average net product. In the case of input *a,*

$$\frac{\delta x}{\delta a} = \frac{x - (bp_b + cp_c)}{a}$$

which implies a maximum average net product but not a maximum average gross product.

isfaction with its supposedly reactionary or antiunion ethical implications. If so, such hesitancy rests on a serious misconception. Few, if any, marginalists of stature have followed John Bates Clark's jointure of marginal-productivity economics with Milton's *Paradise Lost* "to justify the ways of God to Man," although, as we shall see in the next chapter, the neoclassical definition of "exploitation" points in the same direction. A more common position, by no means confined to socialists, is set forth by Hahn:[26]

> The socialist . . . is unhappy with the idea that a man poorly endowed physically, intellectually, and socially, should be further penalized by having a low reward geared to his low productivity. "To each according to his Marginal Product" has not been a socialist doctrine.

We assume in this section that the supplier of each input to the private sector of the economy receives that input's v.m.p., no more and no less, or, in other words, that the adding-up theorem is satisfied with no residual. Let us go on to consider what faults an ethical philosopher, with or without a socialist commitment, might find with this outcome.

(a) Quantitatively speaking, the most important fault is the equating of the productivity of *inputs* with the productivity of their *suppliers*. For land and physical capital, this equation begs the questions of private property and its inheritance, and sanctions implicitly whatever institutional arrangements may prevail at the moment. These arrangements have, of course, been subject to both erratic and secular modification. Socialist critics in particular propose to modify them drastically in the direction of reserving the share imputed to land and capital for public use, including as a "public use" transfer payments to workers. For skilled labor or human capital, the problems are less different than they seem at first glance, insofar as the supplier of highly productive technical, professional, or managerial labor has been educated and trained at the expense of his family under conditions of quasi-inheritance, by philanthropic subsidy, or by the state, rather than by his own investment or by "learning by doing" on less skilled jobs.

(b) Productivity is, for marginal theory, productivity to the employer, not necessarily to society. Divergences, called by welfare economists "externalities," may be substantial in either direction. Extreme examples combining a positive marginal productivity to an employer and a negative one to society involve quasi-criminal activities, as when juvenile delinquents are employed by garages to damage the tires of parked automobiles, or hoodlums are employed by cleaning establishments to send

26. Frank Hahn, "The Battle for Better Britain—How and Why Labour Lost It," *Econ. and Pol. Weekly* (August 27, 1966), p. 88.

clothes (with acid capsules in pockets or linings) to price-cutting competitors. An unpatentable innovation, such as the supermarket principle
in retailing, is and example in the opposite direction, with high productivity to the society and zero or negative productivity to the innovator or
his employer (when rivals can employ it more efficiently than the original
user) . A special form of intra-firm externality may occur[27] when the "productivity" justifying top executive salaries results from the added effort of
lower-bracket executives competing for posts rendered extra-glamorous by
their incomes, while the successful incumbents luxuriate in semiretired
recuperation from corporate rat races.

(c) When the marginal productivity function of an input slopes downward, the measured marginal productivity of this input at any time
depends upon supply as well as demand factors—not only the supply of the
input in question, but the supplies of complementary and competitive
inputs as well. The marginal productivity of the graduate engineer depends on the supply of similar engineers, which may be reduced by "raising professional standards" in ways related only tenuously to the jobs he
does. The engineer's productivity depends favorably on the supply of
draftsmen, workmen, and equipment to test and apply his ideas, and it
depends unfavorably on the availability of technicians and others who can
duplicate his expertise without benefit of diploma. The general fall of the
white-collar differential, culminating in its replacement by a blue-collar
one on the American scene, reflects the increasing availability of high
school and junior college education, the increasing severity of female competition in office work, and the decreasing supply of husky young, male,
semiliterate immigrant blue-collar workers with language handicaps. It
reflects no obvious change in the intrinsic merits of clerical and manual
workers, either absolutely or comparatively.

(d) Limiting attention exclusively to the demand side of the input
markets, it is often difficult to associate ethical superiority with the adap-
tation of one's services to the peculiarities of the pattern of demand for
outputs in each particular time and place. The professional matador, possessed of sufficient skill and luck, can look forward to a high income in
Spain—but not in the United States. The professional baseball pitcher,
with parallel qualifications, will be a money-maker in the United States—
but not in Spain. Which of the two specialized athletes "deserves" the
higher income, in any absolute sense?

Again, to return to our engineer, the demand for his services may be
expected to rise and fall with the vigor of the international arms race,
especially when we include such paramilitary rivalries as space explora-

27. Harry Johnson has suggested that this case involves no externality if we measure
salary income on a lifetime rather than a current basis.

tion. This fluctuating pattern of demand gives him a certain perverse economic interest in Doomsday, for which he may compensate by devotion to pacifist causes or, alternatively, rationalize by hawkish foreign policy positions and macabre humor about "peace breaking out." Our problem here is, which level of relative valuation of this engineer's services should we consider as expressing his relative social merit—wartime affluence, disarmament penury, or some cold-war compromise?

(e) We have argued that marginal productivity determines input demands in the private profit-making sector of a mixed economy, but hardly at all in the public or nonprofit sectors. This gives rise to difficult problems of ethical comparison between public- and private-sector workers, particularly when productivity is rising in the profit sector while remuneration elsewhere is restrained by considerations of tradition. An illustration, which aroused the concern of Lady Barbara Wootton, was the equality of her own academic salary at the University of London with the food and other allowances (fringe benefits?) of a child-carrying and fee-earning elephant in the London Zoo.[28] The disaffected soldier, schoolteacher, and civil servant are all disruptive forces in industrial societies, whether their disaffection leads to military fascism, seditious indoctrination of the nation's youth, or large-scale graft and corruption.

(f) We have mentioned several times that the relation between marginal productivity and labor input remuneration may be a circular one, with high remuneration being a cause as well as an effect of high productivity. Our most recent illustration was the intra-firm externality case of paragraph (b) above. At the lower end of the income scale, the inverse relation is primarily a matter of health, strength, and the length of the working life. At higher levels, it involves morale and incentives. More indirectly, we have productivity reactions if the *enjoyment* or *utility* of given incomes is changed, as by the repeal or enactment of sumptuary restrictions on the consumption of either domestic or imported luxuries, by increasing or decreasing the safety of personal property in durable consumption goods, or by increasing or decreasing the range of income-earning investments permitted private individuals.

(g) Finally, the marginal productivity principle is itself subject to numerous modifications when we have the pure-competition assumptions of the last two chapters and consider (in Chapter 8) certain imperfections of competition.

28. Rudolf Klein and David Haworth, "The Secret World of Salaries," *The Observer* (December 4, 1966). (The illustration would be more apt if the elephant's marginal productivity entered more directly into the comparison!)

CHAPTER EIGHT

Imperfect Competition
and Exploitation

An Introductory Paradigm

1. This chapter traces the influence of a few standard departures from pure competition on the demand for productive inputs and, through demand, on their prices. The departures to be considered are on the supply side of output markets (partial or complete monopoly) as well as the demand side of input markets (partial or complete monopsony). Departures on the demand side of output markets will concern us only in passing. We reserve for Chapter 10 one important departure on the supply side of input markets, namely, trade union collective bargaining.

Much of the chapter is devoted to the derivation and adumbration of a single paradigm and its implications, including the theory of exploitation. This paradigm is presented initially in tabular form, as a focus for the discussion. (Figure 8.2 is a diagrammatic depiction.)

In the last three cases, one or more wedges are introduced to make input prices systematically below the value of their marginal products. The basic equality, holding for all four cases, is between the marginal revenue product and marginal input cost (to be explained shortly). In our notation, this general form is, for input a,

$$p \left(1 - \frac{1}{\eta} \right) \frac{\delta x}{\delta a} = p_a \left(1 + \frac{1}{e} \right) \tag{8.1}$$

where η and e are elasticities, respectively, of the demand for the employer's output of x and the supply of input a to the same firm (not to any larger entity). Both elasticities are defined as positive.

189

Table 8.1   Productivity and Price of Inputs under
Alternative Market Conditions

Case	Market Output	Input Market	Value of Marginal Product (v.m.p.)	Marginal Revenue Product (m.r.p.)	Marginal Input Cost (m.i.c.)	Input Price (a.i.c.)	Exploitation Type (Pigou Criterion)
1.	Competi- tive	Competi- tive	=	=	=		None
2.	Monopo- listic	Competi- tive	>	=	=		Monopolistic
3.	Competi- tive	Monopso- nistic	=	=	>		Monopsonistic
4.	Monopo- listic	Monopso- nistic	>	=	>		Double

The purely competitive case 1, leading to equality of v.m.p. (value of marginal product) and input price, has been the subject of Chapter 6. It is the special case of (8.1) with both elasticities infinite, and with no "wedges" between v.m.p. and input price.

The Monopoly Case

2.   The marginal revenue from the production of an additional unit of x, when its sale requires lowering of p (either gross or net of selling costs and quality improvements), is less than p. Denoting marginal revenue by $d(xp)/dx$, we derive a well-known result, deserving the title of fundamental theorem of imperfect competition theory:

$$\frac{d(xp)}{dx} = p + x\frac{dp}{dx} = p\left(1 + \frac{x}{p}\frac{dp}{dx}\right) = p\left(1 - \frac{1}{\eta}\right) \qquad (8.2)$$

interpreting the demand elasticity for the firm's output in the positive sense. The expression $(1/\eta)$ in (8.2), often written μ, is the "Lerner" measure of the firm's monopoly power, varying from zero to infinity.[1]

Brief reflection will show why marginal revenue plays the same role in determining input demand in monopoly cases that output price plays in competitive ones. Maximum profit (revenue minus cost) implies equating cost and revenue at the margin. While input cost remains input price, as under competition, the relevant revenue function now has changed, involving marginal revenue rather than output price along with the marginal (physical) product of the input.

1. A. P. Lerner, "The Concept of Monopoly and the Measurement of Monopoly Power," *Rev. Econ. Stud.* (June 1934) .

We accordingly define *marginal revenue product* (m.r.p.) as marginal product multiplied by marginal revenue. The result is the left side of (8.1).

3. In exploring the relations between m.r.p. and v.m.p. functions, we make use of yet a third function, *marginal value product* (m.v.p.). This is defined for input *a* as

$$\frac{\delta x}{\delta a} \phi (x)$$

where output price is no longer constant as in v.m.p. but is functionally related to output *x* by the demand function $\phi (x)$, with $\phi' (x)$ normally negative. It should not surprise us that these three closely related notions are often confused with each other, since they are identical under pure competition. We repeat all three for ready reference:

$$\text{v.m.p.} = \frac{\delta x}{\delta a} p$$

$$\text{m.r.p.} = \frac{\delta x}{\delta a} p \left(1 - \frac{1}{\eta}\right)$$

$$\text{m.v.p.} = \frac{\delta x}{\delta a} \phi (x)$$

In words, m.v.p. (and m.r.p.) fall for *two* reasons, falling marginal physical product and falling output price. Only falling marginal physical product affects v.m.p.

The *diagrammatic* relations between v.m.p. and m.r.p. are not those of the conventional average and marginal functions (which we have used in Chapter 6, section 27). Rather, they depend upon the degree of the employer's monopoly power. If the employer has little monopoly power, v.m.p. and m.r.p. will be close together, regardless of the slope of v.m.p. If he has a great deal, the two functions will lie further apart.

4. We carry the geometry a step further in Figure 8.1, limiting ourselves to the linear case. For purposes of this digression, the v.m.p. and m.v.p. functions are taken as given, and an m.r.p. function derived. The steep slope of m.v.p., as compared with v.m.p., embodies the output price effects of input (and therefore output) changes. The intersection at *P* indicates the existing level of employment, and thence (indirectly) both output and output price. An additional broken-line function, labelled (v.m.p.)′ is drawn. It is a shadow v.m.p., with output price constant at the highest price at which any output can be sold. The vertical difference between

(v.m.p.)′ and m.v.p., therefore, shows the effect of falling output price on m.v.p., as distinguished from the effect of falling marginal productivity of input *a*. Once this output price effect is isolated, we may treat it like the falling demand function in determining marginal revenue. By the argument of Chapter 6, section 27, the slope of the marginal revenue function is, in the linear case, double that of the corresponding demand or average revenue function. This condition translates here into the *difference* between the slopes of (m.v.p.)′ and m.r.p. being double the difference between the slopes of (m.v.p.)′ and v.m.p. This completes our construction. Note that m.r.p. exceeds v.m.p. to the left of P′. Also, if the initial (intercept) level of output price had been lower, as indicated by (v.m.p.)″, the range of m.r.p. > v.m.p. would have been less.

While m.r.p. lies completely below m.v.p., it crosses v.m.p. at P′, to the left of P. If we now suppose a competitive price lower than the prevailing monopolistic one which m.v.p. is based, a second shadow v.m.p. function, labeled (v.m.p.)‴, intersects m.r.p. at P‴, to the right of P′. If as in this

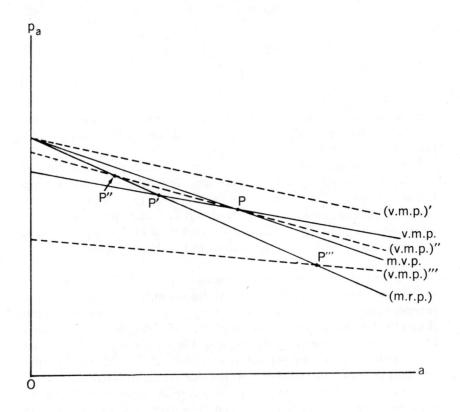

Figure 8.1

illustration, P''' is also to the right of P, we can see how all actual, and some potential, suppliers of input a may gain from the effectiveness of monopoly in the x industry in raising P, despite the implication that monopoly injuries input suppliers which we shall derive from exploitation theories. If a is a labor input, this construction rationalizes the tendency of "labor aristocrats" and "pampered palace slaves" (Lenin's phrase) to collude with employers in establishing or maintaining "orderly" output market conditions.

The Monopsony Case

5. When an employer raises the price of input a against himself by increasing his employment of a, and conversely, the upward-sloping input supply function that faces him may be also called an *average input cost* (a.i.c.) function, with input price equaling average input cost. The a.i.c. function can then be marginalized to obtain a *marginal input cost* (m.i.c.) function along familiar lines, including doubling of the slope if a.i.c. is a straight line. The algebra gives us the right side of (8.1), using the same process that yielded (8.2). We may even write $(1/e)$ in (8.1) as v, and use it as a Lerner-type measure of monopsony power.

The economics underlying this algebra and geometry is the situation of partial or complete monopsony, which is the analogue to monopoly on the demand side of the market. This situation is largely limited, as regards inputs, to local or specialized markets for labor and raw materials. In the case of labor markets, the specialization may be according to function in highly skilled and often highly paid sorts of labor, which are seldom thought of as exploited. Specialization may also be by race, sex, age, nationality, or language in the low-skilled and low-paid sorts more commonly viewed sympathetically.

6. The ordinary calculus of profit maximization suggests for monopsony, with monopoly absent, that while the marginal revenue from employing any input is v.m.p., as under thoroughgoing competition, the marginal cost term is no longer the input price but m.i.c., which now exceeds a.i.c.

If, to end conditions of monopsony, minimum input prices are fixed by some outside force, as is done by minimum wage legislation for unskilled labor, it can be demonstrated that m.i.c. may be lowered over a considerable range of the input supply function at the same time that the input price or a.i.c. is being raised. This is because, for a flattened a.i.c. resulting from minimum-wage legislation, a.i.c. and m.i.c. are brought into equality with each other, whereas previously m.i.c. was higher. It appears to follow that employment, far from falling, may be raised by an adroitly contrived legal minimum wage or collective agreement. Indeed, this proposition is an important one in the theory of both wage regulation and trade unionism. Its applicability is sometimes limited, however, even when monopsony is significant, by the danger that the employer may be driven out of business completely, as when, because of his own irremediable inefficiency or other objective disadvantages, monopsony profit achieved at his workers' expense is the differential between hanging on and outright failure.

Cases Compared

7.   The reader can combine for himself the details of the monopoly and monopsony cases into the form of case 4 in Table 8.1. A graphical comparison of all four tabular cases is presented as Figure 8.2. In each panel of this diagram a focal point F is located at the intersection of m.r.p. and m.i.c. functions, but in cases 3 and 4, including monopsony, p_a is below F.

Also, in these monopsony cases, employment of a may be raised (provided that at the same time monopsony is eliminated but the employer does not quit business) by any rise in input price up to p_a'', with the maximum-employment price being p_a'. (This result is shown for case 3 only.) The effects of monopoly and monopsony are distinguished by different shading patterns.

A case combining monopoly and monopsony elements occurs when the employer's monopoly power relates not to the sale of x but to the sale or rental of food, housing, and other goods to his own employees.[2] This is the "company town" situation, with the employer's monopoly power μ exceeding his monopsony power ν. It will then be profitable for the employer to leave his monopsony power unexercised and to let wages rise to or even above a "competitive" level, letting larger profits on his retailing activities offset smaller profits on his "productive" ones.[3]

Typology of Exploitation

8.   If the term "exploitation" has indeed degenerated from a noun to a noise, as per Bloom's strictures,[4] the noise remains far from chaotic. Three

2. This is one of the curiosa considered in Melvin W. Reder, "Inter-Temporal Relations of Demand and Supply Within the Firm," *Can. Journ. Econ.* (February 1941).

3. Even in competitive cases, it is possible for a wage increase to raise short-run profits for all the enterpreneurs in an industry, if consumer demand for the product is inelastic and nonwage costs are largely fixed or "overhead." This "paradox" was noted by Richard R. Nelson, "Increased Rents from Increased Costs: A Paradox of Value Theory," *J.P.E.* (October 1957). For subsequent discussion and wider implications, see a colloquium on "A Paradox on Profits and Factor Prices," *A.E.R.* (September 1968), participated in by James C. Miller III, Paul B. Trescott, and Paul A. Meyer.

4. Gordon Bloom, "A Reconsideration of the Theory of Exploitation," *Readings,* no. 14, p. 345.

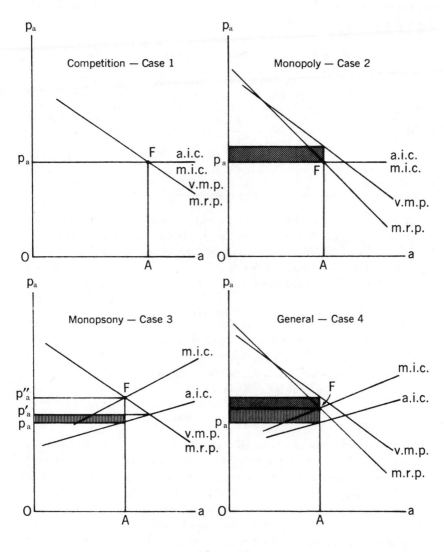

Figure 8.2

main strains (melodies?) are discernible, which we may associate with the names of Marx, Pigou, and Chamberlin. The Pigou definition (used above in Table 8.1) has the strongest claim to orthodoxy, following its development in Joan Robinson's *Imperfect Competition.*[5] To distinguish

5. Joan Robinson, *Economics of Imperfect Competition* (London: Macmillan, 1933), book ix. Prefatory credit is given (*ibid.,* p. v) to R. F. Kahn's contributions in this area.

between the three major exploitation concepts, which should be kept clear if disputants are not to argue at cross-purposes, another simple paradigm is presented as Table 8.2.

Table 8.2.   Alternative Exploitation Concepts

Author	Criterion: Input Price <	Exploitable Inputs	Responsibility Assigned to
Karl Marx	Value of average net product	Labor only	Capitalism, feudalism, or slavery
A. C. Pigou	Value of marginal product	All	Imperfect competition
E. H. Chamberlin	Marginal revenue product	All	Monopsony

9.   The term "exploitation" was applied by Marx to labor inputs as well as natural resources, and its derogatory usage in economic analysis dates from him. The basic idea, however, is at least as old as the Ricardian Socialism of the pre-Marxian generation. One anonymous verse presentation, with stronger ethical overtones than literary merit, is:

> Wages should be the price of goods
>   Yes, wages should be all,
> And we who toil to make the goods
>   Should justly have them all.
>
> But if the price be made of rent
>   Tithes, taxes, profits all,
> Then we who toil to make the goods
>   Shall have—just none at all!

Translated into economics, this is the famous doctrine of *Das Recht auf den vollen Arbeitsertrag* ("the right to the entire product of labor"). Labor is being exploited, in this sense, if the average wage rate is less than net value added per worker, "netness" meaning here, after deduction of depreciation and taxes. Nothing but replacement—no net income whatever—is left for the owners of the other inputs. (The productivity of these inputs is recognized only as that of labor already paid for but applied indirectly.) It is accordingly meaningless, in this framework, to speak of the exploitation of nonlabor inputs apart from the expropriation of private property rights in them. On the contrary, any net income received by their owners constitutes exploitation of labor.

10.   Thanks to its Marxian usage, the concept of "exploitation" of productive inputs, particularly of labor, acquired unfavorable overtones. Apologetic elements are certainly present in the orthodox reformulation

of Pigou's *Economics of Welfare.*[6] This implies that no suppliers of any input are exploited if that input's compensation equals its v.m.p., however low this may be. The orthodox criterion is in one sense broader than the Marxian one, covering nonlabor as well as labor inputs, but at the same time, it is narrower in asserting, by definition, the absence of exploitation under competitive conditions.

With the Pigou criterion, there entered into economic literature the distinction between monopolistic and monopsonistic forms of exploitation. Each form might affect any input, but monopsony is generally thought of as confined in practice to labor and raw material inputs. If A units of an input are supplied (referring back to Figure 8.2), the monopolistic exploitation per unit is (v.m.p. − m.r.p.) and total monopolistic exploitation is this differential multiplied by OA, or the entire diagonally shaded area of cases 2 and 4. Monopsonistic exploitation per unit, on the other hand, is (m.i.c. − a.i.c.); with A units employed, total monopsonistic exploitation is this differential multiplied by OA, or the entire vertically shaded area of cases 3 and 4.

Students may consider this distinction a pedantic quibble. Its principal significance lies in the method by which each type of exploitation can be eliminated, as by a trade union in the case of labor. We have argued that fixation of a minimum or standard wage can replace the lower portion of the supply or a.i.c. function by a horizontal line, with which m.i.c. is identical. It can therefore eliminate monopsonistic exploitation altogether, while possibly raising employment, as from A to B (Fig. 8.3, left panel) if the new wage rate is below AF and if it does not drive the employer out of business.

In the monopolistic exploitation case, however, a rise of p_a (Fig. 8.3, right panel) to p_a', which was the v.m.p. with A employed, will have quite different effects. It shifts the focal point of equality between m.r.p. and m.i.c. from F to F'. Consequently, it contracts employment in the profit-maximizing monopolistic firm to C while retaining an exploitation area (shaded in the diagram) ordinarily smaller than its previous size.[7] To

6. Such apologetic implications are stressed by Gunnar Myrdal, *The Political Element in the Development of Economic Theory*, trans. by Streeten (Cambridge: Harvard University Press, 1954), pp. 10, 127, 130, from a critical Social Democratic viewpoint. Pigou is himself less rigid, distinguishing between "fair" and nonexploitative wages. For example, in *The Economics of Welfare* (4th ad.) (London: Macmillon, 1932), p. 551, he speaks of wages as "unfair, in some place or occupation, because . . . the value of the marginal net product of the labour assembled there . . . [is less than] the value of the marginal net product, and, therefore, the wage rate, of similar labour assembled elsewhere."

7. This diagram includes no adjustments for any output-price increase following upon the input price rise from p_a to p_a'. As it stands, therefore, its application is limited to stringently regulated industries. For such industries, when output price is held constant although input prices rise, input price increases reduce monopolistic exploitation areas.

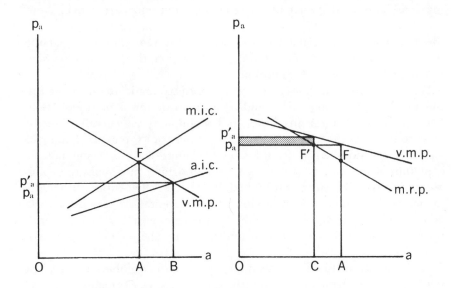

Figure 8.3

eliminate monopolistic exploitation, measures stronger than minimum
wage legislation or ordinary collective bargaining (which we may call
wage bargaining) are required. The monopolistic employer may be forced
off his input demand curve, as by all-or-none bargaining (specifying a
minimum amount of employment) or by such bargaining approaches as
restrictive working rules. An alternative method, which is less favorable
to that part of the labor aristocracy composed of the employees of monopolistic firms, would be to reduce or eliminate the employer's initial monopoly power, as, for example, by output price regulation.

11.   Two major arguments support the more restrictive Chamberlin criterion, included in the later editions of *Monopolistic Competition*,[8] which
leaves monopolistic competition completely out of account, limiting ex-

---

8. Edward H. Chamberlin, "Monopolistic Competition and the Productivity Theory
of Distribution," *Readings*, no. 7. The original edition of *The Theory of Monopolistic
Competition* (Cambridge: Harvard University Press, 1932) concentrates upon output
markets.

   Incidentally, the "exploitation" illustrations in *The Economics of Welfare (op. cit.,*
especially pp. 556–571) are confined to monopsony cases. This suggests that Pigou himself may have had the Chamberlin criterion originally in mind, despite formal statements to the contrary. The distinction between the two criteria is clarified by Joan
Robinson, *Imperfect Competition, op cit.,* pp. 281–283.

ploitation of input suppliers to monopsonistic cases. The first Chamberlin argument associates exploitation with deliberate manipulation or price administration. Only under partial or complete monopsony is there any such manipulation of input markets to the employer's benefit; a monopolist, like a pure competitor, is a price-taker or input markets. Chamberlin's second major argument relates more explicitly to his theory of monopolistic competition. For long-run equilibrium in the large-group cases on which he concentrates attention, output price tends to equality with average cost, although not to marginal cost or minimum average cost. The equality of price and average cost eliminates, in the long run, any monopoly profits otherwise tappable through elimination of monopolistic exploitation. The question may be asked: what has exploitation profited the exploiter? Furthermore, if anyone is exploited deliberated by monopolistic competition, it is the consumers of output, by reason of the higher output prices prevailing under monopolistic competition. (Chamberlin justifies these as costs of the increasing range of choice which affluent consumers supposedly desire among less-standardized outputs.) To speak of input suppliers being exploited as well, therefore, involves double counting, even if we neglect the monopolist's price-taker status in purchasing input.

This writer prefers to think of imperfect competition, including monopolistic competition, as a statically inefficient system that exploits both consumers and input suppliers, sometimes automatically and sometimes through the deliberate price-making that it permits. Whether or not it permits or insures abnormal profits for the immediate beneficiaries of the exploitation is, in this view, irrelevant.

Discriminating Monopsony

12.   Discrimination in employment, as by race, sex, age, religion, national origin, education, or other social bases, in ways unrelated to productivity differentials, is a feature of the demand for labor inputs. The discrimination may take a multitude of forms. It is probably concentrated in imperfectly competitive, regulated, and nonprofit industries and organizations, where the imperatives of efficiency are least overriding.

We consider here only forms of discrimination associated with *monopsony,* where we may distinguish between *employment* and *wage* discrimination. Employment discrimination occurs when, rather than concentrating monopsony power on forcing down wage rates, the employer leaves some part of his monopsony power, which we have called v, potential or unused, so as to confine his staff to workers satisfying his preferences or prejudices, usually at some sacrifice of money profit. This is a leading

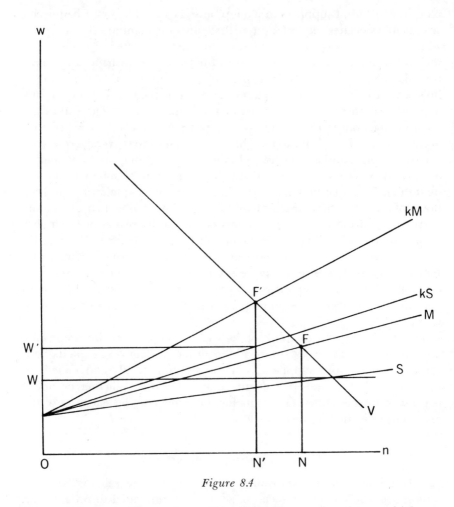

Figure 8.4

theme of Becker's *Economics of Discrimination,* and a theme which we
have ourselves touched upon elsewhere.[9] Analytically, if only *k* per cent
of the labor supply *S* facing the monopsonist (of Figure 8.4) meets his
preferences, he may set the most profitable wage that will permit him to
dispense with the hiring of *Untermenschen* rather than that which will
maximize his unconstrained monopsony profits. In the diagram, *M* being

9. Becker, *Economics of Discrimination* (Chicago: University of Chicago Press, 1957),
chs. 1 and 3. "When an employer discriminates against employees," argues Becker (p.
122), "he acts as if he incurs non-pecuniary, psychic costs of production by employing
them." Compare also M. Bronfenbrenner, "Economics of Collective Bargaining," *Q.J.E.*
(August 1939); and "Potential Monopsony in Labor Markets," *Ind. and Labor Rel.
Review* (July 1956).

his marginal labor cost and V his v.m.p. functions, he prefers the wage W' (with employment of N' preferred workers) to the lower wage W and the higher "mixed bag" employment N. The argument is not affected significantly by the relative positions of kS and M, or by the variability of the proportion k, which may be higher at higher wages than at lower ones.

13. Whereas *employment* discrimination costs the discriminating employer money, *wage* discrimination makes money for him. This is the main reason for distinguishing between the two forms. Wage discrimination involves taking "unfair" advantage of differing elasticities of supply in different segments of the employer's labor market, the disadvantaged segments having in most cases the lower elasticity. The result is that the employer's monopsony power coefficient v and the ratio of v.m.p. (or m.r.p.) to the wage rate are both greater in those segments with lower supply elasticities. The optimal solution for the monopsonist is "sectoral" equality between m.i.c. values, so that no further cost saving remains possible for the employer through shifting employment between sectors. It need not follow that the segment with lower elasticity receives the lower wage, if the productivity differential is sufficiently in its favor. The "disadvantaged" segment may be defined as one with either lower wages or a lower supply elasticity; it need not satisfy both criteria simultaneously.

The special case considered in Figure 8.5 is not only linear, but presumes the v.m.p. of both types of labor to be the same. The linearity property gives us the useful result that the m.i.c. function ΣM_i is marginal to the horizontal sum of the partial or segmental supply functions S_i, or S. We may therefore call it M rather than ΣM_i.[10] Following from this identity, neither the focal point of v.m.p.–m.i.c. intersection (point F, where M and V cross), nor total employment N is affected by the fact of discrimination, but only the profitability of monopsony and the division of employment between different categories of labor suppliers. Taken literally, the diagram's assumption of identical v.m.p.'s gives the result of unequal pay for strictly identical work. This is difficult to realize in practice without some specious geographical-separation or job-specification disguise. A more general interpretation, however, is possible if we think of the several partial input supply functions S_i as somehow "standardized" for productivity differences.

10. This follows because, as we have seen in the linear case, each marginal function is also linear, identical with the corresponding linear average function at its vertical asymptote, and with a double slope.

More general treatments, allowing for differing concavities of partial supply functions, are to be found in Joan Robinson, *Imperfect Competition* (*op. cit.*, pp. 192–195, 302–304), and Edgar O. Edwards, "The Analysis of Output under Discrimination," *Econometrica* (April 1950).

Using this apparatus, let us compare the optimal monopsony solutions with and without wage discrimination. Given the existence of monopsony, we shall find that the group or segment with the higher supply elasticity gains, from the discrimination, in both wage rate and employment, while the disadvantaged group with lower supply elasticity loses on both counts. The employer is also a gainer. The relative size of the several groups makes no difference to the argument.

Without discrimination, employment is clearly N $(= N_1 + N_2)$, while the optimum monopsony wage rate, from the employer's viewpoint, is W. We assume group 1 to have a higher supply elasticity than group 2, so that M_1 (for N_1 employment) is less than M_2 (for N_2 employment) at the uniform rate W. This warns us that monopsony profit can be increased further by shifting employment from group 2 to group 1, until the group m.i.c.'s are equal $(N_1'F_1 = N_2'F_2)$. For group 1, with better

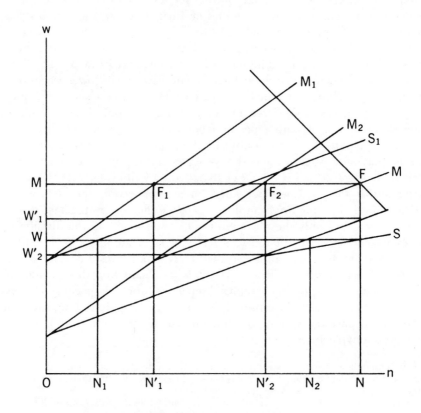

Figure 8.5

alternative opportunities reflected in higher supply elasticity, the discriminatory employment and wage (N_1' and W_1') exceed N_1 and W respectively. For the disadvantaged group 2, $N_2' < N_2$ and $W_2' < W$. In this linear case, total employment N being constant, $\Sigma N_i = \Sigma N_i'$ but the weighted average wage rate falls below W as a condition for increasing the employer's profit.

The reader may extend his command of this analysis by working through an example where the employer's monopsony power is limited to group 2 only, while he is a price-taker on the competitive labor market for group 1. Another extension is to cases of what Pigou called first- and second-degree discrimination.[11] First-degree discrimination involves a separate price for each individual unit of input, and second-degree discrimination, a separate price for each individual supplier. (We have limited our own discussion to the less abnormal third-degree discrimination, between clearly distinguishable groups without possibility of arbitrage between them.)

14. Social implications lurk beneath the surface of this formal argument. If we observe a system of wage discrimination, questions arise as to the responsibility for the underprivileged position of group 2 under discriminating monopsony, particularly if it is disadvantaged simultaneously in the employment and the wage senses. (Such a situation may occur among Negroes, women, foreigners, etc.) Radicals and Socialists blame the monopsonistic employer almost exclusively, particularly if he engages in active operations to keep the working groups hostile to each other and prevent their joining forces (as in, say, a strong union) against his monopsony power. Conservatives, on the other hand, blame the group 1 workers as well, particularly if they have formed a union effectively closed to group 2 workers, or if the group 2 workers originally entered the job competition as economic refugees from still-worse conditions in some other area or industry, like the Mexican *braceros* in California agriculture.

The analysis in section 13 implies that both employers and elastic-supply workers gain from discrimination, as compared with uniform monopsony wage setting. They share joint interests in keeping the disadvantaged workers down, so long as monopsony exists. When it comes to breaking down the monopsony itself, however, the two worker groups have a common interest, with management on the other side. The employer's interest in maintain discriminating monopsony is therefore clearer, sharper,

11. Pigou, *Economics of Welfare, op. cit.,* pp. 278 f.

and less equivocal than the interest of the favored-worker group. The favored workers have still more to gain in absolute terms by completely overthrowing the underlying monopsony than by supporting wage discrimination. (Employment discrimination is quite another matter!) Relative to the disadvantaged group, however, the favored ones have more to gain by playing Macbeth, who

> Wouldst not play false, and yet wouldst wrongly win.

We cannot say a priori which basis for decision weighs most strongly, in any particular instance, with any particular group of favored workers or with their organization. Their optimum position seems often to combine the best of both worlds—breaking down employer monopsony by a strong, closed union that, however, shares his preferences for employment discrimination, or even forces stronger employment-discrimination preferences than he would practice independently.

The Consumer Interest in Monopsony[12]

15. The consumer *qua* consumer has an interest in lower prices, and therefore in lower costs of production, including lower wages and lower raw material prices. Has he also an interest in upholding employers' monopsony power to hold down wages and raw material prices? The ordinary input pressure group would seem to think so, judging by its strictures against "drones" and "idlers" who do not "understand" the problems of the worker, farmer, and miner. A standard example is the Webbs' classical *Industrial Democracy*,[13] which does not distinguish between pure and imperfect competition, short of pure monopoly.

Standard economic analysis, presuming maximizing behavior all round, answers with a forthright negative our questions regarding consumer interest in monopsony. Monopsony power operates by reducing or restricting employment in desired occupations. This reduces not only wage rates but also output. The reduction or restriction of output raises not only profits but prices in the corresponding industries. This effect is clearest and most direct when monopsony and monopoly power are associated, as in the double-exploitation case 4 (Fig. 8.2). It is smaller and less direct in the simple-monopsony case 3. (We may not conclude, however, that

---

12. This section represents a substantial revision of the author's argument in "Monopsony and the Consumer Interest," *Indian Econ. Rev.* (February 1954) .

13. Sidney and Beatrice Webb, *Industrial Democracy* (London: Longmans, 1898) , part iii, ch. 2, entitled "The Higgling of the Market," especially pp. 654–674. (It should be remembered that this volume was written at the trough of a twenty-year deflation.)

monopsony raises the general price level. Workers denied employment in monopsonistic industries may find employment elsewhere, in more competitive and presumably less desirable sectors of the economy, increasing output and lowering both wages and prices there. A similar argument holds with regard to raw material inputs. The vagaries of index-number statistics may move the measured price level in either direction or not at all, monetary conditions remaining the same.)

16.   When we go "beyond supply and demand," the issue of consumer interest in monopsony is further muddied in two general ways: (a) by the possibility of reinvesting imperfectly competitive profits (monopsony profits included) in successful research and development, increasing the pace of economic progress; and (b) by the prevalence of mark-up or full-cost methods of price administration, which may operate to tie posted prices to wage rates, even at the expense of profits. In these conditions, monopsony lowers posted prices, but output markets may not clear at these posted prices. If monopsony lowers posted prices, but output markets do not clear, two subsets of consumers gain. One subset is favored by whatever formal, informal, or aleatory rationing system may develop. The other is willing and able to bear rationing uncertainty. However, another subset of consumers loses, generally including newcomers to the purchase of output and people in a hurry to acquire the goods in question. They are disfavored by the rationing system or are ration-risk averters.

Standard welfare theory, by allowing for reexchange between consumers in our several subsets, professes to prove a net consumer loss from monopsony in case (b), if a two-price system develops with opportunities for mutually profitable arbitrage.[14] The writer is skeptical of the generality and rigor of this demonstration, when no such two-price system does in fact develop. On the other hand, a net consumer gain from markup-price monopsony is less likely than it appears in advance.

17.   While it seems difficult to envisage a case of generalized consumer interest in monopsony, it is by no means impossible. An important example is a monopsony offsetting a monopoly that has no monopsony power itself, or that shares its profits with labor or raw-material suppliers by some process of bargaining. When consumers, or such price-cutting surrogates as discount houses, mail-order houses, chain stores, or "chiselers" not elsewhere classified, challenge the national oligopolies, a favorite ally is the monopsonistic manufacturer from a low-wage area. Even allowing

14. Textbook illustrations abound; see, for example, Stigler, *The Theory of Price*, 3rd ed. (New York: Macmillan, 1966), pp. 81 f.

for the restrictive consequences of such suppliers' monopsony tactics, the net effect of their expansion is to increase output and lower prices, in the interest of consumers otherwise underrepresented in the Galbraith panorama of countervailing power.[15] Even here, of course, the consumer interest would be better served by low costs alone, without the monopsony feature, but this alternative is not always available, and monopsony is "second-best."

Promotion Ladders

18.   Still concentrating on labor-market monopsony, let us now consider systems of long-term or lifetime employment, with promotion primarily from within the employing organization. Under such systems, let the worker enter employment at time t_o. This represents graduation from one or another educational institution, or possibly completition of compulsory military service. Initial productivity may be zero or even negative, as in Figure 8.6. As the worker acquires skill, he may progress from one job to another along one or another of a relatively few and well-defined promotion ladders—the ladder he climbs is usually determined at the time of first employment—until he retires at time t_n; t_n is often age 55–60 in Japan and 65–70 in the United States. Such a worker spends his working life as an organization man in one company, climbing a hierarchical pyramid from within, with few or no possibilities of shifting his employer without financial loss to himself.

A feature of this system is the short-term tenuousness of any relation between v.m.p. and either wage rates or m.i.c. at any random point on the time scale of a diagram like Figure 8.6, or in any specific job. Reder sees the system as one of tacit mutual insurance by participants against the unfavorable consequences of ability differences, so that "the very imperfect attempts at mutual insurance represented by a policy of promotion from within enormously complicate the relation between the value of the marginal contribution of a productive agent and its reward." And he adds, "The points where market forces impinge upon the wage and personnel policies of employers cannot [usually] be predicted in advance, but their occasional collision create crises for 'job evaluation plans' . . . oriented toward maintaining internal equity, irrespective of market conditions."[16]

15. Galbraith sees both organized labor and agriculture as "countervailing" the economic power of big business, rather than cooperating in restrictionist schemes in exchange for a share of the spoils. He has less to say about the consumer interest. *American Capitalism: The Concept of Countervailing Power*, rev. ed. (Boston: Houghton Mifflin, 1956) , ch. 9.

16. "Aspects of the Size Distribution of Earnings," in Marchal and Ducros, *The Distribution of National Income* (London: Macmillan, 1968) , pp. 607 f. Compare also

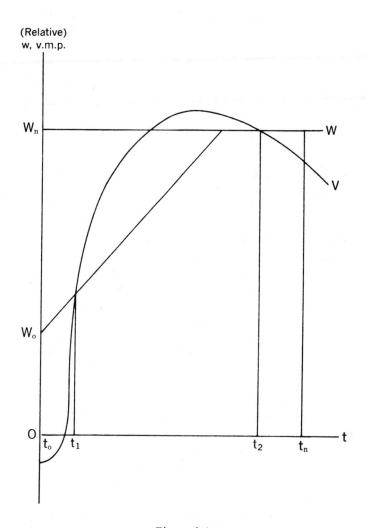

Figure 8.6

In particular, the raw apprentice or trainee (in the neighborhood of t_o) and the tired old *de facto* retiree (in the neighborhood of t_n) are both paid more than they are worth, as is indicated by the anticipated wage or W function lying significantly above the anticipated v.m.p. or V function at both extremes, both W and V being measured *ex ante* at t_o as percent-

Bronfenbrenner, "Potential Monopsony," *op. cit.* (Reder's interest is directed largely toward the "upper tail" of executive compensation; the notion of tacit mutual insurance plays a major part in his thinking.)

ages of expected lifetime earnings on that particular ladder.[17] On the other hand, there is at least one range like $t_1 t_2$ in the diagram, in which the representative worker on the representative promotion ladder is being paid significantly less than he is "worth."

The consequences of monopsony are apparent in the figure because the total area under the V function exceeds that under the W function. The existence of some such institution as monopsony is required to prevent workers being systematically bid away during the interval $t_1 t_2$.[18]

19.   A number of labor-market peculiarities combine to suggest the realism of some such practice as is represented, in simplified form, by our diagram. We mention five of these: (a) The anxiety of firms to avoid hiring unstable "floaters" in their first apprenticeship or trainee jobs (at or near t_o). (b) Their reluctance to extend retirement ages beyond t_n, even in tight labor markets with rising wage rates. (c) Their reluctance to hire even experienced older workers, at or near t_2. (d) Their unwillingness to hire women at the same pay scale as men, when the women may quit at or near t_1 to keep house and raise children. (e) Their desire for more vocationally oriented schools and colleges (the desire being expressed by personnel managers rather than top executives), to cut firms' losses during the interval $t_o t_1$ and to shorten the length of this interval by preparing graduates more specifically for their first assignments. At least, none of these behavior patterns is consistent with strict maximizing behavior at every point on each promotion ladder.

20.   If many large employers in both Japan and the United States have promotion-ladder systems, one wonders why American unemployment is concentrated among the very young, while Japanese unemployment hits harder in the middle years, and both countries have problems at the highest ages at and beyond t_2.[19] One partial explanation stresses the lower living standards of Japan, which force the Japanese worker to seek employment at an earlier t_o and an initial wage W_o that is lower relative to his anticipated lifetime average earnings. This moves t_1 to the left, making the young worker not only a cheaper but a safer investment than his American counterpart. Another partial and quite consistent explanation stresses the traditionally larger size of the Japanese family and the tradi-

17. The picture is complicated further, both by discounting for futurity, allowance for fringe benefits, etc., and by the occasional removal of the exceptional individual from his promotion-ladder for special consideration.

18. Reder seems to be mistaken in supposing all the phenomena of Figure 8.6 compatible with "pure competition in all markets." ("Aspects of Size Distribution," *op. cit.,* p. 584.)

19. Among the writer's Japanese-born students, Koji Taira and Yoichi Niwata have been most persistent in raising this issue and exploring possible answers.

tionally shorter Japanese span of life and health. These factors lead to a steeper rise in "subsistence" wages as the worker assumes family responsibilities, and also to higher final relative wages W_n; in addition, they move both t_2 and t_n to the left in time. These circumstances combine to make the older Japanese worker a worse investment, relative to a younger one, than an American worker of corresponding age.

Insofar as Japanese labor-market conditions are shifting toward the American pattern, rather than the reverse, an economic forecaster may reasonably anticipate future shifts in the Japanese promotion-ladder structure toward the American one, but, again, not the reverse. And if the promotion ladder shifts, so, one might suspect, will the age structure of Japanese unemployment and underemployment.

A Rule of Thumb?

21. We have been using the term "potential" monopoly (or monopsony) in this chapter and the preceding one to describe situations where economic power is left largely unexercised, that is, translated into what Hicks calls "the quiet life," and the behavioral economists call "organizational slack," with plenty of psychic income and quasi-leisure for both management and favored employees. A sign of potential economic power, or organizational slack, is widespread reliance on rarely reexamined, let alone modified, routines or rules of thumb in decision-making on both input and output markets.

On the input markets that concern us here, the labor markets in particular, the simplest of such routines is to keep total payrolls at a certain percentage of gross sales net of all taxes. The writer has suggested previously that the selected percentage may perhaps have approximated an economic optimum in some past period, when the firm in question (or some other firm that serves as its model) was being built up under the guidance of some more active, Schumpeterian entrepreneurial-managerial individual or group.[20] If this surmise is correct in a sufficient number of cases, it operates to explain on a microeconomic level certain phenomena that, when aggregated, form the subject matter of our Chapter 16. These include not only the "Bowley" phenomenon of near-constant labor shares in private sector output, but, more directly, the "Weintraub" phenomenon of constancy in the ratio of aggregate payrolls to total sales.[21]

20. Bronfenbrenner, "Imperfect Competition on a Long-Run Basis," *University of Chicago Journal of Business* (April 1950), pp. 91–93.

21. Sidney Weintraub, *General Theory of the Price Level, Output, Income Distribution and Economic Growth* (Philadelphia: Chilton, 1959), chs. 3–5. This "rule of thumb" explanation for the Weintraub constant (approximately 1/2) is more direct than its explanation for the Bowley constant (between 3/5 and 3/4) because it omits any "reduction" step to carry us from gross sales to total "factor payments."

CHAPTER NINE

The Supply of Inputs

1. Crossing the Great Divide between supply and demand, we return to pure competition on the input markets, and initially consider each individual as supplying a single input in variable quantities per time period. The amount which he supplies may have a technically fixed or structurally fixed upper bound, such as the number of hours of his own labor he can supply in a given interval. (This limitation can be relaxed easily in a more general treatment.) We also assume, when considering the services of capital goods, that suppliers may buy, sell, borrow, or lend these instruments themselves. We do not consider the possibility of arbitrage between the "output markets" for capital goods and the "input markets" for their services.

The Individual Supplier

2. The supplier of the input a receives an income y. Part or all of y consists of payments for a. Part or all of y is also capitalized at an interest rate r, yielding part or all of the supplier's wealth w.

We suppose the supplier governed in his input-market behavior by a continuous utility function U, which we assume measurable:

$$U = U(a, y) \tag{9.1}$$

In the relevant range, which need not encompass all positive values of a and y,[1] the derivative $\delta U/\delta a$ is assumed to be negative, and the derivative $\delta U/\delta y$ to be positive. The second derivatives are both assumed nega-

---

1. We shall subsume, in this chapter, wealth effects in income effects, and use y indiscriminately for y and w alike.

tive, and also the mixed derivative. A plausible rationalization for the last assumption is to suppose "leisure," or the direct-consumption employment of one's stock of potential inputs,[2] to be an ordinary, noninferior good. Its utility, as well as the supplier's own demand for it, rise with the supplier's income. Therefore, his supply of a to others falls as his income increases.

3.   Optimizing behavior is then indicated, in response to a given input price p_a, by a Lagrangian extension of (9.1):

$$U(a, y) - \lambda (ap_a - y) = \text{max.}$$

$$\frac{\delta U}{\delta a} - \lambda p_a = 0, \qquad\qquad \frac{\delta U}{\delta y} + \lambda = 0.$$

Hence, equating values of the Lagrange multiplier,

$$\lambda = \frac{\delta U / \delta a}{p_a} = -\frac{\delta U}{\delta y}. \tag{9.2}$$

As a first-order condition for a maximum: the marginal utility of a unit of income, whose price by definition is unity, equals the marginal utility of a dollar's worth of leisure, or (with opposite sign) the marginal disutility of a dollar's worth of a supplied. The purist will note that, while income y_0 from sources other than a might have been added explicitly to the Lagrangian equation, making its second term

$$- \lambda [a p_a - (y - y_0)],$$

our result (9.2) would have remained the same.

4.   The result of (9.2) can be reformulated and expanded diagrammatically, using either marginal-utility functions (Figure 9.1) or an indifference map (Figure 9.2).

In the marginal-utility diagram, we represent on the left-hand vertical axis the marginal utility of income from each of two alternative employments.[3] The marginal-utility functions themselves are labelled y_1 and y_2. Their differences may reflect different input prices, as where a worker supplies both skilled and unskilled labor, and/or different working con-

2. If there exists an upper limit a^* to the supplier's possible short-run supply per period of input a, "leisure" or "direct-consumption employment" may be defined as the difference $a^* - a$.

3. The marginal utility concerned is that of whatever income may be received from supplying a unit of a in each of the two employments, with differences in irksomeness netted out conceptually. It is not the marginal utility of a unit of income, since the diagram's horizontal scale is in units of input rather than of income. (I owe much of the detail of this diagram to John A. Buttrick.)

ditions, as in the division of an academician's time between teaching, research, and administration. The generalized marginal-utility function for
income, labeled simply y, is the horizontal sum of y_1 and y_2. The maximum endowment of inputs is assumed equal to OO', with no opportunity

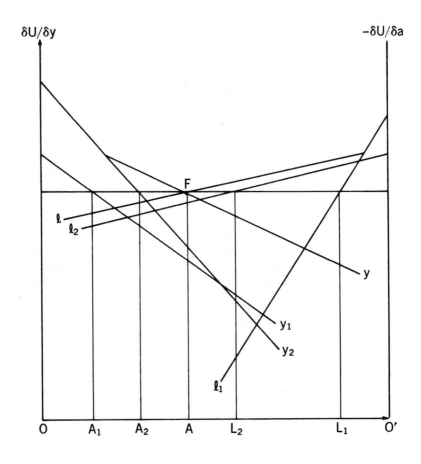

Figure 9.1

for short-term expansion. On the right-hand vertical axis is measured the
marginal utility of leisure, or alternatively, the marginal disutility of employment. Leisure, too, may be utilized in two alternative ways, whose
marginal utilities are indicated by l_1 and l_2, with units of potential input
read from right to left. The first method of leisure utilization may be, in
the case of labor input, sheer *dolce far niente,* the popular meaning of
leisure. The second may be some form of nonmarket or do-it-yourself

work at home. There is again a horizontal sum *l*, representing the generalized marginal utility of leisure.

The upshot of the diagram, assuming given but not necessarily identical input prices in employments 1 and 2, is a focal point *F* between in-

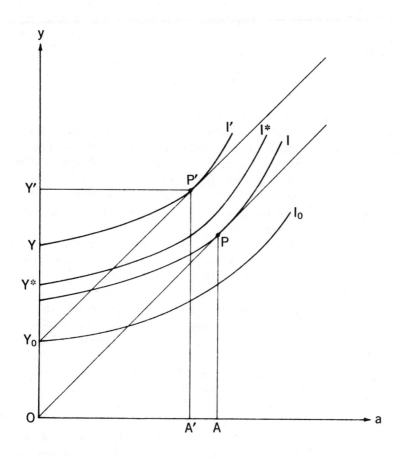

Figure 9.2

come and leisure, with a total of *A* input units (labor hours) devoted to work—A_1 in employment 1 and $A_2 = A_1A$ in employment 2—and AO' units reserved for leisure broadly conceived—L_1O' in form 1 and $L_2O' = AL_1$ in form 2.

5. The indifference map of Figure 9.2 is built around an unconstrained off-diagram optimum point, with an indefinitely large income and a cer-

tain modicum of work (or other input supply) to satisfy Thorstein Veblen's "instinct of workmanship" or its "social consciousness" equivalent in
socialist thinking. Aside from the location of this bliss point, the map is
quite conventional. The slopes of the indifference curves, with signs reversed, are again called marginal rates of substitution, or m.r.s. (this time,
between income and leisure). They may also be interpreted, without sign
reversal, as ratios between the marginal utilities of leisure and income. In
the notation of (9.2), the m.r.s. is

$$-\frac{\delta U}{\delta a}\bigg/\frac{\delta U}{\delta y} \tag{9.3}$$

at any point. The m.r.s. or slope thus defined is presumed to *rise* as a rises
in the relevant range, meaning that the m.r.s. derived from (9.2) is presumed to *fall*. Geometrically, we limit ourselves to the portion of the diagram where those indifference curves that concern us are all upward sloping and concave upward, *i.e.*, where the marginal utility of leisure rises
(and that of further income declines) as we move to the northeast along
a given indifference curve or satisfaction level. The m.r.s. is also presumed to rise, in the relevant range:

(a) With the amount of income received (leisure remaining constant,
as in northward movement on the diagram), so as to make the second
derivative $\delta^2 U/\delta y^2$ clearly negative without reference to the mixed derivative $\delta^2 U/\delta a \delta y$.

(b) With the amount of input supplied (income remaining constant,
as in eastward movement on the diagram), so as to make the second derivative $\delta^2 U/\delta a^2$ clearly negative[4] without reference to the mixed derivative.

By analogy with similar arguments in Chapter 6, these conditions are
required for a maximum. Geometrically, they combine to insure upward
concavity of the indifference curves.

5.   The parallel rays from the origin and the point Y_0 of Figure 9.2 correspond to price and budget lines. They represent exchanges between income and leisure. Their slope is the input price p_a, still assumed given
and constant. The distance Y_0 represents the supplier's income from other
inputs, accumulated wealth, transfer payments, or gifts. The supplier's
optimum point P, with no supplementary income, is at the income level
Y, the satisfaction level I, and the input supply A. His optimum point P',
with supplementary income Y_0, is at the (higher) income level Y', the
(higher) satisfaction level I', but the (lower) input supply A'.

---

4. Sign reversal (as between m.r.s. and slope) and the negative signs of $\delta U/\delta a$ (but
not $\delta U/\delta y$) combine to explain any apparent anomalies in these results.

These results are quite general, given only the concavities of the indifference curves. They can be expanded to cover the consequences of larger and smaller values of Y_0, and also of wealth holdings, which yield flows of either income or of nonincome satisfactions.

Certain social consequences can also be developed readily. The following examples all involve "willingness to work:"

(a) The provision of social security, doles, or other transfer income lowers the quantity of labor supplied by recipients at any wage rate, whether or not accepting a job involves the surrender of the transfer income or any part of it.

(b) If acceptance of a job involves the surrender of transfer income, result (a) is even stronger. If the level of transfer payments (relief) should then be at some level Y^* on Figure 9.2, yielding a satisfaction level $I^* > I$, the recipient will rationally prefer relief to offering any work whatever at the wage rate p_a indicated by the slope of OP, even if jobs are available yielding an income $Y > Y^*$ at this wage rate.

(c) The quantity of labor supplied by a family member, such as a married woman, at a given wage rate, is related inversely to the income and assets of the remainder of the family, particularly the husband. The same is true of young people not living with their parents but supported by them. When affluence increases the transfer income available to these people, without lowering the disutility of the work for which they are qualified, the fluourishing of the perpetual-student, Bohemian, beatnik, hippie, or *stilyagi* ways of life should be less surprising than it was in the 1960s.[5]

(d) When we deal with a large-family or extended-family system, as in many parts of the Far East, the proportion of the potential labor force

5. The economist's standard reaction to such ways of life is viewing-with-alarm. Thus Myrdal, a Socialist, comments on proposals for social dividend and guaranteed income (*Challenge to Affluence;* New York: Pantheon, 1962), p. 40 f.:

Such proposals underestimate how unhealthy and destructive it is for anybody and particularly for young people without much share in the national culture to go idle and live more permanently on doles—this tenet of old-fashioned Puritanism, I believe, is also fully borne out by recent social research. Work is not only, and not even mainly, a "disutility" as conceived by the classical economists. It is, if not always a pleasure, the basis for self-respect and a dignified life. There is no real cure for unemployment except employment.

American "hippies" and "yippies," however, take precisely the opposite view. The quotation below is from an anonymous manifesto of the Youth International Party, distributed in Chicago in August 1968, and reproduced in Norman Mailer, "Miami Beach and Chicago," *Harper's Magazine* (November 1968), p. 96. "Yippie" demands include "A society which works toward and actively promotes the concept of 'full unemployment.' A society in which people are free from the drudgery of work. Adoption of the concept, 'Let the Machines do it.'" See also "Free" (Abbie Hoffman), *Revolution for the Hell of It* (New York: Dial, 1969), p. 167.

affected by the incomes of other family members is greater than under the small, or nuclear, Western family. It is conventional to argue that the large-family system reduces the labor supply. On the other hand, increasing the number of idle family members lowers the value of Y_0 per head, as well as the proportion of each day's wage that can be retained by the actual worker and his own nuclear family. The combined effect of the extended-family system on willingness to work is therefore a complex phenomenon. For larger extended families, perhaps, discouragement is less extreme than for smaller ones.

Input-Offer and Input-Supply Functions

6.   Let us now drop the assumption of a constant input price p_a, while retaining the competitive assumption that no individual supplier can affect it. As the input price varies, the slope of the ray through the origin (or through Y_0) varies proportionately. As p_a rises, the slope of the ray rises, and the amount of a offered by a representative supplier will trace out a roughly bow-shaped pattern, first rising and then falling, like $\Sigma\Sigma$ on Figure 9.3. If we construct a similar function $\Sigma'\Sigma'$, by assuming some extraneous income Y_0, $\Sigma'\Sigma'$ would lie entirely to the northwest of $\Sigma\Sigma$; the two functions would be asymptotic at their upper limits (with y increasing without bound) :

We call functions like $\Sigma\Sigma$ and $\Sigma'\Sigma'$ *input-offer* functions. They are not input-supply functions proper.[6] The movement between any two points on an input-offer function, such as P_1 and P_2 on $\Sigma\Sigma$, can be broken down into an income and a substitution effect, as in the standard case of consumer behavior in output-demand theory. The input-supply and output-demand analyses differ, however, in that income and substitution effects normally work in opposite directions on input supplies. The income effect of an increased wage rate, for example, is to raise incomes. Since income rises and leisure is by hypothesis an ordinary (not an inferior) good, the income effect is to raise the demand for all types of leisure and to reduce the supply of all inputs—not only of the particular labor input a whose price has risen.

The substitution effect results, on the other hand, from raising the price of leisure higher than before, the price of leisure being measured backhandedly by income forgone, in standard opportunity-cost terms. The substitution effect for a given income, therefore, reduces the amount of leisure demanded or reserved, and increases the supply of the particular input whose price we suppose to have risen. Generalization to other in-

---

6. An input-supply function, as we shall soon see, relates the supply of an input to the price paid for it.

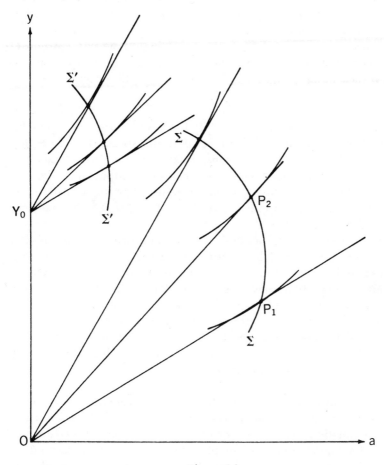

Figure 9.3

puts supplied by the same individual does not follow so simply as with the income effect.

The total or combined effect, and hence the slope of the offer function, may go either way, depending on the relative sizes of the income and the substitution effects.[7] The shape of the $\Sigma\Sigma$ curve, as drawn, illustrates the general or common sense assumption that there exists some tendency for

7. The same result is put in terms of elasticities in Lionel Robbins, "On the Elasticity of Demand for Income in Terms of Efforts," *Readings,* no. 13. Robbins criticizes the positions of earlier writers, particularly the view that input supply functions must slope negatively. Robbins specifies the maximum input offer as the point where the "elasticity of demand for income in terms of effort" is unity. This result is among those derived in the appendix to this chapter on "The Maximum Input Offer."

the positive substitution effect to dominate at lower incomes, and the negative income effect to dominate at higher ones. Two arguments in support of common sense are that little or no supply will be forthcoming at a zero input price, so that $\Sigma\Sigma$ will pass through or near the origin O, and that some input prices normally exist that elicit higher input supplies (and leave less leisure) than are associated with the optimum or bliss point.

7.   The development of an input-supply function SS from an input-offer function $\Sigma\Sigma$ is shown in Figure 9.4. Analytically speaking, the development is a simple matter of linear transformation of the vertical axis from total income to input price.[8] There are no shifts in input quantity, measured along the horizontal axis of the diagram. In particular, the maximum quantity of input supplied is the same for both $\Sigma\Sigma$ on the upper and SS on the lower panels of Figure 9.4.

The distinction between input-offer and input-supply functions is clarified when we assume, for a labor input, the existence of a floor to the wage rate. This may be a legal minimum, a union scale, or some other standard rate maintained tacitly by class or group solidarity. The floor is indicated in the upper panel (input-income function) by a minimum slope of the ray through the origin O. At this ray, indifference curves appear to be kinked; below it, they are irrelevant. On the lower panel (input-supply function) the same ray is transformed to a horizontal line and the wage rate is said to be inflexible downward.

8.   For the input-supply as well as the input-offer functions, the slope is forward-rising for lower input prices, and backward-bending for higher ones. By summation, this result derived for *individual* supply functions holds also for market ones, except that the points of slope reversal are normally different for different individuals, so that the extent of slope reversal is normally less sharp for the market supply functions.

But what is a "low" input price or income, and what is a "high" one, in this connection? Is it, for example, true (as some dualistic development economists have maintained) that, over nearly all relevant wage rates, the upward slope holds for the labor of advanced peoples and the downward one for the labor of primitive peoples? Is it safe to maintain, as is implied when we speak of fixed "production frontiers" for alternative goods exclusive of leisure, that input supplies are so inelastic that they may be taken as given and fixed in all countries at all times?

8. The transformation is not only linear but proportional, when the input supplier has no other income than that received from the sale of input a.

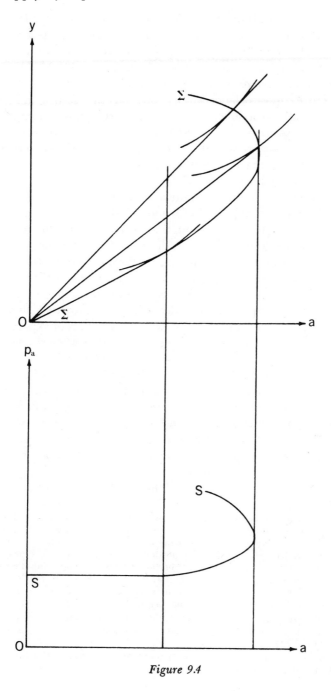

Figure 9.4

The empirical aspects of this problem have been investigated most intensively with reference to the effects of income taxes. These taxes lower effective or "take-home" wage rates. How do thy react upon the propensities to supply labor inputs and "improve human capital"? This is familiar and controversial terrain, with many examples on both sides. Conservatives hold fast to upward labor supply functions in asserting unfavorable tax effects overall, with substitution effects outweighing income effects. Reformists and redistributionists take the opposite view, in asserting favorable tax effects on the overall labor supply, as taxpayers work harder to maintain their living standards after taxes.[9] The empirical issue is, which effect is dominant?

For the income tax problems, we owe to Professor Break our most impressive collection and appraisal of a mounting number of studies from many countries. Their results, though admittedly inconclusive, seem to run in a reformist or redistributionist direction.[10] A later survey of American high-income consumers (excluding rentiers) concludes that no more than 20 to 25 per cent of aggregate income in a given tax bracket is received by those claiming to work less because of taxes. This peak is reached at a bracket whose marginal tax rate is approximately 50 per cent. The percentage declines at higher marginal rates.[11] This unexpected peaking led the researchers to "offer the speculation that when a person's income reaches the level where the federal goverement becomes for the first time the major partner in extra earnings, resentment of the tax becomes intense and disincentives are strong. But after a while the high-income taxpayer becomes used to having only a minority interest in his own extra earnings, and from then on disincentives weaken."[12]

Our main sources of residual doubt, apart from technical questions of statistical significance, are taxpayers' ignorance of how much taxes actually reduce their incomes, considering the existence of widespread tax avoidance among the well-informed. The question the economist hopes

---

9. Formal arguments similar to those for changed income tax rates, apply to proposals for changed income tax *progression,* with increased progression corresponding to an increased rate. Tax progression imparts variable degrees of downward *concavity* to the linear rays from which we derived our input-income functions, whereas proportional income taxation involves only a downward *rotation.* Comparing and combining the two analyses, it is not necessarily true that a progressive tax will reduce an individual's labor supply by more than a proportional tax of the same absolute yield. Robin Barlow and Gordon Sparks, "A Note on Progression and Leisure," *A.E.R.* (June 1964).

10. George F. Break, "Income Taxes, Wage Rates, and the Incentive to Supply Labor Services," *Natl. Tax J.* (December 1963), and "Income Taxes and Incentives to Work," *A.E.R.* (September 1957).

11. Robin Barlow, Harvey E. Brazer, and James N. Morgan, *Economic Behavior of the Affluent* (Washington: Brookings, 1966), pp. 138–145.

12. *Ibid.,* p. 143.

to see answered is, would a completely publicized and fully enforced income tax lower the supplies of labor and other inputs? The qualified reply —that existing taxes seem not to do so to any significant extent—is somewhat biased, insofar as taxpayers either remain ignorant of the post-tax consequences of their working behavior, or effective tax loopholes remain open for their use.

Social Aspects

9. We have postulated in (9.1) individual utility functions defined over incomes and input supplies. This postulate should not be taken to imply that anyone's function is strictly individual, genetic, mechanical, or otherwise impermeable to social influences. The opposite is usually the case.[13] This is clear from the frequent success of massive hortatory campaigns to elicit cheap labor and savings for national emergency, including war. Such a result, when "we" accomplish it successfully, is ascribed to patriotism, idealism, or ideological conviction. When "they" (our enemies) are successful, notions of "forced labor" and "brainwashing" are used instead.

There has arisen, in socialist countries, an active dispute between partisans of "material incentives" and partisans of "moral incentives" as means of eliciting more, or higher quality, labor inputs. The argument for material incentives is, basically, for utilizing existing upward-sloping labor supply functions by raising wages and bonuses for scarce varieties of labor, including the managerial sorts. The argument for moral incentives, on the other hand, dominate in the Chinese and Cuban spheres. The difright, at existing wage rates, by stronger moral suasion. At this writing, proponents of material incentives, including elements of profit-sharing, seem to be winning in the Soviet sphere of influence. Moral incentives, on the other hand, dominate in the Chinese and Cuban spheres. The difference is an important source of the ideological conflicts between the two. Comparing the incentive systems, an American socialist journal points out their distributional implications:[14]

> If material incentives are asigned the dominant role, the result is inevitably the privatization of life, the concentration of individuals on their own affairs, fatalistic acceptance of the status quo. Rulers and managers who also share—and disproportionately at that—in the rewards of the incentive system, can entrench themselves in power and gradually arrogate to themselves the privileges of a ruling class.

13. Compare, for a psychologist's view, Victor H. Vroom, *Work and Motivation* (New York: Wiley, 1964), ch. 3.

14. "The Latin American Revolution: A New Phase," *Monthly Review* (February 1967), pp. 2 f (running quotation; italics in original).

If primacy is placed on moral incentives, the implications are entirely different. Without the active and willing cooperation of the masses a system of moral incentives simply will not work and will have to be replaced by material incentives or coercion. But the cooperation of the masses can be won only if their interest and enthusiasm are aroused *and continuously sustained,* and this in turn is possible only if they are drawn out of their private lives, only if their horizons are widened, only if they participate meaningfully in making the decisions which effect their lives. Moral incentives can be effective, in short, only within a framework of essentially radical and egalitarian policies. Within this framework, material incentives should be used only where their justice is obvious, that is, where there is a palpable relation between reward and the amount and difficulty or unpleasantness of work done. Above all, there should be no special favors or privileges for leaders: such privileges are the greatest breeders of cynicism and disaffection.

10.   Less extreme examples of shifting labor supply functions are reported from developing countries, where both Western and native entrepreneurs entice labor into plantation, mine, and factory employment by shifting their labor supply functions, and their turning points in diagrams like Figure 9.4 to the northeast, by a number of devices. These include demonstrating what workers' wages will buy in terms of goods previously unknown to them, and showing why such goods are rational objects of desire. "Demonstration effects" in the opposite direction are sumptuary legislation. They result from strict rationing, and twist labor supply functions to the southwest by reducing the range of goods that workers can buy. They transform the attractiveness of high wages into the subsidization of absenteeism.

Mention of absenteeism reminds us that individual determination of labor supply seems at first glance inconsistent with the facts of factory or office discipline. If the length of a day or shift is eight hours, how can Jones quit after six hours (or remain for nine) on such fantastic grounds as that, with the going wage rate, the last two hours are not worth their cost in leisure, or an extra hour of leisure is not worth its cost in income forgone?[15] The answer is that the notions expressed in our equations and diagrams are more viable over the longer term, where absenteeism and multiple-jobholding are the adjustment factors, than over the short term where these factors are ruled out. If even the long-run adjustment is incomplete, some writers apply the term "leisure preferrer" to a worker

15. The length of the working day or shift itself takes some account of worker preferences, if a preferred length is a fringe benefit that may lower labor cost by improving productivity or (in monopsony cases) lowering wage rates. The discussion in the text applies primarily to the idiosyncratic individualist or to special circumstances in the life of the conformist worker.

forced by organizational pressures to work more than his optimal amount, and the term "income preferrer" to a worker "unemployed," so to speak, with respect to overtime work or a supplementary job.[16]

Some critics of American society maintain that the typical American worker is in fact pressured (over and beyond any change in his long-run utility function) into working harder and more productively than he consciously wishes to do, and that he is a leisure-preferrer. The higher work and greater productivity lead to higher measured income per capital, as compared with the more leisurely societies of Europe. If this is true (but how can we tell?), there might be a negative correlation between per capita income and satisfaction, both for American data over time, and cross-sectionally between American and European data.[17] A systematic error of this sort would also be a sufficient explanation of the reason why the typical American, enjoying more goods and services than his European contemporary, supposedly enjoys them less. The same sort of argument may be applied against the sort of "growthmanship" that sacrifices leisure heedlessly to the maximization of the growth rate of measured income, either total or per capita.

Further Applications

11. The oldest applications, or perhaps misapplications, of the bow-shaped input-supply function antedate the formal development of this apparatus. Medieval and mercantilist writers, for example, seem to have developed notions of an optimum wage for labor, above which idleness would spread,[18] leading to a decline in the nation's economic and military power. Less attention was paid to the consequences of wages below the optimum, so that the policy outcome of the optimum-wage notion was maximum-wage rather than minimum-wage legislation. Similar arguments have been repeated *ad nauseam* to justify the slavery and peonage of "natives," or collusive monopsony among their Western employers to hold wages down in most of the presently developing countries. Such arguments have contributed to a legacy of hostility against Western economic institutions generally.

Another elementary application that we have mentioned several times in passing, relates to the effects of transfer payments, both in cash and in kind (housing, health, and educational services). The reductions we have

16. Compare Leon Moses, "Income, Leisure, and Wage Pressure," *Ec. J.* (June 1962).

17. This paragraph has been influenced by discussions with John Wise.

18. Adam Smith, interestingly enough, denied that prosperity and good wages increased idleness (*Wealth of Nations;* Cannan edition [New York: Modern Library, 1937], pp. 82 f.), thereby extending his antimercantilism to this point as well.

noted for input-offer functions carry over to input-supply functions as well. This effect rationalizes resistance to humanitarian impulses toward what we have called regressive expenditures for the benefit of unemployed workers for assistance to special classes such as students, retired people, and large families, or for distribution as dividends to everyone. A less comfortable application of the function from the viewpoint of the upper and middle economic classes, is to such private transfer payments as inheritances, gifts, pensions, and the like. Reducing or abolishing such perquisites of the rich, as by taxation, would cause increases in individual input supplies in the same way as would greater harshness to the poor. And conversely, if more leisure would really be better for the middle and upper classes than more conspicuous and vicarious consumption of luxury goods and services, a similar argument might justify a more kindly regard for measures contracting the input-supply functions of the poor as well.

12.   Three somewhat more sophisticated applications of our apparatus occupy this section. Application (1) deals with overtime wage rates; application (2) is an introduction to the special problem of multiple-job-holding or "moonlighting" which results from compulsory reduction in hours of work; application (3) is macroeconomic and takes up "cross-overs" in the choice of techniques in economic planning.

Application (1). To elicit an additional A_0A_1 hours of work (in Figure 9.5) from an individual who is in equilibrium at P_0 and whose offer function $\Sigma\Sigma$ is backward-bending, lowering the wage rate is presumed impossible, while raising it would have a perverse effect, which we shall explore. The device commonly used (illustrated in Fig. 9.5) is to pay an appropriately chosen premium wage for all units above A^* $(A^* \gtrless A_0)$, bending upward the wage ray (drawn through the origin O) at the point P^*. This device moves the worker's equilibrium position from P_0 to P_1. It raises his income from Y_0 to Y_1 and his level of satisfaction from I_0 to I_1, while his working hours rise by A_0A_1.[19] A rise in the standard wage rate, such as would permit straight-time earnings of Y_1 for A_1 hours of work, as per the wage ray P_1, would have cut the worker's hours in this illustration by A_0A_2, but raised him to the still higher satisfaction level $I_2 > I_1$. His income Y_2 would have been intermediate between Y_0 and Y_1. It is an interesting exercise to apply the same analysis of overtime pay to offer functions with non-negative slopes.

The choice of overtime premiums cannot be completely arbitrary. A premium may be either too small or too large to accomplish its purpose.

---

19. Sidney Weintraub points out in correspondence an inconsistency between tax progression and "time-and-a-half for overtime."

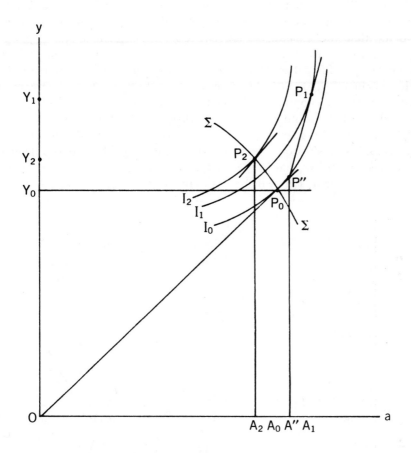

Figure 9.5

The function of our illustration, and of Figure 9.5, is merely to show that at least one premium arrangement generally exists that will increase the labor supply under circumstances when an equivalent rise in the straight-time wage rate would have decreased it.

Application (2). To spread employment opportunities more widely among workers in periods of unemployment, at no cost in wage incomes, it is often suggested by union leaders and labor economists that hours be cut, as from A_0 to A_1 (in Figure 9.6), with wages being raised simultaneously so as to keep the representative worker's income from falling below Y_0. This will move him from P_0 to P_1, raising his satisfaction level from I_0 to I_1; as we are presently on the supply side of the economic dichotomy, we need not consider how the employer can meet the added labor cost.

The only difficulty that concerns us here is that P_1 is not an equilibrium position from the worker's viewpoint. He will therefore seek, at any wage rate less than the slope of the tangent to I_1, a modicum of second-job or moonlighting work. If available, this second job, whether or not it is in the worker's principal trade, and whatever its wage rate, will decrease the effect of the original cut in hours on total employment. In this case, even with a negatively sloping offer function $\Sigma\Sigma$, the amount of moonlighting he seeks is A_1A_2. It might be greater than A_1A_2 for a certain range of higher wages in his second job. Moonlighting raises his total labor income to Y_2 and his satisfaction level to I_2. At the same time, for any supplementary wage rate below that in the worker's primary employment, the moonlighting increment A_1A_2 will be less than the gross reduction A_0A_1 in his

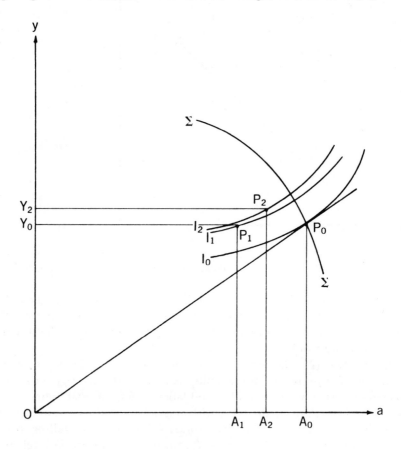

Figure 9.6

working hours on his regular job, even though both $\Sigma\Sigma$ and his corresponding labor supply function slope upward.[20] There remains, therefore, some net reduction in the total labor supply so long as $A_0 A_1 > A_1 A_2$.

Application (3). Suppose the supply function of homogeneous capital to be bow-shaped, while that of homogeneous labor is inelastic. Suppose the v.m.p. of both inputs to be declining functions of their quantities, and equal to the interest and wage rates respectively. Suppose, finally, an Economic Planning Agency (E.P.A.) charged with the maintenance of full employment of both capital and labor, without forcing disguised unemployment of either input at rates exceeding its v.m.p., or exploitation of either input by employment at rates less than its v.m.p.

The question before the E.P.A. relates to its choice of techniques for producing a uniform national income x at three different interest rates, $r_3 > r_2 > r_1$, the middle rate r_2 being the one currently in accord with the equality of voluntary full-employment saving and investment. It is entirely consistent with received doctrine that the technique adapted to the higher interest rate r_3 be less capital-intensive than that adapted to the current rate r_2. (It is less commonplace to recognize that, for full employment of both capital and labor to be maintained, this result also assumes a backward-bending capital supply function over the interval $r_2 r_3$.) Also, if, instead of rising, the interest rate should fall to r_1, the appropriate technique may again be less capital-intensive than at r_2, if the capital-supply function has a positive slope over the interval $r_1 r_2$ and overemployment of capital must be avoided.[21] This combined result, capital-intensity first rising and then falling as interest rates move *either* downward from r_3 to r_1 or upward from r_1 to r_2 is an example of a *technical crossover*.

20. For discussion of the degree to which the conclusions of this paragraph may be generalized, see M. Bronfenbrenner and Jan Mossin, "The Shorter Work Week and the Labor Supply," *So. Ec. J.* (January 1967).

21. If the productivity of capital is also to be lowered to r_1 as its relative quantity decreases, the aggregate production function must shift (or be shifted), from:

$$x = F(a, b) \qquad \text{to} \qquad x = G(a, b)$$

where, at the level of b (capital) elicited by r_1, and for a constant value of a (the labor force):

$$\frac{\delta F}{\delta a} < \frac{\delta G}{\delta a} \qquad \text{and} \qquad \frac{\delta F}{\delta b} > \frac{\delta G}{\delta b}.$$

Or, alternatively, if we drop the assumption of a constant a, function F may be more productive at r_1 and r_3, and function G at r_2, giving us crossover in a different sense.

Harry Johnson points out (in correspondence) that the standard treatment of crossover is "inherent in the influence of the interest rate on the *value* of capital involved in various techniques." This is an alternative mechanism for achieving the same result. Compare Harcourt, "Some Cambridge Controversies in the Theory of Capital," *J.E.L.* (June 1969), pp. 386–395.

Aggregative Influences

13.   In a world of uncertainty, we should also consider the possible impact of the economic climate or conjuncture upon input supplies, again
with particular reference to manpower or labor inputs. Two sets of circumstances, at opposite ends of the business-cycle spectrum, have been said
to increase the labor supply; they can, however, be combined, as we shall
see.

The first circumstance increasing labor supply functions is deep depression. It operates by making any given family income. (Y_0, in diagrams like
Figures 9.2 and 9.3), particularly the labor income of the main breadwinner in his principal employment, both smaller and more precarious than
previously. The conjecture of transitorily inflated labor supplies in depressions, exaggerating both the level of measured unemployment and the
difficulty of eliminating it, became associated, as the "additional-worker"
hypothesis, with the name of W. S. Woytinsky[22] during the 1930s in the
United States. The additional workers are, in the main, relatives who reduce their educational, homemaking, or leisure activities to enter the labor force when a principal breadwinner's job is threatened or lost. If correct, the additional-worker hypothesis relates the aggregate labor supply
function inversely to the national income per capita, or directly to the
unemployment rate.

A different sort of uncertainty, which may also shift labor supply functions to the right, is high prosperity of uncertain duration. This situation
makes birds in the hand—the present working opportunities—look unusually favorable relative to birds in the bush—the future opportunities
that might, or again might not, become available after further education,
after further full-time housekeeping, or in sporadic labor force reentry
after retirement. The conjecture of increased labor supply from this
source appeared in American labor economics in a left-handed form called
the "discouraged-worker" or "hidden-unemployment" hypothesis during
the decade 1955–1964. This hypothesis is phrased in terms of withdrawals
from the measured labor force under conditions variously called high-level
stagnation, partial recovery, and slow growth. The discouraged workers
or hidden unemployed are, once again, relatives of main breadwinners

---

22. Woytinsky, "Controversial Aspects of Unemployment Estimates in the United
States," *Rev. Econ. Stat.* (May 1941). See also Don D. Humphrey, "Alleged 'Additional
Workers' in the Measurement of Unemployment," *J.P.E.* (June 1940), and Woytinsky,
"Additional Workers in the Labor Market in Depression: A Reply to Mr. Humphrey,"
Ibid. (October 1940).

The additional-worker hypothesis may be regarded as a special case of a backward-
sloping offer function with the supplying unit defined as an entire household and "income" reduced to its "certainty-equivalent" values.

who turn or return to school, home, or retirement when employment opportunities decline, particularly after the discouraged workers are laid off. The discouraged-worker hypothesis clearly relates the labor supply function directly to the national income per capita, or inversely to the unemployment rate.[23]

14. Despite their apparently contradictory implications, the additional-worker and discouraged-worker hypotheses can be combined in some such pattern as Figure 9.7. This reverse-bow-shaped diagram plots the measured labor force (horizontal axis) against national income per capita (vertical axis). Full employment may be defined as either some high proportion (96–97 per cent) of A_1 (the Woytinsky concept) or of A_2 (which might be called the growthmanship concept). The lower branch of the bow represents the additional-worker hypothesis. Distrusting both hypotheses, Long's National Bureau study[24] supports the (conventional) rival view, that the two effects cancel each other out at most income levels, making their sum statistically insignificant for "moderate" income changes. The labor force at any time may then be represented by a constant A (the vertical line on the diagram, lying between A_1 and A_2), of which 96 or 97 per cent have jobs under full employment conditions.

15. Statistical verification and testing have been difficult in this field, since the measured labor force differs from the economist's labor supply in excluding responses to changes in wage rates and nonlabor income, not to mention the economic climate or conjuncture. Tentative results for the United States in various periods after World War II appear to confirm Long's results for prime-age male workers (aged 25-64). They locate considerable hidden unemployment, however, among marginal workers, who are defined as females of all ages, plus males under 25 or over 64. Since we lack comparable data for the 1930s, these studies have not simultaneously tested the additional-worker hypothesis, which was applied to periods of depression.

As for the size, location, and significance of hidden unemployment, the studies differ in detail. One estimate for the United States concludes that, as of 1965, an increase of employment of one million would have resulted in "an induced increase of 291,000 in the labor force, and, therefore, a decrease in unemployment of only 709,000," remembering that "each . . . percentage point reduction in the unemployment rate raises the average

23. This case, the converse of that treated in the previous footnote, reduces to an upward-sloping input-offer function.

24. Clarence D. Long, *The Labor Force Under Changing Income and Employment* (Princeton: Princeton University Press, 1958), 29–31 and ch. 10.

work week by 0.16 hours,"[25] a factor damping down any induced increase. (The basic labor force estimate underlying this study was approximately 78 million.)

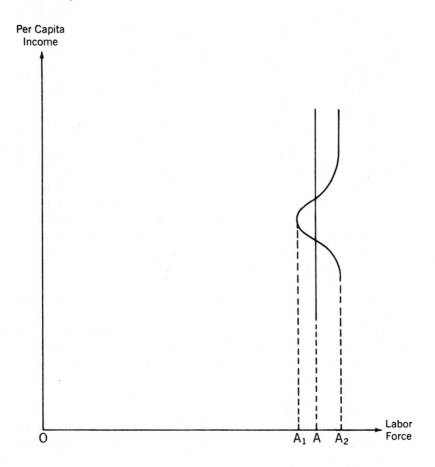

Figure 9.7

25. Lester C. Thurow and L. D. Taylor, "The Interaction Between the Actual and the Potential Rates of Growth," *Rev. Econ. and Stat.* (November 1966), pp. 353 f. Other influential contributions to the discussion include: Alfred Tella, "The Relation of Labor Force to Employment," *I.L.R.R.* (April 1964); Kenneth Strand and Thomas Dernburg, "Cyclical Variation in Labor Force Participation," *Rev. Econ and Stat.* (November 1964); William G. Bowen and T.A. Finegan, "Labor Force Participation and Unemployment," in Arthur M. Ross (ed.), *Employment Policy and the Labor Market* (Berkeley: University of California Press, 1965); Dernburg and Strand, "Hidden Unemployment, 1953–62," *A.E.R.* (March 1966); Jacob Mincer, "Labor Force Participation and Unemployment: A Review of Recent Evidence," in Gordon and Gordon (eds.), *Prosperity and Unemployment* (New York: Wiley, 1966), ch. 3.

A Dynamic Extension

16. We have seen in Chapter 6, at the microeconomic level of the single firm, that any input *a* is complementary, within the substitution area, with at least one other input *b*, and with all other inputs lumped together under the name of input *b*. This proposition also holds for the economy as a whole.

It is tempting to extend the argument one step further, to the comforting proposition that, under pure competition, an increase in the supply of input *a* must increase the total absolute remuneration of at least one other input *b*, and also the total absolute remuneration of all other inputs taken together under this head. (Their relative shares, of course, may fall, since that of *a* may rise by the increase in its own supply, if $\sigma > 1$, or if there are market shifts in favor of *a*-intensive outputs whose relative prices fall because of the increased supply of *a*.)

When we make appropriate allowance for the supply variability of inputs other than *a*, however, the comforting proposition about their absolute remuneration may not hold. For a contrary instance, let us construct a three-input example. The supply of input *a* increases, raising the v.m.p. of the complementary input *b* and lowering the v.m.p. of the competitive input *c*. By hypothesis, p_b rises and p_c falls, but the combined index number of input prices exclusive of p_a will rise. Suppose, however, that the rise in p_b results in a fall in the amount of *b* supplied, so severe as to reduce the total remuneration bp_b despite any further rises engendered in p_b. Suppose also, asymmetrically, that the fall in p_c results in no such rise in the amount of *c* supplied as would prevent the total remuneration cp_c from falling. Our comforting propostion then holds neither for *b* nor for *c*, nor does it hold for *b* and *c* taken together. Nor need such a disharmonious example, however freakish, involve instability on either output or input markets.

17. If, departing from our usual terminology, we suppose input *a* to be capital, input *b* skilled labor, and input *c* unskilled labor, we can envisage a possible application of this last example. An expansion of the effective capital supply, due to both capital accumulation and continued labor-saving technical progress of the sort called automation, may be supposed complementary to skilled labor but competitive with unskilled labor. Then, if our paradox holds, automation will raise the remuneration of skilled labor but reduce the amount supplied, so that the product bp_b will decline. It will also reduce the remuneration of unskilled labor, but without increasing the amount supplied sufficiently to avoid a fall in cp_c. The progress of automation will then, in this paradoxical case, reduce

the absolute and not merely the relative remuneration of both sorts of labor, and hence of labor as a whole. Some such nightmare as this may be of concern to our more extreme "structuralists" or automation-pessimists. To others, it may not seem nightmarish at all, since the suppliers of b —the skilled workers—are better off and have chosen to consume additional leisure.

Appendix to Chapter 9

THE MAXIMUM INPUT OFFER*

We have, from the text:

$$U(a,y) - \lambda(ap_a - y) = \text{max.}$$

Differentiating with respect to a,y, and λ:

$$\frac{\delta U}{\delta a} - \lambda p_a = 0, \qquad \frac{\delta U}{\delta y} + \lambda = 0, \qquad -ap_a + y = 0. \tag{9.i}$$

Differentiating again with respect to p_a:

$$\frac{\delta^2 U}{\delta a^2}\frac{\delta a}{\delta p_a} + \frac{\delta^2 U}{\delta a \delta y}\frac{\delta y}{\delta p_a} - p_a\frac{\delta \lambda}{\delta p_a} = \lambda$$

$$\frac{\delta^2 U}{\delta a \delta y}\frac{\delta a}{\delta p_a} + \frac{\delta^2 U}{\delta y^2}\frac{\delta y}{\delta p_a} + \frac{\delta \lambda}{\delta p_a} = 0 \tag{9.ii}$$

$$-p_a\frac{\delta a}{\delta p_a} + \frac{\delta y}{\delta p_a} = a$$

If the determinant of (9.ii) is D (a positive number, by our second-order conditions), the solution for $\delta a/\delta p_a$ is:

$$\frac{\delta a}{\delta p_a} = \frac{1}{D} \begin{vmatrix} \lambda & \dfrac{\delta^2 U}{\delta a \delta y} & -p_a \\ 0 & \dfrac{\delta^2 U}{\delta y^2} & 1 \\ a & 1 & 0 \end{vmatrix} = \frac{1}{D}\left[a\left(\frac{\delta^2 U}{\delta a \delta y} + \frac{\delta^2 U}{\delta y^2}p_a\right) - \lambda \right]$$

Substituting the first-order conditions (9.i):

$$\frac{\delta a}{\delta p_a} = \frac{1}{D}\left\{ a\left[\frac{\delta^2 U}{\delta a \delta y} - \frac{(\delta U/\delta a)(\delta^2 U/\delta y^2)}{\delta U/\delta y}\right] + \frac{\delta U}{\delta y} \right\}$$

$$= \frac{1}{D}\frac{\delta U}{\delta y}\left\{ a\left[\frac{(\delta U/\delta y)(\delta^2 U/\delta a \delta y) - (\delta U/\delta a)(\delta^2 U/\delta y^2)}{(\delta U/\delta y)^2}\right] + 1 \right\} \tag{9.iii}$$

*This appendix is based on a derivation by Toshihisa Toyoda.

If we differentiate the m.r.s. (9.3) between a and y with respect to a, the result is the expression in square brackets in (9.iii). Therefore, using m for m.r.s., (9.iii) becomes

$$\frac{\delta a}{\delta p_a} = \frac{1}{D} \frac{\delta U}{\delta y} \left(1 - a \frac{\delta m}{\delta a} \right) = \frac{\delta U / \delta y}{D} - \frac{a \, (\delta U / \delta y) \, (\delta m / \delta a)}{D}. \quad (9.iv)$$

The first term of (9.iv) represents the substitution effect, increasing the offer of input a. The second term represents the income effect, which operates in the opposite direction. The total becomes zero (maximum value of a) when

$$a \frac{\delta m}{\delta a} = 1. \quad (9.v)$$

This can be shown to equal the elasticity of the m.r.s., or m, with respect to y. Denote this elasticity by e:

$$e = \frac{\delta m}{\delta y} \frac{y}{m} = \left(\frac{\delta m}{\delta y} \frac{y}{m} \right) \left(\frac{a p_a}{y} \right) = \left(\frac{\delta m}{\delta y} \frac{y}{m} \right) \left(\frac{a \, m}{y} \right).$$

Since $y = a p_a$ and $p_a = m$ from (9.2, 9.3), cancellation of m and y yields (9.v) and completes the proof that a is maximized when e is unity, *i.e.*, that $e = 1$ is the critical point for the slope of input.

Robbins' elasticity (of demand for income in terms of effort) [26] may be denoted by η. It is, in our notation,

$$\eta = \frac{dy}{d \, (1/p_a)} \cdot \frac{1/p_a}{y} = \frac{dy}{dp_a} \cdot \frac{dp_a}{d \, (1/p_a)} \cdot \frac{1/p_a}{y}.$$

Utilizing $y = a p_a$,

$$\eta = - \left(a + p_a \frac{\delta a}{\delta p_a} \right) p_a^2 \cdot \frac{1}{a p_a^2} = - \left(1 + \frac{\delta a}{\delta p_a} \frac{p_a}{a} \right).$$

This also equals unity in absolute value where a is a maximum with respect to p_a and $\delta a / \delta p_a = 0$, but is not generally identical with e. The expression $\left(\dfrac{\delta a}{\delta p_a} \dfrac{p_a}{a} \right)$ is, of course, the conventional supply elasticity of a with respect to its own price. This supply elasticity is zero where a is a maximum with respect to p_a.

26. Lionel Robbins, "The Elasticity of Demand for Income in Terms of Effect," *Readings*, no. 13.

CHAPTER TEN

Collective Bargaining

Imperfections in Input Supply

1. Our entire treatment of input demand, and also our introductory chapter on input supply, have assumed pure competition on the supply side of input markets. We turn now to trade union collective bargaining as the major and standard example of imperfect competition in input supply. (This choice does not deny the existence and importance of "the land monopoly" or "the money trust" in regulating the supply of non-labor inputs at particular times and places.)

Since "imperfect competition," like "monopoly" and "syndicalism," has a pejorative meaning in conventional economics, its mention at the outset of any discussion of trade unionism or collective bargaining arouses immediate suspicion of antiunion, if not antilabor, bias. Economists friendly to the union movement, we know, deny the existence of labor monopoly[1]— at the same time that they credit collective bargaining with raising wage rates. (Their opponents are sometimes guilty of the opposite inconsistency, in accusing unions simultaneously of labor monopoly and of ineffectiveness in raising wages!) The question is worth examination in some detail.

2. Why cannot a trade union be a monopoly? We can isolate five arguments. (a) Labor is not a commodity, and only commodities can be monopolized. (b) Unions are not sellers of labor. (c) Unions as economic

---

1. One such presentation is Richard A. Lester, "Reflections on the 'Labor Monopoly' Issue," *J.P.E.* (December 1947).

organizations do not maximize any identifiable quantity such as profits or income. (d) Indeed, unions are primarily political organizations, concerned with issues of survival, power, and lobbying for their members' interests. (e) In the absence of unions, the bargaining power of monopolistic employers would be strong enough to distort nonunion labor markets further from the economists' "competitive model" than unionized markets actually are.

This superficially impressive case harbors its share of irrelevancies. First, it makes no difference whether or not labor is excluded from the definition of "commodity" for the special purposes of antimonopoly or other statutes—or, for that matter, of Marxian economic theory, which also excludes labor (but not labor-power) from its definition of commodity. If the definition of "commodity" be narrowed to exclude labor, or fish, why cannot the definition of "monopoly" be extended to cover such definitional noncommodities as labor, or fish? Second, an output monopolist may be either itself a seller of the output in question or merely an agent for the actual sellers; it is the latter capacity that a union may occupy on input markets. Third, an output monopolist, too, need not be a strict profit-maximizer; it may "optimize" or "satisfize" a multiple-goal mix of objectives that, like that of the union, defies quantitative amalgamation. Fourth, an output monopoly's concern, like a union's, may concentrate on the political climate of its industry. It may reward its friends and punish its enemies. It may finance or otherwise dominate a political faction or party. Oil interests in developing countries, and defense industries, or "merchants of death," in developed ones have furnished examples that Labor Parties can hardly surpass. Finally, we may admit the possibility of exploitative nonunion labor markets in any of the several senses of Chapter 8, without denying the monopoly status of unions. When a monopoly bargains with a monopsony, the result is called bilateral monopoly, not pure (or even workable) competition.

The Fellner Model

3. A useful introduction to the economics of collective bargaining is provided by a model included in Fellner's *Competition Among the Few*.[2] Figure 10.1 is derived from his work.

No fewer than six alternative solutions are included in this single bilateral-monopoly diagram. The first three are dominated by the union; the last two by the employer. The sixth case is pseudocompetitive. Furthermore, bargaining is limited to two issues, wages (w) and employment (n) ;

2. William Fellner, *op. cit.* (New York: Knopf, 1949) , ch. 10.

other issues are assumed, not always realistically, to be reducible to monetary or employment equivalents.

To start with familiar notions, let r in Figure 10.1 be the employer's
m.r.p. function, and a the value of the average net product of labor.[3] The
four indifference curves I_1, I_2, I_3, and I_0 are ascribed to the union officialdom collectively. If the curves are horizontal, they imply a union concerned only with the wage rate; if vertical, they imply a union concerned
only with the number of its employed (and dues-paying) membership;
if equilateral-hyperbolic, they imply a union concerned with workers'
total income nw. The curve I_1 has been drawn tangent to the employer's

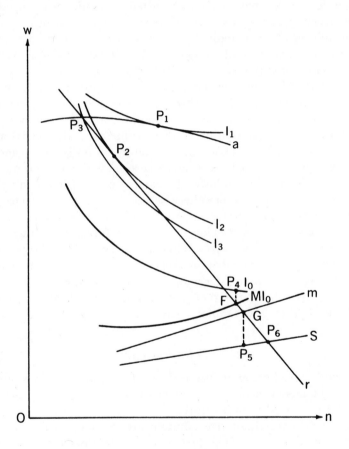

Figure 10.1

3. The average net product of input a is, in our notation:

$$\frac{1}{a}\left[xp - (bp_b + cp_c + \ldots)\right]$$

a curve, which is presumed known to the union. Similarly, I_2 is tangent to the employer's *r* curve. I_3 passes through the maximum value of $a,$[4] while I_0 is a locus of points such that, either below or to the left, the existing union is envisaged as falling apart and being replaced either by individual bargaining, or by some rival union or faction.

4. We can now indicate three union-dominant solutions. The most favorable holds when the union can dictate not only the wage rate but, either directly or through working rules, the volume of employment. This solution is at P_1, to which correspond a wage W_1 and employment N_1 (not included on the crowded diagram). Any outcome more favorable to the union (northwest of I_1, on a higher indifference curve would drive the employer out of business, which we suppose the union does not wish to do.[5] This solution, which has special virtues in overcoming monopolistic exploitation if it exists, is called the union's *optimum all-or-none bargain*. The location of P_1, of course, will differ with the union's preference system.

If the union can dictate only the wage rate but not the volume of employment at that rate, its best move is to P_2, implying a wage of W_2 and employment of N_2. This is inferior to P_1 as regards wage rate or employment or both, but is called the union's *optimum wage bargain*. The maximum wage the union can secure, under our assumptions, is indicated by the point P_3, which is called the union's *maximum wage bargain*. Because of its employment effects, it is generally less desirable than P_2. A common ordering of wage-rate results is $W_3 > (W_1, W_2)$;[6] of employment results, $N_1 > N_2 > N_3$.

In the case of horizontal indifference curves, with the union concerned only with wage rates, the points P_1 and P_2 both converge on P_3, and all three union-dominated bargains are identical.

5. We now shift assumptions to suppose the employer dominant in the bargaining situation. Fellner's analogue to all-or-none bargaining is a desire on the employer's part to retain the existing union, usually in preference to some more militant rival. His strategy is, therefore, to pick the point most favorable to himself on the union's "survival" indifference curve I_0, which we assume is known to the employer as well as to the union

4. The intersection of *a* and *r* on the diagram at the maximum value of *a* expresses graphically the Euler adding-up theorem, which need not hold in practice.

5. A *revolutionary* union may plan to do precisely this, after which the state or the union could itself take over the unprofitable enterprise cheaply. Our analysis abstracts not only from such syndicalist strategy, but also from the possibility that the employer can finance conditions better than P_1 by increasing exploitative pressure on consumers or on suppliers of some nonlabor input.

6. W_1 may be either above or below W_2.

leaders themselves. To locate this point, P_4 in Figure 10.1, the employer considers I_0 an average cost of maintaining his "sweetheart" union; he is pictured as visualizing a corresponding marginal cost function MI_0. The intersection of MI_0 with r gives a focal point F, from which P_4 can be located, with implicit coordinates (W_4, N_4). It is interesting that P_4, like P_1, lies to the right of the m.r.p. function r, so that it combines elements of featherbedding, made work, or disguised unemployment with employer dominance. (These may be looked upon as consequences of union *maintenance*, rather than union *dominance* as in Case 1.)

If the dominant employer is both willing and able to break the union altogether, the situation reduces to the simple monopsony case of Chapter 8. The employer faces a labor supply function s, from which an m.i.c. function m has been derived. The focal point, labeled G on the diagram, is at the intersection of m and r; the equilibrium point P_5 can be readily derived. Comparing the two employer-dominant solutions, it is clear that at least one of (W_4, N_4) must be larger than the corresponding coordinate (W_5, N_5). A competitive solution, incidentally, can also be found at P_6, the intersection of r and s, a point usually lying below and/or to the left of I_0.

Comparing now the extremes of union and employer dominance, it is no surprise to find the former cluster leading to higher wages. Analytically, this result is associated with the downward slopes of the a and r functions. The latter (employer-dominant) cluster, however, leads to higher employment in most cases. The most important exception is all-or-none bargaining as at P_1; inelastic r functions would also produce exceptions.

Two Intermediate Solutions

6.   The Fellner model is of little practical use, both because its informational requirements are extreme and because it indicates only end points of what may be wide ranges of indeterminacy. A model that confines collectively bargained wages between $0.50 and $10 an hour accomplishes little or nothing when the actual range of disagreement is between $2.50 and $2.60 an hour. In the same way, awareness of the consequences of complete dominance is not particularly helpful in bargaining situations where neither side possesses it.

We consider only two of the large number of existing incomplete-dominance bargaining models, an early one by Hicks and a later one by Pen.[7]

7. Hicks, *Theory of Wages, op. cit.*, ch. 7; J. Pen, *The Wage Rate Under Collective Bargaining*, trans. E. S. Preston (Cambridge: Harvard University Press, 1959). An enlightening review of the latter volume is by Carl Stevens, *Rev. Econ. and Stat.* (November 1960), pp. 463–465.

Both these models are best considered with the wage rate the only point at issue and other problems reducible somehow to wage equivalents. Also, both are best considered as *ex ante* models of behavior in advance of any strike or other work stoppage, rather than after such a dispute has begun.

7. In the Hicks model (Figure 10.2), consider first the position of the union bargainer. He desires a wage rate of W_o, usually lower than any of the completely union-dominant solutions worked out by Fellner. Rather than endure a strike of length T_i, however, he is willing to modify his demand to W_i. Similarly, the employer's representative wants a wage W'_o if he can get it without a stoppage, but is willing to offer W'_i rather than endure a strike of length T_i. As the length of the anticipated stoppage t increases, the union's wage coordinates W_i trace out what Hicks calls a

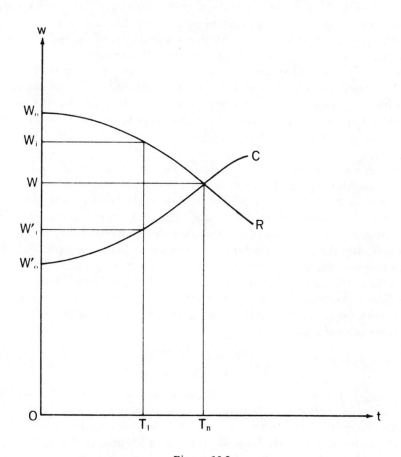

Figure 10.2

union demand function, which we label *R*. As we have suggested, it tends eventually to slope downward. The corresponding *employer's concession function,* labeled *C*, eventually takes on the opposite slope for the same reason, namely, the losses involved in work stoppage. Hicks assumes the two functions to cross only once at some point T_n with wage rate *W*. This, however, means neither that there will be a strike T_n in length, nor that settlement will actually be reached *ex post* at wage *W*, nor that *W* corresponds to the hypothetical competitive solution P_6 of Figure 10.1.

It is safer to regard Hicks' apparatus from the viewpoint of bargaining strategy *ex ante.* The union bargainer's function, formally speaking, is to make the union demand function *R* appear horizontal or upward-sloping, whatever its actual shape, and to frighten the employer into twisting his concession function *C* so as to increase its upward slope as bargaining proceeds. His object is the optimal settlement with the shortest work stoppage, beyond whatever stoppage the union may find useful for morale-building. The employer's representative has similar bluffing and threatening functions on the other side of the table. If a mediator or arbitrator enters the picture, his function is to ascertain the true pattern of the *R* and *C* functions, and then to convince the bargainers that he has done so, that is, that a solution in the neighborhood of *W* will eventually occur. The mediator is expected to do this as soon as possible, so that work stoppage can be averted or abbreviated.

8.   The more ambitious Pen model, which also assumes all macroeconomic variables constant, uses notions derived from game theory. Its basic notions are sets of wage-rate preferences and evaluations of both the risks and the consequences of work stoppage. Thus, the union's preferences are described by a utility function $L(W)$, which has a maximum at $L(W_l)$; both W_l and the $L(W)$ function may shift as the bargaining proceeds. In deciding whether to hold out for W_l instead of accepting some inferior settlement at *W*, a possible gain of $L(W_l) - L(W)$, is balanced by the union bargainer against a possible cost of $L(W_l) - Lc$, where *Lc* is the disutility of a work stoppage. The union's maximum acceptable risk of conflict Pen goes on to define as:

$$\phi_l \left[\frac{L(W_l) - L(W)}{L(W_l) - Lc} \right]$$

where ϕ_l is a union risk-evaluation function, depending on subjective attitudes toward risk, as well as the union's subjective forecast of the outcome of a strike.

If the union rejects the wage *W*, the risk of a stoppage depends on the employer's function $E(W) - Ec$, where *E* is a utility function for the employer (analogous to L) and Ec is the disutility of a stoppage to the employer. (If $E(W) - Ec < 0$, the employer himself will not accept the contract at wage W.) The union representative does not know $E(W)$ or Ec, but forms an estimate $F_l[E(W) - Ec]$, called by Pen a "correspection function," of the actual risk of conflict.

The union will settle at W if the maximum acceptable risk of conflict equals the estimated risk as derived from the correspection function:

$$\phi_l \left[\frac{L(W_l) - L(W)}{L(W_l) - Lc} \right] = F_l[E(W) - Ec] \qquad (10.1)$$

Similarly, the employer's representative will accept a contract at W, rather than holding out for something nearer his side's own optimum W_e,[8] when

$$\phi_e \left[\frac{E(W_e) - E(W)}{E(W_e) - Ec} \right] = F_e[L(W) - Lc]. \qquad (10.2)$$

A determinate contract is reached when and if (10.1) and (10.2) are satisfied simultaneously and the fact of mutual satisfaction can be somehow communicated between the parties, either directly or by the good offices of a third party.

While these collective bargaining models have some expository neatness, it is difficult to conjure up great optimism about their predictive power in specific disputes, their value to practical labor negotiatiors, or their amenability to quantitative statistical fitting. The formal theory of collective bargaining, rather, is still in its early stages of development.

The Incidence of Collective Bargaining[9]

9. The principal economic purpose of collective bargaining (as distinguished from its political or psychological purposes) is to raise wages and improve working conditions for particular groups of workers, or sometimes for workers as a class. The questions of whether it has done so, and at whose expense, may be summarized under the rubric of "the incidence of collective bargaining," modeled on the theory of tax incidence in public finance.

Some of the difficulties of our subject may be clarified by referring to its fiscal prototype. One perennial dispute relates to the question of whether or not one takes account of the expenditure of the tax receipts.

---

8. The subscripts l and e refer to "labor" and "employer" respectively.

9. This discussion leans heavily upon two previous efforts by the present writer, "The Incidence of Collective Bargaining," *A.E.R.* (May 1954), and "The Incidence of Collective Bargaining Once More," *So. Ec. J.* (April 1958).

Another tax-incidence dispute deals with the basis of comparison—a situation in which the tax under discussion is simply repealed, or replaced by some "standard" tax raising the same revenue, like Musgrave's proportional income levy. The analogous question for collective bargaining theory is whether to confine ourselves to collective bargaining construed narrowly or to take account of the political and other activities by which unions try to raise their bargaining power. In this discussion we take the narrower position for the sake of analytical manageability; Kerr has been a spokesman for those denying the realism of any separation between the political and the economic aspects of union activity:[10]

> The term "trade unionism" instead of "collective bargaining" is used deliberately. Unions can and do affect actions of both employers and governments, and some of both kinds of action have potential or actual consequences for distributive shares. To explore the impact of unionism in only the economic sphere . . . is to tell but half the tale.

This is no mere methodological quibble. Suppose one effect of collective bargaining to be the pricing of labor out of certain occupations, and lower wage rates wherever the displaced workers go; this would be a clear case of incidence on workers down graded or disemployed. But suppose that at the same time, the political pressure of the same union increased the employment opportunities of its members, so that the net result of union activities downgrades and disemploys nobody! The situation becomes yet more confusing when we recall that a union's collective bargaining practices may depend on the effectiveness of its political pressures, and vice versa.

10.   There seem to be six main theories of the incidence of collective bargaining in economic literature. They can be subdivided into two groups of three theories each. The first group maintains that incidence exists—unionists make gains through collective bargaining at the expense of one or another outside economic group. The second group of theories maintains that incidence does not exist; either union members make no gains over and beyond what the free market would have given them, or these gains come out of increased productivity and growth, injuring nobody.

(*1*) The redistribution theory. Collective bargaining redistributes income in favor of workers against receivers of profits and property income—"capitalists" in the broad sense. This is the *Machttheorie* ("power

10. Clark Kerr, "Labor's Income Share and the Labor Movement," in George W. Taylor and Frank C. Pierson (eds.) , *New Concepts in Wage Determination* (New York: McGraw-Hill, 1957) , p. 266.

theory") of the German historical and socialist economists, and similarly, the American institutionalists' bargaining theory of wages. It dates back at least to Karl Rodbertus. The great Böhm-Bawerk failed notably to lay the ghost of this theory in his last essay, "Macht oder ökonomisches Gesetz?" It remains the leading normative (if not positive) theory within the organized labor movement.[11]

(2) *The reallocation theory,* perhaps more nearly "orthodox" than any other. The labor share of private national income stays approximately constant—Bowley's Law is interpreted as a statistical wage-fund theory. What strongly organized workers gain is spread "sympathetically" to a number of related trades, industries, and perhaps localities. This process is known as "raising their sights." Outside this penumbra, the labor supply rises, wages fall, and increases are observed in open unemployment, withdrawal from the labor force, and involuntary entrepreneurship of the peanut-stand variety. Another group of losers under this pattern is that subset of consumers whose demands are concentrated on goods and services whose prices have been raised directly or indirectly by collective bargaining. (These are not "consumers as a whole.")

(3) *The inflation theory.* The effect of collective bargaining is to force up money wages and prices. Its incidence is on fixed income receivers and others whose wealth and income lag behind inflation.

Passing to theories denying any incidence of collective bargaining, we find:

(4) *The illusion theory.* Collective bargaining gives members of established unions, at least,[12] no more on the average than they could have expected through the competitive labor market.

(5) *The productivity theory.* Collective bargaining increases the rate of economic growth by "shocking" employers into increasing their efficiency and introducing innovations. It also insures workers against wage cuts and unemployment when their productivity rises, and increases their cooperation with technical progress. A higher growth rate results, out of which it has been possible to increase the pay of organized workers without injuring any other group.

(6) *The consumption theory.* This is usually presented as an exten-

11. A radical variant blames the government for shirking its alleged duty to insure that the positive incidence of collective bargaining follows the normative pattern. An English translation of Böhm-Bawerk's essay, entitled, "Control or Economic Law?" is in *Shorter Classics of Eugen von Böhm-Bawerk* (South Holland: Libertarian Press, 1962), vol. i, pp. 141–199. The German original appeared in *Zeitschrift für Volkswirtschaft, Sozialpolitik, und Verwaltung* (December 1914).

12. An upward fillip to wage rates as an early consequence of organization is often recognized, and attributed to the overcoming of monopsonistic exploitation. By "established" unions we mean those for which this short-run effect has already come and gone.

sion of the redistribution theory (numbered [1] above) but stressing longer-run effects. Collective bargaining redistributes income from capital to labor, hence from the rich to the poor. This raises purchasing power, permits full consumption and full production, and leaves even capitalists no worse off in the long run than they would have been without collective bargaining.

Of these six views, the redistribution, productivity, and consumption theories are prounion in their implications. The reallocation, inflation, and illusion theories share an antiunion flavor. The six theories are by no means mutually exclusive, and it is common to find writers combining more than one. Trade unionists often combine redistribution and consumption theories, sometimes adding productivity theories as well. Antiunion writers tend to combine reallocation and inflation theories, speaking of unemployment and inflation as consequences of union power.

11.   As often happens when ideological issues enter an argument, discussions of the incidence of collective bargaining are not always on a high level. Some writers take their own positions for granted, without rebutting or even mentioning those of others. Their arguments sometimes beg the question and otherwise play fast and loose with the evidence. For instance, when union wages rise faster than nonunion ones, the argument is that this shows that collective bargaining raises them; when they do not do so, it proves that collective bargaining rises nonunion wages as well! One also sees the fact of economic growth—through which all economic groups have enjoyed rising real incomes—used as evidence that collective bargaining has had no incidence and has injured nobody.

Advocates of redistribution theories, and of consumption theories built on them, assume that the share of production workers in private national income has risen as a consequence of collective bargaining. If they can, in fact, isolate no rise, they assume that the share would have fallen without collective bargaining because the capital-labor ratio has risen.[13] Neither proposition is tenable without supporting evidence, and such evidence as this writer has seen (summarized in Chapter 4) is inconclusive.[14] Nor have proponents of productivity theories yet investigated, in particular

13. This argument assumes the elasticity of substitution (σ) between capital and labor to exceed unity. The facts seem to point to the contrary conclusion.

14. See also Kerr, *op. cit.*, pp. 279–294. For the United States in particular (p. 281): "Over the past century [including both periods of union strength and weakness], labor's share has risen primarily as employed persons have become a more important component in our population. In other words, employees are not comparatively better off as individuals; there are, however, many more of them." In terms of Joseph D. Phillips' "Wage Parity" discussion ("Labor's Share and 'Wage Parity.'" *Rev. Econ. Stat.* (May 1960) p. 165), unionism does not seem to have raised the workers' parity ratio.

crafts or industries, the empirical relation between union power and the growth of productivity.[15]

The literature also tends to generalize and to erect universal theories of incidence on the basis of a few specific episodes of recent economic theory. The reallocation theorists seem to have been thinking about 1920–22 or 1929–33 in the United States and Great Britain, when union wage rates were maintained better than others, and when employment shifted from sectors of union strength to sectors of union weakness. The American underemployment inflation of 1936–37, followed by renewed depression in 1937–38, may have been uniquely important in inspiring combinations of misallocation and inflation theories.[16] The inflation of 1945–48 in the United States, following upon four years of wartime suppression, saw the emergence and development of the illusion theory. In periods of apparent cost-push inflation, it is naturally the inflation theory that is most fashionable.

12.   The present writer takes the eclectic position that different theories (or combinations) apply in good times than in bad, and that different theories apply under conditions of monetary ease than under conditions of monetary stringency. We therefore distinguish four cases. To make the problem more difficult, crafts, industries, and localities (and the associated unions) may operate simultaneously under quite different conditions of both prosperity and credit availability.

(*1*) When a craft, industry, or locality is enjoying both prosperity and easy money, the major effect of collective bargaining is inflation of the variety that has come to be known as cost-push or, more specifically, wage-push. Wage increases, above those obtainable under competition, can be both secured and passed on (or magnified) in output price increases.[17] The money supply expands as an adjustment to higher prices, and any rise in velocity of circulation is not offset, so that prosperity continues. The increased wages and prices are not only *financed* but *under-*

---

15. We do not know the relative importance of union encouragement of efficiency (in the use of machinery and raw materials) and union encouragement of featherbedding (in the use of direct manpower). The relevant literature has been reviewed by Kerr, "Productivity and Labor Relations," (Berkeley: University of California Institute of Industrial Relations, n.d.) Reprint 96, as of 1957.

16. Three standard American presentations are Henry C. Simons, "Some Reflections on Syndicalism," in *Economic Policy for a Free Society* (Chicago: University of Chicago Press, 1948), ch. 6; Charles E. Lindblom, *Unions and Capitalism* (New Haven: Yale University Press, 1949), ch. 11; Fritz Machlup, *Political Economy of Monopoly* (Baltimore: Johns Hopkins University Press, 1952), chs. 9–10.

17. Bargaining under an open or tacit understanding that wage increases will be passed on completely, or more than completely, in output prices may be called collusive as well as collective in character.

written or *validated* by easy money, to which is often added loose budget-
ary policy as well.[18]

(2) When times are good but money is tight, any appreciable rise of
wages and prices in a strongly organized economic sector is accompanied
or followed by downward pressures on wages,[19] prices, output, and employment in the economy as a whole. We then have a reallocation effect,
since the original price- and wage-raising sectors are usually protected
by such circumstances as price and income inelasticities of both output
and input demand. Thus, a wage and price rise in steel can lead, through
financial repercussions, to wage cuts or unemployment in textiles or construction rather than in the steel industry itself. The reallocation effect is
heightened if disemployed workers from the steel industry join the textile-
industry labor supply.

(3) When a craft, industry, or locality is itself suffering hard times
and tight money, the major incidence of collective bargaining is again
reallocation, which is sometimes called antideflationary. Money wages are
held at the levels of the last prosperity; they are at least as likely to rise as
to fall. Employment falls off in terms of hours, and usually also in terms
of men. The unemployed go elsewhere; new entrants enter elsewhere;
wages are often forced down elsewhere. The resulting displacment may be
upward, as when coal miners from Kentucky become auto workers in
Michigan. More commonly, displacement will be downward, involving
more unemployment of old skills than development of new ones. Accompanying the displacement and reallocation are assorted price reactions
favorable to some consumers and unfavorable to others, as relative prices
follow the relative wage movements.

(4) If collective bargaining, by raising wages, results indirectly in some
loosening of credit during a recession or depression, recovery may be ini-
tiated through the mechanism of the consumption theory of the incidence,
or rather nonincidence, of collective bargaining. Such cases, however, are
extremely rare and usually involve political rather than economic pressure by the trade unions. They also entail, in most cases, some element of
inflation or "reflation" as well.

---

18. A distinction should be made between that degree of monetary ease which finances
a wage increase in the first instance, and that further degree which underwrites or validates it by providing higher money purchasing power at higher money prices. When we
consider (in chapter 11) the relation between the general wage level and employment,
the lesser degree of monetary ease may support the classical (inverse) relation, whereas
the greater degree supports the Keynesian independence relation or the super-Keynesian
(direct) relation.

19. The pressure on wages is more likely to reduce real wages than money wages in
an inflationary environment.

With limitations, therefore, we may concur with Slichter as to the inflationary bias in current collective bargaining arrangements, if not in his recommendation to accept the inflation passively.[20] The major limitation is to good times with easy money. If times are bad or money is tight, the major effect of collective bargaining is to reallocate labor and to change relative prices rather than the general price level. When hard times are combined with easy money, substantial consumption and purchasing-power increase may be achieved by collective bargaining with minimal inflation.[21] At another extreme, when inflation gets under way for other reasons than cost-push, as in the American episodes of 1945–1948 and 1950–1951, bargained labor markets often inflate no faster, or even slower, than competitive ones, if excess demand for labor is general at prevailing wage rates and if union contracts run for long terms.[22] In these cases, the illusion theory of nonincidence rules the roost.

In both good and bad times, particularly the latter, bargaining probably induces a slight redistribution of income. The empirical evidence was developed for the United States by Levinson, and has been considered in Chapter 4, section 8.[23] There is also supporting evidence from Great Britain and Western Europe, if not from Japan.[24] It is nevertheless unwise

20. Sumner Slichter, "Do the Wage-Fixing Arrangements in the American Labor Market Have an Inflationary Bias?" *A.E.R.* (May 1954), pp. 342–346. See also section 15–19, below, in which we consider the contributions of H. Gregg Lewis.

21. What some unionists desire, in their effort to tap the profit share, are controls to prevent the passing of wage increases through to price increases, without at the same time stiffening employer resistance to the wage increases themselves. Such control systems do not exist in capitalist systems, except where bargaining is replaced or supplemented by public regulation of wages and prices.

22. Albert Rees, "The Economic Impact of Collective Bargaining in the Steel and Coal Industries During the Postwar Period," Industrial Relations Research Association, *Proceedings* (1950), pp. 203–210.

23. N. J. Simler, "Unionism and Labor's Share in Manufacturing Industries," *Rev. Econ. and Stat.* (November 1961), uses a different methodology less sensitive to the choice of beginning and ending dates, and finds rather less redistribution than does Levinson.

24. E. H. Phelps Brown and P. E. Hart, "The Share of Wages in National Income," *Ec. J.* (June 1952), pp. 276 f.; also Phelps Brown, "The Long-Term Movement of Real Wages," in John T. Dunlop (ed.), *Theory of Wage Determination* (London: Macmillan, 1957), pp. 48–65. Phelps Brown sees a conventional element in profit margins, which can be squeezed by the coincidence of a hard labor market (aggressive collective bargaining) with a soft product market (depressed economic conditions and/or vigorous price competition.)

The Japanese evidence (which relates to a boom decade, 1951–1960) relates labor shares (and their first differences) simultaneously to unionization ratios and (average) labor productivity. Most of the "unionization ratio" coefficients in both regressions are statistically insignificant and/or have the "wrong" (negative) sign. Masao Baba, "Economic Growth, Labor Unions, and Income Distribution," in Ryutaro Komiya (ed.)

to base any consumption theory of nonincidence on so small a redistributive effect as any writer has yet isolated.

13.   To summarize: Our eclectic theory of the incidence of collective bargaining stresses price inflation (incidence on fixed-income consumers) for an easy money prosperity, or for a depression with expansionist monetary and fiscal policy; it conforms to an illusion theory once a demand-pull inflation is under way, and to a labor-reallocation theory (incidence on displaced workers) in most other circumstances. A redistributive strain (incidence on "capitalists") underlies the process, but on a scale too small to produce significant consumption effects or otherwise to influence the course of prosperity. The illusion theory also warns us at all times against exaggerating the quantitative significance of other patterns of incidence. As for the productivity theory of nonincidence, the evidence for and against it awaits detailed examination.

The Phillips Curve

14.   Phillips curves are empirical attempts to explain and predict the rate of increase in money wages (or occasionally in real wages) using a number of lagged independent variables, particularly the rate of unemployment, the size and direction of change of business profits, and the rate of living-cost inflation.[25] Phillips curves are relevant here because of their implications regarding the incidence of the collective bargaining institution. We shall revisit them, in other connections, in Chapters 11 and 17, below.

The next diagram (Figure 10.3) represents two simplified two-variable Phillips curves, P_0 and P_1. The horizontal axis is an unemployment rate, either gross or net of the rate of unfilled vacancies, while the vertical axis is the rate of change of either money or real wages. The downward slope of the Phillips curves conforms roughly to expectations. The horizontal

Postwar Economic Growth in Japan (trans. Robert S. Ozaki, Berkeley: University of California Press, 1966), pp. 143–151. G. Tsujimura later related this anomaly to the appearance of excess demand in the lowest-wage (unorganized) labor markets. Rōdōryoku no Yukōryō de Kanari no Seichō wa Kanō," *Ekonomisuto* (Oct. 20, 1967).

25. A. W. Phillips, "The Relation Between Unemployment and the Rate of Change of Money Wage Rates in the United Kingdom, 1962–1957," *Economica* (November 1958). Alternative explanations of Phillips' results are found in E. S. Phelps, "Phillips Curves, Expectations of Inflation, and Optimal Employment Over Time," *Economica* (August 1967); M. Friedman, "The Role of Monetary Policy," *A.E.R.* (March 1968) pp. 8–11; the two main papers (by Solow and Cagan) in Stephen W. Rousseas (ed.), *Inflation: Its Causes, Consequences, and Control* (Wilton, Conn.; Kazanjian Economics Foundation, 1969); also R. E. Lucas and Leonard Rapping, "Real Wages, Employment and Inflation," *J.P.E.* (September-October 1969).

line *A* represents an estimate of the maximum annual rate of wage increase compatible with price-level stability. In the context of the Kennedy-
Johnson "guideposts" in the United States (1962–66), *A* would have been
a 3.2 per cent increase in money wages. The region above *A* is "inflationary." The vertical line *B* represents an estimate of the maximum unemployment rate politically tolerable to the government in power, given the
importance of the labor vote. In the American case, *B* might be 5 per cent.
The area to the right of *B* is "political dynamite." The *A* and *B* lines
cross at a focal point *F*.

Let P_0 be the Phillips curve under weak unionism or no important col-

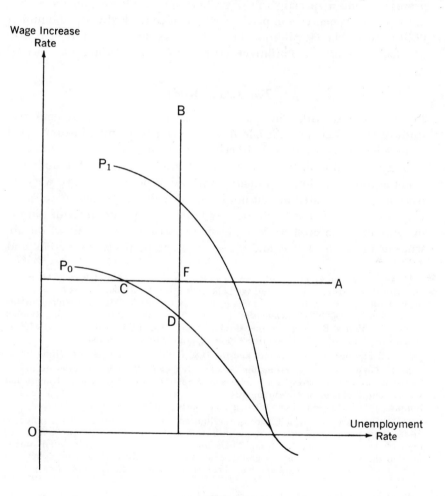

Figure 10.3

lective bargaining, as in the period dominating Phillips' initial study of
1958. It is drawn passing to the southwest of the focal point F, which
means that monetary and fiscal policy makers can maneuver over a considerable range of high-employment, noninflationary policies; the range
is labeled CD on the diagram. This type of Phillips curve is sometimes
called "good." On the other hand, more recent studies of highly unionized
economies suggest "bad" Phillips curves like P_1, passing to the northeast
of the focal point F.[26] Such a situation gives the public the unhappy
choice of inflation and unemployment. In terms of incidence theory, such
a Phillips curve implies inflationary incidence of collective bargaining in
prosperity, and a special form of reallocation incidence (on the unemployed) during depression, particularly when contrasted with a nonunion
Phillips curve like P_0. Additional evidence has been supplied by Pierson,[27]
who has fitted separate Phillips curves to "union" and "nonunion" sectors.

The Lewis Model

15. In contrast with Phillips-curve analysis, the ambitious empirical
study of H. G. Lewis on the effects of collective bargaining in the United
States[28] may be looked upon either as supporting, or as partially discon-
firming,[29] the illusion theory of the incidence of collective bargaining.

Lewis concerns himself primarily with what he calls relative wage effects, which are related to, but not identical with, what others have called
wage distortions. Let w_i be the observed money wage rate in sector i in the
presence of unionism,[30] while w_{io} is the hypothetical wage rate in the absence of unionism. Let v_i and v_{io} be equal, respectively, to $(w_i/\bar{w})$ and

26. An influential American illustration is Paul A. Samuelson and Robert M. Solow,
"Analytical Aspects of Anti-Inflationary Policy," *A.E.R.* (May 1960). See also two papers
by R. J. Bhatia, "Unemployment and the Rate of Change in Money Earnings in the
United States, 1900–1958," *Economica* (August 1961), and "Profits and the Rate of
Change in Money Earnings in the United States, 1935–1959," *Ibid.* (August 1962),
which divide the American experience into separate historical periods.

27. Gail Pierson, "Union Strength and the U.S. 'Phillips Curve,'" *A.E.R.* (June 1968).

28. H. Gregg Lewis, *Unionism and Relative Wages in the United States* (Chicago:
University of Chicago Press, 1963). See also a review article by Reder, "Unions and
Wages: The Problems of Measurement," *J.P.E.* (April 1965). I am indebted to Leonard
Rapping for elucidation of several stages of Lewis' original argument.

29. Milton Friedman, an adherent of the illusion theory, suggests 15–20 per cent as a
probable upper limit to upward wage distortion and 4 per cent as a probable lower
limit of downward wage distortion. These limits seem to embody substantial concessions to the distortion theory. "Significance of Labor Unions for Economic Policy," in
D. M.C. Wright (ed.), *The Impact of the Union*, (New York: Harcourt Brace, 1951)
p. 216.

30. Unionism need not be present in sector i. It suffices that it be present somewhere
in the economy.

$(w_{io}/\overline{w}_o)$, where $\overline{w}$ and $\overline{w}_o$ are weighted means of the w_i and w_{io}. Then R_i, or (v_i/v_{io}), measures what Lewis calls the relative wage effect of unionism on sector i.[31]

16. Lewis' contribution is the devising of procedures for estimating relative wage effects empirically, without knowing either the hypothetical union-free wage rates or the absolute wage effects derived from them. Estimation details differ from one study to another, but what follows may be regarded as a paradigm of the Lewis method. At any time, let

$$w_i = f(s_i, p_i) \tag{10.3}$$

where the s_i are "market-force" or "supply-and-demand" variables acting on sector i, while p_i is a measure of trade union power. For two sectors i and j, likewise:

$$\frac{w_i}{w_j} = f\left(\frac{s_i}{s_j}, \frac{p_i}{p_j}\right).$$

This procedure uses union power p (measured by the proportion of eligible workers covered by collective agreements) as a residual, after such market variables as supply, demand, labor quality, race, age, region, and city size have been allowed for, however imperfectly, under s. Lewis also admits that p, so measured, is an imperfect index of union power. It is also possible that labor quality may be correlated with unionism in ways that lead statistically to ascribing their joint effects entirely to unionism, and so to overestimating union power effects on wages.[32] No adjustments are made for featherbedding, all-or-none bargaining, or other related effects of unionism. Attention is focused strictly on hourly wage rates, which in principle have been adjusted for fringe benefits with pecuniary equivalents, but exclude all other fringe benefits.

17. Divide the American economy into sectors i (strongly organized) and j (weakly organized). The former includes, for Lewis, manufacturing, mining, construction, communications, and public utilities. The latter

---

31. Lewis also defines an *absolute* wage effect A_i, or (w_i/w_{io}). The absolute and relative wage effects are related as follows:

$$R_i = v_i/v_{io} = (w_i/w_{io}) / (\overline{w}/\overline{w}_o) = A_i/A$$

where A is the weighted mean of the absolute wage effects A_i. Given the A_i, we could obtain the R_i directly, but the reverse pattern of estimation is impossible without knowledge of the hypothetical union-free wage rates w_{io}. For this reason, Lewis does not estimate absolute effects.

32. There is an obvious pattern of correlation between unionism and labor quality: unionism leads to higher wages, leading in turn to employment of higher-quality labor (exclusion of lower-quality labor).

includes trade, finance, agriculture, government, and service industries. For the period 1920–1958, Lewis writes his relative wage effect equations (10.3) in exponential form:

$$R_i = \frac{v_i}{v_{io}} = e^{\beta(p_i - \bar{p})} \qquad \text{and} \qquad R_j = e^{\beta(p_j - \bar{p})}.$$

where $\bar{p}$ is a weighted average of p_i and p_j, and the statistical parameter β is the focus of all the analysis that follows. Taking logarithms:

$$\log v_i = \log v_{io} + \beta(p_i - \bar{p})$$
$$\log v_j = \log v_{jo} + \beta(p_j - \bar{p})$$

whence, by subtraction:

$$\log(v_i/v_j) = \log(v_{io}/v_{jo}) + \beta(p_i - p_j).$$

Let $W = (v_i/v_j)$, $W_o = (v_{io}/v_{jo})$, and $p = (p_i - p_j)$:

$$\log W = \log W_o + \beta p \qquad\qquad (10.4)$$

It is clear that β is the estimate of relative wage effects that Lewis seeks, while W_o is his market forces variable. Before fitting (10.4), however, we need an estimate of W_o by years. This estimate Lewis obtains most ingeniously. Let E_d be the labor demanded in sector i (as a percentage of that demanded in sector j). Let E_s be a similar ratio of labor supply in sector i, and let Q be a ratio of average value added per worker in sector i, both relative to sector j. Assume these new variables related by log-linear functions:

$$\log E_d = c_o + c_q \log Q - c_w \log W_o$$
$$\log E_s = C_o + C_w \log W_o$$

where the Q are known, and the terms in c and C are statistical parameters. Equate the last two equations (*i.e.*, assume an equilibrium solution), and solve for $\log W_o$. The result is

$$\log W_o = \frac{c_o - C_o}{c_w + C_w} + \frac{c_q}{c_w + C_w} \log Q.$$

Call the constant term A, and the coefficient of $\log Q$, D. Substituting in (10.4) we obtain (10.5), in observable variables only, with each observation relating to a different year:

$$\log W = A + D \log Q + \beta p. \qquad\qquad (10.5)$$

This procedure, to repeat, avoids problems of labor quality. For example, if the occupation "mix" is getting "richer" in i relative to j, an upward bias is imparted to the coefficient β, and vice versa.

18. Estimates of β are not constant throughout the generation 1920–1958. For example, from a number of results over various subperiods, Lewis finds β to be correlated positively with the growth rate of union power:

$$\beta = \beta_0 + \beta_1 \, (p_t - p_{t-1}) = \beta_0 + \beta_1 \, \Delta p.$$

Positive values of the coefficient β_1 lead Lewis to suspect that, when union strength is rising, the economic climate and possibly the weakening of exploitation permit larger relative wage effects.

Lewis also argues that β tends to fall as a result of inflation, particularly unanticipated inflation. If x is the actual price level, and x^* its expected or "permanent" value as derived from past experience,[33]

$$\beta = g \, [\Delta p, \, (x/x^*) \,]$$

33. The estimation of x^* involves a digression. We assume that the permanent price level adjusts only partially to disturbances of expectations:

$$x^*_t - x^*_{t-1} = b \, (x_t - x^*_{t-1}) \qquad (0 < b < 1)$$
$$x^*_t = bx_t + (1-b) \, x^*_{t-1} \tag{10.i}$$

Similarly:

$$x^*_{t-1} = bx_{t-1} + (1-b) \, x^*_{t-2}, \; x^*_{t-2} = bx_{t-2} + (1-b) \, x^*_{t-3}, \text{ etc.}$$

By mathematical induction, substituting in (10.i):

$$x^*_t = bx_t + b \, (1-b) \, x_{t-1} + b \, (1-b)^2 x_{t-2} + b \, (1-b)^3 x_{t-3} + \ldots$$

with the remainder eventually vanishing for a sufficient number of terms, leaving:

$$x^*_t = b \sum_0^n \, (1-b)^i x_{t-i} \tag{10.ii}$$

To estimate b, we may apply the equation of exchange. If M is the nominal money supply, v the velocity of circulation, and y^* an estimate of long-term (permanent) income:

$$M_t = \frac{(x^* y^*)_t}{v} \quad \text{and} \quad M_{t-1} = \frac{(x^* y^*)_{t-1}}{v} \, .$$

Substitute for x^*_t its value as per (10.i) above, and eliminate x^*_{t-1}:

$$M_t = \left[bx_t + \frac{(1-b) \, v \, M_{t-1}}{y^*_{t-1}} \right] \frac{y^*_t}{v}$$
$$M_t = \frac{b}{v} x_t y^*_t + (1-b) \, (y^*_t / y^*_{t-1}) \, M_{t-1}$$

which gives, in order, $(1-b)$, b, and v, if y^* is known.

If y^* is not known, it too may be estimated from consumption C and the average consumption propensity c. By analogy with (10.i):

$$y^*_t = dy_t + (1-d) \, y^*_{t-1} \qquad (0 < d < 1) \, .$$

We also suppose

$$C_t = cy^*_t \quad \text{and} \quad C_{t-1} = cy^*_{t-1}$$

whence:

$$C_t = c \left[dy_t + \frac{(1-d)}{c} C_{t-1} \right] = cdy_t + (1-d) \, C_{t-1}$$

which gives estimates of $(1-d)$, d, and c in that order. From the resulting estimate of d, by analogy with equation (10.ii):

$$y^*_t = d \sum_0^n \, (1-d)^i y_{t-i}$$

This equation is linearized to

$$\beta = \beta_0 + \beta_1 \Delta p + \beta_2 \ (x/x^*).$$

Substituting in (10.5) gives an equation with multiplicative terms in p:

$$\log W = A + D \log Q + \beta_0 \ p + \beta_1 \ p \Delta p + \beta_2 (x/x^*) \ p. \qquad (10.6)$$

While (10.6) fits the American data well, and the signs are as expected ($\beta_1 > 0$, $\beta_2 < 0$), this equation does not purport to explain interindustry differences within the unionized sector. Neither does it separate out the apparent "compression effect" of inflation upon the wage structure, by which lower incomes tend to outpace the higher ones.

19.   Sections 15–18 have merely sampled the methods of Lewis and his coworkers. On the basis of the entire group of studies, we present a running quotation summarizing Lewis' principal conclusions:[34]

> The majority of workers are employed in industries whose average relative wages have been raised or lowered by unionism by no more than 4 per cent. However, in industries employing a small fraction of the labor force—less than 6 per cent—the relative wage effect is 20 per cent or more. The list includes bituminous coal mining, some building trades in some cities in which the trades are highly unionized, and possibly barbering in a few cities.
>
> There is much uniformity in the evidence that the impact of unionism on the average union/nonunion relative wage varied markedly from one date to another. The peak impact of the last 40 years occurred about 1932-33, near the bottom of the Great Depression. At the peak, the effect of unionism on the average wage of union workers relative to the average wage of nonunion workers may have been above 25 per cent. The relative wage effect declined sharply to a level between 10 and 20 per cent by the end of the 1930's. The decline continued until about 1947 or 1948, the peak of the inflation immediately following World War II. At the trough, the impact of unionism was close to zero—under 5 per cent.
>
> The near-zero relative wage effect of unionism did not persist, however. In recent years the average union/nonunion relative wage was approximately 10 to 15 per cent higher than it would have been in the absence of unionism. During the 1950's, the extent of unionization of the labor force was close to 25 per cent. These figures imply that recently the average wage of union workers was 7 to 11 per cent higher relative to the average wage of all workers, both union and nonunion, than it would have been in the absence of unionism. Similarly, the average wage of nonunion workers was about 3 to 4 per cent lower relative to the average wage of all workers than in the absence of unionism.
>
> Unionism has tended to raise relative wages most in industries with above-average relative wages. Therefore, unionism has been a factor making the rela-

34. Lewis, *op. cit.*, pp. 4–9. (Italics in original.)

tive inequality of wages *among industries* greater than it otherwise would be. In 1958, unionism increased the relative inequality of average wages by about 6 to 10 per cent compared to what [it] would have been in the absence of unionism.

It does not follow, however, that unionism must have increased the relative inequality of wages *among all individual members of the labor force*. The latter depends on both the relative inequality *among* industries and the average relative inequality of wages of individual workers *within* industries. Unionism could have reduced the all-worker inequality by reducing the average inequality *within* industries by more than enough to offset the increase in inequality *among* industries.

It is improbable that unionism has changed within-industry inequality by as much as 5 per cent. If unionism has increased the inequality of average relative wages *among industries* by 8 per cent and has changed the average relative wage inequality *among workers within industries* by not more than 5 per cent, then unionism has changed the relative wage inequality *among all workers* by less than 6 per cent.

20.   In a subsequent study, Lewis extended his analysis to encompass a relative *employment* effect of unionism as well.[35] His basic demand and supply equations, using the variables of section 17, embody lagged-adjustment effects:

Demand:
$$\log E_t - \log E_{t-1} = \gamma \left[a_o + a_q \log Q - a \log W_t - \log E_{t-1} \right]$$
Supply:
$$\log E_t - \log E_{t-1} = \delta \left[c_o + c \log W_t - (a + c)(B_t p_t) - \log E_{t-1} \right]$$

where the new variable B is an estimate of the relative wage effect of unionism as between the union and nonunion sectors, and the new variable E is employment in the union relative to the nonunion sector. The coefficients γ and δ represent partial adjustments. Their values are positive but less than unity.

When the relative wage variable W_t is eliminated between these equations, the result may be written

$$\log E_t = b_o + b_q \log Q_t + b_t \log E_{t-1} + b_u (B_t p_t)$$

with the various coefficients compounded from those of the original pair of equations. Whether the relative-employment variable E_t be measured in terms of man-hours or employees (Lewis uses both series), the b_u coefficient is negative, indicating a tendency of unionism to reduce employment in union sectors relative to nonunion sectors of the economy, and implying some "reallocation" incidence of collective bargaining. More-

35. "Relative Employment Effects of Unionism," Industrial Relations Research Association, *Proceedings* (December 1963).

over, none of the unionism coefficients b_u differed significantly from (-1), suggesting that the order of magnitude of the relative employment effect was roughly the same as the relative wage effect.

21.   Rees, combining the Lewis studies with Harberger's earlier work on enterprise monopoly, estimated the output loss due to union redistribution of labor in the United States at approximately $600 million in 1957, or approximately 0.15 per cent of national output.[36] His argument is reproduced as Figure 10.4. The numerical results are accurate, however, only under the restrictive conditions of the diagram.

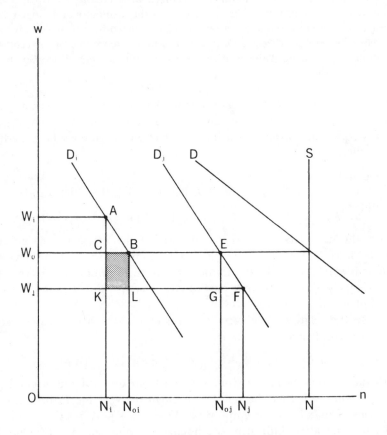

Figure 10.4

36. Albert Rees, "The Effects of Unions on Resource Allocation," *J.L.E.* (October 1963) ; the equivalent study on enterprise monopoly is Arnold Harberger, "Monopoly and Resource Allocation," *A.E.R.* (May 1954) .

The axes of Figure 10.4 are again employment (n) and wage rate (w). S is the labor supply function, which is considered absolutely inelastic. D_i, D_j and D represent, respectively, the demand for labor in the union sector, the nonunion sector, and both combined; D_i and D_j must be parallel. Before the entry to unionism, there is a common uniform wage W_o. If the union raises this rate to W_i in sector i, employment in that sector falls from N_{io} to N_i. This increases the labor supply to the nonunion sector j. Employment in j rises from N_{jo} to N_j, with total employment remaining at N. The wage rate in the nonunion sector, however, is forced down from W_o to W_j.

Since the demand functions are presumed related to marginal productivities, the areas under them are approximations to total products. As a result of the labor reallocation, the output loss in the unionized sector i is the trapezoidal figure ABN_iN_{oi}, while the output gain in the nonunion sector j is the trapezoid $EFN_{oj}N_j$. It remains to compare the gain with the loss.

Because N_iN_{oi} and $N_{oj}N_j$ are equal while D_i and D_j are parallel, both the triangles ABC and EFG and the rectangles KLN_iN_{oi} and $GFN_{oj}N_j$ are congruent. The only difference between the gross output gain and the gross output loss, therefore, is the shaded rectangle $CBKL$, representing a net loss. The base of this rectangle is the employment shift, while the altitude is half the relative wage effect W_jW_i.

Rees traces the arithmetic of his final estimate:[37]

> Union membership in the United States in 1957 was approximately 17 million. A relative employment effect of 15 per cent implies a transfer of about 1.7 million workers out of the union sector as a result of bargaining, and a relative wage effect of 15 per cent implies an absolute wage effect of about $700 per worker per year. One half of $700 times 1.7 million is approximately $600 million.

22. Strong unions and their spokesmen see the role of collective bargaining not as reallocating labor but as raising the sights of the less strongly organized and encouraging them to develop their own bargaining power. We can extend the Lewis-Rees analysis somewhat, to cover this sight-raising effect and the possibly related phenomena of disemployment, including involuntary entrepreneurship.

---

37. Rees, "Effect of Unions on Resource Allocation," *op. cit.*, p. 71. The 15 per cent figures are at the high end of the Lewis estimates. (The 17 million union membership figure, as against nearly 54 million nonunion labor force participants, indicates a union-nonunion employment ratio of 0.31. Had this ratio been 15 per cent higher, or 0.36, union membership would have been 18.8 million. The differential of 1.8 million is comparable with Rees' estimate of 1.7 million.)

Let D_0 and S_0 (in Figure 10.5) be pre-union demand and supply functions for some type of labor. Their intersection results in employment N_0
and a wage rate W_0. Let us now suppose that N' of the labor force orga-
nizes and obtains, through collective bargaining, a higher wage rate W'.
This reduces the remaining (unorganized) labor supply, who are working
at wages below W', by not only N' but some larger amount. (More workers now refuse to work for low wages and disappear from the labor markets into voluntary unemployment.) The difference between the new
supply function S_1 and the dashed function $(S_0 - N')$ measures the sight-
raising effect, which is presumably higher at wages well below W' than at
wages close to W'. The demand function D_1 for unorganized labor is simply $(D_0 - N')$, assuming the union strong enough to prevent its own dis-
establishment. If nothing more happens, the nonunion wage rate rises to
W_1 because of the raising of its sights. Total employment, however, is
$(N' + N_1)$, which is less than the original N_0.

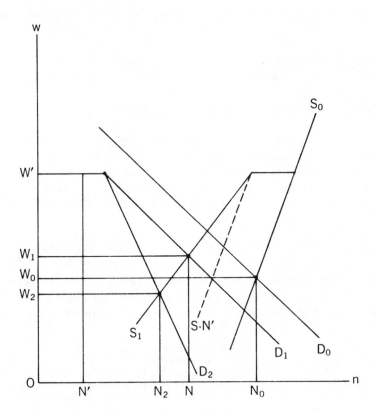

Figure 10.5

But something more is likely to happen. This "something more" is a decrease in the demand for unorganized labor at wages below W', in anticipation of future organization and wage demands, or, more generally, in anticipation of additional raising of the workers' expectations. This effect is indicated on the diagram by a leftward shift in D_1, or $(D_0 - N')$, to D_2. As Figure 10.5 is drawn, this shift is so large, particularly at lower wages, that the nonunion wage W_2 is not only below W_1 but also below W_0, despite the "raising-sights" effect. While this accords with Lewis' conclusions, there is no necessity about it; W_2 may exceed W_0. However, a further fall in employment, denoted on the diagram by N_1N_2, is avoidable, if at all, only by all-or-none bargaining.

Labor Aristocracy, Wage Distortion, Noncompeting Groups

23.   Ideological passion lurks close below the surface of any discussion of the incidence of collective bargaining, especially in the case of labor-reallocation theories. Unionists are naturally sensitive to charges of constituting a labor aristocracy, of being a noncompeting group of pampered palace slaves, or of serving as equal or junior partners in exploiting the proletariat, whether these charges come from the political Right or Left.[38]

24.   What is a labor aristocracy? Discussing the phenomenon in nineteenth-century Britain, for which he estimated the aristocracy at between 10 and 20 per cent of the working class, the labor historian Hobsbawm listed six identifying criteria:[39]

> *First,* the frequency and regularity of a worker's earnings; *second,* his prospects of social security; *third,* his conditions of work, including the way he was treated by foreman and masters; *fourth,* his relations with the social strata above and below him; *fifth,* his general conditions of living; *lastly,* his prospects of future advancement and those of his children.

38. Exemplifying criticism from the Left, we have the long-time American Socialist leader Norman Thomas, proposing that "every union, to be entitled to recognition as the agency of the workers in collective bargaining . . . must conform to certain minimum standards of democracy. Its doors must be open to all qualified workers, regardless of race, creed, or color, under reasonable standards of initiation fees and dues. Next, its constitution, by-laws, and elections must provide for orderly elections at reasonable intervals . . . Disciplinary procedure must . . . protect members of the union from arbitrary punishment more serious than most judges and juries can impose. Possibly some other requirements might be laid down . . . but those which I have mentioned seem to me essential." "How Democratic are Labor Unions?" *Harper's Magazine* (May 1942), quoted by Myrdal, *Challenge to Affluence,* (New York: Pantheon, 1963), p. 80. (Post-1942 legislation has sought to remedy the abuses Thomas had in mind, utilizing remedies less extreme than those he had proposed.)

39. E. J. Hobsbawm, "The Labour Aristocracy in Nineteenth-Century Britain," forming ch. 15 of *Labouring Men: Studies in the History of Labour* (London: Weidenfeld and Nicholson, 1964), p. 273.

Hobsbawm goes on to distinguish between the old (nineteenth century) labor aristocracy, composed primarily of skilled craftsmen, and the new, which includes "the permanent full-time officialdom of trade unions and the full time politicians among labour leaders," "salaried white collar, technical, and similar workers," and "a relatively contented stratum of 'plebeians' promoted to semi-skilled factory work, to secure jobs in and about the vastly swollen apparatus of government and so on,"[40] presumably including in "and so on" unions as well as workers in the strongest, and most strongly unionized private monopolists, oligopolists, and cartel members.

24.   Standard economic theory has concerned itself less with labor-aristocracy issues as such than with the obviously related question—whether the structure of relative wages was primarily to be explained by "equalizing differences" or by "noncompeting groups." Thoroughgoing practitioners of a labor theory of value, such as Ricardo and Marx, are forced by the logic of their position to the former view, according to which higher wages tended to compensate in the long run for various nonpecuniary disadvantages of particular employments, and vice versa. The best-known statement of the equalizing-difference principle is, however, Book i, Chapter 10 of Adam Smith's *Wealth of Nations*. Smith was upholding (in this chapter) a total-cost rather than a labor theory of value; his exposition applies to the rate of profit equally with the wage structure:[41]

> The whole of the advantages and disadvantages of the different employments of labour and stock must, in the same neighborhood, be either perfectly equal or continually tending to equality. If in the same neighborhood, there was any employment evidently either more or less advantageous than the rest, so many people would crowd into it in the one case, and so many would desert it in the other, that its advantages would soon return to the level of other employments . . .
> Pecuniary wages and profit, indeed, are everywhere in Europe extremely different according to the different employments of labour and stock. But this difference arises partly from certain circumstances in the employments themselves, which, either really, or at least in the imaginations of men, make up for a small pecuniary gain in some, and counter-balance a great one in others . . .
> The five following are the principal circumstances which, so far as I have been able to observe, make up for a small pecuniary gain in some employments, and counter-balance a great one in others: first, the agreeableness or disagreeableness of the employments themselves; secondly, the easiness and cheapness, or the difficulty and expense, of learning them; thirdly, the constancy or incon-

40. *Ibid.*, pp. 301 f .
41. Smith, *op. cit.*, pp. 99 f.

stancy of employment in them; fourthly, the small or great trust which must be reposed in those who exercise them; and fifthly, the probability or improbability of success in them.

By contrast, the archetypal statement of the principle of noncompeting groups is from John Stuart Mill's *Principles of Political Economy*. It appeared in 1848, 72 years after the *Wealth of Nations* but well before the great flowering of British trade unionism and collective bargaining. Mill may not have realized the extent to which his wage-structure theory weakened his general theory of value. (That realization, as well as the term "noncompeting groups" and a reformulation of value theory that treated each such group like a separate country in international trade, came with J.F. Cairnes a generation later.) To quote from Mill:[42]

> So complete, indeed, has . . . been the separation, so strongly marked the line of demarcation, between the different grades of labourers, as to be almost equivalent to an hereditary distinction of caste; each employment being chiefly recruited from the children of those already employed in it, or in employments of the same rank with it in social estimation . . . The liberal professions are mostly supplied by the sons of either the professional, or the idle classes; the more highly skilled manual employments are filled up from the sons of skilled artizans, or the class of tradesmen who rank with them; the lower classes of skilled employments are in a similar case; and unskilled labourers, with occasional exceptions, remain from father to son in their pristine condition.

25. With the mushroom growth of wage-structure theory in labor economics,[43] one might have expected a focusing of attention on the comparative validity of these general theories in the nonunion world, and on the impingement of collective bargaining on the balance between them, not to mention the labor-aristocracy issue. Instead, the literature has taken a statistical turn, concentrating on the empirical influence of measurable variables, singly and in groups, on the relative wages of particular groups of workers, and on the question of whether particular relative wage

42. Mill, *Principles of Political Economy*, p. 393. In a number of individual trades and professions, the folkways described by Mill have subsequently been hardened and legalized by closed unions and occupational licensure. Licensure, generally supported by unions and equivalent professional organizations, dates in America (after a half century of near-freedom in Mill's lifetime) from the final quarter of the nineteenth century. Compare Rottenberg, "The Economics of Occupational Licensing," in National Bureau of Economic Research, *Aspect of Labor Economics* (Princeton: Princeton University Press, 1962), Rottenberg's prize example is barbering in Illinois.

43. Concentrating on the American literature are two studies by Melvin Reder, "The Theory of Occupational Wage Differentials," *A.E.R.* (December 1955), and "Wage Differentials: Theory and Measurement," in *Aspects of Labor Economics, op. cit.* A later international study, with special reference to development, is Koji Taira, "Wage Differentials in Developing Countries: A Survey of Findings," *Int. Lab. Rev.* (March 1966).

changes require institutional explanation over and beyond the expectations of standard economic analysis. Two informative examples of the
first sort are Levinson's discussion of the influence of concentration (monopoly) in the employing industry and Blumenthal's variance analysis of
the detailed wage structure of Japanese manufacturing.[44] Levinson concludes that concentration or cartelization enforced by union pressure does
better for its workers than pure employer concentration with substantial
powers of monopsonistic resistance. Blumenthal finds that neither age
alone, education alone, scale alone, nor any other single factor produces
large earnings differentials by itself; some combination is required, so
that a man in his forties or fifties, employed in a salaried position by a
large firm in an expanding heavy industry, who has graduated from a
leading Japanese university, stands the best chance of reaching the highest
pay bracket. An enlightening, analysis of the second sort is McCaffree's
discussion of the reversal of the white-collar differential from positive to
negative between the 1930s and 1950s in the United States.[45] He concludes, contrary to general belief, that collective bargaining played only
a minuscule role as compared with the upgrading of standards for manual jobs, the near-elimination of blue-collar immigration, the rising of
the educational level of the work force, and the entry of women into the
white-collar labor market. Reder's "competitive hypothesis"[46] also fits
into this category.

26.   Despite the burgeoning literature concerning wage structure, the
most pointed attempt to separate noncompeting elements from equalizing-
difference elements remains the Friedman-Kuznets study of independent
professional practice in the United States before and during the great depression of the 1930s,[47] which does not involve collective bargaining by
self-styled trade unions. (The American Medical Association is sometimes

44. H. M. Levinson, "Unionism, Concentration, and Wage Changes: Toward a Unified
Theory," *I.L.R.R.* (January 1967) ; Tuvia Blumenthal, "The Effect of Socio-Economic
Factors on Wage Differentials in Japanese Manufacturing Industries," *Riron-Keizaigaku*
(September 1966) .

45. Kenneth M. McCaffree, "The Earnings Differential Between White Collar and
Manual Occupations," *Rev. Econ. and Stat.* (February 1953) .

46. Reder, "Wage Differentials: Theory and Measurement," *op. cit.,* pp. 264–267, 276–
279, 299–311. In relation to skill differentials, the competitive hypothesis places major
emphasis on investment in and opportunities for education. As between industries, the
hypothesis is that "any industry will pay the same price for a given grade of labor as
any other industry hiring in the same location" (p. 276) , so that interindustry differentials are explainable by skill and location, but "there should be no association between
either the relative growth in the quantity of labor utilized, or the relative growth in
wages (measured by average hourly earnings) in that industry" (p. 278) .

47. Milton Friedman and Simon Kuznets, *Income from Independent Professional
Practice* (New York: National Bureau of Economic Research, 1945) .

referred to by outsiders as a trade union, usually with pejorative implications.) The five professions covered are law, medicine, dentistry, public accounting, and for some purposes, consulting engineering.

Comparing professional workers with nonprofessionals generally, Friedman and Kuznets find average earnings 85 to 180 per cent higher, after adjustment for age and location. (The differential itself varies with time, location, and the like.) Of this differential, they estimate only 70 per cent as "equalizing."[48] In fact, they state, "If the average income of nonprofessional workers is assumed equal to that of skilled workers . . . , the differential needed to make professional and nonprofessional pursuits equally attractive financially is reduced to 55 per cent." Even ascribing some elements of bias to the inevitable inaccuracy of such estimates, this leaves a disconcertingly wide margin explainable primarily by a melange of factors, including ignorance, which may be summarized under the rubric of "noncompeting groups."

Comparing physicians specifically with dentists, Friedman and Kuznets find a 32 per cent income differential, of which slightly more than half (17 per cent) is estimated as "equalizing."[49] Tentatively, then (though omitting the penumbra of qualifications exaggerates the accuracy the writers claim for their estimates) they suggest that a 15 per cent differential between physicians' and dentists' incomes may be explainable primarily by some combination of higher standards and restrictionism in the medical profession.

27.　If we include systems of political and paternalistic planning among alternatives to collective bargaining, as well as pre-union and nonunion labor markets, we do not escape patterns of arbitrariness in wage-setting and labor allocation. We limit ourselves to two examples, a wage schedule set by a Yugoslav workers' council and a labor-reallocation order by the Bulgarian government. Although both these examples come from Socialist countries, parallel examples can be found from the rules of thumb applied by corporate feudalists in capitalist regimes. *De te fabula narratur,* as Marx told his largely German audience about his largely English data.

Our first illustration is an elaborate and, one suspects, unwieldy point system for wage-setting in a Zagreb textile mill, as reported for 1963 by a Zagreb economist.[50] Points evaluation along the lines of Table 10.1 was

48. *Ibid.*, chapters 3.3 and 9.1; Appendix to chapter 4, pp. 142–151. The quotation is from p. 84.

49. *Ibid.*, chapters 4.2 and 9.3; Appendix to chapter 4, pp. 152–173.

50. Rudolf Bičanič, "Some Aspects of the Policy of Workers' Income in Yugoslavia," in E. Stiller (ed), *Lohnpolitik und Vermögensbildung* (Frankfurt: List Gesellschaft, 1964), pp. 214 f.

Table 10.1   Point Evaluation of Selected Textile Mill Positions,
Zagreb, Yugoslavia (1963)

	Educa-tion	Ability and Expe-rience	Manage-ment	Respon-sibil-ity	Physi-cal Effort	Men-tal Effort	Work-ing Condi-tions	Total Points
General Manager	100	170	150	190	10	100	10	730
Technical Manager	100	140	140	160	10	90	10	650
Works Manager	100	130	100	120	10	90	30	580
Foreman	80	60	40	50	10	40	40	320
Skilled Weaver	50	40	–	40	35	30	40	235
Semiskilled Spinner	30	20	–	20	30	10	40	150
Sales Manager	100	130	100	140	10	90	10	580
Bookkeeper	100	100	50	90	10	80	10	440
Truck Driver	80	60	–	70	30	40	40	320
Janitor	20	10	–	10	40	10	40	130

SOURCE: Bičanič, *op. cit.*, note 5.

applied to some 440 different jobs, although the plant employed only 2800 workers! There were also special premiums for cutting costs, improving product quality, and increasing quantitative productivity, plus a 10 per cent premium for top personnel "for successful management." The exchange rate between these points and Yugoslav dinars was subject, finally to constraints set both by the total gross profits of the mill and by the Yugoslav minimum wage law. By Western standards, the results show a surprisingly high white-collar differential; compare the bookkeeper with the weaver, spinner, truck driver, and janitor.

The second illustration, a drastic Bulgarian labor reallocation of 1964, is quoted from a source hostile to the Bulgarian regime:[51]

> In Communist Bulgaria, a government survey showed that 64,000 jobs were going begging in chemical plants and heavy industries. At roughly the same time, another government survey uncovered 65,917 men who were working at desk jobs that could just as well be filled by women. Solution: effective immediately, the Bulgarian government ordered all able-bodied men under 40 who held nonprofessional office jobs for less than ten years to transfer to harder factory work; their jobs will be filled by women.

28. When collective bargaining is compared with the alternatives sketched in the last three sections, it is not surprising to find the hostile charges of wage-distortion and labor-aristocracy difficult to confirm. Mention has been made (in section 25) of Reder's inconclusive statistical tests of conformity between interindustry wage structures and his version of

51. "The Bulgarian Way," *Time* (May 8, 1964).

the competitive model.[52] An institutional approach, reaching equivalent conclusions, has been taken by Reynolds.[53] Rather than following Reder in supposing collective bargaining to approach the competitive model reasonably closely, Reynolds takes an opposite tack and merely denies that it departs from this model more drastically than other real-world systems do.

Assuming—Reder and others might say, exaggerating—the imperfections of nonunion labor markets, Reynolds believes that collective bargaining has shifted wage structures closer to the competitive norm than they would otherwise have been. This "competitive norm" excludes collective bargaining, it is true, as well as monopsony, worker ignorance and immobility, and noncompeting groups of workers privileged for other reasons than union membership. Using this definition, Reynolds concludes, with reservations, that the countervailing power of unions, exercised through collective bargaining, has brought actual wage structures closer to the norm than they previously were.

In our terms, Reynolds may be interpreted as saying that any reallocative incidence of collective bargaining represents mainly the overcoming of exploitation. This makes it, by definition, a movement toward the competitive norm. Also, many who suffer from reallocation (or inflation) effects of bargaining are white-collar folk who previously formed a closed group with respect to recruitment from the ranks of the manual-worker class. These incidence patterns, too, may be represented as competitive rather than the reverse, although Reynolds does not make this point explicitly.

In considering Reynolds' position, we may again subdivide the labor aristocracy into old and new aristocracies, corresponding to the elites of craft and industrial unionism, respectively. The old aristocracy consisted of members of skilled trades, established by old-style collective bargaining as noncompeting groups, sometimes dominant over their small and weakly organized employers. On balance, this kind of collective bargaining was probably an anticompetitive force despite its antimonopsony aspects. Reynolds bases his argument, however, mainly on the new industrial unionism, that is, the new labor aristocracy. This includes workers of all skill grades, united by the good fortune of working for firms with substantial monopoly power and large profits on their output markets, and therefore with substantial ability to pay wage increases. Here, collective

52. For skeptical doubts regarding the Reder model in its interindustry application, see Donald E. Cullen, "Comment" in *Aspects of Labor Economics, op. cit.,* pp. 311–317.

53. Lloyd G. Reynolds, "The Impact of Collective Bargaining on the Wage Structure in the United States," in John T. Dunlop (ed.), *Theory of Wage Determination* (London: Macmillan, 1957), pp. 194–221. Also Lloyd G. Reynolds and Cynthia Taft, *The Evolution of Wage Structure* (New Haven: Yale University Press, 1955), chs. 7, 13.

bargaining by industrial unions has had complex consequences. The antimonopsony effects are clear; it is these that Reynolds stresses. But at the
same time, collective bargaining has raised these employers' costs and
given their workers some share in what would otherwise have been their
monopoly profits. This effect is most marked when monopolistic exploitation is overcome, as by all-or-none bargaining or featherbedding rules.

Should we agree with Reynolds in treating the rise of the new labor
aristocracy as a movement toward the general competitive norm? From
the viewpoint of functional income distribution, his view has much to recommend it. To whatever extent bargaining raises the labor share, it re-
tards the shift to profits that Marx, Joan Robinson, Kalečki and others
have foreseen as the ultimate end of "a world of monopolies."[54] Doubts,
however, spring from both the inflation and the reallocation theories of
incidence of collective bargaining. There seem to be elements of collusion
or conspiracy against consumers of particular products (and fixed income
groups generally), mobilization of labor support for monopolistic restrictions on output markets, cultivation of monopoly profits as pools for wage
increases to strategic groups of organized palace slaves of the business
oligarchy.[55] It is, moreover, uncertain that the injured parties are confined
to the monopsonists and noncompeting groups of yesteryear. What of the
family farmers and unorganized farm workers, unskilled employees in
service trades, widows and orphans, pensioners and annuitants, clients of
relief agencies and career enlisted men in the armed forces, the racial and
religious minorities? Inflation and reallocation, like the biblical rain, fall
alike on the just and the unjust. Reynolds may have conjured up for the
just, by his theory, a better umbrella than the Lord has thus far provided
in reality.

54. Prediction of a trend toward monopoly, coupled with reduction of the labor
share, dates back to Marx and beyond. It is, in fact, one form of his doctrine of increasing misery. Among the turn-of-the-century "distribution" books it appears in John
R. Commons, *Distribution of Wealth* (New York: Macmillan, 1893), pp. 101–107, 198–
200, 229–237; 246–248, and Ch. 6. An explicit statement is found in Joan Robinson,
Imperfect Competition, op. cit., book x. It underlines the aggregative distribution theory of Michal Kalečki, "The Distribution of the National Income," *Readings,* no. 11,
to be considered later in Chapter 16.

55. The author has expressed these views previously in "Wages in Excess of Marginal Revenue Productivity," *So. Ec. J.* (January 1950) pp. 307–309. Similar doubts
were not unknown to the generally pro-union founding fathers of labor economics, as
in the discussion of "capital and labor hunting together, their prey being the people
who needed cheap housing," in Commons, *Economics of Collective Action* (New York:
Macmillan, 1950), pp. 31 f. But as Kerr reminds us ("Labor's Income Share," *op. cit.,*
p. 272), collusive agreements between monopolistic employers and favored employees
antedated trade unionism. "It is very difficult," Kerr concludes, "to keep the employers
indefinitely from giving away their profits in part to their employees, in one way or
another."

CHAPTER ELEVEN

Wages and Employment

Two Controversial Problems

1. The preceding chapters have each considered a variety of topics in microeconomic income distribution or its theory. The present chapter, by contrast, is focused on two controversial macroeconomic problems.

The first of these problems is whether, in a predominantly capitalist world with some involuntary unemployment at going wage rates, a general rise in money and real wages will raise the overall level of employment, lower it, or leave it unaffected. (All three positions have strong supporters.)

The second problem is dynamic, and considers the relation between unemployment and money wage *changes*. Is there a stable inverse relationship—such as the Phillips curve of Chapter 10, section 14—between the unemployment level and the rate of increase of money wages? If so, does this relation preclude the simultaneous achievement of high employment and price-level stability without direct controls over prices and wages?

The Wage-Employment Relation: Introduction

2. We consider first the static wage-employment relation. Disputants generally agree that a horizontal (infinitely elastic) aggregate supply function for labor (in terms of either money or real wage rates), at its intersection with an aggregate demand function for labor, is *sufficient* to open up the possibility of equilibrium at less than full employment of persons willing to accept equilibrium wages. In other words, it opens up

267

the possibility of equilibrium with some involuntary unemployment.[1] It does not matter whether the horizontality of the aggregate labor supply results from individual preference or collective action. The dispute is whether such downward wage rigidity is a *necessary* condition for involuntary unemployment, or whether such unemployment would persist if workers were more pliable and wages fell more readily.

Writers who allege an inverse relation between wages and employment focus on wages as a cost of production, but pay little attention to wages as income or purchasing power. Conversely, writers who allege a direct relation between wages and employment focus on wages-as-income, with little regard to wages-as-cost. The major difficulty of this topic is to consider wages simultaneously as income and as cost.

Classical Theory

1.   Classical and neoclassical economics unite in treating the economy as a firm or industry writ large. For a single firm or industry when involuntary unemployment is present, raising wages reduces employment, and lowering wages increases it.[2] Raising wages reduces employment for three reasons: technical substitution of "input *b*," or capital, for "input *a*," or labor;[3] consumer substitution of less labor-intensive goods in consumption because of relative price changes;[4] increasing concentration of innovative activity in labor-saving directions, as in Chapter 6, section 28.

This classical orthodoxy remains perhaps the most popular of the three positions to be considered, at least outside the world of organized labor. Its popularity is especially marked in business and employer circles, because it is so clearly "practical" in microeconomic terms. A standard macroeconomic translation is Cannan's, which dates from mid-depression 1932:[5]

1. If some or all the unemployed are *indifferent* as between employment and unemployment at the given real wage, should they be described as voluntarily or involuntarily unemployed? (Harry Johnson raises this question; I have no answer.)

2. Although lowering wages increases the demand for labor, as we have seen, whether it also increases employment depends upon supply considerations. If our initial conditions had involved labor shortages (excess demand for labor), our conclusions regarding wages and employment would have been reversed.

3. If capital instruments are ultimately produced by labor, but not vice versa, such substitution is stabilizing in the long run only if the capital-goods industries are themselves more labor-intensive (on a value-added basis) than the remainder of the economy. Compare Hirofumi Uzawa, "On a Two-Sector Growth Model," *Rev. Econ. Stud.* (October 1961) .

4. By "labor-intensive" we mean only "hired-labor intensive." "Do-it-yourself" expedients are often more labor-intensive, by any measure, than commercial outputs.

5. Edwin Cannan, "The Demand for Labour," *Ec. J.* (September 1932) , p. 367.

General unemployment is in reality to be explained almost in the same way as particular unemployment . . . General unemployment appears when asking too much is a general phenomenon.

2. A multiquadrant aggregative model, pointing in the same direction but with an eye to avoiding Cannan's logical fallacies of composition, is presented in Figure 11.1.[6] This figure represents, in four quadrants, five equations in the variables y (national income) and p (price level), as well as n (employment), w (real wage) and w^* (pw, or money wage). A production function F in quadrant (a) assumes given endowments of inputs other than labor, but with diminishing returns throughout; it does not, therefore, presume a labor theory of value, despite the omission of nonlabor inputs. The labor market of quadrant (b) is composed of labor demand and supply functions D_n and S_n. The labor demand function is drawn as dF/dn, and slopes downward on marginal-productivity grounds. The labor supply function S_n may slope in either direction (as per Chapter 9), but preferably not so extremely (if its slope be downward) as to imperil stability. In lieu of an aggregate demand function for output, which classical writers considered illegitimate, we have in quadrant (c) an MV function representing the quantity theory of money; M is the nominal quantity of money and V its velocity of circulation. Since $MV = py$, and we hold both M and V given and constant in strict quantity-theory fashion, the function is a rectangular hyperbola in p and y. Finally, quadrant (d) gives a resultant money-wage function. It relates p and w also in rectangular-hyperbolic forms, since $w^* = pw$ by definition.

All four quadrants are combined as the lower panel of Figure 11.1. In the combined diagram, the production function (a) is the southeast quadrant; the labor market (b) the southwest quadrant; the quantity theory (c) the northeast quadrant; and the money wage (d) the northwest quadrant. The focal point of the equilibrium solution is E, the labor market equilibrium. It determines the equilibrium real wage W and employment N. Given the production function F, N determines equilibrium output Y. Given M and V, according to the quantity theory, Y determines the equilibrium price level P. P and W between them define the equilibrium money wage level W^*, shown as a rectangular hyperbola through the intersection of P and W at Q.

Unemployment, in this model, is a disequilibrium phenomenon due to

6. There have been many models of classical macroeconomics. This one derives from Bronfenbrenner, "Classical and Marxian Macro-Economics in Separate Nutshells," in Tullio Baggiotti (ed.), *Essays in Honour of Marco Fanno* (Padua: CEDAM, 1966), pp. 134–136. Had we assumed a strictly classical "wage-fund" theory of labor demand instead of a neoclassical marginal theory, the labor-demand function D_n would have been a rectangular hyperbola.

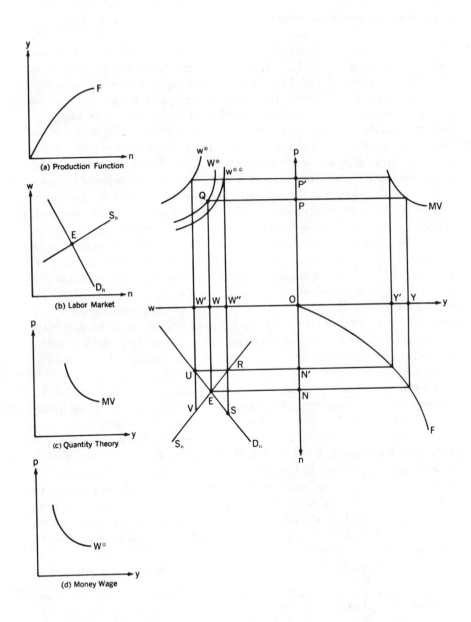

Figure 11.1

real and money wages above W and W^*, respectively. In the presence of unemployment, a further increase in the money wage rate, as to W^* on the northwest quadrant of the lower panel, will lower employment and income (while raising the real wage) ; while a fall in the money wage rate will raise employment and income (while lowering the real wage), provided the new rate is not below the equilibrium one. (With labor shortages and with money wage rates below W^*, we have the opposite effects on employment. This point bears repeating because it is so frequently and conveniently forgotten.)

Specifically, the "too-high" money wage rate w^* will raise real wages to W' and the price level to P', but will lower output and employment to Y' and N' respectively. It will also generate unemployment in an amount UV. A sufficient fall in money wages below W^*,—say, to w^{**},—also lowers output and employment; it may also have an inflationary effect on prices by creating a labor shortage RS, which may be greater than, less than, or equal to UV. Real wages in this case, however, fall to W''.

Unlike disequilibrium at money wage w^*, disequilibrium at money wage w^{**} involves a distributional shift to property income or "gross profits." The two inflationary effects also differ. The inflation at money wage w^* is a once-for-all price rise. Full equilibrium, including the real wage W, can be restored by a rise in MV. The inflation at money wage w^{**} has no such simple solution. It results from a real disequilibrium, with excess real demand for labor reflected in unfilled vacancies.

3. Despite its aggregative setting in diagrams like Figure 11.1, this presentation does not avoid concentration on wages as cost or neglect of wages as income or purchasing power. The maintenance of aggregate demand and expenditure either comes about naturally, according to Say's Law (more accurately, Say's Identity),[7] or is provided by some other branch of economic administration such as monetary or fiscal policy.[8]

Keynesian Theory

4. The intermediate position associated with Keynes and his earlier disciples is (in brief) that neither real nor money wage rates have significant effects on the employment level of a closed economy. The position was stated in opposition to pressure for wage cuts in a depression environ-

7. Say's Law and Say's Identity may be distinguished as follows: the Identity asserts that supply generates its own demand at *any* price level; the Law, that this effect occurs only at the *equilibrium* level (like P in Figure 11.1) .

8. Strictly speaking, fiscal policy must be the senior partner if the quantity of money is held constant, as implied by quadrant (c) of Figure 11.1.

ment.[9] Such cuts exercise their effects, if any, through lowering prices. A
lower price level increases the real quantity of money and hence, by what
has become known as the Keynes Effect, putatively lowers the rate of interest. There may also be expectational and redistributive effects on aggregate expenditures from a given income. The expectational effects of
"nibbling at wages" tend to be unfavorable, inducing postponement of
purchases and investment until wages fall further, unless there is some
mechanism bringing about once-for-all cuts. The redistributive consequences working through the inducement to invest are liable to be favorable (according to the Keynes Effect). Those working through the propensity to consume, however, are apt to be unfavorable because of the
putatively lower marginal propensity to consume of rentiers and fixed-
income receivers, who are the principal beneficiaries of deflation.[10]

5.   The simplest exposition of this skeptical theory uses the Keynesian
cross, an analytical apparatus that has become familiar in elementary textbooks. Here real income y is measured on the horizontal axis of diagrams
like Figure 11.2, and real expenditure x is measured along the vertical
axis. The quantity F (which equals G) represents full-employment income, or "capacity" output, as the case may be. The aggregate expenditure function $C + I$ (often called a demand function despite the absence
of any price term) is the vertical sum of consumption (C) and investment
(I). Consumption is related to disposable income by a consumption function, whose slope is the marginal propensity to consume and must be fractional for stability; the investment-income relation, if any, need not concern us here. Equilibrium is attained at income Y $(\leqq F)$ and expenditure
X $(\leqq G)$, where income generates expenditures sufficient to sustain itself,
as indicated by intersection of the expenditure function with a 45-degree
line through the origin O. Assuming a wage cut to have favorable impact
effects upon employment, output, and income (that is, assuming an elastic impact demand for labor), the increase in real income is indicated by
YY' and the increase in output by XX'. Since the expenditure function has
a fractional slope, the income increment would fail by $X'Y'$ to be maintained by additional expenditure, and would fall back to Y, except when
there are such second-order complications as we have just considered.

    A more extreme argument, not confirmed by statistical analysis, was
that workers could not cut real wage levels even if they wanted to. Be-

    9. John Maynard Keynes, *General Theory of Employment Interest and Money* (New
York: Harcourt Brace, 1936), ch. 19.

    10. A. P. Lerner, "The Relation of Wage Policies and Price Policies," *Readings*, no. 17;
James Tobin, "Money Wage Rates and Employment" in Seymour E. Harris (ed.), *The
New Economics* (New York: Knopf, 1947), ch. 40.

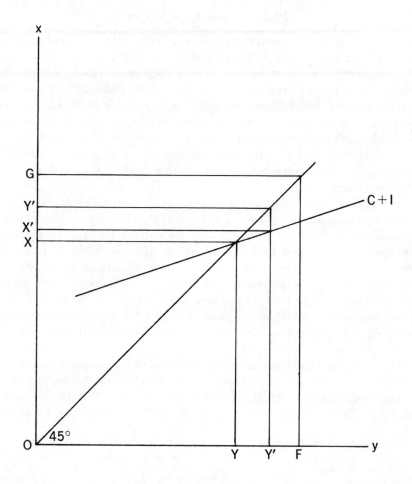

Figure 11.2

cause of the assumed reducibility of marginal costs to wages, and the assumed proportionality between output prices and marginal costs (constant degrees of monopoly), money wage cuts, Keynes believed, would pass through to prices in deflationary fashion, so that real wages would not fall. The empirical weakness of this chain of reasoning was disclosed by the disclosure of a strong positive correlation between money and real wages[11] over periods too short for the correlation to be attributable to long-term growth.

11. John T. Dunlop, "The Movement of Real and Money Wages," *Ec. J.* (September 1938) ; Lorie Tarshis, "Changes in Real and Money Wages," *Readings,* no. 18.

Philosophy of High Wages

6. A third position maintains that the wage rate and the level of employment move together, so that a rise in money and real wages increases employment, while a fall reduces it. There are always practical limits to the amount by which wages can be raised without reducing employment, but these limits are left imprecise, and bear no relation to the economist's notion of labor market equilibrium. It would be ingenious, tortuous, and probably misleading to assimilate the philosophy of high wages to the analysis of Figure 11.1 by the added assumption that actual money and real wages are usually below their equilibrium levels; that is, that they are at points like w^{**} and w''.

The philosophy of high wages is rather at an extreme of unorthodoxy, standing the classical theory upon its head. It should not be confused with generalizations from the ability of superior entrepreneurs to compensate the special talents and higher skills of superior workmen more handsomely than ordinary employers and to secure the pick of the market by offering high wages.[12] In pristine radicalism, the philosophy of high wages has led a long life in trade union and social worker circles. Its basis is a maldistributionist underconsumption theory of business depression, such as we have considered in Chapter 5, section 7. Its initial stress was on maintaining money wage rates in the face of output price reductions during depressions.[13] Since output prices also seem to have become more rigid in depressions, the theory now takes the form of recommending increased money wages as a means of increasing employment. This has been the argument of the "Nathan Reports" and the Conference on Economic

12. Compare Hicks, *Theory of Wages* (New York: Peter Smith, 1948), p. 36.

13. For the long life and status of the doctrine of the desirability of money wage maintenance in depressions, see Sidney and Beatrice Webb, *Industrial Democracy* (London: Longmans, Green, 1902), pp. 417–428, 793–795; John T. Dunlop, *Wage Determination Under Trade Unions*, rev. ed. (Oxford: Blackwell, 1950), pp. 66–70; Arthur M. Ross, *Trade Union Wage Policy* (Berkeley and Los Angeles: University of California Press, 1953), pp. 14 f.

However, the philosophy of high wages has gained its widest appeal from its occasional business advocates, and the term is associated more closely in the public mind with Henry Ford than with any individual labor leader. Ford's belief is quoted as follows:

It is bad financial policy to reduce wages because it also reduces buying power. There is no charity in proper wages. There is something sacred about wages—they represent homes and families and domestic destinies. On the cost sheet, wages are mere figures; out in the world, wages are bread boxes and coal bins, babies' cradles and children's education—family comforts and contentment.

Edwin G. Nourse, *Wages as Cost and as Market* (Washington: Brookings Institution, 1942), p. 15, citing Ford's *My Life and Work* (with Samuel Crowther), p. 163 (running quotation).

Progress in the United States;[14] Lady Wootton's *Social Foundation of Wage Policy* has been a United Kingdom spokesman:[15]

> It now appears that an increase in the general level of wages is as likely to be a cure as a cause of unemployment—at least in circumstances in which for some reason or other there are unused resources lying idle . . . In the event of a slump, the arguments from general welfare would be entirely on the side of wage increase.

This theory regards wages primarily, if not exclusively, as the source of income and purchasing power, while neglecting the problems of wages as cost. It has, however, the merits of its defects. It raises explicitly the issue of wage increases as a redistributive device; its major thrust is that such increases will, or should, be paid from excessive profits rather than from rises in the price-determining cost of production. Direct controls are sometimes urged to force such a redistributive method of raising wages.

Three Theoretical Approaches

7. The reason for the unsatisfactory state of this branch of macroeconomic wage theory is not hard to find. Vested interests are involved, both economic and ideological. Moreover, the analysis is delicate in requiring that attention be paid simultaneously to wages as cost and to wages as income, without overlooking redistribution possibilities.

Starting from the relatively neutral Keynesian position, three extensions were attempted in the 1950s. We shall consider the contributions of Weintraub, Bronfenbrenner, and a Minnesota group.

8. Weintraub's several contributions, beginning with his 1956 "Macroeconomic Approach to the Theory of Wages,"[16] have been based on a special presentation of the Keynesian system with employment (N) as the basic "quantity" variable rather than output or income, and with an aggregate supply function derived from Keynes' cryptic references to an aggregate "proceeds" function Z, such as

14. For the Nathan Reports, see the controversy between Robert R. Nathan and Sumner H. Slichter, "Increasing Wages as a Means of Increasing Employment," *Rev. Econ. and Stat.* (November 1949) . For the Conference on Economic Progress see Leon Keyserling. *The Role of Wages in a Great Society* (Washington: Conference on Economic Progress, 1966) , chs. 2, 4–8.

15. Lady Barbara Wootton, *Social Foundations of Wage Policy* (London: Allen and Unwin, 1955) , pp. 21, 104.

16. Sidney Weintraub, "Macroeconomic Approach to the Theory of Wages," *A.E.R.* (December 1956) , forming the basis of *An Approach to the Theory of Income Distribution,* (Philadelphia: Chilton, 1958) , ch. 6.

$$Z = wN + F + R \tag{11.1}$$

where w denotes the wage rate, F the volume of fixed charges, and R a residual, catch-all category termed "profits."[17] On diagrams like Figure 11.3, Z-functions are drawn in monetary terms, with upward concavity representing increasing costs, while aggregate money demand functions D owe a downward concavity to a falling marginal propensity to spend.

When money wages rise, both Z and D functions are shifted upward (from Z_1 and D_1 to Z_2 and D_2, respectively, in Figure 11.3). The effect on employment may be favorable (northwest panel) or unfavorable (northeast panel). In each case, Weintraub goes on to draw what he considers to be aggregate labor demand curves, using the intersections P_1 and P_2. These curves D_n slope upward in the southwest panel and downward in the southeast.[18] (Later in his presentation, Weintraub concerns himself with the stability issues raised by the "underconsumptionist case" of the two left-hand panels.[19])

For Weintraub's estimate of the empirical probabilities, we turn to another monograph, *Forecasting the Price Level, Income Distribution, and Economic Growth.*[20] Here his proceeds function (11.1) is transformed to

$$Z = PQ = kwN$$

$$P = kw \frac{N}{Q} = k \frac{w}{A}. \tag{11.2}$$

Justifying the shift from (11.1) to (11.2), Weintraub argues that the ratio of business gross product (private national product, without corrections for double counting) to total payrolls wN is approximately constant at 2.0, although a slow fall can be surmised from his American data for 1929–1956.[21] (A, or Q/N, is a measure of average labor productivity.) The implication is that wage increases (in excess of productivity) affect primarily the price level, while distribution remains as before, thanks to the stability of the magic constant k. In the absence of redistribution, it is difficult to see how real demand or employment can change as a result of a wage increase. The movements in Figure 11.3 will represent little beyond inflation or deflation, depending on the unit labor cost quotient

17. Weintraub, "The Micro-Foundations of Aggregate Demand and Supply," *Ec. J.* (September 1957) and *Theory of Income Distribution, op. cit.*, ch. 2.

18. *Ibid.*, Figure 22, p. 111.

19. *Ibid.*, p. 122.

20. (Philadelphia: Chilton, 1959), p. 13. (Another edition bears the title, *A General Theory of the Price Level, Output, Income Distribution, and Economic Growth;* it was also published by Chilton in 1959).

21. *Ibid.*, table 3.1, p. 14.

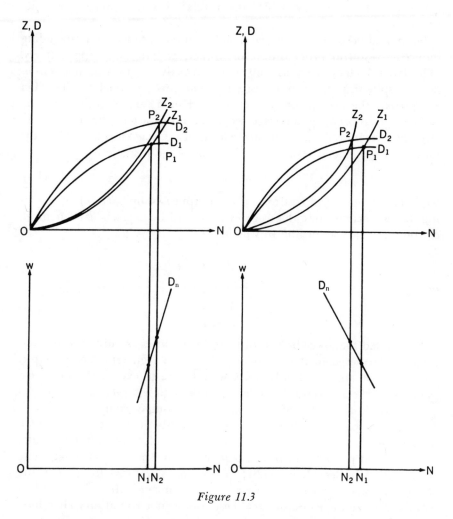

Figure 11.3

w/A, and the D_n functions will approximate vertical lines. Unemployment being left unaffected, the most probable case is the Keynesian one described in sections 4–5 above.

9. The present writer interpreted as expansionary any increment of aggregate money demand resulting from a money wage increase in its redistributive aspects. He interpreted as contractionary any incremental cost of a constant output resulting from the same wage increase. If the expansionary quantity exceeded the contractionary one, the net effect of the

wage increase was expansionary, and would increase employment if unemployed labor were available; the reverse was true in the opposite situation.[22]

Let m and m' represent the marginal spending propensities (including induced-investment propensities) of workers and capitalists respectively. (The latter include firms as well as individuals.) Let us assume $1 > m > m'$, despite firms' high propensity to spend their retained earnings. Let k represent the proportion of each unit of monetary wage increase absorbed by the profit or nonwage sector, and abstract at the outset from any employment-reducing "impact" effects of the wage increase. Then the increment of demand resulting from a unit wage increase is

$$m - km' \tag{11.3}$$

while the increment of cost for a given output is simply $(1-k)$. Comparing the two magnitudes, the wage increase will be expansionary, neutral, or contractionary according to whether

$$m - km' \gtrless 1 - k$$

or

$$k \gtrless \frac{1 - m}{1 - m'}. \tag{11.4}$$

I estimated the lower branch of these inequalities as most realistic, and accordingly veered to the orthodox side of the argument. For example, with m at .95 and m' at only .75, k would have to exceed .20 for an expansionary effect, a result considered unlikely in a capitalist society.

The simple apparatus of (11.3 and 11.4) assumes complete money illusion on the part of both workers and capitalists. It also ignores the real-balance effects upon expenditures. The removal of money illusion would, as Rothschild pointed out in a subsequent criticism,[23] increase aggregate consumption by less than (11.3), as consumers restored the preexisting relation between real consumption and real income after the round of wage and price increases, but real costs would not rise at all. Therefore,

22. Bronfenbrenner, "A Contribution to the Aggregative Theory of Wages," *J.P.E.* (December 1956).

23. Kurt W. Rothschild, "Aggregate Wage Theory and Money Illusion," (October 1957), with reply by Bronfenbrenner. In a later contribution, David C. Rowan claims that both writers had included real-balance effects implicitly, at least in part. Any consumption function (in money terms) that includes a constant (also in money terms) embodies at least a partial real-balance effect, since the real value of the constant term varies inversely with the price level. Interestingly enough, after this and other modifications, Rowan too concludes that the classical outcome is theoretically the most probable alternative. "Note on the Aggregate Theory of Wages," *J.P.E.* (February 1964), with a reply by Rothschild, "Illusions About Money Illusion?" *J.P.E.* (June 1965).

Rothschild believes the philosophy of high wages furnishes the most likely alternative. Real-balance effects, as I argued in reply, work in the opposite direction. My argument might, therefore, be reinterpreted as implying that these secondary effects cancel each other.

10. The "Minnesota" analysis comes out strongly on the orthodox side of the debate.[24] It uses a four-dimensional diagram, like the one on which our Figure 11.1 was modeled. If we turn back to Figure 11.1 and compare it with the "Minnesota" Figure 11.4, we can see that only one quadrant has been changed significantly. This is (c), which relates real national income and the price level, and which we have drawn as northeast. In Figure 11.4, replacing a strict quantity theory of money, we now have an aggregate demand function D. Its downward slope presumes the presence of a real-balance effect. (A vertical D would have meant an insignificant real-balance effect.) Also, D should be considered asymptotic to the y axis, implying that aggregate demand would increase without bound if all prices fell to zero and all goods became free. The aggregate supply function S is derived geometrically in Figure 11.4, and also fits into the northeast quadrant. It will be noted that a different S function must be drawn for each money wage rate, and that all S functions stop short (or become vertical) where labor shortages prevent equality between the real wage rate and the marginal product of labor.

Figure 11.4 has been drawn with its initial position at less than full employment. National income is Y_o, the price level P_o, the real wage rate W_o, the money wage rate W_o^*, and employment N_o. At the money wage rate W_o^*, the appropriate aggregate supply function is S_o. Unemployment is indicated by the segment UV on the southwest or labor market quadrant.

This unemployment can be eliminated by monetary and fiscal means, shifting D to the right. This shift will raise the price level above P_o, even without any rise in the money wage rate above W_o^*. The diagram, however, shows that unemployment can also be eliminated in classical fashion, by a fall in the money wage rate to W^* and no change in the aggregate demand function D.[25] At the same time, output rises to Y because of the rise of employment to its full-employment level N. There is a decline of the price level (to P), but this does not prevent a fall in the real wage to W. The aggregate supply function, finally, shifts to the right; its new position is S.

24. O. H. Brownlee, "Theory of Employment and Stabilization Policy," *J.P.E.* (October 1950); Joseph P. McKenna, *Aggregate Economic Analysis,* 3d. ed. (New York: Holt, Rinehart & Winston, 1964), ch. 13.

25. For this mechanism to operate effectively, it is necessary for D to be asymptotic to the y axis, as specified above.

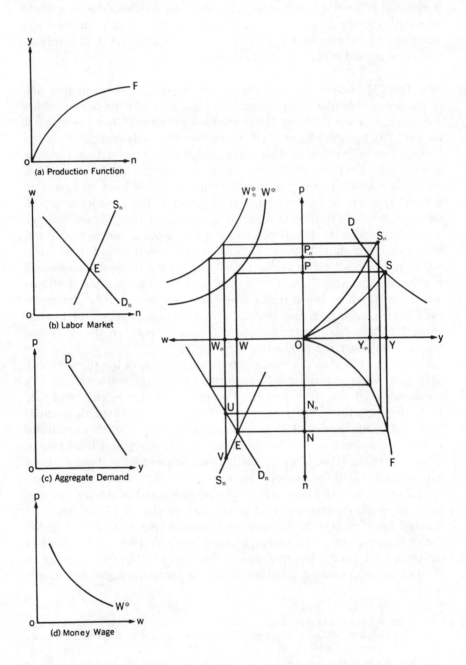

Figure 11.4

The aggregate supply function *S* has not been changed by the wage reduction. Its stability implies either the absence of any significant redistribution of income or the insignificance of the aggregate demand effect of
whatever redistribution does result. Either position has much to support
it, and the two positions can be combined.

Digression on Automation

11.   The apparatus of Figure 11.4 can be used also to analyze the effect
of automation on both wages and employment.[26] Like any other technological improvement, automation raises the total and average product of
labor, shifting production functions upward. At the same time, automation may (if it is very labor-saving) lower the marginal product of all but
the first few units of labor. This effect will occur if the radius of curvature
of the new production function is sufficiently lower than that of the old
one. On the other hand, it need not occur at all, and the marginal product
of labor may rise along with the total and average products.

The two panels of Figure 11.5 illustrate, respectively, optimism and pessimism concerning automation. In the left-hand panel, the shift of the

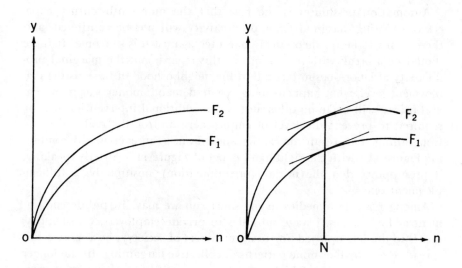

Figure 11.5

26. Bronfenbrenner, "Notes on Aggregate Supply and the Automation Problem,"
Dōshisha Daigaku Keizaigaku Ronsō (October 1964), pp. 6–12.

production function from F_1 to F_2 involves a simultaneous increase in the marginal productivity of labor; for all values of employment (n) the slope of F_2 is higher than that of F_1. This is the optimistic panel. In the right-hand, or pessimistic, panel, the marginal productivity of labor is reduced by the shift of the production function from F_1 to F_2, for employment greater than N. (The two production functions are parallel at this employment level.) To interpret such a panel pessimistically, of course, initial employment must exceed the critical value N.

If the marginal as well as the average product of labor is raised by automation (as it was on the whole by the Industrial Revolution), the result can be increased income, real wages, and (labor supply permitting) employment. There can also be a fall in the general price level, unless it is prevented by rising money supply and rising money wages. Conversely, money wages can rise substantially without output-price inflation. All these benefits will come if aggregate demand is increased sufficiently rapidly or, alternatively, if money wages are curbed adequately. A fall in money wages below their original position, while unlikely, is not ruled out if aggregate demand does not rise. Such a fall in money wages, however, will not prevent real wages from rising. The reader may derive these results quite readily for himself, by combining Figure 11.4 with the left-hand panel of Figure 11.5 as an exercise.

Automation pessimism is the fear that the nineteenth-century experience of rising marginal labor productivity will not be continued—and there seems to be no theoretical guarantee against this outcome. If there should be a break with past trends in this regard, and the marginal productivity of labor does in fact fall in the neighborhood of the existing employment level, what happens to aggregate demand, money wages, or general prices; will make no difference: some additional intervention will be required to prevent the level of employment and/or the real wage rate from falling. This result too can be worked out as an exercise, by combining Figure 11.4 with the right-hand panel of Figure 11.5. Strictly speaking, it presupposes that the initial (preautomation) position be a full-employment one.

Among possible remedies in the short run we may list public employment at high wages,[27] wage subsidies to private employers, transfer payments to the unemployed (or to all members of society), or a more widespread resort to all-or-none patterns of collective bargaining. In the longer run, the combination of higher total income with lower real wage rates (or lower employment) suggests both a redistribution of income in favor

---

27. In standard methods of social accounting, the marginal product of labor in public employment is equal, by definition, to the wage the worker receives.

of capital owners and profit recipients and a high marginal productivity of capital instruments. This combination of circumstances, in its turn, suggests a possible remedy in the form of additional investment, which will raise labor productivity and lower capital productivity all along the line. This remedy assumes, however, not only that on balance the new capital instruments will be complementary (rather than competitive) with labor, but that the pace of new investment is sufficiently rapid to outweigh, over time, the very labor-saving character ascribed to the continuing automation process.

Stability Conditions

12. None of the three theoretical approaches (Sections 7–10) to our problem of wages and employment has reached unequivocal conclusions. Two of the three tended toward the classical inverse solution (wage increases reducing aggregate employment) ; the other toward the Keynesian solution of independence. None, however, really ruled out the philosophy of high wages or, in Weintraub's terms, the underconsumption case.

We leave to the Appendix to this chapter Simler's (unpublished) general equilibrium demonstration that stability requires the classical outcome for money wages, in the short run and under pure competition.[28] The mathematical development is long and involved.

Before beginning his mathematical development, Simler presents two contradictions in literary form: (*1*) The philosophy of high wages works through a rise in the labor share. Under competitive conditions, however, this share is the ratio of the marginal to the average product of labor, which would *fall* if output and employment were to increase in the short run (with capital constant).[29] (*2*) A necessary condition for short-run expansion in output and employment is a decline in the real wage rate. For this to come about through a rise in the money wage rate, prices must

---

28. N. J. Simler, "Wages and Employment in the Short Run" (mimeographed: Minneapolis, n.d.). (All citations are running quotations.)

29. The relative share of input a in output x is $(a \delta x / \delta a) / x$ or $(\delta x / \delta a) / (x/a)$, the ratio of marginal to average product. Let this share be s.

(In the short run, with other inputs constant, $\delta x / \delta a = dx/da = 1/ (da/dx)$. This result is used in the appendix.)

To demonstrate the proposition in the text, determine the sign of ds/dx:

$$\frac{ds}{dx} = \frac{d}{dx}\left(\frac{a \, \delta x / \delta a}{x} \right) = \frac{1}{x^2}\left[\frac{\delta x}{\delta a}\left(x \, \frac{\delta a}{\delta x} - a \right) + ax\frac{\delta^2 x}{\delta a^2} \right].$$

The term within the square brackets must be negative. The first term in brackets cannot be positive, since, if it were, $a \, \delta x / \delta a > x$, and inputs other than a would receive negative returns. We also know that a, x, and $\delta x / \delta a$ are positive, while $\delta^2 x / \delta a^2$ is negative as a stability condition. It follows that the entire expression in square brackets is negative, and so is ds/dx.

rise more than proportionately. "If the system is stable, it is impossible for this condition to obtain, and no increase in the aggregate quantity of goods and services is possible."[30] The mathematics, however, does not rest upon these propositions.

An Unemployment-Wage Change Relation?
The Affirmative Case

13.   The remainder of this chapter is concerned with the observed inverse relation between the rate of unemployment, taken as a causal variable, and the shortly subsequent change in the level of money wages. The issues are whether such a relationship is more than a statistical artifact and whether it is sufficiently stable for use in policy discussions. The principal form to be examined is the Phillips curve, already mentioned in Chapter 10, section 14.

Such an inverse relation as the Phillips curve is plausible on grounds of either economic theory or bargaining theory. We introduced it in Chapter 10 as an aspect of the incidence of collective bargaining. However, for any commodity x with price $p = f(x)$ in a purely competitive market, the Samuelson condition of dynamic stability of the relationship $f(x)$ is that

$$\frac{dp}{dt} = \dot{p} = \lambda E_x$$

where t is time, λ is a positive constant, and E_x is the excess demand for x (quantity demanded less quantity supplied) at price p.

If we rewrite the last expression in terms of a wage rate w and a quantity of labor a, and introduce a positive technical improvement or productivity increase factor w_o:

$$\dot{w} = \dot{w}_o + \lambda E_a \tag{11.5}$$

Let E_a be the excess demand for either some special sort of "standard" labor or for "standard" labor in the aggregate. Even so, the condition $E_a = 0$ is consistent with considerable unemployment of substandard labor (uneducated, inexperienced, handicapped, subject to discrimination). It is therefore consistent also with a positive measured unemployment rate, especially if no allowance is made for unfilled job vacancies. The measured unemployment rate also include the "frictional" unemployment of workers changing jobs.

On a diagram like Figure 11.6 (redrawn from Figure 10.3), the hori-

---

30. Simler, *op. cit.*, p. 6.

zontal line A may serve as an estimate of w_0, with $E_a = 0$. It also represents the annual rise in average and marginal labor productivity, and hence the maximum wage increase consistent with price stability in the absence of functional income redistribution in favor of labor. The vertical line B, it will be remembered, is the maximum "politically feasible" unemployment level, and F is the intersection of the A and B lines. The P_0 and P_1 functions of Figure 10.3 are two-dimensional[31] Phillips curves and serves as estimates of w in (11.5).

P_0, which passes southwest of F, is called a "good" Phillips curve. P_1, which passes northeast of F, is called a "bad" one. When a Phillips curve is good, as in Phillips' original essay about Great Britain, it suggests the existence of a range of policy choices or trade-offs CD, all involving high employment without inflation. (Most economists, given this range of choice, would prefer C to D.) When a Phillips curve is bad, as in most studies related to post-1945 data,[32] the range CD does not exist, and we enter the realm of trade-offs between unemployment and inflation. One writer estimates the cost of consumer price stability as being the unemployment of 10.5–18.8 per cent of the U.S. civilian labor force in 1960, while a further annual increase of 2.1 per cent in the consumers' price index would have sufficed, in the 18.8 per cent variant, to eliminate unemployment entirely. Such terms of trade-off suggest, for most readers, a choice of full employment *über alles*.

14. Less abstruse than (11.5) is a straightforward bargaining model to explain the Phillips curve. In this view, a low level of unemployment increases the bargaining power of trade unions relative to the bargaining power of employers, especially when it is combined with a high level of measured industrial profits. (The profit variable may be a proxy or surrogate for the array of market, nonbargaining variables embodied in w_0 and E_a of [11.5].) An interesting variant of this bargaining explanation concentrates its attention upon a few "key industries," which bargain in "wage rounds." The result of their "key bargains" is alleged to dominate the remainder of the wage structure in manufacturing industries, both union and nonunion.[33]

31. Statistical Phillips curves usually include additional dimensions (variables).

32. Two influential U.S. examples have been Samuelson and Solow, "Analytical Aspects of Anti-Inflationary Policy," *A.E.R.* (May 1960); and George L. Perry, "The Determinants of Wage-Rate Change and the Inflation-Unemployment Trade-Off for the United States," *Rev. Econ. Stud.* (October 1964). The figures cited below are from Ronald Bodkin, *The Wage-Price-Productivity Nexus* (Philadelphia: University of Pennsylvania Press, 1966), pp. 120 f., 211, 278.

33. Otto Eckstein and Thomas A. Wilson, "The Determination of Money Wages in American Industry," *Q.J.E.* (April 1962).

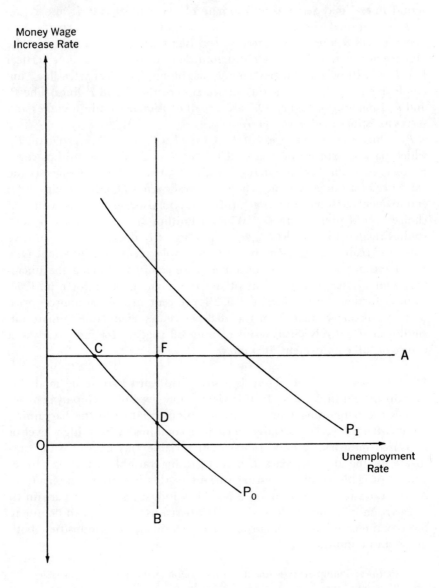

Figure 11.6

An Employment-Wage-Change Relation? The Rebuttals

15.   Both the structure of Phillips curve analysis, and policy trade-offs based on Phillips curves, have been attacked. The attack has been on both

quasi-political and strictly technical grounds. A piece by the present writer exemplifies the first sort of objection; the second sort is more frequent. Several examples are at hand and have already been cited. These arguments do not usually deny that Phillips curves exist, particularly in the short run. What is more generally denied is their stability.

16. On the quasi-political side, an important factor is the actual or expected consequences of wage increases on monetary and fiscal policy, when accompanied by simultaneous unemployment and inflation.[34]

When it is anticipated generally, on the basis of recent experience, that monetary and fiscal policy will be more sensitive to unemployment than to price-level changes, Phillips curves can be expected to be "bad," and lie to the northeast of F (Figure 11.6). They will be high even at high unemployment, and perhaps nearly horizontal. Labor demands in these circumstances will be more insistent than otherwise. Employer resistance will be less insistent, since wage concessions can be passed on easily and higher wage-price structures "validated" by easy money and/or loose budgets.

When it is assumed generally that monetary and fiscal policy will be sensitive primarily to the price level, however, Phillips curves can be expected to be "good." They will lie to the southwest of F. They will be generally low and nearly vertical (above extremely low levels of unemployment).

Supporting evidence for these conjectures of instability in Phillips curves may be found in Phillips' own studies of Great Britain. "Good" curves are derived in periods dominated by classical economics and gold-standard orthodoxy. "Bad" ones, however, appear in periods dominated by "heresies" like Keynesianism, growthmanship, and "full employment at whatever cost."

17. On the technical side, Rees and his coworkers are concerned with the variability of the Phillips curve slope both with the rate of change of unemployment and also with the choice of time period (annually, quarterly, or monthly). For example, when the prior-year unemployment rate U_{t-1} is included as an independent variable, the slope of the Phillips curve is steeper when U_{t-1} is held at the average value of U_t than it is in Bodkin's study cited above, or in the steady-state case of $U_t = U_{t-1}$. The intercorrelations between U_t, U_{t-1}, and $(U_t - U_{t-1})$ are also too great

34. The following argument restates M. Bronfenbrenner and F. D. Holzman, "Survey of Inflation Theory." *A.E.R.* (September 1963), p. 635.

to justify statistically the use of more than one of this trio as independent variables. For these and allied reasons, Rees is[35]

> astounded by how many very different Phillips curves can be constructed on reasonable assumptions from the same body of data. The nature of the relationship between wage changes and unemployment is highly sensitive to the exact choice of the other variables that enter the regression and to the forms of all the variables. For this reason, the authors of Phillips curves would do well to label them conspicuously *"Unstable. Apply with extreme care."*

18.   Another technical argument against the Phillips curve is more basic from the economic point of view, as distinguished from the statistical one. Its simplest presentation is in Friedman's 1967 presidential address to the American Economic Association.[36] Friedman bases the entire Phillips analysis on money illusion; he analyzes a wage-employment relation set off by easy money policies, rather than one set off by any increase in union bargaining strength or militancy. He also assumes an environment without recent inflationary experience.

There is at any time, according to Friedman, an equilibrium rate of unemployment (with equilibrium prices and wages, a given body of labor legislation, a given degree of union strength, etc.). This equilibrium rate need not be zero. Now suppose a rise in the nominal money supply, accompanied by an increase in money wages and followed only later by an (unanticipated) rise in the price level. Workers interpret this initially (*ex ante*) as a *rise* in real wages, and so the amount of labor supplied will initially rise. Because output prices characteristically respond more rapidly to unanticipated rises in nominal demand than to input prices, there is apt to arise instead an *ex post* fall in real wages. This leads to an increase in the amount of labor demanded. The combination of an *ex ante* rise in real wages received and an *ex post* fall in real wages paid increases employment. When the actual price increases become known and the workers take them into account, employment returns, *ceteris paribus,* to its original level, unless there is another monetary expansion and money wage increase commensurate with the first one. If the second monetary expansion is proportionately larger than the first, the level of unemployment may temporarily fall even further. And so it goes, in the Phillips curve pattern to which we are accustomed. A similar argument also applies in a reverse (deflationary) process.

35. Albert Rees and Mary T. Hamilton, "The Price-Wage-Productivity Perplex," *J.P.E.* (February 1967) p. 70. (Italics in original.) The "sensitivity" referred to is sometimes called a lack of "robustness." The difficulty is by no means confined to Phillips curves, but pervades much econometric work.

36. Milton Friedman, "The Role of Monetary Policy," *A.E.R.* (March 1968), pp. 8–11.

When and if brakes are put on monetary expansion after a Phillips curve pattern is under way in an upward direction, Friedman believes that almost a generation may be required for a "real" equilibrium to reestablish itself under conditions of mild inflation, and that unemployment will be higher than normal during much of the readjustment period.[37] This time period will probably be smaller after more rapid inflation and more complete erosion of money illusion.

Statistical evidence for this skeptical view of the longer-run wage-employment relationship has come from Cagan's fitting of Phillips curves to business cycles rather than to years or months. Cagan finds that essentially all the money-wage changes, over and above "productivity" or "improvement" factors like w_0 in (11.5), are accounted for by lagged price movements, so that the influence of unemployment is negligible.[38]

19. To Cagan's argument it can readily be replied that his long run is too long for practical policy considerations, and fault can also be found with his price series. James Tobin, however, developed in his formal rejoinder[39] a sophisticated rationale for a Phillips curve, in terms of delayed adjustments of price change expectations.

For any variable x, the rate of change g_x may be defined as $\dot{x}/x$; the change in g_x over time may be denoted by $\dot{g}_x$. The variables Tobin uses are w (money wage rate), p (price level), π (v.m.p. of labor), and p^e (expected price level). We suppose these relationships:

$$g_w - g_p = g_\pi \tag{11.6}$$
$$\dot{g}_p{}^e = s\ (g_p - g_p{}^e) \qquad (0 < s < 1). \tag{11.7}$$

Tobin also relates wage changes to price expectations by

$$g_w - \alpha g_p{}^e = \beta g_\pi + f(u) \tag{11.8}$$

where u is the unemployment rate and $f(u)$ the Phillips curve. The coefficients α and β are positive, but are otherwise free to vary. If we solve (11.7) for g_p, (11.8) for g_w, and substitute both results in (11.6):

$$\left[\alpha g_p{}^e + \beta g_\pi + f(u)\right] - \left[g_p{}^e + \frac{1}{s}\ \dot{g}_p{}^e\right] = g_\pi$$

whence:

37. ". . . The initial effects of a higher and unanticipated rate of inflation last for something like two to five years; this initial effect then begins to be reversed; a full adjustment to the new rate of inflation takes . . . a couple of decades." *Ibid.*, p. 11.

38. Phillip Cagan, "Theories of Mild, Continuing Inflation," in Stephen W. Rousseas, (ed.), *Inflation: Its Causes, Consequences, and Control* (Wilton, Conn.: Kazanjian Economics Foundation, 1969), pp. 44–47.

39. James Tobin, in Rousseas, *op. cit.*, pp. 49 f. The presentation below is a simplification of Tobin's argument.

$$\frac{1}{s}\dot{g}_p{}^e = [f(u) - g_\pi(1 - \beta)] - g_p{}^e(1 - \alpha). \tag{11.9}$$

When the left side of (11.9) is zero, expectations of inflation or deflation need not be revised; the price level is moving at its equilibrium or expected rate. The equilibrium value of the expected inflation rate $g_p{}^e$ is then:

$$\frac{f(u) - g_\pi(1 - \beta)}{1 - \alpha}. \tag{11.10}$$

This means that, at equilibrium, there normally remains a long-run Phillips curve $f(u)$ unless $\alpha = 1$. If $f(u)$ equals $g_\pi(1 - \beta)$, $g_p{}^e$ is zero with an equilibrium unemployment rate, as Friedman concluded.

20.   Even though, according to (11.10), the Phillips curve is more than a short-term or disequilibrium phenomenon, it may not be stable enough for use in economic policy. Suffice it to say, in ending this chapter, that the "Phillips curve issue" remains far from solution, either *pro* or *contra*.

Appendix to Chapter 11

STABILITY CONDITIONS IN WAGE-EMPLOYMENT RELATIONS

i.   Let X be total real income, composed of W (real wage income) and V (real nonwage income, equal to $X - W$). Let r be the nominal rate of interest and M the real money supply. Let aggregate private saving and investment be $S = S(W, V, r, M)$ and $I = I(W, V, r, M)$.

These two functions are equal at equilibrium, and linearly homogeneous in the neighborhood of equilibrium. Furthermore, let the marginal spending propensity of workers exceed that of nonworkers. This means that

$$\left[\left(1 - \frac{\delta S}{\delta W}\right) + \frac{\delta I}{\delta W}\right] > \left[\left(1 - \frac{\delta S}{\delta V}\right) + \frac{\delta I}{\delta V}\right]$$

$$\text{or}\quad \left(\frac{\delta I}{\delta W} - \frac{\delta S}{\delta W}\right) > \left(\frac{\delta I}{\delta V} - \frac{\delta S}{\delta V}\right).$$

We apply the linear homogeneity properties of S and I at their equilibrium intersection, and solve for X:

$$W\frac{\delta S}{\delta W} + (X - W)\frac{\delta S}{\delta V} + r\frac{\delta S}{\delta r} + M\frac{\delta S}{\delta M} = W\frac{\delta I}{\delta W} + (X - W)\frac{\delta I}{\delta V} + r\frac{\delta I}{\delta r}$$

$$+ M\frac{\delta I}{\delta M}\left(\frac{\delta S}{\delta V} - \frac{\delta I}{\delta V}\right)X = \left[\left(\frac{\delta I}{\delta W} - \frac{\delta S}{\delta W}\right) - \left(\frac{\delta I}{\delta V} - \frac{\delta S}{\delta V}\right]W$$

$$+ \left(\frac{\delta I}{\delta r} - \frac{\delta S}{\delta r}\right)r + \left(\frac{\delta I}{\delta M} - \frac{\delta S}{\delta M}\right)M.$$

Let $W = wn/p$ and $M = m/p$, where w is the money wage level, n the employment level, m the nominal money stock, and p the general price level. In this notation X is

$$X = \frac{1}{\frac{\delta S}{\delta V} - \frac{\delta I}{\delta V}} \left\{ \left[\left(\frac{\delta I}{\delta W} - \frac{\delta S}{\delta W} \right) - \left(\frac{\delta I}{\delta V} - \frac{\delta S}{\delta V} \right) \right] \frac{wn}{p} \right.$$

$$\left. + \left(\frac{\delta I}{\delta r} - \frac{\delta S}{\delta r} \right) r + \left(\frac{\delta I}{\delta M} - \frac{\delta S}{\delta M} \right) \frac{m}{p} \right\}. \quad (11.i)$$

ii. This implies an inverse relation between X and r. The denominator is positive, since $\delta S/\delta V$ is positive and $\delta I/\delta V$ is near zero. The coefficient of wn/p in the numerator is positive, with $\delta S/\delta V > \delta S/\delta W$ and ($\delta I/\delta W$, $\delta I/\delta V$) both near zero. The coefficient of r is negative; we assume a discouraging effect of high interest rates on investment without a significant negative effect on saving. The coefficient of m/p is taken positive on the theory that easy money (plentiful real money) encourages spending for both consumption and investment at the expense of saving.

The graphic translation of this development would be a standard macroeconomic diagram (not shown) using what are called *IS* functions as loci of equality between planned saving and planned investment. Two shift parameters W and M operate positively on *IS*, by the argument of the preceding paragraph, but the slope of each *IS* function reflects $\delta x/\delta r$ and is negative. To quote Simler:[1]

> Movements from one [IS function] to another can be considered as representing some combination of changes in the money wage rate, the level of employment, the price level, and the [nominal] money supply. If the money wage rate increases and the elasticity of demand for labor is greater than unity, the increase in real wage income may offset the decrease in the real value of monetary assets, and enable [the IS function] to shift upward.

iii. This conventional macroeconomic exercise leaves our results indefinite, but Simler does not stop here. He passes on to the demand and supply for money, M^d and M^s respectively. He has $M^d = M^d(X,r)$ and $M^s = m/p$. The M^d function is linear homogeneous in the neighborhood of equilibrium; its partial derivatives with respect to income and the interest rate are positive and negative respectively. To obtain an equilibrium condition, we proceed as in deriving (11.i):

$$X \frac{\delta M^d}{\delta X} + r \frac{\delta M^d}{\delta r} = \frac{m}{p}$$

$$X = \frac{1}{\frac{\delta M^d}{\delta X}} \left(\frac{m}{p} - r \frac{\delta M^d}{\delta r} \right). \quad (11.ii)$$

1. Simler, *op. cit.*, p. 8.

The coefficient of the real money stock is positive, as is the coefficient of the interest rate. Graphically, we may recall, as loci of supply-demand equilibria for money, the standard macroeconomic *LM* function (not reproduced). The slope parameter, given by $\delta X/\delta r$ in (11.ii), is positive. The shift parameter is m/p, or M^s; its effect is also positive. Money wage increases operate indirectly, by raising p and lowering the real money supply (with constant nominal m).

iv.   We next derive an aggregate demand function for real output X, by solving (11.i) and (11.ii) simultaneously for r, and then substituting this equilibrium interest rate in (11.ii). The algebra is tedious,[2] and the result can be abbreviated to

$$X = k_1 \frac{wn}{p} + k_2 \frac{m}{p} \tag{11.iii}$$

with both k_i normally positive,[3] whence $\delta X/\delta w$ is positive and $\delta X/\delta p$ negative.

A standard aggregate-demand diagram would express these ideas. The negative slope of the aggregate demand functions would be determined by $\delta X/\delta p$, and the upward shift by $\delta X/\delta w$; the money wage w is the shift parameter. The downward slope of the aggregate demand functions is entirely orthodox.

v.   On the side of aggregate supply, the volume of employment n becomes an additional unknown, varying with w and p. It is derived from a labor market model (which assumes other inputs constant) and an aggregate production function.

2. Equating the right sides of (11.i) and (11.ii) and solving for r, denote by U the expression:

$$U = \frac{\delta I/\delta r - \delta S/\delta r}{\delta S/\delta V - \delta I/\delta V} + \frac{\delta M/\delta r}{\delta M/\delta X}.$$

The solution for r is, in terms of U,

$$r = -\frac{1}{U}\left[\left(\frac{\delta I/\delta W - \delta S/\delta W}{\delta S/\delta V - \delta I/\delta V} + 1\right)\frac{wn}{p} + \left(\frac{\delta I/\delta M - \delta S/\delta M}{\delta S/\delta V - \delta I/\delta V} - \frac{1}{\delta M/\delta X}\right)\frac{m}{p} \right].$$

Substituting this value in (11.ii), the coefficients of (11.iii) become

$$k_1 = \frac{\delta M/\delta r}{U\delta M/\delta X}\left(\frac{\delta I/\delta W - \delta S/\delta W}{\delta S/\delta V - \delta I/\delta V} + 1\right)$$

$$k_2 = \frac{1}{\delta M/\delta X}\left[\frac{\delta M/\delta r}{U}\left(\frac{\delta I/\delta M - \delta S/\delta M}{\delta S/\delta V - \delta I/\delta V} - \frac{1}{\delta M/\delta X}\right) + 1\right].$$

I am indebted to Yoichi Niwata for assistance at this point.

3. Simler points out that k_1 is negative when the marginal spending propensity of nonworkers is greater than that of workers, while k_2 is negative when a money wage increase sets off a more than proportionate increase in the price level. *Op. cit.*, pp. 21–23.

On the demand side of this labor market model, $n^d = f(w/p)$, with $f'(w/p)$ negative on marginal-productivity grounds. (The partial derivative $\delta n^d/\delta p$ is positive.) On the supply side, n^s is treated as fixed, and actual employment n is n^d or n^s, whichever is smaller. In the standard case, with at least frictional unemployment, $n^d < n^s$.

The short-run production function depends only on n. We have, therefore, $X = F(n)$ with a positive first derivative and a negative second derivative in the relevant range. Substituting the labor market results in the presence of unemployment,

$$X = F\left[f\left(\frac{w}{p}\right)\right]. \qquad (11.iv)$$

This is the aggregate supply function. The signs of $\delta X/\delta w$ and $\delta X/\delta p$ are the same as those of $\delta n^d/\delta w$ (negative) and $\delta n^d/\delta p$ (positive). This function too is often presented graphically with the sign of $\delta X/\delta p$ reflected in the upward slope of aggregate supply functions and the sign of $\delta X/\delta w$ reflected in the direction of shift. (The money wage is again the shift parameter.) This diagram is also omitted here.

vi. In setting aggregate supply and demand in confrontation, we substitute $f(w/p)$ for n (employment) in (11.iii):

$$X = k_1 \frac{w}{p} f\left(\frac{w}{p}\right) + k_2 \left(\frac{m}{p}\right). \qquad (11.v)$$

The quantity X continues to represent aggregate demand, but in an expanded sense "satisfy[ing] the conditions of equilibrium in both the commodity and money markets, with given values for the money wage and the money supply."[4]

The partial derivatives of (11.v) are:

$$\frac{\delta X}{\delta w} = k_1 \frac{1}{p}\left[f\left(\frac{w}{p}\right) + \frac{w}{p} f'\left(\frac{w}{p}\right)\right]$$

$$\frac{\delta X}{\delta p} = -\left\{ k_1 \frac{w}{p^2}\left[f\left(\frac{w}{p}\right) + \frac{w}{p} f'\left(\frac{w}{p}\right)\right] + k_2 \frac{m}{p^2}\right\}.$$

Since $f'(w/p)$ is the (negative) slope of the marginal productivity function, these derivatives take on their conventional values (positive and negative, respectively) only at sufficiently high values of the price level p. On a "confrontation" diagram (Figure 11.7), both the slope and the direction of shift are represented as unconventional at low price levels. Aggregate output "increases [with the money wage w] so long as k_1 times

4. *Ibid.*, p. 16.

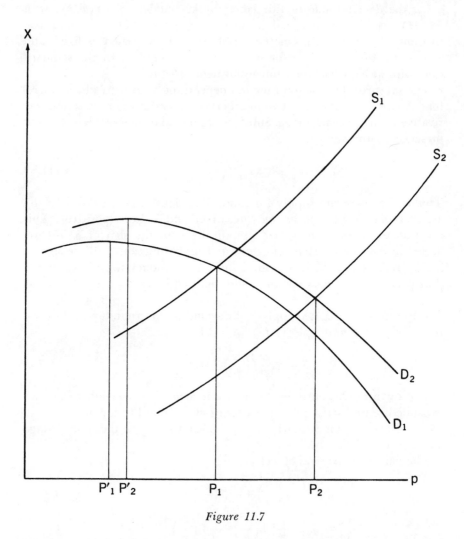

Figure 11.7

the increase in real [wage] income exceeds k_2 times the decrease in real monetary assets. In order for real wage income to increase as the real wage increases, the elasticity of demand for labor must [exceed] unity." Even so, "the positive real income effect is [eventually] offset by the negative 'real balance effect' and X reaches a maximum [at P' in Figure 11.7]. Thereafter it behaves in orthodox fashion."[5]

5. *Ibid.*

vii. We are ready for the discussion of stability. The stability condition is that the slope of each D_i (Figure 11.7) must be less than the slope of the corresponding S_i, at their intersections. But this tells us nothing about wages, since w is only a *shift* parameter of this figure. We turn, therefore, to equations (11.iv) and (11.v), and a marginal-productivity relationship. Rewriting and renumbering, we have the following:

$$X - k_1\left(\frac{wn}{p}\right) - k_2\left(\frac{m}{p}\right) = 0 \qquad \text{(11.vi)}$$

$$X - F(n) = 0 \qquad \text{(11.vii)}$$

$$\frac{\delta X}{\delta n} - \frac{w}{p} = 0 \qquad \text{(11.viii)}$$

Differentiate (11.vi–11.viii) partially with respect to the money wage rate w, with (X, n, p) all variable:

$$\frac{\delta X}{\delta w} - \frac{\delta n}{\delta w}\left(\frac{k_1 w}{p}\right) + \frac{\delta p}{\delta w}\left(\frac{k_1 wn + k_2 m}{p^2}\right) - k_1\frac{n}{p} = 0$$

$$\frac{\delta X}{\delta w} - \frac{\delta n}{\delta w}\frac{dF}{dn} = 0$$

$$\frac{\delta n}{\delta w}\left(\frac{\delta^2 X}{\delta n^2}\right) + \frac{\delta p}{\delta w}\left(\frac{w}{p^2}\right) - \frac{1}{p} = 0.$$

The unknowns of this three-equation system are $(\delta X/\delta w,\ \delta n/\delta w,\ \delta p/\delta w)$. If Δ is the determinant of the system, and dF/dn equals $\delta X/\delta n$, the solutions are:

$$\frac{\delta X}{\delta w} = \frac{-1}{\Delta}\frac{\left(\dfrac{\delta X}{\delta n}\right)k_2 m}{p^3} \qquad \text{(11.ix)}$$

$$\frac{\delta n}{\delta w} = \frac{1}{\Delta}\frac{k_2 m}{p^3} \qquad \text{(11.x)}$$

$$\frac{\delta p}{\delta w} = \frac{1}{\Delta}\frac{k_1\dfrac{w}{p} + k_1 n\dfrac{\delta^2 X}{\delta n^2} - \dfrac{\delta X}{\delta n}}{p} \qquad \text{(11.xi)}$$

and the value of Δ is

$$\frac{1}{p^2}\left[k_1\frac{w^2}{p} + \frac{\delta^2 X}{\delta n^2}(k_1 wn + k_2 m) - w\frac{\delta X}{\delta n}\right].$$

The numerators of (11.ix) and (11.x) are positive. It remains to determine which signs of Δ and of (11.xi) are consistent with stability. We may rewrite (11.vi–11.viii), distinguishing between aggregate *supply* X^s

and aggregate *demand* X^d, and adding a dynamic stability condition as (11.xii) :[6]

$$X^d - k_1\left(\frac{wn}{p}\right) - k_2\left(\frac{m}{p}\right) = 0$$

$$X^s - F(n) = 0$$

$$\frac{\delta X}{\delta n} - \frac{w}{p} = 0$$

$$\frac{dp}{dt} - \lambda(X^d - X^s) = 0 \qquad\qquad (11.\text{xii})$$

This four-equation system (11.xi, 11.vi, 11.vii, and 11.xii) can now be differentiated with respect to time. (Only X, n, and p are direct functions of time, with w changing autonomously.)

$$\dot{X}^d - \dot{n}\frac{k_1 w}{p} + \dot{p}\left(\frac{k_1 wn + k_2 m}{p^2}\right) = 0 \qquad\qquad (11.\text{xiii})$$

$$\dot{X}^s - \dot{n}\frac{\delta X}{\delta n} = 0 \qquad\qquad (11.\text{xiv})$$

$$\dot{n}\frac{\delta^2 X}{\delta n^2} + \dot{p}\frac{w}{p^2} = 0 \qquad\qquad (11.\text{xv})$$

$$-\dot{X}^d + \dot{X}^s = -\ddot{p} \qquad\qquad (11.\text{xvi-a})$$

If this differential-equation system has a solution of the form $p_t = p_0\,e^{ct}$, where c is a constant, $\ddot{p} = c\dot{p}$, and (11.xvi-a) becomes:

$$-\dot{X}^d + \dot{X}^s + c\dot{p} = 0. \qquad\qquad (11.\text{xvi})$$

For a nontrivial (nonzero) solution for the four unknown time derivatives X^d, X^s, n, and p, the determinant of (11.xiii–11.xvi) must itself be zero. Call this determinant D.

$$D = \begin{vmatrix} 1 & 0 & -\dfrac{k_1 w}{p} & \dfrac{k_1 wn + k_2 m}{p^2} \\[2mm] 0 & 1 & -\dfrac{\delta X}{\delta n} & 0 \\[2mm] 0 & 0 & \dfrac{\delta^2 X}{\delta n^2} & \dfrac{w}{p^2} \\[2mm] -1 & 1 & 0 & c \end{vmatrix}$$

For this determinant to vanish, we require:

$$D = c\frac{\delta^2 X}{\delta n^2} + \frac{1}{p^2}\left[k_1\frac{w^2}{p} + \frac{\delta^2 X}{\delta n^2}(k_1 wn + k_2 m) - w\frac{\delta X}{\delta n}\right] = 0.$$

6. The development that follows is simplified by setting $\lambda = 1$ in (11.xii). In words, this equation says that the price level rises with overall excess demand and falls with overall excess supply.

Except for its first term, D equals the determinant Δ of (11.ix–11.xi). Therefore, for D to vanish,

$$c \frac{\delta^2 X}{\delta n^2} + \Delta = 0.$$

This is our condition for nontriviality. For *stability*, however, the price level p_t must approach some equilibrium value $\bar{p}$. This means that the constant c in (11.xvi) must be negative. Diminishing returns suggest that $\delta^2 X / \delta n^2$ is negative also. Therefore, for stability, Δ must be negative.

We return to (11.ix–11.xi). With Δ negative, we have

$$\frac{\delta X}{\delta n} = \frac{1}{\Delta} \frac{\left(\frac{\delta X}{\delta w} \right) k_2 m}{p^3} \qquad \text{negative}$$

$$\frac{\delta n}{\delta w} = \frac{1}{\Delta} \frac{k_2 m}{p^3} \qquad \text{negative}$$

$$\frac{\delta p}{\delta w} = \frac{1}{\Delta} \frac{k_1 \dfrac{w}{p} + k_1 n \dfrac{\delta^2 X}{\delta n^2} - \dfrac{\delta X}{\delta n}}{p} \qquad \text{positive (?)}$$

The second result is most relevant for the purposes of this chapter. It establishes, as a stability condition, the classical proposition that employment moves inversely with the money wage rate. The first result establishes in the same way the related proposition that output moves inversely with the money wage rate. (The third result, that prices and money wages move together under competition, rests on economic common sense. It is not proved rigorously.) [7]

7. If $\delta X / \delta n = w/p$ as per (11.viii), and $\delta^2 X / \delta n^2$ is negative, a positive value of (11.xi) requires a negative value of

$$(k_1 - 1) \frac{w}{p} + k_1 n \frac{\delta^2 X}{\delta n^2}$$

for which we need $k_1 < 1$, or alternatively

$$\frac{\delta^2 X}{\delta n^2} < \frac{1 - k_1}{n k_1} \frac{w}{p}.$$

CHAPTER TWELVE

Classical Interest Theory

Simplifying Assumptions

1. Capital theory is not only an autonomous branch of economics, but perhaps the most difficult branch of all. We do not hope to treat it exhaustively here *en passant,* and so operate from assumptions less justifiable than usual (except for considerations of convenience and simplicity). We dispense with the resulting artificialities only gradually, and less completely than would be required for a treatise on capital theory.

2. Eight of our principal simplifications are the following.

(*1*) "Capital" will mean only reproducible physical capital, not human capital, not research and development, and not land or natural resources. In the present chapter (but not in Chapter 13) we shall commonly ignore the possibility of holding assets in monetary form, so that we shall be considering capital instruments solely. Herein lies the most important difference between classical and postclassical (or monetary) interest theory.

(*2*) Capital instruments, too, will often be homogenized further into all-purpose machines—"putty" or "jelly" or "leets" or "meccano sets"— with uniform lengths of life. That is to say, capital will be treated as malleable and plastic in the long run, and as having uniform marginal productivity. This assumption has often been applied to homogeneous labor as well, if not to land.

(*3*) These homogeneous capital instruments or machines are, moreover, reproducible at constant cost in the long run. This level of cost, while affected by changes in both past and "permanent" capital charges and interest rates, will be treated as only infinitesimally sensitive to present changes in these magnitudes.

(*4*) The price of a machine diverges only temporarily from its cost of production. This assumption, in conjunction with (*3*), permits us to relate changes in the marginal productivity of capital to changes in interest rates over the long run.

(*5*) The homogeneity of capital or machines applies only at a point in time. That is to say, this year's machines are different from (superior to) last year's machines. Such embodied technological progress occurs, however, only at a regular, predictable, and hence discountable rate.

(*6*) We are therefore able to define the quantity of capital, in an index-number sense, as accurately as the quantity of product, the quantity of labor, or the level of prices. We can also define "keeping capital intact,"[1] and likewise define its marginal product net of appropriate allowances for both depreciation and obsolescence. (These allowances depend on the age of the machines, the intensity of their use, and the pace of both technical and product innovation. They, too, are assumed to be only infinitesimally sensitive to changes in present interest rates.)

(*7*) Production processes involve capital inputs as defined above, and also noncapital inputs such as land and labor. The processes are "circular" in the sense that all of them, including the formation of human capital, use as inputs the outputs of other processes. We do not, therefore, follow the tradition that regards labor and land as "original" inputs or factors of production, whose productivity is supposed to embody the productivity of "derived" inputs like capital. In other words, the marginal productivity of capital has meaning apart from the productivities of labor and land.[2]

1. Hicks, *Value and Capital*, 2d ed. (Oxford: Oxford University Press, 1946), ch. 14, is a useful introduction to the difficulties of defining capital, income, and "intactness" when simplifications (2) through (5) are abandoned.

2. It is sometimes useful to distinguish the marginal productivity (called *efficiency* when the complications of long periods and uncertainty are kept in mind) of *capital* from that of *investment*. There are, however, several methods of doing this.

Keynes, for example, calls the "marginal efficiency of capital" the entity which we shall call below the "internal rate of return," and which Irving Fisher called "the rate of return over cost." Another distinction starts from a production function:

$$x = F(a, b), \qquad \text{with} \qquad \frac{dx}{db} = \frac{\delta x}{\delta b} + \frac{\delta x}{\delta a} \frac{da}{db}$$

where, if a is labor and b capital, the (private) marginal efficiency of investment is $\delta x/\delta b$, which is less than the (social) marginal productivity of capital dx/db when labor and capital are complementary, and increasing capital causes wages as well as employment to rise. (This is the "Wicksell effect;" see Mark Blaug, *Economic Theory in Retrospect* (Homewood, Ill.; Irwin, 1962), pp. 510–513.) Harry Johnson points out in correspondence that when wages rise, the net marginal product of capital is $(\delta x/\delta b) - (\delta^2 x/\delta a \delta b)$.

Donald Dewey, *Modern Capital Theory* (New York: Columbia University Press,

Also, circular production processes are of indeterminate or infinite duration; a "production period" has meaning only in terms of the length of an individual investment, which is governed by market rather than technological considerations.

(*8*) The bulk of our theoretical analysis will run in terms of two periods only, the present and "the future," which usually means the next period. (This period, however, is long enough to allow for long-run adjustments!) We shall not, in particular, attempt to treat infinite periods or to cruise developmental turnpikes.

Laymen's Difficulties

3.   Laymen and students, approaching capital theory for the first time, usually bring with them certain errors and misconceptions, or at least confusions. It will be useful to remedy some of these.

(*1*) It is important, first of all, to remember that a firm *demands* capital (machines) by *supplying* securities (including IOU's and commercial paper as well as stocks and bonds), while an individual *supplies* capital indirectly when he *demands* securities.[3] A rise in the price of securities, other things being equal, therefore implies a fall in the price of capital, and vice versa. If p is the price of an asset or security yielding a certain and perpetual real income y when the rate of interest is r and is expected to remain at that level:

1965) , pp. 60–62, bases the distinction between the marginal efficiencies of capital and investment upon a capital-stock-adjustment model of the demand for investment. If K_{t-1} is the actual stock of real capital at time $t-1$ and K^*_{t-1} the desired stock, the net demand for investment I_t in the interval between $t-1$ and time t is

$$I_t = K_t - K_{t-1} = \beta \left(K_{t-1} - K^*_{t-1}\right)$$

with the adjustment coefficient β a positive fraction. When we speak of the marginal efficiency of *capital*, we assume β to be optimal from the demander's viewpoint. When we speak of the marginal efficiency of *investment*, we assume β at its technically feasible value, which is usually smaller. The two are equal under stock equilibrium $(K - K^*)$ or when stock adjustment is feasible at its optimum rate $(\beta = 1)$. Otherwise, the marginal efficiency of capital is the higher.

Incidentally, we do not accept the "mythology" that rules out disinvestment, or negative values of aggregate I_t, or conditions of $K > K^*$, a priori. Compare Friedrich von Hayek: "[A] basic mistake . . . is the idea of capital as a fund which maintains itself automatically, [so] that, in consequence, once an amount of capital has been brought into existence, the necessity of reproducing it represents no economic problem." ("The Mythology of Capital," *Readings*, no. 20, p. 357.) Positive net investment and stock adjustment, Hayek agrees, are normal states of affairs.

3. The identity between demand for securities and supply of capital does not hold for consumption loans, consumer credit, or transfers of old (previously issued) securities.

$$pr = y \quad \text{and} \quad p = \frac{y}{r} \tag{12.1}$$

so that we speak of an asset or security price as the *capitalized value* of its income. Uncertainty about y and r, and also finite maturities of securities, complicate these elementary formulae in practice. (The formulae found in handbooks of financial mathematics treat the complications of finiteness more adequately than they do those of uncertainty.)

(2) Any observed market interest rate r_i is the sum of three parts:

$$r_i = r + r' + r_i''. \tag{12.2}$$

Of these three parts, r is the *pure* or *economic* interest rate, and much discussion of "*the* interest rate" treats it as the only rate in existence. The *general* risk premium r' is called by Fisher "appreciation"; it compensates for actual and prospective capital losses due to inflation or to interest rate increases during the life of the security i. (In case of deflation or falling rates, r' will often be negative, and the security will sell at a premium rather than a discount.) The *particular* risk premium r_i'', which cannot be negative, compensates for the debtor's present or anticipated unwillingness or inability to meet his obligations for paying interest on, or repaying the principal of, security i; it includes allowance for the cost of securing repayment, as well as for default risk proper. If security i is a pure equity, involving no contractual obligations for either principal or interest, r_i'' is correspondingly high.

In a regime of multiple interest rates, the closest approach to the economic rate r is a "bill rate" on the short-term security of a responsible domestic government, on which neither the asset nor its income carries special tax privileges or penalties. This rate is computed, of course, on an annual basis and as a percentage of the security's unregulated market price, which may differ from its face or par value. (The actual bill rate, then, may differ from the stated rate on the face of the bill.) It is sometimes impossible to estimate r with any accuracy, usually because of rapid inflation, stringent control of security prices, and/or serious social unrest. Also, in less developed countries, there may be no organized capital market on which bills are traded—or, for that matter, no bills may exist.

(3) The *formal* distinction between the rate of interest and the rent of capital is that the latter is expressed in monetary units per time interval, whereas the same figure is transformed, in the former measure, to a percentage of the value of a capital instrument. It is to some extent a matter of custom, convention, and convenience that a given contract be expressed in one form rather than the other. (The *rental* form obviates

the need to estimate the values of capital assets; the *interest* form is common when the return per period is measured in units of the item lent, as in money loans and loans of specific goods *in natura*.)

The economic distinction between rent and interest has considerably more substance, especially for short-term problems. Suppose an increase in the marginal productivity, and hence the rental, of a given capital asset. Will this involve a rise in the rate of interest, or will the value of the asset rise while the interest rate remains the same? The second outcome

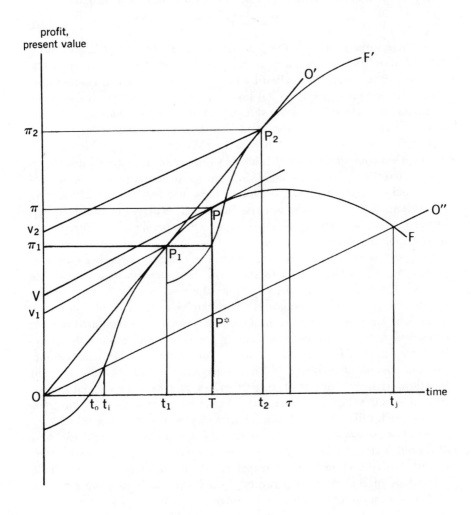

Figure 12.1

is at least equally probable in the short run; the example illustrates the economics of the rent-interest distinction. (To Marshall, and to other writers seeking to reserve the term "rent" for land and the term "interest" for reproducible capital, this situation involves a "quasi-rent.") It is confusing to read of some economic force causing a change in the interest rate because it causes a change in the rent on capital instruments, without some indication of the reason why capital values are not also affected. (See section 2[3] above.)

(*4*) What constitutes optimizing behavior with respect to management of capital assets? Is it to maximize the *rate of return* on the investment or the *present value* of that investment? Does the distinction vanish at equilibrium, or does it persist?

The distinctions and their implications have been shown most clearly by examples involving the investment of a fixed sum (inventory) over variable time intervals and optimizing the *investment period*,[4] as in a biological maturation process like the fermentation of wine or the growing of trees.

The horizontal axis of Figure 12.1 accordingly measures time in years. The vertical axis measures gross profit (returns minus costs), which may be either future, as indicated by the symbol π, or discounted to the preinvestment present, with present values indicated by V or v. The prospective investment yields its returns along function F, which is indeed a production function involving time. As F is drawn, there are heavy investment expenses at the outset, and F involves a loss or deficit until time t_o. There are, however, profits of π_1 and π if liquidation occurs at t_1 and T respectively. The maximum profit (not indicated symbolically) occurs if liquidation is postponed to τ, which may itself be infinite. At an interest rate r indicated by the slope of the line v_1P_1, the present value of π_1 is v_1, which is positive.[5] This implies that investment in the F process, with liquidation at t_1, is not only profitable but more profitable than a loan

---

4. The particular schema used below is derived from Kenneth E. Boulding, *Economic Analysis*, 3rd ed. (New York: Harper, 1955), pp. 862–874. For more rudimentary examples, involving investment of varying quantities of capital over fixed time periods, compare Dewey, *op. cit.*, ch. 8.

5. The relation assumed on this diagram between a gross profit π_t t years hence and its present value v_t is

$$v_t \ (1+r) \ t = \pi_t \qquad \text{or} \qquad v_t = \pi_t / \ (1+r) \ t.$$

This permits discounting to be visualized along a straight line, but it ignores the force of compound interest. More accurate equations would be, for annual compounding:

$$v_t = \frac{\pi_t}{(1+r)^{\ t}};$$

for compounding n times a year:

of the same amount at rate r along the path OO''. (Liquidation before t_i or after t_j would not have been more profitable than simple loans of the same respective lengths.)

But the question before the house is to locate the single most profitable investment period (which we assume to be unique). Three possibilities are t_1, T, and τ, usually in increasing order of length. The attraction of t_1, involving liquidation at t_1, is the maximization of the *internal rate of return* (in Fisher's terminology, the rate of return over cost); geometrically speaking, this condition is expressed by the tangency of F at P_1 to the steepest radius vector from the origin O, the slope of each vector being $(1 + r)$, with r variable. Call the highest internal rate of return ρ, which exceeds the ruling rate of interest r.[6] The attraction of T (liquidation at T) is the maximization of the *present value* of the investment at a given interest rate r; geometrically, this condition is expressed by the tangency of F and P to the highest "discount line" VP with which it is consistent. In particular, liquidation at T is better than at t_1 followed by a loan at rate r over the interval $t_1 T$ along an extension of $v_1 P_1$, since V exceeds v_1. Finally, the attraction of τ is the maximizing of profit (regardless of time), since the liquidation point τ corresponds to the maximum value of F. Liquidation at τ, therefore, is better than liquidation at t_1 or T, followed by no further earnings $(r = 0)$ over the intervals $t_1\tau$ or $T\tau$.

When the market interest rate is strictly positive (>0), the irrelevance of the maximum future income criterion should be obvious. It is, however, by no means equally obvious in a subsistence economy with no organized capital market when τ is short, or for that matter in a planned economy that does not permit the earning of interest and that fixes its eye on the distant future. We shall, assuming a positive interest rate, limit ourselves to the comparison of t_1 and T as optimal investment periods.

$$v_t = \frac{\pi_t}{\left(1 + \dfrac{r}{n}\right)^{nt}};$$

and for continuous compounding, with n increasing without bound:

$$v_t = \pi_t\, e^{-rt}$$

since

$$\lim_{n \to \infty} \left(1 + \frac{r}{n}\right)^n = e^r.$$

If we had used compound interest, the vertical axis of Figure 12.1 might have been the logarithm of profits or present value, and the negative part of the diagram (below the horizontal axis) might have been ignored. This change would have permitted use of straight-line discounting and compound interest simultaneously.

6. If $\rho = r$, the rate-of-return and present-value criteria give identical results; if $\rho < r$, the investment is not worthwhile on economic grounds. The case in the text, $(\rho > r)$, is the only interesting one.

The choice depends, in the first instance, on the nature of the production function F and its alternatives. If F is a unique investment process, to which the only alternative is lending money or goods at rate r per annum, the investor should continue on F for however long the internal rate of return exceeds r, even though it may pass its own peak value of ρ. This consideration leads at once to the present value criterion, as can be seen on Figure 12.1, the maximum present value being V. This is indeed the orthodox view among economists.

Suppose, however, that the investment process is not unique, but can be replicated at internal rates in excess of r.[7] Such capital market imperfections are not uncommon, although they may be less common than professional tipsters would have outsiders believe. When the replication possibility exists at rates higher than r, discounting from T at rate r is no longer the relevant determinant of investment policy. The optimal strategy is rather liquidation at t_1, and then following F' (a replication of F), with a second liquidation at t_2, and so on along the envelope OO'. (Present value, of course, increases without bound so long as the internal rate of return ρ exceeds the market rate of interest r.)

For competitive equilibrium on the capital market, such replication opportunities as we have just discussed, which incline practical business men to the internal-rate criterion of investment optimality, must be absent. Their absence may be due to diminishing returns to single investments or investment types (lowering of ρ to approach r),[8] or to increased demand for resources to take advantages of opportunities with infinite present values (raising r to approach ρ).

Not only this, but competitive capital markets tend toward elimination of capital gains (present-value windfalls) like V on Figure 12.1. They often do so through increases in the interest rate. The only position consistent with the adding-up theorem (6.4) lies on a discount line OO'', at which no such windfalls are possible, *i.e.*, on which the v.m.p. (marginal efficiency) of investment is equal to its average net product.

The adjustment from VP to OO'', however, need not involve changes in r. (In this illustration, it does not; VP and OO'' have been drawn parallel, implying a uniform interest rate.) Rises in input prices or falls in output prices can serve the adjustment purpose by themselves. The simplest example, suggested by Boulding's presentation,[9] applies when

7. In Figure 12.1 the replication is not subject to diminishing returns; the envelope OO', tangent not to F and its successive replications, is a straight line with slope $(1 + \rho) > (1 \div r)$. Diminishing returns would require downward concavity of OO', but not necessarily tangency with any discount line.

8. This adjustment process need not imply diminishing returns to aggregate investment as a whole. See below, section 9 f.

9. *Op. cit.*, p. 854.

process F requires some unique input or opportunity in inelastic supply. Its owner may then charge V as a rent, while the F line is transposed downward vertically by this amount, to tangency with OO'' at P^*. (The transposed F is not shown in the diagram.)

(5) Since so many recipients of interest income are passive rentiers and nonparticipants in direct productive activities, the question naturally arises: What does the rate of interest (as distinguished from the rentier) do? The standard answer has been, for generations, that it equalizes saving and investment while determining the allocation of the national income between present consumption and provision for future growth and change. If, however, as modern macroeconomics tells us, the *ex post* equality between saving and investment is an identity regardless of the rate of interest,[10] and if saving depends more immediately on income than on interest, what is left for the interest rate to do?[11]

The remaining, or rather revised, functions of the interest rate appear to be five in number: (a) to bring *planned* saving and investment into equilibrium *ex ante* (in conjunction, however, with the income level!) ; (b) to ration investment opportunities by cutting off those for which sufficient returns are not forecast; (c) to encourage saving, including the discouraging of dissaving, by cheapening the price of future income relative to present consumption;[12] (d) to determine, in connection with capi-

---

10. An anarchistic closed economy, with neither public nor international sectors, illustrates the point most clearly. Income earned during period t is then the sum of the consumption and investment expenditures of others, and we have an aggregate income *source* equation:

$$Y_t = C_t + I_t.$$

If the interval t is long enough for the planned disposal of income to be accomplished within the period of its receipt, we assume the following *use* equation dividing it between consumption and saving:

$$Y_t = C_t + S_t$$

whence I_t and S_t are equal, as in Keynes, *General Theory, op. cit.*, p. 63. In the more general case, the equality holds if I_t is redefined to include public expenditures (net of transfer payments) , exports, and receipts of foreign aid, while S_t is redefined to include taxes (again net of transfers) , imports, and grants of foreign aid.

11. Compare Henry C. Wallich, "The Changing Significance of the Interest Rate," *A.E.R.* (June 1946).

12. The price of a unit of future income or income "next year" is $1/(1+r)$, which varies inversely with r.

It does not follow that increasing r (and lowering the price of future income) increases either gross or net saving, any more than raising wage rates increases the amount of labor supplied. By analogy with the argument of Chapter 9, substitution effects alone lead to this conclusion, but income effects operate to encourage consumption instead, since consumption is not an inferior good. (See also below, section 6.)

A good collection of economists' surmises about the shape of the net saving function, as related to the interest rate, is Paul H. Douglas, *The Theory of Wages* (New York: Macmillan, 1934) , ch. 17. These surmises run from a negative slope to a high positive elasticity below a certain minimum rate (related to the life expectancy of persons retir-

talization formulae like (12.1), the prices of securities as capitalized values of their yields, of capital instruments as capitalized values of their rents, and, in general, "the price of future income;" (e) to assist in the determination of both personal and functional distributions of income and wealth. Rentiers and their agents, meanwhile, merely shift their portfolios between various assets, or between future income and present consumption.

(6) As for the distributional effect of interest rates, the popular view is that any rise subsidizes the creditor classes, the rich, and the idle, while any fall aids the debtors, the poor, and the active majority of the population. Much of the hostility toward high interest and "tight money" remedies for inflation[13] springs from such distributional concerns, although the effect on investment also arouses opposition from partisans of rapid growth through capital accumulation.

We agree that high interest rates favor creditors on new loans, while low rates favor debtors. The creditor on an outstanding loan or security, however, suffers a capital loss if rates have risen since the loan was made, unless he can hold his paper to maturity; but he can dispose of this paper at a profit if rates have fallen in the same interval.

If elasticities of substitution between capital and labor in production are below unity, high rates tend to increase the property share of the functional income distribution, and vice versa. Elasticities higher than unity operate in the opposite directions, however.

It does not follow that high rates necessarily favor the *idle* rich. The explanation stems from equation (12.1) and the capitalization aspect of interest. If p is the price of an asset yielding a perpetual income y when the interest rate is r, we know that $p = (y/r)$. Let us now distinguish the positions of two classes of participants in the capital-asset market. These are the frequently passive *anciens riches,* with wealth already embalmed in earning assets, and the economically active *nouveaux riches,* seeking to found family dynasties by purchasing earning assets to perpetuate their current high incomes. Both groups have balance sheets as well as income statements, and are concerned with capital gains as well as income flows.

---

ing from active business). Gustav Cassel, including the first element while stressing the second, anticipates a near-infinite positive elasticity at a rate not far from 3 per cent (*Nature and Necessity of Interest* [London: Macmillan, 1903], pp. 146–152). For criticism, see Knut Wicksell, *Lectures on Political Economy* (London: Routledge, 1935), vol. i, pp. 209–211. Martin J. Bailey, "Saving and the Rate of Interest," *J.P.E.* (August 1957) reinterprets the supply function as assuming constant *real,* rather than *money,* income, and therefore derives a positively sloping function involving substitution effects only.

13. A sample of this literature is "The Toll of Rising Interest Rates—The One Great Waste in the Federal Budget" (Washington: Conference on Economic Progress, April 1964).

The interest of the *anciens riches* is in high prices for any earning assets they are induced or required to sell; they stand to make capital gains from low interest rates which raise asset prices. The interest of the *nouveaux riches,* on the other hand, is on the cheapness with which they can buy assets securing any given income stream, or alternatively, in the size of the income stream they can purchase for a given capital outlay. It is the *nouveaux riches,* active rather than passive, possessed of income rather than wealth, who have an economic stake in high interest rates. The idle rentiers, like the poor debtors, prefer to see rates low, except when they are acting as lenders. Since society as a whole is a net holder of earning assets, a rise in the rate of interest, *ceteris paribus,* makes society as a whole worse off.[14]

Individuals on Capital Markets

4. In explaining why the rate of interest is what it is, we turn first to the individual or firm. He (it) may be either buyer or seller in this market, and may even change sides if interest rates change. Our analysis is based on the two-period schema of Irving Fisher,[15] in which "a dollar of future income" means "a dollar next year" rather than, as in many other schemes, "a dollar a year in perpetuity." We suppose our individual or film dividing resources between present consumption and future income, neither of them inferior goods, in accordance with an indifference-curve family J_i (Figure 12.2). These indifference curves ordinarily reflect a "time preference" or "agio" for present over future income. They also may, but need not, reflect some systematic "underestimate of the future," such as was postulated by Böhm-Bawerk.[16] When such an imperfection of rationality actually holds, the J_i curves are steeper than they would be for a more rational individual, who forecasts the future more accurately. It requires more than the "reasonable" amount of future income to compensate an underestimator of his future demands for the loss of a dollar

14. Boris P. Pesek and Thomas R. Saving, *Money, Wealth, and Economic Theory* (New York: Macmillan, 1967), p. 362. See also *ibid.,* pp. 317 n., 361, and R. C. O. Matthews, "Expenditure Plans and the Uncertainty Motive of Holding Money," *J.P.E.* (June 1963), p. 205. Pesek and Saving add that this interest-induced wealth effect causes consumption to move inversely with the interest rate, but see below, section 6.

15. Fisher's two expositions are *The Rate of Interest* (New York: Macmillan, 1907) and *The Theory of Interest* (New York: Macmillan, 1930). More pointed is Jack Hirschleifer's exposition of Fisherian doctrine, "On the Theory of Optimal Investment Decision," *J.P.E.* (August 1958).

16. Böhm-Bawerk, *Positive Theory of Capital,* trans. William Smart (London: Macmillan, 1891), book v, chapter 3. Böhm-Bawerk has in mind a systematic underestimate of future needs, or of the intensity of future demands; an equally systematic *overestimate* of future income serves his argument equally well.

of his present consumption. In terms of economic policy, one can make a case for forcing such a man to save more (or consume less) than he wishes here and now, and hence to substitute "growth" for "choice" at the policy margin. But to repeat, Figure 12.2 involves no such assumption, which has not, to the writer's knowledge, been either confirmed or disconfirmed.

Let us return to our representative economic man or firm. His initial position, including the consequences of past decisions, is at P_0 (coordinates C_0, Y_0) if he abstains from further capital transactions, that is, if he consumes his entire current income but abstains from further borrowing. Further capital transactions, if he embarks on them, may be of two sorts:

(1) He may borrow or lend, at a given interest rate r. If he does so, he is depicted as moving along a straight line through P_0, whose formula is

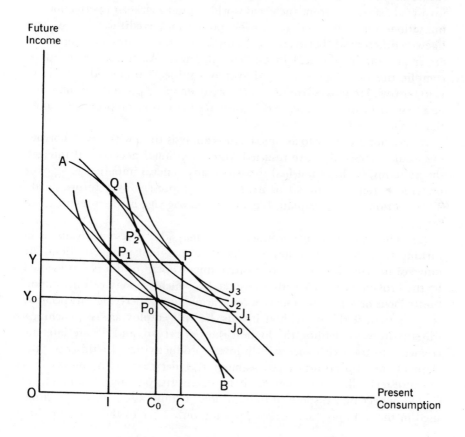

Figure 12.2

$$C + \frac{Y}{1+r} = K_o \qquad \text{or} \qquad Y = (1+r)(K_o - C)$$

where K_o is a constant. There are an infinite number of such loan-market lines, corresponding to different initial positions P_0. Each loan-market line corresponds to a price line in standard consumption theory. The price of a unit of present consumption is defined as unity, and the price of a unit of future income (next year's income, not a perpetual income stream) is $1/(1+r)$. A southeast movement from P_0 along this line represents borrowing for additional present consumption. A movement northwest from P_0 represents lending for additional future income. Rotation of a loan-market lines represents an interest change; a steeper negative slope results from a higher interest rate r (a lower price of a unit of future income), and vice versa. The straightness of the loan-market line involves abstraction from such real-world capital market imperfections as limitations on individual borrowing power and credit-worthiness, and likewise differentials between borrowing and lending rates, both of which are important in practical investment planning. Abstracting from these complications on Figure 12.2 as drawn, our subject's preferred alternative is to borrow. He moves from P_0 to P_1, securing more present consumption at a cost in future income, and improving his utility or preference position from J_0 to J_1.

We are not required to assume for this analysis that, with $r = 0$, borrowing would necessarily have resulted. In conventional neoclassical interest-theory terms, we have not had to assume any general impatience, agio, or preference (either rational or irrational) for present over future goods. These notions, however plausible, are excess baggage in the present treatment.

(2) The representative economic man may also invest or disinvest in earning assets or in machines with positive marginal productivities. The range of internal investment or disinvestment open to him is represented by the broken curve AB with a cusp at P_0, which we may call his opportunity locus or function. The economic argument underlying this peculiar curve is that, if the individual invests, he will employ assets (machines) initially in ways yielding the highest rates of return, and devote later increments to uses with successively lower productivities. In this case, the slope of the opportunity locus segment P_0A decreases as he moves in a northwesterly direction from P_0. If he disinvests, on the other hand, we should expect him dispose initially of low-yielding assets, or of machines used in the least productive ways, passing only later to the more produc-

tive elements of his stock. The slope of the segment P_0B will therefore increase as one moves in a southeasterly direction from P_0. As the figure is drawn, the individual's preferred alternative is to invest, moving from P_0 to P_2, and improving his utility or preference position from J_0 to J_2. In the diagram, J_2 is superior to J_1; but this is not a general outcome.

5.   In the normal case, an individual or firm has both loan-market and investment alternatives open simultaneously. In our figure, therefore, he moves from P_0 beyond P_2 to Q (by investing), until his internal rate of return equals the interest rate r. He simultaneously improves his position further, moving to P (coordinates C, Y) by borrowing, following the loan-market line tangent to the opportunity function AB at Q. His final position P, lying on indifference curve J_3, is preferred to either P_1 or P_2 by itself, let alone the original position P_0. This result holds generally, except for the vacuous cases in which there is no investment or loan-market activity in either direction.

To summarize the entire movement from P_0 to P: At the given interest rate r, the individual or firm has invested IC_0, borrowed IC, dissaved (increased consumption) by C_0C, and consumed C. His new future income is Y, which exceeds Y_0 by YY_0 as a result of his combined capital market activities, in which he has appeared overtly as an entrant on the demand side (*i.e.*, a borrower). The reader may, by varying the slopes and patterns of our various functions, work out numerous qualitatively different outcomes as exercises, confirming our statements about the generality, or lack of it, in our several results.

6.   Let us extend the argument of the last section to encompass the consequences of changed interest rates. This extension will indicate the slopes of individual demand and supply functions in capital markets, which can then be added (with appropriate adjustments for the biases considered in Chapter 6) to apply to capital markets as a whole. In Figure 12.3, therefore, let the unprimed solution at P (C, I, Y) correspond to that of Figure 12.2, which we have just considered. The most significant difference, comparing the two figures, is that in this case we are dealing with a lender, a saver, and a supplier on the capital market.

A once-for-all change now introduced is a substantial fall in the rate of interest, caused by a general change either in other people's time preferences, or in the productivity of their machines, or possibly in the prices of machines with unchanged productivity schedules.[18] This fall raises the

18. We suppose, for simplicity, and at some sacrifice of realism, that none of these changes affect our particular individual's indifference map or opportunity function to any significant degree.

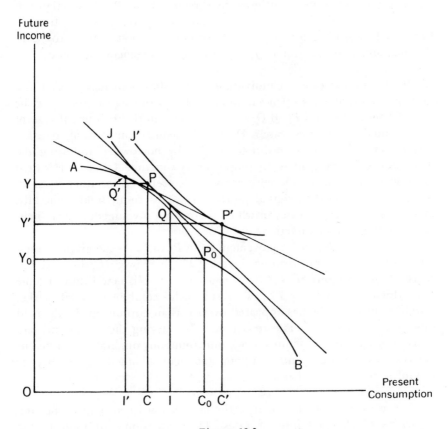

Figure 12.3

price of a unit of future income, which we remember to be $1/(1+r)$. It reduces the slope of the loan-market lines and changes from Q to Q' the tangency point of the family of these lines with the opportunity function AB. There is a new (primed) solution at P' (C', I', Y'). Comparing the two solutions, we find that the change has resulted in more internal investment, less lending (in this case, a shift from the supply to the demand side of the loan market), less saving, more consumption, less future income, and a rise in the satisfaction level. Internal investment has risen from IC_0 to $I'C_0$; lending of IC is replaced by borrowing of $I'C'$; saving of CC_0 is replaced by dissaving of C_0C'; consumption rises from C to C'; future income falls from Y to Y' and its increment from Y_0Y to Y_0Y'; J' lies above J. But which of these results can be considered at all general, and which are dependent upon peculiarities of the figure as drawn?

The first two results (more investment and less lending) are the general ones. The increase in investment will normally involve an increase in the ratio of machinery to labor inputs in producing a given sort of output, but will not necessarily involve any outright displacement of labor. It may also involve some shift in the type of output from a less to a more capital-intensive variety; for example, in our crude "aging" examples, from "greener" to riper wine, tobacco, or lumber. These changes are often called Ricardo Effects and sometimes distinguished as Ricardo Effects I and II, according to whether output is or is not assumed to remain qualitatively uniform. Their importance is in dispute in more advanced capital-theory discussions. Hayek, in particular, probably exaggerated their roles in causing cyclical business expansions when interest rates were held below their equilibrium levels, and cyclical contractions when "natural forces" forced them up again.[19] But here we impinge on the subject matter of the next chapter.

Our second result of lowered interest is less lending, which we may expand to include more borrowing. This result is of more immediate interest at this stage. It implies both an upward-sloping supply function for lenders on capital markets and a downward-sloping demand function for borrowers, if the volume of loans is plotted in the usual fashion against the rate of interest. We accordingly have a standard stable supply-and-demand type of result.

Returning to Figure 12.3, our observed shifts toward less future income and a higher indifference curve when interest rates decline are only semi-general. That is to say, they apply for the entire group of individuals on the P_0A (investing, northwest) segment of the opportunity locus AB. They would be reversed for individuals on the P_0B (disinvesting, southeast) segment of the same locus. The moves may be in either direction for individuals induced by the rate decline to shift from one segment to the other. These conclusions are consistent with common sense, if we concentrate on the opportunity locus aspect of the demonstration. Thus, the fall in r permits the investor a *greater* volume of profitable investment (ranging further from P_0 on P_0A), with a consequent increase in satisfaction. The same fall in r constrains the disinvestor to a *smaller* volume of profitable disinvestment (staying closer to P_0 and P_0B) with a consequent decrease in satisfaction. The difference is not counteracted by the lending aspects of the capital market.

The effects of lower interest on consumption and saving may go either way, depending upon the relative sizes of the offsetting shifts in invest-

19. See, in particular, Hayek, *Prices and Production,* 2d ed. (London: Routledge, 1934), lectures 2–4, and his interchange with Alvin H. Hansen and Herbert Tout, *Econometrica* (April 1933 and April 1934).

ment and lending activities (the first rising and the second falling). It is not necessarily true, as conventionally assumed, that a fall in r will increase consumption or decrease saving, or that a rise in r will have the opposite effects.[20] The solution on the diagram is, however, the conventional one, with the substitution effect of cheaper future income outweighing its income effect.

A Zero Interest Rate?

7. A hoary dispute in capital theory has been whether the zero interest rate advocated, among the faithful, by the Bible and Koran, could be an equilibrium one in a capitalist world. It is indisputable that such a rate, or indeed a negative one, might be enforced at least briefly by formal or informal capital rationing, either in isolation or as part of a more general disequilibrium system.

At the utility-theory level, a negative rate of interest would imply a "time preference" at the margin for future income over present consumption. This is a conceivable situation for a prosperous individual or country on the verge of decline, such as a spendthrift on the eve of retirement or an oil-rich sheikhdom whose wells are running dry (however fantastic it seemed to Böhm-Bawerk in the complacent days of Franz Josef and Queen Victoria).[21] On diagrams like Figures 12.2 and 12.3, the only formal requirement is that the family of loan-market lines be shallow, intersecting the horizontal (consumption) axes at angles of 45 degrees or less, so that that reduction of present consumption by one unit would increase future income by one unit or less. In terms of price, a unit of income next year would be worth one or more units of present consumption this year.

8. A zero or negative interest rate has, however, been said to involve a logical contradiction. This arises, if at all, in connection with the valuation of capital assets (machines). If p is the price of a machine yielding an income stream y when the rate of interest is r, an equilibrium condition is, by (12.1),

$$p = \frac{y}{r}$$

---

20. A strong defense of the conventional view is Martin J. Bailey, *National Income and the Price Level* (New York: McGraw-Hill, 1962), pp. 178–185. Its argument is based on the "Friedman" interpretation of Marshallian demand and supply functions as embodying substitution effects exclusively. M. Friedman, "The Marshallian Demand Curve," *J.P.E.* (October 1949).

21. Böhm-Bawerk, *op. cit.*, pp. 251 f. Böhm-Bawerk's comparisons, however, were between present and future *incomes*, the former of which could in turn be used to provide the latter. This casuistic device introduces an element of tautology into his argument.

or, if the income is equal to the *v.m.p.* of the machine:

$$p = \frac{v.m.p.}{r} \ .$$

If r is zero, must not p be either infinite $(v.m.p. > 0)$ or indeterminate $(v.m.p. = 0)$ regardless of its cost of production? And if r is negative, must not p or $v.m.p.$, but not both, be negative too?

The solution to these conundrums, in the case of a machine, starts with the recollection that *v.m.p.* is taken net of allowances for depreciation Assume p positive from cost considerations, machines being scarce goods with demand exceeding supply at zero price and justifying positive production costs. Then their gross *v.m.p.* may still be positive, but equal to the depreciation allowances for $r = 0$, and falling short of these allowances for a negative r. The problem is not of great moment.

If we are dealing with a nondepreciating asset, like land or money, however, the dilemma returns in full force and the logical contradiction applies again. It is against holders of such assets, lying outside the strict purview of this chapter, that critics like Silvio Gesell have concentrated their appeals for an end to "interest-slavery" or *Zinsknechtschaft*. Here, the dilemma is avoided (in the critics' schemata, at least) by artificial imposition of depreciation equivalents on land and money, to permit the "machine" solution to apply. For land, the *Freiland-Freigeld* reformer's standard device is a heavy tax on the rental value (corresponding to our v.m.p.) after the pattern of the physiocrats' *impôt unique* and Henry George's single tax. For money, the standard device is ordinarily a tax on currency and bank deposits, sometimes taking the form of "stamped money."

Diminishing Returns from Investment?

9. A more general and pervasive problem is whether capital accumulation relative to the growth of other inputs such as land and labor (*pace* the population explosion!) leads in the long run to any significant decline in the marginal productivity of machines. Classical and Marxian political economy can both be interpreted to imply that it does, by analogy with diminishing returns to labor. In production-function terms, with $x = F(a, b, c, \ldots)$ as per (6.1), we assume all the second partial derivatives negative as a stability condition. In the case of input b, which we take to represent machines, a negative $\delta^2 x / \delta b^2$ is, by definition, a falling marginal productivity of b, and represents diminishing returns to investment.

Diminishing returns to investment, or "the tendency of profits to a minimum," would continue, said Ricardo and Mill, until a somnolent stationary state was achieved, in which savings (from incomes higher than nineteenth-century ones) at lower, but probably still positive, interest rates would just suffice to maintain capital intact. Marx and his followers extend the doctrine further to forecast stagnation and collapse rather than any stationary-state Nirvana as the outcome of "Marx's Law" of the falling rate of profit. (Separate consideration of Marx's Law would carry us too far afield from the topic of this chapter. Such monetary considerations as hoarding are required for its operation to bring on stagnation or collapse.)

10.   The historical record in advanced countries, however, shows no clear tendency for interest rates to fall. The applicability of the diminishing returns analysis to capital-in-general has likewise been denied, primarily by Schumpeter and Knight.[22] Schumpeter's argument is an important element of his broader theory of economic development. It relies on innovations, introduced more or less autonomously by the truly creative and entrepreneurial minority of business men, to counteract the diminishing returns prevalent in the static economy. Knight places less stress on spontaneous genius, but sees innovation as largely induced by the investment process itself. Capital accumulation, to Knight, includes an important element of investment in knowledge, including research and development, from which innovation arises in a reasonably predictable manner. (Compare Chapter 6, Sections 28 f.) Capital accumulation also includes investment in the quantitative expansion and qualitative improvement of human capital and natural resources, through, for example, education and exploration. The result is that capital accumulation has thus far brought in its own train the technological progress and increases in complementary inputs required to ward off diminishing returns to investment in the long run, let alone the nonpositive rates of return considered in section 8f. Neither Schumpeter nor Knight can guarantee continuance of any such trend into the future—Schumpeter being particularly pessimistic on the point under conditions of mixed-economy and welfare-capitalism. In the short run, also, dynamic or historical considerations have less pertinence, and the idea of diminishing returns to investment has its principal importance there.

Two Subsequent Extensions

11.   In the tradition of classical interest theory are two later extensions. To both of these, Solow's Rotterdam lectures[23] offer convenient introduc-

22. Joseph A. Schumpeter, *The Theory of Economic Development,* trans. Redvers Opie (Cambridge, Mass.: Harvard University Press, 1934), pp. 157–211; Frank H. Knight, "Diminishing Returns from Investment," *J.P.E.* (February 1944).

23. Solow, *Capital Theory and the Rate of Return* (Amsterdam: North-Holland, 1963).

tion. One extension is to weaken the related assumptions of smooth, algebraic production functions and determinate marginal productivities of capital, in favor of greater generality. The other, more important, extension is to compare explicitly the private and social rates of return to capital, particularly in the presence of embodied technological change.

We need not follow Solow's generalization of classical interest theory to encompass the input-output and linear programming cases so realistic for short-run "practical" problems. He shows, first, how the rate of return to a finite increment of capital (machines) remains determinate in these linear and discontinuous cases when the marginal productivity of an infinitesimal increment becomes indeterminate. He puts the entire argument in terms of consumption-goods output sacrificed in his period 1. (The one-period rate of return is computed from the maximum increase in consumption-goods output obtainable in period 2, without affecting the stream of consumption-goods output in periods 3, 4, . . . , n.) This preserves the essence of classical productivity analysis. It still pays, in Solow's discontinuous angular world, to expand capital so long as its rate of return exceeds the rate of interest, and to contract it in the opposite case, although discontinuity may prevent achievement of strict equality between the two rates as an equilibrium condition.

Embodied technical progress presents a hard welfare-theoretical nut to crack. If progress is embodied only in new machines, owners of old machines can neither share in its advantages nor compete on equal terms with owners of new ones. The value of the old equipment is written off to a level at which its owners can earn the going rate of return. (This write-off, or allowance for obsolescence, we suppose known, as per the argument of Section 2 (5) above.) Like physical depreciation, the allowance for obsolescence is deducted from the *gross* product of machinery to arrive at its net *private* productivity. However, the net *social* productivity of the machinery, in physical terms, is apparently not affected by this accounting manipulation. If investment is adjusted to equate the private productivity of capital with the going interest rate, the social productivity of capital remains higher than the interest rate. This implies a bias in the private economic system, in the presence of embodied technical progress, toward too little investment as compared with an "efficiency" or "welfare" optimum. Or, alternatively, efficiency and welfare might be increased if private managers were replaced by technocratic planners whose investment schemes were based either on "shadow" or "accounting" interest rates systematically lower than market ones, or on marginal efficiencies without deductions for obsolescene.

Solow's answer to this argument for centralized planning is that the social productivity of capital is only superficially unaffected by embodied technical progress. In fact, any discrepancy between the marginal productivity of capital (ignoring obsolescence) and its private return (allowing for obsolescence) "is fully reflected in a parallel difference between the marginal productivity of capital and the social rate of return on saving. So once again the private and social rates of return coincide."[24]

This "social equivalent to obsolescence" is not, as in the private economy, a capital loss, but represents "the fact that it is more costly [in consumption-goods terms] to increase next year's capital stock through this year's saving than it will be to increase the following year's [more productive] capital stock through next year's saving . . . The [social] return to current saving is reduced by the fact that current saving adds less to future consumption potential than next year's saving would,"[25] and is equivalent in this respect to a smaller volume of next year's saving.

The qualitative point can be grasped (once it has been pointed out), but its quantitative equivalence to obsolescence is more complex. Solow, in fact, shows it for the special case of embodiment in capital alone, where (in the notation of Chapter 6 above)

$$x = F[a, \beta(t)\, b] \qquad \text{rather than} \qquad x = F[\alpha(t)\, a, \beta(t)\, b]$$

which is more general. Any more general proof than Solow's gets beyond our mathematical depth; the qualitative point suffices for our present interest.

Summary

12. The reader with an eye to classifications and pigeonholes may well ask, at this point, what sort of interest theory has been presented here? Basically, it has been an attempt to apply the general theory of input pricing, owing more to American writers (Clark, Fisher, and Knight) than to European ones. The key concept on the demand side has been the separate marginal productivity (*v.m.p.*) of capital instruments or machines, viewed on a par with other inputs. This treatment has permitted us to avoid such questionable notions as the roundaboutness of production and the period of production, as well as the classification of inputs into "original" and "derived" categories. On the supply side, a key concept has been time preference, rational and otherwise, as between present consumption and future income. We have tried to avoid such normative ideas as "abstinence," "waiting," and "underestimate of the future," and we have avoided assuming an "agio" operating universally in favor of the present as against the future.

24. *Ibid.*, p. 59.
25. *Ibid.*, p. 63.

As for "exploitation" theories of interest, we must plead guilty to sweeping them under the rug, so to speak, by not raising the question of the basis or validity of capitalists' titles to the existing stock of machines or to the income attributable to them. We have also assumed, without adequate evidence, the measurability of capital (along with other inputs and outputs) within the limits required for meaningful index-number, aggregation, and production function analysis.

13.   What remains to be attempted in Chapter 13 is, primarily, to bring money into the picture. Thus far we have been considering all transactions, loans included, as made in some nebulous, unholdable, and unstorable money of account or *numéraire*.[26] Such a treatment is never complete, or entirely satisfactory, insofar as one alternative to buying or selling any individual output or input is to permit one's money balances to rise or fall, and this alternative is rarely explored explicitly.[27] The omission, however, is most serious when we speak of aggregate consumption, saving, and investment, as we have done here, without considering this alternative, because it is an especially important alternative in these cases. Our "classical" diagrams, in other words, have supposed that nonconsumption means acquisition of future income through purchases of machines or, at most, of claims to their services. This moves us dangerously far in the direction of Say's Identity, by which aggregate supply creates its own demand at any price level. The next chapter will attempt to close, in some degree, the resulting loophole of monetary accumulation and decumulation, and to avoid the implications of Say's Identity.

26. This does not imply that Leon Walras, to whom, more than any other economist, we owe the notion of *numéraire,* used the term to mean an abstract money of account. (The evidence is overwhelmingly to the contrary.)

27. See, however, Boulding, "A Liquidity Preference Theory of Market Prices," *Economica* (May 1944) .

CHAPTER THIRTEEN

Monetary Interest Theory

Introduction

1. We have thus far treated differences between inputs and outputs, or between capital and consumption goods, as matters of black and white. We know gray areas exist, but are seldom important.[1] But we can no longer do this in capital theory. In dealing with problems of capital and interest, it is dangerous to neglect the omnipresence of a special sort of investment good. On the one hand, this good is competitive with other investment goods (and titles to them) on capital markets. One may speak of its productivity, like that of any other intermediate good. On the other hand, the good in question is also valued like consumption goods, for its direct services related only tortuously, if at all, to considerations of productivity or efficiency.

2. This universal-equivalent investment good is, of course, money, held in the form of cash balances (including bank deposits). Interest is paid explicitly for its direct services when it is lent. For its sake, also, machines or inventories are forgone so that cash positions can be maintained or

This chapter was written before I had seen F. A. Lutz, *The Theory of Interest* (Chicago: Aldine, 1968). It overlaps with Lutz' part iii in many respects.

1. One such gray area, more significant than most, arises in consumption theory and concerns the distinction between "permanent" and "measured" consumption. Analysis based on "permanent" income treats consumer durables as capital instruments, with their services (consumption goods) spread over their useful lives. Compare Milton Friedman, *Theory of the Consumption Function* (Princeton: Princeton University Press, 1957), ch. 3.

improved. In these cases, one may think of money as earning *implicit* interest. By "money" we shall mean real money, deflated for price changes, rather than nominal money.

The direct service of money is called *liquidity*. Its formal analogy is with physicians' or attorneys' direct services in wage theory, in that productivity considerations are vague, forced, and strained. Its importance is greater, possibly by an order of magnitude. The demands for both money as such and for its service of liquidity have been combined, since Keynes' *General Theory,* in the rubric of liquidity preference.

Any commodity x is economically liquid, if, with a high probability (approaching unity), its holders can rationally expect to reduce or close out their holdings of x whenever they so desire after an infinitesimal time interval, without risk of loss of real income or wealth. Money includes any x with these properties, whose real value would decline substantially if the liquidity attribute should disappear or be attenuated.[2] We need not draw precise lines for purposes of this study, or make concrete distinctions between moneys, near-moneys, money substitutes, and mere liquid assets, in the absence of "breaks in the chain of substitutes."

3. Because cash balances are significantly competitive in demand with earning assets like machines, postclassical capital theory has focused upon the complications that money introduces. Another reason for this concentration, associated more specifically with Keynes, has been the weakening of the comfortable classical background assumption of constant aggregate real income. If real income, along with the interest rate, is not only variable but is also affected by aggregate saving and investment (and in turn acts on them), and if monetary supply and demand considerations also influence and are influenced by income, the possible direct and indirect relationships between money, interest, and income merit more attention in capital theory than they received in our Chapter 12.

Loanable Funds

4. Historically speaking, the initial stepping-stone between classical and monetary interest theories has been a more complete analysis of the market for loanable funds. It was developed independently by Knut Wicksell in Sweden, Sir Dennis Robertson in Britain, and H. J. Davenport in the United States. Top honors go to Wicksell for both priority and profundity.

Loanable-funds analysis is embryonically macroeconomic. It explores the directly competitive aspects of the demands for liquidity on one hand

---

2. Compare Bronfenbrenner, "Some Fundamentals of Liquidity Theory," *Q.J.E.* (May 1945).

and for earning assets on the other, but it originally abstracted from changes in the level of aggregate income.

Of the numerous diagrammatic simplifications and condensations that have been developed,[3] consider Figure 13.1 as an expository model of the capital market along pre-Keynesian loanable-funds lines. Both (real) investment and (real) saving are shown as planned *ex ante* on the horizontal axis of this diagram. (They are identical *ex post*.) The nominal rate of interest is portrayed on the vertical axis; it includes "appreciation,"

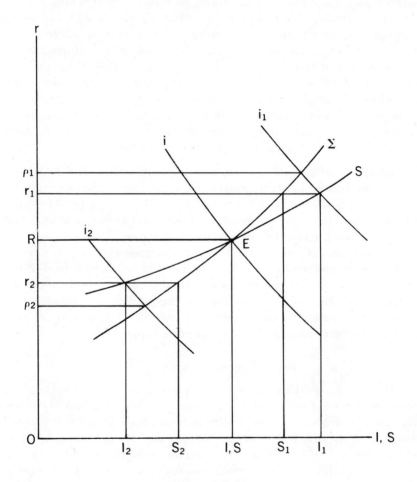

Figure 13.1

3. Compare in particular A. P. Lerner, "Alternative Formulations of the Theory of Interest," in Seymour E. Harris (ed.), *The New Economics* (New York: Knopf, 1948), pp. 637, 639.

that is, the effects of price-level changes. Investment demand functions i_i (which include demands for consumption loans) are drawn with negative slopes according to the argument of Chapter 12. We may base these functions on considerations of both marginal productivity and time preference, the "productivity and thrift" of textbook interest theory.

The textbook savings-supply function of Chapter 12, a "thrift" construct ignoring money, is represented by Σ, but is here only a pseudo-supply function. The true capital-market supply function S may pass to the right of Σ, as with the demand function i_1, or to the left of Σ, as with the demand function i_2. It lies to the right of Σ at high interest rates and to the left at low ones. It may slope upward even when Σ does not. This is because, at high interest rates, the banking system (introduced explicitly by Wicksell) expands its loans by reducing its aggregate reserve ratio. Individuals and firms also "dishoard" by drawing down money balances to make loans and supply capital without contemporaneous saving, waiting, or "abstinence." At lower rates, on the other hand, banks may cancel money and improve their liquidity positions by not renewing loans to the full extent of repayments. Individuals and firms also divert part of their current saving into cash balances. The supply function of loanable funds, then, is more elastic than that of saving. It can also change in either direction without any corresponding change in saving, waiting, abstinence, or thrift.

5.   Wicksell's analysis distinguishes sharply between what he calls natural and market rates of interest. Natural rates ρ_i are set by the equality of investment demand and *voluntary* saving, with the volume of active (unhoarded) money constant. On our diagram, natural rates are determined by the intersections of i_i and Σ. The market rates r_i are set by the equality of actual supply and demand for loanable funds. On our diagram, market rates are determined by the intersections of i_i and S. If we denote by E the intersection of Σ and S at the interest rate R, we observe that the natural rate exceeds the market rate whenever i_i passes northeast of E as in the case of i_1, while the market rate exceeds the natural rate whenever i_i passes southwest of E as in the case of i_2. Only when the investment demand function passes through E, as in the case of i, is there full equilibrium at rate R, with $I = S$ *ex ante*.

At E, as another aspect of full equilibrium, a condition called monetary neutrality prevails. There are no net changes in the money supply, which might otherwise affect interest rates or the division of the social income between present and future. In other words, expansion (or contraction) by banks is offset by net hoarding (or dishoarding) by nonbankers at interest rate R. It does not, however, follow that maintaining full equilibrium and monetary neutrality guarantees stability of the price level, as Wicksell believed.[4]

6.   The investment demand function i_1 represents a boom situation in the sense of accelerated growth. Investment I_1 exceeds its full-equilibrium value I. There is "forced saving" of S_1I_1 as a result of money expansion, dishoarding, or both. Although the market interest rate r_1 is high by comparison with the full-equilibrium or permanent rate R, it remains below the natural rate ρ_1, which would have eliminated the forced saving. The primary result of $\rho_1 > r$ is price inflation, which absorbs the disgorged cash balances and new money created at (I_1, r_1).

This situation cannot, in the view of Wicksell and the Wicksellians, persist. It is brought to an end by some combination of (a) a lack of the reserves required for continued monetary expansion by the banking system, (b) shortages of specialized resources for continued investment activity above the I level, (c) a lack of profitable outlets for the additional output produced with the aid of the community's increasing capital stock, (d) diminishing marginal productivity of new machines with given stocks of cooperant inputs, and (e) adjustments by savers to the fact of continued price inflation.

Of these five changes, (a) moves the S function to the left (in Fig. 13.1), (b), (c), and (d) depress i_1 (move it downward), while (e) moves Σ upward. Assuming full equilibrium to be restored eventually, its new position need not be identical with any prior full-equilibrium position such as E. (We may assume a "Wicksell process" to have been set off by a previous rise in the investment demand function from i to i_1.)

The investment demand function i_2 represents a recession in the limited sense of growth deceleration. Investment falls below its long-term value. There is money cancellation, net hoarding, or both; forced saving is a negative quantity I_2S_2. (One might speak of "forced dissaving" or "abortive saving." Sir Dennis Robertson devised various other terms in *Banking Policy and the Price Level.*[5]) Although the market interest rate r_2 has fallen below R, it is above the natural rate ρ_2, which would have eliminated the (negative) forced saving. There is a decline or deflation of the general price level. Wicksell, it should be remembered, wrote before "downward rigidities" and "bottom stops" became so commonplace as to concentrate deflationary effects on output and employment rather than on prices.

According to pre-1929 versions of loanable-funds theorizing, this situa-

---

4. In a technically progressive world, the price-level trend would probably be downward under neutral money; in a resource-wasting world, or a world with a rising volume of financial intermediation, the price-level trend would probably be upward.

5. D. H. Robertson, *op. cit.,* 3d ed. (London: P. S. King, 1932).

tion, too, could not persist. It could be brought to an end (without significant changes in the real income level) by some combination of (a) the practical limit on the accumulation of idle balances by both banks and nonbankers, or the diminishing marginal utility of additions to liquidity, (b) declines in the prices of inputs specialized for machine production, (c) the eventual need to replace and up-date depreciating and obsolescent equipment to avoid dead loss, (d) a rise in the marginal productivity of machines, as the existing stock grows at a subnormal rate, and (e) adjustments by savers to the fact of continued price deflation. The effects of these five changes are the converses of those considered (for a movement from i to i_1) in the second paragraph of this section.

7.   Several objections may be raised to all this as interest theory. (We do not discuss its implications for the theory of industrial fluctuations.) The effects of such income changes as occur in real-world booms and depressions on the savings and the loan-fund supply functions Σ and S are not shown at all. (They tend likewise to be overlooked in literary presentations of the theory.) The necessary *ex post* equality of saving and investment is not shown explicitly; in fact, the possibility of forced saving at equilibrium appears inconsistent with it. Finally, the analysis runs exclusively in terms of *flows* (in this instance, flows of saving and investment per period). We cannot even be sure that the money *stock* in existence, neither more or less, is being held at the interest rates other than R.

Liquidity Preference

8.   It is precisely on stock analysis and changes in real output that Keynes concentrated his own positive argument in the *General Theory*.[6] To Keynes and the Keynesians, the dominant function of the interest rate is to equate the *ex ante* supply and demand for the money stock. (It goes without saying that, *ex post,* all money in existence—and no more—is held by someone, if we neglect the commercial bank "float," bills burnt in fires, and coins fallen into the water!) The marginal efficiency of investment adjusts to this essentially monetary rate of interest, and not vice versa. The mechanism of adjustment is a change in the volume of investment. This in turn changes real income, and the change in income changes saving, all in the same direction. (Price-level changes are largely ignored, in contrast to Wicksellian analysis.) If the rate of interest is above the marginal efficiency of investment at full employment, the marginal efficiency rises, while investment, income, and savings all fall, dragging down the level of employment.

Keynes' system includes no adjustment mechanism in the opposite direc-

6. See also Keynes "The Theory of the Rate of Interest." *Readings,* no. 22.

tion, of r to m.e.i. It confines the efficacy of the loanable-funds mechanism to the (preliminary) determination of a (tentative) m.e.i. The power of loanable-funds theory is further limited in the Keynesian scheme by the postulated equality of saving and investment, which Keynes sometimes seems to lapse into treating as an identity *ex ante* as well as *ex post*. (If it were such an *ex ante* identity, the S and i functions of Figure 13.1 would have coincided throughout their lengths.)

We call this theory "liquidity preference," not only because Keynes himself did so, but because of its concentration on the demand and supply for stocks of liquid assets. By "liquid assets" we mean primarily money, and often overlook, on first approximation, the complications introduced by the existence of liquid assets such as short-term government securities, which may be complementary with money on the demand side and competitive with earning assets generally, including, of course, machinery.

9. Figure 13.2 is a diagrammatic summary of liquidity preference theory, including a supply function for the money stock. It makes liquidity preference (the demand for money) explicitly dependent on income as well as on the interest rate.[7] The liquidity, or liquidity preference, functions L_i slope downward. The slope indicates greater willingness to dispense with liquidity at higher than at lower alternative costs, in terms of interest earnings forgone. Also, since money is a normal rather than an inferior good, the liquidity function for a higher income is drawn to the right of that for a lower one. (The index i refers to the income level.)

In some of his verbal argument, Keynes modified the downward slope of his liquidity function or functions by introducing a horizontal floor, or bottom stop, at some low but still positive interest rate, possibly in the neighborhood of 2 per cent. This construction is called *absolute* liquidity preference or a liquidity *trap*.[8] The theory is that, at this positive rate, infinite amounts of cash are desired. The interest rate is therefore prevented from falling below this level, even though a still lower rate, conceivably

7. It is customary, and legitimate as a first assumption, to represent Keynes' view by some such function as:

$$M = L_1(Y) + L_2(r) \qquad \left(\frac{\delta L_1}{\delta Y} > 0, \frac{\delta L_2}{\delta r} < 0\right)$$

where M is the money stock, L_1 represents transaction demand for money, and L_2, representing what Keynes called the speculative demand, represents liquidity preference proper.

8. Axel Leijonhufvud, *On Keynesian Economics and the Economics of Keynes* (New York: Oxford University Press, 1968), considers this liquidity trap a part of Keynesian economics not derivable from the economics of Keynes himself. Keynes' own "trap," in Leijonhufvud's view, was little more than refusal of the banking community to let bond prices rise (and interest rates fall) sufficiently.

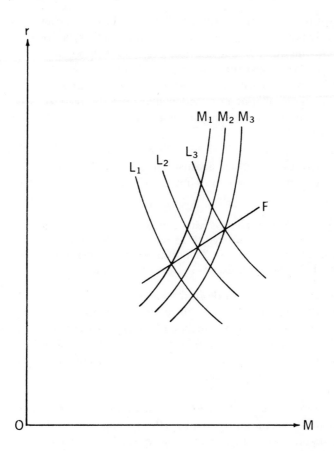

Figure 13.2

even zero or negative, was required during the Great Depression to attract a volume of private investment equal to the full-employment level of saving, and therefore to maintain full employment.

In this writer's view, the empirical evidence to date does not support this particular Keynesian postulate, but the question is far from closed.[9] We can agree that the *slopes* of liquidity functions seem to increase as the interest rate falls, but the increase of their *elasticities* toward the infinite

9. M. Bronfenbrenner and Thomas Mayer, "Liquidity Functions in the American Economy," *Econometrica* (October 1960), pp. 818, 831–834; Robert Eisner, "Another Look at Liquidity Preference," *Econometrica* (July 1963) (with reply by Bronfenbrenner and Mayer and rejoinder by Eisner); Karl Brunner and Allan H. Meltzer, "Liquidity Traps and Money, Bank Credit, and Interest Rates," *J.P.E.* (January 1968).

level required for a true liquidity trap is another matter. (Keynes may conceivably have confused the slope and the elasticity of his liquidity functions.) On the other hand, it is not easy to interpret such phenomena as the persistence of zero interest rates on bank deposits (negative rates, if account is taken of bank service charges!), such as are usual in the United States. Are these phenomena evidence against the trap, or are we observing nothing more than payment for caretaking and bookkeeping services unrelated to liquidity?

Insofar as liquidity is desired only as a safeguard against future rises in interest rates, or rather, against capital losses contingent on them, to holders of earning assets purchased at low rates, Robertson's quip is valid:[10]

> Thus the rate of interest is what it is because it is expected to become other than it is; if it is not expected to become other than it is, there is nothing left to tell us why it is what it is. The organ which secretes it has been amputated, and yet it somehow still exists—a grin without a cat.

But insofar as liquidity is desired as a speculation that some or all asset prices may fall for reasons quite unrelated to the rate of interest, or simply to meet unforeseen large-magnitude obligations such as result from illness or accident—Keynes' "precautionary motive," in a midway limbo between transactions and speculative motives—Robertson misses the point, or perhaps Keynes did not quite make it.

10.   The money supply functions M_i of Figure 13.2 embody only money creation and cancellation by banks. (Public hoarding and dishoarding are covered in liquidity functions.) The upward slopes of the M_i functions are based on profitability arguments. That is to say, net expansion of bank loans is supposed more advantageous at higher than at lower interest rates. An increase in the national income is also expected to increase the safety of expansion at any given interest rate, and also to provide, in the bankers' eyes, a certain ethical justification for expansion. (At higher levels, the "needs of trade" for "productive credit" are higher, and expansion is less "speculative.") For this reason, an M_i function corresponding to a higher level of income will not lie to the left of the function for a lower level.

The locus of intersections between pairs of L_i and M_i functions is indicated by F and is drawn upward-sloping. This is a conventional view, although a strict quantity theorist, to whom the real money supply M/P is a near-constant, would prefer F to be near-vertical. One plausible explanation for the upward slope of the F locus is that, at least after a certain point, shifts in M_i become small, relative to those in L_i, as income

10. D. H. Robertson, "Mr. Keynes and the Rate of Interest," *Readings*, no. 23, p. 448.

rises. This is because of the increasing pressure of statutory and other reserve requirements for nominal fiduciary money. (The monetary base itself is assumed almost insensitive to changes in either Y_i or r.)

11.   A major problem is the one-way causation (which Keynes appears to
assume rather than demonstrate) between the interest rate and the
marginal efficiency of investment. When there is no reverse channel of influence for m.e.i. upon r (as, for example, through the L_i functions themselves), his treatment has the advantages of straightforwardness and simplicity, but this presumption seems rather a special than the general case.
Also, the *ex post* equality of L_i and M_i is purely tautologous. If Keynes
rejects the loanable-funds theory because $I = S$ is an identity rather than
an equilibrium condition, is not liquidity preference equally vulnerable
when the same is true of $L = M$?

Reconciliations

12.   How are these main strands of monetary interest theory related to
each other? Is one right and the other wrong? Are they, perhaps, both
wrong, and on the brink of supersession by some *tertium quid?* Are they,
by any chance, alternative ways of saying the same thing? Under what conditions, if any, do they yield the same concrete results?

Reams of paper and bottles of ink were expended, much of it waste-
fully, upon these questions during the first decade of the *General Theory.*[11] The discussion eventually made it clear that the two theories were
not identical, primarily because of their dimensional incompatibility
(loanable-funds theory concentrates on flows, liquidity-preference on
stocks); that it was easier to propound a case for either view than to dis-
countenance the rival one; and that full equilibrium required the two
theories to yield the same result, so that perhaps income changes and
Walras' Law[12] might play important parts in bringing them together.

11. This discussion is sampled in *Readings,* nos. 22–25.

12. Let D_g and S_g be the demand and supply for goods and services (including both
inputs and outputs, and likewise both consumption and capital goods). Let D_s and S_s
be the demand and supply for new securities. Let D_m and S_m be demand and supply for
the *increment* to the money supply. (We must be careful to avoid stock-flow discrepan-
cies.) Then Walras' Law (or Identity), whose attribution to Walras is questionable,
states, in the flow form we propose to use here,

$$D_g + D_s + D_m = S_g + S_s + S_m.$$

Walras' Law is clearly an expansion of Say's Identity, which involves D_g and D_s alone.
See Oscar Lange, "Say's Law: A Restatement and a Criticism," in Lange, McIntyre, and
Yntema (eds.), *Studies in Mathematical Economics and Econometrics* (Chicago: University of Chicago Press, 1942); and for a contrary view, Robert Clower, "The Keynesian Counterrevolution," in Frank H. Hahn and F.P.R. Brechling (eds.), *The Theory
of Interest Rates* (London: Macmillan, 1965), ch. 5.

13. The "standard" reconciliation appeared early in the discussion. It is found in Hicks' essay, "Mr. Keynes and the 'Classics'; A Suggested Interpretation."[13] It reconciles liquidity preference with the classical (nonmonetary) interest theory of "productivity and thrift," but omits Wicksellian loanable-funds analysis. In this section we derive Hicks' familiar result by a slightly variant analytical process.

Our "reconciliation" diagram comprises the three panels of Figure 13.3. The left panel reproduces part of Figure 13.1, but omits the heart of loanable-funds theorizing, namely, the Wicksellian Σ function. It shows I_0 and S_0 determining an interest rate r_{01}, which Hicks calls an investment rate, at an initial income of Y_0 (not shown on this panel). A rise in income, as from Y_0 to Y, exercises its main effect on the savings function, causing S_0 to shift to the right, as to S. In this diagram we allow for no effect on the investment demand function I; this may be an exaggeration as well as a simplification.[14]

The central, or liquidity-preference, panel of Figure 13.3 is essentially a reproduction of Figure 13.2. At the same assumed income level Y_0, L_0, and M_0 determine an interest rate r_{02}, which Hicks calls a money rate. It

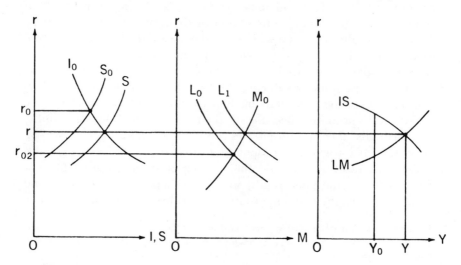

Figure 13.3

13. *Readings*, no. 25. Clower (*op. cit.*, p. 103) regards this essay as having launched "the Keynesian Counterrevolution."

14. Contemporary "acceleration" investment theory makes the location of the I function dependent upon (among other variables) the income change dY, often in a distributed-lag pattern involving dY_t, dY_{t-1}, . . . , dY_{t-n}, but not the income level Y itself. See Dale W. Jorgenson, "Capital Theory and Investment Behavior," *A.E.R.* (May 1963).

is shown as lower than the loanable-funds rate r_{01}. A rise in income, as from Y_0 to Y, exercises its main effect on the liquidity function (demand for money), causing L_0 to shift rightward to L. In the diagram, we include no effect on the money supply function M.

In the third (right) panel we introduce income explicitly into the picture. At our initial value Y_0, $r_{01} > r_{02}$; clearly, two different rates cannot prevail simultaneously. Abstracting from arbitrage, the factor bringing the rates together for full equilibrium at interest rate r is the rise in the national income from Y_0 to Y.[15] A function, labeled *IS*, traces out the course of r_{01} as income changes, and another function, labeled *LM*, does the same for r_{02}. Equality between the two is reached, as we have just seen, at the *IS–LM* intersection, whose coordinates are (Y,r). We have given both *IS* and *LM* their conventional or textbook slopes (downward and upward, respectively), which follow from our neglect of income effects on *I* and *M*. Stability requires only that *IS* lie above *LM* at income levels below Y, and vice versa.

14. It was also pointed out (subsequent to the Hicks essay) that the simple effects of measured income changes in shifting our measured S_0 and L_0 functions to S and L are accompanied by changes in wealth and permanent income. The increased wealth, or the increased level of permanent income, such as often results (at least subjectively) from any rise like Y_0Y in the measured income level, will increase the society's sense of well-being and therefore its measured marginal propensity to consume out of the increment Y_0Y. This increased marginal propensity to consume can also be expressed as a decreased marginal propensity to save. With the reduced propensity to save comes a reduced rightward shift in S_0, and presumably in L_0 as well, insofar as increased saving includes saving in its cash-balance form.

The consequences of these wealth considerations can be traced on diagrams like Figure 13.3. They appear to be concentrated on the size of the income change required to bring about interest-rate equilibrium from any initial (disequilibrium) position. The effect on the equilibrium interest rate itself is not clear. For example, if the wealth effect on *IS* is greater than that on *LM*, the equilibrium interest rate r will be higher than if there were no wealth effects, if one starts from a lower-than-equilibrium initial income position; but the rate will be lower if one starts from a

15. While not germane to distribution theory, the mechanism of change is worth explanation. When the *money* rate of interest is below the *investment* rate, there results a rise in investment and (through the multiplier process) in income. The rise in income shifts the saving function (left panel) to the right, and therefore lowers the investment rate of interest. At the same time, it shifts the liquidity function (center panel) to the right, and therefore raises the money rate of interest. This process eventually brings the two rates together, either immediately or after (damped) oscillations.

higher-than-equilibrium position. The effects in each case will be reversed if the wealth effect is concentrated on *LM*.[16]

15.   The point of Figure 13.3 is the demonstration that, while not identical at all income levels, the classical and liquidity-preference variants of interest theory yield the same result at equilibrium. While this demonstration started from a position of $r_{01} > r_{02}$ at an income level that was eventually shown to be below the equilibrium one, we might equally well have started from a position of $r_{01} < r_{02}$, in which our initial income level would have been above the equilibrium one. Equality of liquidity-preference and loanable-funds interest rates (according to Fig. 13.3) may be looked upon as an equilibrium condition for both the interest rate r and the income level Y.

Readers recalling the Keynesian cross (Figures 11.2, 13.4) and its argument may also inquire as to the relation, if any, between its equilibrium income level Y and the equilibrium level Y derived in Figure 13.3. Life is much easier for the economist when they are the same; Walras' Law has in fact been used to provide another reconciliation.[17] The equilibrium level of Figure 13.4 equates D_g with S_g in Walras' Law. At all points on *IS*, $D_g = S_g$; and at all points on *LM*, $D_m = S_m$. At their intersection, $D_g = S_g$ and $D_m = S_m$ simultaneously. (By Walras' Law, $D_s = S_s$ as well.) If the equilibrium on the Keynesian cross is not coincident with this intersection on the income side, a disequilibrium interest rate has been assumed. In terms of Figure 13.4, the aggregate expenditure function $C + I$ is not uniquely determined. Instead of the single functions labelled $C + I$, there should realistically have been a family of such functions, higher ones corresponding to lower interest rates and lower ones for the higher interest rates; the particular function yielding a Y-value coincident with that on the *IS–LM* diagram (Fig. 13.3, right panel) would then be the function based on the equilibrium interest rate r, and the relevant one for analysis here. In this sense, the intersection of *IS* and *LM* may be thought of as dominating logically the Y value of the Keynesian cross.

16.   Following Patinkin,[18] we can expand this standard reconciliation to include loanable funds, that is, the Σ function of Figure 13.1, while per-

16. H. G. Johnson points out that this discussion is incomplete for the long run, inasmuch as it omits the effects of capital accumulation on marginal-efficiency (*I*) functions. The discussion also assumes that *IS* slopes downward and *LM* upward in the relevant ranges underlying our argument.

17. See footnote 12.

18. Don Patinkin, *Money, Interest, and Prices,* 2nd ed. (New York: Harper and Row, 1965) , ch. 11.

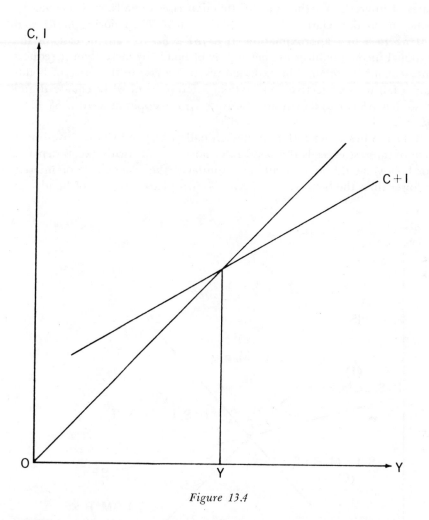

Figure 13.4

mitting both real income and the price level to vary. The key to this expanded reconciliation is explicit consideration of the market for securities, or "bonds" in Patinkin's terminology.

Let B represent the net volume of new bonds supplied when $I > S$; it is negative when $I < S$. Let F represent the net volume of funds supplied to buy bonds—the net volume of demand for new bonds—when $L < M$; it is negative when $L > M$. (This exposition ignores direct interactions between the market for money and the market for goods.)

Let BF (in Figure 13.5) be a locus of (Y,r) values such that $B = F$, and the bond market is in equilibrium. Let the r coordinates be called bond rates of interest. Whether the *BF* function rises or falls with income depends upon the relative sizes of $\delta S/\delta Y$ and $\delta L/\delta Y$, ignoring $\delta I/\delta Y$ and $\delta M/\delta Y$ to a first approximation. If $\delta S/\delta Y > \delta L/\delta Y$, an increase in the national income reduces the net supply of bonds by more than it reduces the demand for them. The expected result is a rise in the price of bonds and a fall in the effective bond rate of interest required to equate *B* and *F*, so that *BF* slopes downward. Conversely, *BF* slopes upward if $\delta S/\delta Y < \delta L/\delta Y$.

When *IS* lies above *LM*, as in the left half of Figure 13.5, the investment rate of interest exceeds the bond rate, since $L < M$ (with excess demand for bonds) at the investment rate. Similarly, the money rate of interest is lower than the bond rate, since $I > S$ (with excess supply of bonds) at

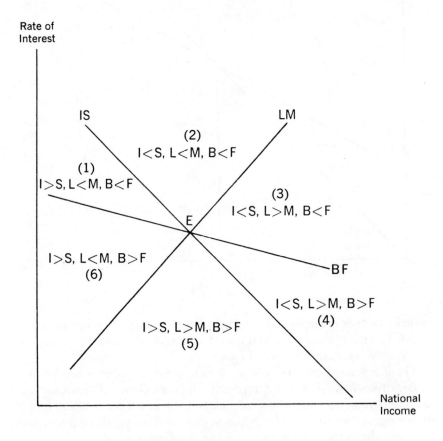

Figure 13.5

the money rate. An identical analysis would apply to the left half of the figure, where *LM* lies above *IS*. It follows that *BF* lies between *IS* and *LM* as drawn in all stable cases. Also, by Walras' Law, *BF* must coincide with *IS* and *LM* at the equilibrium point *E*.

Some Interest-Rate Dynamics

17. A single equilibrium interest rate and income level can be derived from considerations of investment rate, money rate, or bond rate, as we have just seen. The dynamic path to this equilibrium position *E* is, however, different for the three rates, and under the three interest theories underlying them. It remains uncertain which theory is most nearly correct; furthermore, combinations and compromises are possible. A number of alternative initial interest rate adjustments are illustrated in Figure 13.5 and Table 13.1.

Before returning to the diagram or consulting the table, we recall that in the presence of underemployed resources, an interest rate below the investment rate and the *IS* function leaves *ex ante* investment in excess of *ex ante* saving $(I > S)$. This is an expansionary force, tending toward a rise of *Y* and *S*. (The opposite is true for an interest rate above the investment rate and the *IS* function.) Passing now to the money rate, an interest rate below the *LM* function leads to an *ex ante* excess demand for money $(L > M)$. This is a contractionary force, resulting in a shift from earning assets to cash balances. It tends toward a fall in *Y* and *L*. (Again the reverse holds for an interest rate above the money rate and the *LM* function.) Any initial income level Y_0 will tend to rise at interest rates such that $I > S$ and $L < M$, and to fall at rates such that $I < S$ and $L > M$. The uncertain cases are $(I \gtrless S, L \gtrless M)$: they involve "crucial experiments" between these alternative theories.[19] If either of the two inequalities $(I$ and S, L and $M)$ is zero, the other inequality determines the direction of income change.

18. Figure 13.5 embodies the arguments of sections 15 and 16 in six zones. The figure is drawn in orthodox textbook fashion, with *IS* sloping

19. Loanable-funds analysis provides no unequivocal prediction of the direction of income change. Suppose $B > F$ (excess supply of bonds, or excess demand for loanable funds). This leads to a fall in bond prices, or a rise in the bond rate of interest, but what of its income effect? By Walras' Law, the excess supply of bonds may be balanced predominantly by an excess demand for goods, an excess demand for money, or both these excess demands in equally weighted combination. The excess demand for goods is expansionary in its income effect, the excess demand for money is contractionary, and the equally weighted combination is neutral.

downward and *LM* upward.[20] The six zones are bounded by the *IS, LM,*
and *BF* functions intersecting at *E*. In each zone, the direction of income
change is suggested by the directions of the inequalities between *I* and *S*
and between *L* and *M*.

Table 13.1 indicates the directions of interest-rate changes in each
numbered zone in Figure 13.5, for each interest theory under consideration here.

Table 13.1. Initial Interest-Rate Adjustments under
Alternative Interest Theories

Zone (Fig. 13.5)	Productivity and Thrift (Investment Rate)	Liquidity Preference (Money Rate)	Loanable Funds (Bond Rate)
1	Rise	Fall	Fall
2	Fall	Fall	Fall
3	Fall	Rise	Fall
4	Fall	Rise	Rise
5	Rise	Rise	Rise
6	Rise	Fall	Rise

We illustrate the argument: From any arbitrary point (r_0, Y_0) in the
zone indicated by the left-hand column of the table, the initial movement
in the interest rate is to the particular function (*IS, LM,* or *BF* respectively) stressed by one of the theories shown in one of the other columns.
If (r_0, Y_0) is in any of the three zones (1,5,6) where the initial interest
rate r_0 is below the *IS* function, and the investment rate is considered
dominant, the initial interest rate movement will be a vertical rise to *IS*.
All other combinations in the table operate in the same way.

In only two zones (2 and 5) do the three categories give the same results
for the interest rate movement. In these two zones, the investment and
money rate analyses give different answers for the initial direction of income change. Considered in the abstract, Figure 13.5 and Table 13.1 point
to something very like a set of crucial experiments as between the three
alternative interest theories. The problem in practice, however, is to iden-

20. The two functions may also yield stable equilibria if their slopes have the same
sign, provided that *IS* cuts *LM* at *E* from above. If the cutting is from below, or if the
slopes are reversed from those of the figure, instability results. To show such instability,
draw Figure 13.5 with any "unstable" *IS–LM* configuration. Along *LM*, the direction of
the *IS* inequality will lead income away from *E* at all points. Along *IS*, the direction of
the *LM* inequality will do the same. The opposite is true for all *IS–LM* configurations
that we have called stable. Complications of nonintersection, multiple intersection, etc.,
we ignore as lacking economic significance. Compare Patinkin, *op. cit.;* also Thomas F.
Dernburg and Duncan McDougall, *Macro-Economics,* 3d ed. (New York: McGraw-Hill.
1968) , ch. 15.

tify in advance the particular zone in which an economy finds itself at any point in time—assuming that (r_0, Y_0) depart finitely from the equilibrium point E.

19. A related problem is the choice between monetary and fiscal policy as a means of changing the level of national income. It is related because the shapes of our *IS* and *LM* functions are crucial to the final decision, and also because the "Keynesian economics" version of liquidity-preference interest theory leans to the fiscal policy side of the argument.

We shall assume the desired policy to be an increase in the income level, either to eliminate unemployment or to accelerate growth. We can also define as fiscal any policy acting primarily or exclusively upon the aggregate *IS* function.[21] This covers the obvious cases of changing the volume of public expenditures on goods and services, and of changing the volume of public revenues (taxes net of domestic transfer payments). Public expenditures are included in *I* or supplementary to *I;* if we denote them by *G*, our discussion of *I* can be rephrased in terms of $(I + G)$. We shall suppose, therefore, that an increase in *G* moves *I* and (normally) the *IS* function to the right. It ordinarily raises both the income level and the interest rate; at least, it does not lower either of them. Similarly, a decline in *G* normally lowers both *Y* and *r;* at least, it does not raise either of them. As for taxes, a *decrease* operates to raise both private consumption and saving. The *S* and (normally) the *IS* function are again shifted to the right. The effects on *IS, Y,* and *r* are qualitatively the same as the effects of increased expenditures.

Monetary policy, on the other hand, may be defined as any policy acting primarily (exclusively) upon the aggregate *LM* function. This covers the usual varieties of open market, debt management, bank reserve, and printing press operations; there is no implication of constancy in the interest rate. Easy money operates to shift the *M* and (normally) the *LM* functions to the right. It ordinarily raises the income level while lowering the rate of interest; at least, it does not have the opposite effects. Similarly, a tight money policy normally operates to lower *Y* and raise *r;* at least, it does not have the opposite effects.

The weighting of these two policies depends in part on distributional considerations far removed from positive interest theory. Many maldistributionists are averse to high nominal interest rates under almost any conditions. They would include a heavy dose of easy money in any prescrip-

21. An alternative definition of fiscal policy would be this: any policy acting primarily upon *IS,* but including sufficient movement in *LM* to hold the nominal interest rate constant. Since movement in *LM* involves Treasury and central bank action, we do not recommend this usage.

tion for economic expansion, but they oppose the inclusion of tight money in any cooling potion for an overheated economy. Another extraneous condition is the state of the country's foreign balance. A country with a passive or "unfavorable" balance will usually be more chary of easy money for expansion, but more inclined toward tight money for contraction, than another country less concerned with attracting or retaining mobile balances. (We assume capital markets imperfect enough to permit country interest rates higher or lower than international or "world" rates.)

In general, however, a rational choice of weights, as between monetary and fiscal policy, is influenced heavily by one's estimate of the slopes and elasticities of the *IS* and the *LM* functions. We shall illustrate this by considering four extreme cases, in which either *IS* or *LM* may have zero or infinite elasticity.[22] In these cases, one policy or the other is entirely ineffective, and the entire burden should rationally be placed upon the effective one. This is shown in the four panels of Figure 13.6, together with some interest-theory implications of the alternative policies.

20.   The top panels (a) and (b) of Figure 13.6 are pro-fiscal policy. The bottom panels (c) and (d) are pro-monetary policy. The top panels also support a liquidity-preference theory of interest, the bottom ones, one of the other theories. These conclusions are supported below.

(*1*) The upper left panel is a Keynesian liquidity trap. The horizontal *LM* function implies that further monetary expansion affects neither the rate of interest nor the income level, but merely increases cash balances. To put the matter differently, the *LM* function dominates "structurally" because it is immune from downward pressure. The only way to raise income from Y_0 to Y is by fiscal policy, which shifts *IS* to the right. In terms of interest theory, this is an extreme Keynesian or liquidity-preference position.

(*2*) The upper right panel illustrates stagnationism. The vertical IS_0 means that there is a fixed amount of private investment, which will not be exceeded at any positive interest rate. A shift from IS_0 to *IS* is possible only by some fiscal policy change. Monetary policy exercises its entire effect, under the conditions of this diagram, in raising or lowering the interest rate, and has no effect on the level of income. When *IS* not only given but constant, the rate of interest depends entirely upon *LM*. This too is an extreme Keynesian or liquidity-preference position. (Incidentally, the vertical *IS* and horizontal *LM* may be combined on a single diagram, bringing together two strains of the "Left Keynesian" interpretation of the *General Theory* in simplest form.)

---

22. We do not consider cases where *IS* and *LM* are both zero or both infinite, in which no equilibrium income level exists, or in which there is "neutral equilibrium" if the functions coincide.

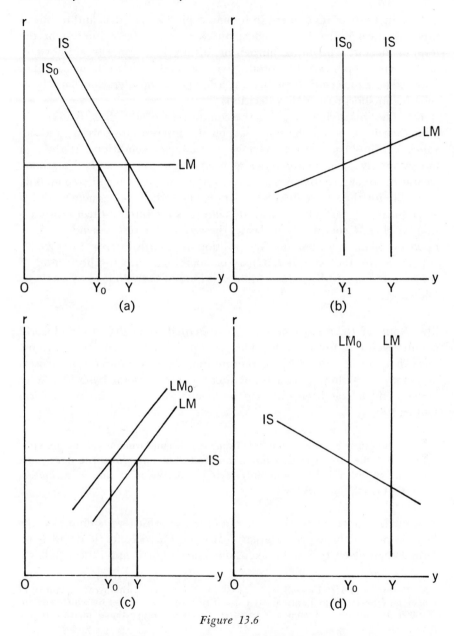

Figure 13.6

(*3*) The lower left panel is the counterpart of (*1*) directly above it. The rate of interest is determined either as a loanable-funds rate or, more probably, by the nonmonetary analysis (productivity and thrift) of Chapter 12. Because *IS* is horizontal and cannot fall, as a result, for example, of the productivity of investment in human capital knowledge, and technical progress, fiscal policy has no effect on either the rate of interest or the level of income. The entire burden of raising the income level above Y_0 is on monetary policy. (The productivity of investment in human capital, knowledge, and technical progress is a long-run consideration, largely irrelevant in short-term policy decisions.)

(*4*) The lower right panel is the counterpart of (*2*) directly above it. This time fiscal policy shatters itself on the interest-rate barrier, and advance can only come from a change in monetary conditions. If the real money supply is considered fixed, as in many intermediate-level textbook treatments of aggregative economics, a vertical segment is quite commonly derivable for the upper interest-rate range of *LM*. This segment is called a "classical range."[23] One "classical" feature is the interest-theory implication. With *LM* completely inelastic, the rate of interest depends entirely upon *IS*. (This is a nonmonetary position as regards interest theory.)

Once again, the vertical *LM* may be combined with the horizontal *IS* function in a single diagram (although it has not been done to this writer's knowledge).

21.   None of these extreme cases is presented as fitting any real-world country well much of the time. The general situation is one of an income level that can be shifted by an infinite number of combinations of fiscal and monetary policy. The menu of alternatives, and some bases for choice between them, has been outlined by Samuelson as a grand neoclassical synthesis:[24]

> A community can have [non-inflationary] full employment, can at the same time have the rate of capital formation [and economic growth] it wants, and can accomplish all this compatibly with the degree of income-redistributing taxation it ethically desires.

Samuelson goes on to cite two examples, of which we summarize the first. As one might expect, a great deal more microeconomic detail is required than given by our blanket "monetary policy" and "fiscal policy":

23. Dernburg and McDougall, *op. cit.*, ch. 10. Constancy of the (real) quantity of money may be taken to imply a strict quantity theory of money, by which any increase in the quantity of money is balanced by an equiproportional increase in the price level.

24. Paul A. Samuelson, "The New Look in Tax and Fiscal Policy," from *Federal Tax Policy for Economic Grown and Stability* (Washington: Government Printing Office, 1955), p. 234. Two noteworthy omissions from Samuelson's Utopian menu are "the balance-of-payments position it wants" and "the degree of downward price and wage rigidity it wants." Samuelson also assumes the existence of numerous alternative fiscal policies with identical macroeconomic effects and different distributional ones.

Suppose that we desire a much higher rate of capital formation but stipulate that it is to be achieved by a tax structure that favors low-income families rather than high-income ones. [This] requires an active expansionary monetary policy (open-market operations, lowering of reserve requirements, lowered rediscount rates, government credit agencies) which will stimulate investment spending. However, with out taxes bearing relatively lightly on the poor, consumption will tend to be high at the same time that investment is high. To obviate the resulting inflationary pressure, an increase in the overall tax take with an overly balanced budget would be needed.

Monetary Expansion and the Interest Rate

22. Monetary interest theory is often interpreted as implying that the interest rate moves in the opposite direction to the *nominal* as well as the real money supply, regardless of the concurrent movement of the price level. This misleading half-truth is reflected in the term "cheap money," used indiscriminately to mean low interest rates and rapid expansion of the money supply.

The proposition is, however, true under a fairly wide variety of circumstances: (a) in a seriously underemployed economy, when the increased nominal money supply does not materially increase prices and is reflected almost entirely in the real money supply; (b) during a period, usually brief, of "money illusion," when price rises are expected to be only temporary; (c) when increased nominal money is reflected significantly in increased real money, despite price increases, and the reported interest rates have been corrected for what Irving Fisher called "appreciation," so that they do not reflect expectations of future price movements.

More generally, the proposition is false, particularly for reported interest rates in the long term. The closest approach to a "standard" reaction pattern of interest rates to increased nominal money is in three stages:[25] In Stage 1, there is a short-term decline. It is followed (Stage 2) by a reaction to approximately the original level, as the market realizes that inflation has nullified the bulk of the change in the real money supply. Finally (Stage 3), interest rates actually advance above their original levels, reflecting Fisherian "appreciation" and anticipations of future price increases. A similar argument applies, *mutatis mutandis,* to deflationary contractions in the nominal money supply, except that Stages 2 and 3 are somewhat more apt to be delayed by downward rigidities and "ratchet effects."

25. The argument in the text assumes an initial position of price-level stability. In an inflationary environment, the discussion of Stage 2 should refer to *"accelerated* inflation" rather than merely "inflation," and the discussion of Stage 3 should refer to "anticipations of *increased rapidity of* future price increases" rather than merely "anticipations of future price increases."

Postscript on the Rate Structure

23.   As everyone knows, but as we nevertheless repeat, there is a multitude of market interest rates, and not just one. Loans differ in size, in length, in purpose, in the risks involved (Chapter 12, section 2) ; these risks depend on the identity of the lender as well as the stated terms of the loan contract or security. It is not unusual, in countries with active credit policies, to attempt regulation of the resulting structure of interest rates. We offer four examples, relevant to the United States: (a) States have established ceiling rates for small loans, which are usually made, with minimal security, for consumption purposes. The ostensible purpose of these ceilings is the protection of poor debtors. (b) Federal monetary authorities have attempted to raise short-term rates on commercial loans (to attract or retain internationally volatile funds) without permitting long-term rates to rise (and possibly discourage investment) as a method of meeting balance-of-payments problems. (c) Federal monetary authorities have permitted particularly favorable (or unfavorable) terms for such special purposes as housing and consumer credit, in connection with housing shortages or incipient inflation in the prices of consumer durable goods. (d) Federal monetary authorities have set maximum rates to be paid by banks on deposits, including a zero rate in the case of demand deposits.

The distributional effects of interest-rate differences are smaller than those of wage-rate differences. On the other hand, distributional considerations have obviously influenced interventions like the four just noted.[26] These considerations are the fact or belief that, at the high end of the income and wealth distributions, the rich as investors can (unlike the mass of society) afford professional advice to earn higher returns at lower risks. In regard to the low end of the income scale, it is argued that the poor as borrowers pay more for either consumer or business credit in a free market than can be justified on grounds of differential risk. This writer knows no evidence to either confirm or deny these widespread beliefs.

24.   Rate structure *theory* has concentrated on the pattern of rates applicable to securities that differ from each other in primarily with respect to

---

26. This is not to deny the relevance of the standard problems of price-fixing to these cases. For example, consider usury laws that set ceilings on consumer-loan rates. At the ceiling rates, the demand for credit exceeds the supply. Borrowers able to obtain accommodation at the legal rates obviously gain. The excluded ones obviously lose either by doing without credit altogether or by having to turn to criminal elements for so-called "juice" loans.

their time to maturity, which does not have obvious distribution-theory implications. The remainder of this chapter, therefore, constitutes a postscript or digression from the main theme of income distribution theory proper.

Three hypotheses have dominated the discussion of the time pattern of interest rates. These are (a) the *expectations* hypothesis; (b) the *liquidity* hypothesis; and (c) the *segmentation* hypothesis. It is not always easy to distinguish between any pair among this trio.

The expectations hypothesis, as formalized by Hicks,[27] would make the short rate (in public securities, the bill rate) the fundamental one, and treat long rates as averages of expected short ones. If ρ is the long rate per period on an n-period security, and the $r_1, r_2, \ldots r_n$ a series of actual or anticipated one-period rates on an otherwise identical one-period security, we have

$$(1 + \rho)^n = (1 + r_1)\ (1 + r_2)\ \ldots\ (1 + r_n) \tag{13.1}$$

or, ignoring the complications of compound interest:

$$(1 + \rho)n = \sum_1^n (1 + r_i) \quad \text{or} \quad \rho n \cong \sum_1^n r_i$$

where r_1 is known but $r_2, \ldots, r_n$ are anticipated values.

The liquidity hypothesis states that ρ will normally be significantly higher than the value suggested by (13.1). The higher rate is required, in this view, to compensate for the loss of liquidity (risk of capital loss, on disposal prior to maturity) involved in holding an n-period security. Indeed, the long rate will almost always exceed the short, regardless of the state of expectations about the future of short rates.

The segmentation hypothesis states, in the present context,[28] that the markets for long- and short-period securities are so disparate, and that arbitrage between them is so minimal, that in the short run, ρ is correlated with the r_i, or with the entire right side of (13.1), only minimally, if at all.

Considerable work has been done to distinguish, compare, combine, and test the implications of the expectations and liquidity hypotheses. A particularly controversial work has been Meiselman's *The Term Structure of Interest Rates*.[29] Our own analysis is based upon a subsequent National

27. Hicks, *Value and Capital, op. cit.*, pp. 144 f. See also F. A. Lutz, "The Structure of Interest Rates," *Readings*, no. 26.

28. The segmentation theory is more applicable to classes of securities differing not only in length but in other characteristics as well; for instance, government short-term bills as against long-term residential mortgages.

29. David Meiselman, *The Term Structure of Interest Rates* (Englewood Cliffs, N.J.: Prentice-Hall, 1962).

Bureau monograph by Kessel.[30] Meiselman plumps for a pure expectations hypothesis, while Kessel (and the author) are impressed by an eclectic combination of expectations and liquidity hypotheses.

25.   To illustrate a pure expectations hypothesis, Kessel provides an arithmetical table that forms the basis of Table 13.2.[31] Suppose that at t_1, the rates on 1-, 2-, 3-, and 4-period securities (maturing at t_2, t_3, t_4 and t_5) are as shown in column (1) of this table.

"Implied forecasts" of the short-term r_2, r_3, r_4, and r_5 are derived in column (2). Now suppose that in the following period t_2 the observed rates are as given in column (3), with implied forecasts for r_3 and r_4 worked out in column (4). An implied downward revision of forecasts is given in column (5), allowing for the fact that the n-year security of t_1 becomes the $(n-1)$-year security of t_2. The principle of computation for columns (2) and (4) is that, if ρ_n be the rate of return on an n-period security and F the "implied forecast" one-year rate,

$$(n-1)\,\rho_{n-1} + F = n\,\rho_n$$

What is illustrated by this exercise with hypothetical data is that[32] "if a realized or actual short term rate is above its predicted level, then the predictions for other rates, yet to be realized, will be raised upward. Conversely, if the actual rate is below the predicted, then other predicted rates will be moved downward during the time interval between observations." This is seen as an important consequence of the expectations hypothesis.

In symbols: $_iR_i$ is an actual short rate at t_i, and $_iE_t$ is an expected short rate for the same year i anticipated at some t prior to i. Then we have, for example, $_2R_2 = 2.0$ per cent (column 3, line 1), whereas $_2E_1 = 3.0$ per cent (column 2, line 2). Since $_2R_2 < {}_2E_1$, the expectations hypothesis suggests that $_3E_2 < {}_3E_1$ and $_4E_2 < {}_4E_1$. More generally, Kessel interprets the expectations hypothesis as implying that, for any $i > 2$:

$$_iE_2 - {}_iE_1 = \beta\,(_2R_2 - {}_2E_1). \tag{13.2}$$

The coefficient β is a positive proper fraction, approaching zero as i increases as a "rationality condition" for anticipations.

But the true expectations $_iE_t$ are actually unknown. All we have are the implied forecasts $_iF_t$, derived in Table 13.2. Pure expectations theorists like Meiselman have taken $_iE_t = {}_iF_t$, as we have done in construct-

30. Reuben Kessel, *The Cyclical Behavior of the Term Structure of Interest Rates* (New York: National Bureau of Economic Research Occasional Paper 91, 1965).

31. *Ibid.*, pp. 13 f. (We have taken the liberty of modifying Kessel's notation and presentation.)

32. *Ibid.*, p. 12.

Table 13.2. *Illustration of Expectations Hypothesis*

Time to Maturity (Years)	At t_1		At t_2		
	Observed Yield (per cent) (1)	Implied Forecast 1-Year Rate $_1F_t$ (per cent) (2)	Observed Yield (per cent) (3)	Implied Forecast 1-Year Rate $_2F_t$ (per cent) (4)	Implied Revision (per cent) (5)
1	1.0	–	2.0	–	–
2	2.0	3.0 $[1.0 + F = 2 \times 2.0]$	3.3	4.6 $[2.0 + F = 2 \times 3.3]$	–0.4 $(4.6 - 5.0)$
3	3.0	5.0 $[(2 \times 2.0) + F = 3 \times 3.0]$	4.0	5.4 $[(2 \times 3.3) + F = 3 \times 4.0]$	–1.6 $(5.4 - 7.0)$
4	4.0	7.0 $[(3 \times 3.0) + F = 4 \times 4.0]$	–	–	–

ing the table, and then gone on from there. The expectations-cum-liquidity theorists like Kessel may be interpreted as adding a liquidity term $_iL_t$, a liquidity premium (illiquidity penalty) for period i as anticipated at the earlier period t, so that

$$_iF_t = {}_iE_t + {}_iL_t \qquad \text{or} \qquad _iE_t = {}_iF_t - {}_iL_t. \tag{13.3}$$

(The $_iL_t$ will normally be positive, but may be negative for persons who already have fixed money debts maturing n years in the future.)

Equation (13.2) may be rewritten, distinguishing E from F terms as per (13.3):

$$({}_iF_2 - {}_iL_2) - ({}_iF_1 - {}_iL_1) = \beta \left[{}_2R_2 - ({}_2F_1 - {}_2L_1) \right]. \tag{13.4}$$

Defining a liquidity-preference shift $\Delta L = {}_iL_2 - {}_iL_1$, we rewrite (13.4):

$$({}_iF_2 - {}_iF_1) = \beta \left({}_2R_2 - {}_2F_1 \right) + \left(\beta \, {}_2L_1 + \Delta L \right). \tag{13.5}$$

To put everything into observable terms by omitting the notional expressions in L and ΔL, we define as α the second parenthetical expression on the right side of (13.5). Rewriting for the last time, we have Meiselman's equation:

$$({}_iF_2 - {}_iF_1) = \alpha + \beta \left({}_2R_2 - {}_2F_1 \right). \tag{13.6}$$

Fitting (13.6) to American public-security data, Meiselman found the α coefficient not significantly different from zero. This result he interpreted as showing that liquidity terms like $_2L_1$ in (13.5) are insignificant, and that the expectational factor tells the whole story. However, as Kessel points out, this ignores any ΔL term and implicitly assumes L to be constant. If ΔL is nonzero, $_iE_t$ may differ significantly from $_iF_t$, and the $_iL_t$ terms be significant as a result.

Kessel's positive reason for accepting the liquidity supplement to the expectational theory is elementary and historical. For American data over the half-century ending in 1954, for example, the average yield on government securities was an increasing function of their term to maturity, although the period was marked by a falling trend of short rates.[33] To repeat: Kessel accepts the expectation theory in its main outlines and is duly impressed by the good fit and low α value of Meiselman's equation (13.6), but insists that a liquidity element also be added.

26.   Demand functions for securities of different maturities normally slope downward. They are seldom perfectly elastic (horizontal), as a care-

33. *Ibid.,* p. 18.

less reading of the foregoing paragraphs might imply.[34] Different potential buyers usually hold different estimates of the future course of short rates; many prefer to hedge in various ways against the probabilities of expectations being erroneous in either direction; on the liquidity side, too, preferences are also far from uniform.

As a result of the nonhorizontality of demand functions for securities, the pattern or structure of their yields is open to influences from the supply side as well as from the basically demand-side influences we have been considering. Borrowers in general, or individual large borrowers (like the public exchequer) with some measure of monopoly power, can vary the rate pattern either voluntarily or unconsciously by "tailoring" or "orchestrating" the time pattern of their own offerings of different maturities, despite the arbitraging efforts of other market participants. For example, by replacing or refunding short-term bills with long-term bonds, the United States Treasury may be able to twist the rate structure appreciably, raising the bill rate and lowering the bond rate. Public authorities can sometimes, even when short-term rates are expected to rise, force the bond below the bill rate in disconfirmation of expectation and liquidity theories of the rate structure. There is often pressure on the monetary authorities, including treasuries and central banks, to manipulate the rate pattern and reduce total interest costs on a public debt of given volume. A common reply to such pressure is exaggerated denial of the authorities' power to affect the pattern, either by ordinary open-market operations on given stocks of outstanding securities or by varying the proportions between different maturities.[35] We can leave to discussions of fiscal and monetary policy any consideration of appropriate debt-management principles and practices, and only point out the frequent possibility of rate-structure manipulation.

34. These demand functions are infinitely elastic when the price of a security is being regulated, as by the open-market operations of a public monetary authority. Supporting the price of a security—keeping the price from falling—imposes a ceiling on its rate of return, and is accomplished by readiness to buy at the support price all that is offered for sale. Enforcing a ceiling on the price of a security, on the other hand, imposes a floor on its rate of return, and is accomplished by readiness to sell at the ceiling price all that buyers desire to purchase.

35. Variation of these proportions (a supply-side operation) has a wider range of effectiveness than ordinary open-market operations (on either side), which are limited by fixed proportions. Ordinary open-market operations, aiming at bank reserves and the monetary base, frequently seek to avoid changing the rate pattern or arousing "speculation." With rate-pattern neutrality in view, open-market operations are sometimes limited to "bills only" or "bills preferably," on the theory that demand functions for the shorter maturities are most nearly horizontal (expectations being subject to a narrower range of uncertainty) with respect to interest rates.

CHAPTER FOURTEEN

Two Theories of Rent

The Varieties of Rent Theory

1. We dealt with wage theory in Chapters 9 through 11 as concerned with the quantity of some input a, the flow of services of labor or human capital, and with its price or wage p_a per unit of time. It would be only natural to deal with rent theory as concerned with the flow of services of another input b, the service of nonhuman or material capital, and with its price p_b per unit of time. Actual rent theory, however, is ordinarily narrower in its coverage and is not a complete counterpart of wage theory. It is limited conventionally to special cases, whose specification varies among writers.

Suggestions have not been lacking for reform through generalization. Johnson, for instance, is concerned that many "concepts of distribution theory no longer match the categories of income distribution; and consequently, the theory of distribution is, to put it mildly, in a rather unsatisfactory state."[1] His remedial proposal, a drastic one, involves completely recasting the theories of wages and rent so as to put them on a par with each other:[2]

> The time has come to sever the link with the classical attempt to identify categories of income with distinctly different kinds of productive factors: . . . a more useful approach would be to lump all factors together as items of capital equipment, created by past investment and rendering current services . . . The current price of a factor's services can be divided conceptually into two ele-

1. Harry G. Johnson, "The Political Economy of Opulence," *Can. J. Econ.* (November 1960), p. 561.

2. *Ibid.*, p. 562. By "scarcity of the factor," Johnson has in mind complete supply inelasticity of individual units, at all prices above transfer costs.

ments: the payment necessary to keep the factor in existence (or in a particular employment) corresponding to the classical notion of "wages"; and a surplus above that necessary payment, arising from scarcity of the factor and corresponding to the classical notion of "rent."

What may be called traditional rent theory, following both the physiocrats and the classical economists, is concerned only with the pricing of the services of those capital instruments whose total stocks are fixed, notably "the original and indestructible powers of the soil," or land, including natural resources. The quotation is from Ricardo, and Ricardian rent theory has the best claim to the title "orthodox." A generalization of the Ricardian rent concept, which is due primarily to Marshall, includes "quasi-rents" to fixed capital instruments like buildings and machinery, whose stocks are constant only in the short run. A similar generalization includes also "rent of ability" to types of labor and personal services that are similarly limited, either naturally or artificially (as by apprenticeship limitations). These are primarily the higher levels of differential skills, whether managerial, athletic, professional, artistic, or technical.

Outside the tradition of Ricardo and Marshall are a congeries of notions that overlap with theirs, which we pass over with relative brevity. To Viner, for example, rent means (in one famous essay) the return to inputs, human and nonhuman alike, that are specialized to a particular industry, in the sense that expansion and contraction of that industry alone affect the input price significantly.[3] (His categorizing of cost as "inclusive" and "exclusive" of rent might be read more precisely as inclusive and exclusive of rent *changes*.) To Schumpeter, rent apparently includes any sort of long-term monopoly gain not traceable to innovation and its accompanying "process of creative destruction"; many other writers speak of "monopoly rents" in the same way. To Pareto, rent is the return to *limitational* inputs, for which the principle of substitution (Chapter 6, section 3) does not apply, inasmuch as the ratio a/x or the ratio a/b is structurally fixed and insensitive to either output or input price changes. Of these heterodox formulations, we shall in this chapter consider only the Paretian one (see sections 12–14).

Seven Ricardian Propositions

2.   Contrasting with the substantial flux of wage and interest theory, rent theory in its textbook versions has tended to ossify where Ricardo left it in the second chapter of his 1819 *Principles of Political Economy*. We

3. Jacob Viner, "Cost Curves and Supply Curves," *Zeitschr. für Nationalökon.* (April 1931). Compare also Joan Robinson, *Imperfect Competition* (London: Macmillan, 1933), ch. 8, 10.

may summarize his treatment in a series of seven interrelated "Ricardian" propositions.

(*1*) Land is significantly different from capital.

(*2*) Land rent is due to the "niggardliness of nature," whence it follows that the economic interests of landlords (who gain from scarcity) are out of harmony with those of the remainder of society.

(*3*) The rent of land is equal to its v.m.p. (Ricardo, of course, does not use this term.)

(*4*) The rent of land is a residual after other inputs have received their v.m.p.[4]

(*5*) The rent of land is exclusively a differential. It would not exist if all land were of uniform quality (in terms of fertility and/or location), or if diminishing returns did not apply to labor and capital on top-quality land.

(*6*) Rent is not a cost, and therefore does not enter into price.[5]

(*7*) Rent is an economic surplus or unearned increment.[6] It is a peculiarly fitting object for differentially high taxation, both because it is unearned by the landlord and because its supply is fixed.

Our discussion of Ricardian rent theory will consider these propositions in order.

3. "Land is significantly different from capital." The difference is that, for nonreproducible goods and their services, there only fixed stocks in existence. This means that their prices may be looked upon as determined from the demand side and so unrelated to supply factors, particularly the cost of production. The Austrian theory of value comes into its own.[7] A mechanism to show this is the so-called "Wicksteed" demand function of Figure 14.1.[8]

---

4. "Other inputs" are, in Ricardo's treatment, "doses" of a single input, namely, labor plus capital, presumably in fixed proportions—a Paretian notion, as we shall see.

5. In a later usage, the argument is restated: Rent is a price-*determined* rather than a price-*determining* cost. One also sees the term "noncost outlay" applied to rent in the Ricardian sense.

6. For most land-taxation enthusiasts, if not for Ricardo, this statement is too weak. They regard land as a monopoly of its owners, and rent as a monopoly profit, because of the fixity of the total stock and not as a reference to possible collusion between landholders. This use of the term "monopoly" is difficult to reconcile with anything else in the economics of either imperfect or monopolistic competition.

7. Austrian value theory assumes implicitly that the stocks of all "original" inputs (including labor as well as land) are fixed. Their prices, and therefore the costs of outputs, are therefore set by demands derived (sometimes by marginal productivity considerations) from the direct demands for outputs. These in turn depend on marginal-utility functions, which become the prime movers of the entire economy.

8. Philip H. Wicksteed, "The Scope and Method of Political Economy," in George J. Stigler and K. E. Boulding (eds.), *Readings in Price Theory* (Homewood, Ill.: Irwin, 1952), pp. 15–19.

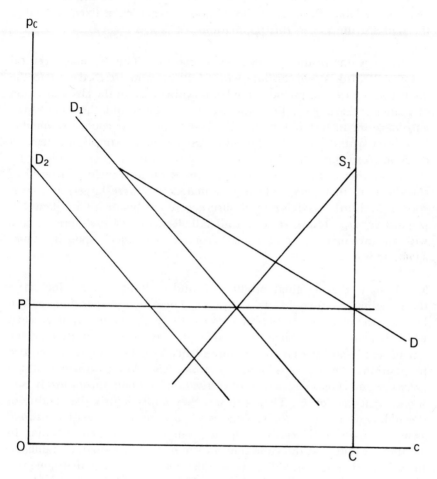

Figure 14.1

In this diagram, let input c be land, or rather the flow of its services per period, p_c its rent, and C the maximum flow available from the constant stock. The demand and supply functions D_1 and S_1 are drawn conventionally, but the quantity $(C - S_1)$ is treated as the "reservation demand" function of the present holders, and labeled D_2. Total demand D in the Wicksteed sense is the sum $(D_1 + D_2)$, and rent is set at R where D crosses C. At the same level, of course, D_1 and S_1 also intersect. Similar analyses cannot, except in the extreme short run, be applied to other outputs and inputs. For example, to apply this analysis to the labor market (as the Austrians appear to have done), we would have to include all nonparticipation in the labor force by working-age individuals and likewise all time away from work (possibly including sleep) in the reservation demand for labor. Population should also be regarded as fixed, as well as the skill-distribution of this population.

4. "Rent is due to the niggardliness of nature." This became a central point of Ricardo's long dispute with Malthus, who ascribed rent to the bounty of nature and included the land-owning class in the classical vision of economic harmoney. Both the Ricardian thesis and the Malthusian antithesis are in fact half-truths. Their two positions could presumably have been synthesized, with the aid of an elementary supply-and-demand diagram like Figure 14.1, by a present-day tyro with an I.Q. decidedly inferior to either of these contending giants. Ricardo is saying, in terms of this diagram, that rent could be eliminated if C were larger, and he is correct. Malthus is saying that, if nature were less bountiful and land less productive, D_1, D, and R would all fall. Rent might therefore be zero with an unchanged C (and a small economy dependent upon it). Once again, he is correct.

5. "Rent is the marginal product of land." "Rent is a residual after the marginal products of other inputs." These two propositions entrap between them the later marginal productivity theory of input pricing, which bore for a time such alternative titles as "a generalization of the law of rent" and "the law of the three rents." At the same time, the two propositions—derivable, respectively, from Ricardo's treatments of the *extensive* and *intensive* margins of cultivation—are only incompletely consistent with each other. That is to say, they imply jointly the validity of the adding-up theorem (6.4). This, as we have seen, is a relatively strong assumption, although legitimate for long-run competitive equilibrium. In addition, if rent is at the same time an v.m.p. and a residual, it is difficult to avoid a "double residual" fallacy under conditions other than long-run competitive equilibrium. If both rent and "pure profits" are residuals, we need a much more satisfactory explanation of the allocation of windfall gains and losses between the two than classical economics was able to provide.

6. "Rent is exclusively a differential." This proposition was abandoned early, even by Ricardo's popularizer and successor John Stuart Mill. It is by no means more generally valid than would be a similar proposition about any other input price. (Could homogeneous labor be expected to have a zero wage?) Assuming all land to be uniform in desirability, it should be clear that whether its rent would be positive or zero depends upon considerations of demand and supply or, more fundamentally, upon the marginal productivity of this land and the stock or acreage available.

It is interesting to speculate on the considerations that led the acute Ricardo to his conclusion. Perhaps he merely equated the hypothetical uniform grade of land with the marginal land of the Scottish Highlands or the American frontier

> Where rolls the Oregon, and hears no sound
> Save its own dashing

and which afforded no rent in his own day. But more significantly, one needs some such assumption to combine a labor theory of value (even a 93 per cent one) with strict proportionality between values and long-run normal prices.[9] For, with such a labor theory and values proportional to prices, not only must value be based on (constant) cost, with demand influences be confined to the quantity side of the market, but the cost-and-supply side must be purged of any extraneous influences from land and capital. In the case of capital, an obvious way out (although not completely satisfactory when there is time discounting) is reduction of machinery and inventory to labor, applied indirectly. In the case of land, Ricardo's solution is to consider value as being determined exclusively at the extensive margin of cultivation, where land is marginal and rent zero. It is deceptively easy to extend this result—value determined where rent is zero—to all cases where land is uniform and then to ascribe the persistence of rent to the lack of uniformity.

7. "Rent is not a cost, and does not enter into price." This is among the most controversial of the Ricardian propositions. It has not, for example, been accepted in the business community. The everyday advertisements, "Out of the High-Rent District—Our Prices Are Lower" and "Up One Flight of Stairs—Save 10 Per Cent," indicate the popularity and effectiveness of the practical or common-sense view.

To clear the air, a preliminary point in this connection is that the "rent" most relevant is rent per unit of output or value added, rather than rent per acre of land or per square foot of floor space. Something similar is equally true of wages, where "labor cost per unit of product" or value added, embodying corrections for productivity differences, is more relevant in discussing wage-price relationships than "wages per hour," with or without fringe benefits. On this basis, it is difficult to see why rent should be treated differently from wages in its price effects, and yet we seldom see advertisements of products "Made by Unskilled Labor—Our Prices Are Lower," or "Workers Illiterate—Save 10 Per Cent." Why the

---

9. Marx, of course, dropped the proportionality postulate. The "93 per cent" reference is to Stigler, "Ricardo and the 93 Per Cent Labor Theory of Value," in *Essays in the History of Economics* (Chicago: University of Chicago Press, 1965), ch. 12.

difference? Can it be explained entirely by considerations of distributional ethics?

A 1929 essay by Buchanan[10] clarifies some of these issues on the basis of what later writers were to call the distinction between micro- and macroeconomics. Briefly, the practical business man is right at the "micro" level; rent, like wages, enters into competitive prices of specific goods, to whatever extent it is not offset by superior productivity. On the other hand, Ricardo is right at the "macro" level; the index number of rents as a whole is determined by the index number of general prices, rather than determining it.

On the microeconomic side, let us follow Buchanan in analyzing an agricultural example. Most agricultural land can be used for a multitude of crops: grains, fruits, vegetables, poultry, livestock, and forest products, singly or in combination. Consider, for example, the potato farmer, operating on land with alternative agricultural uses. When the demand for potato land rises because of expansion in one or more of these rival uses, say, chicken raising, its price and rent rise. To keep potato land from being bid away by poultry farmers to become poultry land, potato growers must pay higher rents. If enough potato land is involved, the higher rents will be reflected in part in higher potato prices, despite compensatory shifts by potato growers to less land-intensive (more labor-intensive) cultivation methods. Potato prices will also rise if, unable to meet the poultry farmers' competition for land, any large number of potato farmers abandon this industry and shift to other occupations, not necessarily agricultural ones. In terms of the standard diagrams of elementary competitive economics, the supply of land to the potato farmers, or to the potato industry, is infinitely elastic at the going rental, quite like the wage rate of unspecialized farm labor or the rate of interest on crop loans. When the going rental rises for reasons unconnected with potato growing, the higher rent is a price-determining cost on the same footing with wages or interest.

At the macroeconomic level, the case becomes different. The flow of services developed from the constant stock of agricultural land to farming as a whole, approximates the vertical line C (Fig. 14.1), except in the neighborhood of reclamation projects (drainage, irrigation, etc.) and suburban sprawl. Its rent is fixed entirely by demand considerations, direct and indirect (v.m.p.), if we treat its supply function as reservation demand à la Wicksteed. Abstracting from both technical change and nonagricultural demand, an increase in the demand for farming land arises

---

10. Daniel H. Buchanan, "The Historical Approach to Rent and Price Theory," *Readings*, no. 31.

from an increase in some index of agricultural prices. Two likely causes for such increase are prosperity and population growth; a third, where the farm bloc has political potency, is a shift in agricultural controls in favor of farmers. Rent is a price-determined cost in the absence of technical change and nonagricultural demand for land; and Ricardo was largely right on his own terms, which, as Buchanan argues, involved the use of "corn" to mean not merely wheat but agricultural produce in general.

This is Buchanan's solution for Davenport's celebrated general-equilibrium paradox in verse, which made better American economics than English poetry:[11]

> The price of pig is something big,
>   And likewise corn, you'll understand,
> Is costly too, because they grew
>   Upon the high-priced farming land.
>
> If you'd know why that land is high,
>   Consider this: its price is big
> Because it pays thereon to raise
>   The costly corn, the high-priced pig.

Land-Value Taxation

8. "Rent is an economic surplus and an unearned increment, and therefore a fitting object for differential taxation." The argument is familiar. The stock of land of any sort being fixed, the flow of returns to its owners can be reduced by taxation without diminution of the stock or decreased efficiency in its allocation. At the same time, and for the same reason, the landlord cannot be said to have earned the rent on his land, other than by such tenuous indirection as speculative shrewdness in selecting appropriate parcels, holding on to them, and, in some cases, bearing whatever costs appertain to their "ripening." This line of argument was, however, developed less by Ricardo than by his physiocratic predecessors and single-tax successors. (The legitimacy of the single-tax claim to succession is open to question.)

Subsidiary and post-Ricardian arguments for such taxation are (1) that it would reduce the profitability of keeping land out of use or in inferior uses while waiting for its price, or capitalized rental value, to rise; and (2) that it would permit reduction of other taxes impinging more directly upon production of specific commodities, or on the supply of

11. H. J. Davenport, *The Economics of Industry* (New York: Macmillan, 1913), p. 107 n.

productive inputs.[12] With land used more efficiently—continuing along the line of (1)—the productivity and remuneration of complementary inputs, including most types of both labor and capital, would rise. So would the national product, so that the growth rate would receive an upward fillip. This fillip would, however, be of the once-for-all variety, unless induced technical progress were stimulated along with other sorts of investments. Reduction of tax rates on other types of incomes—along the line of (2)—would operate in the same directions.

9.   These arguments, both neo-Ricardian and proto-Ricardian, seem empirically sound in a sufficient proportion of cases to justify more serious consideration than they have in fact received. Why, one wonders, have they been relegated so readily to the dumping ground of crank and crackpot gadgetry? A number of reasons may be adduced, with varying degrees of economic relevance and economic content, against the discriminatory taxation of land rents and values. We have collected them under nine heads:

(*1*)   The capital losses imposed by such taxation upon "innocent purchasers for value without notice."[13] It is one thing to impose such losses upon primeval speculators and their heirs, but another to impose them on third parties who bought shortly before land taxes were increased. For this reason, the optimal point of time for inaugurating a system of land-value taxation is at the beginning of settlement. This was done to a great extent in Australia and New Zealand; for this reason, the system has firmer and more widespread roots in Australasia than on other continents.

(*2*)   The ubiquity of land speculation. Landholders and land speculators are not, in advanced countries, a special class readily located and identified for purposes of economic lynching (justified or otherwise). They are more commonly, at least in these countries, a substantial fraction of the influential middle and upper classes generally, the fraction increasing in periods of actual or potential monetary inflation. Every home owner is a conscious or unconscious, voluntary or involuntary, land speculator. The family farm, of which Americans are so proud, has been called (I do not recall by whom) "a losing business financed from the profits of land speculation." It is politically suicidal to fly in the face of so many, and such powerful, elements of the voting public, until clearer benefits

12. It is assumed in this argument that increased returns to labor and capital would in fact increase their supply. This is not necessarily the case; compare Chapter 9, sections 6, 8.

13. Mention of capital losses from higher tax rates does not imply acceptance of the so-called "capitalization" theory of property tax incidence, according to which incidence is *entirely* upon the property holder at the time such taxes are imposed or raised. A *substantial degree* of capitalization is all that we assert.

are visible for most of them as individuals (for example, lower taxes of other sorts) than the disciples of Henry George have yet been able to demonstrate.

(*3*) The rising tendency of the general price level, which has been mentioned obliquely. Land is a classic inflation hedge; conversely, land speculators are called "land poor" in deflationary periods. People will not look kindly on deprivation of so important a hedge unless and until the need for it passes, along with the so-called "age of inflation."

(*4*) The existence of "unearned increment" in so many forms other than land rent. This has always weakened the ethical case for land-value taxation, primarily by shunting reformist sentiment along other lines. The most obvious cases of unearned nonrent increment are the profits of imperfect competition. We have seen that these benefits may be spread among workers and salaried staff as well as managers and shareholders. Other important examples are "rents of ability" to scarce talents of all sorts, particularly when nurtured at public expense, the usufruct of inherited wealth in all its forms, and (in the short run) the quasi-rents accruing to owners of strategic elements of the physical capital stock.

(*5*) The administrative difficulties of determining either the price or the rental value of land, as distinguished from buildings and other improvements (the latter including clearing, drainage, fertilization, and so on), or the true rental value of property held idle and in inferior uses. The mechanical task of estimation is, of course, possible, and is accomplished every day by assessors in numerous localities in North America, Britain, Australasia, and elsewhere. What is questionable is whether assessors' judgments and rules of thumb are, or can be rendered, adequate to bear the strain of a system that imposes much more than the present level of dependence upon their reasonableness and probity.

(*6*) In a changing economy, it is not necessarily inefficient in the long term to use land suboptimally in the short term. Let us construct a hypothetical case in point, without venturing to judge the significance of cases like it. Consider a parcel of land with uses α_1 and β_1 at some time t_1, and uses α_2 and β_2 at some subsequent t_2. Suppose that α_1 is unequivocally superior to β_1 at t_1—as when α_1 involves a positive marginal product and β_1 is complete idleness—but that β_2 is unequivocally superior to α_2 at t_2. Suppose also that there are intertemporal complementarities between uses such that α_1 effectively requires α_2, while β_1 (idleness) is neutral between α_2 and β_2, or possibly even is complementary to β_2 and competitive with α_2. It is not difficult, from such initial conditions, to conjure up instances in which the social interest, however conceived, would be best served (at going rates of time-discounting) by the sequence (β_1,β_2), but in which land-value taxation of the Georgist variety, unless administered with extraordinary finesse and foresight, would impose (in a world of uncertainty and imperfect credit markets) the inferior sequence (α_1, α_2), by taxing the landlord at t_1 at rates appropriate for use α_1. (Under perfect certainty and perfect credit markets, this problem would vanish.)

(7) The association of all land-value taxation schemes with Henry George's single-tax program, as enunciated in *Progress and Poverty* (1879). This lends an aura of unreality to the entire subject. George proposed to finance the public 5 to 10 per cent of the gross national product from the proceeds of a single tax on the rental value of land. This may have been feasible in 1879, but the current 25 to 30 per cent would surely require some additional revenue sources. Land-value taxation accordingly carries with it notions of complete repeal of all other taxes, which "lies not within the prospect of belief," and accordingly receives less than a fair hearing.

(8) The comforting physiocratic doctrine of tax incidence, that all levies fall upon the landowner in any case. The theory is that workers, including independent artisans and small businessmen of the "classe stérile," are already at the subsistence level, and cannot be pushed lower in the long run. Only the landholding aristocracy possesses the surplus above immediate needs out of which the state can be financed. This type of incidence theory is no longer held widely, either by the general public or by specialists in public finance. Unfortunately again, it seems to have been both prevalent and reasonable in the context of eighteenth-century European living standards, at a time when, as per (*1*) above, the ethical case for land-rent taxation was stronger than it now is.

(9) The association of Henry George's views on land-value taxation will his faulty theory of economic development. According to this theory, "progress" led to "poverty" under conventional fiscal systems. By "poverty" George meant (if I understand him correctly) both an increase in the proportion of the population living below some poverty line and a fall in the living standard of the representative man or at least the representative non-landowner.

Issues of Rent Control

10.   Although rent controls, where they exist, apply to commercial rather than economic rent, *i.e.*, to improvements on land as well as to raw land, we shall discuss two interesting issues arising in connection with them. The first issue is the reason for their extraordinary longevity, and the second, their effect upon the prices of property offered for sale rather than for rent. In both instances, we focus our attention on residential rent con-

trols, assuming no controls (or much weaker controls) over the sale prices of property.

The longevity of rent controls is proverbial, at least on "old" housing in "renters'" as distinguished from "home owners'" communities. In Paris, they have been enforced continuously since 1914, and in New York since 1942. In both France and the United States, by contrast, the remainder of the World War II control structures were repealed shortly after the close of hostilities. One reason for the difference may well be the importance of rent in the tenant family's budget—more than any single item of food or clothing. Another is resentment against "unjust enrichment" of landlords, particularly absentee landlords. More important than either of these, however, may be the permanence of tenancy, and the consequent concentration of the burdens of market disequilibrium upon such weakly organized minorities as the transients and the young-marrieds. Once installed in a rent-controlled house or apartment, one has it indefinitely—barring natural or contrived disasters like fire, harassment,[14] or (under looser controls) ostensible conversion of the property from tenancy to ownership, from apartments to rooming houses, and so on. Whereas, in the case of perishables like food, meeting today's demands at controlled prices is no guarantee of equal fortune tomorrow or next week, the durability of housing joins with the difficulty of eviction in confirming present renters in their tenancies. They, often conjoined with their heirs and assigns, constitute the majority. The young and the newcomers form not only a minority but a politically weak minority, and the system lives on.

11. When rent controls are imposed or strengthened, and again when they are removed or weakened, there are forecasts about renters or would-be renters being forced to buy, and about the rents and prices of uncontrolled properties being forced upward. In the case of imposed controls, a dissatisfied fringe forced into the uncontrolled market consists of people unable to find housing at the controlled rent levels. In the case of decontrol, it consists of persons forced out by inability or unwillingness to pay free-market rents. But how, one wonders, can *both* rent control and rent decontrol force up the prices of owned housing? If only one does so, which one is it likely to be?

The dissatisfied fringe at the controlled rental R_0 (in Figure 14.2) is indicated by AC homogenized housing units per period, and the unsatis-

---

14. British cases are reported where landlords, to rid themselves of apartment tenants who "knew their rights" under controls, had their agents remove roofs, play rock-and-roll music all night, and urinate in hallways.

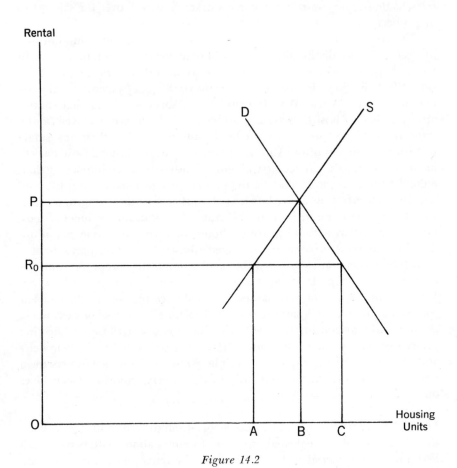

Figure 14.2

fied fringe at the free market rental R is indicated by BC such units. If the demand and supply functions have their normal slopes, AB is strictly positive and $AC > BC$. If the supply of controlled-rental housing is somehow rendered completely inelastic, as by confinement of controls to "old" housing with stringent prohibition of diversion to other segments of the real estate market, AB is zero and $AC = BC$. Shifts between owned and rented quarters, new and old housing, housing and housing substitutes (house trailers, houseboats, rented rooms, doubling-up) seem to guarantee a downward-sloping demand function D. This in turn means that a stable free market rent of R may be presumed to exist, and that negative AB $(BC > AC)$ may be ruled out for the ordinary control situation of $R_0 < R$.

If the same percentage (call it k) of both fringes AC and BC shifts into the free market for housing under control in one instance and under decontrol in the other, it follows from $AC \geqq BC$ that rent control raises the demand and price of uncontrolled units, while decontrol lowers them. (At any rate, we may rule out the reverse effects.) These presumptions may be overthrown, however, if the control fringe is more likely to turn to owned housing than is the decontrol fringe, that is, if $k(BC)$ is sufficiently greater than $k'(AC)$, where k and k' are the two proportions of fringe individuals and families shifting to owned housing. An extreme example might have AC composed of upward-mobile newly married couples able and willing to make down payments on new houses, while BC is composed of old-age pensioners forced by decontrol into sharing the quarters of younger relatives. When several types of housing are left uncontrolled, it is possible for rent control to raise the prices of some types (say, owned houses in the case immediately above), and for decontrol to raise the prices of others (say, house trailers, if the old-age pensioners shift to this type of housing).

Paretian Rent

12. The Paretian theory of rent has little beyond nomenclature in common with the Ricardian one. We have encountered the Paretian theory already, in Chapter 7, section 8. It deals, we said there, with the pricing of limitational inputs, which are used in structurally fixed proportions. There are two classes of these limitational inputs: class 1 involves a fixed ratio of particular inputs to particular outputs or, in our terminology, fixed a/x ratios in physical terms; class 2 involves fixed ratios between two inputs or, in our terminology, fixed a/b ratios, again in physical terms.

Rigidities of either sort may be matters of technology in the strict sense, requiring only the avoidance of outright waste. On the other hand, rigidities of either sort may be matters of institutional working rules, sometimes unilaterally determined managerial rules of thumb, and sometimes collectively bargained agreements between employers and workers' organizations. Many cases in both classes involve inputs of land in the broad sense, including natural resources. Pareto's favorite example, falling in the first class, is the amount of gold in a gold coin.[15] The importance of these

---

15. As has been objected, this example is less happy than it appeared to Pareto. It neglects the margin of substitution between a grain or two of extra gold as a safety margin of full weight and fineness, and a shade of extra expenditure on quality-control measures, gold-dust recovery, and so no. Our discussion will omit these niggling technical points, where Pareto's inaccuracy may be infinitesimal, and concentrate on the economics of rent determination.

natural resource cases in Pareto's thinking may explain the otherwise confusing use of the term "rent" for the problem he has in mind.

Since Pareto's day, linear programming methods have come into vogue
in dealing with the range of problems we call Paretian rent. We can, however, treat both his classes in more nearly orthodox macroeconomic terms,
by inserting limitational inputs more or less directly into aggregate production functions under conditions of long-run competitive equilibrium.
In each type of case, the *prima facie* condition for equilibrium is satisfied
(equality in the numbers of equations and unknowns in the system or
model), while the price of limitational inputs are not related to their
marginal products or v.m.p.

13.   In the first Paretian case, that of input-output fixity, marginal productivity turns out to be measurable, but to have nothing to do with
input pricing. If we take the output price as given (at unity), our production function is modified to treat the limitational input a as an intermediate product rather than a pure input:

$$x = \phi (a; b,c) = ka + F (b,c)$$

where b and c are ordinary (substitutional) inputs, and the constant

$$k \left(= \frac{x - F (b,c)}{a} \right)$$

is given. As for the modified production function F, we assume it tangent
to a linear homogeneous function at its minimum cost point (as per
Chapter 6, section 14). The adding-up theorem also applies in modified
form.

In pecuniary terms (value added) we may rewrite

$$x (1 - kp_a) = F (b,c) \tag{14.1}$$

and, by analogy with the development of Chapter 6,

$$p_b = \frac{\delta x}{\delta b} (1 - kp_a) \tag{14.2}$$

$$p_c = \frac{\delta x}{\delta c} (1 - kp_a). \tag{14.3}$$

These equations give us equality between p_b and p_c and their respective
(modified) v.m.p. However, any equality between price p_a and v.m.p.
$(= k)$ for the limitational input a is suppressed. This suppression is essential to Paretian rent theory. We have instead a modified adding-up
theorem:

$$x (1 - kp_a) = \frac{\delta F}{\delta b} b + \frac{\delta F}{\delta c} c \tag{14.4}$$

or alternatively, for a short-run case in which the unitary output price equals marginal cost but the entire product may not be distributed determinately:

$$1 - kp_a = \frac{p_b}{\frac{\delta F}{\delta b}} + \frac{p_c}{\frac{\delta F}{\delta c}} . \tag{14.4a}$$

On the supply side, we may suppose well-behaved supply functions for all inputs, limitational and substitutional alike:

$$a = S_a(p_a), \tag{14.5}$$

$$b = S_b(p_b), \tag{14.6}$$

$$c = S_c(p_c). \tag{14.7}$$

This miniature system has seven equations. Offsetting or balancing these are seven unknowns (x,a,b,c,p_a,p_b,p_c). To include the output price p as an unknown, we need only have added an output demand function. In short, we have a balanced general-equilibrium system, or rather subsystem.

14. The same is true also in the second class of Paretian cases, that of fixed proportions between inputs, but the subsystem is different. Let us denote by d the composite input $(a + k'b)$, with the constant k' given. Although separate v.m.p. of the separate inputs a and b cannot be estimated (and may not exist), the v.m.p. of the composite input d does exist, and the development resembles that of section 13.

Our aggregated production function is now

$$x = F(a,b,c) = F(c,d) \tag{14.8}$$

and we must take explicit notice of the two relations

$$d = a + k'b \quad \text{and} \quad p_d = p_a + k'p_b. \tag{14.9, 14.10}$$

Our v.m.p. relations become

$$p_c = \frac{\delta x}{\delta c} \quad \text{and} \quad p_a + k'p_b = \frac{\delta x}{\delta d}. \tag{14.11, 14.12}$$

The adding-up theorem now takes the form

$$x = \frac{\delta x}{\delta c}c + \frac{\delta x}{\delta d}(a + k'b), \tag{14.13}$$

and the three input-supply functions (14.5–14.7) hold as in section 13.

The relations (14.5–14.13) now form a nine-equation subsystem. Balancing them are nine unknowns $(x,a,b,c,d,p_a,p_b,p_c,p_d)$, which represent the volume of output and the prices and quantities of all inputs, both the "natural" original inputs and the artificial composite input d, which may comprise, for example, a machine plus its full crew. Again, we have a balanced general-equilibrium system in miniature.

15. The question may be asked, "What has all this to do with rent?" It must be admitted at the outset that the "rent" involved is not the same rent, either economic or commercial, that Ricardo or Marshall had in mind. The similarity or analogy between Paretian and, say, Ricardian rent lies in a vague "residual" notion, whereby the rent is looked upon as a differential between the value of outputs and the income of limitational inputs, all determined by ordinary market forces in a way that rent itself is not.

Perhaps the argument will become clearer if we suppose the fixity, embodied in our "Paretian" coefficients k and k', to be a matter of social determination (legislation or collective bargaining) rather than of technology in any strict sense. We may also suppose that the return to at least one productive input, say, a, is increased by such legislation or collective bargaining, so that it is p_a rather than some lower value, say p'_a, which it would have been on a substitutional market. The analogy between the differential $(p_a - p'_a)$, or dp_a, resulting from *fixed proportions* and other rents fixed by *supply inelasticity*, should be sufficiently obvious to permit an understanding of the reason for selecting the term "rent" to describe them. At the least, Ricardian, Marshallian, and Paretian rents are all incremental incomes due either to rigidities in the supply of strategic inputs to productive processes, or to rigidities in the substitution of other inputs for them.

CHAPTER FIFTEEN

Normal Profits

That Mixed and Vexed Income

1. "Profits" has meant, and continues to mean, all things to all men. To make matters worse, the profits about which A is theorizing in his ivory tower differ from whatever B is measuring for tax or accounting purposes and also from whatever C would like to see raised or lowered by legislation or regulation.

We back into this chaos by indicating five popular meanings of profits to which our chapter will be largely irrelevant:

(*1*) "Profits" comprise all nonlabor income. (In Marxian economics, only the wages of direct labor—production workers—are excluded.)

(*2*) Profits or "business incomes" comprise all implicit returns not actually paid out to other firms or to outside suppliers of inputs. (They may be measured gross or net of reserves for inventory replacement, depreciation of fixed capital, and the like. The reserves, too, may or may not be adjusted for obsolescence, price changes, and so forth.)

(*3*) The profits of an individual or an enterprise comprise the changes in his (or its) net worth in the accounting sense, insofar as they can be associated with the operations of particular business enterprises rather than with "extraneous" changes in asset values.

(*4*) *Monopoly* profits comprise all increments of entrepreneurial income traceable directly to elements of monopoly or monopsony as discussed earlier in Chapter 8. (We postpone to later sections the problem of identifying "entrepreneurship" and "entrepreneurial income" in a corporate situation.)

(*5*) *Windfall* profits (or losses) comprise all elements of entrepreneurial income, positive or negative, arising under pure competition from the slowness of adjustment to changes of all sorts. They are viewed in the textbooks as being subject to elimination by the process of long-run adjustment.

The first three of these meanings lump together disparate elements that we prefer to treat separately; the last two deal with pure residuals.

2.   What is left to form the primary subject matter of this chapter has been called "normal," "pure," and sometimes "necessary" profits under competition in the long run. Profit theory considers such questions as whether normal profits, in this sense, persist or are reduced in the long run to implicit wage, interest, and rent payments. And, if they persist, who does or should receive them?

Naive Profit Theory[1]

3.   We start from a profit theory, possibly naive but worth reconsideration, that enjoyed its heyday in elementary textbooks during the first third of the twentieth century. (Strangely enough, it springs neither from Marshall nor J. B. Clark, the *loci classici* for English-language textbook theoretical chapters of that day.[2]) It survives largely as underpinning for policy pronouncements of a capitalist-apologist variety—a fate possibly worse than death. It can be embodied in a set of five propositions:[3]

(*1*) One of the distributive shares in a competitive economy is normal profits.

(*2*) These are usually positive in the long run, even net of implicit returns to inputs supplied by entrepreneurs to their own firms.

(*3*) Profits are the return to the related entrepreneurial functions of ultimate decision-making and uncertainty-bearing. A maker of ultimate

1. Sections 3–17 of this chapter revise the writer's "Reformulation of Naive Profit Theory," *So.Ec.J.* (April 1960) .

2. Both these writers argued that profits vanish in the long run under competition, Clark more clearly than Marshall. See Alfred Marshall, *Principles of Economics,* 8th ed. (New York: Macmillan, 1920) , pp. 605 f., and J. B. Clark, *Distribution of Wealth* (New York: Macmillan, 1899) , p. 70. Over and beyond business "common sense," the source for the naive theory may be the half-forgotten American profit theorist Hawley, on whom see F. H. Knight, *Risk, Uncertainty, and Profit* (Boston: Houghton Mifflin, 1921) , pp. 41–45, and Richard M. Davis, "Frederick B. Hawley's Income Theory," *J.P.E.* (April 1953) .

3. In Weston's classification of profit theories, this "naive theory" falls in class R— "profits are rewards for bearing uncertainty and risk"—which he himself opposes. J. Fred Weston, "The Profit Concept and Theory: A Restatement," *J.P.E.* (April 1954) , p. 152. Alternative classifications may be found in Knight, *op. cit.,* ch. 2, and R. A. Gordon, "Enterprise, Profits, and the Modern Corporation," *Readings,* no. 29, p. 560.

decisions (bearer of ultimate uncertainties) is an "entrepreneur"; entrepreneurs receive all profits in the long run.

(*4*) The quantity that a firm seeks to maximize in its economic operations is the absolute size of the profit component.

(*5*) In marginalist terms, uncertainty-bearing may be regarded as a separate input or factor of production on the same footing as land, labor, or capital.

4. Of these five propositions, the last is less essential than the others. The first four propositions have intuitive appeal in a world dominated by proprietorships and partnerships. (We shall end by modifying most of them for the corporate case.) The fifth proposition, often omitted from more elementary presentations, represents an attempt to fit profit into the Procrustean bed of marginalism. (We shall abandon it in favor of another formulation in section 13 below.)

Eclipse of the Naive Theory

5. Despite its intuitive plausibility and apologetic usefulness, naive profit theory, as outlined above, was falling into disrepute even before 1929. We assemble here some of the considerations brought against it, and outline some of the alternative positions constructed as rivals to it:

(*1*) In point of time, the initial crack in the structure was implicit in the "adding-up theorem" (6.4). This theorem appears to show that, with a linear homogeneous production function or in conditions of long-run competitive equilibrium, there is simply nothing left over for profits after all explicit and implicit inputs are paid their v.m.p.

Alternatively, the adding-up theorem seemed to require the elevation of uncertainty-bearing to the status of a separate input, as in section 3–(*5*) above. The most ambitious effort in this direction was by Pigou, in his *Economics of Welfare*.[4] This construction was highly tentative and likewise artificial—disembodied uncertainty-bearing being a kind of grin without a cat—and was not followed up seriously.

(*2*) As these formal difficulties became apparent, two attacks on the naive theory developed within the family of neoclassical economics, with the names of Schumpeter and Knight the most prominent.

The Schumpeterian attack came first. It reduced both uncertainty and profit to consequences of innovation—no innovation, no profit (as well as no interest, according to our Chapter 12, section 10). It also defined

4. A. C. Pigou, *op. cit.*, 4th ed. (London: Macmillan, 1932), pp. 161–164, 771–781.

entrepreneurship as the introduction of innovations, replacing the normal or necessary profits of the naive theory with the windfalls of the innovator.[5] Monopoly profits and similar gains, when not traceable to innovation past or present, are defined out of the picture as rents or surpluses rather than as profits.

Knight's position, stated originally in *Risk, Uncertainty and Profit,* provides the basis for the more sophisticated versions of contemporary orthodoxy in profit theory. To paraphrase Knight and his followers (among whom Weston has spelled out his own position most fully),[6] profits stem from uncertainty or noninsurable risk. They pervade the entire society. They are borne not by some special entrepreneurial class but by everyone in the economy. Uncertainty-bearing results in increments or decrements to all incomes from whatever source derived.[7] The positive increments may or may not, in the event, overbalance the decrements due to unfavorable disappointment of expectations. These increments (net of the decrements) Knight calls profits and losses. (They include, for example, "compensating differences" in the wage rates for dangerous, unhealthy, and transitory jobs.) Such elements of profit are not only unplanned but unanticipated. Knight therefore regards them as differences between disequilibrium and equilibrium incomes, or between incomes *ex post* and *ex ante,* rather than as compensations for uncertainty-bearing or any other activity. There is no separate profit component in the income distribution; there are only profit elements in all types of income.[8]

Two corollaries render this theory less vacuous, if no more refutable, than it appears at first glance. One corollary: The attempt to locate within corporate bodies "entrepreneurs" with paramount claims to profit is to look in dark rooms at midnight for black cats that are not there. A second corollary: It is meaningless to speak of a firm maximizing "profits" except

---

5. *Theory of Economic Development,* trans. Redvers Opie (Cambridge, Mass.: Harvard University Press, 1934) , *passim.* In the Weston classification, this theory is placed in category E—"profits are payments for the exercise of managerial or entrepreneurial functions."

Knight pointed out in *Risk, Uncertainty, and Profit (op. cit.,* pp. 32–41) and in "Profit" (*Readings,* no. 27, p. 540) some anticipations of Schumpeter's profit theory in J. B. Clark, *Distribution of Wealth, op. cit.,* ch. 6, pp. 25 f.

6. In the Weston classification, Knight and his followers are placed in category U— "profits are deviations arising from uncertainty" between incomes *ex post* and *ex ante.*

7. J. F. Weston, "Profit as the Payment for the Function of Uncertainty-Bearings," *Journ. of Bus.* (April 1949) ; "Enterprise and Profit," *Journ. of Bus.* (July 1949) ; "A Generalized Uncertainty Theory of Profit" *A.E.R.* (March 1950) ; "The Profit Concept and Theory," *op. cit.*

8. However, "in the case of the owner of the business the difference is the entire income, since under perfect equilibrium the owner as such would have no functions and receive no income" (Knight, "Profit," *op. cit.,* p. 537) .

as shorthand for "enterprise net income" to all implicit inputs taken together.

6.   The naive theory appeared unequal to the ancillary function of identifying entrepreneurship or entrepreneurs in a corporate regime. It included no unequivocal notions on this score. Some versions treat entrepreneurship as primarily a matter of uncertainty-bearing, others as a matter of decision-making, others as a matter of organization of the productive inputs, and yet others as necessary combinations of a number of the above activities.[9] When, as in the modern Western corporation, most ultimate decision-making and input-organization came to rest on salaried managers with no necessary ownership interest, while ultimate uncertainty-bearing came to rest upon stockholders who might be absentees, the distribution of the usufruct is difficult to rationalize with any combination of "uncertainty-bearing," "decision-making," or "factor-organizing" principles. With ownership separated largely from control, to use the catch phrase, any theory of profit that assumes them united now appeared both apologetic and anachronistic, part of "the folklore of capitalism."[10] Nor is a substitute theory that allocates a firm's entrepreneurial functions to that artificial personage, the firm itself, much more helpful.[11] (This theory gives no clue to the allocation of profits among the natural persons comprising the corporate ownership and control groups. It relegates such allocation to the indeterminacy of corporate infighting.)

Largely as a result of the corporate diffusion of entrepreneurship, there has arisen, largely outside the neoclassical family, a set of sociological or institutional profit theories. These take several forms,[12] although no in-

9. For detailed bibliography see Weston, "Enterprise and Profit," *op. cit.*, pp. 158 f.

10. Inapplicability to the corporate regime is a basis of, among others, Gordon's attack upon traditional profit theory (*op. cit.*, pp. 555–570) .

11. James H. Stauss, "The Entrepreneur: The Firm," *J.P.E.* (June 1944) ; Richard M. Davis, "The Current State of Profit Theory," *A.E.R.* (June 1952) , pp. 251 f. In the Weston classification, this strain of thought is related to category Q—"profits are unimputable quasi-rents" ("Profit Concept and Theory," pp. 152, 166–168) .

12. Examples include Paul P. Streeten, "The Theory of Profit," *Manchester School* (September 1949) ; R. G. Hawtrey. "The Nature of Profit," *Ec.J.* (September 1951) ; Jean Marchal, "Construction of a New Theory of Profit," *A.E.R.* (September 1951) ; Peter L. Bernstein, "Profit Theory—Where Do We Go From Here?" *Q.J.E.* (August 1952) ; Anatol Murad, "Questions for Profit Theory," *Am. J. Econ. and Soc.* (October 1953) .

What we call sociological or institutional theories include Weston's categories A, MC, MN, and W—"profits are the difference between accounting revenues and costs," "profits are gains from 'contrived' monopolies and predatory activities," "profits are surpluses or rents resulting from . . . 'natural' barriers to entry," and "profits are payments derived from the ownership of productive assets" ("The Profit Concept and Theory," p. 152) .

stitutionalist Schumpeter or sociological Knight seems yet to have founded a viable school. Writers of these persuasions agree on identifying profits with accountants' "business net income,"[13] including all returns to implicit inputs, whether distributed, retained, or paid in corporate income and profits taxes. They often stress, at the same time, class distinctions between "profit receivers" and such other classes as "wage earners" and "rentiers."[14] (From class considerations arises the main justification for lumping profit receivers' diverse income types together under the single head of profit.) For some of these writers, too, the very notions of entrepreneurship and pure competition smack of apologetics, not science.[15] Their views of profit accordingly include monopoly gains and "exploitation" theorizing in the Marxist tradition.

7. It is difficult to profess full satisfaction with Schumpeter, Knight, or the institutional writers. Payments, generally regarded as profits rather than rents, persist without apparent justification in Schumpeterian innovation. Businessmen and promoters persist in estimating profits *ex ante* despite Knightian usage, and the public continues to think of profits as the special income of a special class. At the same time, accountants' "net income" combines elements so numerous, and weighted so differently in different firms, as to cast doubt on the analytical value of the institutional theories. In this predicament, when both sophistication and iconoclasm fail, can nothing more be done with simple-minded naivete?

Reformulation of the Naive Theory

8. It is particularly important in profit theory to clarify one's assumptions. For our own part, we are considering a society with constant population, tastes, natural resources, and social institutions (of a capitalist sort), and with an unchanging spectrum of technical alternatives for production. The economy is purely competitive, with complete divisibility of both inputs and outputs, mobility and standardization sufficient to assure a single price for all inputs and outputs on each market over each suffi-

13. Contemporary Western accountants shun the controversial term "profit" in favor of the neutral "earnings" or "income" (cf. Weston, "The Profit Concept and Theory," p. 165). Soviet accountants and economists, by contrast, use "profits" freely, and theorize regarding their role in a socialist society.

14. On this point, they were anticipated by, among others, Knight: "Under the enterprise system, a special social class, the business men, direct economic activity; . . . the great mass of the population merely furnish them with productive services, placing their persons and property at the disposal of this class" (*Risk, Uncertainty, and Profit,* p. 271).

15. Marchal, and particularly Murad, are examples.

ciently small unit of time; and full knowledge of existing prices and qualities. The society is not, however, stationary. The capital stock may be accumulating or decumulating. The perfection of knowledge does not extend beyond present prices and qualities, either to cost and production relations or to the future. (We assume all elasticities of expectations[16] to be unitary or fractional, for stability's sake.) We have, in short, uncertainty without innovation.

What is this uncertainty about? Primarily, it is about two matters just mentioned: (1) The amount, nature, and consequences of capital accumulation (even with no change in the spectrum of techniques[17]); and (2) the forms and coefficients of cost and production functions. (We need not forget what we all know of the vagaries of weather, the breakdown of machinery, the incidence of illness and accident, or the variability of motivation and morale.) We are concerned only with that subset of uncertainties that cannot be transformed efficiently into hedgeable, insurable, or otherwise transferable risks.

Following tradition, we consider only a competitive and stable state of things, and only the long run. Imperfect competition, temporary instabilities, and short-run windfalls lie at the heart of concrete problems, but we offer no contribution to their unsatisfactory treatment in economic theory. It also seems desirable to eschew the classical commingling of profits with interest, the Marxian commingling of profits with other elements of surplus value, and the accountant's commingling of profits with implicit returns to any and all inputs.

9. From this compromising sort of framework we derive a compromising sort of profit-theory. Let us divide economic uncertainties, at the outset, into those giving rise to profits and those affecting other incomes. This differentiation, if it stands up, will permit reestablishment of normal profits, positive or negative, as a separate income share. It might produce a "specialized" uncertainty theory, as distinguished from the "generalized" ones of Weston's category U (see above, footnote 6). Given such a specialized uncertainty theory, we can try to make peace with the adding-up theorem, consider the meaningfulness of "profit maximizing," and identify "entrepreneurship" in a corporate setting.

16. An elasticity of expectations is the elasticity of an expected *future* price relative to the *present* one. J. R. Hicks, *Value and Capital,* 2d ed. (Oxford: Oxford University Press, 1946), pp. 205–207.

17. Knight has stated, "Many changes, such as the steady growth of population and capital, are fairly predictable, and to a corresponding extent do not occasion imperfect competition or profit" ("Profit," p. 841; compare *Risk, Uncertainty and Profit,* pp. 35–38). This is more nearly true for the economy as a whole than for particular branches or trades.

But how can uncertainties be divided? Of the thousand natural shocks that flesh is heir to, those compensated by profit are neither the most pervasive nor the most significant. Considerations of uncertainty alter, in both directions, the supply and demand functions for all inputs and outputs; their combined net effect on any price or income is highly uncertain.

We propose to consider profit as compensation for merely that subset of uncertainties arising from *lack of any contractual claim to recompense* either per hour of labor, per "piece" of output, or per unit of land or capital supplied. We concentrate, in other words, upon the incomes of persons who accept, as residual claimants, part or all of whatever is left after contractual claims are honored and contractual claimants paid.[18] We do not imply, at one extreme, that contractual claims are necessarily either honored or enforced. Varying degrees of uncertainty (called "premia" on loan markets) attest to the fact that particular contracts may be neither honored nor enforceable, except at substantial cost. Neither do we imply, at the other extreme, the tautological limitation of the profit receiver's risk to the risk of not making his profit. He bears the additional risk of loss on income account, that is, a smaller income than his inputs would have brought contractually. He may also lose on capital account by the writing down or wiping out of his assets, when a debt investment would have protected him.

Let us, then, reclassify inputs for the special purposes of this chapter into "contractual" and "entrepreneurial" categories, according to whether their incomes are or are not determined contractually.[19] This terminology,

---

18. Knight presents a similar view as a "compromise position" between his own "theoretical" view of profits and a "practical" one that identifies economic profit with "business net income." ("Profit," pp. 537 f.; likewise Weston, "Profit Concept and Theory," pp. 167 f.)

Knight also points out that profits (as defined by him) may be concealed in inflated (contractual) payments to "insiders," while Weston objects that *all* incomes would become gross profits if institutional arrangements should eliminate the possibility of contractual claims. Knight's objection, however, seems to assume imperfect competition; Weston's noncontractual world seems inconsistent with the operation of a capitalistic economy.

19. This classification is not watertight. We may consider a few intermediate cases: (a) The *preferred stockholder* has a contingent contractual claim, like the piece-worker or the salesman on commission. (b) The *convertible bondholder* has a contractual claim, with the privilege of exchanging it for an entrepreneurial one in the future. (c) The *salaried partner* provides entrepreneurial services, since his claim is not in fact enforceable against the partnership in being. If the partnership is dissolved (with his salary in arrears) he may shift to a salaried position vis-à-vis any successor firm. (d) The *executive on a bonus list* has a contractual claim to his salary. His claim to his bonus is entrepreneurial until it has been voted, and contractual thereafter, like the common stockholder's claim to dividends. (e) The *participating preferred stockholder* is in position (a) as a preferred stockholder and in position (d) as regards his participation.

while not implying that all contractual obligations are honored fully, identifies entrepreneurship exclusively with the *extra* precariousness of a noncontractual legal position, rather than with responsibilities innovational, organizational, or managerial. (In a partnership, entrepreneurship is divided among all partners, silent or active. In a corporation, it is allocated to holders of common stock, coupon-clippers included.[20]) Managers and directors are not, in this terminology, entrepreneurs except as they are also stockholders. Still less is the entrepreneur "the firm" or any other entity abstracted from the people encompassed by it.

10. Entrepreneurial inputs frequently have highly imperfect markets, in which different prices (or shadow prices) prevail simultaneously. This is obviously true not only when these inputs are unstandardized; it is also true for special reasons peculiar to entrepreneurship. Many "transactions" are implicit, with an input supplier dealing with himself in his other capacity of businessman (input demander). Demand and supply are identical, and neutral equilibrium prevails. In addition, the "price" or "rate of return" of the entrepreneurial service is seldom, in these cases, set or recorded; it is merely a consensual expectation or shadow price. Expectations are, moreover, imprecise; even when buyer and seller deal at arm's length, they may hold different expectations. Geometrically, any "equilibrium position" involves an unusually large range or zone rather than a single point. We shall, however, use the single-point approximation, on the theory that[21]

> though it may be difficult to read the lessons of an individual trader's experience, those of a whole trade can never be completely hidden, and cannot be hidden at all for very long . . . There is a general agreement among business men that the average rate of profits in a trade cannot rise or fall much without general attention being attracted to the change before long. And though it may sometimes be a more difficult task for a business man than for a skilled labourer to find out whether he could improve his prospects by changing his trade, yet the business man has great opportunities for discovering what can be found out about the present and future of other trades; and if he should wish to change his trade, he will generally be able to do so more easily than the skilled workman could.

Let us accordingly consider in turn each panel of Figure 15.1. The left-hand panel relates the *internal* (implicit) supply and demand for some

---

20. One is reminded of the concept of "drone entrepreneurship" devised by Danhof in a different setting. Compare Yale Brozen, "Entrepreneurship and Technical Change" in Harold F. Williamson and John A. Buttrick (eds.), *Economic Development: Principles and Patterns* (New York: Prentice-Hall, 1954), p. 205.

21. Marshall, *Principles of Economics* (8th ed.), *op. cit.*, pp. 607 f.

entrepreneurial input *e* to its anticipated gross return. The "supply" and
"demand" functions are identical, since each entrepreneur as input demander is "buying" from himself as input supplier. The combined supply-
and-demand function is accordingly represented by a single curve *DS*. This
function is drawn sloping upward, in accordance with the observation
that high profits result in increased business population, increased internal
investment, and similar signs of increased use of productive inputs under
noncontractual conditions.

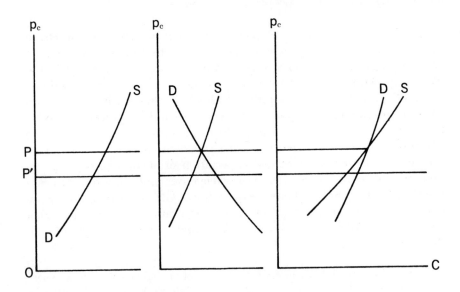

Figure 15.1

The center panel represents the long-term *external* supply and demand
for the same entrepreneurial input *e*. These functions are drawn conventionally, and the ordinate *OP* of their intersection indicates equilibrium
gross profit.

The right-hand panel is the horizontal sum of the other two. It is drawn
with the *internal* market dominant, so that both aggregate supply and demand functions slope upward. (The demand function slopes more steeply,
as a Hicksian stability condition.) This is a common state of affairs where
unincorporated businesses and closed corporations rule. For the publicly-
traded equity securities of corporations, the external market is usually
dominant, and the aggregate demand function slopes downward. (We
remember from Chapter 12 that a company's demand function for equity
capital is manifested by its supply of securities, and the stockholders' supply of equity capital by their demand for securities.)

The aggregate supply-demand functions cross at P (an average value in a zone or range). This makes P a gross profit, or gross return to the entrepreneurial input e. Let P' (on Fig. 15.1) be the return to the physically identical input in contractual uses. (We treat P' as a constant, unchanging with the amount of e used entrepreneurially.)[22] P then represents an implicit contractual return to the entrepreneurial input, and PP' represents the net or normal profit we seek to explain.

In Figure 15.1, P exceeds P', and normal profit PP' is positive. It might equally well have been zero or negative. Its sign depends on many things. What is the relative strength of the "insurance" motives for uncertainty aversion, as against the "gambling" motives for uncertainty preference?[23] We assume that the former motives are stronger at the margin, for entrepreneurs who bear uncertainty as well as for professors who only write about it. This assumption supports the results indicated in the diagram.

11. Positive normal profits may mean that the entrepreneurial supply of inputs need *not* be associated with putative advantages like empire building, tax avoidance, or being-one's-own-boss. (For the small-scale stockholder, no such association exists.) Or, if these attractions of the entrepreneurial way of life are present, they do not suffice to outweigh the aversion to the incremental uncertainty-bearing involved in noncontractual input supplies. The demanding firms or industries may also be facing deflation, obsolescence, or some other prospect making a contractual position, rather than an entrepreneurial alternative, peculiarly attractive to the suppliers of inputs.

On the other hand, to repeat, nothing prevents $P < P'$ either for another entrepreneurial service in the same industries, for the same entrepreneurial service in other industries, or for entrepreneurial services as a group in competitive industries as a group. This may mean that supply of entrepreneurial services is associated strongly with some or all of the attractions mentioned in the last paragraph.[24] Alternatively, it may mean that entrepreneurs, like gamblers, see uncertainty-bearing as a positive pleasure. Or it may mean that the demanding firms or industries face prospects that, like inflation, render entrepreneurial positions particularly attractive to input suppliers.

22. Dropping this assumption would require redrawing of the horizontal line through P' as downward-sloping, to allow for the effects of a falling v.m.p. of input e.

23. Compare, in a quite different context, Milton Friedman and L. J. Savage, "The Utility Analysis of Choices Involving Risk" in Stigler and Boulding (eds.), *Readings in Price Theory* (Homewood, Ill.: Irwin, 1952) no. 3.

24. Peter L. Bernstein, "Profit Theory" (*op. cit.*, pp. 409–411) cites personal banking experience to support the familiar proposition that many small businessmen and farmers accept deliberately, and with full knowledge of alternatives, situations of negative normal profit.

12.   It can also be shown, with the aid of elementary indifference analysis, how a firm's budget for a given productive service may be allocated between contractual and entrepreneurial sources of supply. Both axes of Figure 15.2 measure quantities of a single productive input available to the individual firm on either contractual or entrepreneurial terms. Quantities supplied contractually, at explicit prices on a competitive input market, are measured along the horizontal axis. Quantities supplied entrepreneurially, at implicit prices, are measured along the vertical axis. The family of price lines C_i, drawn with slopes of less than 45 degrees to the horizontal, imply in this case a higher price for entrepreneurial supplies. The family of indifference curves I_i reflect no differences in the productivity of inputs raised by the two methods, since no differences are assumed to exist. Rather, the curves reflect a variety of considerations in the

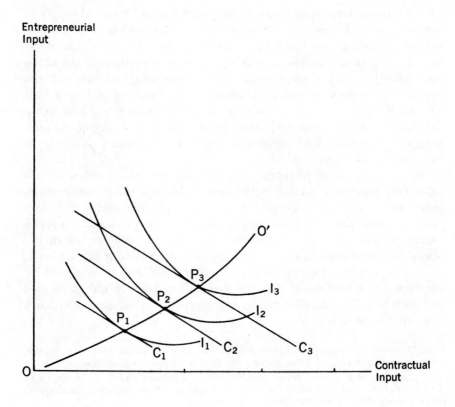

Figure 15.2

minds of management, indicating pervasive uncertainty. There is usually the fear of diluting both control and profits if too many inputs are acquired entrepreneurially. There is usually also the fear of excessive overheads in bad times if too many inputs are acquired contractually. A firm may prefer a "wrong" size with the "right" proportions of entrepreneurial inputs to a right size with the wrong proportions.

A near-conventional form of indifference curves, with some suggestion of closure around an optimum size, appears plausible, and is adopted in the diagram. The points of tangency P_i between price lines and indifference curves represent optimal divisions of different outlays for the input in question. The expansion path OO', connecting the P_i, shows how this optimum proportion may vary with the total outlay on this input. (If this proportion does not vary, OO' is a radius vector.)

With any outlay on this input, a weighted average price can be computed for the input as a whole. This weighted average will generally differ from the explicit contractual market price. In our example, the weighted average price is the higher of the two.

13. Much analysis of the cost of capital can be reformulated along similar lines, but with slightly different assumptions and results. Both axes of Figure 15.3 deal with money capital, the Keynesian "finance." The horizontal axis measures debt and the vertical axis equity capital. Instead of price lines we have iso-cost curves C_i, drawn with downward concavities such that the relative cost of debt increases with the debt-equity ratio, and vice versa, except for the presence of a range—the Modigliani-Miller[25]

---

25. Franco Modigliani and Merton H. Miller, "The Cost of Capital, Corporation Finance, and the Theory of Investment," *A.E.R.* (June 1958). These writers would themselves extend what we have called the "Modigliani-Miller range" to the entire spectrum of choice, in the absence of discriminatory tax treatment of dividends as against interest. A simplified version of their argument is as follows: Let V be the value of a firm, comprising debt securities D and equities E. There are two states of the world, a and b, with probabilities p_a and p_b which add to unity. The firm's income is Y, and the cost of capital ρ is the capitalization rate relating Y and V. Using these symbols, we have

$$V_a = D_a + E_a \qquad V_b = D_b + E_b \qquad V = p_a V_a + p_b V_b = D + E.$$

It follows that

$$V = p_a (D_a + E_a) + p_b (D_b + E_b) = (p_a D_a + p_b D_b) + (p_a E_a + p_b E_b) = D + E$$

which is independent of the debt-equity ratio D/E.

We also have:

$$V = \frac{1}{\rho} (p_a Y_a + p_b Y_b)$$

Since neither the ρ nor the Y terms are affected by the debt-equity ratio, it follows that the capitalization rate of cost of capital ρ is independent of this ratio whenever V is.

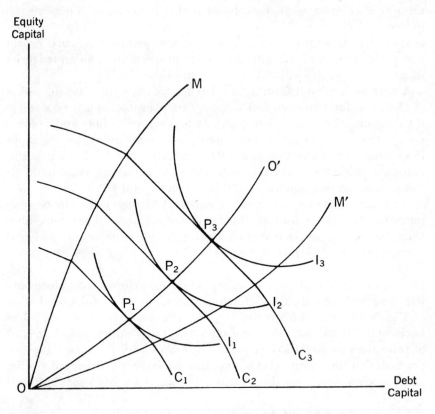

Figure 15.3

or M-M range, bounded by *OM* and *OM'*—where the concavity does not differ significantly from zero. Within this range, moreover, the iso-cost curves become price lines parallel to each other and with slopes close to 45 degrees. This implies local independence of the average capital cost and the debt-equity ratio, with both debt and equity prices presumably above market interest rates by reason of uncertainty premia. These premia are related, in the debt case, to high debt-equity ratios, and in the equity case, to the lack of contractual protection.

Reconciliation with the Adding-Up Theorem

14. We have yet to answer the question of how normal profits can be paid at all. We are dealing with long-run competitive equilibrium and with production at minimum average cost. If each input's suppliers re-

ceive the v.m.p. of that input, the entire output is distributed. How can we simultaneously postulate differentials for profit, either positive or negative? Is there no inconsistency involved?

Fortunately, the weighted average of contractual and entrepreneurial input prices (section 12) assists us in this dilemma. We may look on the competitive entrepreneur as adjusting the use of productive inputs so as to equate their v.m.p. not only to their contractual market prices, but to weighted averages of contractual and entrepreneurial prices, whenever any entrepreneurial inputs are used and whenever the two prices diverge.

This simple device avoids conflict between the persistence of normal profits and the adding-up theorem. It is also consistent with the tendency of so-called "marginal" firms to concentrate on enterpreneurial inputs like "unpaid family labor" and to avoid contractual inputs. This tendency is generally criticized as inefficient; it is an aspect of the losses these marginal enterprises are earning. It is good marginalism for marginal firms to consider entrepreneurial inputs as costing less than the contractual market prices for the same inputs, especially if those inputs would be unemployed at going market input prices, as is the case of much involuntary (disguised unemployed) enterpreneurial labor.

15. A welfare complication results from all this. When the competitive firm expands or contracts its output, the proportions between contractual and entrepreneurial inputs normally change, unless OO' (Figs. 15.2 and 15.3) is linear. If the proportions do change (with OO' curvilinear), the weighted average price of some inputs will change with the firm's output. Even under pure competition, then, the analysis of the firm's expansion and contraction involves the monopsony considerations of Chapter 8. These may include exploitation of (contractual) input suppliers, and output changes inspired by input price changes as well as by "economic efficiency."

The same is true for adjustments of technique, by which contractual, entrepreneurial, and "mixed" inputs must be substituted for each other. Here again, pure and imperfect competition move closer together, in a way that undermines to some extent the conventional welfare economist's preference for pure competition.

Suppose, to make these complications more nearly concrete, that entrepreneurial inputs for a firm all have implicit (shadow) prices higher than the corresponding contractual ones, and that input b always has a higher entrepreneurial component than input a. Suppose also that efficient expansion requires a shift of the firm's input mix in the direction of b. The firm's expansion then causes its input-price ratio p_b/p_a to rise against it, as in the case of an industry for which b is a "specialized" input. The firm will expand less, or contract more, than is required for optimum resource allocation, and it will always operate below its theoretical optimal scale, in order to economize on input b. It will also tend to use too little b and too much a at any given scale of output, since substitution of b for a, even without expansion, raises the ratio p_b/p_a.

If b is capital (machinery) and a is labor, our firm would therefore mechanize less completely than efficiency requires, thus also choosing a smaller scale and a smaller output x.

On Optimizing Profits

16.   We have listed (section 3 in this chapter) five propositions as embodying the substance of naive profit theory. We have accepted or modified the propositions labeled (*1–3*) and rejected proposition (*5*).[26] We have said nothing about proposition (*4*), that firms seek to maximize profits.

We state three views boldly, for later diagrammatic comparison. The naive one we have seen already—the rational entrepreneur maximizing his net profit. Sophisticated (Knightian) profit theory is of firms maximizing net receipts[27]—in our terms, total return to their implicit or entrepreneurial inputs. (It is not immediately clear how this is related to Knight's definition of profits as a nonmaximizable disequilibrium difference between incomes *ex post* and *ex ante*.) In organization theory, the firm maximizes no single quantifiable variable whatever, but rather satisfies simultaneously its multiple goals, which usually include satisfactory net income, size, growth, citizenship, etc.

26. Proposition (*1*) we have accepted; proposition (*2*) we have modified only to allow for "normal losses." Proposition (*3*) is modified more substantially. We have discarded decision-making and generalized uncertainty-bearing as bases for profit. We have limited uncertainty-bearing (in relation to profit theory) to the assumption of noncontractual positions in input supply. And as for entrepreneurship, it is scattered among all noncontractual input suppliers.

Weston, representing the Knightian position, agrees with this treatment of decision-making but not of entrepreneurship: "The principles explaining the compensation of [ultimate decision-making] in a firm are similar to the principles explaining the compensation for other services . . . The exercise of judgment may be sold on a fixed-price basis or on a variable-price basis." However, "non-contractual income receivers [may be] identified as entrepreneurs. The application of this term . . . to a use in which functional activities perform no role is likely to result in confusion." (Generalized Uncertainty Theory of Profit," pp. 48, 47.)

27. Thus Milton Friedman, "The Methodology of Positive Economics," in *Essays on Positive Economics* (Chicago: University of Chicago Press, 1953), p. 21: "Under a wide range of circumstances, individual firms behave *as if* they were seeking rationally to maximize their expected returns (generally if misleadingly called 'profits')." And, as a footnote to this passage, " 'Profits' are a result of uncertainty and . . . cannot be deliberately maximized in advance."

17.   These three alternatives by no means exhaust their field. (Sales maximization, for example, is an alternative stressed particularly by Baumol.) [28] They do, however, lead to different results, which can be compared readily on a diagram like Figure 15.4.[29] The horizontal axis of this diagram measures units of the undifferentiated entrepreneurial input e. The vertical axis measures residual entrepreneurial income y, gross in some cases and net in others. The expected results of various alternatives open to the entrepreneur (who is supplying inputs entrepreneurially) are plotted on three functions, OX, OY, and OZ. OX is a path of expected gross profit; it has a maximum value R when A units of entrepreneurial input are supplied. The ray OY measures return to the same service supplied contractually to outside firms under competitive conditions. The function OZ, or expected normal profits, is the vertical differences between OX and OY. It too has a maximum at S (below R) where B (less than A) units of entrepreneurial input are supplied.[30]

According to the naive theory, the firm will aim at Q, with coordinates (B,S), at which the firm's net profit is maximized. According to the sophisticated theory, more entrepreneurial input will be used if it is available, and the firm will aim at P, with coordinates (A,R), at which the firm's income is maximized. The two theories give the same result when the quantity of entrepreneurial inputs is fixed at some value less than or equal to B. (This may be the case Knight and his followers have in mind.)

Let us now introduce a set of indifference curves I_i, combining a reluctance to supply inputs entrepreneurially—at least beyond a certain point—with a preference for a higher over a lower income from entrepreneurial inputs. Geometrically, the curves slope upward with upward concavity (rising m.r.s.). In economic terms, this construction may illustrate not only an aversion to the bearing of entrepreneurial uncertainty, but also tax considerations, devotion to the rentier's irresponsibility and "quiet life," smallness of scale as an end in itself, or the labor-leisure choices associated with backward-bending labor supply functions in Chapter 9.

There is, in any event, an "optimizing" tangency point π, with coordinates (β,Σ), which we suggest the firm may set as a goal. It is generally southwest of P, involving smaller entrepreneurial supplies of services than

28. William J. Baumol, *Business Behavior, Value and Growth* (New York: Macmillan, 1959), ch. 6.

29. This diagram is based on Tibor Scitovsky, "A Note on Profit Maximization and Its Implications," in Stigler and Boulding, *op. cit.*, fig. 2, p. 354.

30. An elementary generalization of this proposition has many applications: Let $u = f(x)$ be a function with negative second derivatives over the relevant range, and let $v = g(x)$ be any monotone increasing function. Let u have a maximum at x_1 such that $f'(x_1) = 0$, and let $(u - v)$ have a maximum at x_2 such that $f'(x_2) - g'(x_2) = 0$. Then $x_1 > x_2$, from the negative sign of $f''(x)$ and the positive sign of $g'(x)$.

the sophisticated theory indicates. We cannot generalize about the relation between π and Q, or rather Q', which is the projection, on the gross income function OX, of the point Q that the naive theory indicates as the firm's target. On Figure 15.4, π lies between P and Q' on OX; it may well be less than either alternative.

18. An interpretation of an organization theory or satifizing position may also be presented on the same diagram (Fig. 15.4). Suppose that the

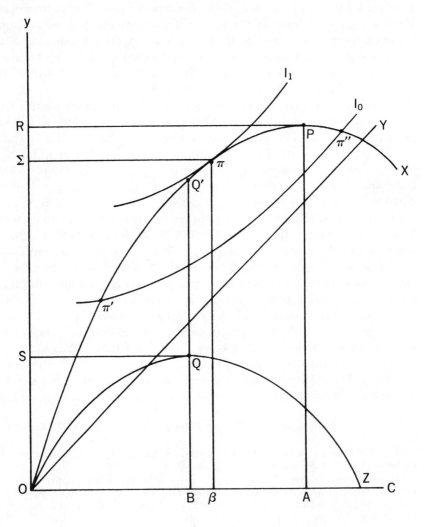

Figure 15.4

firm can fulfill its various goals with reasonable organizational comfort and security by any combination of entrepreneurial inputs and entrepreneurial income on or above a particular indifference curve I_0, which must at least touch OX if the firm is to remain viable. Suppose further that I_0 does in fact cross OX at two points π' and π'', lying, respectively, left and right of π. Then, according to our simplification of organization theory, any point along OX between π' and π'' is a priori as acceptable as any other. Choice between them is a matter of historical accident, rule of thumb, or some additional criterion. The professional bias of the theoretical economist tends to hope for something to narrow the range of "satisfizing" behavior. Baumol's revenue-maximizing hypothesis, for example, may be interpreted as suggesting that the neighborhood immediately left of π'' is more likely to be selected than that immediately right of π'.

Figure 15.4 does not permit depiction of a choice to maximize either gross or net profit *per unit of entrepreneurial input.* This is because OX and OY are drawn concave downward, and pass through the origin O. Inclusion of an inflection point, or permitting OZ to cross the horizontal axis to the right of O, would permit this rather unrealistic choice to be diagrammed also.

19.   This discussion of the goals of a firm has ignored external pressure for profit-maximizing. At least two important sorts of external pressure can operate in this direction. One source originates in the market for equity securities, and the other from the investment policies of any conglomerate or combine to which the firm may belong.

Stockholders dissatisfied with management policy on profit-maximizing, or anything else,[31] can register their protests by selling their shares and investing in other assets, including consumption goods. When enough stockholders sell enough shares, share prices are affected adversely. This reflects on management. It may even expose management control to raiding and take-over by minority interests, or by complete outsiders to the firm.

A second pressure to maximize profits exists if the firm is part of a combine or conglomerate. Part or all of the total profits of the combine members are usually pooled by some central office or headquarters and then redistributed for internal investment—to whatever members promise the most profitable use, which need not be those members who have contributed these profits in the first place! If a firm in such a system wants size or growth through internal investment, it must also provide the profits to

31. The sale of securities is the stockholder's (owner's) main protection, in particular, against appropriation of profits by "insiders" (management) in salaries and bonuses.

justify such investment, as against alternate investments, on some capital-budgeting basis.

The issues and their importance are matters for empirical testing. At the level of the present discussion, the naive theory of profit maximization seems to require modification primarily from notions of optimizing profits and of allowing for the variability of the entrepreneurial inputs, however profits themselves may be defined and estimated.

Profits on Internal Investment

20.   Among the most important entrepreneurial inputs are the reinvested net incomes of the firm itself. The legitimacy of further earnings on such internal investment, particularly "profits" above the going rate of interest, has been called into question for large corporations with substantial separation of ownership from management. The legitimacy of profits on internal investment comes into question in connection with collective bargaining, price fixing in regulated industries, general price control, undistributed-profits taxation, and compensation for nationalized industrial facilities.

The argument against legitimacy is simple, not to say simple-minded. The funds for internal investment came originally from consumers who were charged "too much" and workers who were paid "too little." The abstinence of ordinary saving and the risks of ordinary entrepreneurial investment are, for these funds, largely hypothetical. Management does not bear these burdens completely, because it is not management's money that is being invested. The owners do not usually bear them consciously; they neither pass on the internal investment decision, nor receive even temporary personal title to the funds invested. Consumers and workers, after being squeezed to provide profits for internal investment, are, it seems, squeezed again to produce profits on the investment they provided in the first place. Does this not add insult to injury?

But the actual distinction between internal and external investment is usually weaker than the last paragraph implies. If, instead of being invested internally, funds had been paid in dividends to owners who had then decided to reinvest them in the same companies, or in others equally "exploitative," the formal argument of the last paragraph would have failed, but the condition of consumers and workers would not have been changed. Also, we should not exaggerate the separation of ownership from control (see the arguments of section 19) .

Insofar as these arguments are correct, "the separation of ownership and control" makes an attractive slogan and little more. The phrase should not be worked too hard against internal investment, if the real problem is excess or monopoly profits.

21.   We can do little more than speculate on the macroeconomic results if profits on internal investment were first illegitimized, and then controlled out of existence. Prices could be cut in the industries affected directly; they would probably fall in other industries competitive in demand with these firms, or using their outputs as raw materials for further production. It is, however, by no means certain that any general price index would fall or that total consumption would rise in real terms. Suppose, for example, that price p_i were lowered for output i. Demand for i is inelastic, so that less is spent upon it than before. Income freed from buying i is spent on j, which is in inelastic supply. Its price p_j rises by a higher percentage than p_i has fallen. As a result, the index number of (p_i, p_j) rises, while the total $x_i + x_j$, evaluated at either beginning or ending prices, may actually fall.

Total investment demand would probably fall, since many companies cannot, and others will not, raise funds externally for investment projects that they could otherwise finance out of profits. It is at least doubtful whether the fall in investment (demand for loanable funds) would suffice to keep the interest rate from rising in the face of the concurrent decline in business saving (supply of loanable funds). If the interest rate rises, further declines in investment could be expected to follow.

The combined effect on private-sector income and employment would probably be unfavorable, since we are opposing a small and questionable rise in consumption to a certain fall in investment. The probability of unfavorable effects is even higher on private-sector growth, since growth is usually related to investment rather than to consumption.

It seems to follow that disallowance of profits on private internal investment will require compensatory expansion in the public sector if contractionary effects on income, employment, and growth are to be avoided. If the economy is overheated at the outset, or if disallowance is part of a broader socialization program, these objections lose most or all of their force.

CHAPTER SIXTEEN

Macrodistribution Theory:
The Summing Up

Introduction

1. "Everyone" bewails the unsatisfactory state of distribution theory. One source of tears has been the scientific and ideological deficiencies of the general theories of input demand and supply, as applied to individual input categories. A second source has been a persistent discrepancy between the distributional categories of economic theory, economic statistics, and the real world, a discrepancy that interferes with quantitative verification at numerous points. The main complaint, however, has been that the various pieces of distribution theory do not add up to any generally usable, generally accepted, or generally verified whole. This "adding-up problem" is the problem of macrodistribution.

Macrodistribution, then, is about the relative shares of various functional classes in functional income distribution. It should be distinguished particularly from microdistribution, which is about the pricing of productive inputs or "factors of production."

Neoclassical macrodistribution, in particular, has been based on two major notions aggregated from microdistribution, namely, the production function[1] and the elasticity of substitution. It also uses some form of the

This chapter represents an expansion and updating of the writer's "Neo-Classical Macro-Distribution Theory," Marchal and Ducros, *The Distribution of National Income* (London: Macmillan, 1968), ch. 18.

1. Most, if not all, neoclassical writers would, however, agree with Solow's concession: "I have never thought of the macroeconomic production function as a rigorously justifiable concept. In my mind it is either an illuminating parable or else a mere device for handling data, to be used so long as it gives good empirical results, and to be abandoned as soon as it doesn't, or as soon as something better comes along." (R. M. Solow, review of J. R. Hicks' *Capital and Growth*, *A.E.R.* [December 1966], pp. 1259 f.)

marginal productivity theory of input demand (as in Chapter 6). Rival macrodistribution theories discard one or more of these elements as rubbish, or at least include other elements as more significant. For example, if we suppose all productive inputs ultimately reducible to simple abstract labor, as in the systems of David Ricardo,[2] Karl Marx, Wassily Leontief,[3] and Piero Sraffa, it makes little sense to discuss the marginal productivities of several independent inputs on the basis of substitution among them.

The Cobb-Douglas Function and the Elasticity of Substitution

2. The simplest and still most widely used production function in neoclassical macrodistribution theorizing is the so-called Cobb-Douglas function. It developed in the 1920's from observations by Paul H. Douglas on time series of index numbers of labor, capital, and output in manufacturing industry for the United States and for the state of Massachusetts. These indexes rose in logarithmic straight-line patterns, indicating constant long-term growth rates. The "capital" series rose most rapidly and the "labor" series most slowly. The "product" series followed labor more closely than capital, whether the latter was defined to include or exclude working capital.[4]

Searching for a mathematical formula to summarize these relations, one that might also combine constant returns to scale (linear homogeneity) with diminishing returns to individual inputs, Douglas consulted Charles W. Cobb, a professional mathematician. The result was a formula that has become standard. In our notation:

$$x = x_0 \, a^a \, b^{1-a} \qquad \text{or} \qquad \log\left(\frac{x}{b}\right) = \log x_0 + \alpha \log\left(\frac{a}{b}\right) \qquad (16.1)$$

and in Douglas' notation:

$$P = b \, L^k C^{1-k} \qquad \text{or} \qquad \log\left(\frac{P}{C}\right) = \log b + k \log\left(\frac{L}{C}\right).$$

2. This may be unfair to Ricardo (and some of the other writers mentioned), inasmuch as they treat time along with labor as a component of capital.

3. Formally speaking, the Leontief system may include nonlabor "primary inputs," such as imported raw materials (without domestic substitutes) and indirect taxes. (I am indebted to Toshihisa Toyoda for this emendation, which may apply equally to the other systems mentioned.)

4. Paul H. Douglas, "Comments on the Cobb-Douglas Production Function," in Conference on Research in Income and Wealth, *The Theory and Empirical Analysis of Production,* Studies in Income and Wealth, vol. 31 (New York: Columbia University Press, 1967), pp. 15 f.; Douglas, *Theory of Wages* (New York: Macmillan, 1934), charts 10 and 15 (pp. 135 and 161).

The arguments $(x,a,b$ or $P,L,C)$ represent "homogenized" output, labor, and capital respectively, while the parameters $(x_0,\alpha$ or $b,k)$ are statistical constants, presumably positive, fitted by least squares. The α or k parameter is, as we shall see, the estimated macroeconomic labor share. The simplest interpretation of the x_0 or b parameter is as a statistical catch-all for such omitted variables as land, management, technical progress, and (sometimes) working capital, as well as for imperfect homogeneity of the basic variables (x,a,b).

3.   This function fit Douglas' data with impressively high correlation coefficients. The pattern of deviations between actual and computed index numbers for output was also significant. The function generally overestimated output, as it theoretically should do, in periods of depression characterized by "disguised unemployment" of labor (considered as a quasi-fixed input) and of fixed capital generally. The reverse was generally true, as one would have expected, in periods of boom. In such periods, computed output was less than actual, because labor and capital worked overtime, and inflation sometimes led to understatement of the value of capital.[5] Using index numbers, the parameter x_0 (Douglas' b) was close to unity.

3.   The Cobb-Douglas function's use for macrodistribution theory may have been something of an afterthought. Douglas did, however, compare observed labor shares, which we denote by s_a, with theoretical shares computed along marginal productivity lines, and expressed satisfaction at the closeness of results. In our notation, the theoretical value of the relative share s computed from the Cobb-Douglas function (16.1) is simply α:

$$s_a = \frac{ap_a}{x} = \frac{a}{x}\frac{\delta x}{\delta a} = \frac{a\,(\alpha x_0\,a^{a-1}\,b^{1-a})}{x_0 a^a\,b^{1-a}} = \alpha.$$

In addition to fitting the function as a statistical project, Douglas was interested primarily in estimating the demand elasticity η for labor. This elasticity equals $[-(p_a/a)\,(\delta a/\delta p_a)]$. In terms of the Cobb-Douglas function, with $p_a = (\delta x/\delta a)$ as per marginal productivity theory, we have

$$\eta_a = -\frac{\dfrac{\delta x}{\delta a}}{a\,\dfrac{\delta^2 x}{\delta a^2}} = \frac{-\alpha x_0 a^{a-1} b^{1-a}}{a[\alpha\,(\alpha-1)\,x_0 a^{a-2}b^{1-a}]} = \frac{1}{1-\alpha}.$$

With both measured and computed labor shares in the range 0.65–0.70,[6]

----

5. Douglas, *Theory of Wages, op. cit.*, charts 10-a and 17 (pp. 136 and 164).

6. It is not true that α was selected arbitrarily to equal s_a. (This "circular-reasoning" procedure is sometimes found in fitting other production functions, and this writer has heard it attributed to Douglas himself.)

the estimated elasticity of demand for labor is in the range 2.7–3.3. Indeed, the estimated elasticity must be greater than unity unless the share ratio is negative, an obvious impossibility! Some feature of Douglas' procedure must hold the demand elasticities for productive inputs above unity, a result that makes payrolls, in particular, rise when wages fall, contradicting the "purchasing power" arguments for high wages and wage increases regardless of the facts! (Compare Chapter 11, above.) Douglas did not compare his estimates of η against more direct estimates from wage and employment data.

4.   The Cobb-Douglas function made its formal bow in December 1927.[7] It has subsequently gone around the world, with applications to firms, industries, regional, and national economies. It is applied frequently to production and growth problems, as well as distributional ones. In many cases "[it] was adopted out of convenience, rather than on any evidence of its validity."[8] Moreover, applications have come increasingly to involve modified forms of the functions, most modifications being responses to objections discussed below. The most exhaustive examination of results (up to its own publication date) may be found in a survey article by Walters.[9] Controversy about the meaning and usefulness of the Cobb-Douglas function, and for that matter, of aggregate production functions generally, was inaugurated by the discussants of the original Cobb-Douglas paper. It has never died out.

5.   If only by comparison, the elasticity of substitution (which we encountered at the microeconomic level in Chapter 6) has led a quiet life.

7. C. W. Cobb and Paul H. Douglas, "A Theory of Production," *A.E.R.* (May 1928). For anticipation by Knut Wicksell, see Murray Brown, *Theory and Measurement of Technical Change* (Cambridge, Eng.: Cambridge University Press, 1966), p. 31 n.

Later statements are in Douglas, *Theory of Wages* (*op. cit.*), and "Are There Laws of Production?" *A.E.R.* (March 1948), included as a foreword to *Theory of Wages*, 1957 reprint.

8. E. S. Phelps, "Substitution, Fixed Proportions, Growth, and Distribution," *Int. Econ. Rev.* (September 1963), p. 284. But, Phelps continues, "there is no convincing evidence against it." Compare also Leontief: "For over 30 years, whenever a working economist was called on to describe in numbers or to interpret in analytical terms the relationship between the inputs of capital and labor and the final product of a plant, an industry, or a national economy, he was more likely than not to reach for the Cobb-Douglas function. Theorists questioned the arbitrariness of its form and statisticians the validity of procedures used in fitting it, but despite all criticism the familiar exponential equation was used over and over again, essentially, I think, because of its convenient simplicity." "An International Comparison of Factor Costs and Factor Use," *A.E.R.* (June 1964), p. 335 (running quotation).

9. A. A. Walters, "Production and Cost Functions: An Econometric Survey," *Econometrica* (January-April, 1963). Later data is included in the several empirical articles of Conference on Research in Income and Wealth, *Theory and Empirical Analysis of Production, op. cit.*

In the aggregate domain, as several writers have pointed out,[10] the *economic* elasticity of substitution is a compound of the elasticity of *technical* substitution (between inputs along individual isoquants within individual firms) and the elasticity of *demand* substitution (between the products of different firms and industries with different input-intensities). In microeconomic problems, as we have seen, technical substitution is of primary importance. It is erroneous to assume the same thing for macroeconomic problems, and doubly erroneous to connect aggregative shares directly with elasticities of technical substitution. Under normal circumstances, the economic elasticity of substitution is significantly *higher* than the technical.

It is not difficult to show that, in the Cobb-Douglas case, the elasticity of substitution σ is unitary. This result is required for the constancy of relative shares, since a unitary σ implies that the relative quantities of inputs vary by the same proportions as their relative prices. The algebraic demonstration is

$$x = x_0 a^a\, b^{1-a}$$

(Cobb-Douglas Function, 16.1)

$$\sigma = \frac{(\delta x/\delta a)\,(\delta x/\delta b)}{x\,(\delta^2 x/\delta a \delta b)}$$

(Chapter 6, Appendix A)

$$\frac{\delta x}{\delta a} = \alpha \frac{x}{a},\ \frac{\delta x}{\delta b} = (1-\alpha)\frac{x}{b}$$

$$\frac{\delta^2 x}{\delta a \delta b} = \frac{\alpha \delta x}{a \delta b} = \frac{\alpha\,(1-\alpha)\,x}{ab}$$

$$\sigma = \frac{\alpha\,(1-\alpha)\,(x^2/ab)}{x[\alpha\,(1-\alpha)\,x]/ab} = 1.$$

The elasticity of substitution was, until recently, used more widely in abstract analysis than in empirical work. One early empirical estimate of the elasticity as between labor and capital was published by Kravis in 1959, covering a 58-year range of American data.[11] His estimate of 0.64 added to Kravis' doubts of the validity of Bowley's Law of constant relative shares (Chapter 4). The value significantly below unity implies that labor, which increased less than capital over the period of Kravis' study, should have increased its relative share—as, indeed, it did.

10. A. C. Pigou, "The Elasticity of Substitution," *Ec.J.* (June 1934); Fritz Machlup, "The Common Sense of the Elasticity of Substitution," *R.E.Stud.* (June 1935); Irving Morrissett, "Recent Uses of the Elasticity of Substitution," *Econometrica* (January 1953). (Morrissett's survey article includes an extensive bibliography.)

11. Irving Kravis, "Relative Income Sharles in Fact and Theory," *A.E.R.* (December 1959).

The Cobb-Douglas Function: Economic Objections

6. The Cobb-Douglas "verification" of marginal productivity theory at the aggregative level has seemed since 1927 "too good to be true," in view of the apparent prevalence of imperfect competition, including collective bargaining. Objections have crowded in thick and fast, and we may sort them out arbitrarily as economic and statistical.

One immediate objection was anchored on the facts of technological change, which is conspicuous by its absence from the Cobb-Douglas function. Douglas' critics of 1927–28 [12] saw no economic rationale for forcing into one function the technologies of 1890 or 1900 and 1925. They saw in the Cobb-Douglas function only fortuitous interrelationship between the slopes of trend lines.

7. Somewhat later came the objection that a production function that is linear homogeneous throughout its length, like (16.1), is inconsistent with the atomistic competition assumed for computing the "theoretical" relative share s_a. This is because, for such a function, one scale of plant is as efficient as any other for the competitive firm. There is no optimum, and the scale is indeterminate. At the very least, say the critics, Douglas should have permitted independent estimates for the coefficients of a and b in the Cobb-Douglas function, instead of binding their sum at unity.[13]

8. We have already mentioned the difficulties inherent in measuring "capital" when the capital stock is made up of heterogeneous goods of varying ages. Joan Robinson has been the most articulate spokesman of the so-called neo-Cambridge School in arguing that this problem is insoluble. What can be meant, she wonders, by "a quantity of 'capital' in the abstract?" "What is meant by saying that a quantity of 'capital' remains the same when it changes its form is a mystery that has never been explained to this day."[14] For the purposes of distribution theory, estimating the value of a heterogeneous physical capital stock by some capitalization process involves circularity, when the capitalization factor is itself the return per unit of capital, which cannot be presumed to be known in

---

12. J. M. Clark and Morris Copeland may be mentioned particularly. Clark, "Inductive Evidence on Marginal Productivity," *A.E.R.* (May 1928), and Douglas, *Theory of Wages, op. cit.,* pp. 214–216.

13. The first writer to make this suggestion seems to have been David Durand, "Some Thoughts on Marginal Productivity, with Special Reference to Professor Douglas' Analysis," *J.P.E.* (December 1937).

14. Joan Robinson, *Economic Philosophy* (London: Watts, 1962), p. 60. A fuller statement of her position and its relation to the production function generally, is "The Production Function and the Theory of Capital," in her *Collected Economic Papers,* vol. ii (Oxford: Blackwell, 1960).

advance. To proceed from the opposite direction, estimating capital value
as its cost under "prudent investment" is little, if any, better. The cost
also embodies returns to investment in capital goods production, also
computed at the same supposedly unknown rate, reduced by past depreciation and obsolescence in which the same rate enters.

9.   Measured capital figures—and measured labor figures as well, where
labor is "a quasi-fixed factor"—include variable amounts of inputs available but not in use. For the best results in fitting production functions,
we should limit ourselves to inputs actually in use, depreciated (in the
case of capital) as accurately as possible. In dealing with capital, our input b, Solow adjusts his estimates by assuming equal proportions of capital and labor unemployed, while Massell interpolates in a trend of full-
employment capital-output ratios.[15] Massell obtains less variance than
Solow in the ratio of capital in use to capital available; neither writer
allows for the disguised unemployment of quasi-fixed labor. No writer,
indeed, provides insurance that his observations represent readings from
the production function itself, and not underestimates of x due to any of
the myriad inefficiencies in the use of inputs, particularly capital.

10.   A sophisticated objection is due to Reder.[16] Differentiating (16.1)
with respect to a (labor), we obtain

$$\frac{\delta x}{\delta a} = \alpha\, x_0\, a^{a-1} b^{1-a} = \alpha\, x_0 \left(\frac{a}{b}\right)^{a-1} = \alpha\, \frac{x}{a}\,.$$

As x/a varies (between observations lying on the function) in the same
direction as b and in the opposite direction from a, the marginal productivity $\delta x/\delta a$ should vary (between observations) with the differing quantities of either capital or labor. But the wage rate (which equals $\delta x/\delta a$)
is uniform, as an equilibrium condition. These results seem inconsistent
with the assumption of homogeneity in input units. Perhaps the fitted
functions include the effects of qualitative differences in inputs, or of
exogenous disturbances correlated with time (in a time series) or with
industry size (in a cross-sectional study), along with standard marginal
productivity. At least, this is Reder's concern.

15. Solow, "Technological Change and the Aggregate Production Function," *Rev.
Econ. and Stat.* (August 1958) ; Benton Massell, "Capital Formation and Economic
Change in United States Manufacturing," *Rev. Econ. and Stat.* (May 1960). Compare
Walters, *op. cit.,* pp. 22 f., on parallel problems of "homogenizing" labor and output
data.

16. Melvin Reder, "Alternative Theories of Labor's Share," in Moses Abramovitz
et al., The Allocation of Economic Resources (Stanford: Stanford University Press,
1959), pp. 200 f. Other objections by Reder are included in "An Alternative Interpretation of the Cobb-Douglas Function," *Econometrica* (July 1943).

11. And what, finally, can we say of results "forced" by the form of (16.1) —the elastic demand for labor, the constant labor share, the unitary elasticity of substitution? To quote Nicholas Kaldor, spokesman for a rival macrodistribution theory, the standard view is "unable to account for such constancies as the constant relative functional share of labour except in terms of particular hypotheses (unsupported by any independent evidence) such as the unity-elasticity of substitution between Capital and Labour."[17] Other objections are voiced by Solow, who applies the statistical formula for the standard error of the mean to show that variability of the labor share exists, and that it is no less than would be expected from the share's substantial variability between industries and the number of industries within the entire economy. Using the elasticity of substitution, the author has attempted to show, in partial rebuttal, that relative shares are insensitive to variations in this elasticity, particularly when the values of σ exceed unity.[18]

The Cobb-Douglas Function: Statistical Objections

12. There is little point in reminding readers further of the imperfections of available data. Over and above simple errors of observation and measurement, recorded inputs and outputs vary in composition. Over and above the capital-measurement problems touched on in the last section, there are others involving netness (adjustment for depreciation and obsolescence), and still others in adjusting investments of different ages and efficiencies to a common price level. We have also mentioned the special difficulties arising from the presence of inputs available but used only partially, if at all. These are all real problems for the statistician.[19] Questionable solutions may account for a sizable proportion of the ridiculous results occasionally obtained from production functions in macrodistribution problems (for example, a Cobb-Douglas α lying outside the range between zero and unity).[20] Our present discussion will, however, be concerned with problems of *collinearity* and *identification,* which are of more general interest.

17. Kaldor, "A Model of Economic Growth," *Ec.J.* (December 1957), p. 592.

18. R. M. Solow, "A Skeptical Note on the Constancy of Relative Shares," *A.E.R.* (September 1958) Bronfenbrenner, "A Note on Relative Shares and the Elasticity of Substitution," *J.P.E.* (June 1960). See also Chapter 6, Appendix B, of this book.

19. A broad range of statistical problems is considered in Marc Nerlove, *Estimation and Identification of Cobb-Douglas Production Functions* (Amsterdam: North-Holland, 1965.)

20. Consider, as cases in point, results for Japanese rice-growing reproduced in Walters, *op. cit.,* table iv, or for U.S. agriculture and British cotton-spinning (*ibid.,* Table ii). More generally, fits which include large service sectors, non-profit sectors, and public sectors (along with "ordinary business") tend to be unsatisfactory. (See note 29 to this chapter.)

A standard textbook in econometrics has defined multi-collinearity as "the general problem which arises when the explanatory variables are so largely correlated with one another that it becomes very difficult, if not impossible, to disentangle their separate influences and obtain a reasonably precise estimate of their relative effect."[21] Geometrically speaking, multi-collinearity results from fitting a line through a configuration very close to a point, or fitting a plane through a configuration very close to a pencil in space. Error terms aside, there are an infinite number of solutions, none better than any other. The phenomenon was analyzed at length by Frisch in 1934, and applied to the Cobb-Douglas function by Mendershausen.[22] (The independent variables of Douglas' original data —index numbers of capital and labor inputs—are indeed correlated highly with each other.)

13. A frequent introduction to the identification problem in economics is drawn from the elementary law of supply and demand. Suppose that both the quantity of x demanded per period and the quantity supplied per period depended exclusively upon p_x in that period, but that both demand and supply functions were subject to random shifts. We are given series of price and quantity data on x for a number of periods; we plot these on a graph, and perhaps fit a regression line to them. Without further information about shifts in the functions, we could not tell whether the plotted points and regression line represented a supply function, a demand function, or a hybrid of the two. The identification problem was brought into the econometric forefront by Haavelmo in 1944; Marschak and Andrews applied similar reasoning to the Cobb-Douglas function almost simultaneously.[23]

In addition to the production function (which may be of the Cobb-Douglas type), Marschak and Andrews pointed out, there is another relationship that connects the variables (x, a, b), namely, the cost function. Under long-run competitive equilibrium, with p_x or p set equal to unity, we have

$$x = ap_a + bp_b.$$

21. John Johnston, *Econometric Methods* (New York: McGraw-Hill, 1963), p. 201.

22. Ragnar Frisch, *Statistical Confluence Analysis by Means of Complete Regression Systems* (Oslo: University Economics Institute, 1934); Horst Mendershausen, "On the Significance of Professor Douglas' Production Function," *Econometrica* (April 1938).

23. Trygve Haavelmo, "The Probability Approach in Econometrics," *Econometrica* (Supplement, July 1944); Jacob Marschak and William H. Andrews, "Random Simultaneous Equations and the Theory of Production, *Econometrica* (July-October, 1944). For later developments, see discussion among J. Kmenta, M. E. Joseph, and Irving Hoch, *Econometrica* (July 1963); also Nerlove, *op. cit.*

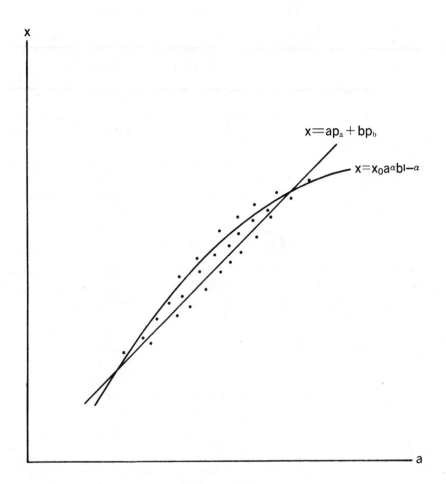

$$x = ap_a + bp_h$$

$$x = x_0 a^\alpha b^{1-\alpha}$$

Figure 16.1

The problem of distinguishing the production function from the cost function is identical with the supply-demand problem of the last paragraph, and is illustrated by Figure 16.1 for two variables a and x (with b constant). Marschak and Andrews concluded, on balance, that Douglas and his several coworkers had fitted hybrid functions and confused them with true production functions. In a later critique,[24] Phelps Brown went even further. He argued that the functions fitted to Australian data were cost functions and not production functions at all.

24. E. H. Phelps Brown, "The Meaning of the Fitted Cobb-Douglas Production Function," *Q.J.E.* (November 1957).

Cobb-Douglas Function: Modifications

14.   Douglas and his staff did not find it difficult to meet objections to binding the coefficient of b at $(1 - \alpha)$, and to refute the suggestion that his results reflected fortuitous coincidences between time series.

$$x = x_0 a^\alpha b^\beta \qquad \text{or} \qquad \log x = \log x_0 + \alpha \log a + \beta \log b \qquad (16.2)$$

and testing the closeness of the sum $(\alpha + \beta)$ to unity.[25] He also began the fitting of cross-section as well as time-servies data, with results no worse than he had achieved earlier with time series.

The freeing of $(\alpha + \beta)$ did not change the assumed elasticity of substitution, which remained equal to unity by the standard formula (section 5, above). The theoretical sum of income payments, assuming marginal productivity analysis to hold, became

$$a \frac{\delta x}{\delta a} + b \frac{\delta x}{\delta b} = (\alpha + \beta) x$$

rather than x itself as under Euler's Theorem with a linear homogeneous function. This meant that the computed relative shares of inputs a and b were not (α, β) unambiguously. One practice was to consider

$$\frac{\alpha}{\alpha + \beta} \text{ and } \frac{\beta}{\alpha + \beta}, \text{ i.e. } \frac{a \dfrac{\delta x}{\delta a}}{a \dfrac{\delta x}{\delta a} + b \dfrac{\delta x}{\delta b}} \text{ and } \frac{b \dfrac{\delta x}{\delta b}}{a \dfrac{\delta x}{\delta a} + b \dfrac{\delta x}{\delta b}}$$

which add to unity. However, the true theoretical shares

$$\frac{a \dfrac{\delta x}{\delta a}}{x} \text{ and } \frac{b \dfrac{\delta x}{\delta b}}{x}$$

remained simply (α, β). The resulting ambiguity or contradiction remains unsolved. One may consider a solution in terms of windfall "profits" and "losses," which are not considered input payments in the usual sense but rather pure residuals. These may possibly make up the positive or negative difference between $(\alpha + \beta)$ and unity, but at the cost of a tautological element.

15.   It has been less easy to relate the Cobb-Douglas function, with its macrodistribution implications and microeconomic anomalies, to micro-

---

25. Walters (*op. cit.*, pp. 5 f.) considers (16.2) as the most representative type of Cobb-Douglas function. It remains homogeneous, but its degree is $(\alpha + \beta)$. This follows since replacement of (a, b) by $(\lambda a, \lambda b)$, where λ is a positive constant, will yield $(\lambda^{\alpha + \beta} x)$ as the value of the dependent variable.

economic production functions for single firms, from which it is supposedly derivable.

The conventional econometrics of this "aggregation problem" assumes macro- and micro-functions of the same mathematical form. It relates the coefficients of the former to sums or averages of the latter.[26] In the present instance, the micro-function may be of a quite different form—since, for example, a micro-production function that is linear homogeneous throughout its length involves major difficulties. In this case the conventional econometrics loses its relevance.

A minority view treats the Cobb-Douglas function, or any other aggregative production function, as an *envelope* of micro-functions.[27] Each of the latter has the standard shape discussed in Chapter 6 and illustrated in Figure 16.2. The macro-function is tangent to all the micro-functions at their equilibrium points, where the two have the same slope. Indeed, the macro-function is the locus of all such tangencies. Even at the points of tangency, the macro-function has the smaller curvature, and therefore the larger elasticity.

In Figure 16.2 we measure a on the horizontal axis and, on the vertical, the net marginal product of all inputs other than a; the macro-function may be of Cobb-Douglas form even if the marginal product of a alone is constant between firms. (Two micro-functions are also shown, indicated by different amounts of b, which is presumably more nearly fixed.)

16. It is difficult to share the contemporary Cambridge School concern with the indefinability of capital, or rather, with the increment of indefin-

---

26. Walters, *op. cit.*, pp. 7–11. A Cobb-Douglas function application is V. N. Murti and V. K. Sastry, "Production Functions for Indian Industry," *Econometrica* (April 1957). These writers average sectoral results to obtain overall estimates.

27. Bronfenbrenner, "Production Functions: Cobb-Douglas, Interfirm, Intrafirm," *Econometrica* (January 1944).

Frankel proposes an alternative distinction between *ex ante* and *realized* production functions in the individual enterprise. The *ex ante* function is, in our notation:

$$x_i = x_{0i} \, \rho_i \, a^a b^{1-a}$$

where ρ is the capital-labor ratio b/a, and the subscript i refers to a firm. Frankel's aggregate or macro-function is:

$$x = x_0 \, \rho^\delta \, a^a b^{1-a} = x_0 \, a^{a-\delta} \, b^{1+\delta-a}.$$

If δ approaches α, both functions reduce to what Frankel calls a "realized Harrodian growth function" of the simple form: $x = x_0 b$, which he feels is often observable. Marvin Frankel, "The Production Function: Allocation and Growth," *A.E.R.* (December 1962).

Yet another alternative approach assumes that, for each firm, both input-output ratios $(a/x, b/x)$ are fixed. For efficient firms, these will be low, and for inefficient ones, high. If the ratios are distributed in a Pareto distribution, Houthakker shows that the resulting macro-function will approach the Cobb-Douglas. Hendrik Houthakker, "The Pareto Distribution and the Cobb-Douglas Production Function in Activity Analysis," *Rev. Econ. Stud.*, vol. 23, no. 1 (1955).

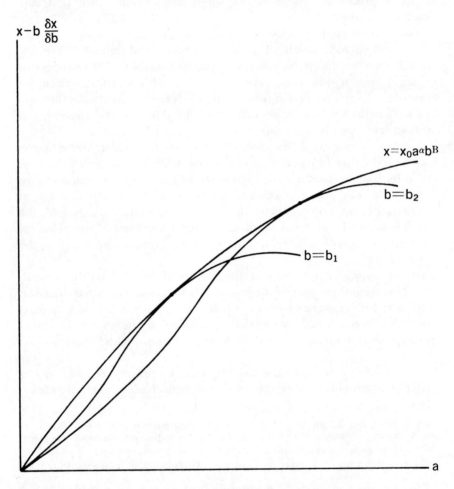

Figure 16.2

ability that is not shared by other economic aggregates like labor or output. All we need argue to avoid circular reasoning,[28] if capital is valued with a capitalized value, is that the capitalization factor at time t is either the (known) prior interest rate r_{t-1} or some "permanent" rate, such as

28. This "circularity" issue is a species of an ancient genus. A familiar member of this genus is the dispute about including money in the utility or preference functions determining money prices. If we include money, at what value should it be included? Does this value not depend upon purchasing power, *i.e.*, upon the unknown money prices? And so we once proceeded round the circle, but (hopefully) need do so no longer. (Much of the credit for clearing up this matter goes to Don Patinkin, *Money, Interest, and Prices,* 2d ed. [New York: Harper and Row, 1965], ch. 5.)

a weighted average of several past rates $(r_{t-1}, r_{t-2}, \ldots, r_{t-n})$, which determine our anticipation of what expected rates will be.

17.   Turning to statistical problems, we may agree that, were the "good" Cobb-Douglas results great rarities and the freakish ones common, we might be justified in assuming, with Mendershausen, a multi-collinear universe that occasionally yields encouraging results by pure chance. The facts now seem clearly otherwise, however they appeared to Mendershausen in 1938. The method gives too many right answers to be accounted for by chance.[29] Something more must be operating.

Quite generally, the multi-collinearity bogey has been laid for sufficiently high multiple correlation coefficients. In the production function case (which Klein uses to illustrate the preceding conclusion[30]), if the multiple correlation is above 0.95 with x dependent and (a,b) dependent variables, there is no real multi-collinearity problem, even when the simple correlation between a and b is as high as 0.90.

18.   A similar argument may perhaps be used against skeptical doubts on the score of improper identification. Instead, however, what is done has been to introduce into the production function terms whose purpose is to allow formally for technical change, either embodied or disembodied. (These terms have been defined in Chapter 6.)

A disembodied change would transform the production function to

$$x = F\ (a,b,t)$$

where the new variable t (time) is a surrogate for technical progress. This change makes the production function identifiable, since there is no t term in the cost identity:

$$x = ap_a + bp_b.$$

An embodied change would transform the production function to:

$$x = F[\alpha\,(t)\,a, \beta\,(t)\,b]$$

---

29. Fits to post-1945 GNP data for the entire economy are as several writers point out, systematically less good than older fits for manufacturing alone. Compare, for the United States, Robert E. Lucas, Jr., "Capacity, Overtime, and Empirical Production Functions," *A.E.R.* (May 1970), Appendices A-B. This result seems to be due primarily to inclusion of public, centrally planned, and other nonprofit sectors. In addition, there is no reason to expect similar production functions to hold for, *e.g.*, agriculture or services on the one hand and manufacturing on the other. A third possible explanation, which would also apply within the manufacturing sector, is an increasing prevalence of all-or-none bargaining or approaches thereto in input markets. (Compare Chapter 10.)

30. L. R. Klein, *Introduction to Econometrics* (Englewood Cliffs, N.J.: Prentice-Hall, 1962), p. 101.

where $\alpha(t)$ and $\beta(t)$ are qualitative improvement factors not found in the cost identity. (The expressions $\alpha(t)$ and $\beta(t)$ should not be confused with the coefficients α and β of the Cobb-Douglas function itself.)

An example, using disembodied change only, is Solow's: [31]

$$x = e^{gt}\, a^{1-\beta}\, b^{\beta} \qquad \text{or} \qquad \log\left(\frac{x}{a}\right) = gt + \beta \log\left(\frac{b}{a}\right). \qquad (16.3)$$

Equation (16.3) retains the Cobb-Douglas unitary elasticity of substitution. It also treats all technical progress as neutral in the Hicksian sense, since the ratio of the marginal productivities of a and b is independent of t. The equation is also subject to criticism for using an entity so colorless as "time" as its surrogate of technical progress.

The Constant Elasticity of Substitution Production Function

19. Solow later participated in a more exciting improvement, which in its turn has given rise to many more developments (generalizations) of production functions. This is the homohypellagic or constant elasticity of substitution (c.e.s.) production function.[32] The c.e.s. function may be regarded as a generalization of the Cobb-Douglas function, so that (16.1) is a special case with $\sigma = 1$. The elasticity of substitution between a and b, while still constant, need no longer be unitary. The function can therefore suggest directions of change in relative shares, without being bound to Bowley's Law.

The formula of the c.e.s. production function is, in a notation close to our own,

$$x = x_0[\,(1-\beta)\, a^{-\rho} + \beta\, b^{-\rho}]^{-\frac{1}{\rho}}. \qquad (16.4)$$

Here ρ is $(1-\sigma)/\sigma$ and not the ratio b/a, which we have been denoting by this symbol. It follows, of course, that the elasticity of substitution σ is $1/(1+\rho)$.

---

31. Solow, "Technical Change and the Aggregate Production Function," *op. cit.* Solow actually did not estimate β, but substituted s_k, the *observed* capital share, thereby rendering his results useless for the verification of distribution theory. If we denote dx/dt, etc., by $\dot{x}$, etc., x/a by y, and b/a by ρ, we derive:

$$\log y = gt + \beta \log \rho$$
$$\frac{d \log y}{dt} = \frac{\dot{y}}{y} = g + \beta \frac{\dot{\rho}}{\rho}.$$

This equation gave rise to Solow's estimate that nearly seven-eighths of the observed improvement in American output per man-hour has arisen from technical change (g) rather than from increase in capital per worker.

32. Kenneth J. Arrow, Hollis B. Chenery, Bagicha Minhas, and Robert M. Solow, "Capital-Labor Substitution and Economic Efficiency," *Rev. Econ. and Stat.* (August 1961). The function has also been called ACMS and SMAC, from the initial letters of the coauthors' names.

Of several possible derivations of (16.4), we present (in the Appendix to this chapter) a derivation considerably longer, but more elementary, than many others.

20. The initial use of the c.e.s. function was, quite naturally, to estimate the elasticity of substitution σ. For the sake of simplicity in curve-fitting, and for maintaining the number of degrees of freedom, such estimates used observed rather than computed values of the capital and labor shares β and $(1 - \beta)$. Their results are therefore not directly useful for distribution theory. They are, nevertheless, useful indirectly because they indicate the extent to which the σ values diverge from the unitary ones assumed by the Cobb-Douglas function (16.1–16.2), and therefore the validity of results derived from such functions.

The Arrow-Chenery-Minhas-Solow group estimated the elasticity of substitution in twenty-four industries on a worldwide basis, with each observation taken from a different country. Results were below unity in twenty-three of these industries.[33] Fuchs, however, added a dummy variable to separate developed from developing countries. With this variable included, his estimates of σ clustered about unity (median 1.04), suggesting constant relative shares.[34] Another Solow study (with observations of ten manufacturing industries across regions within the U.S.) yielded a range of σ values from 0.06 to 1.96; ten values exceed unity, eleven fall in the range 0.60–1.50; the unweighted mean is 1.02, the median 1.01.[35] Discussing these results, Eisner suggests the possibility of an upward bias related to transitory output variations, while Kendrick derives lower results from the Solow sample by an arc-elasticity formula.[36]

In order to limit "capital" to instruments actually in use, Kurz and Manne have used engineering estimates rather than economic observations to estimate an elasticity of substitution for the American metal machinery industry; they derived a value of 0.99, still closer to unity.[37]

---

33. Arrow *et al., op. cit.,* p. 225.

34. Victor Fuchs, "Capital-Labor Substitution: A Note," *Rev. Econ. and Stat.* (November 1963).

35. Solow, "Capital, Labor, and Income in Manufacturing," in National Bureau of Economic Research, *The Behavior of Income Shares* (Princeton: Princeton University Press, 1964), table 2, p. 113. (The Eisner and Kendrick criticisms are on pp. 131–135 and 141 respectively.)

36. We have encountered Kendrick's formula in Chapter 6. It applies empirically only for infinitesimal changes, and only after corrections for possible shifts in input-demand conditions:

$$\sigma = \frac{\text{per cent rise in } (a/b)}{\text{per cent fall in } (p_a/p_b)}.$$

37. Mordecai Kurz and Alan S. Manne, "Engineering Estimates of Capital-Labor Substitution in Metal Machinery," *A.E.R.* (September 1963).

It is no longer justifiable to refer (as did Kaldor in 1957) to the unitary elasticity of substitution as "a particular hypothesis unsupported by independent evidence," especially when we are dealing with long-run data. On the other hand, most short-run estimates remain decidedly below unity, and we have already noted a long-run rising tendency in the measured labor share.

Subsequent Developments

21. Later developments have progressed along several lines, many of them oriented explicitly to macrodistribution theory. In particular: (*1*) Other forms of production function have been devised and fitted, to yield desirable or manageable attributes for the elasticity of substitution, the elasticities of derived input demand, and the like.[38] (*2*) Qualitative or "embodied" technical change, sometimes called factor-augmentation, has been included in functions like (16.1–16.4), either by purely economic adjustments in measured values of *a* and *b* or by mathematical modification, as illustrated below.

An expansion of the c.e.s. function (16.4) is

$$x = x_0 [\,(1 - \beta)\,\alpha\,(t)\,a^{-\rho} + \beta\,\beta\,(t)\,b^{-\rho}]^{-\frac{1}{\rho}} \qquad (16.5)$$

where $\alpha\,(t)$ and $\beta\,(t)$ are improvement factors, and β alone is the measured or computed relative share of capital. An impossibility theorem[39] asserts that at least one of the set $(x_0,\,\alpha\,(t),\,\beta\,(t),\,\sigma)$ must be known or assumed in advance before (16.5) can be fitted. A purely factor-augmenting c.e.s. function can, however, be fitted by assuming $x_0 = 1$ in (16.5):

$$x = [A\,(t)\,a^{-\rho} + B\,(t)\,b^{-\rho}]^{-\frac{1}{\rho}}$$

where $A\,(t) = (1 - \beta)\,\alpha\,(t)$ and $B\,(t) = \beta\beta\,(t)$. If we further assume factor-augmentation or embodied technical change to take a simple exponential form,[40]

$$\alpha\,(t) = e^{\lambda_a t} \qquad \text{and} \qquad \beta\,(t) = e^{\lambda_b t}$$

38. Martin J. Beckmann and Ryuzo Sato, "On a Class of Production Functions Defined by Log-Linear Relationships," presented to Econometric Society (1968); James B. Ramsey and Paul Zarembka, "Alternative Functional Forms and the Aggregate Production Function," Michigan State University Econometrics Workshop Paper 6705 (November, 1967); Ryuzo Sato, "Production Functions with Variable Elasticity of Factor Substitution," *Rev. Econ. and Stat.* (November 1968); Arnold Zellner and N. S. Revankar, "Generalized Production Functions," University of Wisconsin Social Systems Research Institute Paper 6607 (1966).

39. Peter Diamond, Daniel McFadden, and Miguel Rodriguez, "Identification of the Elasticity of Substitution and the Bias of Technical Change," paper presented to the Econometric Society (1965).

40. This procedure follows Paul David and Th. Van de Klundert, "Biased Efficiency Growth and Capital-Labor Substitution in the U. S.," *A.E.R.* (June 1965).

equation (16.5) becomes

$$x = [(1 - \beta) \ e^{\lambda_a t} a^{-\rho} + \beta \ e^{\lambda_b t} b^{-\rho}]^{-\frac{1}{\rho}}. \tag{16.6}$$

When (16.6) is fitted, the difference $(\lambda_a - \lambda_b)$, which may, of course, be negative, may be used as an estimate of the net labor-using or capital-saving bias in technical progress. (A negative value estimates the net capital-using or labor-saving bias.)

22. It is difficult to pick and choose among empirical applications of these advances. Accepting as inevitable the risk of unfairness, let us consider three papers in particular. Most favorable to the Cobb-Douglas function is a study by Griliches. Less favorable is a study by Thurow. An application of (16.6) to the explanation of relative share shifts is a study by Ferguson and Moroney. All these papers are based upon American data.

Griliches expands the Cobb-Douglas function (16.2) to take account of a number of quality changes and allow for dummy variables at the same time.[41] In logarithmic form, and adjusting to our own notation, Griliches' equation is:

$$\log \left(\frac{x}{a} \right) = \log x_0 + \beta \log \left(\frac{b}{a} \right) + (\alpha + \beta - 1) \ \log a + \sum_i \gamma_i z_i + d_i + d_j.$$

The new variables are the z_i (indexes of the quality of one or the other input) and the two d terms (coefficients of industry and state dummy variables). (The γ_i are statistical parameters.) Labor is measured as a man-hour flow of production workers rather than a total stock of persons employed in all capacities. Similarly, capital is measured as a flow of capital services, "defined as the sum of insurance premiums, rental payments, property taxes paid, depreciation and depreciation charged, and 6 per cent of gross book value."[42] As actually fitted (to 417 observations for 1958), Griliches' favored equation is:[43]

$$\log \left(\frac{x}{a} \right) = .348 \log \left(\frac{b}{a} \right) + .109 \log a - .083 z_1 - .083 \log z_2 + 1.485 z_3$$

$$-.304 z_4 + .054 z_5 - .069 z_6 + \text{(state dummies)}. \ (R^2 = .760)$$

The included z_i (quality-change variables) are, in Griliches' order:
1. Proportion of establishments with twenty or more employees.
2. Ratio of net to gross capital stock—measure of the "newness" of equipment.

41. Zvi Griliches, "Production Functions in Manufacturing: Some Preliminary Results," in *Theory and Empirical Analysis of Production, op. cit.*

42. *Ibid.*, p. 280.

43. *Ibid.*, p. 307.

3. Occupational distribution of employees.

4. Median age of male employees.

5. Proportion of white labor employed.

6. Proportion or female labor employed.

In another article coauthored by Griliches, adjustment of measured capital and labor variables by quality-change variables (not identical with those listed) reduced the unexplained "technical change" residual—the A term in (16.3) —to near zero.[44]

An otherwise digressional Section III of the Griliches paper justifies the Cobb-Douglas form by computing by three alternative methods the elasticity of substitution σ for seventeen two-digit industries by states. "In general, all the estimated σ's are not very (statistically) different from unity, the significant deviations if anything occurring above unity rather than below it."[45] The β value of the Griliches equation is higher than the capital share usually observed; it is close to the original result achieved by Cobb and Douglas with such simple formulas as our (16.1) .

23. It is primarily its production function methodology that permits Thurow's "disequilibrium" paper[46] to be classified with the neoclassical theories rather than with the dissidents. Thurow's conclusions are, to say the least, ambiguous. In the real world, where net adjustment to equilibrium occurs only slowly, if at all, Thurow finds the overall marginal product of capital significantly below the average real return to capital. These higher-than-equilibrium, or "monopoly-exploitative," earnings on capital Thurow ascribes to an overall capital-using bias in innovation. This bias, however, he believes to be decreasing over time.[47]

Thurow's production function is, on balance, more complex than any of the others we have encountered. It is basically Cobb-Douglas with onion, pickle, ketchup, and mustard, not to mention icing. It therefore holds the elasticity of substitution at unity, although Thurow claims his results "are valid for a wide range of alternative assumptions about the correct specification of the production function . . . as long as the elasticity

44. Dale W. Jorgenson and Zvi Griliches, "The Explanation of Productivity Change," *Rev. Econ. Stud.* (1967) .

45. Griliches, *op. cit.*, p. 292. See table 3, p. 293, for σ values by industry, computed on Griliches' three alternative bases.

46. Lester Thurow "Disequilibrium and the Marginal Productivity of Capital and Labor," *Rev. Econ. and Stat.* (February 1968) . See also Thurow, *Poverty and Discrimination, op. cit.*, Appendix A.

47. "Disequilibrium and the Marginal Productivity of Capital and Labor," *op. cit.*, p. 30. But is not Thurow proving too much? If the marginal product of labor had been *below* the wage rate, this disequilibrium could also be interpreted as motivating labor-saving (capital-using) innovation!

of substitution of capital for labor is less than five."[48] The complications introduced by Thurow include separate estimates of embodied and disembodied technical progress, explicit introduction of the unemployment rate, and elaborate vintage-type adjustments for the age of the capital stock. It is not easy to translate Thurow's production function into the notation used here. Adding time subscripts, however, we have

$$x_t = e^{f(u_t)} \, x_0 \, e^{gt} [a_t{}^a \, b_t{}^{1-a}]\gamma. \tag{16.7}$$

New symbols used are these:

$u_t =$ Unemployment rate in year t. (The function f is quadratic.)

$g =$ Growth rate (through disembodied technical progress).

$a_t = a \, (1 + \lambda_a)^t$, where λ_a represents embodied progress (quality improvement, factor-augmentation) in labor.

$b_t = \sum\limits_{v=0}^{t} (1 + \lambda_b) \, k \, (t - v) \, I_v$, where λ_b represents embodied progress in capital, and I_v is real investment in year v (prior to t), of which the proportion $k(t-v)$ survives $(t-v)$ years later.

$\gamma =$ a positive parameter indicating economies or diseconomies of scale. (In practice, γ did not differ significantly from unity.)

Function (16.7) cannot be fitted statistically as it stands, since the λ-coefficients required in a_t and b_t cannot be estimated simultaneously with the other unknowns. Thurow overcomes this difficulty by trying a number of alternative pairs of values for λ_a and λ_b, and then selecting the pair that leads to those values of a_t and b_t which, in turn, cause (16.7) to fit most closely. This pair is $\lambda_a = .01$, $\lambda_b = .04$, a result that seems imperfectly consistent with "human-capital" enthusiasm. With these best-fit values for λ_a and λ_b, disembodied technical progress (in real U.S. GNP over the period 1929–1965) is estimated at 1.17 per cent per year.

24. In fitting (16.7) Thurow derives real v.m.p. for labor and capital, which he compares with average wages and capital returns. Relative shares do not enter into the picture. A subset of his results is reproduced as Table 16.1.[49] In addition to the exploitative effects already mentioned, the table indicates a slight rising tendency in the ratio of labor returns to v.m.p. and a more substantial falling tendency in the ratio of capital returns to v.m.p., due largely to a rising trend in v.m.p. itself. On this basis,

48. *Ibid.*, p. 23.
49. *Ibid.*, table 1, p. 25.

Table 16.1.   Marginal Products and Actual Returns
of Labor and Capital (United States, Selected Years,
1929–1965)   (1958 dollars)

	Labor			Capital		
	Marginal Product	Actual Returns	Ratio (2) / (1)	Marginal Product	Actual Returns	Ratio (5) / (4)
Year	(1)	(2)	(3)	(4)	(5)	(6)
1929	$2,678	$1,554	0.58	8.5%	26.0%	3.06
1939	3,110	1,830	0.59	12.6	26.8	2.13
1949	4,398	2,546	0.58	16.5	29.7	1.80
1959	6,052	3,811	0.63	16.7	26.6	1.59
1965	7,236	4,550	0.63	18.2	29.5	1.62

with data for more than one-third of a century, it would apparently require at least a full century for "equilibrium" to be attained if Thurow's
elaborate estimates are correct—possibly less for capital, but certainly
more for labor. Shades of the stationary state!

24.   Our final "conventional" or "neoclassical" paper is by Ferguson and
Moroney.[50] These writers estimate the causes of functional share shifts for
each of the twenty two-digit industry groups into which American manufacturing industry is broken down, over the fifteen-year period 1948–1962
inclusive. For the same data, they also estimate the elasticity of substitution within each two-digit industry, using a relation that expands upon
the naive formula for σ that we have already noted:[51]

$$\log\left(\frac{b}{a}\right) = \left(\frac{b}{a}\right)_0 + \sigma \log\left(\frac{p_a}{p_b}\right) + \text{(other terms)}.$$

(Ferguson and Moroney, incidentally, do not check their results with an
important side relation:

$$\left(\frac{x}{a}\right) = \left(\frac{x}{a}\right)_0 + \sigma\, p_a \tag{16.8}$$

which we shall derive in the Appendix to this chapter, en route to the
c.e.s. function [16.4].)

Another part of the Ferguson-Moroney argument relates to interindustry shifts in the employed labor force. In industry i, the labor share s_i is

50. Charles E. Ferguson and John R. Moroney, "The Sources of Change in Labor's
Relative Share: A Neoclassical Analysis," *So. Ec. J.* (April 1969). Compare Brown,
Technical Change, op. cit., ch. 12.

51. Ferguson and Moroney, *op. cit., equation* (33), p. 315. The "other terms" are
time and the lagged value of (p_a/p_b).

equal to payrolls, denoted by w_i, as a proportion of average labor product y_i. It follows that, using dots for time derivatives,

$$\frac{\dot{s}_i}{s_i} = \frac{\dot{w}_i}{w_i} - \frac{\dot{y}_i}{y_i} .$$

If π_i is an index of the relative importance of industry i in manufacturing as a whole—measured by the relative size of value added—the relative share of labor in all manufacturing, denoted by s, equals $\Sigma \pi_i s_i$. Furthermore:

$$\frac{\dot{s}}{s} = \frac{1}{s} \left(\Sigma s_i \dot{\pi}_i + \Sigma \pi_i \dot{s}_i \right)$$

so that, finally:

$$\frac{\dot{s}}{s} = \Sigma \frac{\dot{s}_i}{s} \pi_i + \Sigma \pi_i \left(\frac{\dot{w}_i}{w_i} - \frac{\dot{y}_i}{y_i} \right) .$$

Combining the results of this equation with the family of twenty production functions of the form (16.6)—yielding λ_a values generally below λ_b—Ferguson and Moroney ascribe to capital deepening the greater part of the observed increase in the relative labor share. The status of the twenty elasticities of substitution, none higher than 0.66, is ambiguous. On the one hand, they seem not to enter directly into the final calculations; on the other hand, the summary sentences (quoted immediately below) implicitly assume $\sigma < 1$.[52]

> Five per cent of the increase in labor's aggregate relative share is attributable to shifts in the composition of demand within the manufacturing sector. The remaining 95 per cent is accounted for by changes within each of the industries. Of the 95 per cent, 10 per cent cannot be imputed statistically, 25 per cent is attributable to labor-using technological progress, while capital deepening accounted for 60 per cent of the increase. The importance of capital deepening should be especially stressed because in its absence the relative share of labor would have decreased. To say this somewhat differently, the predominance of capital-using technological processes would, other things equal, have caused an increase in capital's relative share.

The Dissenters: An Introduction

25. The macrodistribution theory considered thus far in this chapter may be called the Good Old Theory, alias the Conventional Wisdom. As usual, a number of voiciferous dissents have developed, particularly in Western Europe. These dissents appear to have little in common, beyond

52. *Ibid.*, p. 321.

skeptical doubts, sometimes extending to contempt, for the Good Old
Theory in general, and for certain particular pieces of apparatus like the
production function and the marginal productivity concept. The discussion that follows will focus first on selected dissenting positions, and later
on attempts at an electric combination of a number of these dissents with
elements of the Good Old Theory. The chapter will eventually end with
the writer's own tentative position and prejudices.

The selected "dissenting positions" will be five in number, characterized as:

(*1*) Monopoly theories
(*2*) Accounting identities
(*3*) Saving-investment theories
(*4*) Magic Constancy theories
(*5*) Sociological-institutional theories

We shall attempt to be selective, meaning that the great bulk of writing
under each head will be perforce neglected. A more inclusive survey was
prepared by Rothschild in 1961.[53]

Monopoly Theory: Kalečki

26. Let us define "modern times" as the period since 1929 (or, alternatively, the period since the unveiling of the Cobb-Douglas function). The
initial analytical dissent of such "modern times," as distinguished from
historical-institutional dissent, which has never been absent, is the monopoly theory of the distinguished Polish Socialist economist, Michal
Kalečki.[54] This theory dominated British macrodistribution thinking for
nearly a generation—from its original publication in 1938 to the Keynesian (Kaldorian?) saving-investment theory outlined below (sections 33–
34).

Kalečki's notation is idiosyncratic but not difficult. We shall follow it
at the price of inconsistency with our own system:

> Small letters refer to the individual firm, capitals to the entire economy.
> Barred variables are weighted arithmetic means.

53. K. W. Rothschild, "Some Recent Contributions to a Macro-Economic Theory of
Income Distribution," *Scottish Journ. Pol. Econ.* (October 1961). Several later contributions are noted by Wilhelm Krelle, "The Laws of Income Distribution," in Marchal
and Ducros, *op. cit.*, ch. 16.

54. Kalečki, "The Distribution of the National Income," *Readings*, no. 11. This ex-
position follows Rothschild, *The Theory of Wages* (Oxford: Blackwell, 1954), ch. 14.
For a modification of the Kalečki theory, see Ashok Mitra, *The Share of Wages in
National Income* (The Hague: Centraal Planbureau, 1954). The Kalečki and Mitra
versions are compared in Paul Davidson, *Theories of Aggregate Income Distribution*
(New Brunswick: Rutgers University Press, 1960) ch. 5.

Subscript a refers to an average quantity, subscript m to a marginal quantity.

p = output price m = marginal cost
x = output quantity

e,E = entrepreneurial income w,W = wage costs (manual work-
                                      ers only)

o,O = overhead charge (in- r,R = raw material costs
cluding nonmanual wages)

A = real national income T = real gross output $(A + R)$
$(E + O + W)$

η = elasticity of demand (for μ = degree of monopoly $(1/\eta)$
output of single firm)

The development begins at the micro, or individual firm, level. By definition, price is equal to average cost; all profits and losses are absorbed in entrepreneurial costs e:

$$p = e_a + o_a + w_a + r_a.$$

In computing marginal cost, however, Kalečki treats e_m and o_m as near zero, so that only wage and raw material charges enter in:

$$m = w_m + r_m.$$

The difference, $p - m$, between price and marginal cost, is, by subtraction,

$$p - m = e_a + o_a + (w_a - w_m) + (r_a - r_m)$$

but Kalečki discards the terms in parentheses as near zero. This implies that price must exceed marginal cost:

$$p - m = e_a + o_a.$$

By standard formulas of price theory, we remember that

$$m = p \left(1 - \frac{1}{\eta}\right) \quad \text{and} \quad \frac{m}{p} = 1 - \frac{1}{\eta}.$$

Since the term $1/\eta$ is the Lerner definition of degree of monopoly, symbolized by μ, we have at once:

$$\frac{p - m}{p} = \frac{1}{\eta} = \mu,$$

and after a substitution,

$$e_a + o_a = p - m = p\mu.$$

At the macro level, we let $\bar{\mu}$ be a weighted average degree of monopoly in the entire economy, and let p be a general price level.

$$\Sigma\,(e_a + o_a) = E + O = p\,\bar{\mu}$$
$$\Sigma\,xp = pT$$
$$\frac{\Sigma xp\mu}{\Sigma xp} = \bar{\mu} = \frac{E + O}{T}$$

Or, since the national income A is $(E + O + W)$,

$$\bar{\mu} = \frac{A - W}{T}. \tag{16.9}$$

Diagrammatically, supposing $W_a = W_m$ and $R_a = R_m$ for the economy as well as the single firm, we obtain a configuration like Figure 16.3. Such a situation is clearly inconsistent with long-run competitive equilibrium, since price can never equal both average and marginal cost with a finite output. Kalečki argues, however, that the diagram (Fig. 16.3) is a realistic element in the real world, while pure competition is an unrealistic one and competitive equilibrium even more unreal.

In any event, Kalečki goes on to solve (16.9) for the labor share W/A:

$$\frac{\bar{\mu}\,T}{W} = \frac{A}{W} - 1$$

$$\frac{A}{W} = 1 + \bar{\mu}\,\frac{T}{W}$$

$$\frac{W}{A} = \frac{1}{1 + \bar{\mu}\,\dfrac{T}{W}} = \frac{1}{1 + \bar{\mu}\left(\dfrac{T}{A}\dfrac{A}{W}\right)} = \frac{1}{1 + \bar{\mu}\,\dfrac{A}{W}\left(1 + \dfrac{R}{A}\right)} = 1 - \bar{\mu}\left(1 + \dfrac{R}{A}\right). \tag{16.10}$$

27. On the basis of the various forms of (16.10), Kalečki explains the overall stability of the labor share in advanced capitalist countries as a balance between two offsetting tendencies. An (assumed) rise in the degree of output monopoly (rising $\bar{\mu}$) tends to lower the labor share behind the back of the labor market, with or without collective bargaining. Economy in the use of raw materials (combined with exploitation of raw material producers) lowers R/A over time, and hence raises the labor share. Eventually, Kalečki anticipates, R/A will approach some lower limit, but $\bar{\mu}$ will continue to rise. The labor share W/A will then fall, and a Marxian hypothesis—increasing misery of the working class—will be borne out in at least one of its forms, barring drastic reduction in the labor-force population. No empirical verification is offered, barring approximate constancy of the labor share as per Bowley's Law.

On a more mundane level than the Kalečki forecasts for the long-term future, we can derive from (16.10) an implication that does not seem to fit the facts. The labor share is not equal to unity under free competition, as it should be by (16.10). Nor is it a sufficient answer to doubt in purist fashion the existence of perfect competition on the model of a perfect vacuum or absolute zero; the labor share shows no sign of approaching unity in sectors with small degrees of monopoly. In short, the Kalečki formulation is not the answer to any maiden's prayer.

Accounting Identities: Boulding

28. Many theories in many fields make extensive use of algebraic identities and logical tautologies. Macrodistribution is no exception. For exam-

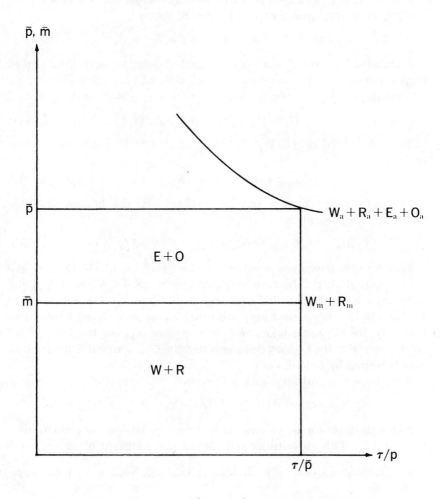

Figure 16.3

ple, we have just seen Kalečki's theory define "entrepreneurial cost" in such a way as to produce identity between price and average cost, and then go on to take advantage of this identity. Boulding's highly original macrodistribution theory is nevertheless distinguished in making use of little more than identity relations. This naturally arouses the question of how causality can be ascribed to his results.

The definitive version of Boulding's theory appears in his ambitious *Reconstruction of Economics*.[55] He starts from balance sheets for a representative business firm and a representative household (Table 16.2, parts a and b). These tables serve simultaneously to present the bulk of his notation.

If we aggregate both sides of Table 16.2 (a) for the entire business community, we obtain (using capital letters for sums)

$$M_b + Q_b + K_b + K_h = K_b' + K_h' + G_b.$$

Since both K_b and K_b' represent the total of debts between firms within the business sector, they are equal to each other. Eliminating these terms, and solving for G_b, we obtain Boulding's "business net worth identity":

$$G_b = M_b + Q_b + (K_h - K_h'). \tag{16.11}$$

The differential of (16.11) Boulding calls the "business saving identity":

$$dG_b = dM_b + dQ_b + dK_h - dK_h'. \tag{16.12}$$

The aggregation process can be repeated for the household sector (Table 16.2[b]), yielding

$$M_h + Q_h + K_{bh} + G_{bh} + K_{hh} = K_{hb}' + K_{hh}' + G_h. \tag{16.13}$$

Four simplifications are possible between (16.11) and (16.13). (*1*) All debts internal to the household sector cancel ($K_{hh} = K_{hh}'$). (*2*) Total debts from households to business appear as K_h in (16.11) and again as K_{hb}' in (16.13). We accordingly substitute K_h for K_{hb}' in the latter equation. (*3*) By the same token, K_h' may replace K_{bh} on the left side of (16.13) (*4*) Finally, G_b may be substituted for G_{bh}, since all firms are ultimately owned by households.

After these four substitutions, we may solve (16.13) for G_h:

$$G_h = M_h + Q_h + G_b - (K_h - K_h').$$

Now substitute for G_b its equivalent from the business net worth identity (16.11). This substitution eliminates the terms involving intersec-

---

55. Kenneth E. Boulding, *Reconstruction of Economics* (New York: Wiley, 1950), ch. 14.

Table 16.2. Balance Sheets for Representative Business and Household

(a) Business

Assets		Liabilities—Net Worth	
Money	m_b	Debts to business	k_b'
Goods	q_b	Debts to households	k_h'
Debts from business	k_b	Net worth	g_b
Debts from households	k_h		

(b) Household

Assets		Liabilities—Net Worth	
Money	m_h	Debts to business	k_{hb}'
Goods	q_h	Debts to households	k_{hh}'
Debts from business	k_{bh}	Net worth	g_h
Net worth of business owned by household	g_{bh}		
Debts from households	k_{hh}		

toral debts, and yields a "household net worth identity" involving simply money and goods:

$$G_h = M_h + Q_h + M_b + Q_b. \qquad (16.14)$$

The differential of the household net worth identity is, as in the similar case in the business sector, the "household savings identity":

$$dG_h = dQ_h + dQ_b + dM_h + dM_b. \qquad (16.15)$$

29.   Let us now indicate by V gross business profits (including all property income), and by D total business distributions of gross profits to households. D includes all interest, dividends, and rent, but includes no wage payments:

$$V = dG_b + D.$$

Substitute for dG_b its value from the business net worth identity (16.12):

$$V = dQ_b + (dM_b + dK_h - dK_h' + D). \qquad (16.16)$$

We can obtain an analogue to (16.16), including the same parenthetical expression, from the household savings identity (16.15). If we abstract from net money creation, so that $dM_h + dM_b$ vanishes, (16.15) simplifies to an expression involving real goods alone:

$$dG_h = dQ_h + dQ_b. \qquad (16.17)$$

But, Boulding points out, an additional identity involving household savings dG_h is

$$dG_h = W + D + dG_b - C_h,$$

where the new symbols W and C_h represent wage payments and household consumption of nondurable goods. If we solve this expression for the wage-bill variable W, after substituting for dG_b and dG_h their respective values from (16.12) and (16.17), the result is:

$$W = C_h + dQ_h - (dM_b + dK_h - dK_h' + D). \qquad (16.18)$$

The expression $(dM_b + dK_h - dK_h' + D)$ is called by Boulding a "transfer factor" and is symbolized by T. This transfer factor enters positively in the gross profit identity (16.16) and negatively in the wage identity (16.18), so that the "transfer" may be looked upon as being from wages to profits. It plays an important role in Boulding's theory.

30.   To show that the sum of W and V exhausts the total product, we may write, from (16.18) and (16.16),

$$W = C_h + dQ_h - T \text{ and } V = dQ_b + T,$$

so that
$$W + V = C_h + dQ_h + dQ_b.$$

The sum $dQ_h + dQ_b$ represents total accumulation of durable goods. Defining total output P_h as the sum of accumulation and consumption, it follows that $W + V = P_h$. Boulding employs this unexciting result in an ingenious diagram (Table 16.3) relating the functional distribution between wages and profits to the breakdown of "absorption" between business and households, by means of the transfer factor T.

*Table 16.3   Relations between Profit-Wage
and Business-Household Income Distributions*

Profits (V)		Wages (W)
Business Accumulation (dQ_b)	Transfer Factor (T)	
	Household Absorption ($C_h + dQ_h$)	

Let us consider this transfer factor in more detail. It is, as we have seen, the sum of four terms: dM_b, dK_h, $- dK_h'$, and D. The first term, dM_b, represents the liquidity preference of business. If the total $M_b + M_h$ is constant, dM_b may be looked upon as the liquidity preference of business relative to that of households, and may be negative. The sum of the next two terms is the net increase in the household debt to business, and may also be negative. The second term, dK_h, is primarily consumer credit. Its extension, by raising T, also raises profits, according to Boulding. Extension of credit therefore pays for itself in the aggregate—one of the numerous Biblical "widow's cruses" (familiar to economists from Keynes' *Treatise on Money*) that enliven *The Reconstruction of Economics*. The third term, dK_h', which enters negatively, represents mainly the sales of business debt securities (bonds) to households. Boulding considers it paradoxical that the sale of securities, motivated by the desire for individual profits, should apparently lower profits as a whole. The fourth and last term, D, is made up of business distributions (dividends, interest, and rent). Their positive effects of T and on V again inspire Boulding to his (and Keynes') favorite "widow's cruse" analogy.

31.   These results can be summarized, widows, cruses, and all, in a table (Table 16.4). They all follow formally from equations (16.16) and (16.18). A group of six factors apparently operate to alter the aggregate income distribution. As in Kalečki's theory, they operate behind the backs of the several input markets, which seem to become irrelevant.

Table 16.4   Factors Influencing Aggregate
Income Distribution between Wages and Profits

Factor Number	Factor	Shift Favorable to: Wages	Profits
1	Household consumption (C_h)	Rise	Fall
2	Household accumulation of durables (dQ_h)	Rise	Fall
3	Business liquidity preference (dM_b)	Fall	Rise
4	Consumer credit extension (dK_h)	Fall	Rise
5	Consumer purchase of debt securities (dK_h')	Rise	Fall
6	Business distributions (D)	Fall	Rise

Boulding then goes on to consider the possible effects of economic growth, technical progress, and various public policy measures upon the course of distribution. Instead of following him, we content ourselves with repeating an important point: these results are all derived from identities, but Boulding interprets them as though they were derived from behavioral relations. While respect is paid to mutual interaction in the best general-equilibrium tradition, the main thrust of Boulding's argument is that these six factors should be considered as important and paradoxical causes for the aggregate income distribution's being what it is.

It has seemed to several critics, including the present writer, more plausible and less paradoxical to regard causation as running almost entirely in the opposite direction. Instead of causes of high wages and profits, may these "factors" not be interpreted more simply and realistically as consequences of the distribution's being as it is?

Under this interpretation, especially when wages rather than profits dominate household income, is it surprising to see high household consumption and accumulation following upon a distributional shift in favor of labor? Or smaller reliance on consumer credit? Or a shift in the money stock from business to households? Or smaller distributions out of the smaller profit pie to be divided?

The problem raised by the Boulding identities is common to much general-equilibrium economics, even without Boulding's reliance upon identities. When one jumps into the air, he comes down to earth—and the earth rises to meet him. Which directions of movement are finite, and which infinitesimal? In our physical analogy, the answer is obvious. In Boulding's reformulation of distribution theory, the answer is less obvious, and Boulding may have been led astray by reconstructional zeal.

Saving-Investment Theories: Kaldor

32.   Reliance on the savings-investment identity suffices to pin the Keynesian label on a distribution theory. Two additional building blocks sup-

port the Kaldorian one.[56] The first of the additional blocks is the stylized fact of a constant marginal capital coefficient or "icor" (incremental capital-output ratio) as a concomitant of economic progress. (This ratio will be discussed in section 33.) The second additional building block is a view of investment at high employment as being determined largely by behavioristic rules of thumb and Keynesian "animal spirits," independent of income distribution, monetary and fiscal policy, or similar aggregative considerations.

33. A necessary prelude to Kaldor's macro distribution theory is the growth equation, or rather identity, propounded by Harrod in 1939.[57] Let national income be Y and its proportionate growth rate G; definitionally, $G = (dy/y)$. Let aggregate saving and investment, both taken net of depreciation and obsolescence, be S and I respectively, while the average saving ratio S/Y is s. (This usage of s is not to be confused with s as a functional share.) Since $S = I$ *ex post* at all times and *ex ante* in equilibrium, we have

$$\frac{dy}{y} = \frac{dy}{I} \frac{S}{Y}$$

But I is also equal to dK, K being the society's capital stock. Let dK/dy be the marginal capital coefficient or "icor," which Harrod calls C, and let s be the saving ratio S/Y. We then have the Harrod equation

$$GC = s. \tag{16.17}$$

Kaldor is by no means alone in regarding C, one of the magic constants or "great ratios" of economic statistics and econometrics,[58] as being approximately constant over the short period. He also accepts Harrod's notion of a "natural" growth rate G_n as a consequence of full employment, resulting from the biological increase in the labor force and from technical progress as reflected in average labor productivity. If we denote

56. Nicholas Kaldor, "Alternative Theories of Distribution" in *Essays in Value and Distribution* (New York: Free Press, 1960), ch. 10. Also reprinted in Joseph E. Stiglitz and Hirofumi Uzawa (eds.), *Readings in the Modern Theory of Economic Growth* (Cambridge, Mass.: M.I.T. Press, 1969), no. 21.

The savings-investment aspect of Kaldor's Keynesian argument was, not too surprisingly, anticipated or parallelled by other writers in the Keynesian tradition. Examples are Josef Steindl, *Maturity and Stagnation in American Capitalism* (Oxford: Blackwell, 1952), ch. 13, and Allan M. Cartter, *Theory of Wages and Employment* (Homewood, Ill.: Irwin, 1959), pp. 155–161. (I am indebted to Arnold Zellner for pointing out the relevance of Steindl's argument in this connection.)

57. R. F. Harrod, "An Essay in Dynamic Theory," in Stiglitz and Uzawa, *op. cit.*, no. 1.

58. Compare Lawrence R. Klein and Richard F. Kosobud, "Some Econometrics of Growth: Great Ratios of Economics," *Q.J.E.* (May 1961). Over the long period, however, C in particular has trended downward in the United States (*ibid.*, p. 197).

by C_r the capital coefficient required to equip the increasing number of workers at full employment, the Harrod equation (16.17) may be rewritten

$$G_n \, C_r = s. \qquad (16.18)$$

Strictly speaking, it may be C_r rather than C that should be thought of as constant in the Kaldorian system.

34.   Given this background, Kaldor's own formal argument can be simplified greatly. Since net income Y is composed of production workers' wages W and gross profits or property income P, we know that

$$Y = W + P.$$

At the same time, total savings are composed of workers' savings $s_w W$ and capitalists' savings $s_p P$, where s_w and s_p are sectoral saving ratios out of wage and profit incomes respectively. Since $S = I$,

$$I = s_w W + s_p P.$$

We can solve the last two equations simultaneously for total profits P and for the profit share (P/Y):

$$P = \frac{I - s_w Y}{s_p - s_w} \quad \text{and} \quad \frac{P}{Y} = \frac{\dfrac{I}{Y} - s_w}{s_p - s_w}. \qquad (16.19 \text{ a-b})$$

The conditions for both positive P and positive P/Y are that the workers' saving ratio s_w be less (or greater) than both the capitalists' saving ratio s_p and the overall investment ratio I/Y. (Only the case of "less" has economic significance.)

Kaldor simplifies (16.19) by ignoring s_w as near zero, so that

$$P = \frac{I}{s_p} \quad \text{and} \quad \frac{P}{Y} = \frac{\dfrac{I}{Y}}{s_p}.$$

By the Harrod growth equation (16.17), $(I/Y) = (S/Y) = s = GC$, and we have, for the profit share,

$$\frac{P}{Y} = \frac{GC - s_w}{s_p - s_w} \quad \text{or} \quad \frac{P}{Y} = \frac{GC}{s_p},$$

depending upon whether or not we disregard s_w as infinitesimal. At full employment, with growth at its "natural" rate, (16.18) applies, so that

$$\frac{P}{Y} = \frac{G_n C_r - s_w}{s_p - s_p} \quad \text{or} \quad \frac{P}{Y} = \frac{G_n C_r}{s_p} \qquad (16.20 \text{ a-b})$$

depending on the size of s_w.

In words: The profit share—or, under socialism, the undistributed or nonlabor share—varies directly with the growth rate, with the capital coefficient, and with the workers' saving ratio, but varies inversely with the capitalists'—or, under socialism, the state's—saving ratio. At full employment, with growth at the natural rate and with the capital coefficient required for that rate, the saving ratios determine the profit share. In terms of the Biblical-Keynesian-Bouldian widow's cruse, the more workers save, the larger their relative share: God helps those who help themselves. In terms of Mandeville's *Fable of the Bees,* the more that capitalists consume, the larger their relative share; private vice is public virtue. In fact, it would appear that capitalists can drive their share close to unity in a Kaldorian world—as close as may avoid starvation and revolution—by a comfortable concentration on living graciously and increasing the scarcity of capital.

A supporting argument stands Say's Law on its head. Full employment is assured by monetary and fiscal policy. The natural growth rate appropriate to full employment, with the required capital coefficient, necessitates a certain quantum of investment. This quantum of investment generates the corresponding amount of saving, acting through the income distribution. If the labor share is too high, steady growth is maintained only through lowering it, for example, through a shift to profits, which Kaldor sees as brought about most easily by price inflation. If the labor share is too low, the shift from profits is less likely to arise from deflation (which would menace full employment) than from a fall in interest rates, as potentially idle savings bid up the prices of existing securities and thereby lower interest and profit rates.

35.   Pasinetti extended the Kaldor model to make the steady-state profit rate r (or P/K) the employment growth rate divided by the capitalists' saving propensity s_p, regardless of the size of s_w.[59] Let N, the volume of (full) employment, grow at rate n, which is also the growth rate of the labor force L, so that $L_t = L_o e^{nt}$. Let K_p be that part of the capital stock which is owned by capitalists proper, while k is the capital-employment ratio K_p/N in capitalist industry. Then, with capitalists' saving equal to capitalists' investment and r the rate of return on K_p,

$$I = \dot{K}_p = s_p r K_p$$
$$\frac{\dot{k}}{k} = \frac{\dot{K}_p}{K_p} - \frac{\dot{N}}{N} = s_p r - n$$
$$\dot{k} = s_p r k - nk.$$

59. Luigi Pasinetti, "Rate of Profit and Income Distribution in Relation to the Rate of Growth," *Rev. Econ. Stud.* (October 1962) .

In the steady state, $\dot{k}$ vanishes, and the profit rate r reduces to (n/s_p), a condition known as "Pasinetti's paradox," since r is independent of s_w. Controversy regarding the significance of this paradox comprised the "two Cambridges" issue of the *Review of Economic Studies* (October 1966),[60] with Samuelson and Modigliani from the American Cambridge downgrading the paradox, and Joan Robinson joining Pasinetti in defense of the English Cambridge view.

36. We have explored in connection with the Boulding macro-distribution theory—equations (16.16) and (16.18), plus Table 16.4—certain doubts about the direction of causation to be read into a particular model. Similar doubts arise regarding the superficially different Kaldor model, including equations (16.19) and (16.20). Do they represent causes or effects of the nonwage, or profit, share being what it is? Unless one accepts two Harrodian notions: a technically predetermined capital coefficient "required" independently of input prices and a "natural" full-employment growth rate independent of the income distribution, plus the Kaldorian inversion of Say's Identity—none of which hold for any branch or sector of the economy[61]—it seems more plausible to interpret these equations as effects rather than as causes, or even as intermediate elements in a general-equilibrium system.

This writer's interpretation of Kaldor's equations runs as follows: With full employment maintained exogenously, a higher nonwage share (plus a wider differential between "class" saving ratios) produces a higher growth rate and/or a higher capital coefficient. There is no reason to sup-

---

60. Paul A. Samuelson and Franco Modigliani, "The Pasinetti Paradox in Neo-Classical and More General Models," *Rev. Econ. Shed.* (October 1966), and in the same issue, Passinetti, "New Results in an Old Framework"; Joan Robinson, "Comment on Samuelson and Modigliani"; Samuelson and Modigliani, "Reply to Pasinetti and Robinson."

61. This is the burden of James Tobin's hilarious "Towards a *General* Kaldorian Theory of Distribution," *Rev. Econ. Stud.* (October 1959), p. 120. "Final output must be divided into n categories: *e.g.*, Aspirin, Binoculars, Cadillacs, Dress suits, Electronic calculators, Football pools, Goose livers, Harrows, . . . Newspapers. Likewise, the population must be split into n mutually exclusive classes. Call them 'factors' if you like, but the distinctive advantage of the theory is that the groups need have nothing at all to do with supplying productive services. Let the classes be, for example, Actors, Birdwatchers, Conservative peers, Dons, Executives, Farmers, Gourmets not elsewhere classified, Hoopers, . . . Nuclear physicists. Class i has income share s_i and divides it in proportions $b_{i1}, b_{i1}, \ldots b_{in} (\Sigma y_j = \Sigma s_i = 1)$. Kindly suppress any neoclassical atavisms suggest that the output of Cadillacs might depend on Executives' share, the output of Goose-livers on the income of Gourmets n.e.c., the production of Harrows on Farmers' fortunes, and so on. The assumption that they don't is just an extension of the two-factor assumption that the division of output between Investment and Consumption is independent of Profits and Wages . . . Now if the Dons will just hurry to make their marginal propensities conform to the fractions in which output is divided (the vector $b_{41}, b_{42}, b_{43}, \ldots b_{4n}$ to equal $y_1, y_2, y_3, \ldots y_n$), centuries of public neglect of education and educators will be avenged."

pose a reverse pattern leading to the income distribution as dependent variable. A number of similar reactions have been assembled in Rothschild's "theme and variations" on the Kaldor model.[62]

A more empirical line of criticism has stemmed from Reder's contribution to the Haley *Festschrift*.[63] The Kaldor formulae, stemming from identities, seem resistant to testing unless interpreted as holding, say, s_p constant. Moreover, their constants apply only to periods of full employment, a condition difficult to identify objectively. Reder, however, is equal to the task. He maintains, after skillful manicuring of American data, that differentiating class saving propensities s_w and s_p does not add significantly (after adjustment for the additional degree of freedom lost) to the accuracy of the undifferentiated saving ratio s in determining the investment-income ratio I/Y. Gallaway, on the other hand, achives results more favorable to the Kaldor theory, focusing his attention on the signs of year-to-year changes in this ratio, and considering the entire period 1929–1960, not merely the high-employment years.[64]

Magic Constancy Theories

37. While magic constants enter Kaldor's macrodistribution theory, they can hardly be said to dominate it. This judgment should perhaps be reversed for the examples that follow. We can divide magic-constancy theories into two groups, according to whether they do, or do not, progress beyond translating Bowley's Law into less familiar terms.

Our example of the first sort (transcending Bowley's Law) is the "simplest" exposition of Krelle's *Verteilungstheorie*.[65] In Kaldor's notation, we have

$$\frac{P}{Y} = \frac{P}{K}\frac{K}{Y},$$

which makes the profit share P/Y an arithmetical product of the profit rate P/K on the capital stock K and the total capital coefficient (not definitionally equal to the marginal one). We have already noted (in Chapter 12) the absence of trend in the long-term interest rate, contrasting sharply with the upward trends of real wages and land rents. In the Kaldorian models, the constancy of the capital coefficient does indeed

---

62. K. W. Rothschild, "Theme and Variations—Remarks on the Kaldorian Distribution Formula," *Kyklos* (Autumn 1965), pp. 653–656.

63. Melvin Reder, "Alternative Theories of Labor's Share," *op. cit.*, p. 191.

64. Lowell E. Gallaway, "The Theory of Relative Shares," *Q.J.E.* (November 1964), pp. 585–589.

65. Wilhelm Krelle, *op. cit.*, ch. 18. Earlier use of the same identity can be found in the literature. An example is William Fellner, *Trends and Cycles in Economic Activity* (New York: Holt, 1956), p. 255.

apply uniformly to total, average, and marginal values. But even so, why should the distributional interpretation above be more valid or relevant than

$$\frac{P}{K}=\frac{P}{Y}\Big/\frac{K}{Y} \qquad \text{or} \qquad \frac{K}{Y}=\frac{P}{Y}\Big/\frac{P}{K}$$

as theories, respectively, of the rate of interest or of the capitalization process? "If any two of [the last three] ratios can be shown to be constant, the remaining one is, by necessity, constant. . . . The chief problem, of course, is the determination of which ratios are fundamental, and which derived. Further it is indeed possible that one or more of the above ratios may be more appropriately explained by the combined effect of factor substitution and technological change, as in the microeconomic theories." [66]

A comment by Modigliani[67] implies that the "true" dependent variable is none of those appearing in the triad comprising the identity, but rather, the rate of progress toward a long-term, permanent, or lifetime value of the wealth-income ratio K/Y. Modigliani assumes a magically constant lifetime ratio K/Y, toward which each economic subject progresses, normally from below. Progress may be faster, slower, or even negative, depending on whether the rate of return P/K exceeds or falls short of its permanent value. In this dynamic adjustment, the profit share P/Y plays a largely passive role. Incidentally, as Denison points out, the "identity" is itself borne out only imperfectly by actual data, inasmuch as the appropriate price deflators for P, K, and Y are imperfectly consistent with each other.[68] (In many countries, including the United States, there is a rising trend in the ratio of capital goods prices to general prices.)

Krelle himself writes with one eye on Kaldor; a graphic illustration of the connection is Figure 16.4. Its basic notion is that, for any income level Y_i, the planned saving ratio is a rising function of the property share P/Y, while the planned investment ratio I/Y depends primarily on other matters. Both S/Y and I/Y functions may tend to move upward as income rises from Y_1 to Y_2 to Y_3. The equilibrium property share FF, connecting the intersections of S/Y and I/Y, may be constant as shown in the figure. The same Krelle locus may, however, trace some other path.[69]

---

66. Charles L. Schultze and Louis Weiner, "Introduction" to National Bureau of Economic Research, *Behavior of Income Shares, op. cit.*, p. 5.

67. Modigliani, "Comment," in *ibid.*, pp. 45–49.

68. E. F. Denison, *ibid.*, pp. 35–39.

69. In "Neo-Classical Macro-Distribution Theory," *op. cit.* (pp. 498 f., Fig. 3), the writer drew FF as bow-shaped, first rising and then falling with income. This form traces out the Kuznets conjecture of Chapter 4, dealing with the paths of relative shares

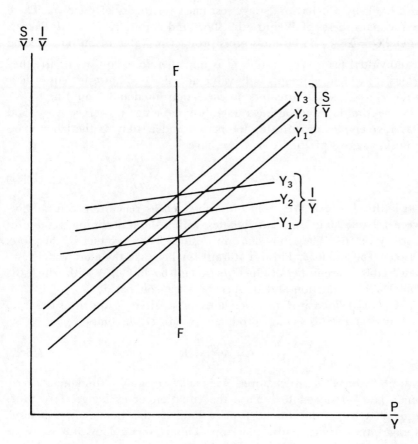

Figure 16.4

38. Closer than Krelle to Bowley's Law is Weintraub's venture into magic constancy.[70] The distributional implications of Weintraub's venture seem originally to have been secondary to his attempted replacement of the Fisherian exchange equation and the quantity theory of money and

---

in the development process. If Kaldor's s_p rises with income and s_w can be neglected, *FF* should slope upward throughout with constant *G* and *C*. (Lowell Gallaway made this point in correspondence.) The figure is adapted from Krelle, *op. cit.*, p. 77, fig. 10.

70. Sidney Weintraub, *A General Theory of the Price Level, Output, Income Distribution, and Economic Growth* (Philadelphia: Chilton, 1959). See also Weintraub, "A Model of the Price Level," in *Some Aspects of Wage Theory and Policy* (Philadelphia: Chilton, 1963), pp. 48 f.

Magic constancy is not the major element in Weintraub's extensive contributions to macrodistribution. These will be considered below (sections 45–49) as our prime example of eclectic theorizing.

price levels by a behavioral wage-cost mark-up theory of his own. These are the main theses of Weintraub's short and ambitious *General Theory*.

Let $PQ = \sum_i p_i q_i$ be business gross product or value of output, i being an individual firm. Weintraub's Q is not, therefore, equivalent to other writers' Y, which represents only value added. Q is, however, equivalent to Kalečki's T, which attempts no correction for double counting.

Let wN be the total business wage bill, w being an average wage, and N average employment during the period under study. If the labor share in business gross product is $1/k$, we have

$$PQ = kwN \qquad \text{or} \qquad P = kw\frac{N}{Q}. \tag{16.21}$$

It is this k which Weintraub has observed as remaining constant between 1.9 and 2.0 in the United States, with a slight declining trend after World War II.[71] The labor share in business gross product is, therefore, between 0.50 and 0.53. This is naturally smaller than the more widely estimated labor share in net product (between 0.65 and 0.75) with which the Cobb-Douglas function and its successors are concerned.

If Q/N is defined as A (average labor productivity), and R as the ratio w/A of wage rate to average productivity, (16.21) becomes

$$P = k\frac{w}{A} = kR \tag{16.22}$$

with no "money" term whatever. This is Weintraub's "fundamental economic law," designed to replace the equation of exchange. His critics argue that it ties the (money) price level to the (money) wage level, average productivity, and a mark-up. This is a tautology, but so is the equation of exchange. Why should either tautology deny the other?

But to return to the "magic constancy" of Weintraub's k. It represents, as we have seen, the reciprocal of the wage share in business *gross* product. Bowley's Law asserts constancy of the wage share in business *net* product, and therefore also of the reciprocal of this share. What Weintraub implicitly adds to Bowley's Law is constancy in the share of net to gross product—a denial of Kalečki's alleged tendency to increasing economy in the use of raw materials. Alternatively, if one questions Bowley's generalization, the constancy of k implies that the rising labor share s is offset systematically by the Kalečki tendency to economy in the use of raw materials, so that k is empirically more reliable in its constancy than is s.

71. Figures covering 1899–1960 are found in Weintraub, "The Constancy of the Wage Share," in *Wage Theory and Policy, op. cit.*, p. 87, table 29. On what Weintraub calls the "postwar sag" in k, see Weintraub, *General Theory, op. cit.*, pp. 41 f.

39. Possible policy implications of (16.21–16.22) are not overlooked by Weintraub. He interprets them as neutral between demand-pull and cost-push theories of inflation, since wages are so important a component of demand. At the same time, the direct cost-push aspect makes wage control (for Weintraub) fundamental to inflation control, and in this he is at one with the cost-pushers. If the wage rate w rises no more rapidly than average labor productivity A, the price level P will take care of itself. Or rather, the constant k will take care of it.[72]

40. The trouble with "magic constants" is that, in the long run, with variable prices, or across national and economic-system boundaries, they seldom remain constant. An overly "stylized" fact is no longer a fact at all. Samuelson has commented, with illustrative reference to some distribution-theory examples,[73]

> . . . The fact that counter-trends have cancelled each other for half a century can be regarded as coincidence, and provides no guarantee of repetition. [I have] learned how treacherous are economic "laws" in economic life: *e.g.*, Bowley's Law of constant relative wage share; Long's Law of constant participation in the labor force; Pareto's Law of unchangeable inequality of income; Modigliani's Law of constant wealth-income ratio; Marx' Law of the falling rate of real-wage and/or the falling rate of profit; Everybody's Law of a constant capital-output ratio. If these be laws, Mother Nature is a criminal. Experience has also taught me to be necessarily suspicious of coincidence; in many cases, even if they do not explain the facts, they do describe the facts, until they cease to describe the facts.

To this line of thought, as expressed by others, Weintraub had already replied:[74]

> It is distressing to find so much discomfort over evidence of certain important consistencies in economics, not least the labor share. Why do we fear them? Why do we refuse to acknowledge them as empirical facts, even as we proceed to understand and explain them? I have even encountered the twisted argument that recognition of a functional relationship imports more insight than

72. Compare Weintraub, "Toward a National Wage Policy," in *Wage Theory and Policy, op. cit.*, ch. 6. Also "In Defense of Wage-Price Guideposts . . . Plus," in Almarin Phillips and Oliver E. Williamson (eds.) , *Prices: Issues in Theory, Practice, and Public Policy* (Philadelphia: University of Pennsylvania Press, 1967) , ch. 5.

73. Paul A. Samuelson, "A Brief Post-Keynesian Survey," in Robert Lekachman (ed.) , *Keynes' General Theory: Reports of Three Decades* (New York: St. Martin's 1964) , p. 336 (running quotation) .

74. Weintraub, "Real versus Price Theories of Distribution," in *Wage Theory and Policy, op. cit.*, p. 243, no. 13 (running quotation) .

an empirical near-constant. Is this anything short of arguing that a horizontal locus in a diagram is a weaker force than a curved locus whose shape we fix only vaguely, whose location is in doubt, and whose stability is in question? Does work with such fuzzy "functions" advance our science in the same way as empirical recognition and analytical utilization of (near) constants?

By this writer's reading of the argument, the Samuelsons come nearer the methodological mark than the Weintraubs, by the absence of analytical explanation of the magical constancy of magic constants. The advantage of fuzzy functions over precise constants does not lie in any greater insight stemming from the fuzziness, mathematical weakness, or fuddydud pedantry of $x = F(y,z)$, but only in the insurance they provide against elaborate theoretical constructions, generalizations, and "fallacies of misplaced concreteness' on no basis beyond strong proportionality observations. Nobody objects to magic constants, black or white, for short-run purposes or for first approximations. Furthermore, the widespread use of approximate linearity and log-linearity, on grounds of empirical convenience and goodness of fit, takes many practicing statisticians and econometricians more than half way between full generalization and magic constants. Let him who is without methodological sin cast the first methodological stone.

Sociological-Institutional Theories

41. A number of sociological and institutional distribution theories, before and since John Stuart Mill's classic summary of distribution as "a matter of human institution solely,"[75] have followed Mill in regarding distribution as institutionally variable within extremely broad limits, even if not "solely." Most such theories still seem, to conventional economists accustomed to neat, tidy, and well-structured theory, somewhat inchoate and formless.[76] Exactly what are the sociologists and institutionalists maintaining, beyond the inapplicability of the Good Old Theory outside the allegedly limited realm of strictly profit-maximizing firms? Exactly what propositions, testable even qualitatively, can be distilled from theory that is sufficiently general to apply both where orthodoxy fits and where it does not—to public employment, subsistence agricul-

75. Mill, *Principles of Political Economy*, Ashley ed. (London: Longmans, 1908), pp. 21, 200. The indeterminacy of income distribution is contrasted, it should be noted, with the determinacy of technical relations of production (*i.e.*, with production functions), and not with any iron determinacy of output price formation.

In the preface to his edition of Mill, W. J. Ashley attributes Mill's views on distributional indeterminacy to the influence of Harriet Taylor, whom Mill later married. (*Ibid.*, p. xxi f.).

76. For a rebuttal to this interpretation, see an interpellation by Emile James in Marchal and Ducros, *op. cit.*, p. 504.

ture,[77] caste systems, and planned economies along with relatively unregulated advanced-country private enterprise? How, and to what extent, are
the sociological conclusions articulated with those of the Good Old
Theory (which most of these critics are willing to retain as a special case
or vermiform appendix) ?

And so one recoils, more puzzled than critical, awaiting the conclusion
of, for instance, the Marchal-Lecaillon treatise,[78] which is written from a
sociological point of view and may rebut these skeptical objections. For
the present, Marchal and Ducros have interpreted the several "country"
papers of the 1964 Palermo Conference on Income Distribution, particularly those prepared by economists in the French tradition, as supporting
the sociological position.[79]

42.   At another extreme stands an idiosyncratic sociological rival to the
Good Old Theory that should be mentioned specially. It is more (rather
than less) highly structured than marginalism, thanks to a whole matrix
full of nearly magic near-constants. It has arisen from the Left-Keynesian
wing of the Cambridge School, the former *fons et origo* of the Marshallian neoclassical tradition. The reference is to Sraffa's Ricardian "commodities by commodities," seconded at a distance by Brahmananda's
"new-classical" economics.[80]

With no influence from the demand side, constant returns to scale,
homogeneous "abstract" labor as the single "original" or "primary" input
or factor of production, and technically fixed production coefficients for
all outputs with respect to all inputs,[81] the wage rate can vary from "sub-

77. A. K. Sen, "Peasants and Dualism with or without Surplus Labor," *J.P.E.* (Oc-
tober 1966) , is one of a number of applications of the Good Old Theory of the specially
inhospitable problems of subsistence agriculture. (See also Pan Yotopoulos' studies of
Greece.) For the even more inhospitable problems of collectivism, see Benjamin Ward,
"The Firm in Illyria: Market Syndicalism," *A.E.R.* (September 1968) , and E. D. Domar,
"The Soviet Collective Farm," *A.E.R.* (September 1966) .

78. Jean Marchal and Jacques Lacaillon, *La Répartition du Revenu National*, 3 vols.
(Paris: Librairie de Médius, n.d.)

79. Jean Marchal and Bernard Ducros, "Introduction" to Marchal and Ducros, *op. cit.*,
pp. xxiv–xxx. "Sociological" country chapters were contributed by Jacques Lecaillon
(France, ch. 2) , M. Falise (Belgium, ch. 5) , Maria Negriponti-Delivanis (Underdeveloped Countries, ch. 12) , and Elias Gannagé (Underdeveloped Countries, ch. 13) .

80. Piero Sraffa, *Production of Commodities by Means of Commodities* (Cambridge:
Cambridge University Press, 1960) ; P. R. Brahmananda, *The New-Classical versus the
Neo-Classical Economics* (Mysore: Prasaranga, 1967) , chs. 14, 16.

81. For an efficient Leontief input-output system without joint production, the fixity
of production coefficients results from the other conditions posited, and need not be
assumed additionally. Paul A. Samuelson, "Abstract of a Theorem Concerning Substi-
tutability in Open Leontief Models," in T. C. Koopmans (ed.) , *Activity Analysis of
Production and Allocation* (New York: Wiley, 1951) . It seems a safe conjecture that
theorem applies also to the Sraffa system.

sistence" as a lower limit to average value added per worker as an upper one, and the labor share can move accordingly (with employment given). These assumptions, however, seem, in F. H. Knight's classroom phrase, "simply not so," to this reactionary critic. Demand makes a difference; constant returns hold only in the small; labor skills result from investment in human capital, somewhat as capital results from the indirect application of human labor; and so on with similar "standard" objections more applicable in developed countries than in developing ones.

43.   It remains to be seen how significant are these doubts as to the variability of the productive shares, and the matter is not one to be decided a priori. Planned economies, with flexible output proportions, can conceivably vary the shares within wide limits. In economies dominated by business enterprises operating under profit constraints, the range of variability seems lower, and attempts to stretch its limits radically may produce inflation, depression, and/or chaos not elsewhere classified. (This is the problem of incomes policy, which must wait for the next chapter.)

Eclectic Theories

44.   "The theory of the distribution of the product of industry between wages and profits which is knocking about in current economic teaching consists of a number of propositions, each of which is quite unexceptionable in itself, but none of which bears any relation to the rest."[82] Statements such as this one by Joan Robinson have inspired the birth of eclectic theories trying, as she puts it, "to fit the pieces together into a coherent whole."

Combinations of two or more elements, orthodox and/or heterodox, in some (hopefully) definitive eclectic macrodistribution theory began in the mid-1950's, when Mrs. Robinson published her "Theory of Distribution." They have continued without pause. Mrs. Robinson goes on to prepare a Kaldor-Kalecki sandwich:[83] "The proposition that the share of profits in income is a function of the ratio of investment in income is perfectly correct, but capacity and the degree of monopoly have to be brought in to determine what income it is that profits are a share of, and investment is related to." Across the Atlantic, Reder has prepared a decidedly different sandwich, suggesting acceptance of Kaldor on the "wage share" of production workers, and of Cobb-Douglas marginalism for the broader functional share of labor as a whole.[84]

82. Joan Robinson, "The Theory of Distribution," in *Collected Economic Papers, op. cit.*, vol. ii, p. 145.

83. *Ibid.*, p. 149.

84. Reder, "Alternative Theories of Labor's Share," *op. cit.*, pp. 200–205.

For introductions to the burgeoning literature, stressing Continental writers, one may turn to Rothschild and Krelle.[85] There are at least two additional Japanese contributions; promising American and Swedish ones appeared too late for consideration by either Rothschild or Krelle.[86]

45. Our exposition will concentrate on Weintraub's *Approach to the Theory of Income Distribution* (1958), with only minor attention to later expansions and emendations. It will borrow freely from Davidson's convenient condensation.[87]

Weintraub's theory sprang from a source that seems at first glance uninviting, namely, his earlier identification of the Keynesian aggregate supply function with the "expected proceeds" function that Keynes has called Z. Let us therefore back-pedal into macroeconomics to explore this function further.

46. When Weintraub expounds Keynesian aggregate demand and supply functions in two-dimensional diagrams (or their literary equivalents), one might expect to find the horizontal axis a quantity of goods (income or GNP per period, perhaps) and the vertical axis some expression for their price (a price index number of some kind, presumably). However, Weintraub's horizontal axis measures not real income, but employment; the vertical axis has the dimension of money income or one of its component parts. Aggregate expected proceeds, or Z, has three dimensions, and so Weintraub writes his aggregate proceeds function, which also serves as an aggregate supply function,

$$Z = Z(N) = wN + F + R. \qquad (16.23)$$

85. Rothschild, "Recent Contributions" and "Theme and Variations," *op. cit.*, are not limited to eclectic theories, but contain copious references to them. The same is true of Krelle, *Verteilungstheorie, op. cit.*, and the later "Laws of Income Distribution in the Short Run and the Long Run," in Marchal and Ducros, *op. cit.*, ch. 16. (The positive arguments of both Krelle essays are species of the genus "eclectic theory.")

86. The Japanese contributions mentioned are Kazu Dodo, "A Study in Macro-Economic Theories of Income Distribution," *Kobe University Econ. Rev.* (1965) and Tetsuhito Nakajima, "Aggregate Supply Function and Income Distribution" (Mimeographed, Kyoto, 1963).

The American offering mentioned is Robert Solow and Joseph Stiglitz, "Output, Employment, and Wages in the Short Run," *Q.J.E.* (November 1968), whose resemblances to Weintraub's work (to be summarized later) prompted Weintraub, "Solow and Stiglitz on Employment and Distribution: A New Romance with an Old Model?" *Q.J.E.* (February 1970). The Swedish offering is Björn Thalberg, "Labour's Share and Economic Development—A Review Article," *Sw. Journ. Econ.* (June 1967), summarizing the theoretical portions of Karl G. Jungenfelt, *Löneandelen och de ekonomiska utvecklingen* (Stockholm: Almquist and Wicksell, 1966), for the benefit of non-Scandinavians and adding suggestions of the reviewer's.

87. Weintraub, *op. cit.*; Davidson, *op. cit.*, ch. 8.

Here N, w, and $W (= wN)$ are as defined in, for example, the Kalečki model (employment, average wage rate, total wage bill). F represents fixed money payments, primarily to rentiers. R is the profit residual; profit maximization requires that dR/dN not be negative.

The Z function passes through the origin O of Figure 16.5, whether or not we follow Weintraub in interpreting it as an aggregate supply as well as a proceeds function. This is because no proceeds are required to justify full unemployment. The function also slopes upward, with an upward concavity. Its upward slope is obvious; positive proceeds are required to justify incremental employment at any positive wage. Its upward concavity seems justified by diminishing returns. Since the v.m.p. of labor falls as employment rises, successively greater amounts of entrepreneurial income or gross profit $(Z - W - F)$ are required to motivate successive increments of employment.[88] In fact, the slope of the Z function (16.23) is

$$\frac{dZ}{dN} = w + \frac{dR}{dN}, \quad \text{where} \quad \frac{dR}{dN} \text{ is non-negative.}$$

With a fixed wage rate w and a given initial employment N_0, we have, in Figure 16.5, the labor share s already determined:

$$s = \frac{AN_0}{BN_0}$$

To measure changes in s with changes in employment (still retaining a constant average wage rate), Weintraub introduces an output supply elasticity which he calls E_z. It is equal to $1/s$ if marginal analysis holds, and is defined as

$$E_z \equiv \frac{EN}{EZ} = \frac{dN}{dZ} \frac{Z}{N}$$

rather than its reciprocal EZ/EN, which we might have anticipated. Returning to the diagram (Fig. 16.5), it follows from diminishing returns and marginal productivity that dZ/dN must exceed Z/N at point B, so that E_z is a proper fraction. Then, with constant w and $dw/dN = 0$.

$$\frac{ds}{dN} = \frac{d}{dN}\left(\frac{wN}{Z}\right) = \frac{1}{Z^2}\left[Z\left(w + N\frac{dw}{dN}\right) - wN\frac{dZ}{dN}\right]$$

$$= \frac{w}{Z} - \frac{w}{Z}\left(\frac{dZ}{dN}\frac{N}{Z}\right) = \frac{w}{Z}\left(1 - \frac{1}{E_z}\right) \tag{16.24}$$

It follows that ds/dN is negative where E_z is less than unity (as per diminishing returns to labor). In words, increasing employment lowers

88. On the other hand, upward concavity of Z implies a rising *share* of entrepreneurial income as employment rises. Can this be verified empirically? It does not follow from the Good Old Theory.

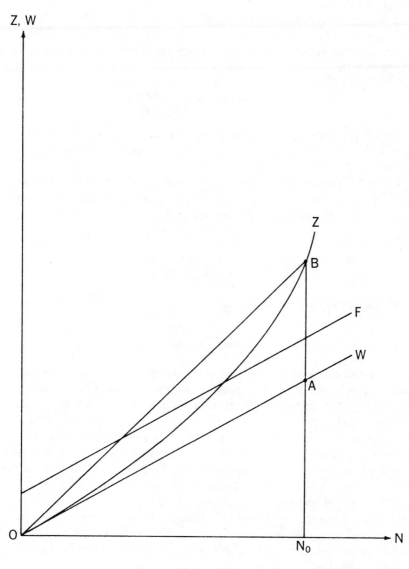

Figure 16.5

the labor share unless the wage rate rises; Bowley's Law must imply some such rise.

46. The next elements to be added to the Weintraub panorama are marginal productivity and the degree of monopoly. (Unlike the English

dissenters whom he admires, Weintraub does not discard conventional marginalism.)

A single competitive firm's wage rate w_i equals labor's v.m.p., or $p_i(dx_i/dn_i)$. (The subscript i refers to the firm, n_i is the firm's employment, and the other terms should be self-explanatory.) It follows, as in Chapter 6, that

$$\frac{dx_i}{dn_i} = \frac{w_i}{p_i}, \qquad \text{and also that} \qquad \frac{w_i n_i}{x_i p_i} = s_i = \frac{dx_i}{dn_i}\frac{n_i}{x_i}.$$

The labor share s_i is the quotient of the marginal product M_i and the average product A_i. In form, it is also an elasticity, which may be called e_p, the firm's elasticity of productivity.

In the aggregate, for a given employment level N (and still assuming competitive conditions), Weintraub aggregates as a weighted average, letting $x_i p_i = Z_i$ and $\sum_i Z_i = Z$, and using E_p as a weighted average value of e_p.

$$\frac{wN}{Z} = s = \sum_i \frac{Z_i}{Z}\left(\frac{M_i}{A_i}\right) = \frac{M}{A} = E_p. \qquad (16.25)$$

When employment is variable:

$$\frac{ds}{dN} = \frac{d}{dN}\left(\frac{M}{A}\right) = \frac{1}{A}\left(\frac{dM}{dN} - \frac{M}{A}\frac{dA}{dN}\right).$$

Both dM/dN and dA/dN are presumably negative (diminishing returns again, applied to an aggregate production function, which Weintraup does not introduce explicitly.) When the proportionate fall of the marginal product exceeds that of the average product, that is, if $[(dM/dN)/M < (dA/dN)/A]$, the aggregate productivity elasticity E_p is a declining function of employment, and the labor share will move in the opposite direction from employment. Conversely, if dE_p/dN is positive, the labor share and employment will move together.

When the (Lerner-Kalečki) degree of monopoly μ_i (for the firm) or μ (for the economy) is introduced into the labor-share equations above, the modifications are relatively simple. We recall from Chapter 8 that the marginal revenue product (m.r.p.) of a monopolistic firm equals its v.m.p. multiplied by the fraction

$$1 - \frac{1}{\eta_i} = 1 - \mu_i$$

where η_i is the elasticity of demand (taken positive), for the value added of firm i. For the economy as a whole, μ is the weighted average value of

μ_i, and E_d (aggregate demand elasticity) is the corresponding weighted average value of η_i. We have, therefore, modifying (16.25),

$$s = \sum_i \frac{Z_i}{Z} \frac{M_i}{A_i} \left(1 - \frac{1}{\eta_i}\right) = \frac{M}{A} (1 - \mu) = E_p (1 - \mu) . \qquad (16.26)$$

The labor share falls, *ceteris paribus*, when the average degree of monopoly rises. This familiar conclusion may be either reinforced or offset by the output-and-employment consequences of monopoly, as summarized in equation (16.24) and Figure 16.5, but not considered explicitly in Kalečki's theory of distribution. A rise in the Z function (resulting from monopoly restriction) operates against the labor share. However, the accompanying fall in employment may carry a certain distributional offset in the form of a decreased output supply elasticity E_z. This elasticity falls insofar as the Z function is concave upward, and the labor share rises since s is the reciprocal of E_z.

Weintraub has a decided disdain for "monetary mischief" as an antiinflationary device. This characteristic disdain is reflected in two arguments, one of which relates directly to the "monopoly" issue:[89]

> Tight money to combat inflation—and central banks seem always to be on a non-triumphal crusade against inflation—must operate to cut the investment volume. Yet unemployment engendered by monopoly pricing requires a *greater* investment volume . . . *In an economy where monopoly power is increasing, inflation can scarcely be countered by monetary policy.* Tighter money can only compound the mischief, and may be disastrous in the final outcome.

47. The perspicacious reader may note that sections 45–46 have not yet dropped the special assumption of a given and constant average wage rate. Weintraub actually drops it expeditiously, although he has little to say about the interest rate on capital.

Much of Weintraub's development can be presented graphically, as an elaboration of Figure 16.5. Replacing the constant wage rate w (and single w-ray through the origin) of that diagram, we may utilize a family of such lines in Figure 16.6, labeled $W_1, W_2, \ldots$.[90] If recession employment is only N_1 at wage w_1, but revival simultaneously raises employment to N_2 and average wage rates to w_2, the overall wage-bill line (W line) can now be drawn through the points A_1 and A_2 (N_1, w_1 and N_2, w_2) . Instead

89. Weintraub, "A Macro-Theory of Pricing, Income Distribution, and Employment," *Weltwirtschaftliches Archiv*, (Spring 1969) , p. 21 (italics mine) . Weintraub's "other" argument combines a "bad" Phillips curve with an ideological unwillingness to inflict unemployment on the working class for the sake of "protecting rentier interests." ("In Defense of Wage-Price Guideposts . . . Plus," *op. cit.,* p. 65 n.)

90. The wage rate w_i is the tangent of the angle between the corresponding W_i line with the horizontal axis.

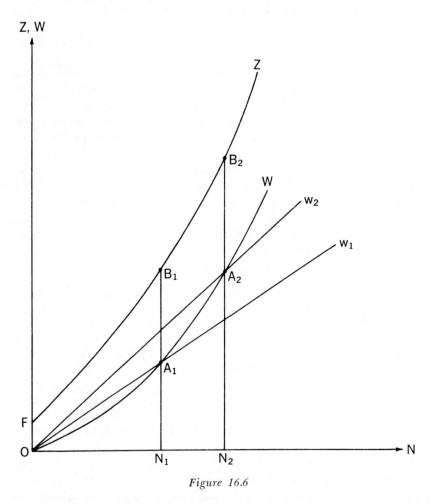

Figure 16.6

of being straight like the W line of Figure 16.5, or like the W_1 and W_2 line of Figure 16.5, or like the W_1 and W_2 lines of Figure 16.6, it takes on an upward concavity of its own. This upward concavity of its W component increases the upward concavity of the total proceeds or supply function Z,[91] and decreases its radius of curvature.

Analytically, we may also examine the path of the nonlabor component $(Z - W)$ or $(A_1B_1, A_2B_2, \ldots)$ as employment and wage rates change simutaneously. Using (16.23),

91. The FF line of Figure 16.5 has been omitted, for clarity and convenience, from Figure 16.6.

$$\frac{d(Z-W)}{dN} = \frac{dZ}{dN} - \frac{dW}{dN} = \left(w + N\frac{dw}{dN} + \frac{dR}{dN}\right) - \left(w + N\frac{dw}{dN}\right) = \frac{dR}{dN},$$

a result neither surprising, informative, nor particularly helpful. Weintraub points out that dR/dN tends upward, and the labor share downward, with capital deepening and also with labor-saving innovation. These changes represent shifts in the aggregate supply function Z, however, and not movements along it.

48. Weintraub's next step introduces aggregate demand, and can be classified as definitely Keynesian. Consumption demand D_c (which may be interpreted to include public and private investment along with consumption proper) depends not only upon disposable income Y_d but also upon asset holdings A. With c the marginal propensity of the society to spend out of disposable income, and λ the similar propensity to spend out of increased asset values, we have

$$D_c = c\,Y_d + \lambda\,A,$$

and in addition,

$$Y_d = wN + F + kR$$

where this k is the proportion of R distributed to individuals, primarily as dividends. (Interest and rent payments are included in F.)

Consumer demand (aggregate demand) D_c may be subdivided into $D_c{}^w$ (workers' demand), which follows roughly the W line of Figure 16.6, and $D_c{}^r$ (capitalists' demand), including rentiers' demand $D_c{}^F$, which receives no separate treatment.

In any case, D_c is dominated by workers' demand $D_c{}^w$, particularly as regards consumption proper. "If it is correct that about 90 per cent of consumer output is purchased by wage- and salary-earners, then the familiar 'consumption-function' is merely . . . a wage-earner outlay-function. The simple implication is that a rise in money wages will raise consumption outlays."[92]

Since aggregate profits rise with employment N, capitalists' demand $D_c{}^r$ is an increasing function of N (on diagrams like Figure 16.7, which does not itself appear in Weintraub's work). However, the upward slope of $D_c{}^r$ is shallower than that of R, because of the saving factor. The wage function W slopes upward, as per Figure 16.6, and may be taken as a first approximation to $D_c{}^w$. In consequence, the sum $D_c{}^w + D_c{}^r$, which equals aggregate demand D_c, slopes upward.

92. Weintraub, "In Defense of Wage-Price Guideposts . . . Plus," *op. cit.,* pp. 71 f.

There will be an equilibrium solution at the intersection (on Figure 16.7) of D_c and the aggregate supply function or Z line of Figure 16.5. This intersection also determines N, the equilibrium level of employment. The equilibrium position, at point B, is stable if, as drawn, the slope of Z exceeds that of D_c at the (presumably) unique intersection B. The "stability" argument is as follows: if the slope of Z exceeds that of D_c at B, Z will lie above D_c to the right of N, that is, for all employment levels greater than N. This juxtaposition of slopes means that, for employment in excess of N, the aggregate proceeds necessary to induce such employment exceed anticipated expenditures D_c, so that the differential employment will be unprofitable and actual employment will revert to N. (The reader can ring the changes on this demonstration for himself.)

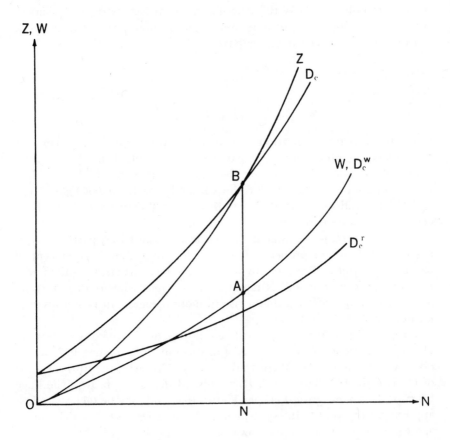

Figure 16.7

The equilibrium labor share, if we may return to macrodistribution theory proper, is indicated by the quotient AN/BN on Figure 16.7 much as we found it previously in Figure 16.5 for a simpler model.

Figure 16.7, as drawn, includes no investment, export, or public expenditure sectors. They may be incorporated implicitly in D_c. Alternatively, we may combine these sectors, to a first approximation, as a horizontal line independent of N. The corresponding amount of expenditures may be added vertically to D_c, obtaining aggregate expenditure D, which intersects Z at B, as we have indicated that D_c does.

49. This is basically a Keynesian theory, although hardly a Kaldorian one. It harbors both marginalist and monopoly-theory adornments. It is not a Kaldorian theory because it makes very little use of the savings-investment identity; neither does it assume full employment. Indeed, by the Sen criterion[93] for distinguishing neo-Keynesian from neoclassical macrodistribution theories, it is neither flesh, fowl, nor good red herring.

The bane of any eclectic system or theory is inconsistency between its several parts. The mathematical translation of inconsistency is overdeterminacy, when the number of equations in a system exceed the number of unknowns to be determined. In the Weintraub system, it is not entirely clear what are the unknowns, and what variables should be taken as given exogenously. However, the Keynesian parts of the system (our sections 46 and 48) seem formally self-contained, and sufficient to determine the distributional unknowns. If so, what are the non-Keynesian (not anti-Keynesian) portions (of section 47) all about? Are they, perhaps, elements of inconsistency or overdeterminacy? Do they, perhaps, represent effects rather than causes of the distribution of income? If so, what mech-

---

93. A. K. Sen, "Neo-Classical and Neo-Keynesian Theories of Distribution," *Ec. Record* (March, 1963). This criterion depends on the equation to be dropped in an overdeterminate macro-system of Sen's devising. In Sen's notation, X is total real output, of which $\overline{X}$ must be used to reproduce itself; L is the labor force and w its real wage rate; W is the total wage bill, and equals Lw; π is total profits, and I total investment. Two saving propensities, s_w and s_p, are taken over from Kaldor. There is also an exogenously determined amount of investment I^*.

There are only four unknowns, S, W, π, and I; the other variables are all given. To solve, however, Sen uses the five equations below. Equation (1) is a production function, assumed linear homogeneous; (2) equates marginal productivity to the wage rate; (3) exhausts total product; (4) equates saving and investment *ex ante*; (5) equates actual with exogenous investment. Neoclassical writers, alleges Sen, avoid overdeterminacy by dropping (4); neo-Keynesian ones drop (2) instead. The equations are:

(1) $X = X\ (L,X)$ $\qquad$ (3) $X = \pi + wL$

$\qquad$ (2) $w = \dfrac{\delta X}{\delta L}$

(4) $I = s_p\pi + s_w W$ $\qquad$ (5) $I = I^*$

The Weintraub system drops (5).

anism brings such effects about? Are they, perhaps, completely irrelevant window-dressing? One misses the fine Lausanne hand of a general-equlibrium economist here and there.

Conclusion

50.   Admitting, as one must, the survival of gaps and ambiguities in neo-classical macrodistribution theory, and also in its statistical supports, we may still anticipate as much progress along its lines as along the more "modernistic" ones that have become fashionable in post-depression generations. In particular, protest seems in order against discarding the Good Old Theory out of hand, and in favor of including it prominently in any future synthesis of macroeconomic distribution models.

Three obvious and mutually related appeals of the Good Old Theory have been: (*1*) its consistency with microdistribution—marginalism and all that; (*2*) its acceptance of the principle of input substitution at the margin, both directly and as a by-product of output substitution, particularly in the long run; and (*3*) its adequate though not conclusive record of empirical testing and application.

As for consistency between micro- and macroeconomics, Machlup has pleaded the methodological case:[94]

> It is not a duty for every macrotheorist to search for the hidden micro-relations that lie at the foot of the macro-relations . . . To specialize in the construction of macro-models without worry about the underlying micro-theories is neither unsound nor dishonorable. But to deny that all macro-theory requires a micro-theoretical underpinning, or to deride the efforts of those who do investigate it, would be unreasonable and obtuse.
>
> While it is, of course, possible to concentrate on macro-theory, taking the micro-relations as given without being concerned about their composition, the macro-theorist wanting to understand his subject more profoundly will proceed to study the micro-theoretical underpinning of his macro-models.

As for the role of input substitution, it may, of course, be negligible in the very short run, in societies with constant relative prices, or in societies insulated from market forces. Under these circumstances, all our elasticities of substitution may be infinitesimal. These cases aside, however, it is of obvious advantage to use a theory that is not so "structural" as to assume these elasticities to be zero a priori, despite evidence to the contrary. (It is admittedly no better implicitly to assume them unitary, as the Cobb-Douglas function does, in the absence of empirical verification.)

94. Fritz Machlup, "Micro- and Macro-Economics: Contested Boundaries and Claims of Superiority," in *Essays on Economic Semantics* (Englewood Cliffs, N.J.: Prentice-Hall, 1963), pp. 109, 140.

With regard to empirical testing, the record of the Good Old Theory is far from spotless, but it remains better than the record of any (nontautological) dissident rivals that have yet come to this writer's attention.

A more controversial reason for anticipating revival for the Good Old Theory is the unpromising character of its dissident alternatives we have encountered. Their principal weaknesses are the converses of the neoclassical virtues. The mid-twentieth century generation of dissident theories suffers from dependence on highly specialized assumptions, tautological characteristics, confusions of cause and effect, shaky micro-foundations and/or general formlessness. Which is not to deny that a later generation of dissident theory may overcome these deficiencies and take over the field.

Appendix to Chapter 16
The C.E.S. Production Function

DERIVATION: INTRODUCTION[1]

i. Let $x = F(a,b)$ be a linear homogeneous production function, so that

$$x = a F\left(\frac{b}{a}, 1\right) = af\left(\frac{b}{a}\right) \quad \text{and} \quad \frac{x}{a} = F\left(\frac{b}{a}, 1\right) = f\left(\frac{b}{a}\right).$$

If we define $y = (x/a)$ and $\rho = (b/a)$,

$$y = f(\rho) \quad \text{and} \quad x = af(\rho)$$

Obtain marginal products of a and b, together with a complementarity measure:

$$\frac{\delta x}{\delta a} = f(\rho) + a \frac{d\rho}{da} f'(\rho) = f(\rho) - \frac{b}{a} f'(\rho) = y - \rho \frac{dy}{d\rho}$$

$$\frac{\delta x}{\delta b} = a \frac{d\rho}{db} f'(\rho) = f'(\rho) = \frac{dy}{d\rho}$$

$$\frac{\delta^2 x}{\delta a \delta b} = \frac{\delta}{\delta a}\left(\frac{\delta x}{\delta b}\right) = \frac{\delta}{\delta a} f'(\rho) = \frac{d\rho}{da} f''(\rho) = -\frac{b}{a^2} f''(\rho) = -\frac{\rho}{a} f''(\rho)$$

If the wage rate $p_a = (\delta x/\delta a)$,

$$p_a = y - \rho \frac{dy}{d\rho} = w(\rho). \tag{16.i}$$

---

1. For an alternative derivation see Brown, *Technical Change, op. cit.*, Appendix A, generalized to n inputs (following a method devised by Uzawa) in Appendix B. A comparison of derivations is found in Morton Kamien, "Comment on Alternative Derivations of the Two Input Production Function with Constant Elasticity of Substitution," *Weltw. Arch.* (Spring 1964).

We also have, as stability conditions,

$$\frac{\delta x}{\delta b} = f'(\rho) > 0 \quad \text{and} \quad \frac{\delta^2 x}{\delta b^2} = f''(\rho)\frac{d\rho}{db} = \frac{f''(\rho)}{a} < 0.$$

Since $x = F(a,b)$, the simplest form of the elasticity of substitution applies (Chapter 6, Appendix A). In simplified notation:

$$\sigma = \frac{\dfrac{\delta x}{\delta a}\dfrac{\delta x}{\delta b}}{x\dfrac{\delta^2 x}{\delta a \delta b}} = -\frac{f'(\rho)[f(\rho) - \rho f'(\rho)]}{\rho f(\rho) f''(\rho)} = -\frac{f'(f - \rho f')}{\rho f f''}. \quad (16.\text{ii})$$

ii. Differentiate (16.i) with respect to the wage rate p_a, remembering that $y = f(\rho)$:

$$1 = \frac{df}{dp_a} - \rho\frac{df'}{dp_a} - f'\frac{d\rho}{dp_a}$$

$$1 = f'\frac{d\rho}{dy}\cdot\frac{dy}{dp_a} - \rho f''\frac{d\rho}{dy}\frac{dy}{dp_a} - f'\frac{d\rho}{dy}\frac{dy}{dp_a}.$$

But $(d\rho/dy) = (1/f')$, so that, after cancellations in the last equation,

$$1 = -\frac{\rho f''}{f'}\frac{dy}{dp_a} \quad \text{and} \quad \frac{dy}{dp_a} = -\frac{f'}{\rho f''}.$$

This enables us to prove that the *price elasticity* of y with respect to p_a is precisely the *elasticity of substitution* σ between a and b, remembering $p_a = (\delta x/\delta a) = (f - \rho f')$ from (16.i):

$$\frac{Ey}{Ep_a} = \frac{dy}{dp_a}\cdot\frac{p_a}{y} = -\frac{p_a}{y}\frac{f'}{\rho f''} = -\frac{f'(f - \rho f')}{\rho f f''} \quad (16.\text{iii})$$

which is precisely σ as derived in (16.ii).

DERIVATION: PRODUCTION-FUNCTION CONSTRUCTION

iii. For a production function to have a constant elasticity of substitution, it suffices, by (16.ii–16.iii), to impose a constant elasticity of y with respect to p_a. (This is also the basis for equation [16.8] in the text.) The most general form of such a c.e.s. function is

$$\log y = \log\frac{x}{a} = \log c_0 + c_1\log p_a = \log c_0 + c_1\log\left(y - \rho\frac{dy}{d\rho}\right) \quad (16.\text{iv})$$

where c_1 is the elasticity of substitution, and $\log c_0$ is a statistical constant. Equation (16.iv) can be fitted by ordinary least squares, if y and p_a are known.

Developing (16.iv) further

$$y = c_0 \left(y - \rho \frac{dy}{d\rho} \right)^{c_1} \quad \text{or} \quad \frac{y}{c_0} = \left(y - \rho \frac{dy}{d\rho} \right)^{c_1}.$$

After solving for the derivative $(dy/d\rho)$, we simplify by defining coefficients (α, γ) such that

$$\frac{dy}{d\rho} = \frac{y}{\rho} - \frac{1}{\rho} \left(\frac{y}{c_0} \right)^{1/c_1} = \frac{y}{\rho} (1 - \alpha y^\gamma).$$

We now have

$$\frac{d\rho}{\rho} = \frac{dy}{y(1 - \alpha y^\gamma)} = \frac{dy}{y} + \frac{\alpha y^{\gamma-1} dy}{1 - \alpha y^\gamma}.$$

(The last step involves partial fractions.)

Integrating:

$$\log \rho = \log y - \frac{1}{\gamma} \log (1 - \alpha y^\gamma) + \frac{1}{\gamma} \log \beta, \qquad (16.\text{iv--a})$$

the last term on the right being a constant of integration.

Taking anti-logs:

$$\rho = y (1 - \alpha y^\gamma)^{-1/\gamma} \beta^{1/\gamma}, \quad \text{whence} \quad \rho^\gamma = \frac{\beta y^\gamma}{1 - \alpha y^\gamma}$$

$$\rho^\gamma - \alpha \rho^\gamma y^\gamma = \beta y^\gamma, \quad \text{whence} \quad y^\gamma (\beta + \alpha \rho^\gamma) = \rho^\gamma$$

$$y = \rho (\beta + \alpha \rho^\gamma)^{-1/\gamma} = (\alpha + \beta \rho^{-\gamma})^{-1/\gamma} \qquad (16.\text{v})$$

since $\rho = (\rho^{-\gamma})^{-1/\gamma}$.

iv. We can rewrite (16.v) in terms of our original production function variables x, a, b, and then solve for σ. From (16.v):

$$\frac{x}{a} = (\alpha + \beta b^{-\gamma} a^\gamma)^{-1/\gamma}, \quad \text{whence} \quad x = (\alpha a^{-\gamma} + \beta b^{-\gamma})^{-1/\gamma} \quad (16.\text{vi})$$

From (16.vi), we can solve for σ, the elasticity of substitution. Proceeding by stages from (16.vi) and its derivatives, and using (16.ii):

$$\frac{\delta x}{\delta a} = -\frac{1}{\gamma} (\alpha a^{-\gamma} + \beta b^{-\gamma})^{-(1+1/\gamma)} \left[-\alpha \gamma a^{-(1+\gamma)} \right]$$

$$= \alpha a^{-(1+\gamma)} (\alpha a^{-\gamma} + \beta b^{-\gamma})^{-(1+1/\gamma)}$$

$$\frac{\delta x}{\delta b} = \beta b^{-(1+\gamma)} (\alpha a^{-\gamma} + \beta b^{-\gamma})^{-(1+1/\gamma)} \qquad \text{(by symmetry)}$$

$$\frac{\delta^2 x}{\delta a \delta b} = -\left(\frac{1+\gamma}{\gamma} \right) (\alpha a^{-\gamma} + \beta b^{-\gamma})^{-(2+1/\gamma)} (\alpha a^{-(1+\gamma)}) (-\beta \gamma b^{-(1+\gamma)})$$

$$= (1 + \gamma) \, [\, (\alpha\beta) \; (ab) \,]^{-(1+\gamma)} \, (\alpha a^{-\gamma} + \beta b^{-\gamma})^{-(2+1/\gamma)}$$

$$\sigma = \frac{\dfrac{\delta x}{\delta a} \dfrac{\delta x}{\delta b}}{x \dfrac{\delta^2 x}{\delta a \delta b}} = \frac{1}{1 + \gamma}. \tag{16.vii}$$

It follows at once that $\gamma = (1 - \sigma) / \sigma$.

DERIVATION: AN EXTENSION

v.   If we define ϵ such that $\alpha + \beta = \epsilon^{-\gamma}$, and δ such that $\alpha\epsilon^\gamma = \delta$, we can solve for α and β in terms of ϵ and δ:

$$\alpha = \delta\epsilon^{-\gamma} \quad \text{and} \quad \beta = (1 - \delta)\,\epsilon^{-\gamma}.$$

Substituting these expressions in (16.vi),

$$x = \{\epsilon^{-\gamma}[\delta a^{-\gamma} + (1 - \delta)\,b^{-\gamma}]\}^{-1/\gamma} = \epsilon[\delta a^{-\gamma} + (1 - \delta)\,b^{-\gamma}]^{-1/\gamma} \tag{16.viii}$$

or, in terms of y and ρ,

$$y = \epsilon[\delta + (1 - \delta)\,\rho^{-\gamma}]^{-1/\gamma}.$$

If δ and ϵ vary with output x or time t (16.viii) becomes

$$x = \epsilon\,(x)\,\{\delta\,(x)\,a^{-\gamma} + [\,(1 - \delta)\,(x)\,]b^{-\gamma}\}^{-1/\gamma}$$

or

$$x = \epsilon\,(t)\,\{\delta\,(t)\,a^{-\gamma} + [\,(1 - \delta)\,(t)\,]b^{-\gamma}\}^{-1/\gamma}$$

The coefficients γ, δ, and ϵ are known as the *substitution, distribution,* and *efficiency* parameters respectively, for obvious reasons.

RELATION TO COBB-DOUGLAS FUNCTION

vi.   In the Cobb-Douglas case, $\sigma = 1$, so that $\gamma = 0$ by (16.vii). Substituting $\gamma = 0$ in (16.viii) yields the indeterminate form $1^{-\infty}$.

To evaluate this indeterminate form, we can apply L'Hopital's Rule, after rewriting (16.viii) as:

$$x = \frac{\epsilon}{\left(\dfrac{\delta}{a^\gamma} + \dfrac{1 - \delta}{b^\gamma} \right)^{1/\gamma}} = \frac{ab\epsilon}{[\delta b^\gamma + (1 - \delta)\,a^\gamma]^{1/\gamma}}. \tag{16.ix}$$

The limit of (16.ix) as γ vanishes depends upon the limit of its denominator, which may also be written as

$$\exp\left\{\frac{1}{\gamma} \log\,[\delta b^\gamma + (1 - \delta)\,a^\gamma]\right\}. \tag{16.x}$$

The expression in curled brackets is also indeterminate $(= \infty \cdot \log 1\infty)$ as γ approaches zero. To evaluate it, we apply L'Hopital's Rule again:

$$\lim_{\gamma \to 0} \frac{\log[\delta b^\gamma + (1 - \delta) a^\gamma]}{\gamma} = \lim_{\gamma \to 0} \frac{\delta b^\gamma \log b + (1 - \delta) a^\gamma \log a}{\delta b^\gamma + (1 - \delta) a^\gamma}$$

$$= \delta \log b + (1 - \delta) \log a.$$

The entire equation (16.x) has, therefore the limiting value as $(\gamma \to 0, \sigma \to 1)$:

$$\exp[\delta \log b + (1 - \delta) \log a] = e^{\delta \log b} e^{(1-\delta) \log a}$$

$$= b^\delta a^{1-\delta}.$$

When this expression is inserted in (16.ix), we can obtain the limiting value of (16.ix) as well, as γ vanishes, and σ approaches unity.

$$\lim_{\gamma \to 0} x = \frac{ab\epsilon}{a^{1-\delta} b^\delta} = \epsilon\, a^\delta\, b^{1-\delta}. \tag{16.xi}$$

If we let $\epsilon = x_0$ and note that $\delta = \alpha$ when $\gamma = o$, (16.xi) becomes precisely the Cobb-Douglas function (16.1):

$$x = x_0\, a^\alpha\, b^{1-\alpha}. \tag{16.1}$$

METHOD OF FITTING[2]

vii. Our "original" c.e.s. function (16.iv) was, to repeat,

$$\log \frac{x}{a} = \log y = \log c_0 + c_1 \log p_a. \tag{16.iv}$$

This may be fitted by least squares as it stands, from data on x, a, and p_a. We can then estimate α and γ from a definition that entered the development leading to (16.iv–a):

$$\frac{y}{\rho} - \frac{1}{\rho}\left(\frac{y}{c_0}\right)^{1/c_1} = \frac{y}{\rho}(1 - \alpha y^\gamma) \qquad \text{or} \qquad \left(\frac{y}{c_0}\right)^{1/c_1} = \alpha y^{1+\gamma}$$

whence $\quad \alpha = (c_0)^{-1/c_1}, \log \alpha = \dfrac{-\log c_0}{c_1}, \quad$ and $\quad \gamma = \dfrac{1}{c_1} - 1.$

Given α and γ, we may estimate β.

$$\log \rho = \log y - \frac{1}{\gamma} \log (1 - \alpha y^\gamma) + \frac{1}{\gamma} \log \beta \tag{16.iv–a}$$

so that, for each observation of $y\, (= x/a)$ and $\rho\, (= b/a)$,

$$\log \beta = \gamma (\log \rho - \log y) + \log (1 - \alpha y^\gamma)$$

$$= \gamma \left(\log \frac{b}{a} - \log \frac{x}{a}\right) + \log\left[1 - \alpha \left(\frac{x}{a}\right)^\gamma\right].$$

2. Brown, *Technical Change* (*op. cit.*, pp. 128–136), indicates three alternative fitting methods.

The mean of the several single-observation estimates of $\log \beta$ is our estimate for the entire set of observations, and leads to an estimate of β itself.

From our estimates of α, β, and γ, we can proceed to estimate ϵ and then δ by the definitions in section v above:

$$\alpha + \beta = \epsilon^{-\gamma}, \quad \text{whence} \quad \log \epsilon = - \frac{\log (\alpha + \beta)}{\gamma} \quad \text{and}$$

$$\gamma \log \epsilon = - \log (\alpha + \beta)$$

$$\alpha \epsilon^{\gamma} = \delta, \quad \text{whence} \quad \log \delta = \log \alpha + \gamma \log \epsilon = \log \alpha - \log (\alpha + \beta)$$

$$= \log \left(\frac{\alpha}{\alpha + \beta} \right).$$

viii.   The method used in section vii arrives at the theoretical shares or distribution parameters δ and $(1 - \delta)$ at the end of a dangerously lofty pyramid of estimates based on estimates based on estimates:

And so proceed *ad infinitum*

To avoid compounding observational errors, many statisticians do not estimate δ at all. In fitting the c.e.s. function (16.viii), they use for δ and $(1 - \delta)$ the (average) *observed* distributive shares over the range of data. When α and γ are estimated by the methods of section vii, a logarithmic form of (16.viii) is:

$$\log x = \log \epsilon - \frac{1}{\gamma} \log [\delta a^{-\gamma} + (1 - \delta) b^{-\gamma}]$$

with $\log \epsilon$ the only unknown. It can be estimated separately for each observation, and a mean value ascribed to the entire distribution. Or, alternatively, we may again use the definitional:

$$\alpha \epsilon^{\gamma} = \delta, \quad \text{whence} \quad \log \epsilon = \frac{\log \delta - \log \alpha}{\gamma}.$$

Such methods, despite the "circularity" charge that can be levied against their use in "verifying" the Good Old Theory, are more usual than the long train of statistical reasoning required for the methods of section vii.

CHAPTER SEVENTEEN

Guidelines, Guideposts, and Incomes Policies

Introduction

1. An application of sociological, institutional, or power theories of aggregate income distribution can be found, within a market economy framework, in numerous mid-twentieth century experiments with direct controls over wages and prices. These are known variously as incomes policies, guidelines, guideposts, guiding lights, etc. "If there is a difference in meaning, it is that the term 'incomes policy' suggests direct or separate measures to restrain profits, interest, and rent, while price-wage guideposts restrain them indirectly and as a group by limiting the margin between prices and wages."[1] We shall ourselves use these terms synonymously. A "standard" guideline or guidepost, in particular, involves a money wage rate rising with average real man-hour or man-week productivity, and therefore also a constant price level.

We speak of these experiments as applications. Some are also tests, albeit incomplete. A test requires estimates of whether some set of controls has altered significantly the long-term course of real wages, or of the labor share. No such test has yet been carried out in any market economy with a satisfactory decisiveness.[2]

---

1. Albert Rees, "An Incomes Policy for the United States," *Journ. of Bus.* (October 1965), p. 374 (running quotation).

2. Domenico Nuti, however, speaks for many socialists in concluding (on a priori grounds, without quantitative testing) that "incomes policy can be acceptable only after the replacement of capitalism with a socialist society." "On Incomes Policy," *Science and Society* (Fall-Winter, 1969), p. 425.

Indeed, with only occasional and partial exceptions,[3] the primary aim of these controls has been neither to maintain nor to reform the distribution of income. The aim has rather been to "talk the Phillips curve down," to increase the level of employment consistent with "reasonable price stability," or to minimize measured inflation under ambitious plans for reconstruction or development. Distributional considerations usually enter, but only as administrative by-products, and sometimes in inconsistent ways.[4] They are introduced by spokesmen for one or another pressure group that is seeking to alter some initial pattern of controls for that group's benefit, which may be either the securing of a distributional gain or the avoidance of a distributional loss.

2.   Direct controls, guideposts included, have become a phoenix of the market economy. They are imposed to meet emergencies, usually of war and/or inflation. They give rise sooner or later—sooner, in peacetime or in an unpopular war—to objections, modifications, evasions, and outright disregard. They are then scrapped amid universal execration, including "requiems" and "post-mortems" from the academic community, only to revive in the next emergency, which may come before the first is over!

Their title of "economic phoenix" must be shared, paradoxically, with

---

3. Of the industrialized countries surveyed by Sheahan, France has departed furthest from distributional neutrality. "The French approach involves explicit decision on how different forms of income should change relative to each other. The annual rate of increase in real wages per worker was projected at 3.3 per cent, and of agricultural real incomes per capita at 4.8 per cent. The growth of total wage payments was projected as falling from 7.3 per cent per year for 1960–65 to 5.0 per cent for 1965–70, while the rate of increase in corporate saving was to go in the opposite direction. The underlying pattern of choice was oriented toward holding back salaries and private consumption . . . in order to permit more rapid relative growth of government services, corporate self-financing, and fixed capital formation." John Sheahan, *The Wage-Price Guideposts* (Washington: Brookings Institution, 1967), p. 115. The French plan also builds in a 1.5 per cent annual rise in the general price level.

In socialist thinking, the distributional effects of controls are normally more sweeping than in any of Sheahan's cases. One such case is the syndicalist combination of monetary expansion with fixed prices, while wages are free to rise and employment may not be curtailed. Capitalists, facing bankruptcy, will hand over their holdings for minimal compensation to worker's cooperatives (syndicates). In another case, practiced in the Soviet Union, receivers of rent and interest may be expropriated by deliberate inflation, while most other prices, and likewise wages, keep approximate pace with monetary expansion. Consider also the Argentine data, footnote 38 below.

4. One accusation of inconsistency, directed specifically at the Kennedy-Johnson guideposts, was made by Denison. He interprets guidepost rulings as fluctuating between three different distributional criteria: (a) Neutrality, meaning an unchanging labor share; (b) Competitive *change*, meaning that wage levels should change in the same way that they would in a purely competitive economy; (c) Competitive *level*, meaning that wage rates should reach whatever levels they would reach under pure competition. E. F. Denison, *Guideposts for Wages and Prices: Criteria and Consistency* (Ann Arbor: University of Michigan Institute of Policy Studies, 1968), pp. 3–6.

the free market itself. Suspended in emergencies, with high administrative hopes for "rational" controls to supplant "anarchy," the market revives every time. The revival is initially *sub rosa* and illegal—black markets, wage drifts, etc.—accompanied by genteel if sometimes corrupt pressure to modify specific regulations. Increasingly, revival takes the form of strikes against controls, and then disregard of controls, until the greater part of the control structure lapses into dead-letter status.

Cases For and Against Controls

3.   The cases for direct controls cover a wide range of sophistication. The crudest, and therefore often the most popular, is administrative directness. To control prices, wage rates, interest rates or profit margin, fix them absolutely or between limits, and that is all. We can then continue the painless paradise of cheap money and loose budgets indefinitely, or so it seems. This view is combined at times with contempt for "the brilliant cybernetics of the private market system,"[5] which is characterized as "jungle law," "pig philosophy," and the like.

A more technical case springs from the economics of imperfect competition and of employment. It has received its standard statement in A. P. Lerner's *Economics of Control*.[6] In the presence of monopoly, maximum prices are to be set at levels consistent simultaneously with supply-demand equilibrium, with marginal costs, and with normal profits. This regulatory magic Lerner calls counterspeculation, meaning speculation directed against the monopolist. In the presence of monopsony, minimum prices are to be set in an analogous way. Furthermore, as an economy approaches full employment, labor shortages develop in different occupations at different times. They begin forcing up prices at a point Lerner calls "low full employment"; at "high full employment" the price increases are not only larger and more rapid, but no longer elicit significant increases in total output. This type of demand-pull inflation, moreover, develops even under pure labor market and output market competition. Lerner therefore proposes an elaborate scheme of wage regulation, embodying both increases in the average productivity of labor as a whole, and excess demands (positive or negative) for each class of labor in each labor market. Problems of administration and enforcement are dealt with only in passing.

A quite different "time-lag" theory of direct controls may be para-

5. "Why Wall Street Is Worried," *Time* (July 18, 1969) , quoting Walter W. Heller.

6. Lerner, *Economics of Control* (New York: Macmillan, 1944) . A fuller treatment of Lerner's wage-control scheme is found in his *Economics of Employment* (New York: McGraw-Hill, 1951) ch. 14–16.

phrased as follows: We admit both the necessity and the efficiency of monetary and fiscal measures, if an inflation is to be checked or prevented. Such measures may, however, take time, first to frame and enact, and then to take effect. Stability may be preserved in such cases by temporary direct controls, usually of the "standstill" or "roll-back" variety. Such controls give the macroeconomic monetary-fiscal system time to work; they substitute constancy of prices and wages for a series of rises, followed by declines and/or (in a system with differential rigidities) by unemployment and slower growth.

Popular in Continental Europe, perhaps particularly among the French school of sociological economics, is a "social equilibrium" theory of direct controls.[7] Let us assume, as these economists often do, an inflationary context with inflationary expectations already built in. Under these circumstances, the restoration of monetary equilibrium would require a prolonged period of tight money, high interest rates, low social expenditures, and high taxes, not to mention increasing disappointment in what were previously rational expectations. Such a shock generates gains for some individuals and some social classes; it generates losses for other individuals and other classes. These gains and losses involve both nominal and real income, both nominal and real capital values, and unemployment as well, when the losses are resisted. The net result may be not only resentment and low morale, but work stoppages, political upheavals, rioting, or actual revolution. Maintenance of what is, perhaps pretentiously, called "social equilibrium"—morale, output, law and order, political tranquillity—is at least as important as monetary equilibrium. It gains in importance in countries that, like post-1939 France, have been plagued by disturbance and upheaval. At any rate, social equilibrium is maintained or restored most readily by precisely those controls least defensible from the viewpoint of monetary equilibrium. Or at least, such as the claim.[8]

4.   There are, at bottom, three major arguments against direct controls.[9] Controls distort the microeconomic allocation patterns of both inputs and outputs; as a result of such misallocation, "suppressed inflation is worse

7. Latin-American *estructuralismo* and *Cepalismo* seem to share this school's aversion to monetary-fiscal anti-inflationary measures, but not its faith in direct controls. Open inflation, rather, is to these writers the least of all evils.

8. Compare H. Brochier, "Income Policy and the French Planning System," in Marchal and Ducros, *The Distribution of National Income* (London: Macmillan, 1968), ch. 24; also Marchal and Ducros, "Introduction," *ibid.*, p. xxx. R. C. Tress, "Incomes Policy in the United Kingdom," *ibid.*, ch. 25, propounds similar arguments in a British setting.

9. Compare Milton Friedman, "What Price Guideposts?" in George P. Shultz and Robert S. Aliber (eds.), *Guidelines: Informal Controls and the Market Place* (Chicago: University of Chicago Press, 1966).

than open inflation." Controls cannot be enforced effectively over prolonged periods, within the limits of conventional "civil rights."[10] Whatever short-term success they may have (or appear to have) operates to
delay appropriate monetary and fiscal solutions to the problems with
which the controls are fumbling.

As to distortion: Any fixation or regulation of a set of complementary
or competitive input or output prices necessarily fixes or regulates the relations between those inputs and outputs. (It is equally impossible simultaneously to regulate a complete set of price interrelations and only a
subset of the individual prices concerned.) Also, there is never any historical "base period" when all the prices and price relationships are recog-
nizably in equilibrium, let alone "fair," and even if there were, that solution would be increasingly meaningless in a changing world.

To impose a disequilibrium system of direct controls on a set of interrelated markets is, therefore, to impose chaos, papered over with rations,
allocations, and subsidies. These in turn work to the benefit of whoever
is in a favorable historical position, whoever is sufficiently insignificant or
nonessential to escape the control network—or whoever is sufficiently influential to warp the control structure "his" way.

As to civil liberties: Like a house divided, an economy divided has difficulty keeping erect in the long run. It cannot indefinitely control only
the essentials, while leaving the nonessentials free. Controls will either
proliferate over the entire economy, or will increasingly limit themselves
to ratifying "market" decisions in regulated areas. When controls spread,
they spread to labor and to entrepreneurship, as well as to other inputs
and outputs.

Here arises the primary conflict of controls with civil liberties. When
people, either individually or collectively (as in a labor union or trade
association) are no longer permitted to withhold their services[11] from essential industry on the controlled terms, whether by striking against controls, by shifting to uncontrolled sectors, or by outright emigration, we
are approaching the army barracks and are halfway to the labor camp.
Serfdom, slavery, and the concentration camp may not be much further
off.

A secondary conflict between a controlled economy and conventional
civil liberties is initially procedural. To enforce a proliferate network of

10. "The usual outcome, pending a complete monetary reform, is an uneasy compromise between official tolerance of evasion . . . and a collectivist economy. The greater
the ingenuity of private individuals in evading the price controls, and the greater the
tolerance of officials in blinking at such evasions, the less the harm that is done; the
more law-abiding the citizens, and the more rigid and effective the government enforcement machinery, the greater the harm." *Ibid.*, p. 32.

11. "Property rights" are not considered here.

unpopular controls, the authorities are tempted to tap wires, censor mail, search without warrant, fabricate evidence, entrap suspects, suborn witnesses, and even excite mobs against black marketeers too smart for the police. We need not claim that the authorities never resist such temptations, or that the entire control structure need' collapse unless they do yield. The argument is only that probability, as distilled from historical records, yields few optimistic conclusions for the Rights of Man and the Citizen.

As to the danger of postponing unpleasant monetary or fiscal measures, which might imperil the social equilbrium—no great elaboration is required.

An Incomes-Policy Dilemma[12]

5.   In the actually or potentially inflationary environment of twentieth-century incomes-policy experiments, the case against incomes policies can be put in dilemma form. If macroeconomic policy is sensible,[13] or so the argument runs, we have no need for these policies. (First horn of dilemma.) If macroeconomic policy is less than sensible, incomes policies do only short-term good or no good at all, and they may do long-term harm, as in the argument in section 4 above. (Second horn of dilemma.)

The history of suppressed and repressed inflations since the outbreak of World War II has sharpened the second horn of this dilemma. It is on the first horn that we venture to operate, at the risk of becoming impaled.

The operation may get us bogged down in spongy economic territory. Like a rice paddy, this territory is at once too soft and too hard. It is soft in the sense of being ill-structured, and therefore imperfectly penetrable by the hard-nosed tank battalions of conventional economic analysis. It is hard in the sense of being abstract, and therefore imperfectly amenable to immanent empiricism, alias fact-finding.

Multiple-Goal Economics

6.   If we regard organizations such as firms and trade unions as rational maximizers of single objectives like profits or sales, wage rates or payrolls, much of the discussion that follows will seem wrong or, if not wrong, irrelevant. Let us, therefore, in line with certain arguments in Chapter 8,

12. The remainder of this chapter represents an expansion and reworking of Bronfenbrenner, "A Guidepost-Mortem," *Ind. Lab. Rel. Rev.* (July 1967), following criticisms by Harry G. Johnson.

13. We shall assume a substantial degree of agreement on the constituents of sensible macroeconomic policy, heroic as this assumption may be.

10, and 15 particularly, view firms and unions as having multiple goals, not all of them economic or quantitative, and as being free to vary the relative weights of these goals in their "utility function" or its equivalent, within such constraints as may be set by the requirements of solvency, the criminal code, "the common conscience of mankind," and so on.[14]

One may possibly interpret guidepost and incomes policies as shifting an imperfectly competitive firm's discretionary behavior toward lower prices, higher output, and higher employment than would have prevailed in their absence. This shift would represent a weakening of the profit or income components of the firm's mix of goals, and a strengthening of the "good citizenship" or public-service components. Similarly, a discretionary union may be induced to shift its preference map (Figure 10.1) away from higher wages and toward higher employment. This shift would represent a similar reweighting of private and public components of the union's mix of goals.

None of this differs greatly from the presumed tasks and successes of advertising, in shifting individual goals away from accumulation and toward consumption, or away from longevity toward assorted enjoyments culminating in lung cancer or highway massacre. Nothing "impractical" about it!

In their capacity of altering (distorting?) the preferences of firms and unions, the more comprehensive and more emotionally advocated guidelines and income policies have approached the French *planification indicative* and the Japanese *yudo-keizai,* in economics generally freer than the French or Japanese. But the weakest of controls translates certain overall macroeconomic targets and directives into terms meaningful at the microeconomic level. Voluntary controls, or even exhortations, indicate to individual firms and unions what the government wants them to do. Sometimes they also suggest the degree of pressure proposed in the future to bend firms' and unions' decisions to the public interest, as interpreted by the government.

Hopefully, but not certainly, increasing what economists might agree to call the reasonableness of the microeconomic control structure will minimize strikes, slowdowns, and flights from essentiality, directed either against individual controls or against the macroeconomic policies that

---

14. Three leading experiments in recasting the theory of the firm along "behavioral" or "organizational" lines have included Richard M. Cyert and James G. March, *A Behavioral Theory of the Firm* (Englewood Cliffs, N.J.: Prentice-Hall, 1963) ; Robin Marris, *The Economic Theory of Managerial Capitalism* (New York: Free Press, 1964) ; and Oliver E. Williamson, *The Economics of Discretionary Behavior* (Englewood Cliffs, N.J.: Prentice-Hall, 1964) .

underlie them.[15] To some extent, controls can improve economic performance in an imperfectly competitive society under (almost) any set of macroeconomic policies in the short term, and under any sensible macroeconomic policies in the longer run as well.

We should not forget the once-for-all character of these improvements in economic performance.[16] Once the gains of restriction and monopoly have been controlled or exhorted away in a finite number of stages, with perhaps a modicum of extraordinary sacrifice in expiation of past sins, the comedy will be over and no further improvements can be expected from further controls.

Controls and Cost-Push Inflation

7. The economic theory of direct controls rests heavily on the theory of cost-push inflation—"seller's inflation" in Lerner's terms. We need not explore this theory in detail here.[17] Briefly, the theory states that the most important factor in inflation is a series of individual price rises, often administered or bargained, in input and output prices. The results of these "wage-price spirals" are then more or less automatically validated by expansive monetary and fiscal policies, in order to maintain production, employment, and industrial peace.

The theory of controls, in its selective versions, contains at least one additional ingredient. This is the belief that restraint on a "key group"[18] of wages and prices will restrain inflation generally, rather than shifting such pressure to non-key industries, penalizing particular firms and unions for the "crime" of essentiality, or verifying (in non-Marshallian context) Marshall's disputed Third Law (Chapter 6) on the advantages of unimportance.

15. Sidney Weintraub, for example, hopes to avoid "involuntary servitude" consequences of comprehensive wage controls by promising long-term increases in real and money wages. "In Defense of Wage-Price Guideposts . . . Plus," in Almaria Phillips and Oliver E. Williamson (eds.), *Prices: Issues in Theory, Practice, and Public Policy* (Philadelphia: University of Pennsylvania Press, 1967), pp. 70 f.

16. This point has been stressed by Harry G. Johnson in correspondence with the writer. He also argues that the case just made supports a *permanent* control organization (since the world is ever-changing) and need not require inflationary pressure as its trigger.

17. See Bronfenbrenner and Holzman, "Survey of Inflation Theory," *A.E.R.* (September 1963), pp. 613–630.

18. This term is associated particularly with Otto Eckstein and Thomas A. Wilson, "The Determination of Money Wages in American Industry," *Q.J.E.* (August 1962), pp. 384 f. For the United States, this key group included the following industries: rubber; stone, clay, and glass; primary metals; fabricated metals; nonelectrical machinery; electrical machinery; transportation equipment; and instruments. (Basic steel is included as a primary metal, while automobiles and aircraft dominate transportation equipment.)

8. Four interrelated elements of control theory seems to be the following:

(*1*) Constraining or inducing firms to leave a larger portion of their monopoly power unexercised—"potential," in the terminology of Chapter 8. (We have discussed the inducement aspects in section 6 above.)

(*2*) Shifting the aggregate supply function of output in anti-inflationary (diagrammatically, a southeasterly) direction.

(*3*) Shifting the Phillips curve (assuming its existence and stability) in an anti-inflationary (diagrammatically, a southwesterly) direction.

(*4*) Reconciliation with the quantity theory of money.

Restraint of Monopoly Power

9. We have had more than one occasion to refer to the standard relation between price p, marginal revenue mr, marginal cost mc, demand elasticity η, and the "Lerner" degree of monopoly power μ, for an individual profit-maximizing firm in imperfect competition:

$$mr = mc = p \left(1 - \frac{1}{\eta} \right) = p \left(1 - \mu \right)$$

from which we have derived

$$\frac{p}{mc} = \frac{1}{1 - \mu}.$$

Guideposts and incomes policies are expected and intended to hold prices closer to marginal costs. They also lower, *ipso facto*, the degree of exercised monopoly power, and keep such power potential only.

10. In so doing, the controls simultaneously assist in exorcising the demon of monopolistic stagnation, associated particularly with the Austrian economist Steindl, whose evidence pertains primarily to the United States.[19]

The American private economy, Steindl argues, is divided into a monopoly–oligopoly sector and a highly competitive sector. The monopoly–oligopoly sector's demand for external investment will not suffice to absorb American savings at high-employment income levels and going interest rates. At the same time, these savings will not be made available to the competitive sector in sufficient volume to take up the resulting slack.

The monopoly–oligopoly sector's demand for external investment is limited by (1) the profitability of restricting output and raising prices in

19. Josef Steindl, *Maturity and Stagnation in American Capitalism* (Oxford: Blackwell, 1952).

lieu of creating excess capacity; and also by (2) the preference of corporate insiders, usually including both top management and principal stockholders, for internal investment out of profits. (Internal investment provides tax savings, as compared with the rival policy of larger dividend distributions and larger external investment. It also involves less risk to the insiders' continuing dominance over corporate affairs.)

No such considerations restrain investment demand from the competitive sector at going interest rates. Indeed, competitive firms often complain about shortages of capital and the difficulties of securing accommodation. At the same time, the supply of investment funds to this sector is disappointingly low. Savers are unwilling to risk investment in this sector, outside their own "family firms." There are several reasons: the high risk of failure; the dangers of unfair direct competition with monopolists and oligopolists; the prospect of exploitation by monopolists and oligopolists, either as suppliers of inputs to small firms or as purchasers of the firms' outputs. Either as a consequence of these reasons, or in addition to them, adequate financial intermediation (brokerage, etc.) has never developed between individual savers and the small would-be investors.

The combined results, still in Steindl's view, will be a level of peacetime private investment well below the level of full-employment private saving.[20] Indeed, he ascribes to the rise of the stock exchange, and to its assistance in creating oligopolies out of competitive firms by "other people's money," the delay of the great depression until 1929.

If one accepts Steindl's diagnosis, which many writers decidedly do not,[21] guidepost, controls, and incomes policies can indeed accomplish a great deal by holding back, or even reversing, the price-raising and output-restricting proclivities of monopolies and cartels, that is, lowering the average size of μ.

Aggregate Supply Effects

11. A conventional manner of relating aggregate real income to the general price level is by plotting aggregate supply and demand functions for real income Y against the price level p, as is done in Figure 17.1.[22] It is also conventional to draw the aggregate supply function S as rising gently,

20. Other writers achieve the same stagnationist result by postulating rigid entrepreneurial insistence on a given *rate* of profit, or a given *profit margin* per unit of output.

21. An unfavorable review by Alvin Hansen (from *Rev. Econ. and Stat.*, November 1954) is reprinted in Arthur Smithies and J. K. Butters, *Readings in Fiscal Policy* (Homewood, Ill.: Irwin, 1955), pp. 548–556.

22. For derivation of aggregate demand and supply functions from more elementary constructions of macroeconomic analysis (which run entirely in real terms), see e.g., Joseph P. McKenna, *Aggregate Economic Analysis*, 3d ed. (New York: Holt, Rinehart and Winston, 1969), pp. 201–208.

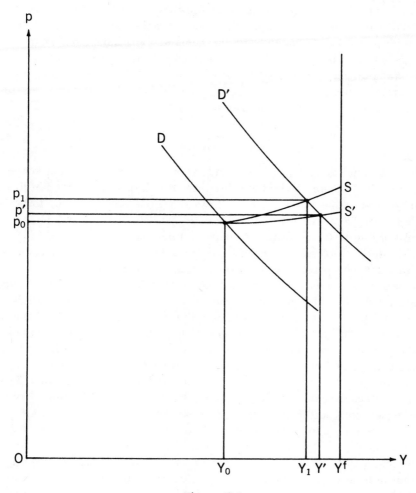

Figure 17.1

if at all, until some income level Y_0 is reached, which corresponds to Lerner's "low full employment." Above Y_0, the slope of S becomes steeper. High, or tight, full employment imposes an absolute ceiling on real income at Y_f. Here S becomes vertical. Well before Y_f is reached, however, expansion of aggregate demand—say, from D to D_1—raises output from Y_0 to Y_1 only at the cost of an inflationary rise in the price level from p_0 to p_1.

Let us relate this apparatus to the problems of this chapter. It is the hope of income-policy makers, starting from a position at or above low full-employment income Y_0, to twist the aggregate supply function—technically, to raise its radius of curvature—so that it assumes the position S'. If successful, this form of "operation twist"[23] raises from $Y_0 Y_1$ to $Y_0 Y'$ the real-income gain associated with the demand expansion from D to D'. It also lowers from $p_0 p_1$ to $p_0 p'$ the price-level increase resulting from the demand-pull DD_1. The purpose of the policy is, of course, to maximize the real income gain resulting from increased aggregate demand, and to minimize its dissipation in higher prices.

Phillips Curve Effects

12.   The analogous construction and argument on the labor market relates to the function devised and fitted to British data by A. W. Phillips, and reproduced as F_0 on Figure 17.2 in its original (two-variable) form.[24] We have previously discussed this function in Chapters 10 and 11.

According to the Phillips formulation, unemployment as a percentage of the labor force—U/L on the diagram's horizontal axis—determines, with a lag, the percentage increase in money wage rates—dw/w on the vertical axis. Subsequent empirical developments of the Phillips curve have added, as independent variables determining wage changes, living costs and their rate of change, corporate profits and their rate of change, the rate of change of unemployment, unfilled vacancies as a percentage of the labor force, and many more. Economists and statisticians have sought to recast the function in terms of real rather than money wage rate changes, "expected" rather than observed variables, and the like. Still another development has been the disaggregation of Phillips curves by region, area, sector (*i.e.*, strongly vs. weakly unionized industries), or time period (*i.e.*, long- vs. short-term), the presence or absence of "full-employment" and "growthmanship" policies, and so forth.

A majority of writers find (even while taking other variables into account in multiple-regression analyses) statistically significant inverse Phil-

23. This "operation twist" is unrelated to the standard one, which "twists" the pattern of interest rates. (See Chapter 13, section 25.)

24. A. W. Phillips, "The Relation Between Unemployment and the Rate of Change of Money Wage Rates in the United Kingdom, 1861–1957," *Economica* (November 1958) represented in M. G. Mueller, *Readings in Macroeconomics* (New York: Holt, Rinehart & Winston, 1966), no. 17. For criticism, a convenient starting point is Bronfenbrenner and Holzman, *op. cit.*, pp. 631–635. An introduction to later (and more sophisticated) literature can be gleaned from three papers (by G. C. Archibald, C. C. Holt, and E. S. Phelps) with accompaning comments (by Frank Brechling, Otto Eckstein, and R. A. Lester) comprising an American Economic Association program on "Wage-Price Dynamics, Inflation, and Unemployment," *A.E.R.* (May 1969); see also Phelps (ed.)., *Microeconomic Foundations of Employment and Inflation Theory* (New York: Norton, 1969).

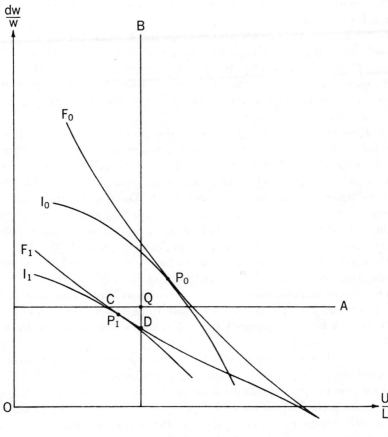

Figure 17.2

lips relationships between dw/w and U/L, at least in the short run. The difficulty is that the parameters (intercepts, slopes, elasticities) of their several Phillips functions have varied so widely as to generate doubt about the stability of these functions, and hence about their usability in applied work. This stability-pessimism sometimes extends to denial that any Phillips function exists.

13. Let us return to Figure 17.2. As in Figure 11.3, a horizontal line labeled *A* and a vertcial line labeled *B* have been included. Line *A* represents an estimate of the maximum percentage money wage change (frequently equal to the percentage increase in man-hour productivity) that the economy can absorb in a manner compatible with price-level stabil-

ity.[25] Line B represents the maximum safe or reservable percentage of unemployment from political and-or "growthmanship" viewpoints.[26] Lines A and B intersect at a point labeled Q.

The diagram also includes community indifference curves, labeled I, whose slopes indicate acceptable trade-offs between employment and prices. These curves are drawn, on plausible grounds, negatively sloped and concave downward.[27] All points on a curve nearer the origin (full employment at falling consumer prices) are preferable to all points on another curve further out.

Let F_0 be the Phillips function in the absence of incomes policy. It is of the type called "bad," meaning that it permits of noninflationary solution at an acceptable level of unemployment. Geometrically, it passes northeast of the focal point Q. (Most influential estimates of the American Phillips function have this characteristic.[28]) On the diagram, the best solution is at P_0, the point of tangency between F_0 and I_0, the relevant community indifference curve. As drawn, P_0 is *both* inflationary (north of A) and insufficiently close to full employment (east of B). Only one of these conditions is necessary for a "bad" curve; P_0 might, in other words, have been located either northwest or southeast of Q.

The role of incomes policy in such a situation is one that proponents of the American guideposts claim to have fulfilled over the period 1962–1965. It is to bend the upper left portion of the Phillips curve from F_0 to F_1, so as to pass southwest of Q. Given a "good" Phillips function like F_1, there will exist a range CD for high-employment, noninflationary wage behavior. This range will include an optimum point like P_1, where F_1 is tangent to I_1, a community indifference curve preferable, by hypothesis, to the pre-guidepost curve I_0. (If P_1 does not lie in the range CD, when such a range exists, it implies that the community's preferences are indeed inconsistent with high employment and price-level stability.)

25. In an American setting, this is the 3.2 (or 3.5) per cent of the Kennedy and Johnson guidelines and guideposts. Its imprecision is admitted by all and sundry.

26. Line B is even less precise than line A. Perhaps 4.5 or 5.0 per cent unemployment would be an intelligent guess under American conditions. The corresponding figures for most Western European countries would be considerably lower.

27. To compensate for higher prices, the community must be provided with more employment, if a loss of utility is to be avoided. To compensate for less employment, the community must be provided with lower prices.

When high unemployment is coupled with deflation (near the horizontal axis), society is assumed to be concerned primarily with reducing unemployment at any cost, and the slope of the community indifference curve I is steep. When rapid inflation is coupled with full or over-full employment (near the vertical axis), society is assumed to be concerned primarily with fighting inflation at any cost, and the slope of I is shallow.

28. The most influential "American Phillips curve" paper was undoubtedly Paul A. Samuelson and Robert M. Solow, "Analytical Aspects of Anti-Inflation Policy," *A.E.R.* (May 1960), reprinted in Mueller, *op. cit.*, no. 27.

14. In the American guidepost case, we owe to George Perry our strongest argument that this set of wage-price controls—primarily wage controls, in actual practice—shifted the American Phillips function from something like P_0 to something like P_1.[29] (Perry puts the argument in terms of deviations from a "pre-guideposts" Phillips function.) We condense Solow's lucid summary of Perry's results:[30]

> [Perry] reconstructs the percentage change in hourly wages in terms of four determinants. The determinants are the unemployment rate, the accompanying change in the Consumer Price Index, the rate of profit on capital, and the change in the rate of profit. Wages will rise more rapidly the lower the unemployment rate, the faster the cost of living has been rising, the higher are profits, and the faster they have been rising. The precise relationship is based on experience from 1948 to 1960; it explains the course of money wages quite well during that period.
>
> When Perry's relationship is used to explain wage changes after 1960, it tells an interesting story. In 1961 and the first half of 1962, wages rose faster than the theory would expect. Beginning in the third quarter of 1962, and without exception for the next 14 quarters to the end of 1965, wages rose more slowly than the theory would expect. Moreover, though the overestimation of wage changes was initially small, it became substantial in 1964 and 1965. In 1965, the annual increase in wage rates was about 1.7 per cent lower than the 1948–60 experience would lead one to expect.

The statistical case sounds convincing, but counterarguments were not long in appearing. Four of these relate to (1) short-term fluctuations in the rate of technical progress; (2) failure of measured unemployment rates to take into account variations in the labor supply, particularly in the labor reserve of marginal and secondary workers; (3) changes in workers' and employers' anticipations of the near-future course of prices, profits, and unemployment; and most generally (4) the short-term variability of fitted Phillips-function parameters under all conditions, which render suspect any "fine-tuned" series of deviations from a single set.[31] The writer sympathizes most strongly with objection (4), without having

29. George L. Perry, "Wages and the Guideposts," *A.E.R.* (September 1967), "The Determinants of Wage Rate Changes and the Inflation-Unemployment Trade-Off for the United States," *Rev. Econ. Stud.* (August 1964) and *Unemployment, Money Wage Rates, and Inflation* (Cambridge, Mass.: M.I.T. Press, 1966), ch. 3.

30. Robert M. Solow, "The Case Against the Case Against the Guideposts," in Shultz and Aliber, *op. cit.*, p. 46 (running quotation)

31. N. J. Simler and Alfred Tella, "Labor Reserves and the Phillips Curve," *Rev. Econ. and Stat.* (February 1968); R. E. Lucas and L. A. Rapping, "Price Expectations and the Phillips Curve," *A.E.R.* (June 1969); H. I. Liebling and A. T. Cluff, "U.S. Postwar Inflation and Phillips Curves," *Kyklos* (Spring 1969); also a series of rejoinders (by P. S. Anderson, M. L. Wachter, and A. W. Throop) to Perry's 1967 essay (with Perry's rebuttal), *A.E.R.* (June 1969).

formed firm convictions as to the principal causes of Phillips-function instability as between (1–3) and other candidates.

Exchange Equation Effects

15.   Equations of exchange relate the quantity of money M and the general price level P in forms that appear to be identities but actually are
not.[32] We shall work in this chapter with a Fisher equation, which also
includes the real income level Y and the income velocity of circulation
of money, denoted by V. This form of the Fisher equation is

$$MV = PY \qquad \text{or} \qquad P = \frac{MV}{Y}.$$

Let us partition the economy into sectors. For our purposes, only two
sectors are required; let us call them simply Sector 1 and Sector 2 for the
present. The partitioning may be on any basis we choose. For example,
production in Sector 1 may be subsidized and that in Sector 2 unsubsi-
dized; Sector 1 may be nationalized while Sector 2 is private; Sector 1 may
be composed of imports and import-competing goods, Sector 2 of export-
ables and home goods. For purposes of incomes policy, it seems relevant
to think of Sector 1 as including the large-scale, highly organized, admin-
istratively priced industries of Eckstein's "key group," and Sector 2 taking
in the remainder of the economy. The problems to be faced are the same
for all bases of partitioning.

In a partitioned economy, each sector produces a separate "product" or
"income," which has a separate "price." Our Fisher equation expands to

$$MV = P_1Y_1 + P_2Y_2, \text{ implying } P = \frac{P_1Y_1 + P_2Y_2}{Y_1 + Y_2} = \frac{MV}{Y_1 + Y_2}.$$

16.   Suppose an inflationary period, with rising P. Suppose further that a
judicious imposition and enforcement of incomes policy restrains the key-
group price level P_1. The question arises, has this policy likewise suc-
ceeded in restraining the rise of P? Or has it instead concentrated inflationary pressure in the non-key sector 2 and raised the non-key price level
P_2 more than it would have risen in a free economy? (The same question

---

32. M and P are measured at particular points in time. One or more of the other
terms in the equation—V and Y in the Fisher equation below—are measured over a
finite time interval, which includes the point at which M and P are measured. The
equation becomes an identity in the limit, as the time interval becomes infinitesimal
or approaches zero. The income term Y should be taken, for exchange equation purposes, to include imports and exclude exports.

may be asked under other partitionings, if P_1 is restrained by lower taxes or increased subsidies, by smaller profits or larger losses in socialized industries, or by similar operations on particular prices and sectoral price levels.)

If the aggregate elasticity of demand for the output of Sector 1—call it Product 1—is greater than unity, P_1Y_1 will rise as P_1 falls relative to P_2. There is then incremental pressure on P_2Y_2 only insofar as Y_1 has reached full capacity and cannot in fact expand. If the elasticity of demand for Product 1 is fractional, P_2Y_2 normally rises, even if some part of the fall in P_1Y_1 is diverted into savings.[33]

17. Mechanisms by which restraint in P_1 may be carried through to the general price level P without dissipation in a higher P_2 can be spelled out with minimal reference to the exchange equation. (The most obvious mechanism is a rise in saving and a fall in velocity.) The point to stress, however, is that there is nothing inevitable about any of these mechanisms. On the contrary, restraints on sectoral price levels are difficult to carry through to the general price level in practice, except by additional controls (allocation, rationing, etc.), once inflationary expectations are operating.

Returning to our two sectors: If there is excess capacity in Sector 1, Y_1 will rise when P_1 is restrained because it has been previously held down by limited demand at higher relative prices.[34] If there is, similarly, excess capacity in Sector 2, a shift in demand to Sector 2 can be met largely by increases in Y_2, meaning that P_2 need not rise to the extent suggested by the rise in P_2Y_2. If Product 1 is an important input of Product 2 (as is the case for much of the key group) and Sector 2 is essentially competitive, P_2 will eventually move in the same direction as P_1, even if demand considerations operate temporarily in the opposite direction. If concern over future inflation can be abated even temporarily, the demand for money (liquidity preference) will rise as expectations change. The change will be reflected in a fall in V.

Perhaps most importantly, guideposts and incomes policies can reduce the "needs of trade" type of pressure to let M rise further as key prices or input prices (including wages) rise, since it is precisely these key prices that the incomes policy has held down.

33. To whatever extent savings on Product 1 are indeed realized, and are saved rather than diverted to Product 2, the result is a fall in V, which restrains P_2 and P along with P_1.

34. If production in Sector 1 has been restrained prior to control (for reasons associated with imperfect competition) or if inventories are being accumulated (in anticipation of future price increases), our argument runs along the same lines as Lerner's "counter-speculation" proposal for monopoly control. See also M. Bronfenbrenner, "Price Control Under Imperfect Competition," *A.E.R.* (March 1947).

The Uneasy Triangle

18.   Certain of the foregoing ideas fit into the framework of the London *Economist*'s "uneasy triangle." [35] A free economy, *The Economist* believes, can maintain one, or two, but not all three, of the following desiderata: full employment, price-level stability, and a strong trade union movement. Expanding the triangle into a rectangle might have been preferable, along with respecifying some of the sides. Let us therefore try again.

An economy can have one, two, or three, but not all four, of the following desiderata, if indeed they are desiderata: a full-employment *policy* or *guarantee* (independent of wage-rate behavior) ; price-level stability (as in the original triangle) ; strong *economic pressure groups* (not merely trade unions) to secure "orderly markets"; and freedom from direct controls over wages and prices (which may extend to rationing and allocation) .

In this setting, incomes policies may be regarded as simultaneously lowering the effectiveness of economic pressure groups at the cost of reduced freedom from direct public control.[36] Furthermore, if incomes policies are coupled with intelligent macroeconomic policy (still left undefined) , they rule out full-employment guarantees in their extreme forms (*i.e.*, guarantees regardless of cost) .

Economic Difficulties

19.   Several sets of economic difficulties result from the microeconomic application of the interrelated aggregative theories just discussed. Each difficulty carries with it certain political overtones.

35. "The Uneasy Triangle," *The Economist* (August 1952) . (Balance of payments considerations are ignored; perhaps balance of payments problems are seen only as consequences of inflation.)

36. We reject the tricky but casuistic argument that "voluntary" adherence to guidelines or guideposts *increases* freedom from whatever involuntary (legislative) controls may be threatened as the next step.

It is also difficult to accept Otto Eckstein's categorical distinction between guideposts and controls on the basis of staffing and procedure as distinguished from economic substance. (It is not immediately obvious where Eckstein would classify other incomes policies.) The following quotation is from Eckstein, "Guideposts and the Prosperity of Our Day," in American Bankers Association, *Symposium on Business–Government Relations* (Washington, 1966) , p. 88 (running quotation) :

Some people maintain that guideposts constitute controls, but this is an unrealistic view. During the Korean War the Economic Stabilization Agency had 16,000 employees, and there were other agencies to help them stabilize prices and wages. The entire staff of the Council of Economic Advisers, the agency with the most direct responsibility for giving guidepost advice, is less than 40. There are no formal reporting requirements for business or labor, no paper work, nothing but a plea to responsible people to consider the national interest in making key decisions.

The first difficulty we can pass over briefly despite its importance. It is the natural confusion of any guidepost figures with a detailed set of floors or ceilings on individual wages or prices, that is, with atrophy of the market's allocation function. Such confusion arose in American labor markets during the Kennedy-Johnson guideposts, because the price-reduction aspects of these guideposts (for industries with supernormal productivity increases) were ignored.

Such confusions between macroeconomics and microeconomics are little more than elementary misinterpretations. The actual nature of guideposts and incomes policies is a sufficient answer, if it is repeated with sufficient frequency, lucidity, and specificity. Microeconomic application, of course, is another matter. It is with microeconomic application that the need for staff arises, which Eckstein (in footnote 36) believes that guideposts can avoid.

Labor-Saving Innovation

20.   A more interesting difficulty may arise in the context of labor-saving innovation, where incomes policy may be a basis for protecting featherbedding and disguised unemployment. This case is dealt with in Figure 17.3, which presents an extreme hypothetical example. (Compare also Figure 6.6.)

This diagram is based on a competitive model of an individual firm or industry. The horizontal axis measures employment n in a firm or industry, while the vertical axis, labeled w, measures both wages and value productivity (average and marginal). In the original, pre-innovation situation (with subscript 0), linear v.a.p. and v.m.p. functions for labor are indicated by a_0 and m_0 respectively, related by the standard economic geometry of Chapter 6. The equilibrium wage rate we suppose to be W_0, so that employment is N_0, while average or man-hour productivity is A_0.

Now, as a result of labor-saving technological progress of an automational type, let the average productivity function a_0 be raised and tilted to a_1. The tilt means that the productivity gain is concentrated on the first few employees—button-pushers, lever-pullers, dial-watchers, maintenance men, etc. The corresponding v.m.p. function becomes m_1. The tilt is exaggerated by the marginalizing process; the rise need not persist for the entire length of the function. In this extreme example (a sort that has concerned us already in Chapters 6 and 11), v.m.p. m_1 actually lies below m_0 with employment constant at N_0, although v.a.p. rises from A_0 to A_1 at N_0.

21.   Let us suppose, however, that the wage rate is increased to W_1; the raise W_0W_1 lies within aggregate incomes-policy guidelines, in view of

the man-hour productivity increase, and perhaps in view of v.m.p. increases elsewhere in the economy. Trouble arises because, at the new wage W_1, optimal employment falls to N_1, reached either by layoffs or by "at-

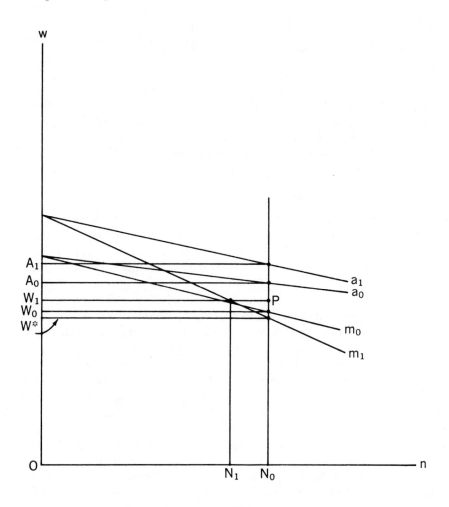

Figure 17.3

trition and pregnancy (A and P)." No wage rate above W^* can be expected to hold employment at N_0, much less increase it. If, however, a union attempts to secure a position with coordinates (N_0, W_1)—point P on the diagram—by all-or-none bargaining, it can plead conformity with aggregate incomes policy as grounds for government and public support.

The Profits Problem

22. Although the problem given in sections 20–21 may seldom appear in the extreme form presented there,[37] the problem that follows arose frequently under the Kennedy-Johnson guideposts. Indeed, it was involved in the airline mechanics' strike (summer, 1966) which may be said, more than any other single dispute, to have broken down the guideposts.

This basic problem is distributional, arising from the heterogeneity of nonlabor income. Specifically, when fixed charges are important, wage awards that maintain the labor share after technical progress will not prevent a shift to profits. This shift will in turn be difficult to justify to the rank-and-file worker.

Let x be the value of output in some firm or industry, which rises to αx because of increased man-hour productivity, with no increase in product price. (This implies $\alpha > 1$.) Let x be composed of a, b, and c. The component a represents payrolls. These rise, after technological progress, to αa, from whatever wage increases are sanctioned by incomes policies, plus changes in the volume of employment. The labor share consequently remains constant by hypothesis, at a/x. The component c represents fixed charges, mainly rent and interest payments. It does not change until long-term contracts are revised or the volume of fixed assets is changed. We treat it as constant. The residual component b represents gross or accounting profits; it becomes βb after technical progress.

It is no accident, and the result of no criminal conspiracy, that the increase ratio β in profits is not only positive but greater than α, thus arousing the wrath of the labor rank and file against the operation of incomes policies. The relation between β and α works out to

$$\beta = \alpha + \frac{(\alpha - 1)\,c}{b}, \tag{17.1}$$

so that, if α is 1.035 (corresponding to a Kennedy-Johnson guidepost 3.5 per cent wage increase) and c/b is 2, β will be 1.105, although .105 is three times .035. (These figures are relevant to the airline-mechanics dispute mentioned before.)

23. The derivation of (17.1) is elementary. In the original situation,

$$x = a + b + c \qquad \text{or} \qquad x - a = b + c.$$

---

37. In less extreme cases, W^* (the wage rate at which employment would remain at N_0 in Figure 17.3) exceeds W_0, although it remains less than the "incomes-policy" rate W_1 in the post-innovation period.

After technical progress, we have, under our assumptions,

$$\alpha\,(a + b + c) = \alpha a + \beta b + c$$
$$\alpha b + (\alpha - 1)\,c = \beta b.$$

Division by b gives (17.1), by which $\beta > \alpha$ for any $\alpha > 1$, provided only that b and c are positive.

Under similar conditions, the labor share will rise if the growth rates of profits and payrolls are each equal to α. In this case, with c constant, the labor share will rise from a/x to

$$\frac{a}{x}\frac{\alpha\,x}{\alpha x - (\alpha - 1)\,c}. \tag{17.2}$$

The increase can be substantial when α and c are both large. In Laborist (Peronist) Argentina, the labor share is reported to have risen in the nine-year period 1945–1954 from 47 to 61 per cent of the national income,[38] largely, though not exclusively, by this mechanism. (Peron's successors lowered the labor share to 51 per cent in four years (1955–1959).)

If α is redefined as the common growth rate of payrolls (a) and gross profits (b), and the value of output after the technological advance is denoted by γx, we have

$$\gamma x = \alpha\,(a + b) + c = \alpha\,(x - c) + c = \alpha\,x - (\alpha - 1)\,c$$
$$\gamma = \alpha - \frac{(\alpha - 1)\,c}{x}, \quad \text{whence} \quad \frac{\gamma}{\alpha} = 1 - \frac{(\alpha - 1)\,c}{\alpha\,x}.$$

The last expression is less than unity under our standard assumptions $(\alpha > 1;\ c,\ x > 0)$. It follows immediately that α/γ exceeds unity under the same conditions.

As for the labor share, it has risen from a/x to

$$\frac{\alpha a}{\gamma x} = \frac{a}{x}\frac{\alpha\,x}{\alpha x - (\alpha - 1)\,c}$$

or (17.2).

Interest Rate Problems

24. Our next case combines substitution and distribution difficulties. Suppose that, in the previous illustration, there has also occurred an increase in the capital-labor ratio, and that this ratio exceeds $\alpha - 1$. Suppose also that incomes policy holds constant the labor share in value added. What then happens to the capital share (as distinguished from other ele-

---

38. Laura Randall, "Economic Development Policies and Argentine Economic Growth," in Randall (ed.), *Economic Development, Evolution or Revolution?* (Boston: D. C. Heath, 1964), p. 141.

ments of gross profits)? With the capital-labor ratio rising by more than $\alpha - 1$ and the interest rate constant, the share must rise. Alternatively, the rate of return on capital, that is, the rate of interest on physical capital, must somehow be forced down.

The first of these alternatives appears "antilabor." The second alternative can hardly be reconciled with productivity analysis, since any capital-labor substitution, with wage rates constant, must have been caused by a rise in the marginal productivity of capital. It is also inflationary, despite its effect on costs, through its effect on the money supply in the absence of credit rationing. Returning to the equation of exchange and taking logarithms,

$$\log M + \log V = \log P + \log Y.$$

Differentiating both sides with respect to the nominal interest rate r:

$$\frac{\frac{dM}{dr}}{M} + \frac{\frac{dV}{dr}}{V} = \frac{\frac{dP}{dr}}{P} + \frac{\frac{dY}{dr}}{Y}.$$

Solving for the price-level change dP/dr:

$$\frac{dP}{dr} = P\left(\frac{\frac{dM}{dr}}{M} + \frac{\frac{dV}{dr}}{V} - \frac{\frac{dY}{dr}}{Y}\right).$$

Experience suggests that dP/dr is normally negative, because dM/dr, the monetary demand effect, is sufficiently large and negative to outweigh dV/dr and dY/dr (both sluggish and near zero under inflationary conditions). This general conclusion does not, of course, deny the existence of sectoral price levels P_i such that dP_i/dr is positive, either by reason of high capital charges to producers or high financing (consumer credit) charges to the consumer.[39]

The Kennedy-Johnson guideposts, with the contemporaneous American balance of payments problems exacerbated by short-term capital flows to higher-interest countries, involved constant or rising interest rates. These were interpreted generally as antilabor. The United Kingdom, however, held down interest rates more consistently, and relied on credit rationing to hold down the money supply at the cost of arbitrariness in the allocation of investment credits.

---

39. George Horwich, in "Tight Money, Monetary Restraint, and the Price Level," *Journ. of Fin.* (March 1966), p. 15, quotes a 1959 questionnaire circulated by Senator William Proxmire directly to the point: "What evidence is there to support or refute a conclusion that 'tight money' serves to limit inflation enough to offset the rising costs of borrowing and the higher total cost of everything that is paid for 'on time?'"

25.   To blunt dilemmas like this one, a number of economists have proposed redefinition of the appropriate productivity increase, for incomes
policy purposes. Rather than using labor man-hour productivity alone,
they propose using the "total tangible factor productivity" or simply "factor productivity" discussed in Chapter 6, sections 31–32.

Suppose that output x depends on two inputs a and b (labor and capital) in accordance with a production function like $x = F(a,b)$, and with
relative shares s_a and s_b which add to unity. Total factor productivity is
then defined as

$$\frac{x}{a}s_a + \frac{x}{b}s_b,$$

and its growth rate is

$$\frac{\frac{d}{dt}\left(\frac{x}{a}s_a + \frac{x}{b}s_b\right)}{\frac{x}{a}s_a + \frac{x}{b}s_b}, \qquad \text{approximated by} \qquad s_a\frac{\frac{d}{dt}\left(\frac{x}{a}\right)}{x/a} + s_b\frac{\frac{d}{dt}\left(\frac{x}{b}\right)}{x/b}.$$

As a result of diminishing returns, it usually happens that the growth
rate of x/a (man-hour productivity) exceeds the growth rate of x/b
(which might be called machine-hour productivity) when the capital-
labor ratio b/a is rising, the normal case in an advanced country. It follows that wage (and interest rate) incomes-policy increases based on total
factor productivity would be substantially more favorable to capital and
less favorable to labor than increases based on man-hour productivity
alone. Kendrick and Sato have estimated a 2.1 per cent figure for the increase rate of total factor productivity during the period 1948–1960 in the
United States, as against 3.2 to 3.6 per cent for man-hour productivity
alone.[40]

The attraction of this proposed revision is its reflection of the relation
between the rise in man-hour productivity and its cause, the availability
of more and better capital instruments to work with. The revision would
operate, however, to lower the measured labor share in output, while
permitting the capital share to rise with the capital-labor ratio.

Dilemma of Partial Failure

26.   Closer to political economy and further from economic theory is a
problem that might be called either partial failure or autonomous shock.
We may identify such a partial failure or autonomous shock as some in-

40. John W. Kendrick and Ryuzo Sato, "Factor Prices, Productivity, and Economic
Growth," *A.E.R.* (December 1963), pp. 978, 983.

flationary rise in workers' living costs, emanating from the uncontrolled Sector 2 of the economy or possibly from abroad, where domestic incomes policies have no direct application. Its cause may be bad crops, acceleration of the world population explosion, higher agricultural price supports, labor shortages in weakly organized service industries, devaluation of the domestic currency, or similar perturbations.

Under such circumstances, organized workers often refuse to accept a real wage increase less than their overall real productivity increase, which equals the incomes-policy or guidepost figure *plus* the rise in living costs. A United Steel Workers economist expressed their case in April 1966, during the Kennedy-Johnson guidepost controversies:[41]

> As we look at 1966, where the Administration has just asked us to again live within the guidelines, we see a situation in which wages and salaries are expected to hold close to the guideline figure in terms of money wages. Yet we have had within the last year an increase in cost of living of 2.5 per cent.
>
> Now 2.5 per cent in one year as compared with the guideline figure of 3.2 per cent leaves labor holding the short end of the stick. It becomes a serious question how you can ask labor to face this kind of a shortfall in its real income. How can you compare real increases in the economy with money income increases on the labor side when there is a shortfall because of increases in the cost of living when the guidelines have failed to hold prices? How can you, under these circumstances, ask labor to accept the guidelines and live within them?
>
> Remember, this is not just a bunch of statistics. This is the bread and meat that go on the table of these people who work in your plants. And believe me, unless they accept the guidelines, it is not going to do any good for me to say "Sure, we will accept them," because our people will not accept them and we cannot live with them.

Moreover, with a situation approaching Lerner's high full employment, unions can obtain higher-than-guidepost increases by some combination of ordinary collective bargaining and what we have called collusive bargaining. There is clearly a strong normative case (put by Brubaker in the preceding quotation) for refusing sacrifices. Employers can usually make an equally strong case against absorbing over-the-line wage increases without passing them on in increased prices.

At the same time—and herein lies the dilemma—bending incomes policies by addition of special allowances for living cost increases on the labor market or for wage increases on the output market, builds what might otherwise have been temporary shocks into the economy's wage and cost

41. Otis Brubaker, in American Bankers Association, *Symposium, op. cit.*, pp. 128 f. (running quotation.)

structure. This means an escalated inflation rate if macroeconomic policy validates these extra wage and price increases by raising M and lowering r, or if liquidity preference and fiscal policy adjust to price increases by various devices that amount to raising V. Replying to the steel workers' representative in his capacity as "guidepost man" on the Council of Economic Advisers, Eckstein argued:[42]

> In the last 12 months consumer prices are up by 2½ per cent. What is the proper response of guideposts to [this?] You need to take the longer term perspective. Prices are up that much essentially because of higher meat prices. Suppose we made full adjustment in the guideposts and had wages rise by productivity plus 2½ per cent. We would be freezing into the industrial cost structure of this country the temporary bulge of meat prices. That is an unreasonable step. Once you correct the guideposts for price changes you are building inflation into the process. You are just mechanizing the wage-price spiral—the very situation we are trying to avoid.

With equal inevitability, the addition of special allowances to incomes-policy guidelines means the generation of unemployment and/or deflation somewhere in the economy if prices rise in the key sector while M, V, and r are all kept stiff and inelastic. The only possible adjustment in this case is a fall in real income Y, which may affect both Y_1 and Y_2.

Political Arguments

27.   We consider next a number of normative arguments, administrative and political, which have been made against incomes policies, or in favor of substantially modifying or weakening them when they are in effect.[43]

When incomes policies are used jointly with monetary and fiscal ones, they function as a stopgap to keep matters under control between the time when the underlying situation changes in the direction of inflation and the time when the authorities have made the necessary policy adjustments and these have actually taken hold; that is, during the combined period of "inside" and "outside" lags. The practical temptation is great to use them as suppressed-inflationary substitutes for unpopular policies like tax increases, expenditure reductions, and tight money. This tendency, with its eventual inflationary bias, seems almost inevitable when elections are frequent, when experts are "on tap but not on top" in economic policy, and when those on top are dominated by "votefare" considerations. It is for this reason that this writer's support of incomes policies

42. Eckstein, *ibid.*, p. 129 (running quotation)

43. Compare the U.S. Council of Economic Advisers list of "Guidepost Exceptions," *Economic Report of the President* (January 1967) , pp. 129–132.

is limited to systems with established fiscal and monetary rules, or with sufficient records of intelligent fiscal and monetary discretion.

28. One frequently hears proposals to increase the political acceptability and administrative workability of incomes policies by greater disaggregation.[44] It is easy to argue that more attention be paid to the special problems of each particular key industry (relatively high or relatively low wages, relatively high or relatively low profits, fast or slow rates of growth, modern or obsolescent capital equipment, and so on.) In addition, the principal parties, or at least unions and management if not stockholders or consumers, should be "represented" when incomes policy is applied to each industry. This apparently means that both labor and management should have veto powers, although the point is seldom explicit.

The *prima facie* case for disaggregation and representation is a strong one. Every firm or industry has its special problems. Moreover, representation opens up issues of income distribution and redistribution, which may otherwise be ignored, postponed, or disregarded. One may, however, question whether the marginal benefits would be worth the additional staffing and other administrative costs involved. Disaggregation and representation introduce dangerous overtones of cartelization and veto. They may sometimes result in a complete deadlock with no policies whatever. They may include indefensible interindustry inconsistencies in incomes policy. More easily, they may be built into engines for escalating inflation by institutionalizing the wage-price spiral. They may also freeze the position of privileged sectors of the economy against intrusions from outside, as by preventing price cuts or by minimizing expansions of plant capacity or of training programs for scarce labor.

29. The basic political question relating to incomes policies is, however, the alleged inconsistency of direct controls, however "informal," with basic economic and political freedoms. We have already listed consistency with these freedoms among our significant criteria for judging economic systems (Chapter 1, section 4).

Incomes policies, like other forms of direct intervention and control, have often involved the "direction" of labor, that is, the civilian equivalent of the military camp or the prison workshop. They have also prevented employers from quitting business, selling their properties, or otherwise lightening (short of bankruptcy) their obligations to meet inflated payrolls or produce unprofitable outputs. Nor have these violations been

44. A standard American expression of this view is John T. Dunlop, "Guideposts, Wages, and Collective Bargaining," in Schultz and Aliber, *op. cit.*

limited either to short-term emergencies or to admitted dictatorships of the Proletariat, the Party, or the Leader. In the United Kingdom, the Attlee cabinet was authorized to require labor direction in the late 1940's, and the Wilson cabinet levied payroll taxes on "nonessential" service employment twenty years later. Neither Clement Attlee nor Harold Wilson had dictatorial ambitions; neither did the British Labour party, which Attlee and Wilson led; the statutes involved were in both cases passed democratically by the Mother of Parliaments. It does not, however, follow from British experience that all experiments with incomes policies will pass through the same stages.[45]

The most likely enforcement methods for incomes policy are neither forced labor nor forced entrepreneurship but milder measures with milder infringements on personal liberties, such as are, after all, unavoidable even in competitive practice. We refer primarily to the selective enforcement of powers and statutes completely general on their face.

In our sub-Utopian world, indirect taxes and bounties are imposed selectively on good x but not on good y. Direct taxes and antimonopoly regulations, are enforced against one man, one firm, or one industry rather than another, given the limitation on the funds available for enforcement in general. All privileges, from profitable public contracts to tariff and immigration protections, are awarded selectively. Public monopoly and monopsony powers, where they exist, may be either exercised against potential "victims" or left potential; the range for potential discrimination seems greater on balance in the monopsony cases (purchase of specialized supplies) than in the monopoly ones (because public outputs are generally undifferentiated). It seems quixotic, therefore, to worry unduly if the amenability of an individual, a company, an industry, or a trade union to incomes-policy controls becomes one among several bases for deciding between leniency and severity, in unavoidably discretionary cases that are also unavoidably discriminatory.

30.   It is likewise Utopian to expect a government to abstain from using its own publicity resources to support its own policies of the moment. Neither can we expect the government to segregate incomes policies from other policies in this connection.

One may rather fault the tendency of many parliamentary governments to criticize and threaten prospective violators sharply in advance of their violations, or before the violations take effect, and then to retreat after

45. The opposite view, which has Hitler or Stalin as end product, is the main thesis of Friedrich von Hayek in *The Road to Serfdom* (Chicago: University of Chicago Press, 1945). It applies not only to incomes policies but to a far wider (and imperfectly defined) range of economic interventions, and is based mainly on the German experience.

the consequences of the violations become clear, however inflationary these consequences may be. This procedure smacks of the paper tiger. Surely, if we are to have effective incomes policies short of dictatorship, the ratio of post-censorship to pre-censorship of violations should be increased. "Post-censorship" means here an explanation of how specific violations have shifted into unemployment inflation the results of policies that might otherwise have produced fuller employment at more stable prices.[46] It also requires retaining one's general policy line, rather than bending it a little to validate extra fillips of inflation. "Pre-censorship," on the other hand, is illustrated by the mixture of threat, denunciation, and entreaty utilized by President John F. Kennedy in the 1962 American steel price crisis.

Post-censorship should identify violations that would require inflationary monetary and fiscal policies to maintain employment. It should identify in particular cases of collusive bargaining between the entrepreneurial aristocracy of some oligopoly or cartel and the labor aristocracy of its employees. At the same time, apparent incomes-policy violations should be condoned if they reflect competitive adjustments between firms, occupations, and industries, or if they are responses to the government's own policies (raising maintenance levels for the unemployed, or minimum wages for public employees). Apparent violations should also be condoned if their effect is purely distributional, as when wage increases are squeezed out of profits without price or subsidy consequences. Incomes policies should (but probably cannot) be neutral as between alternative income distributions. (See the Denison references in footnote 4 of this chapter.)

Penalties for Violation

31. Transcending immediate political feasibility, we may mention certain extensions of the sanctions that might be made available, in a free society, against repeated incomes-policy violators.[47] The "if necessary" clause arises from academic timidity, from the unwisdom of swatting flies with atom bombs, and from an awareness of risks to personal freedom.[48]

46. A case in point antedates the Kennedy-Johnson guideposts. Otto Eckstein and Gary Fromm, "Steel and the Postwar Inflation," Study Paper No. 2, Joint Economic Committee, U.S. Congress (1959) claim to trace 40 per cent of the American postwar inflation directly and indirectly to steel prices. This result was used subsequently as the basis for particularly harsh criticisms of steel industry pricing policies, although it is subject to technical criticism.

47. Compare Weintraub's list of nine similar suggestions, "In Defense of Wage-Price Guideposts . . . Plus," *op. cit.,* pp. 79 f.

48. There are countries in which the death penalty has been imposed for such "economic crimes" as incomes-policy violation.

In addition, fiscal and monetary sanity may themselves make incomes policies easier of enforcement by taking the profits out of violation. References are based on the American scene.

(*1*) Incomes-policy compliance may be made, by legislation, an explicit criterion for judging a firm's "performance" in connection with antitrust and similar proceedings.

(*2*) In many countries, "legitimate" trade unions have secured special privileges. Employers may not discriminate either against them or against their members, and have a duty to bargain collectively "in good faith." Unions are generally exempt from antimonopoly legislation, at least as it affects labor markets. Sometimes the exemption extends to all civil suits, including those by employers, disaffected workers, and even the state. These privileges, as well as the stamp of "legitimacy," may be suspended or withdrawn from unions securing "unreasonable" wage increase.

(*3*) Legislative requirements for "prevailing wages" on public contracts and in public employment may be repealed. Repeal would reduce the hold of union rates in the public sector, and would militate against wage increases that violate incomes policy.

(*4*) If there exists "farm parity" agricultural price-support legislation, the percentage of parity guaranteed may be lowered, and any accompanying production restrictions may be eased, with a view to reducing "dilemmas of partial failure" (section 26, above).

(*5*) Public agencies may be given the power to suspend, wholly or in part, tariff and quota protection for industries that violate incomes-policy requirements on an industry-wide basis. Such provisions would permit the use of imports to hold particular prices down, in a manner analogous to domestic stockpiles and inventories.

(*6*) When immigration laws vary in stringency with the occupation of the prospective immigrant, public agencies may also have the power to suspend or weaken protection against immigrants for trade unions violating the wage-rate provisions of incomes policy. In addition, employers may be given the privilege of recruiting foreign workers on a contract-labor basis, with appropriate safeguards. Along the same lines, the training facilities of the armed services, the vocational schools, and antipoverty programs may be used to break down restrictive apprenticeship and similar practices supporting aristocracies of labor.

(*7*) Public purchases, particularly in defense procurement, are major revenue sources for some oligopolistic industries. The accumulation or decumulation of public stockpiles can affect the profit positions of other such industries.

The government may accordingly be given increased power to defend both the public fisc and the great body of consumers against incomes-policy violations. For example, it may be permitted to engage in do-it-yourself practices for its own protection. This might mean "standby socialism," in such forms as expansible yardstick plants and other facilities, which might compete with private firms for public contracts and construction. These might be staffed largely by military personnel, vocational-school students, or antipoverty trainees. The so-called Seabees of World War II (in public construction) and the Military Air Transport Service (in both passenger and freight transportation) are two obvious American models.

Along similar lines, previously accumulated public stockpiles may be drawn down to restrain price increases. Similarly, the permitted rates of exploitation of publicly owned forest and mineral reserves may be accelerated for the same purposes.

Conclusions

32. Our conclusions may be grouped under a few main heads. Incomes policies should be linked to intelligent monetary and fiscal policy practices, rather than devoted, as they typically are, to maintaining suppressed inflation. They should be enforced to a greater extent by post-censorship rather than pre-censorship methods; if necessary, the range of permissible sanctions should be increased. At the same time, care should be taken to avoid freezing the industrial structure, the price structure, the wage structure, or the income distribution. Mobility and flexibility should be increased on balance, rather than decreased. Even under optimal monetary and fiscal policies, there is a place for optimal incomes policies in addition, if only to "hold the line" in the presence of lagged responses.

These conclusions leave unresolved a number of distributional issues (sections 20–25). There are in fact many difficulties a "guidepost man" must live with in the short term. Consolation is possible for the longer term, possibly along the following lines:

(1) Compliance with incomes-policy guidelines need not be interpreted as guaranteeing the winning of one's case (in collective bargaining), the maintenance of employment (for labor), or the maintenance of one's market position (for output).

(2) Interest rates, nominal and real, need not be regulated. If the overall wage-increase guideline is the growth rate of average labor productivity, the related movements of interest rates and capital intensities will assist in determining the movement of the labor share.

(3) When short-term distributional shifts to profit result from the ex-

istence of long-term contracts (sections 22–23), these contracts must come up eventually for renewal and renegotiation, at which time "constant" incomes become variable.

(4) With continued prosperity, the business population tends to increase. Such an increase, other things equal, operates in the direction of lowering the degrees of employer monopoly and monopsony, which is to say, in the direction of a distribution away from profits to contractual incomes, both of labor and of property.

(5) Perhaps most important, we have not interpreted incomes policy as either requiring or forbidding distributional shifts within sectors or industries, either through market processes or collective bagaining, either toward or away from labor. Neither need they interfere with any of the years' accretions of justifiable and unjustifiable intratype input price differentials, such as the wage or interest rate structures.

Name Index

Subject Index

Adding-up theorem, 123, 136, 156, 163, 237 n, 305, 352, 362, 367, 378–380, 396

Aggregative distribution theory, 22, 267–297, 386–444
See also Keynesian theory of income distribution

Assets, 93, 110, 299–347, 383, 412–416
human, 25, 110
liquid, 25, 320–347

Australia, 29, 128, 356–357, 395

Bowley's Law, 80–89, 142–143, 162, 209, 243, 390, 400, 410, 421–431

Brazil, 29, 46

Britain. *See* United Kingdom

British Labor Party, 3, 71, 472

Bulgaria, 263–264

Business cycles, 104, 228
and income distribution, 29 n–30 n, 76–82, 86

Cambridge School, 142, 397, 420, 427
neo-Cambridge School, 122, 391

Canada, 30, 46, 74, 104

Capital, 1, 31, 79–80, 104–106, 120–188, 227, 244, 268, 283, 298–357, 365–367, 371–372, 377–380, 387–407, 419, 454, 466–467
constant, 31, 88 n
gains, 33–34, 69, 77–79, 83 n, 92, 305, 308
human, 6, 25–26, 31, 58–59, 102, 113, 220, 316, 340, 348–349, 405, 428
marginal efficiency of, 299 n–300 n, 325–329
organic composition of, 88 n, 159 n
-output ratio, 81 n, 155–157, 417–425
theory, 105, 121 n, 298–347
variable, 38, 88 n

Capitalism, 4, 32 n, 67, 96, 104, 110, 117, 196, 242, 244, 247 n, 248, 278, 316, 370, 418–421, 435, 446 n

China, 3 n, 17, 20, 21, 119, 128

Class, 1–2, 11, 15–22, 25, 26, 32 n, 89, 93, 97 n, 98, 101–102, 356, 370, 416–421, 448
working, 5, 16, 21, 29, 88–89, 104, 241, 259, 410, 433 n
See also Workers; Capitalism; Landlord

Classical economics, 3, 121 n, 268–271, 298–319, 321–325, 332, 349–355

Collective bargaining, 112, 117, 164, 175, 198, 234–266, 283–285, 364, 391, 469, 474–476
incidence of, 241–248, 284

Communism, 6, 16, 18

Compensation
criterion, 98
executive, 26

Concentration coefficient, 43–52, 78–79
See also Lorenz curve

Consumption, 104–112, 121, 243–244, 278, 306–347, 385, 412–416
function, 41, 42 n, 107–110, 272, 435
propensity to consume, 81 n, 104 n, 107–109, 272, 331, 418–421

Czechoslovakia, 5 n–6 n

Democracy, 4, 6, 12–22

Denmark, 46

Depreciation Allowances, 31, 88 n, 299, 315, 365

Depression, 2–3, 34, 78–79, 104, 107–112, 245–248, 268, 271, 274, 428

Distribution
bases, 26–31
formula, 50
functional, 6, 26–28, 33, 35–38, 73, 76–93, 94, 110, 120, 307, 386–444

483